SEASONS OF GRACE

A HISTORY OF THE

CATHOLIC ARCHDIOCESE

OF DETROIT

LESLIE WOODCOCK TENTLER

Foreword by Edmund Cardinal Szoka

WAYNE STATE UNIVERSITY PRESS   DETROIT

LIBRARY OF CONGRESS CATALOGING-IN-PUBLICATION DATA

TENTLER, LESLIE WOODCOCK.
    SEASONS OF GRACE : A HISTORY OF THE CATHOLIC ARCHDIOCESE OF
DETROIT / LESLIE WOODCOCK TENTLER.
        P.   CM. — (GREAT LAKES BOOKS)
    BIBLIOGRAPHY: P.
    INCLUDES INDEX.
    ISBN 0-8143-2105-4.
    1. CATHOLIC CHURCH. ARCHDIOCESE OF DETROIT (MICH.) — HISTORY.
    2. DETROIT REGION (MICH.) — CHURCH HISTORY.   I. TITLE.   II. SERIES.
BX1417.D.4T46   1990
282′.77434 — dc20   89-34282
                                                            CIP
PAPERBACK ISBN 0-8143-2106-2

ALL THE PHOTOGRAPHS IN THIS VOLUME ARE USED WITH
THE COURTESY OF THE ARCHDIOCESE OF DETROIT.

GREAT LAKES BOOKS

CONTENTS

PART III: 1919–1958

Illustrations follow pages 161, 361, 467, and 515.

FOREWORD

In 1983 the Archdiocese of Detroit celebrated its 150th Anniversary. In conjunction with that sesquicentennial observance, Wayne State University Press reprinted Father George Paré's *The Catholic Church in Detroit: 1701–1888*. The Archdiocese also took the occasion of the jubilee celebration to announce the commissioning of a new volume which would continue the history of the Archdiocese from 1888–1958, that is, to the death of Edward Cardinal Mooney and the eve of the Second Vatican Council. Envisioned was a work of both social and institutional history which would be of interest to a wide-reading audience, especially Catholics.

With the publication of the present volume, these high hopes have been admirably fulfilled. The author has provided us with an extremely well researched and very readable account of the remarkable development of the Catholic Church in Detroit over the past century. She has also opened up new horizons for Catholic historical studies in the United States. While by no means neglecting the contribution of bishops and centralized institutions which have been the traditional focus of diocesan histories, she has also succeeded in bringing to life the world of the Catholic family, neighborhood, and local parish within the context of the wider community.

This approach responds to a number of developments within the Catholic Church in recent years. The renewal of the Second Vatican Council has led to a greater appreciation of the vital contribution of all members of the Church: laity, religious, and clergy alike. This development in turn has generated greater interest in the historical and social dimensions of the Church's mission as it has been carried out by individuals and by groups of men and women.

The history of the Catholic Church in the United States is long and inspiring. This year marks the 424th year of the continuous presence of the Catholic Church on the soil of our nation, as well as the 200th anniversary of the establishment of the first American diocese. A growing appreciation of this history has led to renewed efforts to preserve ecclesiastical archives and to make them available for research. Without the archives program established in the Archdiocese of Detroit over the past decade, a history of this kind would have been virtually impossible.

It has been said that the historian's most useful contribution is to reveal the past in such complexity that it resembles the confusion of the present. I am confident that both specialists and general readers, whatever their religious faith, will derive from this volume a much deeper understanding of the complex events that have shaped an important segment of American society in one of our nation's major cities. Catholic readers will no doubt be struck by the fact that certain tensions within the Church, which have come to be associated with the post-conciliar era, were also present in the past. Some of these tensions were due to strong differences of opinion. Others serve to remind us of a truth as old as the Gospel, namely, that the Church is made up of both saints and sinners.

I am confident that the Catholic people of the Archdiocese of Detroit and their fellow citizens in Southeast Michigan will be well served by this volume. May we derive from it the wisdom and insight needed to meet the complex challenges of our own day.

Edmund Cardinal Szoka, J.C.L., D.D.
Archbishop of Detroit

March 8, 1989

ACKNOWLEDGMENTS

This book could not have been written without the generous support of Cardinal Edmund Szoka, who was throughout its research and writing the very best sort of disinterested benefactor. It is the rare diocesan historian who enjoys the kind of freedom that was mine in Detroit, with unrestricted access to the archives and full editorial independence. Needless to say, I alone am responsible for any errors that remain in the text and for the interpretations found therein.

My work in the Archdiocesan archives was made immensely easier by Elizabeth Yakel, whose achievement in organizing said archives was little short of miraculous. I am indebted especially to her unfailing patience and good humor, for we worked in what were sometimes uncomfortably close quarters. Roman Godzak, Beth's successor, has continued her tradition of gracious service. Thanks go as well to Sister Celeste Rabaut, IHM, who was a near-omniscient guide to the archives of her congregation, and to Sister Mary Ann Travers, SSJ, who introduced me to the archives at Nazareth. No less helpful were the staffs at the Bentley Historical Library in Ann Arbor, the Cushwa Center for the Study of American Catholicism, Wayne State University's Reuther Archives, and the library of Sacred Heart Seminary in Detroit.

If archivists and librarians were of critical importance, so too were those friends and colleagues whose conversation over the past few years has shaped my thinking about Church history. Thanks, then, to Fathers Leonard Blair and Earl Boyea, Sister Claudia Carlen, IHM, and Monsignor Francis Canfield, to Professors Francis Blouin and Jonathan Marwil, to Justine L'Esperance Murphy and Sister Amadeus Dowd, IHM, to Helen Kern Morris and Margaret Lynch Gibson, to Fathers Bohdan Kosicki, Norman Thomas, Raymond Van Deveire, and Daniel Fox, OFM Cap., and to the members of the Cushwa Center seminar in American religion. Tom Tentler deserves separate mention and special thanks, for he has lived with the history of the Archdiocese for some six years now, and this book is much the better for his insights and his criticism. Finally, I want to express my gratitude to the people of St. Boniface-St. Vincent's and St. Cecilia's parishes in Detroit. They brought the Church to life for me in all its variety and showed me that the Light does indeed shine forth in darkness. My children have been lucky to grow up in such company; perhaps one day they will thank their mother.

INTRODUCTION

This is not the first attempt to write a history of the Archdiocese of Detroit. Bishop Michael Gallagher appointed a diocesan historian in 1922 — he was Father George Paré, then on the faculty at Detroit's Sacred Heart Seminary — and asked not long after that he prepare a book-length history for publication in 1933, the centennial of the Diocese (its designation as an archdiocese came in 1937). But the project did not come to fruition, not, at least, in the form in which it had initially been envisioned. By 1933, after four years of depression, the Diocese of Detroit was in financial crisis. Little money could be spared with which to celebrate the past. Some of Father Paré's research was published, but in much-abbreviated form, in a commemorative edition of the diocesan weekly, the *Michigan Catholic*. Publication of a book-length history was deferred indefinitely.[1]

The death of Bishop Gallagher in 1937 was a further blow to Father Paré's hopes, for Gallagher had been the patron of the projected history. His successor, Archbishop Edward Mooney, who surely sympathized with Father Paré's work, nevertheless assigned the priest to a parish, where he remained throughout the Second World War. Mooney inherited a fiscal disaster when he came to Detroit, and the rapid growth of the city and its environs during the war created a serious shortage of clergy. It made sense to concentrate on the job at hand and to postpone still further the publication of a full-fledged diocesan history. Father Paré worked fitfully on his book during the 1940s, uncertain that it would ever be published. It finally appeared in 1951, the 250th anniversary of the founding of Detroit, to commemorate the considerable Catholic role in the history of that city.[2]

Father Paré's long-delayed book deals with the history of the Catholic Church in Detroit and Michigan from the first Indian missions in the seventeenth century until the appointment of Detroit's fourth bishop, John Samuel Foley, in 1888. The story he tells, and tells admirably, is a long one, and he had presumably no great desire to embark on another long volume in the last years of his life. It was Father Paré's belief that the "pioneer stage" in the history of the Archdiocese was over by 1888, and that subsequent decades belonged to a distinct second stage of diocesan history. He himself had lived through much of this second stage—as a child in St. Anne's parish in Detroit, as a seminarian, and as a priest—and he was aware that writing essentially contemporary history is a difficult task, and one that invites controversy of an especially vexing sort. He hesitated, he wrote, "to delve into modern complexities."

These "modern complexities" became, in 1983, my assignment as the author of a newly commissioned history of the Archdiocese of Detroit on the occasion of its sesquicentennial. This new history is undertaken both as an extension of Father Paré's work—a second volume, in effect—and as an effort to examine the history of the Archdiocese in social as well as institutional terms. Father Paré's book was necessarily devoted mainly to the growth of the institutional Church, for his work was focused on a period for which the evidence is anything but plentiful. It is only because of his years of painstaking labor that we have today a coherent view of the way in which the Church developed in Detroit and Michigan. By the late nineteenth century, however, the Diocese of Detroit was much smaller geographically than it had been at its founding, and sufficiently well organized that the records pertaining to institutional growth are fairly complete. Freed, then, from the necessity of historical detective work, I was able to explore questions of particular interest to a new generation of Church historians—questions having to do with religious belief and practice, with the social dimension of parish life, with the impact of ethnic and racial and class divisions on the Church, with the relationship between Catholics and non-Catholics in politics and community life. I have tried, as far as my sources will allow, to create a portrait of the people who built the institutions that we call the Church in the Archdiocese of Detroit, and to place them, and the institutions that they built, in the context of one of the nation's most turbulent industrial cities and its developing hinterland. It is, inevitably, an imperfect portrait, and incomplete in many ways. The astonishing variety of the Catholic population is a principal reason for this.

I have assumed from the first that this book would address two audiences. There will be readers whose main concern is local history, who are more interested in the particulars of Church history in the Archdiocese of Detroit than in the ways in which that history reflects the history of the Catholic Church in the United States or Europe. For their sakes I have tried to work with a sensitive eye to local detail. For those readers whose interest is the history of Roman Catholicism in the United States, I have tried to make clear the ways in which developments in the Archdiocese of Detroit parallel and diverge from those in other large industrial dioceses. Detroit could not be called a typical American diocese—what diocese could claim that distinction?—but the Church in Detroit faced problems similar to those encountered in Chicago, Cleveland, Milwaukee, or even New York, and worked to resolve those problems with much the same store of assumptions and resources. Detroit is, moreover, a particularly advantageous location from which to examine the Church in the context of rapid urban growth and almost equally rapid decline, and to explore the role that the

Church has played in the industrial union and civil rights movements of the past fifty years.

This is a local history, then, but a local history that aims to shed light on the Church as a national, even occasionally as an international, institution. To give this larger focus to my narrative, I have chosen certain organizing themes that will be followed throughout. These themes, as it happens, are relevant to a number of debates that are currently underway within the Church. But the scope and contents of this book have not been determined by any preoccupation with these debates on my own part. Like Father Paré, I am shy of "modern complexities," and these lie, for me, in the years since the Second Vatican Council. The American Church has changed enormously in these years — that much is clear. We, however, for all our having acted in the drama, have as yet an imperfect understanding of what has happened, much less why it did. This will likely be the case for at least another decade. I could hardly ignore the reality of post-conciliar change as I researched and thought about the history of the Arch-diocese. But I tried not to view the past through the lens of present-day concerns. If the experience of past generations speaks to our problems, that is our good fortune — and a reminder that we are neither as free of the past nor as different from our forebears as many post-conciliar Catholics seem to believe.

The overriding theme of this history, as of the history of any American diocese, must be the slow, often troubled development of a unified and coherent American Catholicism. The Church in Detroit in the mid-nineteenth century was, organizationally at least, little more than a loose assemblage of fractious ethnic parishes. There was not much sense in the polyglot Catholic population of a common religious identity; even the liturgy might vary from one parish to the next. The Church was still a heavily immigrant institution in the early decades of the twentieth century: the Gospel was preached in twenty-two languages in Detroit's parishes as late as 1933. But even before the turn of the century, we can see the emergence of truly American parishes and a fully assimilated American Catholic mentality. Detroit's priests and its bishops had some small hand in this, being, for the most part, proponents of Americanization. The change, however, had more fundamentally to do with the growing wealth and education of the older Catholic population, and the slow growth of a pragmatic religious tolerance in the larger society. As assimilation proceeded in the generations after 1890, the Church in Detroit became gradually more uniform in its religious practice and its organizational life, and increasingly marked by a sense of confessional identity that transcended ethnic boundaries and even, on occasion, class and racial lines. Still, progress was uneven, and the flood of new immigrants — stemmed only in the mid-1920s — made for powerful pressures toward organizational fragmentation and the most narrowly parochial of mentalities.

By the late 1940s, however, we can speak with confidence of a wholly American Church in the Archdiocese of Detroit. For the process of assimilation was greatly intensified after the First World War, and the last wave of immigrants was Americanized more swiftly than their predecessors had been. The end of

unrestricted immigration was important here; so was the nationalization of political life that was wrought by depression and war. During these same years,
moreover, episcopal power in Detroit was at last effectively centralized and bu-
reaucratized. A largely assimilated Catholic population and a mature organization in the Chancery made possible the triumphs of the 1950s — the expansion
of an already large Catholic school system, the building of a major seminary,
the proliferation of Catholic social services, an easy Catholic confidence in state
and local politics. These are the years remembered, generally, when unhappy
Catholics speak of what was lost after Vatican II. But they rarely see that the
uniformity and confidence of American Catholicism in the 1950s was a recent
achievement and, very likely, an inevitably temporary one. The successes of the
Church in the 1950s obscured for many people some very real divisions in the
Catholic population, based now more on age and education and occupation than
ethnicity. These divisions emerged after Vatican II, all the more disturbing for
being unexpected.

Closely related to the slow emergence of a truly American Catholicism is a
second broad theme — a history of changing sacramental practice. Mid-nineteenth-
century Catholics, for the most part, went infrequently to confession and communion. A minority among them were decidedly irregular in their attendance
at Mass. By the middle of the twentieth century, however, American Catholics
were remarkable for their disciplined piety — remarkable, at least, in the context
of the Universal Church — and for their frequent recourse to the sacraments.
The change in religious practice affected every ethnic group, and helped to make
Catholics more alike in their religious behavior and more conscious of their common religious identity. It made men and women more similar too, at least when
it came to religious behavior, for the American Church had unusual success with
its male members, not only holding their loyalty but persuading many of them
to accept strict standards of religious practice. Those strict standards meant, in
turn, that American Catholicism remained centered on the clergy, even as the
wealth and education of American Catholics increased over the generations.
Only in the 1960s was the role of the priest in the worshiping community called
into serious question, and then by a distinct minority among the laity.

The relationship of the priest to his people constitutes a third important focus
of this study. Those charged with the education of priests have, since at least
the sixteenth century, tried to create a distinctive clerical persona and such
strong bonds of loyalty among priests that a priest can serve his people in the
world but still remain a man apart. Detroit's priests until very recently were
trained by men steeped in this tradition. The demands of parish life, however,
have often worked against the integrity of what we might call a "clerical culture":
the busy priest may find himself cut off from frequent contact with his fellow
clergy and immersed in the lives of his parishioners. Broadly speaking, we can
say that the clerical world became progressively more insulated and self-contained
as the number of priests in the Archdiocese grew and as its central institutions
were developed. Detroit's nineteenth-century bishops were in fact inclined to a

more ascetic view of the priesthood than their successors were. But they were less capable than their twentieth-century counterparts of closely governing the lives of their clergy. A priest serving in the Diocese of Detroit under Bishop Caspar Borgess (1870–1887), a notoriously stern disciplinarian, almost invariably had more independence in the practice of his priesthood than did a priest serving under the more genial Cardinal Edward Mooney (1937–1958). The increasingly effective authority emanating from the Chancery affected the laity as well as the clergy. It affected the clergy much more directly, however, and the changing relationship of Detroit's bishops to their priests will be an important subtheme throughout this book.

A priest's relationship to his people was sometimes complicated by the insistence of at least some of the laity that they be permitted an active role in parish administration. Often the roles they claimed for themselves violated the laws governing the Archdiocese and ran counter to the priest's own assumptions about the scope of clerical authority. We are accustomed to thinking of parish "democracy"—in the form of elected parish councils—as an innovation of the American Church in the years after Vatican II. But comparably democratic modes of parish government were common in the nineteenth century and survived into the twentieth century in many ethnic parishes. The history of this "democratic" tradition in American Catholicism is important, not only because it speaks to present practice in the Church, but because it helps us to understand both the vitality of immigrant Catholicism and the difficulties faced by the American bishops as they tried, over the generations, to create a disciplined and uniform Church in this country. The governance of the parish, then, constitutes a fourth important topic which will be examined periodically throughout the book.

No less relevant to present-day concerns is a fifth topic—the role and status of women in the American Church. But here too my focus is dictated not by contemporary problems but by the realities of the world our great-grandparents knew. Catholicism, and not simply its American branch, seems to me much more likely than Protestantism of any variety to insist that the world be segregated on the basis of gender—to insist that the laity are best organized for social and devotional purposes as men and as women, rather than as couples or as members of families. The well-run Catholic parish in the 1880s as in the 1940s featured a wide range of organizations for men and for women, for boys and for girls, and it was expected that many if not most parishioners would receive communion regularly as members of these groups. A celibate clergy and celibate religious simply confirmed the Church as a world where men and women occupied mutually exclusive spheres, as a world distinct in an important way from the world of the family, no matter how genuinely the Church praised family life as a full expression of Christian virtue.

A pervasive consciousness of gender was integral to Catholicism, then, and Catholics were inevitably concerned with the place of women in the Church. That "place," moreover, was a perennial source of tension in many parishes. Catholic women in the United States have historically been more devout than men — a pattern common to the rest of the world — but the need to build churches and schools, without government aid, put a special premium on their loyalty. Women's unpaid labor was critical to the survival of many parishes, just as the work of women religious was essential to the maintenance of Catholic schools and social welfare institutions. And, at least in the Archdiocese of Detroit, lay-women were more important than laymen in the development and support of Catholic charities and in the development of religious education outside the parochial schools.

The Catholic preoccupation with segregating the sexes did give women the opportunity to develop leadership skills and to work independently in the service of the Church. But the very success of their work in each generation emphasized the contradictions attendant on the subordination of women in the Church: lay and religious women were subject to male authority, and yet the Church was dependent to an important degree on the voluntary work of women. A successful pastor was generally able to accommodate this complex reality, which may have done more than anything else to inhibit misogyny in the American Church. And, for a time, better-educated Catholic women found outlets for their talents in the growing number of diocesan and even national Catholic women's organizations. One rarely finds, before Vatican II, a direct challenge to the legitimacy of exclusively male authority; even educated women accepted, to all appearances, the exercise of personal authority within the considerable sphere of Church activities tacitly conceded to women. (This sphere, as one would expect, was quietly expanded in each generation.) The open challenge to male authority in the Church since Vatican II has roots in the feminist renaissance of the late 1960s. But it also reflects a much older tension about the role and status of women in the American Church, the history of which can lend some perspective to the current debate.

Finally I will consider throughout this study the relationship of Catholics to the non-Catholic world around them. Detroit's bishops, like bishops throughout the nation, tried hard to make Catholics a people protected from extensive contact with "outsiders." They insisted that parochial schools be built and that Catholic children attend them; they helped to found Catholic colleges as soon as the community could provide students; they sponsored in each generation various institutions and organizations designed to be Catholic alternatives to Protestant or secular undertakings — Catholic versions of the YMCA and the Scouts, women's social and charitable groups, organizations for Catholic trade unionists and Catholic professional men. But the bishops were never wholly successful. The incidence of mixed marriage in the Diocese of Detroit rose from the late nineteenth century until the Depression, when it steadied at what Catholic spokesmen regarded as an unacceptable rate. A good many individual Catholics clearly moved with some ease beyond the Catholic world the bishops nurtured.

As a group, however, Catholics found it difficult to come to terms with the non-Catholic majority in Detroit and the rest of the Archdiocese. Although the city had been founded by Catholics, who dominated its political and social life into the early nineteenth century, the politics of Detroit by the 1850s were deeply colored by anti-Catholicism. Virulent anti-Catholicism was episodic: the debates of the 1850s were revived in the 1890s and again in the early 1920s. But anti-Catholic sentiment was an important political reality in Detroit and Michigan until the Great Depression, when Catholics — mainly Democrats in a traditionally Republican state — inherited political power. Anti-Catholicism had economic as well as political consequences: some local employers in the nineteenth century refused to hire Catholics, and discrimination in public and private employment lingered in some cases into the twentieth century.

Still, despite a history of mistrust and conflict, Catholics and non-Catholics in the Archdiocese developed over the years a tradition of cooperation that worked effectively to avert communal violence. Interreligious cooperation in Detroit occurred mainly in charitable work, and generally involved Catholics who were relatively well-to-do. But in the countryside and in small towns, precisely where we would expect to find the most entrenched anti-Catholic sentiment, there was in the late-nineteenth and early-twentieth centuries a remarkable degree of Catholic-Protestant cooperation in civic and even religious life. The history of this "practical ecumenism" in the rural portions of the Archdiocese and the rather different course of Catholic-Protestant relations in Detroit is an important topic, and will be examined in some detail. I will look too at the important effects of war on intergroup relations, and on Catholics' sense of themselves in relation to the world around them.

The book that follows has three sections, each divided into chapters of varying length that deal, respectively, with the growth and administration of the Archdiocese in a particular period, with the education and work of the clergy in that same period, with religious and social life in the parish, with Catholic schools and colleges, and with the relationship of Catholics to the larger society. The first section of the book covers the history of the Diocese of Detroit from its founding in 1833 to the resignation of its third bishop in 1887. Since these are years that Father Paré's history discusses in detail, my treatment of them is relatively brief, although it incorporates new research and deals with topics not found in his book. Readers who want an extensive account of the institutional development of the Diocese in these years are referred to Father Paré's excellent volume.

The second section of my book covers the episcopate of Bishop John Samuel Foley, who came to Detroit in 1888 and died in 1918. His long tenure spanned important transitional years in diocesan history, when significant changes occurred in many areas of Catholic life. The third section deals with the episcopates of Foley's successor, Bishop Michael Gallagher (1918–1937), and of Cardinal Edward Mooney, who followed Gallagher and died in 1958. Their episcopates saw the Church in the Archdiocese achieve the maturity in its organization and the discipline in its religious practice that were its hallmarks on the eve of the Second Vatican Council. A brief epilogue attempts to describe the sea change in the Church in Detroit after the early 1960s, but since the personal papers of

Cardinal John Dearden (1959–1980) are not yet open for research, this section of the book is best described as a quite speculative essay.

I should like to speak briefly to the sources on which this book is based. The papers of Detroit's bishops, housed in the Archdiocesan Archives in Detroit, are, on the whole, disappointing. Many documents from the early episcopates have been lost, apparently due to careless management in the distant past. A good portion of the Gallagher papers, moreover, were probably destroyed deliberately, presumably because of Gallagher's close association with the controversial Father Charles Coughlin. The Cardinal Mooney papers are voluminous and contain much of interest with regard to his work as chairman of the Administrative Board of the National Catholic Welfare Conference, but rather less of interest with regard to his work in the Archdiocese. Had I been inclined to write a history that focused principally on the lives and achievements of Detroit's bishops, I would have found it difficult to do so.

More fruitful were the collections of parish records housed in the Archdiocesan Archives, and the records, although often incomplete, of the various Catholic organizations that were active in Detroit. The sheer volume of parish material meant that while holdings for individual parishes might be limited, I was able to compile a good deal of information about parish life and the lives of the clergy. The *Michigan Catholic* was useful in this respect as well. A weekly newspaper that began as the *Western Home Journal* in 1872, the *Michigan Catholic* was lay owned and edited until 1920, when it was bought by the Bishop of Detroit. Especially before the First World War, the paper was a source of lively information about parish social and devotional life, and about the work of local Catholic organizations.

The Archdiocesan Archives contain relatively little material on parochial schools before the 1950s. But fortunately the Sisters, Servants of the Immaculate Heart of Mary of Monroe, Michigan, have maintained an excellent archives, and because they have been, since shortly after their founding in 1845, the largest teaching order in the Archdiocese, their files are an invaluable source of information about Catholic education in Detroit and Michigan. Similarly, papers at the Reuther Archives in Labor and Urban History at Wayne State University in Detroit supplemented the limited material in the Archdiocesan Archives on the Association of Catholic Trade Unionists and the work of various "labor priests" in the 1930s and after. Of no less value, particularly for understanding the education of the clergy and the religious experience of the nineteenth-century laity, were books and documents housed at Notre Dame University, at Sacred Heart Seminary in Detroit, at the Motherhouse of the Sisters of St. Joseph at Nazareth, and at the Michigan Historical Collections in Ann Arbor.

No body of sources, however, could do justice to an institution as large and as diverse as the Catholic Church in the Archdiocese of Detroit. There were Catholics in all social classes and in nearly all occupations. There were immigrant Catholics, poor and despised, and Catholics descended from the founders of Detroit. There were devout Catholics, and Catholic families that produced, generation after generation, sons for the priesthood and daughters for the convent. And there were Catholics who seemed largely indifferent to their religion, whose family traditions were informed more by anticlericalism than by loyalty to the Church. To define these disparate human beings as a community and to attempt to write their collective history was a perilous venture, to be undertaken with good stores of humility and scholarly caution. But it was undertaken too with the conviction that their shared religion, even when lightly valued, gave the varied Catholic population something powerful in common. Ultimately, the venture proved to be as fraught with pleasure as with peril, for the variety of Catholic life in the Archdiocese was, for me, a source of continual delight. I wish my readers the same pleasure as they turn to this story of Catholics "such as they are — very good, good, indifferent, bad, very bad, and the worst," as Father James Ronayne wrote — about his own parishioners — in 1911.[3]

PART I

1833–1887

1

THREE BISHOPS

The Diocese of Detroit was created by Pope Gregory XVI on March 8, 1833, in belated response to the promptings of Cincinnati's Bishop Edward Fenwick, OP, whose domain, before his death in 1832, had included the Michigan Territory. The new Diocese was coextensive with that Territory, which in 1833 encompassed what is now Michigan and Wisconsin as well as a portion of Minnesota. The land was still mostly wilderness, the only access to much of it being by water, and the Catholic population was widely scattered.[1]

In the area that is now the state of Michigan, there were in 1833 perhaps as many as 15,000 Catholics. The majority were French-speaking, for the great migrations that brought thousands of Irish and German Catholics to Michigan had not yet begun. There were enough Irish and German Catholics in Detroit in 1834 to require an English and a German sermon every Sunday at St. Anne's Cathedral, but they were not yet sufficiently numerous to support their own parishes. A sizable minority in the Catholic population of the Diocese were Indians, living mostly in the northern half of Michigan and in Wisconsin. Their presence was a vivid reminder that the United States was mission territory, and that the priests and bishops who served there needed to be gifted linguists, physically strong, and tempermentally able to minister to congregations from widely varying cultures.[2]

The priest chosen to head the new Diocese of Detroit, Father Frederic Rese, would seem to have been an ideal choice as a missionary bishop. Born in Vienenburg in north-central Germany, Rese was orphaned early in life and raised in poverty. He was apprenticed to a tailor while still a boy, practiced his trade as an itinerant journeyman, and later fought in the Napoleonic Wars. At the age of twenty-five he decided to become a priest, although his scant education had hardly fitted him for the seminary. Advised that a willingness to serve in the foreign missions might make him acceptable to the College of the Propaganda at Rome, Rese traveled on foot to that city, where he was ordained in 1823. Fluent by then in French and Italian, he was subsequently sent to an African mission. His normally robust health, however, could not withstand the climate there, and in 1824, having met Bishop Fenwick in Rome, he came to Ohio to minister to German-speaking Catholics.[3]

Bishop Fenwick soon discovered in his new recruit a considerable administrative ability. Father Rese served as secretary to the bishop, and then as vicar-general of the Diocese of Cincinnati. He was Fenwick's principal intermediary in Rome in the later 1820s, and played a major role, in 1828, in the creation of the Leopoldine Society—an organization, based in Germany and Austria, that raised generous funds for missionary work in North America. It was Father Rese whom Bishop Fenwick dispatched on an extensive visitation of the northern missions of the Diocese of Cincinnati in 1830. And when Bishop Fenwick died of cholera, it was Father Rese who was named administrator of the Cincinnati Diocese.[4]

It was no surprise, then, despite his youth—Rese was only forty-three in 1833—that Frederic Rese was chosen first bishop of Detroit. He arrived in Detroit on January 7, 1834, having been consecrated in Cincinnati several months earlier, and evidently found a warm welcome. But he did not find a prepossessing see city: Detroit in 1834 had a population of perhaps 4,500. There was only one Catholic church in the city, St. Anne's, which, modest though it was, had necessarily to be made the cathedral. As for the episcopal residence, it was a single-story frame dwelling, where, as Rese wrote in 1834, he lived "with three priests . . . and with four seminarians, a cook, a handy man and a carpenter." However unaccustomed these arrangements must have been for the new bishop, coming as he did from an established Catholic center at Cincinnati, they seem in keeping with the ambience of early Detroit, with its small log and clapboard houses, its plain commercial buildings, and unpaved streets too often deep in mud.[5]

Bishop Rese was apparently undaunted by the meanness of his new surroundings, and his early months in Detroit sparked notable Catholic activity. The cathedral was renovated, and a church was bought for English-speaking Catholics in the city. Plans were made to establish a third parish, this time for Germans, and steps were taken toward the eventual establishment of a Catholic paper. In all these activities, the Bishop's leadership seems to have been an essential element. Father Florimond Bonduel wrote glowingly of Rese's work early in 1834: "Since the appointment of our Reverend Bishop . . . we have witnessed a flourishing revival of religion. . . . What a magnificent future lies before us!"[6]

For all its auspicious beginning, however, Rese's was a failed episcopate. By 1837, he was in such serious trouble with certain of his fellow bishops that he tendered his resignation to the Holy See. That resignation was accepted in 1840, apparently against Rese's wishes. The hapless Rese did remain Bishop of Detroit by title until his death, in Germany, in 1871. But he had long since ceded full authority over the Diocese to his successors.

The reasons for Rese's essentially forced resignation are virtually impossible to discover. Almost no documents survive from his years in Detroit. Relevant documents do exist in Rome, for the Rese affair was twice deliberated in the Congregation for the Propagation of the Faith—commonly called the Propaganda. But these documents speak in vague and contradictory terms about

Rese's character and his performance as bishop. All that we know with much certainty is that Rese had managed to antagonize a number of influential churchmen both at home and abroad.[7]

There is fragmentary evidence to suggest that Rese had also alienated certain of his own clergy. "The person in question is not overburthened with probity and consequently no slave to truth," Father Stephen Badin wrote of Rese in 1840, "he is rather conspicuous for human wisdom and policy than the simplicity of the dove." Father Badin's grievances were vague indeed, although he clearly held Rese responsible for a crisis in diocesan finances that was acute by 1840. Other priests agreed that Rese was devious and excessively ambitious; like the Badin complaints, their assessments are vague although the bitterness is palpable. Against this, however, we must set the testimony of Father John DeBruyn, a vicar-general under Rese, to the Propaganda in 1839. Father DeBruyn had observed his bishop "at close range for many years with a sort of distrust." But he had "never been able to discover in him any canonical cause that would suffice to have him removed from his position."[8]

Some resentment of the young bishop by his clergy was probably inevitable. Rese had come in 1834 to a frontier region whose priests had been accustomed to a fair degree of independence, and it is likely that any first bishop would have had difficulties with the clergy. But the slight evidence that remains to us suggests that something in Bishop Rese's personality worked to heighten, intolerably for some, the natural tensions that prevail when new authority relations are established. Perhaps his evident ambition for himself and his diocese provides a clue. Rese had hoped to succeed Bishop Fenwick in Cincinnati, then a diocese of greater wealth and prestige than Detroit. Upon coming to Detroit, he was quick to establish — or to try to establish — those institutions appropriate to an old and well-developed see: a college, a young ladies' seminary, a Catholic newspaper. In the process, he may well have been financially imprudent, and less than attentive to the counsel of his priests.

Bishop Rese's time in Detroit was too brief to encompass a significant growth in the local Church. Indeed, quite apart from his own crisis of leadership, his tenure spanned a period when the obstacles to growth were formidable. A devastating cholera epidemic swept Detroit in the summer of 1834. About 700 people died, and economic life took months to recover. The growth of the Church was also restrained by financial panics in 1837 and 1839, by the deep economic depression of the early 1840s, and by a still very limited Catholic immigration into the state of Michigan. Detroit was a frontier trading post and Michigan a mostly impenetrable wilderness for the whole of Rese's episcopate.

Still, Detroit was able to support a second parish by 1835. This was Most Holy Trinity parish for English-speaking Catholics, whose rolls in 1840 contained the names of 202 heads of families, nearly all of them of Irish birth or descent. No separate parish was established under Bishop Rese for Detroit's German Catholics, although a small group of German immigrants had built a log chapel east of the city in the early 1830s. The Chapel of the Assumption, as it was called, was visited by traveling missionary priests and by Father Martin Kundig from Detroit. From this rough country church grew Detroit's Assumption (Grotto) parish.[9]

Outside Detroit there was equally limited progress. Only one priest was resident in the sparsely settled region between Detroit and Port Huron. South of Detroit, along the Detroit River and Lake Erie to the Ohio border, were a string of French settlements, but only two churches—at Monroe and at Erie—in 1833. By 1840 there were two more—a church dedicated to St. Vincent de Paul and a log chapel at Swan Creek—but neither had a resident priest. Catholics living near Ecorse had also organized themselves as a congregation, hearing Mass in a private house when a priest was in the neighborhood.[10]

West of Detroit, the mainly Irish settlements in the vicinity of Ann Arbor were served for most of the 1830s by priests from St. Patrick's parish in Northfield. But in 1839 Father Thomas Cullen moved his residence to Ann Arbor, where St. Thomas parish eventually became one of the more important in the Diocese, located as it was near the state's oldest and most prestigious public university. West of Ann Arbor there were only two resident priests in the interior of the state of Michigan in the 1830s. One was based at the Indian mission in Grand Rapids, the other at Westphalia, a German Catholic settlement that gained a resident priest in 1839.[11]

Bishop Rese did oversee the founding of the first Catholic church in Milwaukee—St. Peter's Church in 1839—and, largely through the efforts of the remarkable Father Frederic Baraga, some extension of the Indian missions in northern Michigan and Wisconsin. He can also take credit for the addition of perhaps five priests to the local clergy, raising the total of priests in the Diocese to something like twenty-two. The best efforts of this small group, however, could have relatively little effect in so vast a diocese as Detroit. A good many Michigan Catholics in the 1830s had only infrequent contact with a priest.

A successor to Bishop Rese was not named until the summer of 1841. He was Peter Paul Lefevere, already a veteran of the North American missions, but living now in Belgium. Having accepted appointment as Administrator of Detroit and Coadjutor Bishop with right of succession, Lefevere left for the United States in the fall of 1841. He was consecrated at Philadelphia and then made his way to Detroit, arriving in the city a few days before Christmas.[12]

The long absence of a bishop from Detroit had worsened the financial troubles that were Rese's legacy to his young diocese. Bishop Rese had bought a good deal of land in and around Detroit, apparently intending it as future security for the local Church. But he incurred a heavy debt as a result, and a heavy tax burden as well. By the late 1830s, moreover, Rese's relations with the various European mission societies were seriously strained—and it was on the gifts of those societies that the Diocese had largely depended. What limited charitable and educational work had been begun under Bishop Rese was mostly abandoned in 1840 and 1841. Bishop Lefevere thus came to a diocese that was deeply in debt and nearly as underdeveloped as it had been at its founding.[13]

Fortunately for the new Bishop, the Diocese of Detroit was to become much smaller geographically during his years in office. The creation of the Diocese of Dubuque in 1837 had already removed from his jurisdiction the portion of Minnesota initially given to Detroit; the creation in 1843 of the Diocese of Milwaukee would remove the territory that is now Wisconsin. And in 1852 the Vicariate of Sault Ste. Marie — later the Diocese of Marquette — was established, encompassing the Upper Peninsula of Michigan. Frederic Baraga, first bishop of Marquette, also assumed responsibility for the Indian missions in the northern counties of the lower peninsula. Within little more than a decade of his coming to Detroit, Bishop Lefevere was left with a manageable diocese — at least in a geographic sense. Still, throughout his long tenure, Lefevere headed what is best described as a missionary see.

That long tenure was by all accounts a successful one: it is Bishop Lefevere who is properly credited with laying the institutional foundations of the Church in the Diocese of Detroit. Circumstances did work to favor him. Heavy Catholic immigration into Michigan after the mid-1840s gave Lefevere a base of support for institution building that his predecessor never had. This new Catholic population, however, was mostly poor and ethnically divided; much still depended on the quality of episcopal leadership. And Lefevere possessed the requisite gifts of mind and heart. Like Bishop Rese, he was young and vigorous and adept at languages, but he was also modest in his vision of the future and, for the most part, sensibly accommodating in his dealings with the clergy and the laity.

Born in Belgium in 1804, Peter Paul Lefevere was the son of a prosperous farmer. He entered the preparatory seminary in his native town of Roulers at the age of sixteen, and in 1825 went to Paris to study in the Lazarist seminary. The Lazarists were active at this time in the Diocese of St. Louis; the young seminarian, acquainted with their work, decided to serve in the American missions. He finished his theological course at the Barrens in Missouri, was ordained at St. Louis in 1831, and began his missionary career, serving first at New Madrid (Missouri) and then, from 1833 until 1838, as pastor of the Salt River mission, a vast tract of wilderness in Missouri and Illinois. Father Lefevere worked there alone, almost continually on the move — "so much so that in the course of the year I cannot remain one week steady at home." It was a life of great physical hardship, requiring enormous stamina, personal discipline, and a deep devotion to pastoral duty.[14]

Lefevere continued very much the pastor during his years in Detroit and seems never to have been much interested in the pomp and privileges enjoyed by bishops in more established sees. (As late as 1855, he was attributing belated correspondence to having been "much engaged in the Confessional.") He lived simply, almost austerely, and kept to a strenuous round of pastoral obligations. Fittingly, he appears to have contracted his last illness while traveling among the Indian missions in the outlying portions of the Diocese. The *Western Catholic* remembered him at his death in 1869 as "one of the kindest men it has ever been our fortune to know."[15]

But if Lefevere was the kindly pastor, he was also a fierce ascetic. In this sense he was a divided man. In 1850 he warned his flock against the evils of social dancing—it was, he paraphrased Cicero, the worst of vices—and reminded the faithful that "the world is hastening to its perdition" and that "the greater part of even Christians will be lost." Let us conform our lives to the Gospel, the bishop urged—"that Gospel which commands us to mortify all our senses . . . that Gospel which promises the Kingdom of Heaven only to those who do themselves violence." Five years later, however, writing to Cincinnati's Archbishop Purcell, Lefevere favored a gentle approach to Catholics entering mixed marriages. "We cannot oppose them with harshness without doing an immense injury to religion." With a certain rueful insight he added, "I feel obliged to confess that, although in all my ministry, either as priest in the mission or as bishop, I have always labored hard in dissuading Catholic parties from engaging [*sic*] into mixed marriages, yet I say it with grief, I have never to my knowledge succeeded in one single case."[16]

Undoubtedly Lefevere, like most bishops, tended to address the public in uncompromising terms, saving his nuanced views for personal correspondence. But the whole of the record that survives from his episcopacy suggests a tension in the man between the fierce, almost self-immolating religious sensibility of the missionary and the compassion and tolerance of the good pastor. Perhaps his success as a bishop lies here. He worked doggedly at imposing discipline on the clergy—and, to a lesser extent, on the laity—but seemed instinctively to know the extent to which he might reasonably expect complaince. (In the view of his successor, Lefevere was too lax.) But Lefevere was able, as his successor was not, to expand his own authority without causing deep and lasting divisions between the bishop and his priests. This was an important achievement, and one not approximated by every prelate of his time.

Lefevere's preoccupation with discipline was a natural outgrowth of frontier conditions. In the absence of strong episcopal authority the clergy and laity in the Diocese of Detroit had grown accustomed to a generous autonomy in parish life. Fundamental to the success of his episcopate, Lefevere believed, was a sustained challenge to that autonomy; he was determined to secure for himself and his successors the undisputed right to make decisions about the location of churches and schools, their cost and design, and to be regularly informed about the financial and spiritual health of the various parishes. The struggle was by no means over when Lefevere died in 1869. But the bishop had succeeded by then in establishing the mechanisms by which effective episcopal authority could be wielded and in legitimizing, for most of his flock, the rights of the bishop as defined in Church law.

Establishing the legitimacy of strong episcopal authority was, in Lefevere's view, fundamentally a spiritual endeavor, at least when it came to the laity. Piety and deference to episcopal authority were virtually synonymous for the bishop, who complained in 1847 of "infidel Germans" in Detroit who "want to have the Church and its management in their own hands." It made sense, then, to adopt the long view where the laity were concerned, to avoid confrontation and concentrate instead on reviving religious devotion. But certain challenges to episcopal authority required immediate action. These mainly involved efforts on the part of laymen to vest title to parish properties in themselves — generally as a corporation — rather than in the bishop. Lefevere insisted from the outset that all property bought for Church purposes be ceded to him — to be held in his name in trust for his successors — and would not give permission for any construction where this was not done. The building of St. Mary's Church in Detroit, the first church in the city for German-speaking Catholics, was delayed for more than three years because of bitter controversy within the congregation over whether or not to grant the bishop title to the land on which the new church was to stand.[17]

The one parish where Lefevere could not demand his "rights of ownership" was, ironically, his cathedral. St. Anne's parish was a legal corporation, governed by a board of lay trustees. Those trustees had leased the properties of the parish to Bishop Rese and his successors, but they were still a troublesome lot, at least from a bishop's perspective. Bishop Lefevere dealt tactfully with the group during his first years in Detroit. As soon as he could afford to, however, he began to build a new cathedral, one that was wholly under his control. This was the church of SS. Peter and Paul. Built on Jefferson Avenue between 1844 and 1848, it served as Detroit's cathedral until 1877.[18]

Bishop Lefevere succeeded in 1867 in having his status as sole owner of church properties in his diocese recognized and protected under Michigan law. His main concern by this time was not his ability to compel the laity to surrender title — "I now hold the most of the Church property here, in fee absolute," as he wrote to Archbishop Purcell — but the safe bequest of that property to his successor. The law passed in 1867 has governed the tenure of Church property in the Diocese to the present day, although it was challenged on a number of occasions — by disgruntled Catholics as well as Protestants — in the late nineteenth century. Those who objected to the law were championing an essentially congregational model of the Church, where the authority of the bishop was limited largely to doctrinal matters and the management of a few diocesan institutions. Bishop Lefevere and his successors, however, did not doubt that such an understanding of the Church was, even in the democratic atmosphere of nineteenth-century America, wholly incompatible with Catholic teaching.[19]

Lefevere's essentially monarchical vision of the Church had implications for the clergy as well as for the laity. The bishop was naturally anxious to recruit priests into his sprawling and underdeveloped diocese. He was even more anxious to impose on those priests a view of the Church — and of their own role in it — that embraced the legitimacy of a strong and centralized episcopal authority. The conditions of frontier life, however, made both objectives hard to achieve. Many priests were unable or unwilling to endure the hardships of service in missionary dioceses; some who were recruited into the Diocese of Detroit served only a short time before they left. The number of priests in the Diocese had shrunk to perhaps fifteen in 1842, and Bishop Lefevere was probably correct when he said that many of the Catholics in his charge had "not seen a clergyman for some number of years."[20]

Frontier conditions also made for clerical independence. Most priests worked alone, far from Detroit, and were often on the move around a mission circuit. Bishops, in such circumstances, were apt to be dim and distant figures. Knowing this to be the case, Bishop Lefevere in 1843 issued the first diocesan regulations, to which he periodically added. (Lefevere's regulations were the heart of the code that governed the Diocese until the 1960s.) Lefevere's priests were soon required to report annually—and in careful detail—on parish finances and spiritual life, and to conform to the rules laid down for priests at the provincial councils of Baltimore and Cincinnati.[21]

The convening of the first diocesan synod in 1859 was the culmination of Lefevere's efforts at forming his clergy into a loyal and disciplined body. The bishop's conciliatory side was in evidence here: he assured the assembled priests that he would not remove pastors from their parishes save for grave canonical reasons. And he announced the establishment of a board of consultors—an advisory body to the bishop and a means by which he might keep abreast of the needs and grievances of his clergy. Neither reform was a radical one. But Lefevere's clergy still had reason to be grateful, for the law governing the American Church in 1859 gave virtually no rights to priests. As a missionary nation, in the eyes of Rome, the United States was subject until 1907 to the governance of the Propaganda. The American bishops possessed in the circumstances an ill-defined but seemingly vast authority, at least with regard to their priests. That authority was not necessarily as great in practice as it looked to be in theory. But it was great enough to cause considerable trouble in the nineteenth century between the American hierarchy and more restive members of the clergy.[22]

Like most bishops, Lefevere regarded a diocesan seminary as critical to the promotion of clerical discipline—and critical too as a stimulus to religious vocations. Accordingly he opened a seminary in 1846 at his new episcopal residence. Nine students were enrolled there two years later. Household seminaries of this sort were common in antebellum America—Bishop Rese had trained seminarians at his residence—and Bishop Lefevere himself was probably a principal instructor. St. Thomas Seminary, as Lefevere had christened it, survived until 1854, when the still-small number of seminarians from the Diocese began to be sent to schools at Cincinnati, Bardstown, and Baltimore. A seminary was apparently too costly an undertaking for a diocese as poor as Detroit. And Bishop Lefevere was probably disappointed that it had drawn so few local students.[23]

There were plentiful vocations to the priesthood, however, in Lefevere's native Belgium, and he had friends among that nation's bishops. As a consequence, the Diocese of Detroit imported priests and seminarians from Belgium for nearly the whole of Lefevere's episcopate. (Thirty-nine of the eighty-eight priests in the Diocese in 1870 were Belgian-born; only six had been born in the United

States.) The "Belgian connection" was strengthened especially after 1857, with opening of the American College at Louvain—an institution that Lefevere was instrumental in founding. The first four rectors of the college were priests who had served with Lefevere in Detroit.[24]

Lefevere seems not to have worried that his Belgian priests came to a diocese where there were few Belgian Catholics. His Belgian clergy spoke French, and he encouraged the study of English and German during their seminary years. Catholics had a right to a priest who spoke their language, in Lefevere's view, but not to a priest of the same ethnic origins. "I know, as you say, that some Irish have complained about their not having an Irish priest," he wrote to Covington's Bishop Carroll in 1861, "but I must say with you, that such complaints are unjust and unreasonable: they cannot but proceed from a spirit of irreligion and of the most loathsome pride." Lefevere does not appear, however, to have been anxious to Americanize his polyglot flock. He demanded loyalty to the Church—no ethnic allegiance could be prior to that—but did not see his mostly immigrant clergy as agents of assimilation.[25]

The development of the Diocese under Bishop Lefevere was made possible in part by his recruitment of priests, but was caused more fundamentally by heavy Catholic immigration into Detroit and Michigan. Irish immigrants came in large numbers after 1847, followed shortly by even larger numbers of Germans, about one-third of whom were Catholics. From 1860 until 1890, Germans were the largest foreign-born group in Detroit. The city itself increased in population from 21,000 in 1850 to 80,000 in 1870. Catholics were a substantial minority in the city by the early 1850s.

As the Catholic population grew, so too did the number of Catholic churches. There were only two Catholic churches in Detroit in 1841; by 1869, the year that Bishop Lefevere died, there were nine. Four of these—St. Mary's (1843), St. Joseph's (1855), St. Anthony's (1857), and St. Boniface (1869)—served German-speaking Catholics. (St. Anthony's served a rural population east of the city proper.) Three others—St. Patrick's (1862), St. Vincent's (1866), and Our Lady of Help (1867)—joined Holy Trinity parish as English-speaking—in fact, Irish—congregations. Bishop Lefevere's cathedral was, effectively, a fifth parish for English-speaking Catholics, one favored especially by the well-to-do. French-speakers, however, were a dwindling portion of the city's Catholic population. No French parishes were founded in Detroit during the Lefevere episcopate.

Outside Detroit, church growth was equally impressive. The *Catholic Almanac* for 1840 lists thirty churches in the Diocese. By 1870 there were seventy churches—these with resident priests—and at least as many missions. Many of these new congregations were multiethnic, especially outside the larger towns. "In almost all the parishes or missions which are now to be supplied," Lefevere noted in 1866, "a priest who does not speak the English and the German, and in many places also the French, could but be of little use."[26]

The development of the Diocese before 1870 was confined mainly to the southern half of the Lower Peninsula, for vast stretches of the north were still heavily forested. But in its southern reaches, the map of the Diocese was, by 1870, surprisingly well filled in. Parishes had been established in those villages and towns that would become, in time, small cities along the principal rail and highway routes between Detroit and Chicago. A resident priest was sent to Marshall in 1852, to Kalamazoo in 1856, to Jackson in 1857, to Ypsilanti in 1858, and to Battle Creek in 1869. Hudson had a resident priest by 1859, Adrian by 1865, and Coldwater by 1867. A second parish was established at Monroe, south of Detroit, as early as 1846. A resident priest was sent to Flint in 1848, to Pontiac in 1851, and to Port Huron in 1857. During the Lefevere years, then, the institutional Church in southern Michigan assumed in rough outline the shape it bears today. New parishes were to appear, the parochial school system was still to be built. But subsequent development proceeded mainly from the growth of centers already settled.

The bishop's death, on March 4, 1869, brought the fruitful Lefevere era to a close. He was succeeded by Caspar Henry Borgess, former chancellor of the Archdiocese of Cincinnati, who came to his new see city in the spring of 1870. A protégé of Archbishop Purcell, Borgess was apparently recommended for Detroit on the strength of his administrative record. He played almost no role in the ecclesiastical politics of the period; insofar as he did, he is best described as a cautious proponent of Americanization.

It was as an administrator that Borgess made his most enduring contribution to the church in Detroit. He had a passion for order and system far greater than that of his predecessor. Although he was bishop in Detroit for only seventeen years, Borgess convened five synods (a subsequent synod was not held until 1944), extended the scope of diocesan regulations, laid the foundation of the parochial school system, and established a diocesan seminary. He instituted a system of parish taxation to support the perennially struggling orphanages. He established the first Catholic school board and tried, though without success, to impose a uniform curriculum on the schools.

The Borgess years, however, are notable for conflict as well as achievement. In his single-minded pursuit of order, Bishop Borgess embroiled himself in a series of acrimonious disputes—with both the clergy and the laity. Ultimately he resigned his office, in April 1887. It was not without cause that he wrote to the bishop-elect of Davenport, in 1881, "to express my heartfelt sympathy for the crown of thorns in store for you."[27]

The man who became Detroit's third bishop was born in 1826, the son of tenant farmers in Westphalia. The Borgess family emigrated to the United States when Caspar was twelve; they lived for a time in Philadelphia and then in Cincinnati. It was at this latter place that young Caspar attended St. Xavier's College and Mt. St. Mary's Seminary. He was ordained by the then Bishop Purcell in 1848, and eventually—in 1860—named chancellor of the archdiocese. For the next ten years, until his appointment as bishop, he worked in the Cincinnati Chancery, helping to administer a diocese that was both older and more thoroughly organized than Detroit. His experience there may have caused him to underestimate the difficulties he was to face as he tried to extend and consolidate episcopal authority in his new diocese.

Borgess was apparently an intensely private man, reserved—even cold—in his public demeanor. Probably because of this, his friendships in the Diocese seem to have been quite limited. He preferred seclusion to what he called "the endless turmoil of city life," and in 1880 bought a villa on the shores of Lake St. Clair, where he generally spent much of the summer. He was certainly hard-working—even his detractors conceded that he was a conscientious bishop. But his solitary preferences meant that he was sometimes wholly out of touch with the life of the diocese he governed—and at a time when the population of that diocese was becoming more heterogeneous. On more than one occasion, ill-informed judgments on the bishop's part exacerbated the already troublesome conflicts in which the Chancery was engaged.[28]

For all his reserve, however, Borgess was a man whose faith was animated by an ardent spirituality and who was capable of great kindness. "After my ordination, and before receiving my appointment to a mission, I staid with him for a few days," the future Monsignor Frank O'Brien remembered of his bishop after Borgess had died in 1890. "I served his Mass in the little chappel and he in turn served mine. Just from the Seminary, I was at first somewhat embarrassed having the bishop serve my Mass, but observing his manner of earnest fidelity to his task, I could not help admiring him. After supper he invariably invited me into his room to have a social chat up to the time of retiring. On these occasions he would talk about his childhood days, his parents, his College and missionary life as familiarly as only a man of generous and unsuspicious nature could do."[29]

Borgess was also a conscientious family man, corresponding regularly with his siblings and their children. It was as "Uncle Caspar" that he played host to the teenage daughters of a widowed sister in the summer of 1883, when he endured—as bishops rarely do—the trials of adolescent loutishness. Borgess endeavored at the close of that memorable summer to correct the more egregious faults of the two girls, perhaps the most thankless task he undertook in the course of his episcopal career. "When coming into the house, the bonnet—cape—shawl, etc. must not be thrown onto the first convenient place," the Bishop pointed out, "but at once taken to the right and proper place where they belong."

> In the private room the wearing apparel must not hang about on chairs and remain unfolded, but be carefully put into their own proper place, and properly folded. Waste articles, such as paper, cords, prices of muslin, etc., must not be thrown on the floor of the room and left to the servants to pick up in vexation. Above all a person should never lay down on the top of a bed with dirty shoes on her feet, soiling the white spread on the bed, and giving unnecessary hard labor to the servants.[30]

It was to the elder of these nieces that Borgess wrote, in the fall of 1883, a series of letters on the spiritual life that illuminate, as no other documents do, his own religious sensibilities. Neither girl had impressed her uncle with her piety: "They speak of religious matters in as indifferent a way as they would of any other ordinary disagreeable or painful duty. The spirit of a conscious-living-individual faith and its practices seem[s] to be entirely unknown to them." The girls' apparent lack of interest makes these letters the more remarkable, for Borgess spoke therein of highly personal matters. "No doubt, we do well," he told his niece, "if we are exact and earnest in the performance of our ordinary religious duties, such as saying our morning and evening prayers, attending Mass on Sundays and Holy days of obligation, and frequenting the Sacraments. But the Christian who contents himself with that, is too apt to grow very lax, spiritually cold, and finally so indifferent that he scarcely knows what he is doing." As an antidote to spiritual coldness, the bishop urged daily devotions, especially to the Blessed Virgin but also to favorite saints. "These special devotions of our own choosing supply, as it were, the fuel to man's interior fire of divine love, assure the graces necessary to love and serve God in the proper spirit, as well as to aid us to advance in Sanctity of Heart and mind." The Christian is thus made ready for a "frequent and devout and profitable" reception of the eucharist, "the Sacrament of Love," to which Borgess devoted his most passionate rhetoric:

> The Soul . . . now enters into the real Living Communion with her divine Spouse —
> He lives in her and she lives in Him — they are united in the most holy mystery of divine Love. . . . At this moment the devout Soul is in possession of Him who is her only and supreme source of happiness in this life, and who, freed from the humble Sacramental veil, will fill her with insatiable delight in the mansion of never ending love. It is heaven on earth for the truly devout Soul — and like St. Paul she now begins to experience the longing "to be dissolved and live with Christ." No wonder, then, that the devout Soul yearns for this frequent union with her divine Spouse in Holy Communion; no wonder, that she yearns to be constantly in the midst of this flame of sweetest love; no wonder that she sobs: "Lord, my sweetest love, remain always with me!"[31]

The extravagance of the Bishop's language may disturb us today. That language, however, reflects certain conventions of late Victorian spiritual writing. Borgess's more pious contemporaries would have been familiar with the style. What might have surprised Detroiters is the depth of feeling in the letters, Borgess being so reserved a man in his public and even his private relations. (Significantly, he advised his niece on her spiritual life by mail rather than in person.) Borgess was in fact a man of strong emotions, capable of both intense affection and swift, almost paralyzing, anger. But his personality and his role permitted rather little in the way of emotional expression.

Perhaps this uneasy conjunction of deep inner feeling and habitual reserve provides the key to the trait responsible for both the bishop's greatest successes and his greatest failures. That trait was a veritable obsession with discipline. Borgess aspired to a more thorough control of his diocese than Bishop Lefevere had attempted and than Borgess's own successor would think possible. And he suffered more than any other bishop in the history of the Diocese from one of the most serious occupational hazards of the episcopacy — the tendency to conflate his own will and the will of God. The single most vivid instance of this dates from 1880. Thirteen altar boys from Holy Trinity parish were drowned that summer when their pleasure boat sank in the river off Detroit. Bishop Borgess, as it happened, had some years earlier prohibited parish excursions on Sundays and discouraged such outings on weekdays as well. And so the bishop concluded that disregard for episcopal authority had been the cause of the tragedy. Although the excursion had taken place on a Thursday, Borgess wrote to Trinity's distraught pastor, it had violated the spirit of the diocesan regulation. "The hand of God has chastized you for this public act of disloyalty to the Church, and given you a frightful lesson, that He does not allow his ministers to mock her authority, and thus prove a scandal to his people." Shortly thereafter, Borgess forbade parish picnics and excursions on weekdays as well as Sundays.[32]

Borgess, it should be noted, was not the only bishop in this period to restrict parish entertainments, although he was probably unusual in the scope of his prohibitions. His predecessor had forbidden Catholics in the Diocese to attend balls and dancing parties; Borgess forbade not only dancing but picnics, fairs, and bazaars under parish auspices or on parish property or under the sponsorship of lay Catholic societies. Catholics, moreover, were forbidden to attend public picnics and excursions "gotten up by others, on Sunday, Holy Day, or any other day of the week." "In the face of many lamentable facts, it is surely unnecessary to point out . . . the innumerable and not seldom unavoidable dangers to which all expose themselves by attending the pic-nics, excursions and similar public amusements," Borgess chided his flock. "The flaming advertisements setting forth the varied features of the amusements, the unseasonable hours, the unholy associations, and the several other inducements offered, furnish more than sufficient proofs."[33]

Those bishops who, like Borgess, tried to impose puritanical mores on a largely unwilling Catholic laity were motivated partly by a desire to court Protestant approval—to win respect and good will for a Church often stigmatized as a foreign institution, out of sympathy with American values. But these bishops were more fundamentally motivated by the stern moral code they shared with many Protestants. Bishop Borgess possessed as dark a view of human nature— especially the proclivity to sexual sin—as the sternest Calvinist, and his restrictions on parish life were, in his view, simply his pastoral duty. Most of the laity and many of the clergy disagreed with him, and during the tenure of his immediate successor the typical parish in the Diocese sponsored an annual round of picnics, fairs, bazaars, and card parties—and was thought enterprising to so do. But there were certainly Catholics who regarded the Borgess stand on these issues as brave and admirable.

The Bishop himself was by no means the only cause of the conflict that marked his tenure. During his time in Detroit, the pace of foreign immigration accelerated sharply and the Catholic population became more heterogeneous. The most important new group, both in Detroit and in its hinterland, were Polish immigrants, the pioneers of a migration that eventually made Poles the single

largest European-born group in Detroit. (The most damaging dispute of the
Borgess years involved a sizable segment of Detroit's Polish community.) It fell
to Bishop Borgess, moreover, to establish a system of parochial schools. Not all
parents or even all priests were initially eager to support such an expensive
undertaking.

Finally, Borgess inherited from his predecessor a lingering tension between
episcopal prerogatives and the customs of local autonomy. (The coming of new
immigrant groups to the Diocese in fact gave new life to the notion of congregational "rights.") The hand of the bishop was strengthened by the creation in 1882
of the Diocese of Grand Rapids, which left under Borgess's jurisdiction only
twenty-nine counties in southern lower Michigan—a diocese which, even in
1882, was fairly easy to traverse and which would not be further reduced in size
until 1937. "Deo gratias! that our responsibility of that vast northern region has
been removed, and put on fresher shoulders," Borgess wrote at the time. "Deo
volente, we can pay more attention to the proper cultivation of the small field
left . . . " But if Borgess was better able than his predecessors to extend his authority over his diocese, he was thereby the more likely to encounter resistance.
These would not have been easy years even for the most tactful and adept of
men.[34]

Borgess's efforts as a reformer are most fully revealed in the legislation enacted by the five diocesan synods convened during his episcopate. It was at the
various synods that the obligation of parishes to establish schools and of parents
to use and support them was formally articulated for the Diocese. It was at the
synods that the first efforts were made to ensure regular financial support of certain diocesan charitable obligations, namely the principal orphan asylums—St.
Vincent's for girls, founded in 1851, and St. Anthony's for boys, which dates
from 1867—and the small number of incapacitated and retired priests. Borgess
also used the synods to impose on the Diocese an expanded code of regulations
and a uniform liturgy, although he had only limited success in this regard. The
sixth synod, in 1885, was devoted in part to enlisting support for a new cathedral. (Borgess had surrendered the cathedral church of SS. Peter and Paul to
the Jesuits in 1877, when he brought that order to Detroit to found an academy
for boys. The bishop was seated thereafter at the exceedingly modest pro-cathedral
of St. Aloysius.) The assembled clergy voiced their support for a new and presumably much grander structure, but the project was never realized.[35]

The final synod of the Borgess years instituted certain important administrative reforms. The clerical Board of Consultors was given permanent status—this
on the instruction of the Third Plenary Council of Baltimore—and priests were
permitted to participate in its selection, a right they retained until the promulga-
tion of the 1918 Code of Canon Law. (Consultors were thereafter chosen by the
bishop alone.) The Diocese was also divided into deaneries—four were created
in addition to Detroit. The deanery was a means of increasing both the administrative efficiency of the Chancery and the ability of the bishop to supervise and
discipline his clergy. With trusted senior priests as deans, a bishop could reason-

ably expect that regulations and other Chancery initiatives would be implemented and enforced throughout the Diocese.[36]

If the synods testify to Borgess's ambitions as a reformer, the various disputes in which he was embroiled reveal the conditions that limited the extent to which reform could be achieved. With this in mind, let us look in some detail at two of these disputes. Both illustrate the resentment of that minority of priests in the Diocese who were angered by the bishop's efforts to tighten control over parish life. Both make clear that at least some of those same priests were unwilling to recognize Borgess's understanding of episcopal authority as wholly legitimate. And both disputes indicate that a portion of the laity in these same years was also inclined to question the legitimacy of a rigidly hierarchical model of the Church. Although they considered themselves good Catholics, the laity involved in both conflicts insisted that Borgess recognize, as their right, certain prerogatives which Church law clearly reserved to a bishop. They were willing to appeal, in the one case, to secular authority in pursuit of these putative rights, and, in the other, to Rome. That Borgess failed in both cases to win his objectives suggests the magnitude of the obstacles he faced as a would-be consolidator of episcopal power.

The case of Father Desiderius Callaert falls into two distinct chapters, connected only by the frustration each caused the unhappy Bishop Borgess. The Belgian-born Callaert had been ordained in 1858 by Bishop Lefevere, who had brought the young seminarian from Belgium at the completion of his studies. He served for about a year as an assistant in Monroe, and then, from 1860 to 1868, as pastor of what is today St. Patrick's parish in Carleton. He was made pastor of Immaculate Conception parish in Marshall in 1868.

Although he had served under Bishop Lefevere with no apparent difficulties, Father Callaert's independent, even arrogant ways attracted the unfavorable notice of Bishop Borgess not long after his advent in the Diocese. Callaert incurred an automatic suspension in 1873 by failing to publish in his parish the newly revised diocesan regulations, as every priest had been ordered to do. He was reprimanded by the bishop in 1874 for dismissing the sisters who taught in his school and negotiating for the services of another religious community, all without a word to the Chancery. In 1876 he was again in trouble, this time for failing to pay the assessments on his parish for the Infirm Priests' Fund and the Cathedraticum. Callaert's parish had been deeply in debt since at least 1874 and its membership had declined, although we do not know why.[37]

It was ostensibly because of this indebtedness that Father Callaert was transferred late in 1876 to Traverse City, in those days a remote mission in the northernmost reaches of the Diocese. The transfer was clearly punitive, and an angry Father Callaert appealed to Rome against the Bishop's decision. He argued that his removal from Marshall had been arbitrary, that he had been unjustly punished for a condition in his parish over which he had little control. By the standards that governed the clergy in Europe, Callaert was essentially right. But Borgess believed that the body of law governing the American Church supported his behavior in the Callaert case. And he believed that the unusual latitude granted to a bishop in the American Church was essential to the creation of a well-ordered *ecclesia* in the United States.[38]

Borgess was thus unpleasantly surprised when the decision from Rome upheld Father Callaert's argument. Since the bishop had offered no strictly canonical reason justifying Callaert's removal, he was asked by Rome to reinstate him as pastor at Marshall. Borgess did so. But subsequently, and as a direct consequence of the Callaert decision, he tendered his resignation to the Holy See, on January 31, 1879. The disposition of the Callaert affair, Borgess was convinced, had undermined all future efforts on his part to discipline his clergy.

The Borgess resignation was not welcomed in Rome, and, two months later, he agreed to withdraw it. In the interim, most of his clergy had signed a petition to the Pope, urging him to reject the Borgess resignation. Not all of them, certainly, were motivated by affection. They were worried, perhaps, that the prestige of the Diocese would suffer if its bishop resigned, and younger priests, especially, were susceptible to pressure from their colleagues. But Borgess apparently had the respect of most of his clergy. His administrative abilities were widely admired, and many priests shared their bishop's desire to bring greater system to parish and diocesan affairs. (Weak episcopal authority in certain other dioceses had led to embarrassing financial scandals and to a few scandals of an even more distressing sort.) The support of his priests at this juncture indicates that Borgess's authority had not been unduly undermined by the Callaert decision, and their support may well have persuaded him to stay on in Detroit.[39]

The logic of the Callaert decision, indeed, had little to do with Borgess personally. By the later nineteenth century, there was growing concern at the Propaganda about the incidence of conflict in the United States between bishops and priests, conflict which generally stemmed from the vague but unusually generous definition of episcopal authority that prevailed here. Hoping to resolve old disputes and prevent new ones, the Propaganda increasingly functioned as a counterweight to the American hierarchy, directing the bishops on various occasions to institute administrative reforms in their dioceses and occasionally serving as a court of final appeal for aggrieved priests—as in the case of Father Callaert. That the Propaganda sometimes upheld the priest in such cases does not indicate a particular concern for the rights of the lower clergy. It had to do, rather, with a growing uneasiness in Rome with regard to the American hierarchy, for the most prominent of American bishops in this period showed a worrisome independence of mind on such issues as church-state relations. This larger power struggle, to which Bishop Borgess and Father Callaert were momentarily parties, reached critical proportions in the 1890s, when it had notable repercussions in Detroit.

The second chapter in the Callaert case opened in 1880. Father Callaert had by then alienated at least a portion of his congregation at Marshall. Unhappy with what they regarded as his autocratic ways, these parishioners petitioned Borgess on several occasions to transfer their pastor. Borgess refused to do so until supplied with unassailable canonical grounds for Callaert's removal. Presumably because they could not force the Chancery to remove Father Callaert, some of the Marshall parishioners became active in — may indeed have initiated — a campaign to change the conditions under which Catholic Church property was owned and administered in Michigan. The vehicle of reform was a bill sponsored by James H. Campbell, member from Marshall of the Michigan House of Representatives.

The Campbell bill, introduced into the House in 1881, represents in extreme form the notion of congregational rights that periodically sparked conflict between the laity and the Chancery. Section Four of the bill stipulated that boards of lay trustees, holding office for five-year terms, "shall have absolute control and direction of all property, real and personal, held for the uses of their congregations, and may remove an occupant therefrom at their pleasure." Under the terms of the bill, the unhappy congregation at Marshall might simply evict Father Callaert — and any other priest who failed to please. Bishop Borgess, certain that the Campbell bill was "fraught with the most disastrous consequences," pledged, in the event of its passage, "the interdict of as many congregations as would introduce the system."[40]

The Campbell bill finally died in committee, a casualty of the legislature's general reluctance to intervene in religious disputes. Shortly thereafter, Father Callaert agreed to be transferred from Marshall; he served as pastor at Manistee until poor health caused his return to Belgium in the mid-1880s. A certain irony attended his replacement at Marshall by Father Peter A. Baart, soon to be widely known as an advocate of expanded legal rights for priests in the American Church and of a modified form of lay ownership of Church property. Baart's career — he died in 1908 — indicates that the issues at the heart of the Callaert case remained very much alive. The same issues, indeed, were fundamental to the most notorious conflict of the Borgess years, that series of sometimes violent events known collectively as the "Kolasinski affair."

Central to the Kolasinski case, as to the Callaert case, was the issue of a priest's right to security of tenure as a pastor. In both cases Bishop Borgess was accused of exceeding his authority by arbitrarily removing a priest from his parish. And in both cases the bishop found himself — although for different reasons — confronted by a laity possessed of a strong sense of violated congregational rights. But there is a critical difference between the two episodes. Father Callaert's opponents, most of them Irish, may have regarded him as a foreigner, but the ethnic antagonisms in the Callaert case pale in comparison to the Kolasinski crisis. Bishop Borgess was driven to his second, and final, decision to resign in good part by the seemingly insuperable troubles that followed Father Kolasinski's dismissal.[41]

The Polish population of Detroit had begun to grow in the mid-1860s. By 1871 there were sufficient numbers to support a priest — Father Simon Wieczorek became pastor of St. Albertus parish, then on the eastern fringes of the city, in September of that year. This parish, eventually the largest in Detroit, had a troubled history from nearly its beginning. Father Wieczorek was dismissed and the parish placed under interdict by Bishop Borgess in 1873, because Wieczorek and a lay committee had begun construction of a school without complying with certain conditions imposed by the bishop. A second priest, Father Alfons Dombrowski, was dismissed by Bishop Borgess in 1879, because of a parishioner's highly publicized charge that the priest had seduced his wife. (Since Dombrowski had apparently offered to pay damages to the aggrieved husband, there were grounds for the bishop's believing that the charge was true.) Many parishioners believed it too: an angry mob stormed the rectory shortly after Dombrowski's dismissal became known, intent on evicting the priest by force. Fortunately for him, he was not at home at the time.[42]

Since the parish was plunged again into turmoil in 1885, when Father Kolasinski was dismissed, we might usefully consider why it was so volatile. St. Albertus was in fact a fairly typical Polish parish. Its large congregation was composed mainly of recent immigrants, and most of these were unskilled laborers, Poles being the poorest group in Detroit in the late nineteenth century. They were an isolated group as well, more segregated residentially than any other local population. (A prominent Detroit Catholic could speak in 1891 of the "terra incognita of the Polish quarter.") Their isolation, coupled with a fierce nationalism bred of oppression in Europe, made them generally suspicious of, and often hostile to, what they regarded as "outside" authority. Life was centered on the neighborhood—on its institutions and its influential men. The priest was naturally a dominant figure in the community—a leader in secular as well as religious matters—and the church was a community center in the widest possible sense.[43]

For all these reasons, the East Side Polish community had from the beginning devoted extraordinary resources to its parish. The first church, completed in 1873, had been partly built by the men of the congregation; the second church, finished in 1885, was the largest Catholic church in Michigan and one of the most sumptuous. As was often the case in immigrant communities, the parishioners of St. Albertus developed a distinct sense of proprietorship with regard to the properties that had exacted such sacrifice. They were never disposed to see as wholly legitimate the bishop's claim to be owner and ultimate administrator of these same properties. Proprietary emotions seem also to have affected the congregation's relations with its clergy. Priests were normally accorded great deference in the Polish community. Still, certain lay leaders in the Kolasinski crisis were willing to argue that the priest's relationship to his people was a contractual one, and that the laity possessed the right to hire and dismiss the clergy.

Many parishioners at St. Albertus, then—and at other immigrant parishes too—understood Church authority very differently than their bishop did. For the most part, these divergent views had little impact on the course of diocesan history. Within the immigrant parish, the sense of lay proprietorship generally manifested itself in strong boards of lay trustees, elected by the congregation, and if this mode of parish government violated the statutes of the Diocese, even the stern Bishop Borgess was not inclined to interfere. (Pastors in immigrant parishes seem generally to have accommodated this custom, sometimes virtually ceding administration of the parish to a lay committee.) But should the Chancery impose an unpopular decision on such a parish—whether the removal of a venerated priest or the revision of a too-ambitious construction budget—this fundamental disagreement about the scope of episcopal authority could lead in short order to intransigence on both sides and to intense and bitter conflict. This is essentially what happened in the Kolasinski affair.

Father Dominic Kolasinski, a priest of the Diocese of Cracow, came to St. Albertus in 1882. His was initially a great success; even his opponents conceded his charismatic aura and his eloquent preaching. It was Father Kolasinski who induced the congregation to build the lavish church that was dedicated in 1885, when the parish counted about 7,000 members. The building of the church, however, had caused division among the lay trustees, a majority of whom believed that the debt on the new church was dangerously large. (Bishop Borgess was not, to all appearances, accurately informed about the costs of construction.) Tensions came to a head in November 1885, when certain of the trustees lodged complaints with the bishop against Father Kolasinski. The priest was accused of mismanaging parish finances, of demanding excessive fees for marriages and funerals, and charged with several counts of sexual immorality. Bishop Borgess dismissed him without a hearing, and ordered him to leave his parish at once.

The bishop's hasty action in the case—and his refusal to permit an investigation—stemmed from his conviction that Kolasinski had indeed been guilty of sexual transgressions. In fact the evidence in this regard was faulty, perhaps perjured, as a careful investigation would have revealed. Father Kolasinski was certainly a careless keeper of records, and his parish finances, by his own admission, were too confused to bear immediate scrutiny by the bishop. But slipshod records, assuming that they did not conceal dishonesty, were grounds for a reprimand rather than a summary dismissal.

Because Kolasinski was popular in the parish and because the bishop's action was widely perceived in the Polish community as unjust, there was broad support when Kolasinski called on his people to protest his dismissal. (Kolasinski also played effectively on the hostility most Poles felt for Germans, since Borgess was of German birth.) The priest himself refused to leave the St. Albertus rectory—he was guarded there for months by members of a parish military company—and he clearly helped to orchestrate the events that followed. There were violent demonstrations at St. Albertus church early in December, as large crowds of parishioners—most of them women—tried to keep Kolasinski's newly appointed successor from saying mass. The same angry mob evicted the Sisters from the parish school. In response, Bishop Borgess pronounced an interdict on the parish and announced the excommunication of all who had participated in or supported the pro-Kolasinski demonstrations.

With the church and school closed, the violent demonstrations ended. On Christmas day, however, a throng of parishioners marched to the bishop's residence on Washington Street to demand the opening of their church. Borgess refused to receive them, angering what had been a peaceful assembly, and later that day there was a confrontation between pro- and anti-Kolasinski forces in the neighborhood of the Polish church—a confrontation that left one man dead. Several of the Detroit papers blamed Borgess for this unhappy turn of events. Certainly the violence of Christmas Day doomed all chances for an amicable settlement of the dispute, at least as far as Bishop Borgess was concerned.

The parish remained bitterly divided for months thereafter. Father Kolasinski left Detroit in the spring of 1886, but armed with a testimonial from Bishop Borgess that permitted him to work as a priest in another diocese—a concession elicted by Cincinnati's Archbishop William Elder. Kolasinski went to the Dakota Territory, where there was a pressing need for Polish priests. From his parish there he wrote regularly to the now-diminished ranks of his supporters, encouraging them to prevent the reopening of St. Albertus church unless he was allowed to return as pastor. For this reason the church remained closed until the summer of 1887, rumors of its reopening having led twice in the interim to violent demonstrations. During this same period, Kolasinski's most ardent supporters organized a school, and began to gather on Sunday mornings for prayers and hymns.

By the time that St. Albertus church was finally reopened, Bishop Borgess had left Detroit, and was living in retirement at his lakeside villa. The Kolasinski trouble was certainly a factor in his resignation, which was tendered to the Holy See in January 1887 and made public early in May. But there were other causes too. The bishop had been angered by yet another effort in the Michigan legislature to place the ownership of Catholic Church property in the hands of the laity, and he was troubled as well by criticisms of his administration from dissident priests and certain lay leaders. "The best and most robust constitution cannot stand an uninterrupted battle," he explained to Cincinnati's Archbishop Elder. The Borgess resignation meant that resolution of the Kolasinski affair was left to the bishop's successor. It was John Samuel Foley who was eventually compelled by Rome to accept Father Kolasinski as a priest in good standing, although Kolasinski had been functioning irregularly as the pastor of a schismatic congregation in Detroit since 1888.[44]

Bishop Borgess did not live to see this unexpected denouement; he died on May 3, 1890. Perhaps in his brief retirement he was consoled by reflecting on his considerable achievements as bishop. He left to his successor a diocese both better organized and better developed institutionally than the one he had inherited in 1870. At the close of 1887 there were in the Diocese ninety churches with resident pastors and a total of 131 priests—roughly one priest for every 900 Catholics. There were still rural populations too scattered or too isolated to support a resident priest, but few Catholics were now denied regular access to the sacraments. And in the larger towns especially, Catholic institutional life was well developed. There were sixty Catholic schools in the Diocese by 1888, plus a Jesuit academy and college. The Diocese also boasted a minor seminary, which had opened in Monroe in 1886. This seminary, Borgess hoped, would eventually make possible a diocesan clergy that was mostly American-born.

The achievements of the Borgess years were particularly visible in Detroit, which had become by the late 1880s a manufacturing center of nearly 200,000. The city's new factories attracted an increasingly varied immigrant population, and Detroit's bishop was generous in his response: of the ten parishes organized in Detroit under Bishop Borgess, eight were foreign-language parishes. The first to be opened, in 1870, was St. Wenceslaus, for the local Bohemian population. St. Albertus parish, as we have seen, began to serve the East Side Polish community in 1871, and a second Polish church, St. Casimir's, was opened on the west side of the city in 1882. A new parish for French-speaking Catholics—St. Joachim's—dates from 1874, and Sacred Heart parish for Germans was established in 1875. The last distinctively German parish to be organized in Detroit also dates from the Borgess era—St. Elizabeth's, founded in 1884. Finally, the number of Belgian immigrants grew sufficiently in the Borgess years to warrant the establishment of two Belgian churches. Our Lady of Sorrows was opened in 1884, and St. Charles in 1887. This latter church was soon serving a multi-ethnic congregation, a sign that the city's immigrant districts were generally characterized by mobility and change.

The turmoil of the Borgess years was, then, only a part of the story. These were also years of accomplishment. By the close of the Borgess episcopate, Detroit was no longer in any sense a frontier diocese. The institutional and disciplinary foundations of the Church were firmly in place by the time that Borgess died, although his successor would discover that, in some respects, the Borgess vision of the episcopacy was not yet capable of full realization. Confiding to Archbishop Elder his reasons for resignation, Borgess had in 1887 evaluated his episcopacy with characteristic terseness. "I am proud to believe, that I will leave the diocese and hand it over to my successor in as good a condition, as an almost uninterrupted struggle of seventeen years could present it." He was right to identify his own hard work as a major cause of progress, but far too modest when it came to assessing the historic importance of his labors.[45]

2

THE DIOCESAN CLERGY: *THE FIRST FIFTY YEARS*

In 1834, when Bishop Rese first arrived in Detroit, there were probably 14 priests in his new diocese, which extended into Minnesota and as far north as Lake Superior. In 1887, when Bishop Borgess retired, there were 132 priests in the Diocese of Detroit, which now comprised just twenty-nine counties in southern lower Michigan. During this span of little more than half a century, the life and work of priests in the Diocese changed profoundly. The missionary priests of the early years lived and worked under conditions of extraordinary hardship, and with a necessarily generous degree of independence. Toward the end of this fifty-year period, both the physical hardship of priestly work and the independence possible in earlier years had been substantially reduced.

Still, even in the 1880s many of the rural clergy lived austerely, tending outlying missions — often several of these — much as their missionary predecessors had done. And most priests possessed, by mid-twentieth-century standards, a fair degree of personal independence, for most priests still worked alone. (Only 11 of the 132 priests in the Diocese in 1887 were assistant priests.) The great majority, even in the Borgess years, became pastors immediately upon ordination. Those who were assigned as assistants could expect to be pastors in no more than two or three years. By contrast, priests ordained under Cardinal Mooney (1937–1958) waited eighteen to twenty years before they had parishes of their own.

Despite the conditions that made for independence, Detroit's nineteenth-century bishops held to a view of the priesthood that centered on obedience and on a code of strictly regulated conduct. Bishops Lefevere and Borgess in particular understood the priestly life in terms of its radical opposition to life in the world. Like later bishops, they expected their priests to maintain a disciplined spirituality and to avoid close friendships with the laity, but they were more rigid in their definition of acceptable behavior for the clergy. The good priest should not drink, according to Bishop Lefevere, not even in moderation. (Bishop Borgess was willing to permit an occasional drink at the rectory, but never in the company of laymen.) The priest should not engage in sports or games — not, at least, in public — nor participate in even the most innocent of lay festivities. Pastoral visits, Bishop Borgess warned his priests, ought never to assume the aspects of a social call. The priest should not frequent theaters or music halls, no matter how respectable, nor be seen in taverns or saloons, even if he was widely known as a temperance man. The recently ordained Father Frank Kennedy gave earnest voice to the ideal in 1891: the priest must always be conscious that "he is nearer to heaven than he is to earth . . . more an angel than he is a man." Not surprisingly, the ideal was elusive of realization, at least among a portion of the clergy.[1]

We can best examine the lives of priests in the Diocese before 1888 by dividing these early years, somewhat arbitrarily, into two periods. The first, from the foundation of the Diocese until the death of Bishop Lefevere in 1869, can be seen as essentially a missionary period. The Diocese was large in these years — coextensive with the Lower Peninsula of Michigan after 1852 — and many of its priests served scattered and isolated rural populations. Under Bishop Borgess, however, and especially after the creation of the Diocese of Grand Rapids in 1882, the diocesan clergy typically ministered to well-organized parishes and to a laity accustomed to a regular religious practice, and they were increasingly brought under the effective discipline of their no-longer-distant bishop. The process of change, of course, was gradual, and did not begin abruptly with the advent of Bishop Borgess in Detroit. The clergy experienced substantial changes in their lives and work during the long episcopate of Bishop Lefevere.

The world of the diocesan priest in the 1830s, in Detroit and elsewhere on the advancing frontier, was far removed in many ways from the realities of rectory life even thirty years later. The handful of priests who worked in the Diocese in the 1830s had all been born abroad — the first American-born priest would not be ordained until 1850 — and they were variously of French, Italian, Flemish, German, Swiss, Irish, Hungarian, and Slavic origins. Their dissimilar backgrounds and training worked against the development of a clerical esprit de corps. The conditions of their work also inhibited the growth of a strong sense of solidarity. Even the priests assigned to the city of Detroit made regular journeys to Catholic settlements in the hinterland, and most of the priests in the Diocese worked alone in vast mission territories.

A number of priests who came into the Diocese in its early years, moreover, remained only briefly. Some were unable to endure the privations, both physical and psychological, of missionary work. Many others, apparently, came to Detroit and other frontier dioceses in this period to escape troubled pasts, and it was usually not long before they were in difficulty with their new bishops. Probably most were alcoholics, for whom the isolation and poverty of frontier life proved an especially powerful incentive to drink. Bishop Lefevere claimed in 1861 that he had "received not less than fifty Irish priests coming from other Dioceses, well recommended" during his years in Detroit. "But I am sorry to say that I have not succeeded with one of them, for all have done more harm than good, whilst many of them have given the most dreadful scandals." Lefevere may have exaggerated, but what was indisputably a troubled and transient element in the clerical ranks in the early years could not help but undermine whatever sense of community prevailed among priests.[2]

Priests in the very earliest years of the Diocese were not even distinguished from the rest of the population by their clothing or form of address. They wore distinctive clerical garb only in church and were customarily addressed as "Mister" rather than "Father." (This was true not only in Michigan but in much of the nation.) Beginning in 1829, the various councils of the American Church endorsed distinctive dress for priests, and the first diocesan synod in Detroit in 1859 required that priests in the Diocese wear the Roman collar in public and a black soutane that reached at least to the knees. Bishop Borgess was evidently willing to dispense at least some of his priests from the soutane for street wear, but he reminded his clergy in 1882 "that no priest within our jurisdiction is allowed to wear clothes made after the fashion of the day, and which are not of a strictly black color . . . nor is any priest dispensed from wearing the Roman collar at home or abroad." As for the manner of addressing the clergy, this seems to have changed gradually during the middle decades of the nineteenth century. As late as 1869 a petition from a parish in the northern part of the state referred to the local pastor as "Mister," but the custom of addressing priests as "Father" probably prevailed by then in the more populous portions of the Diocese.[3]

The physical hardships endured by the frontier priest were also likely to diminish, at least in the eyes of the laity, the distance between the priest and themselves. Especially outside Detroit, the early clergy seem often to have lived at bare subsistence level, sometimes in greater poverty than certain members of their congregations. Father Andrew Viszoczky, a priest from the Diocese of Szepes—then in northeastern Hungary—arrived in St. Clair in 1834 to find "a frame Chapel with a frame annex consisting of one room, the one more poverty-stricken than the other." His food that first winter was mostly potatoes and beans; "water was my drink, is yet, and likely to remain so." He lived alone—"I have no school, no school teacher, no sexton, no mass server"—and although his one-room dwelling "was not in a bad state of preservation," he was troubled by unwanted guests: "rats and mice are my fellow companions." Bishop Lefevere confessed in 1834 that "the support of the clergy in all places of this Diocese is very poor and scanty," but hastened to reassure a prospective recruit to the ranks of his priests: "A good missionary will never suffer for want of food and raiment. . . . I would rather suffer myself than see one of my clergy suffer."[4]

As the Catholic population of Michigan increased, as it did substantially after the middle 1840s, and as the economy of the state developed, the conditions of priestly work in the Diocese improved markedly. Especially in Detroit and the larger towns, priests came to live considerably better than most of their parishioners. By the later nineteenth century, the spacious, well-appointed rectory—often larger than the parish convent—was a fixture of immigrant neighborhoods in Detroit, making clear to all who passed by that the priest's status differed fundamentally from that of his flock. The salaries of priests in the Diocese—set in 1873 at $700 a year for pastors and $300 for assistants—confirmed this difference in status, for wage-earners in Detroit in the late nineteenth century rarely earned more than $500 a year, and many earned substantially less. Polish molders at the Michigan Stove Company in 1890 earned an average of only $344, although they were skilled workers in what was economically a very good year. Most of them had large families to support and, unlike their priests, all of them were obliged to pay for their housing.[5]

Still, throughout the nineteenth century the chancery had recurrent problems with congregations that could not or would not provide their priests with anything close to the stipulated salary. This was especially true of rural parishes. Frequently the parishioners were so poor that the need to build and maintain a church largely depleted their resources. Rural Catholics were often so short of currency, even later in the century, that they could pay a priest only in provisions or labor. Occasionally Catholics who had been for years without a priest were reluctant to contribute generously when a resident priest was finally assigned to them. Largely because of their poverty, rural parishes were unpopular with most priests, and were often given as first assignments to the newly ordained or, on occasion, to men who had failed—administratively or in their personal conduct—in more prosperous parishes.

A substantial number of Catholics in the nineteenth century apparently thought it right to withhold support from the parish when they were unhappy with their priest, and sometimes a disaffected minority did real economic damage. Father Edward Dumont, later Bishop of Tournai, was pastor at St. Mary's parish in Redford, then a rural settlement west of Detroit, from 1859 to 1861. The parish was poor—"there is not one rich family, and only 30 in all can be said to be in comfort"—and had sustained its share of misfortune, for the church was destroyed by fire in the spring of 1859. Struggling to raise money to rebuild the church, this time in brick, Father Dumont discovered that certain French-speaking parishioners were refusing to contribute unless the new church was built in a location pleasing to them, even though a majority in the congregation favored the existing site. The church was finally completed, in 1860, but at a heavy cost to its pastor: "I had to sell my horse, which would have been very useful to me. Besides raffling a watch left me by my parents, I have spent $700 given me by my father." Dumont lived austerely while he was at St. Mary's—"that I may not burden my people." "And when I go into the city, I remind myself that poverty is not a crime, so that I may not be ashamed of my shabby clothes."[6]

Regardless of the wealth of the congregation, the work of the priest in parishes throughout the Diocese was the same, at least in its fundamentals. Priests were expected to say Mass on Sundays at their church of residence, and, if at all possible, at the various mission churches in their care. Widely scattered or inaccessible missions were necessarily tended less often, with Mass perhaps once a month on Sunday or even at midweek. The weekday Mass was understandably unpopular with many Catholics. "We are nearly all farmers or tradespeople," a layman from tiny Portland told Bishop Borgess. "You well know how hard it is for us to leave our work for week day masses." Portland's Catholics were willing to pay generously for a Sunday Mass each month. "But no one is willing to pay for mass on week days." Still, as late as 1885, fifty-six mission churches in the Diocese had Mass on weekdays only.[7]

Priests were also expected to say a daily Mass, and there were certainly Catholics who attended these. But daily attendance at Mass, much less daily communion, was a good deal less frequent in the nineteenth century than it was in the middle decades of the twentieth. Attendance at vespers, however, was probably more frequent, save in the countryside, and priests normally said vespers in the late afternoon on Sunday. Confessions were heard at least once a week. Bishop Lefevere ordered a Detroit priest who had been neglecting his duties to be in his confessional "on all Saturdays in the afternoon and Sunday mornings, as also on the vigils and mornings of all holidays of obligation," although many Catholics in the nineteenth century confessed no oftener than once a year. And priests were always obliged to respond to sick calls, whatever the hour of the night or the rigors of the weather.[8]

Detroit's nineteenth-century bishops placed a high value on the work of their priests as religious teachers, in part because most Catholic children in this period were still without access to parochial schools. They expected their priests under ordinary circumstances to teach the parish catechism classes themselves. "I would recommend to your pious endeavors, in a special manner, the children of the Congregation, that you would spare no pains in catechising them and to habituate them to an early and frequent participation of the holy Sacraments," wrote Bishop Lefevere to Father George Godez when he assumed charge of the parish at Westphalia in 1843. Priests did indeed often teach the catechism, certainly in the parishes where they lived and sometimes in their missions too, although this work might require formidable linguistic skills. "I had catechism for children 3 times a week, in three languages, for about six months," reported the pastor at Immaculate Conception in Anchorville in 1869. (During the other six months of the year, bad weather and poor roads kept the children at home.) The nineteenth-century priest, in fact, was probably more likely than his twentieth-century counterpart to be directly engaged in teaching the young, for as the Diocese developed, the work of catechizing children was increasingly given over to women, both lay and religious.[9]

The work of the priest as a preacher also appears — admittedly on limited evidence — to have been more demanding in the nineteenth century than it would later be. Priests were not expected to write their own sermons; books of sermons for the entire Church year were readily available, Bishop Lefevere in 1858 ordering twelve copies of "short sermons by Canon Thomas." Notwithstanding Canon Thomas, however, many Catholics, especially before the Civil War, were accustomed to long sermons. Father Peter Carrabin is said to have preached to his Monroe congregation in the 1830s for close to an hour each Sunday, despite the sometimes bitter cold in his poorly heated church. He, like most of his confreres in the nineteenth century, was probably held to a fairly high standard of oratory, for Catholics were very much part of an age when oratory was something of a spectator sport. ("Although I had heard some excellent Catholic Sermons preached," a rural Michiganian wrote to his wife in 1860, "it does seam to me that yesterday I heard the Flower of them all.") Certain priests in the later nineteenth century were widely known for their oratorical skills, and were much in demand as preachers and lecturers at gatherings of local Catholic societies. The laity could not, of course, expect that their priests would regularly scale the rhetorical heights. But they evidently did see good preaching as essential to a successful ministry. The people of St. John's parish in Monroe were in 1881 sufficiently disturbed by the poor sermons of a new priest to complain to Bishop Borgess. Although Borgess seldom sympathized with complaints from the laity, he instructed the young man to improve his delivery forthwith—"the only remedy for this would be to submit to training"—and reminded him firmly that the preaching office was of immense importance. "Please, do not excuse yourself, that 'good preaching' is not 'de essentia' etc.; for we must consider the state of things as they are, and not as they ought to be."[10]

The arrival, after midcentury, of large numbers of immigrants had mixed effects on the priest's work as a preacher and teacher. There were many immigrant congregations where the long, florid sermon was immensely popular. (Father Kolasinski's initial success at St. Albertus parish had much to do with his fervid preaching.) Indeed, the centrality of oral tradition to their cultures probably disposed immigrants in a special way to enthusiasm for a vivid style of pulpit oratory. But there were many immigrant Catholics who were inclined to meet their religious obligations—when they met them at all—as minimally as possible. Father Walter Elliott, the Detroit-born Paulist, recalled in 1892 how the late Father Peter Hennaert had brought sermons to one such group of reluctant worshipers. "I remember the time when the old order began to pass away early in the fifties, and whereas it was before then the duty of all, if not by law, at least by custom and tradition, to go High Mass, a great many began to go to Low Mass." Unable to lure the mostly Irish newcomers to High Mass, Father Hennaert did his priestly duty and began to preach sermons at his low masses as well. (Other priests in Detroit soon followed his example, although the sermon at Low Mass was normally a brief instruction.) Hennaert correctly saw that the largely illiterate immigrant population in his parish had no means of religious and moral instruction other than the weekly sermon. Accordingly, he preached not only doctrine, but the application of doctrine to "practical good living"—in the words of Father Elliott—and even, on at least one occasion, to the condition of the working class under a harsh and acquisitive capitalism. "All the world, Catholic and non-Catholic, has recently been electrified by Pope Leo's great Encyclical on The Condition of Labor," Elliott pointed out. "I remember it must be more than thirty years ago Father Hennaert preaching a magnificent sermon on the condition of labor."

> I never will forget the dignity of labor as he portrayed it, the excellence of the common working man, the beauty of his family life, the right he had to fair hours and honest pay, and the protest that the little but powerful man—small in body but great in soul—made against those who poured out the sweat and blood of the common

laborer into the molds that make the coins, the millionaire. Nor was he before his
time, but just abreast of his time, and he was the one we thought over-conservative! [11]

Father Hennaert's "labor sermon" was surely not typical, either of his own
or other priests' concerns as preachers. Although there is little evidence from
the nineteenth century about the content of sermons preached in the Diocese,
most priests there, as elsewhere, probably devoted their Sunday sermons to
simple exposition of the catechism. American priests generally lacked the intellectual training—and the intellectual confidence—to move easily from the exposition of doctrine to its social and political applications. The flood tide of immigrants, moreover, many of them with little or no religious training, made the
preacher's task as a catechist seem all the more urgent. It may well be that a
small minority of the clergy were moved, in times of political unrest, to speak
to their mostly working-class congregations about trade unions, strikes, and the
various reform movements of the later nineteenth century. A number of American priests by 1905 were active opponents of socialism, and their antisocialist
sermons and lectures often included an alternative "Catholic" strategy for reform
of an unregulated capitalism. But these relatively few efforts were essentially re-
active: the nineteenth- and early twentieth-century clergy, like the clergy in the
1930s, spoke to political questions only after the rush of events threatened to win
the loyalties of many Catholics away from mainstream politics. Very possibly Father Hennaert had preached on the exploitation of labor in just such a moment
of crisis.

Indeed, the fullest flowering of priestly oratory in the nineteenth century took
place in a forum where the emphasis in preaching was almost exclusively on individual piety and moral conduct. This was the parish mission, which grew enormously in popularity in the United States in the second half of the nineteenth
century. A typical parish mission lasted about two weeks, included daily Mass
and instruction as well as an evening sermon, and was conducted by visiting
priests—usually members of a religious order. (The Redemptorists, Jesuits, and
Capuchins probably preached most of the missions in the Diocese of Detroit in
the nineteenth century.) The purpose of the mission—to stimulate remorse for
sin and religious laxity and to promote a more fervent religious practice—was
accomplished primarily through the nightly sermon, a sermon that, according
to Father Walter Elliott, "ought to be a masterpiece, arousing the emotions of
fear, reverence, awe, hatred of sin and the love of God." The mission preacher
was something of a revivalist, then, and precisely because the mission was so
emotional in its emphases, it was ideal for a frontier Catholicism perennially
short of clergy. Catholics who had no regular contact with a priest could be visited periodically by itinerant missioners, given a course of sermons aimed at reviving piety, and receive the sacraments. The intensity of the experience, it was
hoped, would keep faith and devotion alive until a priest could visit the region
again. [12]

Detroit's Bishop Lefevere was an early partisan of the parish mission. Distressed by what he saw as widespread religious indifference in his new diocese, Lefevere dispatched his own vicar-general and a Belgian Redemptorist in the summer of 1843 to conduct a series of missions in French-speaking centers. The two men traveled extensively in the Diocese, apparently with gratifying results. "Children of 16 or 17 years, born in these parts, have never seen a Catholic priest," Lefevere reported of a mission preached in the vicinity of Saginaw. "Husbands with their wives and children devoted themselves to learning the catechism, and after an assiduous preparation of eight days, all approached the sacraments shedding tears of joy." At Lefevere's urging, the Redemptorists agreed to continue the work of mission preaching in the Diocese, establishing a community at Monroe in 1844. In 1846 a quartet of German-speaking Redemptorists came to the Diocese to work as missioners with German immigrants. They assumed charge of St. Mary's parish in Detroit the next year.[13]

It was as a means of preserving the faith among scattered Catholic populations that the parish mission initially gained episcopal notice and approval. (The Second Provincial Council of Cincinnati, which Bishop Lefevere attended in 1858, was the first episcopal assembly in the United States to give formal support to the parish mission.) But as Catholic immigrants streamed into the United States in the second half of the nineteenth century, the parish mission came increasingly to be seen as a necessary adjunct to the work of an overburdened clergy, even where Catholics had regular access to the sacraments. The number of missions preached in the United States increased substantially during the 1850s, and by the close of the Civil War the parish mission was a regular feature of Catholic religious life in nearly every region of the country. Certainly this was true in the Diocese of Detroit. By the late nineteenth century, most parishes in the Diocese were accustomed to have missions every four or five years—just the interval most commonly recommended by priests on the mission circuit.[14]

The diocesan clergy did not normally preach missions, but the skill and fire of the visiting preacher offered a standard of eloquence that the diocesan clergy could hardly ignore. Those naturally inclined to extravagant pulpit oratory gained a certain legitimacy from the success of the mission preacher, for the parish mission effectively Catholicized a preaching style that might otherwise, at least in the United States, have looked suspiciously Protestant. And the demonstrable effectiveness of mission preaching emphasized the importance of the preaching office for all the clergy, even those who rarely went beyond simple doctrinal instruction in their sermons. Father Cornelius Moutard, preparing in 1865 to travel from his parish in Jackson to an infrequently visited community of Catholics at Bunkerhill, conceived of his visit as a mission in miniature, and informed the group that a course of sermons would precede administration of the sacraments: "I will not hear Confessions on Monday for I am going to preach to you for a few days and stir you up a little so that you can approach the Sacraments with a warmer heart." The parish mission, in short, may have helped to set higher standards for Catholic preaching in the United States than might otherwise have prevailed. As missions became increasingly routinized, however—and this was happening even in the 1890s—their effects on parish preaching were almost certainly diminished.[15]

Nineteenth-century priests did not invariably define their preaching role as a demanding one. But especially in the early years of the Diocese, when the shortage of clergy was acute, many priests were troubled by the enormity of the work required of them, and convinced that their best efforts could not erase what they saw as a widespread religious indifference. When Catholics could not attend Mass regularly, many priests believed, they often neglected personal devotions and eventually grew cold to religion altogether. Father Edward Dumont, pastor in 1860 of the rural parish at Redford, was especially disturbed that a generation of children had grown up in his parish without religious training or the experience of a disciplined religious practice. The Redford church had been visited irregularly by missionary priests before Dumont's arrival as pastor in 1859, and for a period of three years—evidently in the 1850s—it had been closed because of a dispute between Bishop Lefevere and the congregation. "Oh, how painful it is for a Priest to see his dear children, the only hope of his congregation, grow up in ignorance of their faith and to realize his helplessness in the matter due to lack of resources," Dumont lamented. "Children living near to Church may be taught during the week, but those living two or three miles away often do not come even on Sunday." The difficulties of life in his parish and his resentment at his often recalcitrant parishioners were at least on occasion sources of profound discouragement to the priest. "Ah for two years I have resisted what I regarded as a temptation of the devil; namely the abandoning of these children to irreligion." Nor were conditions in the city of Detroit necessarily less daunting. Walter Elliott recalled that the influx of desperately poor immigrants into the city after the late 1840s had "buried our clergy in a very deluge of incessant and terrific labors."[16]

Not every priest who served in the Diocese was able to bear the physical and emotional costs of such "terrific labors." We have already seen that many clergy—their number is unknown—remained only briefly in the Diocese. Many of these were men whose psychological troubles had been apparent long before they turned their hands to missionary work. But others may simply have been overwhelmed by the rigors of life and labor in a newly settled region. Whatever the cause of their transiency, we know almost nothing about them. About those priests who succeeded in the Diocese, who endured and sometimes thrived on the difficulties of frontier life, we know little more. Some of them were evidently possessed of a passionately ascetic religious sensibility, and in the adversities of the missionary life they found, at least at times, deep peace of soul and the realization of their longing for heroic religious commitment. Father Andrew Viszoczky, living in destitution at St. Clair, was nonetheless "well and contented," as he wrote in 1834. "Yes, far more contented than I ever was in my own native land. For what are all my sufferings compared with those of Paul?"[17]

For men of this bent, the appalling shortage of priests on the frontier was not simply a source of hardship and frustration, but a condition that gave their lives and work a singular drama and importance. Father Viszoczky remained at St. Clair for less than year, and by his own admission had only limited success with his parishioners, whom he described as "the worst possible Catholics imaginable." But he was not ultimately discouraged. Life was a fierce battle against sin, and in this skirmish the priest believed that he had brought salvation to some who would otherwise have perished. He had baptized sixty-eight persons "of various ages and classes . . . All of these would still be in the state of original sin, as the parents hereabouts care very little about having their children baptized, and one is constrained to seek for them far and wide in the wilderness." He had heard 425 confessions, "and what confessions? I too cried, at least inwardly, when I saw these hardened sinners shedding such copious tears over their past misdeeds." He had married three couples who "otherwise would undoubtedly have cohabited in an illicit manner." And he had buried fifteen of his parishioners, "who but for me would have been laid by after the manner of dead beasts." Father Viszoczky left St. Clair for the Indian mission at Grand Rapids confirmed in his priesthood and secure in his conviction that "Almighty God used me" in a vineyard with a "rich harvest, and yet so few laborers." His fellow laborer in the Indian missions, Father Louis Baroux, sustained himself in times of discouragement by seeing his work as a prelude to the eventual conversion of a continent destined to displace Europe as a center of Catholic vitality. His own weariness and frustrations were easy to bear compared to the burdens of the clergy in his native France, "many of whom see with grief the sterility of their labors." Despite the enormity of the task at hand, the missionary must "wait patiently and courageously," he counseled. "I can see in the distance a brilliant horizon expanding."[18]

We cannot understand the work of any priest apart from the faith that defines his vocation. But not all priests—nor even all missionary priests—are "souls on fire," able to thrive in difficult circumstances with few visible sources of emotional support. We must assume that most of the priests who worked in the Diocese during its first half century, like those who came after, needed the sustenance and sympathy of friends as they engaged in what was often an emotionally depleting round of work. But the early priests of the Diocese have left us few clues about their private lives. We know that the itinerant missionary priests of the 1830s and 1840s could not easily turn to other priests for companionship, regardless of the ideal of priestly friendship urged on them in the seminary. And we know that their contacts with at least some of the laity were more intimate than most priests of later generations were accustomed to, for missionaries lodged with members of their congregations when they were on the road, and often said Mass in these same houses. Father Thomas Cullen, traveling in Washtenaw County in 1836, had a church at Northfield but said Mass in private homes when he visited Catholics at Ann Arbor, Dixboro, Base Lake, and Freedom. The farmhouse of the Esper family in Greenfield, west of Detroit, was the center of Catholic religious life in the village when Redemptorist priests began to visit in 1852. The Espers' parlor served as a chapel, an adjoining room as a sacristy and confessional, and a third room as a bedroom for the visiting priest. "In this way the good family surrendered the entire ground floor of their wooden farm home for Church purposes." The family's five sons slept in the barn until a church was built.[19]

Whether the relationships that developed between priests and their parishioners under these circumstances were warm and natural is almost impossible to determine. The pious laity—those most likely to offer hospitality—may well have tended to reserve and deference, even when they knew a priest well. But a priest's desire for friendship might sometimes have breached the barrier, as might the growth of mutual trust and affection as visits continued for months and even years. Father Cornelius Moutard, who periodically visited the village of Bunkerhill from his parish in Jackson, had friendships among the mostly Irish families there which he obviously valued greatly. "I want you to come out here Easter Sunday bring some of the family along," he wrote to James Birney in 1865, "then after Mass I go with you to Bunkerhill. . . . My best respects to all my friends." He anticipated a visit in the spring of 1869 after what had evidently been an absence of some duration. "As soon as the roads are practicable I come and stay a few days." He was anxious to tend to the spiritual needs of these distant parishioners, but nearly as anxious to renew old friendships, especially his affectionate relationship with Birney. "I want to see all very much. . . . What a long long long talk we will have and what nonsense we will talk. . . . PS Jim are we getting better the older we grow . . . I think I am getting worse the old devil never sleeps I wish they would chain him up in Hell the old rascal." Father Louis Baroux, pastor in 1862 at Silver Creek in the southwestern corner of the state, expressed a similar affection for his parishioners. The parish and its missions served an unlikely population of Potawatomi Indians and Irish immigrants, who had become for their French-born pastor his only real family. "I have been established in this mission for so many years that my life has been united to theirs," he explained to a fellow priest. "I partake of their sorrows and consolations, and we, if I may so speak, have become necessary to each other, and this union makes for our mutual happiness."[20]

As the Diocese was developed after midcentury, the life of its priests, even outside the major towns, became gradually more settled. Many still tended mission churches, but these were often easily reached by train or improved roads and priests were less and less dependent on the laity for hospitality. As the number of priests in the Diocese increased, moreover, the possibilities of priestly companionship increased too. By the later nineteenth century, a growing minority had been at seminary together—always an important bond—and surely the large number of Belgian priests recruited into the Diocese by Bishop Lefevere enjoyed a natural solidarity with one another. Finally, there was an increase under Bishop Borgess in the number of priests assigned as assistants in the larger parishes, where priests lived together much as they would in twentieth-century rectories. Friendships were sometimes bred in these circumstances, and certain predictable tensions too. "He is unable to do his work," the assistant at

St. Anne's in Detroit complained about his pastor in 1885, "and however he will direct everything and he does not allow his assistant to undertake any necessary improvements."[21]

By the 1880s, then, the lives of many priests in the Diocese were notably different from those of the priests who had served there in the early years. The world of the priest in the 1880s was closer, in certain significant respects, to the clerical world of the twentieth century than to the world of the mission frontier. But even in the 1880s, most priests were probably not yet members of a well-articulated clerical subculture. There were still too few priests in the Diocese, and they were still too deeply divided by nationality. Friendship among priests certainly existed — so did rivalry and mistrust — but not many priests could confine their social lives to a world inhabited solely by other clergy. Compared to the clergy under Cardinal Edward Mooney, most of whom had attended at least minor seminary together and who served long terms as assistants, the priest of the 1880s was united to his fellows by relatively weak social bonds. To be sure, he shared with them a sense of being set apart for holy purposes. But his life not infrequently proceeded at far remove from the lives of his brother clergy.

We have already seen that bishops Lefevere and Borgess regarded the imposition of a uniform discipline on the clergy as an essential task of their administrations. They were anxious both to gain greater control over the administration of parishes and to regulate the personal behavior of priests. Neither goal was achieved quickly, but by the close of the Borgess years it was the rare priest who still contested his bishop's right to oversee parish finances. Priests of the 1880s would have been nearly as astonished as priests today by the conduct of Father Martin Kundig, who in the early 1840s founded some seventeen parishes in Wisconsin without the knowledge or approval of his distant bishop.[22]

Priests by the 1880s were also under greater contraints in their personal behavior than priests had been in the early years of the Diocese. A body of legislation governing their conduct had been promulgated by the 1860s — issuing variously from provincial councils at Baltimore and Cincinnati and from Lefevere's diocesan synods — and the standards of priestly behavior embodied in these regulations were stringent. Clergy were to wear distinctive garb at all times, to avoid saloons and taverns, as well as plays, musicals, dances, horse races, and hunting. Both bishops Lefevere and Borgess, moreover, endorsed for their clergy an ideal of priestly conduct that was even more exacting than the standards demanded by law. Lefevere was a champion of total abstinence, not only for the clergy but for the laity. Shortly after he came to Detroit, he "took the temperance pledge myself, after high mass, with my few seminarians, and had the soul-moving pleasure of being followed by upwards of two hundred of the French congregation of St. Ann." Borgess too was anxious that his clergy at least appear to be abstainers. "The zealous and prudent priest will never allow himself to be treated to beer, wine, or any liquor" when making a pastoral visit, he warned in 1876, "no matter what the real or pretended custom may be."[23]

Neither Lefevere nor Borgess was able to eliminate drinking among the clergy; like other bishops, each had to deal with a handful of priests who regularly drank to excess. But the ideal of priestly conduct so forcibly articulated by the two bishops—and imparted in the seminaries of the period—had real effect on most priests. Some internalized it completely. Many others were increasingly cautious when it came to public behavior, lest they offend the more conservative members of their congregations. It is possible too that as these stringent norms of clerical conduct were more and more widely disseminated, the conservative elements in the Catholic population may have become more rigid in what they regarded as acceptable behavior in a priest. When certain members of St. Joseph's parish in Detroit complained to Bishop Lefevere about their pastor in 1863, they were disturbed not only by his drinking—"to the great disedification of the people, you drank to excess, at the late pic-nic held for the benefit of St. Anthony's Church"—but because he played ball on Sunday, had "been seen playing at cards," and rarely said his Office. Lefevere was in full sympathy with the petitioners, warning the priest—who left the Diocese shortly thereafter—that he was forbidden by regulations to frequent taverns and saloons. "We hereby also strictly prohibit you to play at cards and other amusements," he added, "which, in this country a priest cannot do without giving scandal . . . ." An 1876 complaint, evidently from a layman, apprised Bishop Borgess that "some of the young clergymen of this city 'play at cards for money—for the sake of gain—even with laymen, and at unseasonable hours (even to 3 o'clock in the morning.)'" Borgess, in this instance less severe than his predecessor, forbade the priests in question to play cards for money or at "unseasonable hours." "It would be best," he advised, "not to play cards at all, especially with laymen."[24]

Not all Catholics were so easily scandalized, and we should not assume that every priest in the later nineteenth century felt obliged to forego cards and sports and drinking with friends—even with laymen. There is almost no evidence that bears on the question, but a 1902 letter from the Belgian-born and educated pastor of Immaculate Conception parish in Anchorville—he was ordained in 1889—expressed astonishment at rumors that his chances for securing a larger parish were hindered by "my sports of sailing, hunting and iceboating" and his fondness for poker. "I must say, I never saw a great deal of harm in it," Father Henry DeGryse wrote to the Chancery, "even thought it was alright . . . ." He knew, to be sure, that certain of his fellow priests thought differently. Father Fridolin Baumgartner, chancellor of the Diocese, had earlier warned DeGryse to give up "that foolish business of ice-boating," and DeGryse refers as well to the "friendly advice of Fr. Ryan of Pontiac to avoid that poker playing and keep away from it." Still, the Anchorville pastor seemed genuinely surprised to learn that he had jeopardized his chances for advancement. Presumably his parishioners were of the same mind, for none of them had complained to the Chancery about their pastor. Other congregations—and other priests—may have been equally liberal when it came to defining acceptable conduct for the clergy.[25]

Men like Father DeGryse might be bewildered, even resentful, at the growing reach of episcopal discipline. But probably a majority of priests in the Diocese were pleased by the progressive consolidation of authority at the Chancery. One goal of Detroit's nineteenth-century bishops was to strengthen the hand of their priests with regard to the laity. (The efforts to limit the powers of lay trustees are but one example of this.) The growth of episcopal power brought other benefits as well. It was good to know that extravagant priests would be kept from incurring embarrassing debts in their parishes, that scandalous behavior would be quickly and firmly punished. And a well-organized Chancery could provide the clergy with at least a modicum of financial security. It was Bishop Borgess who inaugurated the "Infirm Priests' Fund" in 1871, by which he hoped to support those priests who were too ill or feeble to be assigned to a parish. It is true that the fund was so poorly subscribed in its early years that it did not always provide its recipients with adequate support. It is also true that the fund had disciplinary as well as charitable purposes: stipends were available, according to the 1871 legislation, only to priests in good standing, "of which the Ordinary shall be the judge." (The fund was administered after 1878 by an elected committee of priests, but these too granted stipends only to priests whom they judged to be worthy.) Still, the fund was apparently welcomed by most priests as a source of essential protection, especially for those who served in the poorer parishes. The fund was not an entitlement, however, even for priests in good standing, and its advent did not mean that most priests could expect eventually to retire. Until a change in diocesan policy in the 1960s, retirement was something a priest requested — or was asked to take — only when poor health made the performance of his duties impossible.[26]

Those priests who did resent the growth in episcopal power might find themselves in occasional conflict with a bishop. They might complain privately to friends. But only a handful were active in the cause of expanded legal rights for priests in the American Church. Prominent among their number were two priests from the Diocese of Detroit — fathers Peter A. Baart and Charles Ormand Reilly, each of whom played a colorful role in late-nineteenth-century diocesan history. Baart, a noted canonist, was pastor at Marshall from 1881 until his death in 1908. Reilly served as pastor of St. Patrick's parish in Detroit from 1875 until 1890, and was subsequently pastor at Adrian. Both men had been born in Michigan, Baart at Coldwater and Reilly at Chelsea, and both had attended St. Mary's Seminary in Baltimore. Each had the confidence, then, that came with native birth and a superior education. Baart's considerable legal prowess and Reilly's reputation as an orator further enhanced their visibility in the Diocese, and even beyond its boundaries.

The two men came to their interest in the legal status of American priests in quite different ways. Reilly's political activities brought him into conflict with Bishop Borgess in the mid-1880s, when Reilly was serving as treasurer of the Irish National League in the United States. Borgess had ordered Reilly to quit the league post, but without success, and by 1886 the bishop was ready to suspend the defiant priest from his pastorate. To have done so would surely have precipitated a row of international proportions, as Kalamazoo's Father Frank O'Brien was all too well aware. Reilly was prepared to go to Rome to appeal the suspension, O'Brien warned his bishop. "He will bring to Rome with him, the entire weight of the Irish Hierarchy. . . . He will go endorsed by at least six U.S Bps and many priests. The war cry will be one of nationality, 'the best part of the world against a bigoted Dutchman.'"[27]

Under the circumstances, Borgess backed down, and made no move to discipline Reilly. The priest was a prominent figure in Irish-American political circles into the early twentieth century. Priest and bishop remained at odds, however, until Borgess died in 1890, by which time Reilly was already in conflict with Bishop John Foley, successor to Borgess, and himself a partisan of the Irish cause. Reilly's antagonism toward Foley, as indeed toward Bishop Borgess, had much to do with the priest's abrasive personality: Reilly was an aggressive, egocentric man, deeply resentful of any authority but his own. But he translated his essentially personal animus against his bishops into political terms, and was an ardent spokesman, not only for embattled Ireland, but for a principled defense of clerical rights against a growing episcopal power.[28]

Peter Baart, by contrast, seems to have had only passing interest in secular politics, although he, like Reilly, had a pronounced autocratic streak. His passion was the canon law. Baart was one of the few priests in the Diocese to have had any legal training, and he was, as a consequence, drawn repeatedly into disputes between Detroit's priests and their bishops. Baart was distinguished from the first by his insistence that the ill-defined rights of American priests be interpreted as liberally as possible in such conflicts, something that brought him into quick disfavor with both the bishops under whom he served. Not surprisingly, he was increasingly alienated from the episcopate and more and more committed to a generous vision of clerical rights. By the 1890s he had a nationwide reputation as a canonist, and a nationwide clientele among disaffected priests, on whose behalf he prosecuted a number of cases in American and Roman ecclesiastical courts. Still, it was no accident that several of his most celebrated cases came from the Diocese of Detroit.[29]

Baart's career, like Reilly's, is best understood in the context of a larger movement among American priests in the later nineteenth century to reform the laws governing the American Church, a movement that enjoyed some limited success, despite its small numbers. Both men defined their work in larger-than-diocesan terms, and both believed that they defended the true spirit of canon law against the autocratic vision of the American hierarchy. Both had friends and allies in many other American dioceses, and even abroad. But neither Baart nor Reilly commanded a substantial following among priests in the Diocese of Detroit. When the clergy assembled at Detroit for the Sixth Diocesan Synod in 1885 and were asked to elect a Commission of Inquiry, neither Baart nor Reilly was chosen, although the ballot was evidently a secret one. Reilly received seventeen votes, Baart only ten—well behind the leading candidates, who polled between thirty-eight and forty-nine votes each. Commissions of inquiry, established in the 1880s at the behest of the Propaganda, were meant to provide pastors with protection against arbitrary removal from their parishes by a bishop. Still, the radicals' candidacies had little appeal; cautiously moderate men were elected instead. Presumably most priests in the Diocese in 1885 had greater confidence in the judgment and integrity of their bishop than Baart and Reilly did. At any event, most were not on this or subsequent occasions prepared to endorse the openly adversarial stance of the two priests.[30]

THE EDUCATION OF THE CLERGY

We have already seen that bishops Rese and Lefevere had each maintained a seminary at the episcopal residence in Detroit, Lefevere abandoning the project only in 1854. Certain pastors in the early years of the Diocese were also involved in clerical education. "There arrived today a Seminarian who is to study his theology and teach English to the children," Father Viszoczky wrote from St. Clair late in 1834. "Indeed a great blessing for me, although all this is to be accomplished in one and the same building, and although we do not know what we are going to eat." Training of this sort was in the nature of an apprenticeship, and if it was not very thorough in an academic sense, it undoubtedly had considerable practical value. Seminarians learned first-hand what it meant to care for a parish, and had ample opportunity to be of service — to teach catechism, for example, or to accompany a priest on his round of sick calls. Ironically, the makeshift arrangements of these early years provided a preparation for the priesthood that was similar, in many respects, to what certain reformers proposed in the wake of Vatican II as healthy alternatives to conventional seminary training.[31]

Few of the seminarians in the Diocese in the 1840s and the 1850s were American-born, the great majority having been recruited from Europe. The dearth of native vocations was principally caused by the poverty of most Catholics in the Diocese in these years, and by the still-rudimentary nature of Michigan's public schools. Both bishops Rese and Lefevere required that boys have completed the study of "classics" — roughly equivalent to a high school education — before they could enroll as seminarians, and Lefevere, at least, rejected a good many applicants to his Detroit seminary. "For two years past there have been many applications of students who seemingly had all the talents and virtues required by the ecclesiastical state," he wrote in 1850, "but upon examination it was found that they had not even the most common acquirements necessary." Apparently the deficiencies uncovered "upon examination" were not only academic. Not surprisingly, perhaps, for a man who later lamented "the love of independence in this country," Lefevere regretted that all too many of these would-be seminarians "were far from having that spirit of humility, patience, obedience and disinterestedness and that truly Apostolic zeal which are so necessary in the ministry."[32]

By 1856, however, Lefevere had managed to recruit a group of acceptable seminarians from within the Diocese, and these were sent, in the autumn of that year, to St. Thomas Seminary in Bardstown, Kentucky. The bishop himself accompanied the group on its journey, though it was hardly necessary for him to do so, since the boys ranged in age from thirteen to twenty-one. (The mix of ages at the Bardstown seminary was typical of many American secondary schools and colleges in this period.) Six of the Bishop's young recruits were of German birth or descent; two were Irish. Four of the eight eventually served as priests in the Diocese of Detroit, two of them having completed their seminary training at the American College in Louvain.

Bishop Lefevere apparently provided tuition and living expenses for each of these students out of diocesan funds, although the Diocese was still in precarious financial health. "For the future I wish you would not charge to my account anything extra which the children do not absolutely need," he wrote to the Superior at Bardstown in 1857, "such as pocket money, skates, etc., for if these children want anything extra they can easily write for it to their parents and friends." He had written in a similar vein in 1855 to a student whose expenses he was paying at St. Mary's Seminary in Baltimore, gently reminding the youth that poverty had spiritual benefits: "Your merit will be the greater before God and your preparation for his holy ministry all the better for it," adding in characteristic fashion, "I send you $20 to buy what you absolutely stand in need of, but endeavor to economize as much as possible." Neither the bishop's generosity, however, nor his paternal concern for his seminarians resulted in an appreciable increase in vocations from the Diocese in the 1850s and the 1860s. The great majority of priests in the Lefevere years were born and trained abroad.[33]

Bishop Borgess arrived in Detroit in 1870 determined to reverse Lefevere's policy of looking to Europe for clergy. He withdrew diocesan support from the American College at Louvain, and at the Third Diocesan Synod, convened in 1873, he led the assembled priests in a resolution to begin an annual seminary collection, monies from which would provide for the education of local seminarians and eventually for the establishment of a diocesan seminary. The collection yielded only modest sums at first — just over $4,000 in 1873, slightly more than $5,000 in 1875. Because of this, Borgess in 1876 inaugurated the practice of devoting a full month to soliciting contributions, the pastor in each parish being required to appoint lay canvassers to make a house-to-house collection. (This was the manner in which the seminary collection was subsequently taken until it was discontinued in 1920.) There were fifty seminarians in 1876 who were studying for the Diocese of Detroit, the majority of them at diocesan expense. They represented a considerable drain on the bishop's slender resources, and this in turn made it hard to put money aside for the purpose of opening a seminary in the Diocese itself. For most of the Borgess years, as a consequence, Detroit's seminarians were educated elsewhere. In 1876 they were studying at Mt. St. Mary's near Cincinnati; at St. Francis in Milwaukee — then a distinctively German institution; at Assumption College in Sandwich, Ontario; at prestigious St. Mary's in Baltimore; and at St. Vincent's College in Westmoreland, Pennsylvania.[34]

Still, the annual seminary collection did increase after the mid-1870s, and the bishop's dream of a seminary in his own jurisdiction was finally realized in 1886. St. Francis Seminary opened in Monroe in September of that year, under the rectorship of Father Peter Leavy. The initial enrollment was only thirty-five, but the school grew rapidly, with close to 180 students reportedly attending classes by late 1887. The institution was something of a hybrid: it served not only as a preparatory seminary, but as a much-needed secondary school for Catholic families in and around Monroe. Probably a majority of its pupils had no particular interest in the priesthood. Nonetheless, the school was conducted along the rigid lines of a minor seminary, and the faculty consisted of priests from the Diocese and of advanced theological students, whose stint at St. Francis substituted for a portion of their time in major seminary. The faculty lived on the premises, although each of the priests was also responsible for parish work in the vicinity.[35]

For all its promising beginning, however, St. Francis Seminary had only a brief life. It was simply too expensive to sustain, even though the seminary building itself had been donated to the Diocese. Bishop Borgess was too firmly committed to the seminary to see matters in this light, but his successor was of a different mind. Bishop John Foley decided in the spring of 1889 to close St. Francis Seminary permanently. It had already proved difficult to staff the school with a competent faculty, he pointed out. It withdrew priests from full-time parish work, although the Diocese was short of clergy. It deprived the theological students on the faculty of necessary academic training. And it was much too costly. The expense of maintaining the seminary, Foley noted at the time, "is eating up the seminary fund and makes it a question of a few years when we would be forced to close it or place an extra burden on the diocese to sustain it." The closing of St. Francis left the Diocese without a seminary of its own until 1919, shortly after Foley's death, when his successor opened Sacred Heart Seminary in Detroit.[36]

Bishop Borgess had surely known that his seminary would cost the Diocese dearly. By his lights, however, the expense was an essential one. Like many of his episcopal confreres, Borgess took seriously the injunction of the Council of Trent to establish a seminary in every diocese. A measure of ambition and vanity was naturally involved: a bishop's prestige was gauged in good part by the completeness of institutional development in his diocese. And Borgess was motivated, as other bishops have been, by the hope that his own seminary, closely governed, might generate students who embodied as fully as possible his own understanding of what a priest should be. It was Borgess himself who drew up the rules for faculty conduct at St. Francis, and he kept a careful eye on the day-to-day workings of the institution.[37]

The seminary faculty, under the bishop's rules, were to offer an example of highly disciplined piety to their students. "All the Professors must attend all of the spiritual exercises of the Seminary." These included morning prayers and a half-hour meditation in the chapel before Mass, a visit to the Blessed Sacrament at noon "at which one of the Professors may read aloud from the 'Visitete' by Liguori," and evening prayers followed by "strict silence." The faculty were also to give an example of priestly obedience: "If any one of the Professors desires to leave the premises of the Seminary grounds, he must first inform the Rector of his intention, and name the place he wishes to go. If the Rector gives an advice to the applicant, it would be cheerfully obeyed." Borgess never expressed more succinctly his conviction that the good priest was before all else a man of thoroughly regular life and willing obedience to ecclesiastical authority.[38]

The faculty at St. Francis, however, were no more easily ruled than faculties generally are, and the bishop was soon imploring them to set a better example. "Recalling all permissions given by us to any one of the Professors, we beg of you to insist that they all rise in the morning at the appointed hour, and attend morning prayers and meditation, and that no exception be made except in case of real sickness," he wrote to the rector in the winter of 1887. Members of the faculty were traveling to Detroit entirely too often, he continued. "Once a month we would consider too frequent, except for very good reasons." Professors were, moreover, leaving the seminary on private errands, in casual and apparently habitual disregard for the rules. "Finally you will not permit a Professor to go out after dark, unless there is good reason, and you know where he is going." The rector had also ignored certain instructions of the bishop with regard to curriculum. "We regret to learn that the class on 'politeness' has not been regular and that 'on singing' has not even been begun." Whether Borgess was devoted to liturgical music we simply do not know, but his concern for his seminarians' deportment was of long standing. Distressed by an 1882 encounter with a student from the Diocese who "proved to be as void of 'good breeding' as an Indian," he had urged the rector of St. Francis Seminary in Milwaukee to prescribe for his students a well-known manual of priestly conduct. "The world has a right to expect a priest to be a gentleman in the true sense of the word."[39]

Monroe's St. Francis Seminary, then, proved to be for Bishop Borgess yet another bitter reminder that the powers of the sternest bishop are limited by circumstance and the stubborn individuality of the human beings with whom he must deal. It never became the model seminary he envisioned, and he himself lived to see its demise. But Bishop Borgess did assist at the birth of a seminary that has survived to this day, and one that has played a significant role in the history of the American Church. This was the Seminary of SS. Cyril and Methodius, opened in Detroit in 1886 to train students of Polish birth or descent for priestly work among Poles in the United States.[40]

The idea for the seminary and much of the work that attended its founding belonged to Father Joseph Dombrowski, a Polish-born priest who had come to the Diocese of Detroit in 1882. Dombrowski approached Borgess early in 1884 with a request to locate a "College for the Poles" in Detroit, assuring the bishop that funds for the College would come from the ordinaries of the many dioceses that would need the services of its graduates. Borgess gave a ready blessing to the project, and followed the plans for its development with considerable interest. His enthusiasm had much to do with the difficulties he was currently experiencing with Father Kolasinski and his supporters in St. Albertus parish, as Borgess explained in an 1887 letter: "You are, no doubt, familiar with the storms, riots, scandals, murders etc. among the Polish Catholics in the United States, caused by the bad priests of their nationality. This can only be remedied by the education of young men to the priesthood in America." In what was apparently an effort to ensure a rigorous regime at the new seminary, Borgess tried to secure Polish Jesuits for its faculty, but without success. Even *sans* Jesuits, however, the "Polish Seminary," as it was called locally, proved to be a source of well-disciplined priests, most of them as loyal to their bishops as they were to the Polish language and culture in which they were carefully instructed. The seminary, which remained under the rectorship of Father Dombrowski until his death in 1903, moved to its present site at Orchard Lake, Michigan, in 1910. Even in Cardinal Mooney's time, seminarians of Polish descent in the Diocese were frequently sent there for a portion of their training.[41]

The quality of Catholic seminary education in the nineteenth century has often been characterized as narrow and parochial — very nearly anti-intellectual in its indifference to the life of the mind. "The ecclesiastical seminary is not a school of intellectual culture, either here in America or elsewhere," Bishop John Lancaster Spalding pointed out in a famous sermon at the Third Plenary Council. "Its methods are not such as one would choose who desires to open his mind, to give it breadth, flexibility, strength, refinement, and grace." Spalding was under no illusion that the seminary could be easily reformed — he was making the case for establishing a Catholic university — and most of his fellow bishops had such need of priests that they were more than satisfied if the seminaries produced large numbers of reasonably competent and obedient men. Bishop Lefevere revealed the low priority he had necessarily assigned to advanced theological study in an 1863 letter to the rector of St. Francis Seminary in Milwaukee. "I should have been glad and anxious to comply with your wishes by returning Rev. Mr. Schmittdiel to the Seminary for six months longer; but the great want of Clergymen compelled me to ordain him priest and send him on the missions," he explained. "However in consideration of what you wrote to me I have sent him to Monroe in a small German congregation, for the time being, where he will have plenty of time to review his Theology, and where there is a good experienced priest and great Theologian whom he may consult every day." Bishop Borgess, for his part, seemed concerned mainly that his students adhere strictly to the rules of whatever seminary they attended. "If you find, that Mr. D.M. Laughlin was really under the influence of liquor," ran a typical Borgess letter, "you will please dismiss him from the Seminary, because if a seminarian cannot resist the temptation, knowing it to be the sure cause of expulsion, he is not fit to enter the holy ministry." The "spirit of obedience" was "the essential requisite" for the priesthood, Borgess told a seminarian in 1879. The "intellectual culture" that Bishop Spalding proposed for an elite among American priests was, in Borgess's view, utterly unnecessary in ordinary pastoral work. Nearly all of his fellow bishops agreed.[42]

The bishops assembled at the Third Plenary Council did, however, inaugurate two reforms that were meant to promote a modest spirit of study among the clergy. The first required an annual examination for all priests who had been ordained less than six years. The second directed the bishops to hold conferences for the clergy in their dioceses four times each year, at which priests would discuss a variety of topics in dogmatic and moral theology, Scripture, canon law, and liturgy. The junior clergy were to be examined annually in each of these subjects, and in Church history as well.[43]

The quarterly conferences were duly begun in the Diocese of Detroit early in 1887, with Bishop Borgess presiding at the inaugural conference in each of the deaneries. But the conferences were unpopular with many of the clergy, who apparently regarded them as irrelevant to pastoral work, and a waste of time and money. The deans were eventually obliged to institute fines for unexcused absences, which nonetheless remained a problem until the conferences were quietly abandoned in the first decade of the twentieth century. Nor did the junior clergy much like their annual examinations, or perform therein with any particular facility. "Enclosed please find my report of the Examination papers written by the young priests of the diocese," wrote Father Ernest Van Dyke to the Chancery in the fall of 1887. "I find it extremely unpleasant to submit to you my personal and private criticism of the same. Many of the papers actually raised feelings of grief at the low standards of their authors in matters of the gravest importance to themselves and the souls committed to their charge." Still, there is evidence to suggest that bishops Lefevere and Borgess were not necessarily wrong to discount intellectual attainments in their seminarians. Several of the priests who failed their examinations in 1887 had fruitful careers as much-admired pastors.[44]

The young priests struggling with their examinations in 1887 were far removed from the world and the consciousness of the missionary priests who had worked in the Diocese just fifty years earlier. They were probably closer in many ways to the expectations and assumptions of those priests who would be ordained fifty years later, in the midst of depression and rumors of war. But these young men still possessed an important bond to their missionary predecessors — the bond that invariably connects one generation of priests to the next, although that bond is stronger at certain times and places than it is at others. Recent studies have shown that the example and encouragement of priests they admire is an important — often the most important — spur to vocations among young men. And even in this early period in the history of the Diocese, when the number of priests was relatively small, it is likely that one generation of priests inspired the next, both in the realization of a vocation and as it was lived in adulthood.

Certainly this was true for Walter Elliott, the well-known Paulist, who was born and raised in Detroit. His pastor there was Father Peter Hennaert, who had come to Detroit as a seminarian in 1845 and remained until his death in 1892. Elliott came home to preach at Hennaert's funeral, where he eulogized him as the inspiration of his own vocation and of his mature priesthood:

> And I would remember, O, so tenderly, how eloquent he was, not only from the pulpit, but upon the altar. As far back as I can trace the very beginnings of my own vocation, a drawing from the world to the priesthood, the very first element that attracted me were the musical tones of Father Hennaert's voice singing the plain chants of the Church, so humble, so religious, so elevating, so plaintive, so eloquent were they. I can remember on one occasion, when during Holy Week, I think Palm Sunday, he passed down in the procession of the palms through the aisle, and as he came next to us in the pew I heard his voice singing and it seemed to sink in my heart. It seemed to lift my thoughts above the common-place things, even of the religious world, to place in its language a standard which, alas, I am yet far from reaching.

Here is a reality which transcends the economic, social and demographic changes that transformed the Diocese and the lives of its clergy over the course of a scant half-century. Elliott understood, as should we, that without an appreciation of this reality the history of the Church in Detroit cannot be fully comprehended.[45]

3

RELIGION AND PARISH LIFE:
THE EXPERIENCE OF THE LAITY

For the historian, the laity are an even more difficult group to study than the clergy. They are a more varied population, for one thing: the laity includes women and children as well as men, a broad range of occupations, and widely varying degrees of wealth and status. And if the ethnic variety in the laity is often replicated among the clergy, the laity bear a more complicated relationship to the institutional Church than the clergy generally do. There are devout laypersons; there are those — normally the great majority — who perform the required religious observances but betray no ardent attachment to the Church; and there are those who are alienated from or indifferent to the Church into which they were born. To make matters more difficult, individuals may be, over the course of their lives, indifferent or lukewarm Catholics at one period and quite fervent Catholics at another. The lay state may be succinctly defined in canon law, but in the flesh the laity are so diverse that it is extremely hard to generalize about their experience of the Church.

The evidence that might illuminate even isolated portions of that experience is, moreover, none-too-abundant and often flawed. We rarely hear our forebears among the laity speak of their faith or the Church in their own words. Most often we see the laity through the eyes of the clergy, in parish reports, for example, which are among the most numerous documents relating to nineteenth-century parish life. But the clergy tend to see the laity in terms of their own particular values and expectations, and the conclusions they draw are not always apt. A priest is likely to assume that Catholics whose religious observance is neither as regular nor as recollected as he has been trained to expect lack faith as well as interest in religious questions, although this may not be true. His definition of moral conduct may be too narrow to permit him to make adequate judgments about the behavior of the laity, most of whom govern their lives by standards that deviate in important ways from the standards taught the clergy. We should not discountenance priests' testimony when it comes to parish life; it is often of great value. But we should understand that such testimony sometimes tells us nearly as much about the clergy as it does about the laity.

We can look to the records of social and devotional organizations in the parish for indirect testimony to the faith of at least a portion of the laity and to their understanding of the Church and its place in their lives. We can look as well at the churches they built, for these churches both reflected and helped to shape the faith and religious practice of the laity over many generations. We must remember, however, that not all Catholics, nor even most Catholics, were active members of Church organizations at any point in their lives. Nor are church interiors, no matter how evocative, necessarily adequate representations of the faith of every member of a congregation. There are many religious sensibilities that can legitimately be accorded a place in the Catholic tradition, and if we can predict with some confidence that ethnicity, social class, age, and gender will predispose a person to a particular set of religious attitudes and practices, the matter is still very much an individual choice.

Despite these daunting problems of definition and evidence, it is still possible to trace, in broad outline, two important lines of change in the experience of the nineteenth-century laity. The first — and the more significant — concerns the gradual incorporation of ever-growing numbers of the laity into a disciplined religious practice. In the earliest years of the Diocese, as we will see, large numbers of Catholics only rarely attended Mass and received the sacraments, and, in the view of the clergy, at least, many of them were ignorant of the basic tenets of their religion. But as the number of priests in the Diocese grew, and as churches and schools were built, more and more Catholics were able to attend church regularly and to educate their children in the faith. By 1887, at the retirement of Bishop Borgess, the majority of Catholics in the Diocese lived within reasonable distance of a church with a resident priest. Most of them were regularly present at Mass and, at the very least, they fulfilled the obligation to go to confession once a year and receive communion in the Easter season. A growing minority, moreover, were conspicuously devout, many of them active in the various devotional confraternities that spread throughout the United States during and after the mid-nineteenth century.

The second area of change concerns the relationship of the laity to the parish as a social rather than a religious institution, and to the priest in his administrative rather than his sacramental role. Every bishop who has served in the Diocese — and especially those who served during the years of heavy foreign immigration — has been confronted by demands from the laity for greater autonomy in the governance of the parish than the bishop has been willing to allow. These demands have always been premised on the assumption that the laity, because they support the parish financially, have the right to govern its "temporal affairs" with little or no clerical interference. "The Church belongs to the Congregation," according to an 1869 petition from Alpena. "We have built the Church with our own money or hard labor." The sixty-three laymen who signed the petition were unhappy with their pastor and wanted him replaced; should Bishop Lefevere fail to send them an acceptable priest, the petitioners threatened to withhold support from the parish and force the closing of the church. "Mr. Murry says he is stationed here for Life (now God forbid) but should this be the case, we now write in sorrow and humility, we would endeavor to have the church shut up."[1]

The understanding of Church authority that animates the Alpena petition was the understanding that had fueled the well-known struggles over trusteeism in eastern dioceses before the Civil War. And it was an understanding that was very much alive, especially in the Midwest, in the second half of the nineteenth century. It was partly the product of frontier conditions: a generous definition of the role of the laity in parish affairs usually developed in the absence of a resident priest, or where the authority of the bishop was so weak or distant that priests had no effective allies as they attempted to consolidate their own authority. For a variety of reasons, moreover, many immigrant Catholics held to similarly liberal views on matters pertaining to parish government. Thus, despite the growing numbers of priests and the increasingly effective reach of episcopal power, the role that the laity might play in the parish was a source of conflict, not only in Detroit but in most other dioceses, even as late as the Second World War.

But it is nonetheless true that the tendency of the laity to assert their putative authority in the Church declined markedly over time. Immigrants were generally more interested in who would govern the parish than their children were, and considerably more interested than their grandchildren were likely to be. The coming of a resident priest to a hitherto isolated mission nearly always resulted in the eventual ceding of a good deal of administrative authority to that priest, or at least to his successors. And social mobility nearly always meant a growing indifference to matters of parish governance. By the 1920s, what we might reasonably call a tradition of democratic parish government survived mostly in working-class parishes with substantial numbers of immigrant members. The wealthiest parishes, on the other hand, were invariably among those where the authority of the priest in the administrative sphere was virtually never challenged.

Broadly stated, then, the laity after the mid-nineteenth century were increasingly likely to be regular in their religious practice and to cede authority to the clergy in ecclesiastical matters. From the perspective of the Chancery and the rectory, this would seem to constitute a heartening progress: it is not too much to say that over time an essentially clerical vision of the Church gained ascendance among large numbers of the laity. But at the same time, the laity were much affected by changes in the world around them. The United States between the mid-nineteenth and the mid-twentieth centuries evolved into a thoroughly secular society. No matter how hard Catholics tried to build institutional and intellectual barriers between themselves and that society, they never fully succeeded. Thus Catholics, like other Americans, were deeply affected by the process of secularization, both in terms of the beliefs they held and the behavior they accepted for themselves and others. The clergy were naturally affected by the same broad currents of social change, but to a much lesser extent, for their training did not change appreciably from the mid-nineteenth to the mid-twentieth centuries. Their lives after ordination, moreover, became in this period gradually more isolated from the world of the laity. The gulf between lay experience and the intellectual world of the clergy was widening, then, especially after the turn of the century. The tensions bred by this uncomfortable reality help to explain the rapidity of change in the Church in the years after Vatican II.

SACRAMENTAL PRACTICE AND DEVOTIONAL LIFE

A good many Catholics who lived in the Diocese of Detroit in its earliest years had only occasional access to the sacraments. Even in 1860, there were no more than forty-three priests at work in the Diocese, which then encompassed Michigan's entire Lower Peninsula. Such circumstances were hardly propitious for the maintenance of faith, but there were numerous Catholics, apparently, who retained a deep devotion to the Church, despite their isolation on the Michigan frontier. "During my sojourn in Detroit," the Redemptorist Father Simon Saenderl recorded in 1832, "Germans have come to me daily, of whom the majority have not been to confession for years since there is no priest for them. Here and in the neighborhood the Germans are so numerous that we preach to them in German every Sunday to their great joy." His colleague, Father Francis Xavier Hätscher, had much the same experience: "Every Sunday I teach catechism and preach to the Germans living in the woods. . . . When I go out on a missionary tour five or six of them accompany me on horseback so that they may freely converse with me about their spiritual welfare."[2]

Still, there were many Catholics for whom the absence of an organized religious life led eventually to religious indifference, or so most missionary priests believed. Father Andrew Viszoczky was horrified by the spiritual condition of his parishioners when he came as pastor to St. Clair in 1834. "They do not know the holy days of obligation, neither do they observe them, even though I announce them," the hapless priest reported. "Only a few appear at Mass on Sunday, and these too, behave in a most unbecoming manner; they neither sing nor pray, lounge about in their seats as if in a saloon, and chew tobacco; none enter the church before the Introit and leave pallmall at the last Gospel as if driven with a whip." The want of piety among his parishioners was matched by their worldliness, according to Father Viszoczky. "My parishioners are as a rule very lazy, fond of luxuries and delicacies, a circumstance which coupled with an unbridled license, produces results upon which I need not waste many words."[3]

The congregation at St. Clair in 1834 was mostly French-speaking, and their pastor evidently believed that this accounted for most of his troubles, the French inclining almost by nature to impiety and anticlericalism. Viszoczky's prejudice was widely shared: the French were regarded by the clergy in this period much as Italian immigrants would later be, and indeed in both cases it seems that the men of the group were often reluctant to go regularly to church and were wary of, if not hostile to, most members of the clergy. But priests in these early years found religious indifference and ignorance among other ethnic groups as well, and they complained on various occasions about impiety among the Germans and the Belgians and the Czechs in the Diocese, and among the increasingly numerous Irish. Bishop Lefevere himself was moved in 1862 to denounce a portion of the Irish population in his jurisdiction. They were, according to the Bishop, "men . . . who boastingly call themselves Catholics and yet who are most stupidly ignorant of the first principles and most practical part of the Catholic Religion — men who have been most grossly neglected by their clergy at home . . . men whose all and every sentiment of religion seems to be based upon nothing, but a deep-rooted hatred against England, and all other nations of the world but their own."[4]

No doubt the bishop and his clergy assessed the situation in excessively gloomy terms. What they saw as infidelity was often nothing more than ignorance and want of discipline. And not every Catholic of lax religious habits had abandoned a Christian view of life, or lost his sense of belonging to the Church. Still, there can be little doubt that many Catholics on the Michigan frontier did abandon their religion, although it is impossible to say how large their numbers might have been. Some joined the ranks of the unchurched; others became Protestants, either because of intermarriage or the availability of a church and minister in the vicinity. Among the most devoted supporters of the first Protestant church in Michigan — a Methodist church founded at River Rouge in 1817 — were two French women, both of them former Catholics who had married across confessional lines.[5]

The solution to the problem of widespread religious indifference, according to Bishop Lefevere, lay with an increase in the number of priests in the Diocese. And their numbers did grow substantially during Lefevere's tenure: in 1869, the year Lefevere died, there were 82 priests in the Diocese of Detroit, nearly double the number reported for 1860. The ratio of priests to the Catholic population may have been as low as 1 to 1,300 in 1869 and perhaps as low as 1 to 900 by 1888. Not all Catholics, however, lived in or near a sizeable center of Catholic settlement. As a consequence, there were numerous mission churches in the Diocese even in the 1880s — 104, at mid-decade, compared to only 65 churches with resident priests. And in these missions, according to the clergy, indifference and lax religious practice continued to be problems. Father Charles Bolte was typically alarmed by the adolescents and young adults in one of the missions he tended from his parish in Ionia, as he explained to the Chancery in 1883:

> I feel obliged to acquaint you with the state of affairs of St. Mary's Congregation at Otisco, it being such that it seems to me those people cannot be left without a priest on Sunday much longer without serious consequences. My week-day visits are indeed pretty well attended, but it is only by the aged and some *little* children; the young people, of whom there is a *large* number, can scarcely be prevailed upon to come, and the damaging result of their having the whole Sunday to themselves without Mass and instructions is becoming so patent already, that their parents are being justly very much alarmed about it![6]

Certainly a majority of the Catholics in the Diocese by the mid-1880s lived near a church with a resident priest. Most of the mission churches had very small congregations. And reports of laxity in the mission parishes tell only a portion of the story, for those parishes were also home to many Catholics who took their religion seriously. Both Bishop Lefevere and Bishop Borgess were acutely aware that they could not provide a priest to every congregation that wanted one. "From every part of the Country people are constantly writing and entreating me to send them a priest, saying that a number of Catholic families have settled there, and are without the help of religion, that they have built or are about to build a Church, and are willing to support a priest," Lefevere lamented in 1866. "But to my great grief I have none to hand."[7]

For most of the laity in the mission congregations, the eventual arrival of a resident priest was something to be welcomed joyfully. But there were others—a distinct minority, to be sure—who resented not only the cost of supporting a priest, but the values and habits that he represented. These were the Catholics who resisted the imposition of religious discipline, and if they were a clear minority in the Catholic population, their numbers were probably not small. So it is indicated, at least, in certain of the parish reports that have survived from the 1860s and the 1870s, wherein pastors detail their difficulties with the stubbornly irreligious. The situation at Anchorville was apparently not atypical: 1,100 persons had made their Easter communion in 1869, while 250 had failed to do so. An even larger proportion of Catholics in the missions served by the Anchorville pastor had neglected to perform the "Easter duty," and for the usual reason: "they have been, for years, without a priest."[8]

Usually those who stayed away from the sacraments were men: "very few of the female portion are neglectful," reported the pastor at St. Mary's in Monroe in 1870, and he spoke for most of his fellow clergy. But at St. Charles in Newport, where nearly 40 percent of the parish had failed to make the Easter communion in 1868, "about fifty mans and fifty womans" had not received the sacraments "for years," according to Father Adrien de Montauberg, who said Mass at Newport every other Sunday. Conditions in this mission were especially discouraging: "I have to tell you that the parents are very neglecting for the instruction of the children, and the people is generaly inclined to go ad Square [i.e., "to the Squire" or justice of the peace] for marriage. Last year 6 marriages were made by the Square." Father Louis Van Straelen of Marine City was not much more optimistic about some of the souls in his care, although in his case the members of the troublesome mission lived fairly close to the village where the priest had his residence. "My mission in Algonac is in a miserable condition," Van Straelen confided to the Chancery in 1874. "A great many don't attend when I go there, and they hardly ever come to Marine City, even when weather and roads are good and in spite of living but 6 or 7 miles from here."[9]

Even in Detroit, with its numerous parishes and Catholic institutions, there was in this period a not insignificant population of alienated and indifferent Catholics, although it is impossible to estimate its size. Sometimes the problem was caused, or at least exacerbated, by the scarcity of priests of certain nationalities. A number of Czechs in Detroit in the late 1870s stopped attending St.

Wenceslaus church, evidently because they were unhappy with their pastor, Father Wenceslaus Tilek. Of the 200 Czech families in the city in 1878, according to Father Tilek, "about 30 families attend the Church; the others are freemasons." Attendance at the Sunday catechism class at St. Wenceslaus in 1878 averaged only six children. "A many times I could not give instructions at all for want of attendance." Father Tilek had faced a difficult task upon his arrival at St. Wenceslaus in 1877: for a variety of reasons, Czech Catholics both in this country and in their homeland were easily alienated from the Church. It has been estimated that between one-half and two-thirds of Czech Catholic immigrants to the United States in the nineteenth century eventually abandoned Catholicism. But Tilek's apparently abrasive personality further diminished an already small congregation, and because Czech priests were scarce in the United States in this period there was little that Bishop Borgess could do to improve the situation. Father Tilek was assigned to a church in Grand Rapids in 1879; his former parish did without a pastor until 1884. The lack of a church for Dutch and Flemish Catholics in Detroit apparently contributed to a decline in that group's religious observance. "Of the 230 families of Dutchmen and Belgians in Detroit City, nearly 100 fell away from the Church, but can be brought back by a pastor, who will attend to their wants," according to Father W. J. Hendrickx, founding pastor of Detroit's first Belgian parish.[10]

But even among a group as well supplied with churches and priests as Detroit's Germans, there were a number of Catholics who were estranged from their religion. The success of an 1884 mission preached in St. Joseph's (German) church in Detroit was measured by the nearly 400 men "who had not confessed for periods of from three to forty years," and who, under the influence of the mission, "reconciled themselves with God and returned penitently to Mother Church." An 1884 census in the mostly Irish St. Augustine's parish in Kalamazoo revealed an alarming number of indifferent Catholics, perhaps in part because Catholics were a small and distinctly low status minority in this western Michigan town. ("Catholics to a great extent are ashamed of being Catholics," Father Frank O'Brien wrote of his Kalamazoo parishioners in 1885, "especially is this so with the young men.") There were 2,324 persons in St. Augustine's parish, according to the 1884 census. Fully 502 had not made their Easter duty for "from 1 to 30 years."[11]

Notwithstanding such gloomy reports, the clergy had, by the 1880s, lived through a transitional time in the history of religious practice in the Diocese. A majority of Catholics by then were regularly present at Mass, and the great majority confessed and received communion at least once a year. This represents a substantial change over conditions prevailing even twenty-five years earlier. A growing and increasingly visible minority, moreover, were considerably more devout. Usually members of devotional societies or confraternities, they received the sacraments as frequently as once a month, and thereby provided a model of highly disciplined spirituality to the rest of the congregation. They did not generally succeed in persuading the rest of the congregation to join them — most

Catholics in this period were content with a less rigorous practice. But this devout minority still had important effect, for they helped to alter the popular understanding of what religious behavior defined a good Catholic.

We know very little about parish devotional societies in the Diocese in the years before the Civil War. Few parish reports survive from these years, and the two diocesan papers that were founded in this period had brief lives. The *Catholic Almanac* for 1857 does note that "the 'Living Rosary' and Association of the Immaculate Heart of Mary, for the Conversion of Sinners, are established in various churches in the Diocese." And we know that the Confraternity of the Sacred Heart of Jesus had been established at Holy Trinity parish in Detroit by 1842. There may well have been branches of this confraternity in other parishes in the 1840s and the 1850s. Detroit and probably Monroe, the most populous Catholic centers in the state, supported other societies in these years too, societies of a less strictly devotional but still religious nature. The St. Cecilia Society was established in 1837 "for the purpose of organizing choirs for the Catholic churches of Detroit," and a Christian Doctrine Society was established in Detroit in 1838. This latter group had as its purpose the promotion and support of Catholic Sunday schools, a work that apparently spread to Monroe, for the 1849 *Almanac* lists Sunday schools there as well as in Detroit. The *Catholic Almanacs* from 1843 until 1858 also mention "a society among the German Catholics of Detroit, that has as its object principally to sustain their Sunday school, library, and church music."[12]

The earliest devotional societies in the Diocese probably differed little from their counterparts in the later nineteenth century, at least in terms of the goals they promoted and the spirituality they fostered. The devout among antebellum Catholics, like the devout in succeeding generations, were drawn principally to Marian and Eucharistic devotions. These stressed especially the reparation for sin — not simply personal sin but the sins of the world — that was the obligation of those relatively few Christians who were sufficiently imbued with the love of God to be more than perfunctory in their religious observance. Bishop Lefevere's warning in an 1850 pastoral letter that "the world is hastening to its perdition" and that "the greater part even of Christians will be lost" reflects the view of human nature and human society that animated these early devotional groups. This mentality was generated in part by recurrent episodes of anti-Catholic political activity in the middle decades of the nineteenth century and by the evident vulnerability of Catholics in what was still a missionary country to assaults on their beliefs and on their institutions by a confident Protestant majority. But it may have reflected deeper cultural tensions as well. American Protestantism in the thirty years before the Civil War was convulsed by a number of apocalyptic movements which proclaimed the imminent end of the world — or at the very least its utter corruption — and called a spiritual elite to lives of penance and purification.[13]

The Sacred Heart Confraternity that was organized at Detroit's Holy Trinity parish in the late 1830s or early 1840s exemplifies both this pessimistic view of

humanity and the disciplined spirituality characteristic of devotional societies
in general. Sacred Heart devotions in the United States seem not to have had
the right-wing political overtones they possessed in nineteenth-century Europe,
but the devotion emphasized consciousness of personal sin and the sins of the
world fully as much as it stressed a deep interior love for Christ in the Eucharist.
The devotee was "to make reparation for the offenses committed against [Christ]
in this Sacrament of Love" by the recitation of certain daily prayers; by special
devotions, usually including confession and communion on the first Friday of
each month; and by receiving communion with other members of the confraternity on the Feast of the Sacred Heart in June. The Feast, especially, was a
time of contrition: "On the day of the feast, approach the sacraments of penance
and the Eucharist. In your confession accuse yourself and detest your irrever-
ences and infidelities toward the most holy Sacrament of the altar. You ought
to communicate with peculiar fervor, as your intention should be to repair the
negligence and tepidity of your former communions."[14]

The devotional exercises which this confraternity enjoined not only accustomed its members to a regular sacramental practice but encouraged a devotional life that was heavily dependent on ecclesiastical authority. The devotee
was to be always conscious of his personal failings — if his conduct was virtuous
he might still lack the requisite ardor as he performed his devotions and approached the sacraments. The various exercises were presented to the devotee
as powerful antidotes to his weakness, and he was urged to follow the annual
round of minutely prescribed devotions exactly. The religious practice that resulted was not only highly disciplined but very much centered on the Church.
In varying degrees, other nineteenth-century devotional groups promoted a similarly disciplined and clerically dominated spirituality.

Parish reports from the 1860s and succeeding decades allow us to trace the
spread of devotional societies throughout the Diocese, as new parishes were
founded and an ever-increasing number of resident priests were assigned to
towns and villages across the state. Most of these priests spent considerable effort
in promoting the devotional life, for the number and size of confraternities in
his parish was a principal measure of a pastor's success. Even in small parishes,
then, the typical priest tried to establish at least one devotional society for married women and one for married men, as well as groups for single males and
females in their late teens and twenties. The clergy met with varying responses,
however, and only rarely secured a majority of adult parishioners as active confraternity members. Married women were the most cooperative group: their societies were characterized by a regular round of devotional activities, centering
mainly on the Rosary and other Marian prayers. But men, whose ostensibly devotional confraternities were in fact often Church-sanctioned benefit societies,
were seldom attracted to devotions outside of Sunday Mass. Their societies, as
a consequence, aimed mainly at ensuring that members received the sacraments
at least once a year. St. Peter's parish in Mt. Clemens was a fairly representative
small-town parish in 1870 when it supported a Sodality of the Immaculate Vir-

gin Mary for married women that claimed 104 members and a "St. Peter's Society for Gentlemen" with 45 members, which was almost certainly a benefit society. A Young Ladies Sodality had been established by 1880, but the young men of the parish, always the most difficult group to organize, had no society of their own until after the turn of the century.[15]

We know rather little about which nineteenth-century Catholics were members of devotional societies. Women were clearly attracted to such groups in significantly larger numbers than men. And certain ethnic groups appear to have supported devotional confraternities more zealously than others. German and Polish parishes in the Diocese normally sustained a wider variety and a greater number of organizations—both strictly devotional and of a more social nature—than other parishes did. Both Poles and German Catholics tended to resist assimilation with a tenacity not always possible among smaller ethnic groups, and both looked to the Church as the institution through which language and culture might be most effectively passed on to succeeding generations. (By contrast, Irish nationalists in the Diocese by the later nineteenth century had spawned a network of largely secular organizations to promote a cause which they defined primarily as a political one.) Assuming that the cultural integrity of the community depended on a broad participation in parish life, both the clergy and lay leaders among the Germans and Poles promoted membership in parish societies as a cultural as well as a religious obligation, and they often achieved impressive results. The 400 married women who were members of the Confraternity of the Holy Family at St. Mary's (German) church in Detroit in 1885 represented about 80 percent of the adult women in the congregation.[16]

Even at well-organized St. Mary's, however, women were the more active sex. Only 145 men in the parish were members of the Holy Family Confraternity in 1885. (It had 240 "young lady members" and 125 youths in its ranks.) Contemporaries would probably have attributed the preponderance of women to their "naturally" greater interest in religion, and perhaps to their role—in all ethnic groups—as the principal custodians of morality. What is striking from our own perspective is the palpably feminine tenor of nineteenth-century devotional life. The most popular observances emphasized passivity, self-abnegation, renunciation of a threatening world; the language and imagery they employed were highly sentimental. The devotionalism of the period thus celebrated virtues and states of mind that were widely considered appropriate to women, and which might easily be construed as antithetical to masculinity, even subversive of it. Then too, the domination of devotional life by women tended to be self-perpetuating, especially since women were usually the first to organize when a parish was established. Daughters learned from experience that the Church offered an acceptable arena for women's voluntary work and sociability, while their brothers often concluded that the Church was, observably, an institution to which men were attached, if at all, mainly by attendance at Mass.

That the most devout members of a parish were likely to be women created certain difficulties for the clergy. Most of them were uneasily aware that the

Church in Europe was losing its authority with large numbers of the working class and especially with working-class men, and they probably knew that many Protestant denominations in the United States were increasingly concerned about the preponderance of women in their congregations. A conscientious pastor naturally wished to encourage his parishioners to receive the sacraments regularly and to live orderly lives. But he had to be careful that he was not perceived by the men of the parish as an advocate of essentially feminine standards of religious practice and personal conduct. For much of the nineteenth century the clergy in the United States tacitly ceded the higher devotional ground to women — the disciplined religious practice they encouraged for men was nearly always less rigorous than the standards proposed for the female sex. This was less and less true, however, in the opening decades of the twentieth century, when, as we will later see, the clergy had remarkable success in raising the standards of religious practice for their male parishioners. Church-sponsored athletics and social clubs played an important role in this endeavor, which was one of the signal triumphs of the Church in the United States.

Before the end of the nineteenth century, however, the Catholic clergy relied mainly on benefit societies — as well as sermons and the good offices of wives and daughters — to bind men to the Church and to an acceptable standard of religious discipline. In a few parishes, to be sure, men were drawn in substantial numbers to societies that were purely devotional in nature. But men were much more likely to join a church society when it offered insurance benefits in the event of sickness or death — necessary protection in a world without even rudimentary social welfare programs. Probably the great majority of parish organizations for men in the nineteenth century were benefit societies, although many of these functioned as social clubs as well. And all of them had a religious component, this being the price of Church endorsement. Church-approved benefit societies in the nineteenth century required at the very least that their members receive communion in the Easter season. Toward the end of the century, reflecting a generally heightened standard of religious observance, some of these societies began to require more frequent reception of the sacraments.

The St. Joseph's Liebesbund, founded in 1856 at St. Joseph's (German) parish in Detroit, is a case in point. The society initially required that its members receive communion together at Easter; in the early 1860s, the officers expelled 22 men — nearly half the membership — because they objected to the religious character of the society and especially to the obligatory Easter communion. The Easter obligation remained in force until the mid-1890s, when the membership — now 300 strong — decided to receive communion together four times a year. The society thus endorsed, and enforced, for its members a more disciplined religious practice, and on their corporate communion Sundays those members provided an example of visibly masculine piety to the rest of the congregation. The members did not thereby identify themselves as part of a spiritual elite: the notably devout in the congregation received communion at least once a month, and probably most were women. But the men of the Liebesbund were probably more frequent communicants than their fathers had been. Their own sons, in turn, were likely to be even more disciplined in their sacramental practice.[17]

"I CAN REST SECURE IN THE CATHOLIC FAITH": RELIGIOUS EXPERIENCE IN A MICHIGAN VILLAGE

It is well to bear in mind that individual religious experience often defies easy categorization. The indisputable trend in the nineteenth century toward a more disciplined religious practice did indeed affect most Catholics, and many of them found important supports for belief in their closer ties to the institutional Church. But a deep and reasoned faith does not necessarily depend on ready access to a priest, nor does regular attendance at Mass guarantee that the worshiper knows or cares very much about his religion. He may be in church for any number of reasons, some of which have little to do with belief or a need for religious solace. Historians, however, generally work with evidence that speaks to religious behavior in the aggregate; they seldom encounter documents that illuminate individual religious experience. This is especially true of the historian whose subject is the Catholic laity in the United States, until quite recently a mostly working-class and indifferently educated population—one that has left little in the way of letters or diaries that explore religious questions. But remarkably enough, one such series of letters from the Diocese of Detroit has survived from the mid-nineteenth century. These provide a rare picture of religious life in a rural Catholic family, and remind us in an especially poignant way that the religious experience of individual men and women can never be fully understood in terms of trends in religious practice.

James Birney, one of the principals in this correspondence, was born in Vermont in 1821 of Irish immigrant parents. The Birney family subsequently moved to Ohio, and then, in about 1840, to a farm in south-central Michigan near the village of Bunkerhill. There James met Bridget McClear, born in County Tyrone in 1820, who had come to the United States with her family at about the age of twelve, and had evidently worked for a number of years in the carpet-weaving mills of Connecticut. The McClear family moved to a farm in the neighborhood of Bunkerhill in 1836, although Bridget returned to Connecticut for a stint in the mills in the early 1840s. She was by this time engaged to James Birney. The couple were finally married, in Michigan, in the spring of 1845.

James and Bridget settled in Bunkerhill after their marriage and eventually had three children—a son and two daughters. In 1858, when the youngest child was seven, James and one of his brothers left Michigan for California to prospect for gold, apparently because the Birneys were earning at best a modest living at farming. The pair made a second trip to California about one year later, and this time James's brother decided to settle there. James, however, returned permanently to Michigan in 1861, having had little success as a prospector. He lived in Bunkerhill until his death several decades later.

There were not many Catholics living in and around Bunkerhill at mid-

century: only twenty-three families volunteered to help build a church there in
the early 1860s. The village, moreover, was far away from any substantial center
of Catholic settlement. As a consequence, it was only occasionally visited by
itinerant priests between 1845, when Mass was first said at Bunkerhill, and the
late 1850s. Bridget wrote to James in 1858 that "we had the Priest here this week
for the first time in six months." Later that same year, however, the pastor at
Jackson agreed to visit Bunkerhill at three-month intervals, an arrangement that
continued until 1867, when the Jackson pastor promised to send his assistant
to the village every other Sunday. A resident priest was assigned to Bunkerhill
in 1868, but the parish reverted to mission status between 1873 and 1905, during
which time it was visited by the priest at Williamston, some fifteen miles to the
north.[18]

For more than twenty years of their marriage, then—and for a number of
years preceeding it—James and Bridget Birney lived in a village where Mass was
at best an occasional event. Their daughter Jane, born in 1846, wrote to her father after her confirmation in Jackson in 1859 that "saturday knight was the first
time that i ever was in a catholic church." It would hardly be surprising if the
Birney family had drifted away from Catholicism during these years, for Bunkerhill lay in militant Protestant territory. But James and Bridget remained staunch
Catholics, and handed on a lively faith to the rising generation. Their children's
children included two girls who joined religious orders and a boy who became
a priest.[19]

James and Bridget did, however, each pass through a period of religious
doubt early in adulthood. Bridget was twenty-three when she wrote to James
from Tariffville, Connecticut—where she was working in the mills—that she had
resolved most of the doubts which the two of them had discussed at length some
time previously. Her father had recently died, but it is not clear whether the
doubts that had troubled her concerned only doctrines peculiar to Catholicism
or the very existence of God and personal immortality. Certainly her identity as
a Catholic was at issue during this crisis. Whatever the nature of her doubts,
they had probably been resolved without the help of a priest, for there was no
priest living in Tariffville in 1843. "You will recollect that I entertained many
doubts in matters of faith," she wrote to James. "I think I can rejoice to say that
I have found a resting place for them all. I found by sincere examinasion that
I can rest secure in the Catholic faith. I am preparing to receive communion
as soon as I can." James welcomed her news and added assurances of his own:
"I think that I can tell you with pleasure that all my doubts are about to be
moved but I dont pretend to say I [k]now as mutch about it as I hope i shall
in time and soon."[20]

The young couple were aware as they wrote of certain millennial movements
in American Protestantism that had manifestations in both Tariffville and Bunkerhill. "The most talk is about the world coming to an end," James informed
Bridget. "Som[e] are very strong in the believe. . . . Theire has been grate re-
vivels round this place." The general religious excitement may have caused both

James and Bridget to question childhood beliefs hitherto rather uncritically accepted; it also seems to have caused them to wonder whether Protestantism did not represent as vital and grace-filled a tradition as Catholicism, for the revivals and remarkable conversions they were witnessing were Protestant affairs. Bridget was evidently shaken — and finally repelled — by the emotionalism of the revivals in and around Tariffville, where "there has been a great deal of Millerism and Mormonism and such like fooleries. Miller and his desipels have got people so far prursuaded into his doctrine that many have give up work and are preparing to leave this world on or before the first or third day of April." Established denominations in the vicinity were unusually active as well: "the babtist are holding protracted me[e]ting[s] here now the[y] dipped thirteen last Sunday." But the very extravagance of the competing claims of rival evangelists and Bridget's conviction that at least a few of the conversions were spurious — "their must be some wolves in sheeps clothing" — caused her to take refuge finally in Catholicism, whose doctrines, under the circumstances, may have seemed eminently rational. "The[y] cannot be all right," she commented on the local religious scene. "There is but one way to heaven."[21]

Almost no family records have survived from the years between the Birney's marriage in 1845 and James's first departure for California in 1858. The couple had been married by a priest — the wedding took place in a private house in the village of Dexter — and their children were probably baptized by the priests who periodically visited Bunkerhill. The growing family was apparently a healthy one, but their neighbors were not all so fortunate. "There has been one funerl nearly every day at Field's schoolhouse for the last week," John Birney wrote to his absent brother during an especially virulent spell of sickness in 1859 or 1860. "They are mostly children under ten years old." Catholic funerals in the village were presumably presided over by laymen, and presumably proceeded according to a recognizably Catholic ritual. For confessional lines were clearly drawn in Bunkerhill at the moment of death, with the Catholics maintaining their own cemetery. "The Catholics of this place has been fencing the burying ground . . . all turned out and dowe the work it is done nice and it is filling up fast," Bridget informed James in the spring of 1858. Local Catholics also made at least intermittent efforts to sustain a Sunday school. Catechism classes met regularly during the summer of 1858 in the home of the oldest Catholic settler in the vicinity, but do not seem to have survived beyond the autumn. "We have no sunday school here now," Sarah Ann Birney wrote to her father at Christmas during one of his trips to California. Probably the scattered Catholic population could support a catechism class only during those relatively few months when the primitive rural roads were clear and dry. "You did not say w[h]ether you had Sunday School there now or not," James wrote to his daughters. "I hope that will make no difference with you but that you will study your Catechism at home and be sure not to neglect it."[22]

When James and Bridget admitted in their letters to concern about the infrequency of priests' visits to Bunkerhill, they worried not about their own faith but that of their children. "I am very sorry to here that you did not have the priest there any oftener then you have," James wrote to Bridget from California in 1859. "To be sure it does not make so mutch diferns for those that are growen up. But whene there is so many children they ought to have the privlage of being at Mass oftener then that." Bridget, alone with the children, confided to James at about the same time that she felt unable on her own to give them an adequate religious training. "The children attends to their religious duties as well as could be expected. You know children ne[e]ds a great deal of instructions. More than I am capable of giving them. . . . god grant that I may do my duty to my children. It is more concern to me than anything else I have to do." Despite their misgivings, however, both parents were capable religious teachers. Bridget prepared the two older children for confirmation and first communion — both sacraments were generally received in those days at about the age of thirteen — with the aid of catechisms sent by the priest at Jackson. James, for his part, frequently spoke to the children in his letters about what it meant to live the Christian faith. "I hope you will be good and to be good children you must be kind to your parents and obey them . . . and also you must be kind to each other — and say your prayers every knight and morning and remember it is no good to say prayers . . . but you think of what you say and act accordingley.[23]

The Birneys were persuasive teachers largely because each possessed a deep and intelligent religious faith. The maturity of that faith was especially evident during the year between the summers of 1859 and 1860, when epidemic disease, including malaria, repeatedly swept the Bunkerhill region. Many inhabitants died, among them James Birney's brother Charles. "Dear husband before this reaches you I suppose you [will] have heard of your Brother Charles death he is gone I hope where pain and suffering is no more," Bridget wrote at the end of August in 1859. She feared that James would mourn his brother all the more bitterly for being so far from Michigan. "It is hard to part with friends when we are with them in their last momments but I think it is harder to bear when we mourn their loss in a strange land where home and friends are far from us." Charles had been visited by a priest and received the last sacraments before he died, Bridget assured her husband. This was the second letter of the summer to carry sad news from Bunkerhill to California. James had recently been informed that a child of close family friends had died.[24]

Grief-stricken, anxious about their own health and that of their children, and lonely after many months of separation, James and Bridget were confronted with what was evidently a severe test of their belief in a merciful God. Each struggled to comprehend the tragedies suffered by Bunkerhill's families in religious terms, and each seems to have succeeded, although the language with which James in particular addressed the religious meaning of his life during this crisis is nowhere peculiarly Catholic. Neither he nor Bridget ever referred in their correspondence to the Virgin Mary or the saints, nor did they conceive of their relationship to God in terms of intermediaries, either human or supernatural. Neither mentioned the necessity or virtue of praying for the dead, despite the sad news conveyed by letters from Bunkerhill. And while James did not doubt that God ordered the world to His own good purposes—"we are assured that a hair will not drop from our heads without his knowing it"—he spoke always in terms of a transcendent God whose ways were mysterious. His austere religious imagination seems far removed from the sensibility underlying many popular devotions, which peopled the religious landscape with friendly intercessors and imagined God in terms readily analogous to the human experience of love and intimacy.[25]

James responded to the news of his brother's death by reminding Bridget that as Christians they must place their confidence in the promise of eternal life. "I hope our sorrow is his joy and that the blessing of god may be with us now and forever," he wrote. "And I hope god will have mercy and grant his soul peace in heaven." He missed his family deeply and was evidently apprehensive about the future. "We must trust in god and help will come when least expected," he consoled Bridget, rather undermining his assurances by adding, "as also death when least looked for." A month later James wrote again, concerned to place the sufferings of his family and their neighbors in the context of God's providential but undeniably mysterious care for the world. He found a clue to the mystery in human sinfulness, and advised his wife that patience in adversity and trust in God were necessary regardless of what lay ahead. "I am very sorry to here that it is so sickley there this fall but we must be recondscylde to the will of a mercyfull god and receive the afflictions, trubles and difcultyes that may come our way as a just chastisement for what we have done or left undone. If we do so all is well for be assured nothing hapens without the knowledge of god and his will. And it is not unfrequent that the grates afflictions in this world turn out to be the gratest blessings." For her part, Bridget looked for comfort to the hoped-for consolations of the next life. "It seems to me that this world is but a dream at best and if we can prepare for the next it is the thing most needful," she wrote to James, evidently in the midst of the family troubles in 1859. She, like her husband, seems far removed at this point from the religious doubts of her youth, despite the darkness in which her faith came to maturity. James too was increasingly inclined to look beyond the boundaries of this life for answers to their manifold trials. "We should always look forward and hope and trust in God," he told his wife, "that we shall all meet again in a better place."[26]

PARISH LIFE: GOVERNMENT AND FINANCE

The Birney letters, when they address religious matters, deal almost exclusively with the most profound religious questions—the meaning of life, the mystery of death and evil, the transmission of a living faith to the next generation. They have rather little to say about the local church as a social community. We catch only occasional glimpses of Bunkerhill's Catholics as they tax themselves to maintain their cemetery, as they meet to discuss the building of a church, as they welcome the priest on one of his all-too-infrequent visits to the village. If these same Catholics sustained a more or less exclusive social life, the Birney letters give no hint of it. Nor do they mention that late in 1860 — or possibly early in 1861 — a portion of the congregation at Bunkerhill elected a building committee that proceded to raise money and draw up plans for a church, but without consulting the bishop. An angry Bishop Lefevere wrote to James Markey, Bunkerhill's oldest Catholic settler, denouncing the committee's work and declaring that any building "erected by said committee or any other individuals, without our previous permission or sanction, shall never be considered a Catholic Church nor shall Mass be celebrated within." The committeemen were directed to give all the money and subscriptions collected for the new church to Father Moutard at Jackson, "whose duty it is to see to the erection of said Church, and who himself will select and appoint proper persons to assist him in the building of the same." In the absence of further admonitions from the Chancery, we must assume that matters were resolved to the bishop's satisfaction, perhaps through the good offices of the genial Father Moutard, who, because he was only occasionally in Bunkerhill, would have had to rely on local Catholics to see the project to completion. But even his nominal supervision of that project would have upheld the principle of strong episcopal authority which, as we have seen, Bishop Lefevere tried hard to establish during his nearly thirty years in the Diocese.[27]

Bunkerhill, of course, was not the only village in the Diocese where Bishop Lefevere had troubles of this sort. He, like his successor, met with a fairly widespread resistance as he tried to implement his vision of a well-ordered Church. This resistance was mainly encountered in disputes over parish government and parish financial administration, with regard to which there were two quite distinct schools of thought in the nineteenth century. Many of the laity assumed that the parish ought to be governed essentially like the towns in which they lived or the public schools for which they were taxed: the constituents, in this case the adult men in the congregation, should elect a representative body which would in turn be accountable to the community for its performance in office. The committee thus elected was to be responsible especially, although not exclusively, for the administration of parish finances. The American bishops, on the other hand, were united in their insistence that the laity enjoyed no rights with regard to parish government. Authority in the parish, in their view, rested with the priest, who was himself a delegate of the bishop. Individual laymen might be requested by a bishop or priest to play a consultative role in parish administration. But the laity could claim no right to participate in, much less dominate, parish decision making.

Because their views on parish government were not widely shared by the laity, however, most bishops found it difficult, even impossible, to eliminate democratic procedures from all the parishes in their dioceses. Some even seemed to realize that representative government in the parish could be useful to the Chancery, both as a means of defusing conflict and as a check on excessive clerical independence. Bishop Lefevere, for example, not only tolerated the election of church committees in his diocese but, at least on occasion, encouraged the practice. When the men of St. Joseph's (German) parish assembled in 1857 to elect a six-member committee to "take in hand the administration of the temporalities of the congregation," they did so, according to the minutes of the meeting, "by the special command of the most Revd. P. P. Lefevere." The early history of St. Joseph's was a troubled one, and its pastor in the late 1850s was in disfavor at the Chancery. Bishop Lefevere probably wanted a lay committee there to whom he could turn for information on factions in the congregation and which could ensure the integrity of parish finances. But Lefevere did not thereby endorse a democratic theory of parish government. Although St. Joseph's committemen were "elected by the people," their election was subject to approval by the bishop. It was from this approval, in Lefevere's view, that their authority derived. Subsequent parish by-laws, evidently drawn up in consultation with the bishop, gave him the right to nominate a slate of eighteen candidates, from which the church committee would be elected. No other men were eligible for office.[28]

Lefevere's pragmatic approach to parish government was endorsed in 1861 by the bishops at the Third Provincial Council of Cincinnati. Every parish should have a committee or board of "wardens," the council resolved, and up to half the members might be elected by the congregation, if the ordinary so desired. Bishop Lefevere was generous in his interpretation of the council's ruling, while still making clear that authority in the parish derived from those in Holy Orders. Regulations issued in 1862 instructed pastors to nominate slates of candidates, "containing not less than three times the number of councilmen to be elected," from among whom the men of the congregation would choose a church committee. Those elected were to serve for two-year terms, half the committee being up for election at the annual meeting of the congregation. The bishop, however, retained the right to dismiss any committee member who failed "in the discharge of his duties or in the respect due to the Priest" or who gave "any public scandal." Indeed, since a man could neither vote nor be eligible for office unless he received the sacraments at least once a year and supported the parish financially, the reforms of the Cincinnati council might be understood as disciplinary measures fully as much as concessions to democratic sentiment. It should also be noted that, reforms or no, Lefevere was apparently opposed to the introduction of democratic procedures in parishes where they had not previously been the norm. "I do not see the least advantage or utility in having the Congregation to elect the members of the Committee," he wrote to the pastor at Grand Rapids in the summer of 1862, "on the contrary, for it may not infrequently happen that some members or others thus elected, may not only be of no assistance, but prove a serious annoyance both to pastor and congregation." The pastor himself should select the members of the church committee, Lefevere advised, and he as bishop would approve them.[29]

Bishop Borgess was initially less willing than his predecessor had been to countenance even the most limited sharing of authority in the parish. "If there are Wardens in any of those congregations," he wrote in 1871 to the priest he had just assigned to the churches at Newport, Huron, Trenton, and Grosse Ile, "we desire it to be strictly understood that *they must not presume to do anything* in the administration of the temporal affairs of the church *without your consent and approbation,* and *that you* are held responsible *not they.*" Regulations published for the whole of the Diocese in 1873 prohibited the election of church committemen, who were henceforth to be appointed by their pastors and confirmed by the bishop. Revised regulations in 1875 called on pastors to nominate annually "ten good and competent persons," from whose number the bishop himself would select the church committee."[30]

But despite the new regulations, many parishes in the Diocese continued to elect their church committees. It was not unusual, apparently, for pastors to forward slates of candidates who had been elected by the men of the parish—and the Chancery was generally willing to confirm the appointments of those with the largest number of votes. Bishop Borgess had presumably decided to play a waiting game, upholding in principle the right of the clergy to govern without interference, but conceding the manifold obstacles that stood in the way of reform. Indeed, on at least one occasion, the bishop consented in writing to a set of parish by-laws that gave quite generous protection to lay "rights." The parish in question was located at Parisville, and was the oldest Polish parish in the state. The badly factionalized congregation was told by the Chancery in 1886 that it might elect an eight-man slate of candidates for the church committee, from which the bishop would choose four. The Chancery also gave its blessing to a distinctly collaborative approach to parish fiscal management. "The safe for all money of the parish," according to the 1886 rules, "shall be fastened with a double lock with two different keys, one of which will be kept by the Pastor and the other by the treasurer."[31]

Parishes that had existed for a time without a resident priest often developed democratic modes of government which they might be slow to relinquish once a pastor was assigned to them. Other circumstances too could lead to an insistence on democratic procedures. Immigrants, especially, were often mistrustful of episcopal authority, for their bishops were usually assimilated men, only rarely conversant with the customs of the newer ethnic populations in their charge. As parish-founders and church-builders, moreover, immigrants had unusual opportunity for conflict with the Chancery. An immigrant community typically gained a new sense of identity and power as it established its first institutions. But forming a parish entailed certain rituals of submission: any land or buildings already acquired had to be deeded to the bishop, whose approval was needed for any future construction. Requirements like these were widely resented, and could easily lead to a sense of violated rights. We might say that immigrant Catholics democratized the ancient right of patronage as it existed in many parts of Europe, and assumed that the congregation, as the collective donors of the church and the land on which it stood, were entitled to govern the temporal affairs of the parish without episcopal interference.

Where parish committees were active, they had no more important task than tending to parish finances. This meant not only the management of revenue, but also the raising of money—a burden that the typical pastor was more than happy to share. For it was not an easy job, save in the most prosperous congregations. Most nineteenth-century parishes depended for revenue mainly on pew rents, although these were generally supplemented by weekly seat collections. In principle, at least, all but the poorest members of the congregation were expected to rent pews, remitting the "rent" in four annual installments. (The advantage of the system, in theory, was the predictable flow of revenue.) In every parish, the most expensive pews were those closest to the altar, the cheapest those at the rear of the church. Usually the difference in cost was considerable. At Holy Cross in Marine City, for example, the "best" pews rented for $24 a year in 1884, while the least expensive were priced at $8.[32]

A system of pew rents naturally resulted in a congregation seated according to wealth and status. It assumed the existence of a stable population, and one with a steady income. As a consequence, the pew rent system was never widely popular among the laity, many of whom were irregularly employed and some of whom moved frequently. Pastors often had trouble renting all their available pews, and found it hard to collect the rents from poorer members of the congregation. "Sixty-one families paid," reported the pastor at Emmet in 1868. "The remainder say that they are willing but they are not able to pay anything." His counterpart at St. Michael's in Monroe had similar problems. "Perhaps it would be in the interests of religion in my district," he proposed in 1876, "if I published those from the pulpit . . . who are in arrears with their pew rent and school fees, and continued to do so until they would pay up."[33]

Nearly all parishes supplemented pew rents with a weekly seat collection, sometimes taken at the door of the church, to which persons who did not rent pews were expected to contribute. A second Sunday collection was generally taken as well. Pastors sometimes tried to establish a minimum level of church support for all but their poorest parishioners. Families who did not rent pews at St. Peter's church in Mt. Clemens, for example, were expected to contribute $2 a year in 1870, although "not one paid this year," according to the pastor. All heads of household in St. Mary's parish at St. Clair were expected to contribute $10 a year if they did not rent a pew, according to regulations published in 1888. Single wage-earners were expected to contribute $5 annually. But enforcement was always a problem. Some pastors simply accepted whatever support their parishioners gave. "I have no system, I am left to the will of the people," reported the pastor at Emmet in 1868. "They can give me what they please." Others, though few in number, verged on the draconian. Father Robert Doman, who was assigned to a debt-ridden Holy Trinity parish in 1883, was prepared to deny the last sacraments to those parishioners "who do not hold at least one sitting in the church, or, if not holding a sitting, do not donate to its support according to their means." Most pastors, however, probably worked informally to promote a fairly broad participation in church support. They were fortunate men if they could rely for help on a vigorous lay leadership.[34]

Probably no parish in the Diocese depended exclusively on pew rents and Sunday collections to make ends meet. At least until 1881, when Bishop Borgess forbade nearly all parish-sponsored entertainments, most parishes were supported in part by an annual round of bazaars, fairs, and picnics. Events like these, which were often highly profitable, were usually the work of parish women. ("The Parishioners' meeting to consult further about the coming Festival was again conspicuous by the absence of the 'Male Man,'" the *Michigan Catholic* once noted sardonically, in an item concerning the Jesuit parish in Detroit.) It was not the prominence of women in such activities, presumably, that caused Bishop Borgess to prohibit them, but his fear of "the abuses, unavoidably incidental" to large social gatherings and his anger that many Catholics would not adequately support the church unless they could exchange their money for entertainment. The Borgess prohibition, however, may not have been widely observed in the Diocese, at least in parishes distant from Detroit. "All my neighbors had festivals and etc., and were let alone," Kalamazoo's Father Frank O'Brien complained to the Chancery in 1886. "Herein is an advantage of being out of Detroit and with neighbors who keep mum, for they are all in the same boat."[35]

LAY CHARITABLE SOCIETIES

Important as fund-raisers in many parishes, women also played a principal role in the charitable work of the Catholic laity. To be sure, that work in the nineteenth century was extremely modest. But it is nonetheless worthy of note, if only because of the precedents set for later generations. Even in this early period, moreover, it is apparent that Catholic women found in charitable work a means by which to expand their role and achieve a degree of political influence. Lay charities, then, are an important chapter in the still-unwritten history of Catholic women in the United States.

Unfortunately, the activities of lay charity workers in the nineteenth century are poorly documented, and nowhere more so than in the Archdiocese of Detroit. We have detailed records for only a single organization. The group in question was the Catholic Female Benevolent Society of Detroit, organized early in 1834 by Father Martin Kundig, and having as its purpose the care of the city's "deserving" poor and especially its orphans. Father Kundig was responding to an evident need, for Detroit had neither a hospital nor an orphanage, despite recurrent epidemics. Catholic honor was at stake as well. Protestants in Detroit had organized a Moral and Humane Society in 1817 to provide relief to the worthy poor. The women who met to form the Catholic Female Benevolent Society were anxious, as they tell us, to "remove the stigma attached to the Roman Catholic character by Protestants, from their want of sufficient energy to follow [the Protestant] example."[36]

The Catholic Female Benevolent Society of Detroit survived only to 1836, although it may have continued under a different name until the mid-1840s. But during its brief life the society helped to realize an impressive record of reform, sponsoring the establishment of an orphanage and a cholera hospital in 1834 and assuming partial responsibility for the County Poor House in that same year. The society's achievements were due in part to the leadership of Father Kundig, who during his years in Detroit was a tireless champion of the poor — he served as County Superintendent of the Poor from 1834 until 1839 — and who burdened himself with a lifetime's debt in order to provide for the victims of the 1834 cholera epidemic. But the women of the society soon discovered their own capacities for initiative and leadership, not only within the organization but in the community as well. The group's first president had initially been reluctant to chair its meetings: "as yet unacquainted with the duties assigned to her," she prevailed on Father Kundig to preside. By the fall of 1834, however, the society, now wholly under lay leadership, was publicly reprimanding the Wayne County Board of Supervisors for its neglect of the County Poor House. Five months later, the members quite casually dispatched a delegation to see Detroit's mayor, apparently with regard to the care of certain mentally impaired women who were dependent on charity.[37]

The benevolent society was never a large organization — the fifty women at its founding meeting were probably the largest group that ever assembled under its auspices. Only twenty women attended the second meeting, and the group was so plagued by absenteeism that it quickly instituted a twelve-and-a-half-cent fine for members who missed the regular sewing sessions without a good excuse. Probably most of the members were young and single — of the fifty women at the founding meeting, only fourteen were married — and most were probably fairly well-to-do. Several members are known to have contributed to the group's various charities out of their own pockets. The group's active members understood themselves to be motivated by a sense of Christian responsibility for the poor: "No Catholic Christian can take a retrospective view of the condition of the church of St. Anne, for years past, and the situation of the poor and sick members in Detroit — the suffering and neglect of the rising generation among them without feeling an ardent desire to aid in their relief," according to the preamble of the society's minute book. But the members also believed that charity ought to be tempered with prudence. "The commissioners reported that they visited one poor woman whom they considered neither sick or distressed enough to require their assistance," according to the minutes of the second meeting. "Other poor they found indeed distressed but living in idleness, therefore considered them unworthy [of] the exercise of their charity." In these views, of course, the society's members were as one with nearly all the charity workers and reformers of their generation.[38]

Beyond a sense of Christian obligation, however, the women who were the mainstay of the society seem to have been motivated, perhaps not wholly consciously, by a desire to move in a larger world than the narrow sphere of conventional domesticity. They were delighted at Father Kundig's suggestion that the society assist him in his administration of the County Poor House: upon learning that the County Board of Supervisors had given assent to this plan, "the ladies without exception were much gratified at hearing such pleasing intelligence, and were animated with the hope of making themselves useful." The prospect of being useful in so unusual a role seems rapidly to have altered the members' sense of themselves. The recorder at this meeting referred indirectly in her notes to women as "citizens," and the group resolved "that a particular dress should be adopted to be worn by all the members whenever they appeared in public." (The costume finally decided upon was a compromise between worldly dress and that of certain religious orders: "a black dress, white cape, straw bonnet *fashionable* with black ribbon.") The women obviously wished to be identified as quasi-public servants, and their distinctive dress enabled them to be approached by the needy as they moved about the city. This surely broadened the social contacts to which these women were accustomed — they seem, indeed, to have taken pride in their encounters with misery and degradation precisely because these experiences enlarged the world they knew. An excursion to the County Poor House in the fall of 1834 to deliver "4 sheets, 9 shirts, 14 pillow cases and 5 towels" was remarkable, if we look to the minute book, less for the work of mercy performed than for the personal confrontation with destitution and the public admiration that the excursion earned its genteel participants. "It . . . raised them in the estimation of the citizens, and they were taught a lesson, which cannot easily be forgotten, having witnessed that which never before was imagined by any of these ladies."[39]

The reappearance of cholera in 1834 meant new opportunities for heroism — and for public approbation. Distress was apparent by late summer: the society's commissioners reported on August 3 "that they had found many families in distress and many sick, whom they assisted with various things such as coffee, tea, cloth, etc." It soon became clear that the city faced an epidemic, and at this point Father Kundig enlisted the society's more stalwart members in an ambitious campaign of reform. The women helped Kundig convert a former Presbyterian church into a public hospital, successfully petitioning the Detroit Common Council for money to furnish it and to provide nurses. By the end of August they had resolved to raise funds to establish an orphanage. "Many mothers had fallen victim to the cholera since the first of August," according to the minutes of August 27, "and some of the ladies who had witnessed the awful sight which the children in different parts of the city presented to them deeply felt their distress and deplorable situation and therefore begged of the society to make immediate arrangements for a temporary orphan asylum." Father Kundig secured a house, and it was soon converted for use as an orphanage. Sixteen children were living there by mid-September.[40]

The orphanage was placed on a less makeshift footing early in 1836, when it was relocated to newly constructed premises adjacent to the County Poor House, where Father Kundig himself had taken up residence. The new orphanage was a modest structure, but it was large enough to house a free school for the orphans and for poor children who lived in the vicinity. Two fairs sponsored by the benevolent society had helped to make the new orphanage possible, and members of the society continued to offer fine sewing for sale to aid in its support. Their work was not confined, however, to such conventionally feminine pursuits. Together with Father Kundig, the society had petitioned the mayor and the aldermen in 1835 for funds to establish a public hospital, an initiative that was welcomed by city authorities but not given the necessary financial support. A more successful venture was inaugurated shortly thereafter. Reflecting a long-standing concern to provide education for poor children and an uneasy awareness of Protestant activism, the society resolved to establish a Sunday school in Detroit, "since all denominations had undertaken it and with so much success." The school was apparently opened in the spring of 1835.[41]

The minute book of the Catholic Female Benevolent Society ends abruptly in August 1836. The membership had evidently dwindled by this time—those who attended the meeting of August 29 decided against holding a fair "principally because, the number of those who would interest themselves in it, were too small." So few members had been attending meetings, indeed, that the group resolved to meet henceforth only once a month. Still, the faithful members present proceeded to elect commissioners, whose task it was to visit the infirmary at the County Poor House as well as the orphanage. Both institutions were now in the care of "Sisters who stand in need of encouragement"—Poor Clares from a convent that existed in Detroit from 1833 until 1839. Perhaps it was the work of the Sisters at these institutions that had diminished for many members of the society a sense of urgency with regard to reform. The handful of women who attended the society's last recorded meeting evidently saw themselves as auxiliaries to the Poor Clares: the elected commissioners were "to encourage the Sisters and to see what is wanting and deficient, and to report to the Society upon the same."[42]

The benevolent society may well have continued beyond 1836, notwithstanding the absence of minutes and other proofs of its existence. The departure of the Poor Clares from Detroit in 1839, however, brought an end to the orphanage that Father Kundig and his coworkers had done so much to establish. If the society still survived, it was too small and weak to repeat the triumphs of the mid-1830s. But individual members may have continued their friendly visiting among the poor, perhaps even after Father Kundig left Detroit in the early 1840s. The *Catholic Almanac* for 1841 makes mention of two women's charitable organizations in Detroit, either or both of which may have grown out of the Catholic Female Benevolent Society. But neither the Ladies of Providence nor the Young Ladies Charitable Society, which claimed thirty-five members in 1841, is mentioned in the *Almanac* after 1844.

This apparent lull on the charity front was of short duration. There was renewed activity as early as 1845, as we will shortly see. But this activity took place mainly under the direction of women's religious orders, which meant that lay charity work was increasingly confined to the business of fund-raising and providing auxiliary services to the Sisters. Such seem to have been the principal tasks of the various parish societies that devoted themselves in subsequent decades to charity sewing and arranging bazaars and other entertainments. Nearly all of these were women's organizations, but at least four parish conferences of the St. Vincent de Paul Society were founded in Detroit between 1875 and 1885, indicating a quickening interest in charity work among a small group of Catholic men.[43]

It is not, indeed, until the early twentieth century that we again find among the Catholic laity a charitable organization comparable in its impact on Detroit to the Catholic Female Benevolent Society of the 1830s. In part this is explained by the slow growth of a Catholic middle class in what continued to be a heavily immigrant city. But it is explained as well by the growing presence of women religious in Detroit, which clearly limited the range of charitable activities that were open to Catholic women. This limited in turn the chances that Catholic women would move from pioneering ventures in charity work to an overtly political interest in reform, a journey that characterizes the careers of some major Protestant figures in American women's history. On the other hand, the religious orders provided their recruits with an education that was likely to be superior to that of the vast majority of Catholics, and gave them the experience and the authority they needed to ameliorate social conditions among their own people. As generations of Sisters went about this task, they demonstrated the possibilities of female capacity and female influence to a broad lay audience.

CATHOLICS AND TEMPERANCE

Certain parish societies that we would not call "charitable" today were widely regarded by Catholics in the nineteenth century as having essentially charitable functions. Benefit societies, for example, were often praised as a source of assistance to widows and orphans: it was the truly charitable man who paid his weekly dues, and thus gave protection to those who were dependent on him. In a poor community, it was necessary for charity to begin, and usually end, at home. We might even see the flourishing Catholic temperance movement of the mid-nineteenth century as an expression of the family and community-centered charity that Catholics valued. Certainly the movement's leaders believed that their cause, if widely embraced, would substantially reduce the incidence and severity of poverty.

We have already seen that Bishop Lefevere was an ardent proponent of temperance, which he defined as total abstinence from alcoholic drinks. He carefully recorded in the *Catholic Almanac* the growing membership of the temperance societies that developed in the Diocese mainly after his arrival: these societies had, he claimed, 6,000 members in 1845, 9,000 in 1847, and 10,000 in 1849, a figure that remained unchanged until the entry ceased in 1858. The *Western Catholic Register,* a weekly published in the Diocese during 1842, placed membership in the "Trinity Church Temperance Society" in Detroit at 1,002 and that at St. Anne's at 900, "including 600 Indians and French at the Upper Lakes missions to whom the pledge was administered by the Rt. Rev. Bishop Lefevere on his recent visit to that quarter." The Temperance Society of Milwaukee, still within the Diocese of Detroit, was said to number between 600 and 700. Evidently some of Lefevere's priests were as persuasive in the cause as the bishop was proving to be. The *Register* noted that Father Lawrence Kilroy "on a mission to Connor's Creek a few days since, administered the pledge to 12 persons. One, a Mr. Dalton, emptied several gallons of whiskey on the ground which he had purchased a few days before for his workmen." The remarkable Father Martin Kundig founded the Detroit Catholic Temperance Society probably in the late 1830s. Its membership book, which spans the years between the society's founding and about 1846, contains the names of 1,972 Catholics who had taken the temperance pledge.[44]

The temperance societies in the Diocese in the years before the Civil War appear to have differed in some important ways from those which existed in the latter decades of the nineteenth century. They were certainly larger, even assuming that the impressive figures sent to the *Catholic Almanac* by Bishop Lefevere were exaggerated. The antebellum societies also included many women, and it appears that this was much less true in the 1870s and after. As many as one-third of the members of the Detroit Catholic Temperance Society in the 1840s were female. Probably the severe economic depression of the early 1840s accounted for many converts to temperance: temperance advocates promised a hard-drinking society that abstinence was the key to economic success. In a time of widespread hardship, their message may well have been especially persuasive, not only to men but also to women, who hoped that their example would inspire sons and husbands to sobriety. When Bridget McClear, later the wife of James Birney, took the pledge in Ann Arbor in 1842, she promised not only "to abstain from all spirituous and intoxicating liquors unless used medicinally and by order of a medical man," but "to prevent the use of them in all others, as far as it lies in my power."[45]

The insecurity of working-class life is not, of course, an adequate explanation for the rise of Catholic temperance. Hard times may have driven more men to drink than were led to take the pledge. And hard times in the latter decades of the century did not result in a resurrection of the massive temperance organizations of the 1840s. Ethnicity was certainly a factor, however, with the Irish being far and away the most hospitable group to the temperance cause. Nearly all of the members of the Detroit Catholic Temperance Society in the 1840s had Irish names, and the Irish parishes continued after the Civil War to be the places where Catholic temperance organizations were most likely to be found. The Germans, the French, and the Poles, on the other hand, were generally hostile to the cause of total abstinence and even, in many cases, to proposals for regulation of the liquor trade. With the rise of heavy European immigration after the late 1840s, temperance quickly became a divisive issue among Catholics, not only in the Diocese but throughout the nation.

Catholic temperance advocates lost none of their fervor in the later nineteenth century, despite the relatively smaller size of the Catholic temperance ranks. And

they appear to have gained numerous clerical allies: the clergy as a group were almost certainly more disposed to temperance than the laity were in the latter decades of the century. Most of the temperance priests were Irish, at least in the Diocese of Detroit. But the cause attracted men from other groups as well — men like
the Polish-born pastor of St. Albertus parish, who proposed to the Chancery in
1874 a series of reforms that bespoke great expectations of his immigrant flock:
"I would suggest it important to build a Higher Polish Catholic School (College) — erecting and founding [a] Polish Catholic Library, Polish Literary Lectures, etc., etc., establishing of a Polish Catholic Temperance Confraternity."[46]

Still, the Catholic temperance movement in the Diocese never achieved much
organizational success beyond the Irish-American community. Nor did it affect
the political behavior of most of the Irish population. Detroit's Catholics voted
heavily Democratic throughout the nineteenth century, although most local elections turned on temperance issues and the Democrats were prominently associated with the saloon and the liquor trade. And despite an upsurge in temperance
activity in the depression-ridden 1890s, the Catholic temperance movement lost
much of its élan after the turn of the century. This had largely to do with the
growing militance of the Prohibition forces — many Catholic temperance advocates stopped short of endorsing Prohibition — and with the increasingly exclusive identification of the temperance cause with evangelical Protestantism. But
the values of the Catholic temperance movement were neither discredited nor
abandoned. The ideal of Catholic manhood that informed such twentieth-century
organizations as the Holy Name Society embodied the essential values of the
earlier temperance organizations — self-control, a disciplined piety, a strong
sense of obligation to the family. Indeed, because they did not preach the divisive gospel of total abstinence, these later Catholic organizations were better
able than the temperance movement to reach a wide Catholic audience.

Had Catholics living in the Diocese in the late 1880s been asked what changes
had taken place since Bishop Rese first came to Detroit, they would probably
have dwelt on the remarkable proliferation of churches, schools, and charitable
institutions. Perhaps they would also have mentioned the greater ethnic variety
in the local Catholic population. But these same Catholics would probably have
been less aware of the changes that had taken place with regard to religious
behavior. Like most of us today, they were inclined to see their grandparents'
generation as more godly than their own, and certainly more godly than that
of their children. But the trend in the Diocese, as we have seen, was in these
fifty years toward a greater regularity in religious observance and a more disciplined sacramental practice. The growing number of priests and religious,
churches and schools had made this more disciplined practice possible. But the
proliferation of Catholic institutions was also an effect of this altered behavior.
As we look toward the twentieth century, and see there an astonishing variety
of lay Catholic organizations and a flourishing lay piety, we must remember that
the roots of this flowering lie deep in the nineteenth century.

4

CATHOLIC EDUCATION: *THE FOUNDATION YEARS*

The history of Catholic education in the territory that became the Diocese of Detroit is a long one: Catholics in Detroit and other Michigan settlements had established schools many years before the erection of the Diocese in 1833. The first fifty years of diocesan history, however, were of particular importance for the development of the parochial schools and the evolution of Catholic educational policy. For it was principally during the episcopates of Peter Paul Lefevere and Caspar Borgess that the significant battles were fought — both within the Catholic community and in the larger political arena — by which Catholics came to be committed to a separate, privately funded system of schools. During this same period, those schools moved increasingly away from lay control, and became the domain of the various religious orders. Finally, it was during the Borgess episcopate that the first efforts were made to bring the emerging network of schools under centralized administrative control, and to establish uniform standards for the curriculum and for instructional competence. These reforms were too ambitious to be immediately sustained. But they point toward the eventual creation of a highly centralized system of parochial education.

As Catholics in the Diocese in the nineteenth century built their schools and deliberated school policy, they were affected in significant ways by developments beyond the boundaries of Michigan's Catholic community. The impetus to parochial school building came in some measure from the pronouncements of the American hierarchy at its various national and provincial councils. These pronouncements gave special weight to the demands of individual bishops that Catholics under their jurisdiction create and use a system of parochial schools, and this was important, for there were Catholic laity and even priests in virtually all dioceses who were not convinced that parochial schools were necessary or even desirable. And Catholics were affected in their thinking about schools by the values and behavior of those who established and periodically reformed the public school systems which had their birth in most parts of the United States in the middle decades of the nineteenth century. Much has been made of the gulf that purportedly separates the Catholic school from its secular counterpart, for both friend and foe of the parochial school have been eager to believe that it differs significantly from public institutions. But despite certain obvious differences, to be explored in a later chapter, we will discover that Catholic schools have been shaped in important ways by the same educational philosophies and policies that have shaped the public schools, and that they have largely reflected the values of the dominant culture. It is no exaggeration to say that Catholic schools in the Diocese of Detroit had more in common with the public schools of Michigan than with the Catholic schools, say, of France.

The early history of parochial education in the Diocese can usefully be divided into two periods, though we must also make mention of certain developments in the late eighteenth and early nineteenth centuries. The first period is roughly congruent with the episcopates of bishops Rese and Lefevere. Catholic schools in the Diocese in these years were for the most part rudimentary, often short-lived, and frequently taught by laity. The episcopate of Bishop Borgess spans a second period of development, for the number of parochial schools increased steadily during his tenure, while the number of teaching Sisters grew dramatically. And besides the administrative reforms already alluded to, it was during the Borgess years that the Chancery moved decisively to compel Catholics, at least in the more populous areas of the Diocese, to establish schools where they had not previously existed and to support and use those schools. The question of state support for Catholic schools had been vigorously championed by Bishop Lefevere and a mobilized Catholic constituency in the early 1850s and just as vigorously rejected by the voters of Detroit and the members of the Michigan Legislature. Bishop Borgess, like his successors, assumed that the parochial school system he was determined to advance would be financed by Catholics themselves.

Because Detroit was for many generations a largely Catholic community, its earliest educational history was essentially a history of Catholic schools. We know that St. Anne's parish in Detroit supported a school from about 1760 until 1791; taught by a layman, this school was probably a primitive affair, geared only to instruction in the catechism and the rudiments of literacy. There is no evidence of a school under Catholic auspices in Detroit between 1791 and 1804, but in this latter year the redoubtable Father Gabriel Richard began his nearly thirty years of public and private labors in the cause of education. A "College or clergy school," presumably a preparatory seminary, was opened by Richard and a fellow priest in Detroit in 1804, although it survived for only a year. "We have met great difficulties and oppositions to the establishment of a school for the latin and the sciences," he wrote early in 1805. "The most material difficulty is the scarcity of Scholars." By 1808, however, Richard was not only petitioning the Territorial Legislature to establish an academy for boys "in which the high branches of Mathematics, most important languages, Geography, History, Natural and moral Philosophy should be taught," but had already helped to found an "academy for young ladies" in Detroit, where "better than thirty young girls" were being taught by Elizabeth Williams, a Detroit woman who worked closely with Richard in his early educational endeavors. Miss Williams was one of three laywomen whom Father Richard had organized into something like a religious community by 1815, through which he hoped eventually to create a network of Catholic schools in the Michigan Territory. This ambitious project failed of realization, but before his death in 1832 Richard had served as vice-president of the state-supported academy known as the University of Michigania, attempted to open a school for deaf-mutes in Detroit, promoted the cause of Indian education as Michigan's territorial delegate to the Congress, and doubtless played a role in the opening of a free school for girls in St. Anne's parish in the spring of 1832 — credit for which he gave to the "ladies of the Cath. Charity Society." Shortly before his death he was writing to the Superior-General of the Sulpicians in Paris, outlining plans for a college in Detroit. "I have many things wherewith to begin a college," he noted, "even on a grand scale: an electrical machine, a pneumatic machine, an organ for the church, an extensive, well-chosen library, a printing press with 800 pounds of type. . . . All this will belong to the college, which has been planned for a long time."[1]

Thus when Bishop Rese arrived in Detroit in 1833, he came to a diocese poor in priests and churches and Catholic population, but already rich in educational history. Still, the schools established under his own auspices were no more certain in their tenure than most schools were in this formative period of American education. The first of the Rese-sponsored schools was an academy for girls in Detroit, which was opened by the Colletine Poor Clares in 1833. It survived until the Sisters left the Diocese in 1839. (As fashionable a school as Detroit's frontier condition would allow, the majority of the academy's pupils appear to have been non-Catholics.) The Poor Clares also conducted a school for the children of St. Anne's parish, for which they apparently charged a modest tuition. The free school begun in the last months of Father Richard's life seems to have survived, under lay auspices, for a better part of the decade. Bishop Rese also sponsored the establishment, probably in 1835, of the St. Anne's Classical Academy for boys, which was closed by Bishop Lefevere for financial reasons in 1841. Initially taught by a layman, its instructors after 1837 were seminarians studying in the Diocese. And the ambitious Rese opened a Catholic college in 1837 in a picturesque locale east of Detroit, where young men of all denominations were offered the benefits of "a proper literary and classical establishment." St. Philip Neri's College, as it was called, was closed in 1841 and its building destroyed by fire the next year, but according to the reminiscences of a prominent non-Catholic Detroiter, "this school was quite celebrated in its day, and many scions of our first families used to attend it."[2]

What little progress was made in the establishment of Catholic schools outside Detroit during the Rese episcopate was largely the work of the laity. Very little is known about these few schools, save that they were, like the public schools emerging in Michigan in this same decade, capable of imparting little more than the fundamentals of literacy. Typically these early Catholic schools were taught in the same rude building that served the congregation as a church, and in at least one instance the school preceded the church by a number of years. This happened at Flint, where a Catholic layman opened a school, the first in the village, in 1834. Flint's Catholics were visited infrequently by priests in the 1830s, and they did not complete their first church until 1848. Indeed, it is not certain that what had apparently begun as a Catholic school remained an identifiably Catholic institution. There is no question, however, that the school that was opened in 1838 in a crude log church in the village of Westphalia was thoroughly Catholic. Westphalia was something of an anomaly among Michigan communities, populated as it was almost wholly by Catholics, and its first school was both "parochial" and "public." Father Anton Kopp, who taught school there for several months in 1840, received about $8 in salary from the state for his services. The Westphalia school was subsequently taught by laymen, save for a few years in the 1860s, until the advent of the Sisters of Christian Charity in 1874.[3]

Lay teachers played an important role in the parochial schools of the Diocese throughout the long episcopate of Rese's successor, especially outside the city of Detroit. Bishop Lefevere brought five teaching orders into the Diocese — this between 1844 and 1852 — and he presided, in 1845, over the creation of the order that eventually became the largest of those that taught in the Diocese. (This was the Sisters, Servants of the Immaculate Heart of Mary, popularly known as the "IHMs." They were founded at Monroe, under the sponsorship of Redemptorist Father Louis Gillet.) Despite the bishop's best efforts, however, the Diocese was acutely short of teaching Sisters, and remained so for some years after his death. At least half of the forty-odd parochial schools in the Diocese in 1869 were conducted by lay teachers.[4]

The limited progress of the schools in these years should not obscure for us Lefevere's deep commitment to Catholic education. He hoped to lay the groundwork for a veritable system of parochial schools in his Diocese, and looked forward to the day when each of those schools would be taught by members of a religious order. Like many of his fellow bishops, Lefevere regarded the emerging public schools as subversive of Catholic faith and morals. "The Government has erected schools in all parts of the city, and in every village and hamlet, where children receive free instruction, but where it is forbidden to speak of religion in any manner whatsoever," the bishop explained to a French correspondent in 1848. "What disastrous impressions will not Protestant teachers make on Catholic children, either from their indifference in matters of religion, or by their railleries against the Catholic faith." The only remedy was the establishment of Catholic schools throughout the Diocese "to snatch at least our Catholics from the disastrous influence of these infidel schools," Lefevere continued. "But where shall I find the means to support them? And how shall I meet the expenses of establishing them in all these localities? We have so many other things to do."[5]

The poverty of most Catholics in this period meant that the attractions of state-supported free schools were considerable, and a good many Catholics evidently made use of them. Recognizing this, Bishop Lefevere was concerned throughout his episcopate to provide free parochial education for as many children as possible, despite the limited resources at his disposal. The Daughters of Charity, who opened St. Vincent's Select School for Girls in 1844, were required by the bishop to teach two free schools in Detroit as well, one for boys and one for girls. Lefevere even requested the Religious of the Sacred Heart, whose mission had historically been to the daughters of the well-to-do, to keep "a free school for the poorer girls" in addition to their fashionable academy, which was opened in Detroit in 1851. "The Cath. population of Detroit [is] principally composed of the laboring class of people," the bishop explained.[6]

Lefevere was in fact unable to impose a policy of free tuition on most of his schools. (The most successful efforts in this direction came under Bishop Borgess.) But there were free Catholic schools in Detroit and Monroe throughout the Lefevere years, and perhaps in other locations as well. The demand for free Catholic schooling, of course, far exceeded the supply. The Daughters of Charity maintained a free school in Detroit from the mid-1840s until 1871. But when the IHM Sisters came to Detroit in 1864, they found that "the want of a Catholic school had long been felt by the laboring class who, owing to their limited means, could not send their children to a select school, and consequently, were obliged either to have them attend the public schools or have them remain ignorant." The IHMs accordingly established a free school at the cathedral, in addition to the "select school" they taught there, "in which these poor children would receive an education suited to their station in life, and at the same time be well instructed in their religious duties, of which the greater number, even at the advanced age of sixteen and seventeen, were totally ignorant."[7]

Bishop Lefevere's desire to provide a Catholic education for even the poorest members of his Diocese was doubtless the principal motivation for his efforts in 1853 to secure public funding for Catholic schools in Michigan. His was not the first such attempt in the state's history, however: the parishioners of Detroit's Holy Trinity parish, probably inspired by the well-publicized campaign of Bishop John Hughes in New York, petitioned the legislature in 1840 for a subsidy to their parish school equal to the amount of school tax they paid as residents of Detroit. The committee that received the petition looked favorably on their cause, and recommended that the legislature make an annual grant in support of Trinity school "equal to the amount that the petitioners would be entitled to as component parts of the several districts in which they reside." But there is no record of any such subsidy having been paid, presumably because Detroit's voters in 1841 chose candidates committed to the establishment of a city-wide system of nonsectarian, publicly funded schools. When Bishop Lefevere revived the issue of state support in 1853, no parochial school in the Diocese was receiving any monies from the state.[8]

The 1853 campaign was conducted in two political arenas. The more important was the Michigan Legislature, to which many of the parishes in the state sent petitions—at the behest of Bishop Lefevere—decrying "the oppressive nature of our present School laws, the injustice of which is equalled only by the laws of England, which compel the people of all denominations to support a church, the doctrines of which they do not believe." The petitions were followed by intensive lobbying, if we can believe the testimony of mostly hostile witnesses, one of whom referred in the *Daily Free Press* to "a spectacle, new in our day, of the Bishop and Priests of the Catholic Church haunting the lobbies of the halls of legislature." Certainly Bishop Lefevere was determined to orchestrate a highly visible campaign, and he seems to have been little concerned that his aggressive and uncompromising public stance would stimulate an anti-Catholic reaction among even moderate members of the electorate. But this is what happened, and in fairly short order. Petitions and remonstrances from groups opposed to any division of the school funds poured into the legislature and intemperate editorials filled the columns of the mostly Protestant local press. The House Committee on Education subsequently rejected a bill granting subsidies to the state's Catholic schools, a move which the entire House upheld by a decisive margin.[9]

The second battle over public aid to Catholic education was waged in Detroit, which by this time had an autonomous school system. It too took place in the early months of 1853, with Bishop Lefevere playing as prominent and controversial a role as he did in the contest with the legislature. Lefevere may have believed that Catholics constituted a majority of Detroit's population—he made such a claim in an 1850 letter—and because Michigan for much of the nineteenth century permitted aliens with two years' residence in the state to vote, he would naturally have assumed that most of Detroit's Catholic men had the franchise. But Catholics were not in the majority in Detroit in the 1850s, although they doubtless made up a large minority in the city's population.[10]

Whether or not the battle was joined on mistaken assumptions, it proved to be one of unprecedented bitterness. The issue of public funds for Catholic schools was at the center of the March 1853 municipal elections, in which a "regular" Democratic ticket, reputed to be sympathetic to Catholic demands, was opposed by an anti-Catholic "independent" coalition of Democrats and Whigs. The "independents" played in their campaign on familiar and widely popular themes. They warned against episcopal tyranny, both in the Church and especially in politics. They invoked the dangers of an immigrant population kept separate from the democratizing influence of the common schools. They questioned whether the recently established public schools could long survive if public funds were diverted to parochial education. The more extreme among them spoke darkly of foreign plots, evoking the specter of a Catholic community acting "in obedience to the commands and suggestions of a foreign despotic sovereign," in the words of a remonstrance from the elders and deacons of Detroit's First Presbyterian Church. Campaigning "in the true spirit of '76," as one enthusiast had it, the "independent" coalition overwhelmed the "Catholic" slate at the polls and effectively ended, for many generations, serious political discussion in Michigan of state support for parochial education.[11]

That a city with as large a Catholic population as Detroit's could have voted so decisively against such aid raises an important question. To what extent were ordinary Catholics in the mid-nineteenth century committed to the creation of a separate system of parochial schools? Certainly many Catholics voted against the "Catholic ticket" in the Detroit election of 1853, although the vote split generally along religious lines. The "independents" carried the heavily German fourth ward, which was at least 57 percent Catholic in 1853, with 70 percent of the vote. Even the mainly Irish eighth ward, the only ward in the city carried by the "regulars," returned a significantly smaller-than-usual margin of victory to the Democratic organization. That the Irish voted more heavily for the "Catholic" slate than German Catholics did is something of a puzzle, for Germans looked to the parochial schools to preserve their language. Perhaps the Germans were less willing than the Irish, for reasons having to do with the European experience of both groups, to disrupt what had hitherto been a remarkable if precarious history of Catholic-Protestant cooperation in Detroit on school issues. The establishment of the school system in the early 1840s had been, after all, the fruit of a multireligious movement.[12]

It is also possible that Bishop Lefevere had alienated certain Catholics by his strident and highly visible campaign against the public schools. The *Michigan Christian Herald,* staunchly anti-Catholic, was gleefully convinced of this: the bishop's conduct, the paper claimed, had roused resentment among "many of his flock," especially the French and the Germans. It is true that some of the city's Catholics had previously opposed their bishop when he asserted his authority in purely Church affairs. St. Mary's (German) congregation, as we have seen, was bitterly divided in the mid-1840s over whether to grant the bishop title to its parish property. Perhaps memories of this conflict, which culminated in the excommunication of some who had opposed the Chancery, affected a portion of German votes in 1853. In a more general sense, we might reasonably assume that Catholics who inclined to a "congregational" model of the church, with all that this implied in the way of lay rights, would be hostile to clerical involvement in politics.[13]

Finally, it is clear that at least some Catholics disagreed with their bishop when he called the public schools "infidel" institutions — this despite the near-monopoly Protestants enjoyed when it came to teaching in those schools. The public schools were free and open to all, which doubtless did much to commend them to an impoverished immigrant population. (Perhaps some Catholics did not believe that parochial schools would ever be tuition-free, even with the advent of state support.) And we have already seen that a significant minority among the laity in this period were much less disciplined in their religious practice than the clergy would have them be. Their view of the world was bound to be tempered by this. The divison between Christians and "infidels," between the orthodox and the indifferent, was probably less distinct for many lay Catholics than it was for the missionary priest who was their bishop. But whatever the reason, it is evident that Detroit's Catholics at midcentury were far from unanimous in their commitment to parochial education. This was likely the case in other dioceses as well, or so it would seem from the urgent tones in which the American bishops in the later nineteenth century addressed the subject of schools.

That urgency was increasingly manifest among the bishops of the Cincinnati Province, even in the 1850s. The First and Second Provincial Councils of Cincinnati, held respectively in 1855 and 1858, declared it the duty of pastors to prevent the children in their charge from attending schools that endangered Catholic faith. The bishops took a further step at the Second Provincial Council, affirming that pastors "were bound, under pain of mortal sin, to provide a Catholic school in every parish or congregation subject to them, where this can be done." The pastoral letter issuing from that council was especially emphatic on this point. "No good pastor will neglect his duty in this regard. In our minds it is a test of his fidelity, or infidelity, to his God." Detroit's First Diocesan Synod, convened in 1859, reaffirmed the mandate of the Second Provincial Council of Cincinnati with regard to parochial education, formally committing the clergy of the Diocese to the proposition that every parish ought, ideally, to maintain a school. But the poverty of most Catholics in the Diocese, the sparse and scattered population of rural Catholics and the shortage of teaching Sisters meant that Bishop Lefevere could implement this policy in only a limited way, even in Detroit and the larger towns.[14]

When Bishop Borgess came to Detroit in 1870, however, he was determined, against all obstacles, to advance the progress of parochial schooling in every part of the Diocese. "I urged the necessity of having a Catholic school," the bishop noted in his diary of an 1872 visit to St. John's parish in Jackson, "[and] refused to permit the proposed enlarging of the church until the school is established." New diocesan regulations, published in 1873, reiterated the point: a Catholic school was to be established "in every parish or mission at the earliest practical moment, if the strict economy of the revenues and other resources of the congregation can possibly justify it." Catholics, moreover, were obliged to use these schools: "If a Catholic school is attached to the congregation, the pastor or missionary shall not admit a child to prepare for its first Holy Communion which does not attend the parish school." Borgess subsequently ruled, in 1877, that parents who sent their children to public schools "without good and substantial reasons" should be refused the sacraments. The Fourth Diocesan Synod in 1878 rather uneasily ratified this policy, but not without noting that confessors had necessarily to exercise considerable discretion in judging individual cases. This same synod urged unanimously "that our parochial schools must be absolutely free to all our poor children, and that it is highly desirable that they should be free to all our Catholic children as far as circumstances will allow," by placing the burden of school support on the entire congregation. "None of our children should be debarred from our schools for not paying, under any circumstance," the synod resolved.[15]

Enforcement of these ambitious policies was often difficult. Catholics married to Protestants sometimes claimed that the non-Catholic spouse objected to parochial education, and most priests evidently accepted this, especially where it was the father who was not a Catholic. Rural Catholics often lived far from the parish school and refused to use it for this reason. (Bishop Borgess ruled in 1882 that families living more than three miles from a Catholic school were not obliged under most circumstances to send their children there.) Parents who wanted their children to have a secondary education generally had no choice but to use the public schools. Despite the difficulties of enforcement, however, the tenor of diocesan policy with regard to school attendance was firmly set in the Borgess years. His successor, as we shall see, had no difficulty in the 1890s extinguishing the last flicker of articulate Catholic opposition to parochial education.[16]

The Borgess years also saw a significant increase in the number of teaching Sisters in the Diocese: more than 80 percent of the teachers in the Catholic schools in 1887 were members of religious orders. The IHMs accounted for almost half the total, which presumably pleased their bishop, for the order maintained notably high standards of training and pedagogy. Other orders too grew in numbers during this episcopate, and Borgess added eight new orders to those already brought into the Diocese by Bishop Lefevere. (The Borgess recruits included the Felician Sisters, who came to Detroit in 1880 to teach at St. Albertus [Polish] school, and whose first American motherhouse was moved to the city in 1881.) Still, the Diocese suffered a shortage of teaching Sisters throughout the Borgess years, mainly because the number of schools and their enrollment continued to increase. By 1887, the year that Bishop Borgess retired, nearly two-thirds of his parishes had schools of their own.[17]

Beyond the number of schools and teachers, Bishop Borgess was concerned throughout his episcopate with the quality of education offered under Catholic auspices. His concern was warranted, for the rapid development of parochial schooling, coupled with the poverty of many Catholics, meant that the Catholic schools were often overcrowded, ill-equipped, and sometimes taught by marginally qualified teachers. This was especially true in the middle decades of the century. The school at Marshall, for example, was so overcrowded in 1867 that "order was impossible," in the judgment of the IHMs who taught there. The Sisters of Christian Charity took charge of the school at Westphalia in 1874 only to find that many pupils were attending irregularly, largely because of overcrowding. No efforts had yet been made to group the children according to age or ability. Conditions improved toward the end of the century, but congested classrooms were still the norm, especially in Detroit. St. Joseph's school, widely regarded as among the best in the city, had an average of nearly eighty pupils per room in 1889.[18]

The pupils at St. Joseph's were apparently well instructed: "The examinations in each department proved to be very satisfactory," according to a delegation of priests who visited the school in 1889, "and the knowledge of many branches of studies is more than can be expected in a parochial school." But not all teachers were prepared to do so admirable a job. This was particularly true in the newest ethnic parishes, where the demand for teachers was so great that certain orders regularly sent novices into the classroom, although those novices were hardly more than girls. There were orders too whose members were mainly European-born and trained, and where the command of English was far from certain. The sisters at St. Joachim's school "are French, with scarcely a sufficient knowledge of English," according to Father Francis Van Antwerp, who visited the Detroit school in 1887. The pupils there performed "better in French than in English. Pronunciation of English is poor." As for the school at Ionia, where the sisters had quite recently come from Germany, "only one of the teachers speaks English passably," according to an irate—and non-German—parishioner in 1887. (He had complaints about the students too: "The school is attended by many children who use very profane language, who steel from stores on their way to and from school, and whose general behavior is such that they are a disgrace to the school and the Church.") Bishop Borgess put it succinctly in 1881: "It seems a pity that we are obliged to ask for the service of Religious at such a rate, and deprive ourselves of the right of demanding competent teachers, for our experience confirms, that the wearing of a Religious Habit is no guarantee of competency to teach a Catholic school."[19]

The majority of teachers in the Diocese, of course, were reasonably well trained. Some, the IHMs premier among them, ranked with the best that the public schools could offer. And many immigrant children were probably better served by their foreign-born teachers than they would have been by instruction in English. (No less pedagogically astute an order than the IHMs maintained a "dual" school in the parish at Carleton from 1868 to 1891, where Irish and German children were instructed separately.) Most parochial schools, moreover, were not in the nineteenth century notably more crowded or poorly housed than the public schools in their vicinity. But no matter how balanced a view we take, Bishop Borgess still had good cause to enlist as an educational reformer.[20]

The bishop chose a diocesan school board as his principal instrument of reform. Such boards were a Midwestern innovation: Fort Wayne's Joseph Dwenger had been a pioneer in 1879 when he established a school board in his diocese and gave it authority to prescribe texts and curriculum and to establish qualifications for teachers. The bishops of the Cincinnati Province were sufficiently impressed that they endorsed the Fort Wayne plan as a model when they met at their Fourth Provincial Council in 1882. But even before this council, the merits of a school board had been debated in Detroit at the Fifth Diocesan Synod, which sat in 1881. A bare majority of the committee to which the question was assigned recommended the establishment of a board composed of three priests and three laymen, all to be elected "by the Rectors of parishes in Detroit." The board would serve mainly to certify teachers, although the proviso that "teachers belonging to religious orders will not be examined" meant that the board would have little to do. The recommendation was ultimately rejected by the synod; since it was discussed in secret session we do not know the reasons why. But this particular proposal probably satisfied no one. The bishop would surely have objected to an elected board and probably to the equal weight given to its lay members, while the clergy, who were generally loath to surrender any of the autonomy they enjoyed in their parishes, were most of them reluctant to see a central board established and not much disarmed by the franchise given, after all, only to the pastors in Detroit.[21]

The eventual establishment of a diocesan school board, in 1886, was facilitated by the actions of the Third Plenary Council in 1884, where the American bishops ruled that all dioceses must establish boards of examination for parochial school teachers within two years. (These same boards, according to the council, might also inspect schools and approve textbooks.) The reforming vision of Bishop Borgess was still a critical factor, however, for in 1886 Detroit became one of only eight dioceses to establish a central school board before the turn of the century. The board created by the Seventh Diocesan Synod in 1886 was composed of five priests, chosen at the synod but presumably to be appointed thereafter by the bishop. Their commission was a liberal one: the members "by special regulation were to have charge not only of the examination of teachers and the selection of textbooks, but also of the visitation of all the schools of the Diocese." The first members of the board, moreover, were so diligent that they effectively broadened the board's already generous authority. Within the first year of its operation, the board instituted qualifying examinations for all teachers in the Diocese with less than five years' experience, prescribed a list of textbooks to be used by all schools, embarked on an ambitious program of school inspections, and drafted a detailed course of studies to be followed throughout the Diocese.[22]

Whether the board could fully have implemented its reforms had Bishop Borgess not resigned in the spring of 1887 is difficult to say. But it seems unlikely. For the board was challenging both the authority of the pastor in his parish and the traditional autonomy of the religious orders in the conduct of their particular works of service. Neither group was likely to cede its prerogatives without resistance. The clergy were apparently the more forthright: an outraged Father William Hendrickx, denied permission to hire an experienced teacher who had not been certified by the board, vented his anger directly. "All right Sir," he addressed the Board's secretary, Father Peter Baart. "Mind well however I do not believe in arbitrary rulings and moreover, *if it is from mistrust in me,* that said license was not given, I will never in my life build up a school again." His letter indicates how many issues besides those of school quality were involved in what was correctly seen as an effort, in the cause of reform, to diminish the independence of pastors in the conduct of their parishes. As for the teaching orders, the board's reforms threatened their autonomy even more directly, for the larger orders, especially, prided themselves on their distinctive traditions of pedagogy. And Sisters were accustomed, in nearly all parishes, to conducting their schools with minimal interference from the pastor, who, although he clung to his status as head of the parish school, was generally happy to surrender its direction to an experienced religious.[23]

The diocesan school board, as it was initially constituted, lasted only to 1889.

Bishop John Foley, successor to Borgess, moved quickly to diminish its considerable powers, leaving the board with nothing more than authority to examine and
certify teachers. The inspection of schools was given to newly created "district
boards," composed of the more prominent pastors in each of the five deaneries,
and efforts at standardizing texts and curriculum were quietly abandoned. The
new bishop was evidently responding to popular demand: the Foley measures
were widely applauded, even by priests who had long been concerned about the
quality of Catholic schooling.[24]

The controversy over the powers of the diocesan school board reminds us yet
again of how difficult it was for the American bishops to consolidate in practice
the enormous authority they possessed under Church law. In the case of the
schools, the bishops of Detroit, and of other dioceses as well, faced a particularly
daunting opposition: the clergy, the teaching orders, the members of the ethnic
parishes all had compelling reason to prefer a system of school governance that
permitted a good deal of local autonomy. Given the heterogeneity of the Catholic
population, a decentralized system of the sort that prevailed in the Diocese as
late as the 1920s probably worked to minimize conflict, especially between the
Chancery and the heavily immigrant parishes. Certainly the defeat of an early
centralization of the school system gave the teaching orders much greater control than they would otherwise have had over the training of their members, the
development of curriculum, and the management of the schools. In a good many
cases, this independence probably enhanced the quality of Catholic education,
for the more ambitious orders set high standards for themselves, and worked
hard to improve the instructional skills of their members. In other cases, the
want of centralization clearly slowed the improvement of curriculum and teaching. These developments will be explored in a later chapter. But it is important
to appreciate at the outset the limits to school reform that the Borgess experiment and its undoing represented, for the history of parochial education was
shaped for many years by the realities from which these limits sprang.

Secondary schooling and higher education

Nearly the whole of the educational history of the Diocese between 1833 and
1888 is a history of primary schooling. Most Catholic children, like most Protestant children in these years, left school before or during early adolescence, completing at most an eighth grade education. A miniscule minority went on to college: fewer than 3 percent of the college-aged population of the United States
in 1870 were enrolled in a college or university. Young Catholics, of course, were
less likely than Protestants to receive extended education. Detroit's first public
high school was opened in 1863, but it was not until the 1890s that the city's
parochial schools offered much in the way of instruction beyond the eighth
grade.

Interestingly enough, it was girls who were the more favored sex when it came
to Catholic secondary schooling. Bishop Borgess throughout his episcopate for-

bade female teachers, whether lay or religious, to instruct boys over the age of twelve. Once they had reached their teens and made their first communion, boys were required to leave the parish school unless a male teacher was secured for them. But because relatively few boys came from families that could do without their adolescent wages, it was uneconomical in most parishes to hire a layman to teach the boys in the upper grades. The policy created a painful dilemma for those parents who wished to give their sons extended training but who could not afford a Catholic academy or boarding school. At least some of them, presumably, had recourse to the public high schools, despite repeated episcopal warnings not to do so. Bishop Borgess did eventually modify his position on attendance at public secondary schools, granting a precedent-setting dispensation in 1885 for those graduates of St. Augustine's school in Kalamazoo who wished to attend the local high school. But he never altered his rule on the age at which boys were required to have male instructors, believing himself bound in the matter by a ruling of the Propaganda. A change of policy did not come until 1890, after a collective decision by the bishops of the Cincinnati province. Boys were permitted thereafter to remain with their female teachers until the age of fourteen. At least in the Diocese of Detroit, however, the Chancery after the late 1890s simply ceased to enforce the rule.[25]

For all his unwillingness to bend a cumbersome Roman policy, Bishop Borgess was deeply interested in extended schooling for Catholic boys, or at least for the sons of the well-to-do. He was proud to have brought Jesuits from St. Louis to found a Catholic academy in Detroit, and had even surrendered his cathedral in the process. The Jesuit's Detroit College was opened in the former cathedral school in the fall of 1877 with an initial enrollment of sixty students, nearly all of whom were under seventeen. (College-level courses were not introduced until 1879.) The rigorous classical education offered by the Jesuits cost $40 a year, beyond the reach of most working-class families, but this does not seem to have worried the bishop. Nor was he worried, apparently, by the exclusively academic content of the curriculum, although this proved unpopular with many students and their parents. Pressure from both groups resulted in the addition of commercial courses to the curriculum in the 1880s, but these were discontinued with the advent of a new president in 1893.[26]

Detroit College did undergo a significant change in the years around the turn of the century. The high school became a wholly separate institution, while the college evolved into a university—one that emphasized professional training and offered an extensive evening curriculum. The University of Detroit, as it was eventually known, was an important avenue to social mobility for generations of boys from the lower-middle and the working classes. But in the nineteenth century, the school's effects in this regard were relatively limited.

Secondary education under Catholic auspices had been available to girls to the Diocese fully thirty years before Detroit College opened its doors. St. Mary's Academy in Monroe was founded early in 1847 by the Immaculate Heart of Mary Sisters. The new school had both day and boarding pupils, and included

the primary as well as the higher grades. The emphasis, however, was on a genteel secondary education. That education was costly: board and tuition stood
at $70 a year in 1847, while tuition alone for a "more advanced" day student
amounted to $24 annually.[27]

For much of the nineteenth century, the IHMs presented St. Mary's Academy
to the public as an oasis of piety and gentility, emphasizing in their annual announcements the various courses in music and the decorative arts. Students
might choose from among such classes as "Grecian and Oriental Pearl Painting"
and "Wax Flowers and Fruit," according to an 1877 brochure. But the educational aspirations and achievement of the IHMs, unusually high from the order's beginning, meant that St. Mary's was in fact more rigorous and academic
in its curriculum than the typical young ladies' academy of the period. By the
1890s, the school had largely shed its genteel image, boasting now of its strict
academic standards and thorough instruction in the sciences. Not long after, the
academy offered its first college-level courses, the beginnings of what became
St. Mary's College in 1910. The transformation of St. Mary's Academy in the
final years of the century both reflected and helped to stimulate an important
change in consciousness among an elite group of Catholic women. We will later
see just how this came about.[28]

The network of Catholic schools that existed in the Diocese in 1888 could not
properly be called a "system." A fair number of parishes did not yet have schools,
though it must be conceded that most of these parishes were very small. Few
provisions had been made for the secondary education of girls, and even less
had been done for boys. Despite the establishment of a diocesan school board
in 1886, there was little in the way of centralized control over curriculum or
teacher training. And despite the uncompromising stance of Bishop Borgess on
the necessity of parochial education, there were still significant numbers of Catholics who were, for various reasons, reluctant to support and use the Catholic
schools.

But if the educational achievements of this period were limited, they were still
sufficient to make this the true "foundation time" of parochial education in the
Diocese. Although unanimity on the question did not prevail, most Catholics
by the 1880s were persuaded that Catholic schools were necessary and desirable.
The first steps toward secondary education in the parishes had been taken by
1888, and if girls were to predominate in Catholic secondary schools for some
years beyond the turn of the century, the same was true in most public secondary
schools, not only in Michigan but across the nation. Steps had also been taken
to establish a minimum level of competency for parochial school teachers in the
Diocese. If it proved difficult, even impossible, to enforce these standards rigidly,
the principle of accountability to a central diocesan educational authority had
been established, and the teaching orders responded as quickly as they could
by improving and extending the education of their members.

Finally, the numbers of teaching Sisters in the Diocese had increased significantly by 1888, by which time they had largely displaced the lay teachers who had been so important in the decades before the 1870s. The proliferation of religious is what made possible the steady growth in the number of schools that marks the Borgess years, for by the late nineteenth century lay teachers were considerably more expensive than their religious counterparts. And it was the presence of Sisters, more than anything in the general curriculum, that gave Catholic schools the distinctive qualities they possessed before the reforms of the 1960s. Bishop Borgess went so far as to argue that a school could not be truly Catholic unless it was taught by religious. Virtue was effectively inculcated only by force of example, the Bishop explained. "In this Religious seem to be alone successful." It was a reflection, perhaps, of the increasingly disciplined religious behavior of the laity that a good many Catholics appear to have agreed with him.[29]

5

CATHOLICS IN A NON-CATHOLIC WORLD

Detroit and much of its hinterland was once colonized almost exclusively by the French, who were Catholics, if sometimes only nominally so. By the early nineteenth century, however, Catholics were in the minority in southeastern Michigan, and had to learn how to coexist with a growing and economically powerful Protestant population. Coexistence in a literal sense was certainly achieved: there was almost no communal violence in Michigan between Catholics and other religious groups. But the state's political history reveals an electorate in the nineteenth century that was deeply divided on religious lines. Nearly all of Michigan's Catholics between the late 1830s and the mid-1890s were Democrats; the Republican party in the state, after its emergence in the early 1850s, drew heavily on the votes of evangelical Protestants. And from the elections in 1837, the year in which Michigan entered the Union, until the political crises of the 1890s, campaigns in Michigan turned mainly on religious questions, although these took such various forms as the enfranchisement of aliens, the wisdom of Prohibition, and the desirability of Sabbatarian laws. If we look to the political history of the nineteenth century, in short, we cannot but conclude that most Catholics saw the world in a very different way from the majority of Protestants.

That Catholics behaved politically as if they possessed a common set of interests and values does not mean, however, that Catholics in the Diocese saw themselves as part of a community that transcended ethnic lines. Probably most did not. For if the Catholics of the Diocese between 1840 and the early 1890s were more seriously alienated from non-Catholics than ever before or since, they were also more deeply divided among themselves. We will see that even in Detroit the numerous Catholic population was unable before the 1890s to sustain any enduring Catholic organization that drew its members from more than a single national group.

It was largely as members of discrete ethnic communities, then, that Catholics surveyed the larger society and determined what their relations with that society would be. It may well have semed to many of them an inhospitable world at best. But the history of Catholic-Protestant relations in the Diocese of Detroit has never been simply a history of institutionalized antipathies, whatever an examination of politics alone might suggest. Individual Catholics were sometimes quite at home among non-Catholics: Bishop Borgess found it necessary to inveigh repeatedly against what was almost certainly a rising incidence of religiously mixed marriage. Catholics and Protestants shared important moral and political values, even as they fought bitterly over others. And the charitable work of the various religious orders was an increasingly powerful antidote to bigotry, especially in Detroit. The extent to which individual Catholics moved with ease in the world beyond the religious group did vary enormously, as did the extent to which Catholics were led to alter their view of themselves and their religion because of encounters with Protestants or—much more rarely—Jews. We can never know this history in all its variety. But we can bear in mind that it was a complicated one.

INTERMARRIAGE

The extent to which Catholics marry outside the religious group perhaps best measures their isolation—or insulation—from the non-Catholic world around them. It is unfortunate, then, that we have so little information about the rate of intermarriage in the Diocese before the end of the nineteenth century. Records of dispensations granted for marriages to non-Catholics have been kept only since 1870, and the Chancery did not record the numbers of marriages performed by priests in the Diocese until 1884. The proportion of mixed marriages in the total recorded for that year was low—just under 7 percent. It was even lower in the following year, when fewer than 5 percent of the marriages involved a non-Catholic partner.[1]

There is reason to suspect, however, that these low figures do not accurately reflect the extent to which Catholics in the 1880s wanted to, and probably did, marry outside their religion. For it is likely that the Chancery made it harder for Catholics to secure dispensations in that decade than had previously been the case, and that this was especially true between 1884 and 1887. The evidence is as follows. The number of dispensations granted by the Chancery rose sharply during the 1870s, from 35 in 1870 to 130 in 1880, a nearly fourfold increase, although the Catholic population in the Diocese grew only modestly in this same period. The upsurge in mixed marriage clearly troubled Bishop Borgess, who issued no less than three pastoral letters in the 1870s condemning "marriages between Catholics and Protestants and infidels." But he was not pleased by the response: "So far from being consoled by the proofs manifesting a more docile spirit in the observance of the Laws of the Church of God," he scolded in 1878, "the evil [of mixed marriage] has steadily grown, and in the year, just ended, we have been obliged to grant more dispensations for such unfortunate marriages than in any one of the previous seven." The decline in dispensations granted after 1880, reaching a dramatic low of 35 in 1886, might be taken to mean that Catholics had finally learned obedience, were it not for the sharp increase in dispensations issued once Borgess resigned in the spring of 1887. In 1889, the first year in the episcopate of John Samuel Foley, 211 dispensations were granted. The proportion of mixed marriages recorded in 1889 was a startling 22 percent.[2]

Other more fragmentary evidence indicates that a relatively high rate of intermarriage may have prevailed in at least some parishes well before the end of the century. The pastor at St. Mary's in Redford reported in 1879 that fully one-third of the 150 families in his parish were "mixed families, and of these fifty only a few families attend church." Redford was then a rural settlement with a sizable Protestant population, and the congregation had a history of conflict with ecclesiastical authority. Perhaps the proximity of Protestants and the evident alienation of a portion of Redford's Catholics accounts for this unusually high figure. A surprisingly large proportion of mixed marriages was reported in 1884 for St. Augustine's in Kalamazoo, a congregation with a less troubled history than the one at Redford, but similarly marooned in a Protestant sea. The St. Augustine parish census claimed that 16 percent of the families in the parish were "mixed"; had all of the 180 mixed marriages located in the census been included, even those where the Catholic party had left the Church, the proportion of mixed marriages in the parish would have risen to 30 percent. The Kalamazoo experience appears to demonstrate the futility of preaching against mixed marriage, for the pastor there was an unusually vigorous opponent of the practice, even producing a pamphlet on the subject. His conviction that temporal unhappiness as well as spiritual danger was attendant on marriage to a non-Catholic was artlessly conveyed in his 1884 census report. "Among the mixed marriages only 5 claimed to be happy," he noted in the margin, "and I feel sure 3 of them lied."[3]

The reports from Redford and Kalamazoo suggest a dimension to the mixed marriage question that Chancery figures do not reveal. Given the large numbers of mixed marriages in these parishes, especially when compared to the numbers of dispensations being issued in Detroit, and given the frequency with which the Catholic party in these marriages abandoned his religion, we can reasonably assume that some of these Catholics had been married in Protestant or civil ceremonies. Bishop Borgess evidently believed that Catholics in his jurisdiction were sometimes married in non-Catholic services, for in 1882 he ordered his priests to announce to their congregations that marriages before ministers or justices of the peace were grounds for excommunication. The offender could be reconciled with the Church only after "he shall make a public reparation in the presence of the congregation or mission to which he belongs." No uniform discipline, apparently, had prevailed before this time. The pastor at Marine City suggested in 1874 that Borgess ask his priests to note in their annual reports "How many got married during the year by the Squire or by a Protestant minister? What is your practice with such ones afterwards?"[4]

We have no way of knowing how common it was for Catholics entering mixed marriages to forgo a Catholic ceremony. But it would not be surprising if the practice were relatively more frequent in the priest-poor Diocese of the mid-nineteenth century than it was several generations later. Indeed, the sharp rise in the 1870s in dispensations granted for mixed marriages may reflect less an increase in the number of Catholics marrying non-Catholics than an increase in the number of Catholics entering mixed marriages who chose to be married by a priest. If this were true, then what Bishop Borgess saw as a decline in discipline and loyalty to the Church among the laity would actually have represented a trend in just the opposite direction. In any event, we must bear in mind that the extent to which Catholics married non-Catholics was certainly greater, both in the nineteenth century and after, than the Chancery's records alone would indicate.

CONTRACEPTION AND ABORTION

We have long been accustomed to regard Catholics — or at least their spokesmen — as at odds with the larger society over fundamental questions of sexual morality. But this was not the case in the nineteenth century. Even as late as 1914, it is possible to speak of something like a Christian consensus on such matters as contraception, abortion, and divorce. This does not mean that nineteenth-century Protestants — or Catholics, for that matter — never practiced birth control or had recourse to abortion, for there is ample evidence that they did. But their churches either condemned these practices or, in the case of the more liberal denominations, maintained a prudent silence. Virtually no mainstream Protestant clergy in the nineteenth century publicly defended the morality of contraception or abortion, and clergy from the more conservative denominations espoused as unyielding a position on these issues as did the Catholic Church. True, the Catholic press in the later nineteenth century sometimes claimed that Protestants and Catholics behaved quite differently when it came to contraception, with affluent Protestants, especially, portrayed as regular practitioners of birth control. But if Catholic publicists were sure that their Church was better able to discipline the faithful than those denominations that had abandoned an infallible teaching authority and the practice of confession, they assumed nonetheless that most Protestant clergy shared their views on sexual ethics.[5]

Contraception was not, however, nearly as frequent a topic in Catholic sermons and periodicals in the nineteenth century as it would become by the 1920s. Since birth control was widely assumed to be a mainly, even an exclusively, Protestant vice, most bishops and priests concluded that frequent discussion of the matter was both unnecessary and potentially dangerous. Bishop Borgess in 1882 cautioned his clergy against too-explicit questioning in the confessional with regard to contraception, apparently to keep penitents from learning of sinful practices hitherto unknown to them. Bishop Camillus Maes of Covington, who had served as a priest in the Diocese of Detroit from 1869 to 1884, did issue a pastoral letter in 1890 that dealt in part with the evils of contraception. But his warning against the practice was directed solely to men, probably on the assumption that *coitus interruptus,* reputed to be widely employed in France, was the means of contraception most likely to be known among Catholics in the United States. The *Michigan Catholic* reprinted the letter in full, but claimed two years later that contraceptive practices were unknown among Catholics. "It [contraception] will be found among our Protestant fellow citizens; it will not be found among our Catholic fellow citizens. In the highest social strata among them it is absent; it does not appear in the intermediate or in the lowest." For the most part, however, the *Michigan Catholic* was silent on the matter. The paper contains very few references to contraception before the turn of the century.[6]

The Catholic clergy were apparently as little inclined to public discussion of abortion as they were of contraception, although the issue of abortion was after midcentury increasingly the stuff of political controversy. For there is little doubt that the incidence of abortion in the United States rose sharply in the 1840s, and remained at high levels through the 1880s. A survey of physicians in Michigan conducted by a special committee of the State Board of Health resulted in 1882 in the claim that one-third of all pregnancies in the state were terminated by abortion. Similar estimates were made by physicians' groups in other parts of the country. Many, perhaps most, Americans in the nineteenth century appear to have regarded early abortion as less than a grave moral wrong. "There is very generally current among the people the notion that before a pregnant woman 'quickens,' ie before the fourth month of pregnancy, there is no real life in the foetus, or at least that it is not a 'living soul,' and to destroy it is not a real crime," a witness informed the Michigan State Board of Health in 1876.[7]

It was physicians who, in the late 1860s, initiated the first sustained campaigns to alter this popular view of abortion and to broaden the powers of the state to curtail, if not eliminate, the thriving abortion trade. Laws proved easier to change than attitudes, at least in the beginning. Michigan outlawed the advertisement of abortifacients in 1869 — these were usually disguised as cures for various "female complaints" — and in 1873 the state forbade the sale of "drugs and medicines designed to procure illegal abortions." The actual performing of an abortion had been illegal in Michigan since 1846, but popular tolerance of the practice and widespread belief in the "quickening doctrine" meant that the law was little enforced as late as the 1880s. Only with a gradual shift in opinion on the issue, a shift that was largely accomplished by 1900, did abortion come to be regularly prosecuted as a serious criminal offense.[8]

The crusading physicians of Michigan, as elsewhere in the nation, were overwhelmingly of the opinion in the nineteenth century that abortion was not a Catholic problem. The increase in abortion after 1840, they claimed, had been caused mainly by middle-class women of Protestant descent, who were using abortion as a means of family limitation. This is presumably why the Catholic clergy, at least in Michigan, kept largely aloof from the growing policy debate. Their Protestant counterparts in the state were even more inclined to silence, or so a committee of antiabortion physicians charged in the late 1870s. Here, however, the motivation was thought to be primarily self-serving: the Protestant clergy, according to their more bitter medical opponents, were afraid to confront the numerous sinners in their own respectable congregations.[9]

The unanimity of the testimony about Catholic women and abortion is so impressive that one hesitates to suggest that nineteenth-century observers may have been wrong when they claimed that virtually all of the women who sought abortions before the very end of the century were Protestants. The composition of the Catholic population adds weight to the testimony, for that population was heavily immigrant and mostly poor — made up, in short, mainly of those individuals whom historical demographers tell us were the least likely to try to limit family size and space the birth of children. But two pieces of evidence from the Diocese of Detroit suggest that Catholic women in the nineteenth century did sometimes seek abortions, or perhaps, since the evidence dates from the 1880s, that the behavior of Catholics in this regard had begun to change from earlier decades.

First, Bishop Borgess announced in 1882 that both actual and attempted abortion were henceforth reserved sins, for which absolution could be secured only by application to the bishop. He did so, he informed his clergy, because "the spirit of infidelity, of impiety, and of crime, so rampant in our day, has invaded the sanctuary of Catholic hearts, and in many cases succeeded in obliterating the horror and infamy of the brutal crime of murdering the innocent, not yet able to utter a cry for pity." This alone is not necessarily compelling evidence, for Bishop Borgess took a gloomy view of human nature and was ready to suspect serious sin, especially sexual sin, with very little provocation. In 1885, however, a Redemptorist priest who had just preached a mission at Kalamazoo wrote to Bishop Borgess requesting permission to absolve penitents of those sins which the Bishop had declared to be *casus reservati*. He expressed no surprise that in a total of 1,303 adult confessions he had 49 cases of actual or attempted abortion. Not all of these, presumably, had occurred within the year, for missions were occasions when persons alienated from the Church, sometimes for many years, were moved to confess and receive communion. But they were also occasions during which men normally went to confession in large numbers. It is reasonable to assume that close to half of the 1,303 confessions heard in Kalamazoo were those of men. It is difficult, then, to regard the number of abortions confessed at Kalamazoo as anything but startlingly large.[10]

We could, of course, conclude that the Catholics of Kalamazoo were different in their attitudes and behavior with regard to abortion from Catholics elsewhere in the Diocese. The Chancery archives contain no reports from other parishes where abortions were confessed in large numbers. But those archives are notoriously incomplete for the nineteenth century. There is, moreover, no additional evidence to suggest that the Catholics of Kalamazoo were a peculiar population. It seems more sensible to conclude, albeit very tentatively, that the practice of abortion among native-born Catholics was more widespread than most observers believed, at least by the 1880s. Perhaps Catholic women were less likely than Protestant women to turn for abortions or the resultant complications to those well-credentialed physicians whose testimony formed most of the evidence in the public campaign against abortion. Perhaps many of them had recourse to patent medicines, which painful and dangerous though they were, generally had little effect on the course of a pregnancy. A Paulist priest working in the Diocese requested permission in 1883 to absolve a penitent "who twice took medicine to prevent pregnancy though not at all sure she was in that condition. No perceptible result followed, but the intention was there." Against his request, however, we must set the request of Kalamazoo's Father Frank O'Brien in that same year for permission to absolve "four cases of abortion (Complete.)"[11]

The missioner at Kalamazoo in 1885 did not indicate whether the women who confessed there to abortion and attempted abortion were married or single. But the number of abortions he reported seems awfully large to have been primarily the acts of desperate unmarried women. Very possibly, then, there were Catholics by the 1880s who, like their Protestant neighbors, used abortion as a means of family limitation, presumably after failed attempts at contraception. An essentially "contraceptive" motive might make it easier, at least for a time, for a married woman to persuade herself that abortion was not necessarily a mortal sin. The reluctance of the Catholic clergy to preach on contraception and their apparent circumspection in the confessional may have led some Catholics to think that birth control was not invariably wrong. But in the heat of a mission sermon, even an indifferent Catholic would presumably know that abortion was indeed grave matter for confession.[12]

RELIGION AND POLITICS

If contraception was not yet an issue that deeply divided Catholics and Protestants, they disagreed on other questions of fundamental importance. Political historians in recent years have documented the enormous importance of religion and ethnicity in nineteenth-century politics, and they have emphasized especially the conflicting worldviews which distinguished most Catholics from the majority of Protestants. Many Protestants, particularly those belonging to denominations that stressed a radical experience of conversion, looked to politics as a means of imposing godly behavior on the general population. They wanted a culturally homogeneous society, although they were willing for the most part to accept foreigners whose Protestant traditions were similar to their own. They were attracted in large numbers to temperance reform, to Sabbatarianism, and to anti-Catholicism — sometimes in its most virulent forms.

Catholics, on the other hand, and especially foreign-born Catholics, were generally repelled by what they saw as efforts by evangelical Protestants to unite their own sectarian values to the machinery of the state. Their distaste was shared in Michigan to a greater or lesser degree by those Protestants whose ritualistic traditions or foreign birth made them wary of the reformism and nativist zeal that permeated first the Whig and subsequently the Republican party. Catholics and those Protestants who were attracted to the Democratic party generally possessed a more tolerant and pragmatic orientation to politics than their opponents did. Politics was for them a means of dividing patronage and resolving conflict among the many religious and ethnic and interest groups that comprised the population. Politics was decidedly not a means of imposing the moral standards of one group upon all others; if the state had an activist role to play, it lay in protecting the ability of various groups in the population to live according to their particular values. Thus most Democrats opposed temperance and Sabbatarian laws, favored the enfranchisement of aliens, and—in the case of Catholics—defended the propriety of state support for sectarian schools.[13]

Not all nineteenth-century voters, of course, could articulate their vision of the good society in any great detail. What fueled partisanship in many, perhaps most, cases was intense dislike of the ethnic and religious groups that made up the opposition. For this reason candidates and party leaders regularly regaled the party faithful with unflattering stereotypes of their opponents. One might plausibly argue that politics exacerbated the considerable tensions inherent in a multiethnic society: in Michigan, for example, the political divide between Catholics and Protestants became more rather than less extreme between 1850 and the early 1890s. But it is also true that politics provided an arena where ethnic and religious antagonisms could be indulged without recourse to violence. Because many of Michigan's alien residents could vote and because voter participation was high in the nineteenth century, even the more marginal members of the population were involved in what was clearly a cathartic ritual. In Michigan, at least, politics probably functioned more effectively to defuse ethnic and religious tensions than it did to aggravate them.[14]

The anti-Catholicism that was evident first among Michigan's Whigs and then in the Republican party intermittently assumed intense and bitter proportions. A wave of anti-Catholicism swept the nation in the mid-1840s, and its effects were widely felt in Michigan. An avowedly nativist newspaper was founded in Detroit in 1845; a similar paper appeared in Ann Arbor the following year. Both were short-lived, however, presumably because of their editors' Whig loyalties: the importance of alien voters in the Michigan electorate caused many of the state's Whig leaders to work against displays of blatant nativism. Perhaps partly because of this, there was no religious rioting in Michigan during these turbulent years, although Philadelphia was wracked by anti-Catholic violence in the spring and summer of 1844. By 1847 the surge of extreme anti-Catholicism had spent itself locally, leaving in its wake no damage but those invisible wounds that bigotry inflicts on vulnerable psychologies.[15]

The late 1840s and the early 1850s were years of relative good feeling between Catholics and Protestants in the state. By 1850, indeed, the Whig party in Michigan was actively courting the Catholic vote. (Zachariah Chandler was elected Whig mayor of Detroit in 1851 after a campaign in which he made repeated overtures to the local Irish community.) But Bishop Lefevere's 1853 campaign to secure state support for Michigan's Catholic schools brought an end to this brief interlude of uneasy peace, and doomed further efforts at a politics that transcended religious division. The more moderate elements in the Whig party were overwhelmed by the anti-Catholic forces, which, as "Independents" or "Know-Nothings," came increasingly to dominate the anti-Democratic coalition that succeeded the disintegration of the Whig party in Michigan in the early 1850s. When this coalition assumed something like the form of a political party in 1854, from which event the birth of the Republican party is generally dated, the intense anti-Catholicism of its more extreme members was an integral part of the nascent party's ideology. The elections in that same year produced a Michigan legislature dominated by evangelical reformers, who not only instituted "Maine Law" prohibition — a law that was little enforced in Detroit — but empowered lay trustees to hold title to parish properties, effectively affirming the precedence of state over ecclesiastical law. This legislation proved only a minor irritant to Bishop Lefevere in his efforts to gain legal ownership of all Church properties in the Diocese. But it indicates the intensity of the anti-Catholicism that fueled Michigan politics in the mid-1850s. The legislature even considered a bill in 1855 "for the regulation of Roman Catholic nunneries and schools," but never passed it into law.[16]

Michigan's Catholics were by no means a quiescent population during the political storms of the 1850s. The defeats of 1853 gave rise to a Catholic paper in Detroit, one geared especially to defending Irish Catholic interests and points of view. The *Detroit Catholic Vindicator,* as it was called, was initially a diocesan paper, lay edited but enjoying the sponsorship of Bishop Lefevere. Its tone, however, was anything but irenic. Strident, sometimes hysterical, in the cause of "Catholic rights," it reflected the tenor of the more extreme anti-Catholic publications of the day, revealing in the process the psychic wounds that the Irish, in particular, had sustained in the political wars. (It was the Irish who were the favorite target of anti-Catholic orators and publicists in these years, and not only in Michigan.) The *Vindicator* continued as a diocesan organ until 1856, when its defensiveness acquired an overtly partisan cast, something its editor believed to be consonant with the paper's religious mission. Bishop Lefevere disagreed, however, and withdrew his sponsorship. For the rest of its short life, the paper functioned as an organ of the Democratic party. As for the Catholic population generally, its already strong predilection for the Democrats intensified in the 1850s, even as significant numbers of hitherto Democratic Protestants moved into the Republican camp.[17]

The coming of the Civil War forced a hiatus in Michigan's institutionalized religious warfare, and for several decades afterwards, the politics of the state were characterized by a relatively muted anti-Catholic sentiment. The electorate, however, continued to be deeply divided along religious lines, with the state emerging as predominantly Republican in its allegiances. Moral reforms like Prohibition and Sabbatarian laws continued to be issues in both state and local elections, and to reinforce existing religious divisions. The parochial school remained an issue too. Continued denial of state aid to their schools was a source of grievance for many Catholics, while Republicans made it a point of principle to praise the public schools as the sole hope of achieving a homogenized and disciplined society.

Also important as an occasional vehicle for anti-Catholicism was the question of who should own church property. In the 1870s and again in the 1880s there were efforts made to repeal the law, passed in 1867, that recognized the Bishop of Detroit as sole owner of all ecclesiastical properties in his diocese, and to substitute instead a scheme of corporate ownership that included representatives of the laity. There were certainly Catholics who favored these measures, and who were willing to work on their behalf. But each was defeated by a concerted lobbying campaign that was organized at the Chancery in Detroit. Bishop Borgess, writing to the bishop of Grand Rapids in 1887 with regard to the rumored introduction of yet another bill to reform the tenure of church property, indicated the kind of response that had greeted earlier attempts in this direction. "As soon as it [the bill] is introduced," Borgess warned, "a flood of protests from the churches in this State has to be poured into the House and Senate, and if necessary lobbying among the representatives must be done. When the famous 'Campbell Bill' threatened us, it required all our energy (and all our spare money too) to defeat it." There is no evidence, however, that the political skills being honed at the Chancery were employed for any but limited defensive purposes. Catholics were a numerically important minority after midcentury in portions of Michigan and especially in Detroit, but their bishops were not important political actors, not, at least, after the abortive school campaigns of 1853.[18]

"A BODY OF CHRISTIAN GENTLEMEN":
ORGANIZED CHARITY AND INTERRELIGIOUS COOPERATION

If the confessional divide in nineteenth-century Detroit was deep, it was not unbridgeable. Various factors account for this, the most important of which was the slow but steady assimilation of the city's immigrants. Of greater visibility, however, and of no small importance when it came to the question of religious tolerance, was the charitable work of the various Catholic religious orders. Their work brought needed services to a city that even at midcentury had made almost no provision for the welfare of its inhabitants. Their work, moreover, commanded the reluctant admiration of all but the most confirmed anti-Catholics, and helped to generate a modest tradition of interreligious cooperation in the realm of charity and public welfare.

We have already surveyed the pioneering work of Father Martin Kundig, who founded a cholera hospital and an orphanage in Detroit in 1834. Both institutions, it will be recalled, were substantially run by women religious—members of the Colletine Poor Clares, who served in the Diocese from 1833 until 1839. The Poor Clares were eventually succeeded by the Daughters of Charity, who opened St. Vincent's—later St. Mary's—hospital in Detroit in 1845. This same order was responsible for St. Vincent's Orphan Asylum for girls (1851), for the Michigan Retreat for the Insane (1860), and for the House of Providence, a foundling home and hospital for unwed mothers, which was opened in Detroit in 1869. During the Civil War, the Daughters of Charity also conducted a small-pox hospital in Detroit, where most of the patients were soldiers. The order apparently continued to provide nurses to the city's smallpox hospitals until the 1890s.[19]

The Daughters of Charity were the most important of the religious orders locally when it came to charity and social service. The Detroit convent gave up the last of its schools in 1874, and the Sisters devoted themselves thereafter wholly to the work of charity. Bishop Borgess had perhaps encouraged them to do so, for it was he who brought the Little Sisters of the Poor and the Sisters of the Good Shepherd to Detroit. Both were orders that defined their mission exclusively in terms of social service. The Little Sisters opened a Home for the Aged Poor in Detroit in 1872. The work of the Good Shepherd Sisters was more controversial, involving as it did the reclamation of prostitutes and the care of delinquent girls. Their House of the Good Shepherd, opened in Detroit in 1883, was a target of anti-Catholic propaganda as late as the time of the First World War.

The various teaching orders in the Diocese in the nineteenth century were also drawn to the work of charity. Their principal contribution was the care of homeless girls: at least four teaching orders in the latter half of the century had convents that doubled as orphanages. (In the case of the Felician Sisters, an initially modest undertaking grew to be a ministry of some importance. Their Detroit convent was home to nearly one hundred girls by the early twentieth century.) Hospital work was attractive too: the School Sisters of Notre Dame were widely praised for their brave response to the 1856 cholera epidemic. Teachers in Detroit's St. Mary's parish, the Sisters converted both their convent and the school to a temporary children's hospital. The Adrian Dominicans established what they hoped would be a more permanent facility in 1886, when they opened St. Joseph's Hospital. And by the 1880s, plans were underway for what would soon be the thriving Borgess Hospital at Kalamazoo, in the charge of the Sisters of St. Joseph at Nazareth.[20]

By the close of the Borgess episcopate, then, the various religious orders in the Diocese had given rise to four hospitals and at least six orphanages, as well as institutions for the aged poor and for troubled women and girls. And certain orders had distinguished themselves for heroic service in times of war and epidemic. Detroit was still, for all these labors, a veritable sea of misery: epidemic disease and high rates of infant mortality were facts of city life beyond the century's end. But the charitable work of the religious orders was, in the circumstances, highly visible, and it was widely admired. The local press bears witness to this: even papers with marked Protestant sympathies were often warm in their praise of the Sisters and their charitable institutions. With the exception of the orphanages, moreover, the various Catholic institutions were open to all comers, and seem to have had a good many clients who were not Catholic. (The *Michigan Catholic* was proud to note in 1894 that one of the 215 inmates of the Home for the Aged Poor was "a Hebrew.") Even in the late nineteenth century, Detroit's public welfare institutions were few in number and poorly developed. Most Detroiters, as a consequence, had reason to see the work of the Sisters as essential to the city's wellbeing—and perhaps, indeed, to their own.[21]

Largely because of this, there was even in the nineteenth century a certain amount of interreligious cooperation when it came to supporting local charities. At least a few Catholics were active in the Detroit Association of Charities, which was founded in 1879 as an avowedly interdenominational body. Catholic and Protestant women in Detroit regularly cooperated in the later nineteenth century in various fund-raising efforts to benefit the Catholic hospitals. Kalamazoo's Father Frank O'Brien was named to the Michigan Board of Charities and Corrections in the late 1880s. Perhaps partly out of deference to him—he was a popular member—the group invited Detroit's Bishop John Foley to address its convention in 1889. The bishop was pleased to do so, noting in his address that he entered "most heartily into the aims and aspirations" of the gathering. "We meet here as a body of Christian gentlemen," the Bishop told his audience, "men indeed with different views as far as religion is concerned, but who, nevertheless, are all actuated by the common motive of alleviating suffering and of softening sorrow." This is tepid ecumenism by present-day standards. But in the deeply divided religious world of the late nineteenth century, the bishop's words had real significance. For he implicitly endorsed the kind of ecumenism that concerned itself with practical tasks rather than with theology. In the good work of charity, the bishop's cordial greetings seemed to say, we can recognize one another as fellow Christians. Some Detroiters had already come to this conclusion, which could only contribute to the cause of interreligious peace.[22]

CATHOLICS AS A COMMUNITY:
THE SIGNIFICANCE OF ETHNIC DIVISIONS

The beginning of mass immigration in the late 1840s brought an end to French cultural hegemony among Michigan's Catholics, and inaugurated a lengthy period of growing ethnic diversity in the local Church. Detroit's bishops, like most of their confreres, accommodated the newcomers in each generation by authorizing the establishment of "national" or foreign-language parishes, at least in the larger Catholic centers. Detroit's nineteenth-century bishops almost certainly envisioned the eventual assimilation of ethnic Catholics into an English-speaking Catholic community. But they assumed that the process of assimilation would be slow, and they rarely took steps to hasten the decline of the national parishes. Each understood that he was shepherd to a divided flock.

Still, these same bishops were anxious to see a real solidarity among the Catholics of their diocese, both for political purposes and because they were offended by the ethnic antagonisms that belied the catholicity of the Church. As early as 1853, Bishop Lefevere appealed through the *Detroit Catholic Vindicator* for the establishment in the city of "an institution that shall be neither *French,* nor *German,* nor *English,* but Catholic." Writing in the aftermath of the school campaigns, Lefevere envisioned a society that would not only promote Catholic political interests but erode those ethnic enmities that had apparently divided the Detroit Catholic vote on the school question. There was little response to his appeal, however. It was not until 1873 that such a society was founded, and even then the group suffered badly from recurrent ethnic rivalries.[23]

The society in question was the Catholic Union of Detroit, founded under mainly Irish auspices, but with the purpose of promoting among Catholic men a sense of religious identity that transcended ethnic divisions. (An ancillary purpose, according to a spokesman in 1881, was to provide young Catholic men with an alternative to "the society of nominal Protestant or infidel associates.") But the union's demise, some fifteen years after its founding, was caused largely by competition from ethnic social and benefit societies, at least according to one of its most prominent sponsors. A successor organization, the Catholic Club of Detroit, was even shorter-lived, despite an almost exclusively social orientation. It survived from 1888 until 1896, but was obliged in 1894 — in the depths of a severe depression — to recruit non-Catholic members. This "true liberality," as the *Michigan Catholic* had it, was not able to save the club financially, and ran counter to the organization's efforts to be "a center of Catholic sociability in which parish lines do not prevail, but where Catholics in the whole city may meet and become acquainted."[24]

That so few men were interested in a sociability of this sort bespeaks both the relatively small size of the Catholic middle class and the intensely parochial view of the Church that prevailed among nearly all Catholics. Even those assimilated men who moved with ease in business or politics were inclined to identify "the Church" with "the parish." And the mass of Catholics, for whom the world was largely defined by ethnic and neighborhood loyalties, were surely unable to imagine in any meaningful way a "church" that looked much different from the parish in which they lived. It is hardly surprising, then, that parish and ethnic organizations should have flourished at the expense of larger "Catholic" societies. But it was disappointing nonetheless to that handful of laymen who wished to see Catholics organized on a citywide, even a diocesan, basis. Piqued, perhaps, by the somnolence of the local Catholic Union, the editor of what was then the unofficial diocesan paper noted in 1877 that "there is more enterprise in a shoe-peg factory than there is in all the Catholics of this Diocese."[25]

Still, there is evidence that Catholics in the Diocese were moving toward a gradual easing of ethnic tensions by the later nineteenth century. The appearance in Detroit of ethnically heterogeneous parishes bears witness to this. Detroit in the 1890s was still a city segregated primarily on the basis of ethnicity, but in certain of its outlying districts the shape of a city segregated largely by class could already be seen. "The parish is a mixed one," the *Michigan Catholic* informed its readers in 1889 with regard to St. Charles parish on Detroit's far east side. "There are Irish, Flemish, Dutch, and Polanders, all of whom are harmoniously working for the common cause — the benefit of their church and parish." A later account of the parish, in 1896, added Italian and German and French Catholics to the population living in the large area which St. Charles parish then encompassed — so large that the Dutch-born pastor had taken to riding a bicycle when making parochial visits. St. Charles was not a typical Detroit parish in the 1890s, but it stood for the future. The St. Charles experience was repeated again and again in the so-called "suburban" parishes that appeared in large numbers in Detroit after 1900.[26]

Even in the national parishes of Detroit there were growing indications by the later nineteenth century that Catholic solidarity was an ideal worth at least occasional recognition. Detroit's Catholics, like the city's Protestants, were in the nineteenth century a people who delighted in parades, and processions typically marked even minor events in the history of the city's parishes. Toward the end of the century, we find that these parades were more and more often composed of representatives from a variety of ethnic groups. As early as 1873 a parade to commemorate the blessing of a banner acquired by the Christian Doctrine Society of St. Vincent's (Irish) parish included delegations from French and German parish societies as well as Irish organizations. The Chancery evidently approved of these periodic displays of Catholic unity, for the *Michigan Catholic* in the 1880s and 1890s frequently encouraged parish organizations to turn out in large numbers for ceremonies and parades, especially those which celebrated the church-and-school-building accomplishments of Detroit's growing Polish community. That enthusiasm for interparochial celebration might have gone too far was the worry of one correspondent to the *Michigan Catholic* in 1899. Detroit's Irish-Americans, he claimed, had grown so indifferent to their special obligation to commemorate St. Patrick's Day that the recent parade in Detroit had lacked a distinctively Irish flavor. "The majority of 'Irishmen in line' on that day was made up of our German and Polish fellow citizens."[27]

None of this suggests more than the gradual waning of ethnic antagonisms as growing numbers of Catholics in the Diocese were American-born and raised. Ethnic divisions among Catholics remained real and deep, well into the twentieth century. But by the end of the nineteenth century, the growing ranks of assimilated Catholics provided a seedbed for what ultimately became not only diocesan but regional and even national lay Catholic organizations. The growth of the Knights of Columbus from what was initially a federation of Irish-American benefit societies to a powerful national Catholic organization is but one case in point. Such groups gave Catholics a greater visibility and a more respected voice in politics than they had previously possessed, and were integral to the creation of an American Catholic identity.

The shape of changes yet to come was visible, then, in the divided Catholic population of the Diocese at the end of the nineteenth century. Indeed, the last fifteen years of the century were for many assimilated Catholics a time when it seemed possible as never before to be both fully American and fully Catholic. In Detroit, this heady period was marked by an unprecedented flowering of intellectual and cultural life in the wealthier parishes, by a growing interest in the role of the laity in the Church, and — after 1888 — by the excitement associated with a popular bishop, whose connections in his See city were more cosmopolitan than those of his predecessor. At least in the early years of his episcopate, the urbane and eloquent John Samuel Foley (1888–1918) represented assimilated Catholics as they longed to be seen by their non-Catholic peers. That he was Detroit's first American-born bishop simply underscores the changes that were taking place in the Catholic population of the Diocese and the nation.

It is to the Foley years that we now turn. They were years of enormous change: Detroit and its hinterland were transformed by the advent of the automobile, and the Catholic population of the Diocese grew dramatically as a consequence. And although the intellectual excitement of the 1890s did ebb in the wake of theological reaction in Rome, a Catholic middle class began during the Foley episcopate to make its mark on the political and social life of numerous communities in the Diocese. By the time of Bishop Foley's death in 1918, a sizable population of Catholics had assumed for themselves an easy American identity. That they had emerged from a world where ethnic and religious divisions were deep and pervasive was to them but confirmation of the true catholicity of America and the truly American spirit of Catholicism.

PART II

1888–1918

6

THE FOLEY EPISCOPATE

THE MAN AND HIS CITY

When Bishop John Samuel Foley came to his new see city on November 23, 1888, he was welcomed by the most lavish parade that Catholic Detroit had ever organized. The procession began at the Union Station, where the bishop's train arrived, and moved along Jefferson Avenue, which was bedecked "as far as the eye could see" with "torches, Chinese lanterns, electric lights and illuminated windows." Thousands of men, including uniformed companies from the various parish military societies, accompanied the bishop's carriage through the downtown to the episcopal residence on Washington Street. The residence itself "was hung with the Papal colors, and from cornice to basement was a glory of Edison lights in many colored globes," while nearby on Washington Street stood an immense arch of evergreens, "gloriously festooned and lighted," and bearing "on each face a gigantic portrait of the Bishop surrounded with words of welcome."

Upon Bishop Foley's arrival at his new home, he and his party were conducted to an outdoor reviewing stand to watch the rest of the parade. "The immense procession moved past," an observer recorded, "and some divisions . . . sent off rockets and colored lights in thousands. At the same time the legend, 'Leo XIII, our Pope,' in front of St. Aloysius church burst out in many colored flame, the band struck up in glorious harmony, the Catholic knights drew their sabres . . . and then the procession kept moving past, and kept on moving past until near midnight." Bishop Foley patiently reviewed the parade until the very end, to the delight of the still-numerous crowds that lined the downtown streets. Those who had caught even a glimpse of the new bishop, it was subsequently reported, were certain of Detroit's good fortune. A delegation of prominent Catholics who had met the bishop's train at Toledo pronounced what was apparently the judgment of the crowd: "All were satisfied with his appearance, and all voted him 'every inch a Bishop.'"[1]

The man who became Bishop of Detroit in 1888 was indeed a man whose appearance and history were almost bound to impress. John Foley was fifty-five when he came to Detroit, but still a youthful man—handsome, gregarious, possessed of an urbane charm. He had been raised in notably easy circumstances in a genteel Baltimore family, had studied at St. Mary's College in Baltimore and at St. Mary's Seminary in that same city. His preparation was capped by study in Rome, where he received a licentiate in Sacred Theology from the Appollinaire in 1857. He had been ordained in Rome the previous year.

Roman training was still rare among the American clergy, and Foley's education marked him as a man destined for advancement in the Church. So did his family and personal connections. His elder brother Thomas served as secretary to Baltimore's Archbishop Francis Kenrick and then, from 1870 until his death in 1879, as coadjutor bishop and administrator of the Diocese of Chicago. John Foley was a boyhood friend of Baltimore's Archbishop—later Cardinal—James Gibbons and a confidant and advisor to Gibbons until Foley left Baltimore for Detroit. Through Gibbons's influence, Foley had served as a secretary at the Third Plenary Council in 1884 and helped to write the famous *Baltimore Catechism* that issued from it. By 1888, Foley was an intimate friend of many of the most prominent personalities in the American Church—of Bishop John J. Keane, first rector of the Catholic University, of Msgr.—later Bishop—Dennis O'Connell, rector of the American College in Rome, and of Archbishop John Ireland of St. Paul. These men were at the height of their influence in the late 1880s, with well-placed friends in Rome and important admirers at home, including many non-Catholic journalists, educators, and politicians.

It is hardly surprising, then, that when the consultors of the Diocese of Detroit convened to nominate a successor to Bishop Caspar Borgess, their first choice was John Samuel Foley. The bishops of the Cincinnati Province concurred unanimously, and Foley's name headed the "terna" sent to Rome in the summer of 1887. The long delay that followed, however, indicates that at least some members of the Propaganda were not so easily persuaded of Foley's merits. Foley had in fact been nominated in 1886 as Bishop of Wilmington, only to have his name rejected in Rome. The trouble on that occasion stemmed from the claims of several well-connected American priests that Foley was an arrogant man of mediocre intellect, rumored to drink excessively, and overly fond of worldly pleasures. Gibbons had defended his friend against all these charges, but to no apparent avail.[2]

Gibbons's support, however, was apparently crucial in securing Foley's appointment to Detroit, carrying weight with Pope Leo XIII if not with the Propaganda. The Propaganda had decided by May of 1888 to name Dennis O'Connell to Detroit, even recommending that Gibbons be told in confidence that Foley should never again be nominated for a see. But Leo, evidently reluctant to offend the man regarded as honorific primate of the American Church, delayed the decision, citing a need for more information, especially from Gibbons. Ultimately the Foley nomination was approved, and he was named Bishop of Detroit on August 8, 1888. His consecration at the hands of Cardinal Gibbons took place in Baltimore on November 4. The new bishop left shortly thereafter for Detroit, and the tumultuous welcome that greeted him there.[3]

The Detroit to which Foley came could not match the charm and elegance of his native Baltimore, but it was nonetheless a city in the full flush of economic growth and civic optimism. With a population of close to 200,000, Detroit was a prosperous city in the late 1880s, possessed of a diverse economic base. Its still-tranquil downtown belied the manufacturing on which the city's population increasingly depended for their livelihoods. Detroit's wealthy families had not yet abandoned the mansions they had built in previous decades along Jefferson and Woodward avenues and the adjacent streets, and Bishop Foley found that the episcopal residence on Washington Street was very much a fashionable address. Save for a poor and disreputable "sailor's quarter" along the river, most of Detroit's working-class neighborhoods were located well beyond the downtown, mainly but not exclusively on the city's heavily immigrant East Side. Detroit was not yet, however, a city segregated primarily on the basis of class and race. Its immigrant districts—and its immigrant parishes—housed both poor and prosperous families, for ethnicity was significantly more important than class in determining the location of Detroit's population in the 1880s. The small black population of the city—less than 2 percent of the total population—was concentrated on the near east side but not yet rigidly segregated from the European immigrants among whom they lived.[4]

If nineteenth-century Detroit is best understood as a collection of ethnic communities, each with its complement of churches and voluntary associations, it was not a city without conflict and serious social problems. Its politics was fundamentally a politics of religious division, and the early 1890s saw a resurgence of overt and acrimonious anti-Catholicism, a response in part to an influx of poor Catholic immigrants from Poland and Italy and Austria-Hungary. And although Detroit was notably free of the tenements that horrified housing reformers in New York and Chicago, its immigrant districts were still marked by squalor and disease. Nor had the city been able to provide its residents with what contemporaries regarded as an acceptable level of basic services. The newer immigrant districts were as bereft of urban amenities as a peasant hamlet.[5]

But if the problems of Detroit seem by our standards to have been very nearly overwhelming, the city's leaders in the late 1880s looked with confidence to the future. Their buoyant optimism apparently infected Detroit's new bishop, who immersed himself in the city's life immediately on his arrival, visiting churches and social institutions with an enthusiasm his predecessor had never displayed, and ingratiating himself with its Catholic and non-Catholic men of affairs. Like the city fathers, Bishop Foley appeared to believe that he could master existing problems and whatever difficulties the future might bring. Despite his confidence and his considerable charm, however, John Foley was not by most accounts a successful Bishop of Detroit. Like many of the civic leaders whose easy assurance he shared in the late 1880s, his career in Detroit was eventually overwhelmed by the remarkable course of the city's history.

For the Detroit to which a confident, still-youthful Foley had come in 1888 was a city destined to undergo as profound a transformation as any American city before or since. The cause, of course, was the essentially accidental concentration in and near southeastern Michigan of entrepreneurs who were interested in developing a marketable automobile. By 1914, auto workers constituted 40 percent of Detroit's rapidly expanding population of factory employees, and the explosive growth of the auto industry had already brought enormous social change. The city's population reached 750,000 in 1914. By 1918, the year that Foley died, the population of Detroit was approaching one million, and its ethnic variety was greater than ever before. The once-small Polish community had grown so impressively that even in 1910 Poles were the largest European-born group in Detroit. Significant Italian and Hungarian communities appeared in the city after 1900, as well as smaller concentrations of peoples from Russia and the Balkans and even from the Middle East. A majority of the newcomers were at least nominally Catholic; they were also disproportionately young adult men. The Catholic population was thus changed in important ways in these years, for if earlier Catholic immigrants to Detroit had been mostly poor, they had also come mainly in family groups. To be sure, this new population represented opportunities for evangelization and church-building. But it represented more immediate, and formidable, problems for Detroit's clergy and its bishop. Much the same could be said of the city as a whole: if its almost fantastic growth in size and wealth generated an excitement and an energy unknown in the quiet manufacturing town of the 1880s, the same growth brought with it a level of social disorder reminiscent of frontier days.

By the time that Foley died, then, the city to which he had come as a newly consecrated bishop was not even a memory for most Detroiters. The face-to-face world of the urban elite where he had initially moved with such aplomb had been transformed: the men who shaped Detroit after 1900 were increasingly those who had few ties to the old manufacturing city and who were equally at home in New York or Chicago. Nor were they any longer the bishop's neighbors: Foley's episcopal residence was by 1918 an anomaly in what was now a busy commercial district. The city had already assumed in broad outline the class-segregated and racially segregated organization that it bears to this day, and its wealthy residents had begun in large numbers to move toward its outlying districts and suburbs. By 1918 the Chancery was already concerned about the future of those parishes that lay in the innermost regions of the city, now increasingly dominated by commerce and light industry or settled mostly by blacks, a rapidly growing population after 1914 and an increasingly segregated one.

Like his episcopal residence, Bishop Foley himself was something of an anachronism by the time he died—a withered, incapacitated relic of a former age. He had not been much of a figure in the city's life since the early days of the century, nor had he ever been a "builder bishop" like those who were, by the early twentieth century, transforming the institutional life of the Church in other large dioceses. The latter half of the Foley episcopate was hostage, in a very real sense, to the explosive growth of Detroit and its environs after 1900. Even a relatively young man, full of energy and ambition, would have found it hard in these years to provide Catholic Detroit with the institutions it suddenly required. But Foley was not young in 1900 and he was apparently in poor health for most of the fifteen years before his death. He was a virtual invalid after about 1914.

Because Foley failed so signally to fulfill the promise of his privileged and well-connected youth, it is tempting to ascribe his troubles as bishop to personal defects as well as to accidents of health and circumstance. No less an authority than John Tracy Ellis has concluded that Cardinal Gibbons's support of Foley as a candidate for Detroit was an unfortunate instance of the Cardinal's affections overruling his judgment. And even as friendly a witness as Kalamazoo's Father Francis O'Brien was led to confess, in 1897, that Foley was an ineffective bishop, lax in the administration of his diocese and frequently absent from his duties because of deteriorating health. O'Brien alluded on this occasion to Foley's problems with drink, which reference, taken in conjunction with earlier rumors, does raise a serious question about the bishop's habits. But there is not much evidence with which to address the matter. (So many of Foley's personal papers were lost, ostensibly during the moving of the Chancery offices in 1922, that it is impossible to reconstruct his career in Detroit in any great detail.) If Foley did have a drinking problem, he seems to have controlled it in public, at least in the earlier part of his episcopate. He was by all accounts a popular bishop in the 1890s, admired especially by Irish-Americans but liked by many non-Catholics too, and at a time of resurgent anti-Catholicism.[6]

Whatever the truth about his drinking, Foley does seem to have had certain weaknesses that might have compromised his ability to govern effectively. He was a vain man, and inclined to see opposition to Chancery policies as motivated almost solely by dislike or jealousy of him personally. He was not above vindictive behavior toward those who had, in his view, been wanting in loyalty to him. He found it hard to forgive, much less forget, old grievances. And he was not the intellectual equal of his more celebrated friends in the episcopate. Certainly by the mid-1890s the affability and charm that endeared him to a large lay audience, and presumably to such lifelong friends as Cardinal Gibbons, had ceased to protect him from the criticism, even the contempt, of certain American bishops and of influential figures in Rome. "You surely would be surprised at the bad repute in which Bp. Foley is held all around here," wrote a jubilant Father Peter Baart—long a Foley antagonist—from New York in 1896. "I imagined I had a secret, but was freely informed—one informant being a bishop—that Bishop Foley was so lectured at the Propaganda when called to Rome that the only question was 'Has Mgr. Ciasca not been too hard?'" Not long after, the various Detroit papers reported that Foley might be replaced by an apostolic vicar. The hapless Foley cabled to Rome to learn if the rumor was true. (It was "false and absurd," Keane cabled in reply.) That Foley was so unsure of his standing in Rome by 1897 suggests the extent to which his reputation had suffered. "You have indeed your cross to carry; but after Good Friday comes Easter," Cincinnati's Archbishop Elder consoled him. "The cross for a time—the crown forever."[7]

But despite Foley's troubles with Rome, it is not wholly clear that the defects in his character were notably greater than, or much different from, the faults that characterized other of his less notorious fellow bishops. Foley was surely not the only American bishop of his day to see resistance to his policies in personal terms or to behave in petty and occasionally vindictive ways toward those who crossed him. Nor were most of his peers in the episcopate noted for their intellectual attainments. One can, in fact, quite reasonably argue that the failure which Foley's episcopate is generally judged to have been had as much to do with forces beyond his control as it did with his shortcomings. Leaving questions of health aside for the moment, let us consider why this might be true.

The Foley episcopate was marred in the 1890s by several widely publicized disputes between Foley and certain of his priests, disputes that were adjudicated either by the Propaganda in Rome or the Apostolic Delegate in Washington. It was these difficulties which evidently earned him the contempt that Father Baart had discovered in certain quarters by 1896. But these troubles were not, on the whole, of the bishop's making — indeed he inherited two of the more vexing cases from his predecessors. And it is difficult to see that most of his peers in the episcopate would have handled these disputes much differently than he did, for they shared with Foley an essentially absolutist view of the episcopal office. That Foley came so frequently into conflict with Roman authority, then, must be attributed in some measure to simple bad fortune, and in large measure to his having been bishop at a time when relations between Rome and the American episcopate were unusually tense.

We have already seen that Roman authorities were increasingly willing by the late nineteenth century to intervene in disputes between American bishops and their priests. The case of Father Callaert and Bishop Borgess in 1878 stands as a local example. The fundamental intent of such intervention was to limit what Rome saw as the growing independence of the American hierarchy — to bind the American bishops more closely to Roman views and purposes even as these same bishops consolidated their authority in their own dioceses. The establishment of a permanent apostolic delegation in Washington in 1893 made Roman supervision of the American Church considerably easier, and for this reason conservative and liberal bishops alike were alarmed by the event. Archbishop Francesco Satolli, the first delegate, was an active party to a number of quarrels between priests and their bishops, and in many of these cases he forced bishops to accept compromises that entailed, in the eyes of the prelates involved, a serious loss of prestige. Often the unhappy bishop had indeed behaved toward the aggrieved priest in question in an autocratic fashion, ignoring what limited provisions for priests' rights existed in the late nineteenth century. But the facts of particular cases are less important than the principle which Satolli's intervention represented — that the American bishops were subject in the exercise of their authority, even in purely diocesan affairs, to a higher authority centered in Rome. No bishop would have disputed the premise, but none was happy at the prospect of restrictions on what had hitherto been virtual episcopal autonomy in matters of diocesan administration.[8]

Because Bishop Foley was intimately associated with the "Americanist" or "liberal" faction in the American hierarchy, his difficulties with Rome were caused not only by the changed circumstances that Satolli's advent symbolized but also by the waning fortunes of the liberal bishops in Rome after 1895. The rise and fall of the "Americanists" has been told in detail in other sources, and cannot detain us here. But it is likely that Foley's reputation beyond his diocese suffered in part because his powerful patrons—indeed his Roman connections—fell into disfavor as their views on politics, education, and especially religious liberty were increasingly criticized in Rome. Foley's rise in the hierarchy, as we have seen, had been occasioned primarily by the influential friends he possessed. Once these friends became vulnerable to Roman censure, Foley himself was vulnerable to the innuendo and outright vilification that fueled ecclesiastical politics at the end of the century. And because Foley was obviously a less talented man than his better-known allies, his reputation suffered accordingly.

Still, for all his inadequacies, Foley might well have been remembered as an ordinarily competent bishop during the first half of his tenure had not the circumstances of the 1890s brought him repeatedly into conflict with Rome. His continued popularity with the laity in his diocese is an argument in his favor here. His misfortune in the latter half of his episcopate, as we have already seen, was to live to such an advanced age—and in such impaired health—that he could not adequately govern a diocese, much less a diocese growing as prodigiously as Detroit. Here again Roman policies contributed to Foley's failure, for the Vatican refused to appoint a coadjutor bishop to Detroit although Foley, with Gibbons's support, had apparently asked for a coadjutor, presumably with right of succession, in 1908 and again in 1915. Rome did appoint an auxiliary bishop to Detroit in 1911 in the person of Edward Kelly, who had been pastor of St. Thomas parish in Ann Arbor since 1891. But although Bishop Kelly carried on virtually all the business of the Diocese after his consecration, he never possessed the authority to make independent decisions about the development of the Diocese in what was a crucial period in its history.[9]

Thus it was that the institutional development of the Diocese failed to keep pace with the growth of its population for much of the Foley episcopate. The number of priests in the Diocese increased by nearly two and a half times between 1888 and 1918 and the number of parishes nearly doubled, but the Catholic population more than trebled in the same period. Foley's successor was required to recruit outside the Diocese to meet the need for priests in the early 1920s. The shortage of clergy was sometimes ascribed, though perhaps unfairly, to the lack of a diocesan seminary. Detroit was indeed a sufficiently populous diocese after 1900 to warrant a seminary of its own. But the initiative and energy required to found one were presumably beyond the abilities of its ailing and aging bishop.

Health and age also explain, in all likelihood, why Foley died without establishing any central agencies to coordinate Catholic charities and to supervise the growing network of parochial schools, why he failed to hold a single diocesan synod, and why he seemingly neglected the development of secondary and postsecondary education in the Diocese. (The deep depression of the mid-1890s effectively prevented development of the Diocese during several of Foley's most vigorous years.) But this does not mean that Foley had no ambitions for his diocese when he first came to Detroit, for he obviously did. It is to those ambitions that we now turn, and to the limited achievements of his long tenure.

Aspirations and modest achievements

Not long after his arrival in Detroit, Bishop Foley began to identify what he regarded as the more pressing problems in the Diocese and to take steps to remedy them. He closed the costly diocesan seminary at Monroe, assigning its buildings to the St. Anthony's Male Orphan Asylum, which had long since outgrown its original premises. He laid plans for a new cathedral, evidently of considerable dimensions—"about 200 feet in length," he wrote in 1889. "As to the style, gothic or romanesque, I am undecided." By the spring of 1892 he had acquired a large plot of land at the corner of Cass Avenue and Parsons Street in what was then a fashionable section of Detroit, where he planned to build a school as well as a cathedral. He had in the meantime, in 1890, designated St. Patrick's Church to serve temporarily as his cathedral. In deference to the memory of Bishop Lefevere, it was renamed in honor of Saints Peter and Paul.[10]

St. Patrick's was by no means the largest or most lavish of Detroit's churches when it became the cathedral in 1890. But it was the church where Father Charles Reilly was pastor, and Reilly, as we have seen, was well known as an opponent of strong episcopal authority. He was also a popular figure among the Irish and, as such, a particularly potent rival to his new bishop. Foley was well aware of this, and apparently chose St. Patrick's for the single purpose of removing Reilly from Detroit. Father Reilly was subsequently assigned to Adrian, in which small town he spent the rest of his career. The remainder of the story, however, did not proceed according to plan. The depression of the mid-1890s postponed the building of a new cathedral, and the project was apparently abandoned during the long administrative twilight of the Foley episcopate. Uncertainty about the future of the proposed cathedral "district" may have inhibited the aging bishop. When his successor revived plans for a new cathedral in the early 1920s, he bought land for the project at a location much farther from the downtown.[11]

Bishop Foley did oversee the establishment, in 1893, of a lavishly appointed school at the proposed cathedral site. It served as a parish school for the families of the former St. Patrick's Church, who had never had a school of their own, Father Reilly counting himself among that tiny minority of priests in the late nineteenth century who were opposed in principle to parochial education. The new Cathedral Academy proved to be Bishop Foley's most eloquent statement of his ambitions for Catholic education in his diocese. Its facilities and curriculum rivaled the best that the public schools could offer, and he was justly proud of the achievement. More intimate socially with the prosperous Catholics of Detroit than his predecessor had been, Foley well understood the importance of removing from parochial education the identification it had already acquired, in some quarters at least, with inferior academic quality and inferior social status.[12]

Despite his evident commitment to the maintenance of a separate Catholic school system, however, there were occasions in the 1890s when Bishop Foley betrayed what looked to be a relatively latitudinarian stance on matters of school policy. When Archbishop Francesco Satolli, who was appointed Apostolic Delegate in 1893, issued a statement in 1892 that endorsed Archbishop Ireland's cautiously tolerant attitude toward the public schools, Foley was the only bishop in the Cincinnati Province to refuse to sign a letter of protest. His own diocesan paper had defended Ireland's experiments in cooperation with the public schools, albeit in guarded terms. Foley himself had early in his episcopate lent encouragement to a Catholic students' organization at the University of Michigan—called the "Foley Guild" by its grateful members—thereby implicitly sanctioning Catholic attendance at that secular institution. Indeed he was able in 1889 to tell an Ann Arbor audience that the University of Michigan and the nascent Catholic University of America, on whose board of trustees he served, had "both the same aim and mission."

> When our University is opened at the capital of the United States, it will be with the most kindly feeling and with the desire of cultivating the greatest intimacy with those gentlemen whose reputation for learning is so renowned throughout the whole of the United States—the professors of Ann Arbor.

The bishop was the happy inhabitant of a world where, as he assured his hearers, "true science will ever be the handmaid of Revelation." And he knew that if Catholics were to shun the state's most prestigious university, they would deprive themselves of an important avenue to wealth and influence. As late as 1899, the *Michigan Catholic* was rejoicing that Catholic young men could be found at all the nation's most celebrated colleges—"isolation is not always a good policy."[13]

As Foley aged, however, and as the climate of opinion among the American bishops grew more conservative after the turn of the century, his views on education lost the liberality he occasionally displayed in the 1890s. Nor did his policies even in the 1890s betray any lack of commitment to separate Catholic schools. Foley knew that nearly all the American bishops of his day were ardent supporters of the parochial school, and unlike John Ireland and Boston's Archbishop John Williams, he lacked the temperament to stand against this strong majority tide. Indeed, there is little evidence to suggest that Foley ever thought deeply about the meaning of parochial schools for Catholic life in America. But given his optimism about American society and his desire that Catholics participate

in that society as fully as possible, he was inevitably less inclined than his predecessor to see public education as always inimical to Catholic faith. And in the
liberal climate of the 1890s, he was willing, on occasion, to allow his pronouncements on schooling to be colored by his conviction that the destiny of Catholics
in America was nothing less than full integration into the larger society.[14]

If Foley's optimism and openness to American society could not find full expression in his educational policies, concerned as these necessarily were with segregating Catholics from other Americans, he devoted much of his public life in the 1890s
to a celebration of what he saw as the peculiar genius of American institutions.
Patriotic themes ran through many of the sermons and speeches he delivered to
Catholic audiences and especially to immigrants. Foley was an enthusiastic proponent of assimilation for ethnic Catholics, and like other liberal bishops he was
alarmed at the growing assertiveness of German and Polish Catholics in the American Church. Their vision of a Church which not only tolerated but promoted enduring ethnic loyalties was to Foley not simply foolhardy—in that it ensured continued Protestant suspicion of Catholics—but very nearly treasonous. Catholicism
rightly understood, Foley was certain, was not only compatible with loyalty to
America but virtually demanded it. And this was so not despite the religious
neutrality of the American government but precisely because of it. "We have
everything to admire in the glorious Constitution under which we live," he told
an Ann Arbor audience in 1889. "The church needs not, nor does she seek, the
support of the civil government. . . . We can live together in amity and charity
with our fellow citizens, each one pursuing his course, all striving for the great
goal for which God has created us." Foley assured his Cathedral parishioners in
1895 that none other than Leo XIII had given his blessing to American religious
pluralism. "He evinced the most intense interest in everything regarding religion," Foley informed the congregation with reference to his own recent audience with the pope, "and when told of the liberty that we enjoyed under the Constitution of the United States he was earnest in his admiration of our condition."[15]

The theme of religious liberty was felicitously interwoven into many of Foley's
patriotic sermons and addresses. It served not only to reassure non-Catholics
that Catholics were loyal to American institutions but to make the case for an
American identity with the most recalcitrant cultural nationalists. Speaking in
1889 at the blessing of St. Casimir's (Polish) Church in Detroit, Foley argued
that American liberty must be prized and defended by all Catholics, for it was
this tradition of liberty that had made America a sanctuary for the oppressed
peoples of Europe. ("Here there is no bitter Czar to crush you beneath his feet
and say you shall not serve God but in the way he dictates.") And American liberty, he urged his hearers, could only be defended by a people who placed loyalty
to the United States before any other national loyalty. "We Poles, Irish, Germans, French, Bohemians are here—Americans," Foley pointed out. "Can any
other nation under God's high heavens evidence a scene like this?" And the
Bishop proceeded to explain the veritably providential circumstances that made
Catholic Detroit possible:

It is easy for me to tell you my friends, because we live under that glorious flag, that flag that protects every man in the worship of God, and gives liberty, true liberty that we should prize so highly, that we should esteem, that we should defend even with the last drop of life's blood. . . . Here we are equals, free men. All that is asked of us is that we should be good citizens, and as I stand here a Bishop of the Catholic Church, I can pledge myself that there are no better citizens of this Republic than the Catholics of every nationality who stand around this corner-stone. For in this church will be taught the truths of Jesus Christ, but at the same time there will be taught loyalty, fidelity and devotion to that flag that flies over the most beautiful nation that God ever deigned to place upon the face of the earth.[16]

Foley surely intended that the burden of this and similar sermons be heard well beyond the bounds of the Catholic community. More than any of his predecessors, he was anxious to address, and allay, the fear that the heavily immigrant Catholic population was hostile to American political values. Largely for this reason, Foley was the first Catholic bishop to play a conspicuous role in the civic life of Detroit. Whether leading citizens had assembled to decry the Turkish persecution of Armenians in 1896 or, in 1898, to call for the liberation of Cuba, Bishop Foley was prominent among the speakers, sharing the platform with Protestant ministers and even, on occasion, with a rabbi. This was a novel experience for Catholic Detroit, but evidently a satisfying one, at least for the more assimilated. Foley's public pronouncements were not remotely controversial, nor was his a pioneering voice when it came to the problems of city or nation. (During the depression of the 1890s, which spawned a good deal of labor unrest, Foley limited his public statements to florid condemnations of anarchism and socialism.) But Foley's ability to function as a celebrant of "civil religion" almost certainly facilitated the rapprochement between assimilated Catholics and the larger society that was so significant a part of Catholic life at the end of the nineteenth century.[17]

Indeed it is not too much to say that Foley made his most important contribution to the Diocese in his role as a champion of a truly American Catholicism. He was the first Bishop of Detroit to be seen by large numbers of non-Catholics as a thoroughly American figure, and the first to move with ease among the city's elite. (His 1907 Golden Jubilee celebration was notable for the large attendance of non-Catholics, especially the local Protestant clergy.) Insofar as Foley was able to bolster the confidence of those Catholics who wanted to see themselves as fully American and to reassure non-Catholics about the political values of his flock, he strengthened the uneasy tradition of religious toleration in the Diocese. That he did so at a time when the growing size and ethnic diversity of the Catholic population in the Diocese threatened to create a strong anti-Catholic reaction indicates the special importance of his role. Nor should he be faulted here for insensitivity to the needs of ethnic Catholics. For despite his assimilationist rhetoric, Foley was as generous as his predecessors had been in permitting the establishment of foreign-language parishes. And because he abandoned the Borgess experiment in centralized government of the parochial schools, he permitted the schools in ethnic parishes a considerable autonomy in matters of curriculum. Indeed, the long decline in administrative efficiency during the later years of the Foley episcopate probably enhanced the independence of pastors and lay parish committees throughout the Diocese.[18]

Finally, the Bishop must be given at least some credit for those social and educational institutions in the Diocese that were founded or expanded during his episcopate. He initiated the drive for funds that resulted in 1908 in the opening of a spacious new facility to house the boys' orphan asylum, and was apparently instrumental in bringing the Xaverian Brothers to the Diocese in 1904 to found a home for working boys in Detroit. At Foley's request, a group of Detroit laywomen established a home for working girls in the city that survived from 1894 until 1907. Four Catholic hospitals were opened during the Foley years, as well as a Catholic college for women and four Catholic academies. And toward the end of the Foley episcopate, Detroit College moved toward full university status. If the rapidly growing size of the Catholic population in the Diocese after 1900 rather dwarfed these accomplishments, they were nonetheless important.

WHO IS THE CHURCH? CONFLICT IN THE FOLEY YEARS

If Foley was genuinely committed to democratic values in political life, he was no more disposed than other "Americanist" bishops to countenance democracy in the Church. Particularly with regard to his clergy, he assumed that episcopal authority was absolute, and he resented—as most other bishops did—even such limited, Vatican-initiated reforms as the election of consultors. Nor did he willingly tolerate dissent among his priests. Still, he moved early in his episcopate to eliminate certain sources of tension between the Chancery and the clergy, tensions that dated mainly from the Borgess years. We have already seen that his decision to strip the diocesan school board of most of its powers pleased nearly every pastor in the Diocese. And Foley quietly discontinued the Borgess ban on parish entertainments, which had been a potent cause of friction. Because the latter years of the Foley episcopate were characterized by administrative inertia, Foley's administrative decisions in the 1890s have sometimes been described as lax or irresponsible. But one could just as plausibly argue that Foley behaved prudently by mitigating what had been an overcentralization of administrative authority during the Borgess years.

Foley's administrative prudence, however, did not save him from serious conflict with several of his priests. These conflicts exemplify the tensions that prevailed by the 1890s between the Vatican and the American hierarchy; they also provide insight into the Foley personality and his understanding of episcopal authority. For these reasons we will look in some detail at three much-publicized disputes of the Foley years, each of which was adjudicated by Roman authorities. We begin with the conclusion of the Kolasinski case, initiated in such spectacular fashion under Bishop Borgess.

The Kolasinski Case

As we have already seen, Bishop Borgess dismissed Father Dominic Kolasinski as pastor of St. Albertus (Polish) parish in the waning days of 1885. The dismissal had resulted in protests and rioting, and in the imposition of an interdict on the church, which remained closed until the summer of 1887. Kolasinski himself left Detroit in the spring of 1886, leaving behind a small but deeply aggrieved community of supporters, who proceeded to establish a school and what was in effect a church of their own. They gathered on Sundays, under the direction of the lay schoolmaster, to sing hymns and say the rosary, although many of them had at least occasional recourse to the sacraments at various Catholic churches in the city. The members of this dissident community were not, to all appearances, much worried that their continued defiance of episcopal authority had in any way affected their standing in the Church. Their leaders maintained that they and their aggrieved constituents were excellent Catholics, that it was not they but two successive bishops of Detroit who had violated Church law. Arguments like these suggest that the Kolasinski dispute involved more than a quarrel between the Chancery and a provocative priest. It had fundamentally to do with a serious disagreement between the Chancery and an ultimately sizable group of lay people over the nature of Church authority.[19]

When Bishop Foley succeeded to the Diocese of Detroit in 1888, he inherited the troublesome after-effects of the Kolasinski dismissal. The dissident congregation of Kolasinski loyalists probably numbered no more than a few hundred souls by the close of 1888, but it constituted an embarrassment as well as a pastoral problem for the new bishop. Accordingly, Foley turned his attention to the difficulty almost as soon as he came to Detroit. Convinced, it seems, that his predecessor's impersonal style had exacerbated the almost inevitable tensions between the Chancery and the local Polish community, Foley himself twice visited the neighborhood where most of the dissidents lived, and pleaded with them to return to St. Albertus Church. Many of the dissidents had initially hoped that Foley would permit Kolasinski to return to the Diocese. But they were so moved by his visits that their leaders feared wholesale defections from the absent priest's cause. These fears brought Kolasinski to Detroit in December 1888, to make a personal appeal to Bishop Foley for reinstatement at St. Albertus. When Foley refused to reinstate him at any church in his diocese, Kolasinski rallied his wavering supporters and announced that he would remain in Detroit, build a grand — and wholly Catholic — church there, and serve as its pastor.[20]

Kolasinski's grand church was substantially completed at the close of 1893, when his congregation was estimated to number as many as 10,000 souls. (The group had previously worshipped in a combination church-school building that dated from the summer of 1889.) The new church was even larger than St. Albertus Church, which stood just four blocks distant, and it was lavishly decorated — a monument to the parishioners' generosity and to their conviction that they labored in a just and holy cause. For Sweetest Heart of Mary was a Roman

Catholic Church, according to its 1889 by-laws. That its parishioners had been publicly excommunicated by Bishop Foley seemed not to matter in the slightest. Nor did it matter that the democratic mode of parish government prescribed in the by-laws — Kolasinski was actually elected pastor by the church trustees — was wholly at odds with Diocesan regulations. Alarmed and angered by this stubborn defiance, Bishop Foley apparently washed his hands of the dispute in 1889. His parting shot was the establishment of a new Polish church, St. Josaphat, a few blocks to the west of Sweetest Heart of Mary. This new church, Foley hoped, would draw members from Kolasinski's congregation and worsen what he correctly anticipated would be serious financial problems caused by Kolasinski's ambitious building program.[21]

Bishop Foley was presumably comforted in these years by the realization that "Polish troubles" were not peculiar to the Diocese of Detroit. Poles in a number of American dioceses were embroiled after 1880 in sometimes violent conflict with their bishops over what were essentially issues of parish autonomy. In the neighboring Diocese of Grand Rapids, for example, the Polish parish in Bay City was disrupted between 1896 and 1898 by a dispute over the ownership of parish property that was intermittently as violent as the worst incidents in the Kolasinski affair. We have already discussed the circumstances that made Poles in the late nineteenth century unusually suspicious of episcopal authority. And we have also discussed the reasons that virtually all American bishops resisted ethnic demands for autonomy in the conduct of their parishes. Bishop Foley understood the Kolasinski crisis much as his fellow bishops would have done. Uneasily aware that his polyglot diocese had only recently been brought under effective episcopal control, Foley believed that compromise with Kolasinski would not only violate Church law but signal to every restive priest and congregation in his jurisdiction that episcopal authority could be flouted at will. Perhaps because so much was at stake, at least from his perspective, Foley seems to have convinced himself that Kolasinski was guilty of the sexual delinquencies that had been alleged before Bishop Borgess in 1885. Certainly he made no effort to ascertain the truth of what were claimed by some to have been perjured accusations.[22]

Certain of the rightness of his stand and aware that the "Polish problem" was wider than his own diocese, Foley was astonished to learn in 1893 that the Apostolic Delegate was interested in negotiating a compromise settlement to the Kolasinski case. The delegate was concerned about the great and still-growing size of Kolasinski's congregation, and concerned as well about the increasing frequency and violence of disputes between Polish congregations and their American bishops. From his point of view, moreover, the American bishops suffered less from uncertain authority in their own dioceses than from a tendency toward an arrogant independence that made them a growing worry in Rome. Since Delegate Satolli had recently forced as powerful a prelate as New York's Michael Corrigan to reinstate a priest whom he had suspended and then excommunicated in what had been a nationally publicized case, he was clearly not loath to impose a settlement to the Kolasinski affair on the much less influential Foley. Nonetheless, Foley resisted. And because Kolasinski was equally resistant to anything less than complete vindication, Satolli's task was a difficult one. Negotiations extended for the better part of a year, eventually involving the Propaganda in Rome. A decision was finally reached on the last day of 1893, when the Propaganda instructed Foley to accept Kolasinski as a priest in the Diocese of Detroit once Kolasinski had made a penitent retreat and confessed publicly, before his congregation, to disobedience of lawful authority.[23]

Foley was deeply angered by the decision, as were his closest clerical advisors. And probably many of his priests, embarrassed by the more flamboyant aspects of Kolasinski's career, were almost as deeply distressed. But Foley had no effective appeal from the judgment of the Propaganda. Kolasinski was officially reconciled with the Church in February 1894, when, in the presence of Satolli's personal representative and of a vast congregation, he read the prescribed confession — but in a whisper! With this astonishing last defiance of authority, he seemed to have emerged from the long dispute the uncontested victor. For by the terms of the agreement that Satolli had negotiated, Kolasinski was to remain pastor of his enormous if debt-ridden church.[24]

But it was Kolasinski's parishioners who in the end succeeded in imposing their understanding of authority in the Church on the other parties to the dispute. The congregation continued after 1894 to elect a governing board of trustees at its annual meeting, Bishop Foley knowing better than to intervene in the affairs of this particular parish, despite the violation of diocesan statute. Then, in 1897, the men of Sweetest Heart of Mary parish extended the vote in congregational elections to women. (They were almost certainly the first in the Diocese to do so.) The decision to enfranchise women was apparently related to a growing financial crisis in the parish, which reached a head early in 1897, when the church was sold, by court order, to pay outstanding debts. The parish trustees subsequently secured a loan and bought back the church, but not without resolving to keep Kolasinski from any future participation in parish financial affairs. The outraged priest brought his case to the congregation, urging them to elect a slate of trustees at their next meeting who would treat him with the deference due a pastor. But early in 1898, the congregation voted overwhelmingly to retain the trustees who had ordered their priest to busy himself with the spiritual rather than the temporal affairs of the parish — a division of labor that the 1889 parish by-laws in fact prescribed.[25]

Kolasinski died not long after. Bishop Foley himself brought the last sacraments to the deathbed, according to the local papers, and the two former enemies were reconciled at last. Perhaps by this time each man understood that he had been as much a prisoner of events as a free agent in the long conflict known as the Kolasinski affair. Certainly this was true of Bishop Foley, who not only inherited the case from his predecessor but was caught up in its latter stages in a Roman political struggle where he was more pawn than actor. It is easy to say — as Foley's critics said at the time — that he was too much concerned with the maintenance of his own authority and too little concerned about the scandal and the danger to souls represented by Kolasinski's enormous schismatic congregation. And it was perhaps especially easy to say that Foley behaved in this way because he too readily confused the satisfaction of his own desires with legitimate defense of episcopal authority. "He considered and even said to me and others 'that he was the diocese,'" Father Peter Baart, no admirer of Foley, wrote of his bishop to the Apostolic Delegate. "Therefore instead of considering cases official, he considered them personal." This may well have been true. But Father Baart was more than a little disingenuous in this exchange with Satolli, for what he objected to was less the Foley personality than the definition of the episcopal office to which Foley and nearly all his fellow bishops were committed. And in the final analysis, the Kolasinski affair was as much a conflict between differing views of authority in the Church as it was a clash of egocentric personalities.[26]

The "Church Farm" Case

The legitimate extent of a bishop's authority was the question at the heart of a second much-publicized case which began in Detroit in 1892. The "Church Farm" suit was initiated in that year by Father Christian Denissen, pastor of the recently established St. Charles parish on the eastern fringes of Detroit. Quite by accident, Father Denissen had discovered that the land on which his parish buildings stood had once been diocesan property, part of a large parcel with a remarkably complex history of ownership. This history began in 1808, when the parcel was deeded to Catholics living in the "Côte du Nord-Est," a territory stretching along the Detroit River and Lake St. Clair northeast of what was then the village of Detroit. The property was to be used by said inhabitants and their descendants for "literary and religious purposes." Subsequently, in 1833, the land was deeded to Bishop Frederic Rese, apparently to be held in trust by him and his successors for the beneficiaries and purposes designated in the original transaction.

Unfortunately, the 1833 deed was never registered. Nor could it be found after Bishop Rese left Detroit, which led in 1857 to a court challenge to Bishop Lefevere's putative claim to the property. Lefevere's title to the land was eventually upheld, but only after an agreement was reached by which the bishop surrendered a part of the original parcel to various claimants and agreed with regard to the land that remained to abide by what were assumed to be the strictures of the 1833 deed. To this end, Lefevere established St. Anthony's Church and school on a portion of the property, selling additional lots to pay for the parish buildings. The small but increasingly valuable parcel of the "Church Farm" that still remained was deeded in time to Bishop Borgess and then to Bishop Foley. It was this land, or the money to be realized from its sale, that interested Father Denissen in 1892. He was convinced, he told the Foley Chancery, that St. Charles parish was the sole legitimate heir of the 1808 bequest to the inhabitants of the "Côte du Nord-Est."[27]

The protracted dispute that followed Father Denissen's discovery is of interest mostly for what it reveals about the principal parties. Father Denissen's motives were perhaps the simplest. Pastor of a new and financially straitened parish, he was anxious to stake his claim to the Church Farm because—in the words of the "Bill of Complaint" submitted on his behalf to Archbishop Elder—"he very badly needs the income or proceeds of this property for the purpose of paying for the erection of new church, school and rectory buildings." If he came in the course of the suit to dislike and mistrust his bishop, he had not, to all appearances, initiated the suit with a view to challenging episcopal authority for principled purposes. Not so his lawyer, the already well-known canonist Father Peter Baart. Baart's interest in the case seems to have stemmed mainly from his concern for what he regarded as the eroding rights of pastors in the American Church. The issue in the Church Farm case, he asserted at one point, was the canonical right of pastors to administer the property of their parishes. The ownership of Church property might rest with the bishop, in Baart's view, but the bishop's freedom to make use of that property was strictly limited by law. Father Denissen, as pastor of the congregation that was rightful heir to the Church Farm bequest, was free to do with that property as he saw fit. The Church Farm case was thus of a piece with the logic of Baart's legal career, for his interest was always to establish or strengthen legal limits to episcopal authority, not for the benefit of the laity—who were of little interest to him—but for the benefit of the clergy.[28]

Bishop Foley, for his part, saw the case from the first as a threat to his ability to administer his diocese. He argued both privately and in two ecclesiastical courts that he could not, for the good of the Diocese, be bound by the conditions of a legal transaction so old that its very terms had no contemporary meaning. The descendants of the families of the "Côte du Nord-Est" had long been dispersed, and since the original beneficiaries of the Church Farm bequest had lived in a geographically large area, there were many parishes besides St. Charles that might legitimately claim to be heirs. Because of this, the bishop contended, it was both sensible and equitable for him to use the proceeds of the Farm for the good of the whole Diocese, specifically to finance the building of a cathedral. Beyond this, and more fundamentally, Foley feared that this challenge to his administrative authority would weaken him in the eyes of the clergy. This was especially true as the case was adjudicated wholly outside the Diocese. Although Foley claimed that his own diocesan court ought properly to hear the case, Cincinnati's Archbishop Elder accepted Baart's argument that Foley's status as defendant in the suit meant that the Metropolitan Court in Cincinnati was the rightful court of first instance. Should this precedent be upheld, Foley wrote to his friend Dennis O'Connell, he "would be useless in this administration of Detroit and every Tom, Dick and Harry could go before the Metropolitan Court, such as it is." Subsequently appealing the jurisdictional question to the Propaganda in Rome, Foley gave voice to the same fears. "If priests can easily appeal their cases to Cincinnati or to Rome," he demanded, "where will this thing end?

If they can write any combination of facts they please in a bill, and load the Diocese with expense to show their fraud and falsehood, what will become of order in the Church?"[29]

Because the case was finally heard in Rome, a verdict was slow in coming—the Propaganda did not render a decision in the matter until early in 1897. The verdict was essentially a compromise, although the logic of the decision gave more support to Foley's view of episcopal authority than it did to Baart's. The bishop was ordered to use the proceeds of the Church Farm not for the benefit of St. Charles parish alone but for the benefit of all the parishes and Catholic institutions located in the old "Côte du Nord-Est." The bishop's status as owner and administrator of the property was specifically recognized and a subsequent clarification by the Propaganda gave Bishop Foley the right to determine the geographic area defined by the term "Côte du Nord-Est"—a hotly disputed question—and the responsibility of administering any monies realized from the sale of Church Farm property.[30]

Bishop Foley had apparently hoped for a more thoroughgoing vindication of his episcopal rights, for he was unduly disappointed by what was clearly a more than partial victory in the case. His distress was doubtless compounded when he learned from the local papers that Father Denissen considered the decision an unqualified triumph for St. Charles parish, which, the euphoric priest announced, would "at once erect a handsome church, modern school buildings and other buildings required." Just how Father Denissen arrived at this unwarranted conclusion is not clear. Probably he assumed that the case turned more fundamentally on the question of the extent of a bishop's authority than on the rather dubious claim of St. Charles parish to represent the descendants of the original Church Farm heirs. Father Baart was disposed to think this way and indeed, the verdict did limit Foley's freedom to dispose of land that the Propaganda had recognized as his.[31]

Father Denissen, however, was not long able to sustain the illusion of victory. By early April, Bishop Keane could assure his friend Foley that certain Roman authorities "have already written to Fr. Denissen that his claim—that the money should go only to St. Charles Church, cannot be entertained." The last word, moreover, rested with the bishop's side. The long-lost deed of 1833 was found in 1915, and it made no mention of the "Côte du Nord-Est." The Church Farm, according to the deed, was simply to be used for "literary and religious purposes." Foley did nothing with this new evidence, but in 1920 his successor appealed to the Propaganda and received permission to use for diocesan purposes that remnant of the Church Farm still held in trust.[32]

If Foley's authority in his own diocese was not much undermined by the Church Farm case, his standing in Rome was surely affected. Both Foley and his attorney, Father Robert Doman, behaved throughout the case in an almost reckless fashion. Foley was convinced that the case had developed only at the instigation of Peter Baart, and only, in Foley's words, "for the simple purpose of [Baart's] advancing himself and gaining notoriety." Father Doman thought so too. "Rev. Denissen is not the real plaintiff in this case," he warned Archbishop Elder, "he is the tool." Both Foley and Doman had a penchant, from the outset of the case, for scurrilous personal argument, as Baart himself noted — not without a certain satisfaction — in a letter to Foley's secretary. "From the appearance of things, the Bishop takes the case pretty hard, and feels quite mad at me, but when he has been through as many cases as you and I he probably will take them philosophically." Not so in this instance, however. "This man Baart . . . is physically a little shriveled creature," Foley informed the Propaganda in an 1892 brief that was largely devoted to a savage attack on Baart's probity. "He has always been an agitator in this Diocese. . . . We cannot rely on a word he says or writes." But Baart was in fact a respected canonist, and Foley would have done better to confine his argument to the considerable legal and historical precedent that favored his case. That Foley and Doman insisted on arguing in this fashion may explain some of the dislike Archbishop Satolli had conceived for Foley by the time the Kolasinski case was in its final stages. It is noteworthy in this regard that it was Father Baart to whom Satolli turned in 1893 to secure what Satolli described as an unbiased history of the Kolasinski affair.[33]

Why Foley behaved so imprudently in the Church Farm case is far from clear. Certainly he misread the situation in Rome, where his arguments for essentially unchecked episcopal authority were more likely to feed anxieties about the American Church than to strike a responsive chord. And he may have been so uncertain of his actual authority in his own diocese that Baart's cool and skillful challenge of that authority — much publicized in the local press — caused Foley to lash out angrily at the man he believed was deliberately undermining his status in the eyes of the clergy. Or perhaps he was simply the man Baart alleged him to be — vindictive, mean-spirited, unable to tolerate even disinterested opposition to his own policies. It is worth remarking, however, that Foley's position in this case was a good deal more generous, with regard to the whole of the Diocese, than that of Fathers Denissen and Baart.

The Father Francis Kennedy Case

The antagonisms and alliances that grew out of the Church Farm affair had a bearing on the later case of Father Francis Kennedy. Here the least attractive side of the bishop's character was much in evidence; if one wanted to argue that Foley was fundamentally an arrogant and vindictive man — and not a very competent administrator — one would do well to center the argument on this particular case. It began in the spring of 1896, when the young Father Kennedy, pastor of St. John's parish in Ypsilanti, was abruptly transferred by his bishop to a pastorate in Niles, a small village in the far western part of the state. Kennedy had recently given Foley some cause for displeasure: the priest, evidently interceding in a family quarrel, had spent the better part of a day in the unchaperoned company of a young woman, even registering under an assumed name at a hotel in the town to which both had gone. A local reporter had recognized Father Kennedy and then informed Bishop Foley, who was disturbed by the young priest's imprudence if apparently convinced that he was innocent of more serious wrong-doing. Foley claimed that his subsequent transfer of Kennedy from Ypsilanti to Niles was not by way of punishment but simply to avoid a scandal. Had the Niles parish not been smaller and poorer than the prosperous parish at Ypsilanti, and had Foley not immediately given the Ypsilanti pastorate to his friend Father Robert Doman, Kennedy might not have contested the decision. But under the circumstances, he was angry and ready to fight.[34]

Father Kennedy had not been a radical during his short career as a priest; indeed it was partly his loyalty to episcopal authority that had brought him so early to as desirable a parish as St. John's. And his initial attempt to contest the transfer was characteristically respectful: he asked the venerable Father James Doherty, longtime pastor of St. Vincent's in Detroit, to intercede for him at the Chancery. Doherty was plainly puzzled by Foley's conduct with regard to the promising young priest. "It is strange the Bishop would order you so without any understanding," he wrote to Kennedy. "He generally has an understanding with the pastors he moves." Whether Doherty subsequently sought to change the bishop's mind we do not know. In any event, Foley did not rescind Kennedy's transfer.[35]

Kennedy next turned to Father Peter Baart, already widely known for his legal work on behalf of aggrieved priests—and nearly as widely known as an antagonist of Bishop Foley. Baart gladly received the case, and filed an appeal with the Apostolic Delegate on May 28. It was surely one of the easier briefs he had ever prepared, for Foley had disregarded what were generally recognized as the procedures to be followed when a pastor was moved. A pastor was not to be subject to a punitive transfer if he was not guilty of a canonical offense, Baart argued. And Foley himself had admitted that Kennedy had done no serious wrong. Still, he had transferred Father Kennedy, against the priest's will, to a demonstrably inferior post. The Niles parish, Baart pointed out, was not only smaller and poorer than the parish at Ypsilanti, but did not even provide its priest with a rectory. Father Kennedy would suffer economically from the transfer—"the perquisites of your orator would be thus diminished by about half"—and his reputation would suffer as well. No matter what statements were issued to the contrary, Baart claimed, the clergy of the Diocese would consider that Kennedy was being punished, simply because the Niles pastorate was so inferior to his previous one. And Kennedy would suffer socially in Niles, a parish "without city advantages" and considerably farther than Ypsilanti from Detroit. "Moreover the people of Niles are inferior to those of Ypsilanti," Baart continued uncharitably, "and the clergy of that section are not so intimately known to your orator." The real motivation for the Kennedy transfer, Baart concluded, was Foley's desire to accommodate his friend Doman—who had by this time published attacks on both Baart and the Apostolic Delegate, as Baart was careful to mention. "And now, forsooth, to make room for a person of such demerit instead of merit your orator is forced to leave his parish, his home, and go to a much inferior parish, and into practical banishment? Is this fairness? Is this equity?"[36]

The case was decided by the Apostolic Delegate just two months later. Foley's arguments on his own behalf were summarily rejected—the decision "is really dreadful on the Bishop," crowed a delighted Baart, hoping perhaps that this outcome would affect the course of the Church Farm case, still pending in Rome. Foley was ordered to reinstate Kennedy immediately as pastor at Ypsilanti, and the bishop did so. A now thoroughly politicized Father Kennedy sent his thanks to the Apostolic Delegate, repenting of his previously uncritical loyalty to Foley. He especially regretted having signed a petition in 1893 which objected in strong language to the rumored reinstatement of Father Kolasinski as a priest in the Diocese—a petition that Father Baart had pointedly refused to sign. "It was done under pressure and from misinformation," Kennedy explained, "and now the feeling grows that Father Baart's advocacy is testimony to the justice of any cause."[37]

Foley's already poor standing in the estimation of the now-Cardinal Satolli was further eroded by the Kennedy affair, and at a time when his ecclesiastical allies were under increasing attack in Rome. When Father Baart wrote from New York in the wake of the Kennedy decision to rejoice at the "bad répute in which Bishop Foley is held all around here," he also had occasion to note that "Cardinal Gibbons was practically told to leave Rome and today has absolutely no influence there." It cannot have contributed to the equilibrium of the vain and rather quick-tempered Foley to have learned, in this ominous political climate, that the Kennedy case had, in Baart's words, "surely attracted attention." But whatever his personal distress, there can be no justification for Foley's subsequent behavior toward Father Kennedy. Foley quite deliberately refused to approve a teaching order for Kennedy's parish school, causing the school to be closed in the autumn of 1896, apparently hoping in this way to turn the congregation at Ypsilanti against the reinstated priest. That Kennedy was not moved from Ypsilanti in later years may also have been due to Foley's animosity rather than the priest's own preference. Certainly Kennedy's considerable talents had led many to expect that he would finish his career at a large parish in Detroit—as Father Robert Doman did.[38]

If these three cases reveal a side to Foley that was narrow, vindictive, and resistant to compromise, they also reveal the unusually difficult circumstances under which he served in the 1890s. That the Kolasinski and Church Farm cases originated in his diocese was simply bad luck. And that he counted among his priests the redoubtable Peter Baart was likewise—from a bishop's point of view—an instance of misfortune. For Baart was not only a skilled and aggressive canonist with a distinctly minimalist understanding of the episcopal office, he was also a friend of the powerful Cardinal Satolli. And Satolli, as we have seen, had his own agenda in the 1890s, into which Baart's attacks on Foley fitted neatly. This is not to excuse Foley's conduct in the Kennedy case or to argue that his administration of the Diocese in the 1890s was notably adept. But our judgment of his episcopate must be tempered by an understanding of its context.

Bishop Foley died on January 5, 1918. His funeral at Detroit's cathedral was a major civic event—the mayor and the City Council attended the requiem

Mass, and more than 100,000 mourners were said to have passed by the bier where the body lay in state. Foley was eighty-four when he died, and had been only a shadowy presence in Detroit for the better part of a decade. Relatively few Detroiters in 1918 had memories of Foley in his vigorous middle years. Catholics bade farewell, then, less to a man than to the embodiment of their own high Victorian past. And as they did this, they celebrated a coming-of-age for Catholics throughout the Diocese. If organized anti-Catholicism was poised in 1918 for a last major appearance in Michigan politics, Catholics were nonetheless more fully integrated into their communities than they had ever been before. John Foley had served as bishop during an important transition in Catholic life, and for many older Catholics he had himself been a symbol and even a cause of that change.[39]

Many of those who paid their last respects to the bishop were probably at least dimly aware that much had remained undone during his long episcopate. Detroit had only a modest cathedral and it had no seminary. Both were institutions that, for a great many Catholics, gauged the status and progress of a diocese. But if these same Catholics also sensed that the Foley years had been a time of growth and change, they were quite right. For the Foley episcopate encompassed not only significant change in the religious lives of many Catholics in the Diocese, it was a period of greatly increased lay activity in parish and in interparochial organizations. These developments, it is true, had generally been initiated and sustained by forces outside the Chancery. But this did not prevent most Catholics in 1918 from associating the advent of a more disciplined and vigorous Catholicism with "the Foley years."

7

THE DIOCESAN CLERGY: *THE FOLEY YEARS*

The number of priests in the Diocese of Detroit grew substantially in the Foley years. The bishop inherited 131 priests when he came to Detroit in 1888; when he died, early in 1918, his clergy numbered 318. It was during this episcopate too that the diocesan clergy ceased to be a mostly foreign-born population. Fully 75 percent of the priests ordained in the Foley years had been born in the United States or in English-speaking Canada. Episcopal policy was generally geared to the creation of an "indigenous" clergy: the bishop recruited only a relative handful of priests from abroad. And although Foley permitted nine men's religious orders to establish foundations in the Diocese, he may have tried to limit their size. For the ranks of religious order priests, who were the more likely to be foreign-born, grew more slowly in the Foley years than did the diocesan clergy. Religious order priests made up nearly 25 percent of the local clergy in 1887, but just under 20 percent in 1917 — this despite a major expansion of the Jesuit university in Detroit in the years after 1910.[1]

The increasingly American cast to the diocesan clergy had several consequences. It almost certainly helped to ease tensions between Catholics and Protestants in the Diocese, perhaps especially in the small towns. It probably disposed the clergy to an instinctive sympathy for assimilationist policies with regard to liturgical reform and parochial education. And it meant that priests in the Diocese were better able than ever before to create something close to a cohesive subculture. More and more of them seem to have inhabited an emotional and intellectual world that not only differed in important ways from the world of even the pious laity but was a world where priests alone were fully welcome and at ease.

To some extent, of course, the priests of the Diocese had always inhabited a separate emotional world. Their celibacy in itself virtually insured this. But until the 1880s, the priests in the Diocese were too few in number and too deeply divided by ethnicity to feel that they belonged to a genuine clerical community. There was certainly friendship between individual priests, and every priest had been taught, and doubtless believed, that "the priest is separated from the mass of men by the Divine office of Holy Orders"—as Bishop Foley told his *ordinandi* in 1889. Under what were essentially missionary conditions, however, many priests, especially outside Detroit, found it hard to have regular contact with their fellows. Whether they lived mainly to themselves or moved with ease among the laity depended largely on individual temperament.[2]

It was during the Foley years that this situation changed fundamentally. By the time of Foley's death, most priests in the Diocese belonged in fact as well as theory to a separate clerical world. (The Polish clergy were sufficiently numerous by the early twentieth century that they maintained a largely exclusive community of their own.) The lives of the diocesan clergy were by this time more similar than ever before. Their training was more uniform than it had hitherto been, and young men came to ordination with a greater store of common experiences and expectations than had their missionary predecessors. Their lives after ordination still varied enormously, but the priest in Detroit was no longer as far removed from the world of the country pastor as had once been the case, for rural parishes grew progressively less isolated in the Foley years. The growing ease of travel — and the growing number of priests — meant that the clergy were increasingly able to socialize among themselves. And priests throughout the Diocese were bound together by the discipline that was integral to their calling. The American-born clergy, especially, had internalized the norms that certain of their predecessors had resisted, and this simply confirmed, for themselves and for others, their status as men set apart.

The changes of the Foley years, however, represent only the beginning of a longer period of transition in the lives of the clergy. By the middle decades of the twentieth century, the clergy in the Diocese were characterized by a greater uniformity in experience, outlook and discipline than had ever prevailed in the Foley era. Indeed, by the standards of Cardinal Edward Mooney, who came to Detroit in 1937, the priests of the Foley years look like a dangerously atomized lot — capriciously governed by an inept Chancery, riven by resentments and rivalries, lacking in esprit de corps. But if great changes lay in the future, the Foley years still form a critical chapter in the history of the diocesan clergy. To more fully understand why this was so, we must examine the varieties of priestly experience that lie at the heart of this transitional period.

"AN INWARD CALL": RECRUITMENT AND TRAINING

Although the number of priests in the Diocese increased by nearly two and a half times between 1888 and 1918, the Catholic population grew even more rapidly. There was probably about 1 priest for every 900 Catholics in 1888; thirty years later the ratio stood at something like 1 to 1,200. The imbalance developed largely after 1900, for it was then that ordinations failed in a signal way to keep pace with growth in the Catholic population. The class of 1899, with thirteen members, was Bishop Foley's largest group of *ordinandi*. Between 1900 and 1918, classes ranged in size from two (in 1905) to twelve (in 1909 and again in 1912), averaging just under eight members each. (Classes between 1889 and 1899 had averaged just under seven members.) Moderate population growth in the 1890s, however, was succeeded after 1900 by explosive growth in Detroit and its hinterland.

The *Michigan Catholic* was worried even in the 1890s by what it believed was an incipient crisis in native vocations. "If spirituality glowed more brightly here we should have more vocations to the sacred ministry," ran an 1895 editorial, "and our prelates would not be obliged to seek volunteers to serve at the altar from the Catholic countries of Europe." Population growth after 1900 introduced a strident note to the paper's analysis of the problem. It was the fault of Catholic mothers, an editorialist argued in 1901, that so few young men in America were drawn to the priesthood. "In this country, and we speak plainly and truthfully when we say it, Catholic mothers spend too much of their time affecting the airs and graces of their Protestant neighbors to look after the spiritual welfare of their off-spring." By 1916, fathers too had come under indictment: "The blame for this dereliction may be laid to the money-grasping, society-loving fathers and mothers, who give scant attention to the fostering of vocations in the hearts of their little ones and too much time to frivolity."[3]

A good many Catholics probably found this a persuasive line of argument. But the shortage of vocations during the latter years of the Foley episcopate had more to do with the nature of Detroit's population growth than with a decline in the integrity of Catholic family life. The heavily immigrant population that flooded Detroit and other manufacturing cities in Michigan after 1900 contained relatively few young men with the education — or the means to the education — necessary to enter seminary. But at the same time, the influx of this largely Catholic population created an alarming shortage of priests, especially in Detroit. Once the members of this vast migration had achieved a modest degree of security, however, the situation changed. Their sons swelled the large ordination classes of the late 1920s and the 1930s. Since the population of the Diocese actually declined during the early years of the Depression, what the Chancery regarded as an acceptable ratio of priests to Catholic population was achieved before that decade was out.

We know little about most of the men who were ordained in the Foley years. As *ordinandi*, they were a youthful group: of the 197 whose birthdates are known, only 24 were thirty or older at the time of their ordination. The median age of the Foley *ordinandi* was twenty-six; their modal age was twenty-five. Most had apparently set their sights on the priesthood when they were boys. Indeed, for most of these young men an early decision had been nearly essential, for relatively few came from families where extended schooling for boys was a matter of course. And it was widely assumed that a vocation to the priesthood was something that was normally recognized in childhood — a conviction held by many Catholics as late as the 1960s. Priests in the Foley years were certainly disposed to speak of their own vocations in this way. "In his early boyhood he receives an inward call from God, to set himself apart to His service," explained Father Francis Van Antwerp in 1894 of what he apparently regarded as a typical priest's career.[4]

Just what disposed a boy to this "inward call" is a question that is almost never addressed in the historical record. A family history of piety and devotion to the Church was clearly important. Few priests at any time in the history of the Diocese have been the offspring of mixed marriages. And there have always been families that have produced priests and religious in much the same way that other families have produced generations of doctors or lawyers or teachers. That "vocations run in families" was surely borne out in the Foley years, when the phenomenon was probably more pronounced than it was at any other time in the history of the Diocese. Bishop Foley ordained eight pairs of brothers during his episcopate, as well as a pair of twins and their younger brother, two men whose brothers were religious order priests, one man whose brother had been ordained by Bishop Borgess, and two men whose brothers would later be ordained by Bishop Michael Gallagher.[5]

For the exemplary family life that nurtured these vocations—and indeed nearly all vocations—we must give particular credit to mothers, at least according to popular wisdom. "How many of us would be in darkness today," Cardinal Gibbons asked the graduating class at St. Mary's Academy in Monroe in 1911, "in how many hearts would not the grace of faith have died, if it had not been kept alive by the flame of piety enkindled in the home. This is the work of daughters and wives and mothers." The pious mother provided her child with his first religious training, fostered a devotional atmosphere in the home, and ensured that he received a Catholic education. It was her tender vigilance that preserved the aspiring seminarian in purity and rectitude while he was in her care. And if she finally surrendered her son to the closed male world of the seminary, his ordination day was still her day of triumph. The first Mass of Father Michael Bourke at Detroit's Holy Trinity Church in 1914 occasioned a poetic effusion on just this theme. Although the verses are called "The First Mass," it is the mother and not her newly ordained son who is the subject. She, like her son, has been "separated from the mass of men" by virtue of his ordination; she is a vicarious participant in his priesthood. For all its cloying sentimentality, "The First Mass" captures something of the emotional world in which many vocations were nutured. It reminds us too that this world was not without compensations for women.

> She kneels in the aisle, the mother,
> Head high, tho' her lips move in prayer,
> With eyes fast fixed on the altar
> For a priest, her baby, is there.
> How far away seem the voices
> That are singing the Kyrie;
> E'en at the gate of high Heaven
> Seems the heart of the mother today.
>
> Lights blaze from the cross to the table
> They flash between flower and palm,
> Some tremble and bend in devotion

Some burn in the holiest calm.
Her eyes have seen through the darkness
Of many a silent night.
She could see the priest, her baby,
Were there never an altar light.

"Sanctus" they sing, and the music
Dies away on the trembling air,
In the hush his voice sounds triumphant,
A word, and the Godhead is there.
Dear Christ! Save the heart of the Mother.
It must break in this moment of joy;
She is tasting the first sweets of Heaven
Brought down to the earth by her boy.[6]

Father Bourke had worked as an attorney before deciding to become a priest —
his was a "late vocation" — and he surely did not choose the priesthood in order
to assure himself a secure and comfortable life. But were other aspirants to the
priesthood in these years as evidently free of material motivation? We know little
about the families from which the Foley *ordinandi* came, but what evidence we
have indicates that many of them were raised in working-class homes. And even
in the upper reaches of the working class at the turn of the century, life was a
cramped and precarious affair. Most working-class boys looked ahead to long
years of hard work — beginning, generally, in their midteens — and to the same
chronic economic insecurity that plagued their fathers. The priesthood, by contrast, offered not just security and freedom from manual labor but the respect
of the community and even, perhaps, the spice of adventure. For many boys,
the journey to Baltimore or Milwaukee or Cincinnati for major seminary was
the longest of their young lives.

This is not to say that escape from the working class was ever the sole — or
even the major — motivation for choosing to become a priest. The years of preparation were too long, the regime of the seminary too irksome to be borne by
a young man who did not possess a generous vision of his calling. But for a
working-class boy, the choice of the priesthood was a decision for social mobility,
and this could not help but affect the way a boy thought about the prospect of
becoming a priest. It affected as well the expectations that the newly ordained
brought to their careers. Most priests in the Foley years, it seems, expected to
live comfortably, and they were inclined, at least among themselves, to speak
of their lives in terms of a struggle for place — for good assignments, generous
perquisites, the recognition of their peers. There were those among them, to be
sure, who willingly embraced hardship, much in the spirit of the earliest missionaries in the Diocese, and there was genuine admiration for the charitable
priest. But there was little inclination on the part of most priests to see poverty
as a priestly virtue or to see in their comfortable rectories any challenge to the
priestly calling. Very occasionally this troubled a sensitive observer. Father —
later Bishop — Francis Kelley, who served in the Diocese of Detroit from 1893

until 1908, gave a controversial speech in Chicago in 1908 in his capacity as president and founder of the Catholic Church Extension Society, an organization that sponsored mission work in those parts of the United States where there were few Catholics. Father Kelley worried about what he saw as a lack of "missionary spirit" among American seminarians. "Someone has said that young men in our seminaries are too prone to speak of good places and prosperous dioceses. . . . Let the bishop of a missionary diocese appeal for students, and here and there amongst his hearers a hard young face looks up at him with the query 'How much?' written plainly upon it." By way of corrective, Father Kelley urged upon his audience a broader vision of seminary education and indeed of the priesthood itself. Our students, he noted, "are taught the value of prayers and of knowledge. I fear, however, there is not sufficient training given to that unselfish spirit which makes the great missionaries upon whom the Church relies for great results."[7]

If the typical seminarian hoped eventually to live comfortably and to bask in the admiration of the community, he was surely taught that the meaning of his priesthood lay elsewhere. His was above all else a sacramental ministry. The average Catholic in Foley's day was probably ill-equipped to argue the details of sacramental theology. But even the most indifferent Catholic understood that the role of the priest was to make God quite literally present among men. "He can command the Eternal Son of the Eternal God to come down from His high throne in heaven and to be present on the altar, to become food and drink for the faithful," Bishop Foley told the congregation at an ordination in 1889. "More than this, that same power that Jesus exercised when He forgave the sins of Magdalen, does the duly authorised and empowered priest exercise when he frees souls from the chains of mortal sin, a cure which is a greater miracle than the restoration of the lepers at the wayside by the hands of Jesus." By virtue of his ordination, then, the priest became "another Christ." And at the heart of nearly all vocations, it is reasonable to say, was the sometimes inarticulate but very real desire to stand "prominent between God and man"—in the words of the newly ordained Father Frank Kennedy. "The priest is God's representative in our midst," Father Kennedy told a Dearborn congregation in 1891. "On the altar and in the confessional, he is simply omnipotent, simply divine."[8]

Language like this is rarely heard today, nor has it been since the Second Vatican Council. But pre-conciliar Catholics inhabited a world where custom and rhetoric made plain that the priest possessed what Bishop Foley called a "stupendous dignity." And during the Foley years, this vision of the priesthood took on an increasingly personal meaning for many Catholics. For it was during the Foley years that frequent communion and frequent confession were urged on the mass of American Catholics for the first time—and with impressive results. The frequency with which many, probably most, Catholics approached the sacraments increased noticeably in the Foley years, and continued to increase thereafter. This growth in what was essentially a priest-centered piety was an important source of the confidence and vitality that characterized the priestly ranks, and filled the seminaries, between the late nineteenth century and the early 1960s. The young priests of the Foley years, in short, began their careers at an auspicious time.

The certainties of their lives as priests were rooted in part in the closed and static intellectual world of the seminary. With no seminary in the Diocese itself, the aspiring priests of the Foley era were educated at a number of different institutions. But the seminary experience differed rather little from one institution to the next. Having completed the better part of a college course — often at the Jesuits' Detroit College or the Basilians' Assumption College in Windsor — the aspirant was sent to a major seminary, usually outside Michigan. The largest number in the Foley years — seventy-four of those *ordinandi* whose seminary is known — were trained by the Sulpicians at St. Mary's in Baltimore. Bishop Foley himself had been a student there. Forty-eight are known to have attended Mt. St. Mary's in Norwood, Ohio — the seminary of the Cincinnati Archdiocese. Seventeen of the men whom Foley ordained for his diocese were from SS. Cyril and Methodius Seminary, the "Polish Seminary" located in Detroit and then, after 1910, in Orchard Lake, Michigan. Fifteen had attended St. Francis Seminary in Milwaukee, which had apparently lost by the early twentieth century some of its Germanic aura. Bishop Foley sent students there who were not, to all appearances, of German descent. And seventeen of Foley's priests were alumni of the archdiocesan seminary in St. Paul, Minnesota, an institution especially favored by Bishop Foley during the last years of his episcopate. An occasional student was trained elsewhere — in Montreal, Toronto, Dunwoodie (N.Y.), Rochester (N.Y.), St. Louis, even Denver. Despite Foley's own Roman training, however, he sent only four of his seminarians to study in Rome.

The curriculum of the major seminary, generally spanning five or six years, was by the late nineteenth century nearly identical in most institutions throughout the United States. The Third Plenary Council in 1884 had instructed American seminaries to abide strictly by the terms of Pope Leo's recent encyclical on the revival of Thomistic philosophy. The seminary course was to be conducted in Latin, from textbooks approved by the bishop of the diocese in which the seminary was located, and to adhere faithfully to the methods and principles of Thomism. The effect of this, as John Tracy Ellis has noted, was to make even more rigid what was already a mode of education that discouraged flexibility in teaching and experiment in thought. And if it can be said that a handful of American seminaries were briefly marked at the turn of the century by something like intellectual liveliness, they were not among the seminaries to which Detroit's students were normally sent. Those students arrived at ordination, we can reasonably assume, at least competent in dogma and moral theology, but with almost no knowledge of their wider intellectual inheritance as Catholics or of the intellectual ferment that characterized their age. "I was brought up in a system where the teachers neither directed the energy of the student, nor solved his difficulties by force of reason," a priest told Henry Brownson, a prominent Detroit layman, in 1904. As a consequence, he concluded — certainly too pessimistically—"I know almost nothing." As for Roman seminary education, meant then—as now—for an intellectual elite, it was as hostile to most contemporary thought as it was to intellectual independence. "Here they go on the plan that the less clear their matter is the better exercise it gives the student while he is untangling the web," a student at the American College wrote in 1890 to Detroit's future bishop Michael Gallagher. "A brilliant idea, is it not?"[9]

It was not the purpose of the seminary, of course, to produce intellectuals. The seminary was intended primarily to instill in its students a habitual self-discipline, a regular piety, and a firm loyalty to the Church and to their fellow priests. And this the American seminary did admirably well. Its rigid discipline both accustomed the student to a minutely regulated life—which, it was hoped, would become second nature by the time of ordination—and provided in its very irksomeness a bond to one's suffering fellows. Seminary discipline was a prolonged rite of passage, and if there was attrition along the way, so much stronger was the sense of solidarity among those who endured. But the seminary also encouraged a boyish camaraderie that defused the tensions of close living, and served to induct the students into what their mentors hoped would become, after ordination, an exclusively clerical social world. Another of Michael Gallagher's friends at the American College in Rome conveyed to him in 1890 something of the vitality of student sociability there, although what he had to say was probably true, in essence, of life in all but the strictest American seminaries. The young man wrote specifically about the College summer villa in the Alban hills, where, as he noted, "there is greater liberty in everything":

> There is a much livelier set of boys here, out of about 50 who are here at present, I believe there are only three, who don't play ball. The evenings are very pleasant— we have singing by anybody who's called upon, dancing—Virginia Reel and the Quadrille and general rough and tumble. The general tone is not as high as I had imagined, great familiarity among all the boys prevails. You hear as much slang here as at Innsbruck and in recreation it's not Mer-Mer-etc-but Pat, Mike, Jack, etc. A very good spirit prevails among the boys. I felt at home here the very first evening, though a perfect stranger. That eve I made or rather was kindly forced to make my debut as a Tyrolese warbler and the following as the champion third baseman from Innsbruck. Last week I enjoyed a fine swim in Lake Albano. I joined an excursion to Montebano to see the sunrise mentioned in Wiseman's *Fabiola*, it was, indeed, the finest I've ever seen. Last week the Scotch College came over for a game of cricket, in which your friend Horan distinguished himself. By the way Pat and I are great friends, our tastes in the line of a smoke and a good glass of wine perfectly agree. . . . You remember that I left Innsbruck not without some slight touch of regret—but I must say it was only an agreeable transition of from one room to the other in the same house.[10]

If priestly formation was concerned in part with establishing a student's ties to his own generation of priests, it was concerned as well with establishing the authority of experienced priests over those about to be ordained. The discipline enforced by the seminary faculty helped to accomplish this, as did the practice of assigning to the parish priests of vacationing seminarians the task of supervising them over the summer. Father—later Bishop—William Stang, author of a widely read manual of pastoral theology first published in 1896, warned pastors in his book about the gravity of this particular responsibility and listed its special difficulties. "Many temptations beset the young candidate during vacation," Stang cautioned. "He is loved and admired by all; he is the pride of the congregation, and the promising boast of friends and relatives." The seminarian was almost bound to think too well of himself as a consequence. "There is a period in his student's life when he is liable to be haughty, carrying his head high, not exactly inflated with philosophy, but with harmless dreams and foolish flattery. . . . The priest must patiently bear with his apparent insolence until the transition is finished and the young man finds his level." The seminarian must be carefully watched for any "weakness toward female charms or . . . intoxicating liquors" and should not be permitted "to give himself up to absolute inertness." He must attend Mass every day and visit the Blessed Sacrament, read selected books and assist in teaching the catechism—but only to boys. "Frequently invite him to your table, where you can observe his manners and perhaps correct them. Make an occasional excursion with him." We catch a glimpse locally of such an excursion in the summer of 1893, when three vacationing seminarians accompanied as many priests and the entire Young Ladies' Sodality of Detroit's St. Vincent's parish on a trip to Lake Erie's Put-in-Bay. One hundred and thirty-five young ladies was perhaps more temptation than the conservative Father Stang would have thought prudent, but the three seminarians were safely ordained over the next four years.[11]

With ordination, the rigors of the seminary were at an end and the promising expanse of the priesthood opened before the young candidate. On the day of his ordination and at his first Mass, he was more than ever "the pride of the congregation" and of his family. The first Mass of Father Theodore Lindemann at Detroit's St. Boniface parish in 1900 conveys the excitement that typically surrounded the ordination of a parish boy. "Long before the Mass crowds flocked the streets around the church in an effort to get a glimpse of the privileged priest," the *Michigan Catholic* reported. "Early in the morning the young men of the parish presented him with a golden chalice and the women with a beautiful sick-call outfit." The most senior of Detroit's German priests preached at the mass on the "Duties and Hardships of the Life of a Priest," and while the text of his sermon has not survived, he apparently painted the priesthood in bold and heroic strokes. "No doubt his efforts will inspire all who heard him to a greater respect and devotion to so sacrificing a state," the *Michigan Catholic* noted with evident satisfaction.[12]

Young Father Lindemann left Detroit shortly thereafter to take up his first assignment—as an assistant at St. Augustine's parish in Kalamazoo. Whether his experiences there and in later assignments fulfilled the hopes of his ordination day we do not know. But if the correspondence that has survived from Foley's day is any guide, at least some priests found in their work a fair measure of frustration. Not all the laity, they discovered, were promising material when it came to the spiritual life. And the highly public nature of the priestly role could take its toll as well. "The discomfiture of the first months of ministry will soon pass away," Father Frank O'Brien assured a newly-ordained friend in the summer of 1886. "We have all felt them. Be earnest. Take things easy. *Don't fret.* Trust in God and it will come out right." Father O'Brien would presumably have offered the same advice to a man whose distress was rooted in the disappointments of his middle years or the fatigue and discouragement of old age.[13]

THE PRIEST'S CAREER

The course of a typical priest's career underwent an important change during the Foley years. The priests who were ordained in the Diocese between 1889 and 1899 became pastors nearly as quickly as their predecessors had done. Of the sixty-four priests ordained in this decade whose assignments are known, more than half became pastors within eighteen months of ordination. But of those priests ordained between 1900 and 1917, only 17 percent became pastors in so short a time. In this period the median number of years spent as an assistant rose to just under 4.5. The lengthening years of assistantship—still brief by the standards of later generations—spelled a gradual end to the kind of independence young priests had known in the nineteenth century and, despite the conflicts endemic to rectory life, strengthened the bonds that defined priests as members of an exclusive social group.

The rapidity with which a young man became a pastor in the Foley era seems to have had little to do with the promise the Chancery judged him to possess. Indeed, it appears that Bishop Foley sometimes assigned especially bright and personable young priests as assistants—sometimes for many years—in large and well-managed parishes. There they were groomed to assume, in due time, large parishes of their own. Some of the priests who became pastors immediately after ordination, on the other hand, remained for the rest of their careers in small rural parishes. Quite apart from his talents, a priest's ethnicity affected the shape of his career. Even if he were American-born, a man of Polish descent could expect to serve only in Polish parishes, for there was a shortage of Polish-speaking priests in the Diocese well into the Gallagher years. By the turn of the century, however, the German-American priest had a greater measure of freedom. Their numbers were now quite large, and a goodly portion of the German-American population had been assimilated. Hence the German-American priest could reasonably expect to pass a part of his career in a mostly English-speaking parish, although he was likely to be assigned at some point to a historically German church. Priests of French origin seem to have been more restricted in their careers, although they were not assigned exclusively to ethnic parishes. Religious order priests had charge of the two French parishes in Detroit by 1889, but of the eight priests known to be of French descent who were ordained by Bishop Foley, all but one—who died shortly after ordination—spent at least a part of their careers in the old French parishes that stretched along the eastern shore of Michigan from the Ohio line into the Thumb. As for those priests who were recruited into the Diocese to serve one of the growing number of new ethnic populations there, they could expect to minister only to Catholics of their own nationality, no matter how long or admirable their service might be.

Whatever their ethnic background, most priests agreed that success led in fairly short order to a prosperous city parish. The small rural parish, where a good many priests began their careers, was widely disliked for its isolation — both from one's fellow clergy and the vibrant Church life of Detroit — and for its poverty. It was the rare rural parish, by the turn of the century, that was either as remote or as poor as the typical country parish of earlier decades, but young priests naturally measured their lot by the standards of their own rather than a previous generation. And it still happened that priests in small parishes were sometimes unable to collect their full salaries, especially when times were hard. "The people are very poor in this place," wrote the French-born Father Benedict Gery of Algonac's Catholics in 1901. "No work to do during winter, very little during summer and fall, so I understand well that I cannot collect my salary." Father Gery did not say what his pay had actually been that year, but in 1897 — a year of recovery from a devastating depression — he had received only about $300 of his $700 annual salary. (Since his housing was provided and he had no family to support, Father Gery could live — albeit very simply — on a sum that would have meant destitution for a family with two or three young children.) Father John Command was apparently living austerely too as the pastor of St. Joseph's parish in the village of Trenton. "Not a dozen men of this parish earn three dollars a day," he explained in 1909. "The average wage when there is plenty of work is one dollar and sixty-five cents. The parish priest can hardly get much out of people who have only this small income."[14]

Poor as they were, Trenton's wage-earners saw more cash in the course of the year than did many small farmers, who even at the turn of the century tended to be an economically marginal population. "You, having lived in this part of the country, know by experience how much farmers do towards church and school, especially towards a new parish house," wrote the pastor at St. Clement's in rural Centerline in 1895. "'The house is as good as ours,' etc.: You know what that means." What it meant at St. Clement's, at least according to Father Kramer, was a rectory "much too small for its purposes. I cannot even harbor a priest overnight, much less several, as on the occasion of a mission or other special devotions. The furniture is the most ancient, unfit for the poorest laboring man." Father William DeBever, pastor in 1895 at St. Mary's in Redford, had a different set of grievances, but they too were caused by the poverty of his rural congregation. He had been able to collect only $415 of his salary that year, and was decidedly gloomy about his future in the parish. "The revenue will not cover the expenses, unless the priest does his own chores, takes care of his horse (he cannot do without it), split[s] his own stove wood for Church and House, shovels snow, keeps the Church clean etc. etc. and bring[s] himself down to the level of a common laborer." At the age of sixty, the Dutch-born DeBever was emphatic in his refusal to work as the parish hired hand, but his young American-born successor actually served as sexton as well as pastor for more than six years. "No charge for painting barn and outbuildings, nor for painting roof of the wing of the house and cementing same," Father Andrew Dooling wrote in the parish accounts for 1903, "this having been done by the pastor."[15]

The city parish, with its large congregation, stood in contrast to the poverty of the country pastorate, for priests in large parishes nearly always lived well, collecting their full salaries and often additional fees besides and supplied with a spacious, even luxurious, rectory. And if the work of managing the large parish was considerable, it was work appropriate to an educated man. A successful city pastor was necessarily a good administrator, proud of "his good name, business ability and reputation," in the words of Father John Dempsey. His was a way of life removed from the level of the common laborer; it fulfilled the promise of social mobility that the priesthood held out to a working-class boy. And the young assistant in the large parish shared in the glory, although he generally carried a heavy burden of work. The busy city pastor, "engaged in building . . . or fighting a heavy debt" was obliged to "throw upon the shoulders of his assistant, the visitation of the sick, and much of the labor, which, under more favorable circumstances, would devolve on the parish priest," at least according to an 1896 account of priestly life.[16]

Despite his many responsibilities, the assistant priest did not generally enjoy the same independence in his work that his peers in country pastorates did. Occasionally an assistant was assigned to a pastor with whom he worked in something like equality: Father Maurice Chawke was an assistant to Father James Doherty at St. Vincent's in Detroit for more than twenty years, the two men functioning, to all appearances, almost like co-pastors in the care of that enormous parish. But even where relations were amicable, pastors seem normally to have looked on their assistants as priests-in-training. Nor did harmony always prevail. The peace of the rectory was easily disturbed, at least according to a popular manual for priests published in 1909. Pastors should take care not to "show themselves unkind, cold and unfriendly toward their curates," the manual warned. They should not "find fault with everything" nor "overburden others unduly and spare themselves most conscientiously," still less frustrate an assistant's efforts out of jealousy or "go so far as to lay down for them stringent rules of conduct, as if their curates were children in the nursery." For their part, assistants were cautioned to be discreet with outsiders, considerate of the housekeeper, conscientious in their duties, frugal, and punctual. Above all they should cultivate a spirit of willing obedience, striving to overcome "a certain haughtiness of manner which repels the offer of advice and paternal instruction."[17]

The delicate relationship between pastor and assistant was apt to be complicated, according to this particular manual, by any but the most tactful of rectory housekeepers. "Self-willed and overbearing" women were especially to be avoided, for "the assistant priests will seriously complain of the haughty treatment to which they are subjected." Most housekeepers were hardly so formidable, but a handful of rectories in the Foley years were clearly run by women. "He was dominated by his housekeeper, a young woman, who assumed management of the parish," Bishop Foley explained of a priest whose career had not fulfilled its early promise. "This displeased his congregation and though there was no moral charge, I had to remove him on account of the boycott." Foley apparently enforced no rules with regard to the age of rectory housekeepers—his successors insisted on older women only—and on occasion a priest and his housekeeper grew old together. In such circumstances, a priest might develop a strong emotional dependence on the woman who ran his household. One priest ordained late in Foley's episcopate had lived with the same housekeeper for many years by the time he became a prominent pastor in Detroit. "She has a strong influence on the pastor and for the good," a Chancery investigator told Cardinal Mooney in the early 1950s. "If anything should happen to her he could very easily go into a[n] emotional tailspin." What a close relationship between a pastor and his housekeeper meant for the assistants who lived at the rectory obviously depended on the personalities involved. But assistant priests did sometimes "seriously complain" that the housekeeper played a role in the rectory and the parish that undermined their own authority as adult males and even as priests.[18]

Even in an unhappy rectory, however, the assitant learned that his lot was cast with the clerical world and not with the world of the laity. Under a stricter discipline than a priest living alone, he was expected to conform to what his pastor defined as acceptable behavior, earning as recompense the approval of more senior priests and, if he was fortunate, a reputation as a promising young man. The norm to which young priests were expected to hew was not precisely an ascetic one. But it was a code of conduct that defined the priest as a member of what was essentially a closed fraternity. The gregarious Bishop Foley might endorse for his priests a more genial public presence than Bishop Borgess had ever done, but Foley, like his predecessor, believed that a priest's relations with the laity should be characterized by a fundamental emotional reserve. Nor should one's manner of life in any way betray the dignity of the priestly calling. The prudent priest confined his friendships to the circle of his fellow clergy, met the laity on clearly defined grounds, and avoided the more obviously worldly pastimes. If Bishop Foley was not, on the surviving evidence, the ascetic his predecessor had been, his priests were still wise to avoid drinking in public and attendance at most popular amusements.

But the Foley years were also marked by a growing concern among priests that their approved way of life was too formidable a barrier between themselves and a portion of their male parishioners. They worried especially about young men. "There is, it seems, a natural timidity on the part of youth as it grows into manhood to meet a priest," admitted Kalamazoo's Father Francis O'Brien in 1896. "With many there is a shyness which makes them feel reluctant to be seen in the company of a priest." This was a painful experience for any priest, according to Father O'Brien, but particularly for the young one, who "feels this restraint, this shyness which causes the young men to avoid him, most keenly." The gulf might be narrowed, Father O'Brien believed, if younger priests were to enter in a limited way into the secular male world. "Make them feel that you are made of the same material that they are," he advised. "Talk baseball, billiards, and even prize-fighting if necessary." But Father O'Brien could not countenance a whole-sale abandoning of priestly dignity. "Rarely if ever join in their sports," he cautioned. "By doing so you lessen your influence."[19]

Certain of O'Brien's colleagues were even in the 1890s inclined to more liberal views. Father John Schreiber, for example, did not scruple to enter—and win—an 1893 bowling tournament sponsored by Detroit's St. Boniface parish, where he had been pastor since 1890. And eventually the boyish, athletic priest became, for even conservative Catholics, a much-loved fixture of parish life. What Father O'Brien typified was the uneasiness felt by those many priests who were, in the Foley years, caught between conflicting expectations. They were, on the one hand, heirs to the successful efforts of Detroit's nineteenth-century bishops to impose a uniform discipline on their clergy. Nearly all of them had accepted a view of the priesthood—and of priestly behavior—that emphasized their status as men set apart. But at the same time, they were members of a generation with higher hopes than any before it of incorporating the mass of the laity into a disciplined religious practice. And this task seemed often to require that the priest abandon his reserve, that he meet the more alienated laity on their own ground. Thus Father O'Brien, like many of his contemporaries, was trying to balance the dignity appropriate to his exalted calling with the need to be, for pastoral reasons, all things to all men—if not necessarily to all women, whose loyalty to the Church was much less problematic.[20]

Father O'Brien's candor in 1896 was possible, perhaps, because he was known to be a highly successful pastor. He had charge of St. Augustine's parish in Kalamazoo from 1883 until his death in 1921, and during that time he built not only a widely admired parochial school but was instrumental in the founding of a hospital, a college, an academy for girls, a boarding school for boys, and a school for the "feeble-minded." He had, moreover, been among the first in the Diocese to build a fully equipped clubhouse for the young men of his parish—an innovation he recommended to all priests as a means of countering the alienation of youth from the Church. Whatever discouragement he met in his long career, he was surely comforted by the support of his large congregation and the admiration of his fellow clergy. But what of those priests—the great majority—whose careers were marked by less obvious signs of success? Were their modest achievements enough to compensate for the frustrations they encountered? The Chancery archives are of little help to us here, speaking as they do almost exclusively to the grievances and disappointments that occasionally moved a priest—or his parishioners—to write in protest to the Bishop. These grievances provide a certain insight into the clerical world of Foley's day, and for that reason they merit some attention. But they tell only a portion of the story, and perhaps a very small portion at that.

The bitterness that occasionally took possession of a priest as his career passed into its middle stages had most often to do with what he took to be the poverty or low status of his parish. His more successful contemporaries had long since moved into prosperous pastorates, and their good fortune made the austere conditions of his life all the harder to bear. Sometimes, as we have seen, priests did live in genuinely straitened circumstances. "My income here since I am in the parish is all in all about $2.00 per week and from that the housekeeper must be paid and from the rest I can buy bread no butter," Father Henri Meuffels complained during the depression of the 1890s. (He was pastor at St. John the Evangelist parish on the outskirts of Detroit, still too sparsely populated a region to give adequate support to a priest.) But the marked discrepancy in priests' incomes in the Foley years could cause resentment even where a priest could not honestly claim that his life was not reasonably comfortable. "In my service of nearly 26 years I have never been able to take a trip to Europe and around the world as some others have done more than once," the pastor of a rural parish near Detroit told Bishop Foley in 1912. Neither had any of his parishioners, in all likelihood, been world travelers, but he measured his circumstances only against those of his fellow clergy. The relative poverty of many rural clergy led in the Foley years to frequent irritation between neighboring pastors. Father Joseph Seybold, pastor in the village of Maybee, registered in 1897 what was evidently a common complaint when he accused the priest at nearby Stony Creek of baptizing, marrying, and burying Catholics who lived within the Maybee parochial limits. A priest was normally paid for these services, and Father Seybold was aggrieved at what he regarded as a violation of canon law as well as a drain on his income. "I cannot and will not any longer patiently tolerate the free-methodist church performances of Rev. Ronayne," he warned the Chancery.[21]

The resentments nursed by an unhappy priest might be turned in a more general way against his fellow clergy, especially those who were foreign-born or of a different ethnic background. Father John Kramer was disturbed to hear in 1895 that a priest only recently come from Germany was to be assigned to the flourishing St. Anthony's parish on the eastern edge of Detroit. "Now I ask you, as an honest man and as an American who has always done his duty as well as he could, is this right?" he demanded of Bishop Foley. "An imported foreigner, not knowing the customs and manners of this country; not even knowing the language preferred to a priest more than nine years in the service of God without complaint from anyone? An American who spent his time and money for this diocese, a child of the diocese who took the trouble to learn the German language and that well to be of service to his bishop?" (Father Kramer tried on several subsequent occasions to be moved from his rural parish, but to no avail. He was stationed there until his death in 1929.) A German-born priest, however, accused Bishop Foley in 1914 of a long history of animosity against his German clergy. "As a German I am open, frank, truthful, fearless to tell the truth," he wrote to his bishop, presumably to justify the intemperate attack that followed, "and not deceitful like many Irish, whom I have learned to know who are so fine and nice and friendly to one's face but so treacherous as to stab one from behind." He was unhappy with the Wyandotte parish to which he had come in 1906, and from which Foley had since refused to move him. "When nearly 9 years ago, You requested me to go to St. Joseph's Parish in Wyandotte, I asked You, riding in Your carriage with You from Your residence toward the M[ichigan] C[entral] Depot, 'Your Lordship, is this change really a promotion for me?' You assured me then, that it was, when really and indeed, as I found out, it was not, as those priests know well, who are acquainted with the deplorable condition St. Joseph's parish was in when you sent me here." Foley's most recent refusal to appoint him to a better parish had convinced him, he wrote, that what he had heard from various disgruntled priests in the Diocese was really true: Foley disliked his German priests and did not deal equitably with them. As for those who secured the best places, they were invariably the bishop's cronies, the "flatterers" and the "tale-bearers." This impassioned denunciation of a corrupt Chancery can hardly be read as a sober account of Foley's administration, although it does reflect a simmering tension between Foley and certain of his German clergy, who feared that the bishop's "Americanist" loyalties put him out of sympathy with their own vision of the Church. And it reflects in a distorted way the less attractive realities of the clerical world, where we find the same rivalries and festering resentments that all too often characterize life in the secular professions.[22]

Priests also complained about their parishioners, who were seldom as docile or as devout as the clergy would have them be. A good many parishes in the Foley years still had strong boards of trustees, and pastors sometimes found themselves in conflict with their trustees—or with a faction in the congregation—over the extent to which the laity might govern the parish. "One of my former defunct trustees had the hardihood to tell me to my face: I don't see why a bishop or a priest would not do what the people expect him to do since they are paid by the people," an indignant Father Alphonse Bertele told Bishop Foley in 1916. Ethnic rivalries complicated the pastoral role for many priests, especially in small town parishes where several ethnic groups were likely to belong to a single congregation. "New Baltimore people is a very particular people, especially the German element," Father Henry DeGryse explained in 1895. "They want the priest just so! Otherwise they will criticize and fight him pretty badly." In the parish at St. Joseph it was "a certain few polanders and Germans" who made life hard for their Irish-American pastor, whom they wanted to "work on a salary paid him at their discretion," at least according to an irate partisan of Father James Gore. "This I consider an insult not alone to our beloved paster but to our holy religeon thereby placing us on a leval with the country cross roads Methodists." The tensions at St. Joseph, however, were apparently slight when compared to the situation in 1895 at Detroit's St. Joachim parish, whose French-Canadian members were unhappy with their "Franco-German" priest. "The people do not like Rev. Roth," an anonymous parishioner informed Bishop Foley. "They do not want the Order of the Holy Ghost to have control of the Church any more. The trustees wants to run the church themselves and the people wants [a] French Canadian priest. Secret meetings are being held on the quiet and if the church is again rented to the order of the Holy Ghost there is going to be some serious trouble."[23]

Priests of unusually ascetic sensibilities were perhaps especially likely to have difficulties with their parishioners, at least where those priests had not cultivated the art of compromise. Father William Sinn had apparently not done so: just one year past ordination, he spoke sternly in the regulations he published in 1890 for his parishioners at Lapeer. "It is very inconsistent to invite Our Lord to attend and bless your marriage in the morning and ask the devil to the feast in the evening," Sinn warned. "If you have made up your mind that you cannot get along at the wedding without dancing and strong drink, do not profane the Sacrament by your hypocrisy. If you prefer the devil's blessing to God's blessing please keep away from the church." Father Sinn did not stay long at Lapeer — ill health forced his resignation in 1892 and he died just two years later. But his uncompromising stand against drinking and dancing almost certainly caused the kind of resentment at Lapeer that such rules had generally caused in the Diocese wherever and whenever they were imposed. Perhaps significantly, Father Sinn had been unable, according to his 1890 parish report, to establish any societies among the men and boys of the parish.[24]

Had young Father Sinn lived longer, he might conceivably have modified his views. But maturity and even broad-mindedness did not guarantee a priest an amicable relationship with every group in his congregation. The *Michigan Catholic* columnist known as "Rosaleen" was the recipient, in the early years of the twentieth century, of many priests' complaints about the ingratitude and intractability of a troublesome minority among their parishioners. "It is the 'progressive up-to-date-know-it-all Catholic' in a parish who is generally the head spokesman when it comes to meddling [with] the pastor," she charged in 1906. "There are a few of these cheap Catholics in every community." Things had been different in the past, she believed, as ignorant of local Church history as most of her contemporaries. "The Irish and German people of the forties and fifties, the builders of churches in this country, were not such meddlers — they would not criticize their pastor."[25]

A priest's life, however, was not normally centered on rivalries and resentments. The vast majority of his congregation were deferential to him, and many priests enjoyed great popularity among their parishioners, who were eager to honor their pastor on the anniversary of his ordination or the feast-day of his patron saint and certainly at Christmas. His comings and goings were of interest to a broad community. When Father James Doherty, pastor of St. Vincent's parish in Detroit, returned from a trip to Ireland in 1895, "a large and enthusiastic crowd greeted him at the railroad station; he was escorted to St. Vincent rectory by a deputation of 12 carriages." Fully 8,000 persons were said to have been waiting in the vicinity of the church, not only members of the parish but Catholics from other parts of Detroit as well. (The band from the neighboring German parish of St. Boniface was on hand to play Irish and American songs.) The return of Father Joseph Joos to St. Mary's parish in Monroe in 1905 was nearly as lavishly celebrated. Father Joos had gone home to Belgium for six months "in quest of health," and his parishioners were delighted that he was well enough again to resume his pastorate. "A large assemblage" of parish men met him at the depot and — together with the Monroe Cornet Band — accompanied his carriage to St. Mary's Church, where "a vast congregation had been awaiting the Father's arrival since early in the evening." Speeches of welcome followed, and then the presentation of "a basket of flowers in which was concealed a check of $723.00, a donation and thank-offering of St. Mary's congregation." The Catholics of St. Mary's parish in the village of Chelsea were too few to mount such grand demonstrations, but Father William Considine must have understood in what affection he was held there. "We parted today with our dearly beloved Father Considine," wrote young Johanna Devereaux in 1895. "He was my Sunday School teacher. When the news came to our house I did not cry as bitterly as mamma and my sisters, but . . . you know I felt just as bad, he was the best teacher the Catechism class ever had."[26]

If the affection of their people was perhaps the most critical source of sustenance for many priests, their work had other compensations as well. Priests were often important as local men of affairs, as we will have occasion to see when we examine Protestant-Catholic relations in the Diocese. Those many priests who came from working-class families, especially, could hardly help but be gratified by their inclusion in the local elite. The evidently greater discipline in the religious practice of the mass of Catholics in the Foley years was a source of comfort and pride to the clergy, particularly when their own hard work and appealing personalities appeared to be a major stimulus to a new religious fervor among their parishioners. "The pastor, Rev. Father James Stapleton, who came to organize this parish seven months ago has done wonders with the material at hand," an early member of Annunciation parish in Detroit wrote in 1906. The temporary church, housed in a former public school building, "accommodates 300 people and is crowded to the very doors at each of the three Masses on Sunday. So popular has Father Stapleton become in the parish that people who have not thought of religion for years past, have become regular attendants and have rented pews." And priests were obviously sustained in their work by their own religious faith, however little evidence they have left us with regard to their interior lives. A new emphasis on an emotional Eucharistic piety in the 1890s and after was important to the spiritual lives of many priests, and it helped to confirm for them an already strong sense of the exalted nature of their calling.[27]

The typical priest's career in the Foley years did not end in retirement. The majority of priests evidently served as pastors until they died. Retirement was something that a man requested only if his health was so poor that continued work was impossible, and it was apparently something that a conscientious priest sought with some reluctance. "I find myself forced against my will to ask you to retire me from all active duties," Father Charles Thomas wrote from his parish in Erie in the fall of 1897. He was then about to celebrate his seventy-ninth birthday, but wanted to stay on in the parish through the end of the year, in order to balance the books and collect at least a portion of the salary owed him. "If it please your Lordship I should wish to remain pastor until Jan. 1st to collect back pew rent, as we are very much behind. I have been able to pay until now all ordinary expenses; but I have not received anything yet on my salary for '97."[28]

Father Thomas had served at Erie since 1850, and had obviously not grown rich there. He had no recourse, he told Bishop Foley, but "to hope that you will grant me a small pension on the infirm fund." This the bishop did, although we do not know whether Father Thomas drew the full $500 annual stipend that was the maximum granted a priest from the Infirm Fund in the 1890s. This fund was apparently in a perennially precarious state: $2,920 was received in 1898, for example, from the tax that was levied for this purpose on all parishes, while $2,878 was expended on pensions. For this reason, the priests who served as directors of the fund were expected to scrutinize each case that came before them, and not to assume that old age alone was sufficient cause for retirement. When Father James Wheeler, longtime pastor of Our Lady of Help parish in Detroit, asked in 1919 to be retired — on the grounds that he was "advanced in years and in feeble health" — the diocesan consultors, to whom such matters were apparently now referred, were not disposed to grant the request. Father Wheeler was just days shy of his seventy-first birthday, but this was evidently an age when a priest could still be expected to be of service. "It was thought well to get the opinion of his physician," the consultors decided. "If the doctor thinks a vacation of several months will improve his health sufficiently to resume his duties, Father Wheeler is to be asked to reconsider his resignation." Not surprisingly, perhaps, Father Wheeler was pastor at Our Lady of Help when he died in 1923.[29]

Still, it was necessary at times to permit priests to retire at unusually early ages, when their physical — or occasionally mental — incapacity left the Chancery no alternative. And this could be expensive. The member of the ordination class of 1901, for example, who retired for reasons of health at the age of forty-four lived until he was sixty-nine. But most priests not only remained healthy enough to work well into old age; they seem to have accepted without complaint a view of the priesthood that had no place for mandatory retirement. The very meaning of their lives was so bound up with the work they did in the parish — which was also home — that retirement may well have seemed an uneasy, even a frightening, prospect to many of them.

We know almost nothing about how those priests who did retire spent their inactive years. Only the most limited public role was apparently permitted them. "You are allowed to say Mass in your private chapel, without in any way making it a place of worship for Catholics or those living in the neighborhood of said private chapel," Bishop Foley told Father Amandus Vandendriessche, who was "honorably retired" in 1892, just before his fifty-sixth birthday. "You are moreover allowed to say Mass in any church or chapel in our diocese with the permission of the pastor or superior. But you are *not* allowed to preach or make announcements in any church or chapel in our diocese without our special permission." The American-born among the retired priests probably often lived with family members, but those who had come to the Diocese from Europe as seminarians or as young priests might find themselves alone. Occasionally a priest retired to his European homeland, but changes there — and in himself — might prove to have been so great that he was in many ways a foreigner in his native place. This happened to Father George Laugel, born in Alsace in 1843, who came to the Diocese of Detroit about four years after his ordination in Paris in 1875. Father Laugel had returned to France when he retired, and was living at the Seminaire Colonial in Paris in the early 1920s. But he found little in the way of happiness there, at least of an earthly sort: "There are 20 holy Masses said every morning in the Chapel and I attend them all. I have nothing else to do — My existence is sad enough here: Cold, Solitude, inactivity, nostalgy of friends of dear America." The spiritual condition of France, moreover, caused him no end of distress, especially when compared to what he remembered as the spiritual health of his former American diocese. "O happy and dear America!!" he wrote to a friend in Detroit, apparently on the Feast of St. Blaise. "Surely you have been giving the blessing of Saint 'Blaise' from your first holy mass till late. Here, alas! in the whole of France, it is unknown, except in Alsace. There is a great deal of piety in Paris, but, too sad to behold, only one third of the people practices their religion — the laborers are mostly Socialists." Father Laugel's mind was lively, and he maintained an interest in French and American politics, as well as in the theological politics that were so much a part of European ecclesiastical life. (The recent condemnation of Brossac's commentaries on scripture, he noted, had "created a sensation in France," adding wryly, "is it not astonishing that so many learned and deep Sulpicians, the great Tanquerey 'en tete' should not find out those errors in 25 years? Sed Roma locuta est —") But for all his interest in the European scene, his heart was still in the United States, where the active days of his priestly life had been spent — days that he remembered with a wistful nostalgia. "America is now the most beautiful land to live in, after the Kingdom of Heaven," he told his Detroit correspondent.[30]

PRIESTS IN TROUBLE

In every generation of priests who have served in the Diocese, there have been a few men whose careers have been notably troubled. Most often the problem has been alcoholism. Sexual scandals, traditional grist for the anti-Catholic mill, have been surprisingly infrequent, at least if we credit the records that have survived in the Chancery archives. And there were only a handful of men in the generations before Vatican II who are known to have left the priesthood, either by applying for laicization or simply abandoning their careers. We know almost nothing about those who did, save that drink was a factor in many of the cases.[31]

Perhaps the single most notorious instance of a troubled career in the late nineteenth century was that of Father John Busche, who came to the Diocese in 1864 from the American College at Louvain and served as pastor at Lapeer until 1890. Father Busche apparently lost his faith as he became progressively more preoccupied with what a worried Bishop Borgess described as "intricate and difficult questions of science and philosophy," questions that Father Busche was by the early 1880s attempting to explore in his sermons. "It is not only false, 'that Herbert Spencer, Tindall, Darwin, etc., etc. are the great thinkers and philosophers of this century,'" Borgess warned him in 1883, "but it is wrong to laud the leaders of the rankest infidelity from the altar of God; for the very Catholic instinct rebels against the praise bestowed on such heroes of impiety and crime." Father Busche should in future confine his preaching "to simple and solid explanations of Catholic faith and morals," the bishop continued. "In so doing, all hazardous expressions must be scrupulously avoided, such as 'it has been my aim these three or four last years to make religion less galling and burdensome as may have been noticed.'" Any subsequent reformation on the priest's part was short-lived, for Bishop Foley felt compelled to suspend Busche from all priestly duties in 1890. He was never reconciled with the Church, but subsequently married—in a civil ceremony—and apparently lived in the vicinity of Lapeer until his death in 1905, giving occasional vent to his rationalist views in the local press.[32]

Colorful though he was, Father Busche was hardly typical of the troubled priests who made life difficult for their bishops, and, often enough, for their parishioners. ("Recently on two occasions he has been unable to officiate at funerals when the corpse was brought to church and people had assembled at church," an aggrieved parishioner told Bishop Foley about his pastor, who had a history of heavy drinking. "We have had no lenten services this yr after announcing he would hold such services weekly.") We have already seen that alcoholic priests were a serious problem in the early days of the Diocese, when bishops Rese and Lefevere were forced to recruit their clergy from whatever quarter they could, and to accept priests on the slenderest of recommendations. Once Bishop Lefevere had established avenues of recruitment in his native Belgium, however, the incidence of alcoholism among the diocesan clergy seems to have declined markedly. Lefevere, like his successors, inquired closely after the character of those seminarians being trained for the Diocese, and was quick to withdraw support from any young man who evinced a weakness for liquor. But even the most intrusive episcopal vigilance could not prevent the ordination of an occasional man who had, perhaps still unbeknownst to himself, a disposition to alcoholism. A mere handful of alcoholic priests in his diocese could create such problems for a bishop that it was hard for him to see that the problems he faced in this regard were probably much less severe than those encountered by his predecessors in frontier days. "So many young priests in this country have become a disgrace to themselves and to the Church by the excessive use of liquor," an unhappy Bishop Borgess told a priest whom he suspected of heavy drinking, "that the possibility of another victim horrifies us."[33]

Bishop Borgess dealt with the alcoholics among his clergy much as his predecessor had done and much as Bishop Foley would later do. Each bishop was constantly alert to rumors that certain priests were suspected of heavy drinking, and each was quick to warn the priest in question to mend his ways. "When you met us at the depot in Jackson on the 11th ult., your face had the appearance of a confirmed drunkard," Bishop Borgess wrote to one of his priests. "No doubt, you may have a satisfactory explanation for that, but that unfortunately does not remove the public 'signboard.' We were, moreover, told last year by a priest, that 'before long you would be on the drunkard's list — that the opinion of priests on the line.' We beg of you, therefore, for the sake of your own soul and the honor of religion, 'ut sobrinis sis.' We ask for no explanations."[34]

Should a priest ignore his bishop's admonitions and particularly if he were to be drunk in public, his bishop would almost certainly remove him from his parish, although in some cases — most notably in a large Detroit parish in the 1880s — that removal came only after repeated offenses. What to do with a priest once he had been removed was problematic. A period of penance was nearly always required — perhaps a retreat of several weeks' duration at a secluded monastery — and the offending priest had to pledge that he would never drink again. If he seemed penitent and determined to reform, he was generally assigned to a new parish, sometimes as an assistant to a mature and respected priest but more often — at least in the Borgess years — as the pastor of a country church. (Several of the smallest and poorest of the rural parishes in the Diocese were host in the nineteenth century to considerably more than their share of alcoholic priests.) In a rural parish, the Chancery apparently calculated, any future misconduct on the part of the priest would scandalize the fewest people, and the priest himself understood that his new post — poor in revenues and in status — was a punishment for his prior misbehavior. Punishment was called for, at least as far as his bishop was concerned. Lefevere, Borgess, and Foley alike believed that excessive drinking was caused by a failure of will — that it was a sin rather than the manifestation of deep-seated psychological or physical problems. This was especially true of bishops Lefevere and Borgess, both of them well known as temperance men.

Because they understood problem drinking in this way, Detroit's bishops responded to chronic alcoholism among their priests by imposing upon the offenders a round of progressively more severe and isolating penances. If an alcoholic priest resumed drinking in his new parish, he might be sent to an even poorer and more remote pastorate. If he failed there — as he almost invariably did — he would probably be ordered to make yet another penitential retreat, and then be reassigned — perhaps as an assistant, perhaps as a country pastor — but this time in a different quarter of the Diocese. Eventually he was likely to be sent to one of a handful of institutions run by religious orders, generally as adjuncts to asylums for the insane, where alcoholic priests were confined and subjected to an essentially monastic discipline. St. Joseph's Retreat in rural Dearborn was one possibility; St. Benoit-Joseph Asylum near Montreal, founded in 1884, was another. "As your Lordship is aware, I am almost eleven months at Long Point," an unhappy priest wrote to Bishop Foley from this latter establishment late in 1896, "and I am in great dread of the approaching severe weather. . . . I most imploringly beg and entreat you to grant me permission to come home. I trust your Lordship is well satisfied with the long retirement and penance which I was obliged to endure for my past transgressions." This particular priest, whose problems with drink went back at least to 1881, was apparently kept at St. Benoit-Joseph Asylum until 1898, when he was assigned as an assistant in a small-town parish in the Diocese. He did not last long there, however, reverting in short order to the behavior that had caused him so much grief over the course of his career. Bishop Foley never assigned him to a parish again, and he seems to have lived with relatives until his death in 1903. He had at an earlier point in his career been sent to his relatives, for Bishop Borgess had finally despaired of him. "Experience has repeatedly proved that the best promises and even the solemn 'oath' of Rev. ———— cannot be relied upon, for his 'oath' he kept only *one* single month, after he went to Dearborn," Borgess told a priest who still believed that his hard-drinking friend was capable of reformation. "Hence, if you believe him to be sincere in his intention of saving his soul, you ought to encourage him to free himself from every temptation by retiring forever into a religious community."[35]

The point of this dispiriting narrative is not to insinuate that alcoholism was more prevalent among the clergy than it was among the men of other professions, for this was almost certainly not the case. But it was a particularly vexing problem for the Church, because an alcoholic priest remained a priest—and hence the responsibility of the Diocese—no matter how seriously his drinking interfered with the performance of his duties. He could not be laicized, or even sent to another diocese, unless he himself consented. And although a bishop was not obliged to assign a troubled priest to a parish, Detroit's bishops were apparently reluctant to abjure all financial responsibility for even the most confirmed and long-term alcoholics. The priest whose problems were such that—in the words of an understandably unhappy parishioner—he was "no longer responsible for his actions or able to perform his duties as pastor," was still some twenty years later the financial responsibility of the Diocese as an inmate of St. Joseph's Retreat. (Incardinated into the Diocese from Ireland in the early 1890s, this particular priest quickly proved to be a bad bargain for Bishop Foley.) An alcoholic priest was, for his ordinary, rather like the burden of an alcoholic in the family, and Detroit's bishops responded to their troubled clergy with much the same mixture of patience and rage that often characterizes the long-suffering kin of a chronic drinker.

Detroit's bishops did not differ much from their episcopal contemporaries in their response to alcoholism among the clergy. Other bishops too saw the genesis of the problem in a want of virtue, and prescribed for it the kind of penitential remedies that in most cases simply aggravated the deep psychological problems of the alcoholic priest. What finally distinguished Detroit in this regard was the attitude of Cardinal Edward Mooney, who in 1953 gave permission to Austin Ripley to establish "Guest House" in the Archdiocese of Detroit. A lay-run institution for the treatment of alcoholic priests, Guest House operated on the assumption that alcoholism was a "disease of the whole man" and that its clients were "patients, not penitents." Its program, initially controversial, has proved over the years to be remarkably successful. We will later look in more detail at the inauguration and development of Guest House in the Archdiocese, for its history has much to say about the way in which most Catholics — and the clergy themselves — understood the priesthood and the psychology of the priest in the years immediately preceding the Second Vatican Council. Suffice it to say here that most Catholics in the mid-1950s seem to have regarded the alcoholic priest in terms that even the stern Bishop Borgess would have immediately recognized.

It would be wrong to end this chapter on a gloomy note, for the Foley years were a time of significant progress for the clergy of the Diocese. They were, by 1918, a mostly American-born population, and this alone represented a major change from the time when Bishop Borgess arrived in his new Diocese to find that fewer than 7 percent of his priests had been born in the United States. The priests of the Foley years, moreover, were a reasonably disciplined and cohesive lot, despite the personal rivalries and ethnic animosities that sometimes disturbed their relations with one another. The great majority of them were loyal to the Chancery, well conducted and hard working, and seem to have possessed a deeply spiritual vision of their calling. The "true priest" was "a sign of hope and reconciliation" in the world, Father Frank Kennedy told a congregation in 1891, and nearly all of his clerical contemporaries would surely have agreed. Indeed, if we look beyond the Foley years to the ordination classes of the 1920s and the 1930s — some of which were among the largest in the history of the Diocese — we can see that the priests whom Bishop Foley had ordained had proved to be compelling signs of "hope and reconciliation" for a good many young men. Those same priests had helped to stimulate a new religious fervor among many of the laity, whose religious practice by 1918 was more disciplined than it had ever been before. "What a blessing it is then, my dear friends, to have this priesthood among us," the Jesuit William Mitchell told a congregation at St. Vincent's Church in Detroit in 1899. "How grateful we should be to Almighty God for the blessings He gives His ministers." The occasion was the first Mass of Father Richard Grace, who had grown up in the parish and whose friends and family had turned out for the happy event. But they were not the only members of the congregation who gave their full assent to what Father Mitchell had to say in his sermon in praise of the priestly life.[36]

ILLUSTRATIONS

Children at St. Vincent's Asylum, Detroit, probably in the 1890s.

Students at St. Francis Seminary, Monroe, in 1886.

Bishop John Foley, seated left, with Cardinal James Gibbons, seated center.

Interior of Sweetest Heart of Mary Church, Detroit. The church was built between 1890 and 1893, during the pastorate of Father Dominic Kolasinski.

St. Joseph's Hospital, Mt. Clemens, under construction in 1900.

The episcopal residence on Washington Boulevard, c. 1918.

8

THE LAITY: *A TIME OF TRANSITION*

The long episcopate of John Samuel Foley spanned years of significant change for the Catholics of the Diocese. The religious practice of many Catholics was altered more dramatically in these years than at any time before Vatican II. The typical parish in Detroit, moreover, came in this period to resemble more and more, in its social composition, the parishes that eventually characterized a thoroughly suburbanized Church. Many of the social and religious organizations that did so much to shape Detroit Catholicism in the decades after the First World War have their roots in the Foley era: the Holy Name Society, the Knights of Columbus, the League of Catholic Women, the Catholic Instruction League, the Catholic Youth Organization. Finally, despite heavy foreign immigration, the Foley years saw significant progress toward the assimilation of the polyglot Catholic population.

Because this period in the history of the Diocese is so critical a time of transition, it is worth an extended discussion. We will look in turn at changes in sacramental practice and popular devotions, at developments in religious education, at the social life of the Catholic parish, at various modes of parish government, and at the evolution of educational, charitable, and social service organizations among the laity. Naturally, the most important of these changes have to do with religious practice. Catholics in the Foley years came to center their religious lives more than ever before on frequent confession and communion. They became a more disciplined population with regard to religion, and their more disciplined practice seems to have lent a new vitality to a variety of traditional devotions. To some extent these developments are but an extension of changes we have already discussed—a growing number of priests in the Diocese had since the mid-nineteenth century made possible the incorporation of a growing number of Catholics into a regular religious practice. But in the Foley years this progress accelerated dramatically, and as it did, the character of Catholic life was fundamentally altered.

SACRAMENTAL PRACTICE

Catholic youngsters at the turn of the century began their active sacramental lives at about the age of seven, when they were expected to go to confession for the first time. They were instructed thereafter to confess four times a year, and pastors were obliged, by the terms of the Third Provincial Council of Cincinnati, to make provision at least that often for hearing children's confessions. In many if not most parishes this meant time reserved for children's confessions alone, a practice recommended as conducive to a priest's hearing children's confessions in a suitably patient and sympathetic way. "Never scold a child or interrupt him harshly," a popular pastoral manual of the 1890s advised.

> On the contrary, when you notice timidity or bashfulness promise him that you will neither scold nor get angry, but will help him through. Encourage the silent by mentioning a big sin which he certainly did not commit: did you steal a horse? Did you kill a fellow? Use utmost prudence and discretion in questioning children *de sexto*. Do not teach evil. It is often better to be silent on this matter, and to permit a defective integrity in the juvenile confession.[1]

Almost no evidence remains to suggest how frequently children in the Diocese actually went to confession. Those who attended parochial school were presumably subject to a strict regime, although this was not invariably the case, at least in the late nineteenth century. "The majority of children in the school under 12 years of age have never been to confession," a distressed Father Frank O'Brien reported from Kalamazoo in 1884. O'Brien was a new arrival in the parish that year, and he lost no time in establishing a sterner discipline than that of his predecessor. Still, there may well have been other parishes in this period where the pastor, or perhaps the parishioners, were equally casual when it came to regular attendance at confession.[2]

Despite their early introduction to the confessional, Catholic children at the turn of the century did not receive the Eucharist until early adolescence. Youngsters in the Diocese of Detroit generally made their first communion at the age of twelve or thirteen. No child younger than twelve could receive communion, according to regulations established in the Borgess years, and in 1909 Bishop Foley directed "that no child attending a Polish parochial school shall be admitted to the First Holy Communion under the age of fourteen years." He did this at the behest of the Polish clergy, many of whose parishioners thought that children could be withdrawn from school once they had made their first communion. Other ethnic groups too appear to have regarded first communion as a symbolic end to childhood, for working-class children at the turn of the century often began their working lives in early adolescence. And the practice of administering confirmation at about the same time as first communion—often, in fact, on the same day—gave first communion added flavor as a rite of passage. Confirmation has never figured in a vivid way in the religious imagination of American Catholics, but Catholics in the Foley years seem generally to have regarded it as the formal conferring of adult status in the Church.[3]

First communion, then, was a solemn event, but it was also, and preeminently, a festive one. No parish was so small that it failed to mount a lavish celebration. Festivities typically began at an early Mass, out of deference to the rigors of the long precommunion fast. "It was a beautiful sight," confided young Helena

Drawe of Marine City to the readers of the children's page of the *Michigan Catho-lic* in 1898. "The girls were all dressed in white with wreaths and veils, while the boys wore dark suits with little bouquets on their coats. It was the first time I ever witnessed anything so grand." A breakfast in the parish hall usually fol-lowed the Mass, with confirmation — if it was to be administered that day — at a later Mass or in the afternoon. Confirmation, of course, required the presence of a bishop, and this was always cause for excitement, as the many accounts of confirmation from the Foley years attest. Bishop Foley was escorted to a con-firmation at Detroit's Holy Redeemer parish in 1891 by uniformed members of the Holy Redeemer Greys and the Knights of St. John, as well as a large con-tingent of other parish men. Heading the procession was the Hiawatha Brass Band, "which discoursed sweet music along the line of march," according to the *Michigan Catholic*. As the parade neared the church, "it was swelled by the first communicants, the Sodalities of St. Joseph, Children of Mary and the Young Ladies Division of the Children of Mary who fell into line immediately after the men of the parish."[4]

An integral part of the first communion ceremony in nearly all parishes was induction of the young communicants into the boys' and girls' sodalities. They were henceforth to receive communion once a month in the company of their fellow sodalists. And in many parishes, the boys and sometimes the girls as well were required to pledge themselves to temperance until they were adults. "One feature of the occasion was the public pledging of children to abstain from all intoxicating drink until they reached the age of twenty-one," a parishioner from St. Anthony's in Hillsdale quite typically reported in 1909. "With lighted candle in left hand and right hand raised, they repeated aloud and distinctly the words of their Pastor, after which each one, kissing the Missal book, made the scene doubly impressive." (A first communicant from Dowagiac in 1895 had recounted his own experience rather more insouciantly. "There were four girls and six boys that received that day, and the boys took the pledge until they were twenty-one years of age. Father Joos did not have the girls take it, for I guess he thought they would break it.") The pastor at Dearborn's Sacred Heart parish in 1898 had his first communicants promise as well "that they would not contract a mixed marriage," and in 1911 the first communicants at Holy Rosary in Detroit "took the usual pledge to refrain from all intoxicating beverages and the use of tobacco, not to frequent bad places of amusement and the reading of bad books." But in most parishes the children were pledged only to temperance, and this practice was less common after 1911, when children began to make their first communion at about age seven. It seems to have virtually disappeared with the advent of legal prohibition in Michigan in 1918.[5]

The point of such practices was not simply to restrain the behavior of children as they moved into the dangerous teenage years. Pastors naturally hoped to ac-complish this, but they also hoped that the young would serve as models of piety and right behavior for adults. First communion was a time when the heart of the most indifferent Catholic was peculiarly open to the workings of grace, or so it was widely believed, and the good pastor took the occasion to preach a powerful sermon in word and deed. Whether the various promises elicted at first communion had much effect on the subsequent behavior of the young—or of their elders—we cannot say. But that is less important, perhaps, than the aura of high seriousness that surrounded the celebration of the sacrament, and the mingled emotions of anxiety, hope, and joy it evoked in its young recipients, poised on the brink of maturity. A child in early adolescence approached the sacrament with a greater capacity for introspection and a more developed moral sense than the child of seven who would later be the typical first communicant. "Our Sister says that our whole future life depends on our First Communion," reported a girl from Detroit's Holy Rosary parish in 1906. "I am trying to be as good and kind as it is in my power." Occasionally a burden of anxiety seems to have troubled the more scrupulous—or ineptly instructed—youngster. "I am going to make my First Communion this year and, Auntie, will you pray that I won't be the Judas," a child wrote to the *Michigan Catholic's* children's page in 1902. "Our Sunday school sister says there is always a Judas in every First Communion class." But by most accounts the event was a joyful one. "It was the happiest day of my 12 years of life," confided a Detroit girl in 1906.

> When night came I was sorry I only wished I could have had the day for a longer time. In the morning when I awoke it was only 4 o'clock, and mama told me I had better go back to bed, but I could not sleep any more, I was so excited. The day dawned beautifully and our church seemed like a little heaven. Every light in the church was lit. Eight sweet little girls were dressed as angels; two knelt at the foot of the altar and one accompanied each girl and boy to the altar to receive and be confirmed.[6]

When pastors urged the young to receive communion every month and to lead disciplined lives, they were not advocating anything new. But there were still many Catholics in the late nineteenth century who received the sacraments as infrequently as once or twice a year, and did so in good conscience. This was especially true of men, at least according to contemporary testimony. Troubled by what they saw as a want of fervor in Catholic religious life, the priests of the Diocese began, toward the end of the nineteenth century, to preach with a new urgency on the need for Catholics to receive the sacraments regularly, once a month generally being the recommended interval. And what had been in effect a double standard with regard to piety came under increasing attack: men as well as women were expected to go regularly to confession and communion. "Men make no profession of piety; they are rather rebellious against the practice of religion, leaving it if possible to the women folks," admitted a late-nineteenth-century pastoral manual. "And yet with zeal and tact a priest will succeed in bringing men to confession once a month, and thereby making them sober, honest, industrious, and practical members of the Church." Many priests in the Diocese seem to have shared these sentiments, if not the author's confidence, by the closing years of the century. Among the American-born clergy, at least, it was more and more a mark of integrity to preach frequent confession and communion as a manly ideal.[7]

That monthly communion should be the norm for Catholics was an expectation made possible by the growing number of priests in the Diocese. But it was not a matter of numbers alone. American priests, like their European brethren, were much affected in the late nineteenth century by a revival of Eucharistic devotion. The Priests' Eucharistic League, founded in Germany in 1879, was emblematic of this style of piety: its members promised to spend at least one hour a week in prayer before the Blessed Sacrament. The league was established in the United States in 1894 and was soon a thriving organization.

A branch of the Priests' Eucharistic League was organized in the Diocese of Detroit probably in 1895. Father John Dempsey, pastor at the cathedral, was the director in 1897, and in that same year the indefatigable Father Frank O'Brien delivered a paper at the league's second national convention, held at Notre Dame. Father O'Brien addressed the topic "How the members of the Priests' Eucharistic League ought to act concerning the growing tendency to miss Mass on Sundays and Holydays." His anxieties on this score were typical of the clergy who were drawn to the league in its earliest years. Their own spirituality firmly centered on Eucharistic devotion, these earnest priests looked to this mode of piety as a means of revitalizing faith among the laity. "There is a movement on foot among the Bishops and priests of the whole world which must be noted as one of the most hopeful signs of these modern times," Bishop Camillus Maes informed a convention of the German Catholic Association of Michigan in 1895. "I refer to the stirring revival of the devotion to the Most Blessed Sacrament of the Altar." Maes urged his all-male audience to increase their own reverence for the Eucharist — to begin to receive communion once a month, to attend Benediction weekly, to pray each week before the Blessed Sacrament and especially in times of trouble or difficult decisions.[8]

The popularization of Eucharistic piety received enormous impetus during the papacy of Pius X (1903-1914). The Pope himself had early in his reign endorsed weekly communion for the laity. And the Sacred Congregation in 1905 decreed that daily communion, hitherto regarded as the prerogative of a spiritual elite, "should be open to all the faithful of whatever rank and condition of life." A few priests in the Diocese responded with enthusiasm to this reformed vision of sacramental practice, which was at once more liberal and more highly disciplined than the norm they had been accustomed to preach. Father Francis Van Antwerp urged the first communion class at Detroit's Holy Rosary parish in 1907 to receive communion every Sunday. "On a previous occasion he said that he had asked them to go once a month," the *Michigan Catholic* noted, "but under present conditions it would be well for them to go weekly." And Van Antwerp was soon encouraging his parishioners to become daily communicants, even when it meant receiving communion without attending Mass. "Daily communion will be given every half hour commencing at 5 o'clock A.M.," according to a Holy Rosary announcement in 1908. "The parishioners are urged to participate in this great privilege of receiving our Blessed Lord every morning and as our Holy Father Pius X highly recommends this pious practice, every one who can should take advantage of this great means of grace."[9]

It does not appear that Father Van Antwerp was joined by many of his fellow priests in urging daily or even weekly communion. (As late as 1908, the "academic"—or pre-seminary—students at SS. Cyril and Methodius [Polish] Seminary in Detroit were required to go to communion only once a month.) An occasional priest may have been opposed in principle to frequent communion for the laity, seeing in the pope's pronouncements a dangerous narrowing of the gulf that separated priest from people. But most were simply too overburdened to pay much heed to the statements coming out of Rome. Many, indeed, were still trying to persuade the more recalcitrant members of their congregations to receive the sacraments more than once or twice a year.[10]

In the autumn of 1910, however, the pope issued a decree on the Eucharist that affected the practice of the entire clergy. In that decree, Pius instructed pastors to admit children to communion at the "age of reason," generally understood to be about the age of seven. Consistent as this instruction was with pope's own spirituality, it took Bishop Foley and the priests of the Diocese wholly by surprise. And it was met with a notable lack of enthusiasm, for priests were worried that, under this new dispensation, many parents would withdraw their children from the parochial schools after the early primary grades. (The pope's decree had in fact made attendance at the public schools a sin reserved to a bishop, but this was hardly a practical means of enforcing parochial school attendance in a diocese as populous as Detroit.) "The new decree of the Holy Father was discussed" at a meeting of the diocesan consultors in September 1910, "and although various opinions prevailed, the question resolved itself into a matter of mere obedience to the Head of the Church."[11]

Despite the trepidation that greeted its advent, the practice of early communion soon became a popular one. It was not simply that the little first communicants charmed nearly all beholders. The practice spoke to widespread cultural anxieties: early communion was seen by growing numbers of Catholics as an antidote to the increasingly aggressive sexual content of popular culture. (The decade before 1914 was indeed marked by a loosening of restraints on female behavior and by a more explicit sexuality in popular entertainment.) Such changes were perhaps especially striking in a city like Detroit, where explosive growth meant a sharp increase in social disorder. But Catholic spokesmen throughout the nation voiced their trepidation. In 1911, for example, the bishops of the Cincinnati Province commended the practice of early communion on the grounds that children of twelve or thirteen were often hardened by sin and tempted by religious doubt. Did not the conscientious priest, they asked, find all too frequently that in preparing older children for first commuion "his words fall upon hearts [in] which, with difficulty, he can awaken pious sentiments? May not all this be frequently traced to the fact that the hearts of these boys and girls, having already been seared by sin, or chilled by the beginning of unbelief, do not readily respond to his efforts or to the grace of the Eucharist?" The *Michigan Catholic* was ready by 1913 to see in even quite young children the deleterious effects of what it had taken to calling a pagan culture. "By eight or ten years, American children, as a rule, are sadly precocious, and too often at that tender age they have lost their baptismal innocence and have made terrible acquaintances with sin and vice. Early communion is necessary to guard against this sad precocity."[12]

Whether or not early communion prevented precocity, it seems to have had a decisive effect on sacramental practice in the Diocese. The reform focused renewed attention on the efforts of Pius X on behalf of frequent communion, and the number of priests in the Diocese who preached the need for weekly or even daily communion seems to have grown dramatically in the wake of the early communion decree. The *Michigan Catholic* in 1917 could note with approval that one priest in the Diocese had recently told his parishioners that those Catholics who received the sacraments only once a year "are in reality not practical Catholics." The extent to which the mass of the laity altered their practice in these years is nearly impossible to determine, but it is clear that significant change occurred. Younger Catholics especially were reported to be receiving the sacraments more frequently than ever before, and this was true of boys as well as girls. Young men at the Jesuit's Detroit College flocked to the Ichthus Club—an organization for the promotion of frequent communion—upon its establishment at the school in 1911. "Nearly every student in the institution is now a member," the *Michigan Catholic* rejoiced. "It is not unlikely that 1000 Holy Communions a month will be received by members . . . in the near future." Younger children, introduced now to the sacraments at an early age, could be habituated to their frequent reception by means of the parochial school. The pupils of St. Mary's school in Adrian in 1913 attended Mass daily and received communion every Friday, a regime that was probably typical of most schools in the Diocese. At Annunciation parish in Detroit, the pastor was employing the children's sodalities to promote even more frequent communion. "There is an interesting race between the girls of the Children of Mary and the boys of the Junior Holy Name Society as to which has the largest number of communicants each month. The boys have a small margin the best of it at present."[13]

Older Catholics were often less willing than the young to conform to what was a major change in Catholic religious practice. This was especially true of men. ("Why, oh! why are the rear end of our churches so crowded with standing men during the hours of Sunday Mass?" the *Michigan Catholic* wondered in 1914, irritated by the want of devotion that seemed all too often to characterize Catholic males.) The leaders of the Holy Name Society assumed at the time of the First World War that most men in the Diocese were not yet receiving the sacraments monthly. "If, through our organization, we can get the great body of Catholic men to approach Holy Communion once a month," a member of the group's executive board explained in 1915, "we will be doing probably the very best thing that can be done to promote the cause of our religion and to honor God and His Holy Name." A good many Catholics, apparently, continued to receive the sacraments only once or twice a year, although their numbers clearly declined over the course of the Foley episcopate. Their numbers remained strong, however, in many of the ethnic parishes, where any change in religious practice was likely to be greeted with suspicion if not open hostility.[14]

The resistance of what we might call these traditional Catholics to the new sacramental regime was in part a defense of customs learned in childhood. But it was also caused by the reluctance of many older Catholics to go regularly to confession. Yearly confession, as required by the Church, was in their view sufficient unless one fell into serious sin. And that, their behavior seemed to say, was something that happened infrequently. Most priests, of course, held to more rigorous views on the matter, and male "traditionalists," especially, were not anxious to submit themselves, through frequent confession, to the sterner clerical standard. But neither were they accustomed to receive communion without confessing first. The unnamed pastor whom the *Michigan Catholic* had commended in 1917 for his denunciation of "Easter duty" Catholics was familiar with the type. "He said that some people who go to Confession and Communion only one time in twelve months often say they have not felt the need of going more frequently, because they have not committed any grievous sins during the year." Not surprisingly, "he thought that their faith must be weak and their devotion slight."[15]

The Foley years, then, were a time of transition to the disciplined sacramental practice that characterized the American Church in the middle decades of the twentieth century. The children who were accustomed in these years to receive communion weekly and to confess at least once a month — not necessarily as a consequence of serious sin, but out of devotion — matured for the most part into adults who went regularly to confession and communion. And many of their elders were led by the changes of the Foley years to receive the sacraments more frequently than their own parents had done. Thus what had begun in the early years of the Diocese as a gradual trend toward a more disciplined religious practice accelerated mightily in the early twentieth century. (By the 1950s, it is fair to say, no large Catholic population had ever been as regular in its sacramental practice as that of the American Church.) Many priests in the Foley years were delighted by the spiritual progress they saw around them, despite their anxieties over trends in the larger culture. "The faith of priests and people in the Real Presence is stronger, deeper, more Catholic, more satisfactory than ever before," Detroit's Auxiliary Bishop Edward Kelly announced in 1911.[16]

But in their enthusiasm for equating faith with the number of communions dispensed each week, the priests of the Diocese were in danger of misreading their own religious past. The men and women who persisted in receiving the sacraments only once or twice a year were not necessarily lacking in faith and devotion. This is nicely conveyed in a letter from an elderly German at Port Huron's St. Joseph's parish in 1925. He wrote to ask Bishop Michael Gallagher to send a priest to St. Joseph's who could hear German confessions, for, as he told his bishop, "there are to my estimation about one-half of the congregation

that cannot make theyr confession in English." Neither he nor his contemporaries seem normally to have confessed more than once or twice a year, but his
letter was hardly the product of a man whose faith was weak and devotion slight.
"I heard one Mann say to me: I will have to go to Detroit before Easter and
before Christmass to make my Confession. Now what will it be, of those unfor-
tionable ones on their Dying Bett may God help us all." His was a world with
its own sacramental rhythms, its own expressions of devotion, its own modes of
discipline—and a world quite capable of sustaining a deep religious faith.[17]

Liturgy and Devotions

The liturgy in the Foley years was less uniform throughout the Diocese than
it would later be, for the Mass in the various ethnic parishes was accompanied
by distinctive rituals and customs. But the round of services and devotions over
the course of the Church year was similar, even in the 1890s, to that which prevailed on the eve of Vatican II. Besides daily and Sunday Mass, the typical parish offered Sunday vespers, Marian devotions in May and Rosary devotions in
October, Sacred Heart devotions in June and often on the first Friday of each
month, weekly sermons and the Way of the Cross during Lent, and the traditional services in Holy Week. The annual Forty Hours devotion, celebrated only
occasionally in the early 1880s, seems by the 1890s to have been regularly observed throughout the Diocese—one more example of the growing popularity
of Eucharistic piety in the waning years of the century. The same style of piety
can be seen in the introduction of the weekly Holy Hour at a growing number
of parishes during and after the 1890s.[18]

Perhaps the most vivid manifestation of Eucharistic piety is the Eucharistic
procession, and these appear to have increased both in size and number as the
century drew toward its close. Some parishes in the Foley years had Blessed Sacrament processions as often as once a month. Nearly all parishes celebrated the
great Eucharistic feasts in this way. Feast-day processions, especially, were sometimes very large, and attracted numerous spectators. But they were nearly always confined to the church or to its grounds, presumably at Chancery behest
and out of deference to Protestant sensibilities. ("Our unbelieving surroundings
prevent the solemn processions which grace the streets of Catholic countries,"
according to Covington's Bishop Camillus Maes in 1895.) The Corpus Christi
procession on the grounds of Detroit's Holy Redeemer Church regularly drew
large crowds—4,000 were said to have been present in 1889. And the annual
Corpus Christi procession at St. Mary's Academy in Monroe was for many years
an event of note for the city's Catholics and even for a number of Protestants.
An academy student in 1893 did her earnest best to describe this "most beautiful
occasion" for the *Michigan Catholic.* Convinced, as she wrote, that "I could never
do it justice," she has nonetheless bequeathed to us a lively picture of the day's
proceedings, which were apparently flavored by patriotism as well as by religion:

Long before the appointed time crowds gather around St. Mary's church from all parts of the city, many drawn there by devotion, others out of mere curiosity.

At three o'clock sharp the procession starts, headed by the Knights of St. John, and following them are the men, women and children's societies, of which the three churches are composed.

Then come the pupils of St. Mary's Academy, boarders and day pupils and their teachers. All these carry banners while over all the emblem of our country, the Stars and Stripes, float[s] in the breeze from St. Mary's church spire and from the dome of the academy directly across the street.

Next come the little girls in white, carrying flowers, which they strew thickly along the ground. Surrounding them are serving boys swinging incense, and lastly the Rt. Rev. Mgr. Joos, V.G., with the Blessed Sacrament, sheltered by a beautiful silk canopy and surrounded by the clergy of the city.

The procession winds its way along the serpentine walks of the handsome ground surrounding the academy, stopping a short time at the grotto of our Blessed Mother. At the termination of the march the procession enters the church, where benediction is given and the ceremony is ended.[19]

The vitality that marks religion in these years was due in good part to the growing number of priests in the Diocese. But their work was greatly facilitated by the growing number of laity who were models of devout behavior for the mass of Catholics. Membership in devotional confraternities in the Diocese appears to have risen significantly toward the end of the century. The *Michigan Catholic,* for example, reported in 1891 that the League of the Sacred Heart had some 1,500 members at Detroit's Holy Trinity parish, 800 members at St. Vincent's, 700 at St. Anne's, and 230 at the recently established Holy Rosary parish on the northern edge of the city. Probably most of the members were women. But by the 1890s, we find growing numbers of men being drawn to the disciplined piety associated with the various confraternities. The Men's League of the Sacred Heart, founded in 1890, claimed 400 members that same year, with excellent attendance at its monthly meetings in the Jesuit church of SS. Peter and Paul. ("One feature of these meetings is so encouraging to the Catholic heart that we cannot help noting it here," the *Michigan Catholic* confided. "It is the presence at them of so large a number of young men.") The Jesuit church was already known as a local center for men's devotions. Its priests were able to attract nearly as many men as women to the popular retreats they preached at the church in the mid-1890s. "Almost one thousand communions this morning," the house chronicle noted of a men's retreat in 1894. The *Michigan Catholic* was equally impressed by the turnout: "The great crowd in attendance filled the large church, many having to stand."[20]

We cannot know with any precision just what sorts of men were responsive to the vigorous piety preached by the Jesuits. SS. Peter and Paul's was a fashionable parish in the late nineteenth century, and it is likely that many of the men who attended retreats and devotions there were relatively well-to-do. Certainly the experience of groups like the Holy Name Society and the Knights of Columbus suggests that middle-class men were more drawn than their working-class brothers to a highly disciplined style of piety. But if working-class Catholics were underrepresented at the Jesuit church in the 1890s, they were ultimately affected by developments there. For the Jesuits were helping to generate a standard of piety that would eventually be applied to all men in the Diocese.

The religious vitality of the Foley years was marked by more than Jesuit retreats and a quickening of Eucharistic devotion. Marian piety and the cults of various saints also attracted a growing clientele. Such devotions were not new to the Diocese, of course. But they acquired a new visibility in the later nineteenth century, in part because of the growing number of religious orders that had foundations in Detroit. (The great novenas in Detroit were nearly all initiated by religious order clergy.) The Foley years were not the high point for this particular style of piety, which probably had its broadest appeal in the bleak years of the early 1930s. Still, this style of piety does seem to have assumed a more prominent place in Catholic life in the Foley years than it had done before.

Marian devotions have traditionally been the most popular of the many non-Eucharistic devotions in the Church. We have already seen that Rosary confraternities existed in the Diocese from virtually the time of its founding. Marian piety, however, assumed a more public aspect in the late nineteenth century. Lourdes grottoes were built on the grounds of Assumption Church in 1881 and Holy Redeemer Church in 1899, and in Detroit's St. Mary's Church in 1895. Pilgrimages to these sites became increasingly popular in the 1890s and after, with St. Mary's grotto eventually becoming a site for miraculous cures. The Redemptorist Fathers introduced the Mother of Perpetual Help novena into the Diocese in 1880, and built a Perpetual Help shrine at Holy Redeemer Church in 1888. By the late 1880s, the annual novena was attracting Catholics not only from Detroit but from outlying communities as well. Some 4,000 persons were said to have participated in the closing exercises at the 1888 novena, which took place — in highly visible fashion — on the church's spacious grounds. Other aspects of Marian piety in the Foley years were much less public, but no less pervasive, apparently, than they were in the middle decades of the twentieth century. Rosary devotions in the parish church, May altars at home and in school, the consecration of children to the Blessed Mother, Marian prayers and hymns at Mass and at missions — these were familiar to nearly all Catholics in the late nineteenth century. "I have a May altar, on which I keep fresh flowers all the time," a twelve-year-old girl wrote, quite typically, from the village of Pinckney in 1893. "My little sister is 13 months old, and when we tell her to say her prayers she will make her lips go and hold her hands as if she had a rosary in them."[21]

Of the various saints to whom Catholics in the Foley years showed a special devotion, St. Anne — the patron of Detroit's French founders — was almost certainly the most popular. Novenas to St. Anne were increasingly well attended in the Foley years. And at St. Anne's parish, in the care of the Basilian Fathers after 1886, the annual novena was widely claimed by the mid-1890s to be an occasion of miraculous cures and other extraordinary favors. The shrine seems to have enjoyed a mostly local reputation until about 1910, when reports of a series of remarkable cures brought thousands of hopeful clients to the church for what had become a series of novenas held throughout the year. "The five Masses are all well attended with an average at Holy Communion of about 1400," the *Michigan Catholic* reported in the fall of 1911. "There are pilgrims now from nearly every town and city of Michigan and Canada, and also from farther places. . . . It looks very astonishing to see them standing in crowds at the church doors at about 4:30 in the morning, awaiting the coming of the sexton, and when the doors open they file in quickly to take their places by the confessional." The Basilian Fathers had taken, by this time, to calling their church "Ste. Anne de Detroit," engagingly frank in their hopes of displacing the famed Ste. Anne de Beaupré in Quebec as a pilgrimage site for midwestern Catholics.[22]

Despite the growing reputation of "Ste. Anne de Detroit," the more famous Quebec shrine retained its pride of place. Father Francis Van Antwerp began in 1890 to lead an annual pilgrimage from Detroit to Ste. Anne de Beaupré, and a number of cures and favors locally were even in the 1890s attributed to prayer at the Beaupré basilica and veneration of its famous relic. He knew "positively" of two cures which had been effected in the course of a just-completed pilgrimage, Father Van Antwerp told the *Michigan Catholic* in 1892, and he had heard from reputable sources of two more. A young man born blind had received his sight; "another young boy of Trinity parish, Detroit, who accompanied us and could not take a step without his crutch, left the church at Beaupré and now walks perfectly strong." The great majority of the pilgrims in Van Antwerp's charge were women, at least according to the *Michigan Catholic*. And they were presumably mostly well-to-do, for the Beaupré trip was a long and costly one. There were those, however, for whom the trip was worth considerable sacrifice. Nine-year-old Daniel Cronin of Detroit made his second Beaupré pilgrimage in 1893 in the company of his mother, a widow who ran a grocery from her home on decidedly unfashionable Franklin Street. "There were many cured, including myself," according to Daniel. "I thank good Ste. Anne for her kindness to me. My arm has improved very much and I hope to be completely cured next year as it will be my third visit."[23]

St. Anthony of Padua was nearly as popular, in the Foley years, as the redoubtable St. Anne. The principal center for St. Anthony devotions was St. Bonaventure's (Capuchin) monastery, which had been established in 1883 on Detroit's far east side. Special devotions to St. Anthony were inaugurated there in 1898. The Capuchin's St. Anthony's Guild had some 700 members by 1900, and the monastery's novenas were widely reputed to be a fruitful source of favors. Employment secured, debts paid, sickness cured, lost articles found — these and other achievements were credited to the saint by his Detroit clients in 1898.[24]

The success of the Capuchin novenas sparked a boom in parish devotions to St. Anthony; the Basilian Fathers were sponsoring joint novenas to SS. Anne and Anthony by 1911. The Anthony cult was sufficiently popular that petitions to the saint had by 1908 absorbed most of the space once devoted to children's correspondence in the *Michigan Catholic*. The editor of the children's page was herself a devotee of the saint, and a patron of St. Anthony's Orphan Asylum in Detroit. Anxious to raise funds for this struggling institution, she began to promote its inmates as especially favored clients of the saint. (The children would pray for a reader's particular intention, on the understanding that answered prayers required a donation to the orphanage.) The editor was soon inundated by petitions for favors that ranged from success in school to cures for serious illness. "Dear Aunt Rowena," ran a letter typical of many that appeared in 1911. "My husband was badly hurt in a streetcar accident last fall. I am anxious that the company settle with us, without bringing the suit into court and that the settlement may be generous. If petition is granted, I will send $5 at once to the orphan's fund."[25]

Other religious orders besides the Capuchins and the Basilians actively promoted devotion to particular saints in the Foley years. The Sisters of St. Joseph at Nazareth offered prayers and good works to St. Joseph for clients throughout the Diocese. "The sick claim to have been healed, extraordinary vocations have been obtained, unhappy marriages were blessed, sin was overcome and virtue acquired," the Sisters announced in 1897. The Jesuits naturally stressed devotion to St. Ignatius and, at least in the 1890s, recommended St. Ignatius' Holy Water as a source of protection "in difficult cases of childbirth." "Numerous miracles have rewarded the earnest faith and pious confidence of persons claiming the intercession of the great saint," the *Michigan Catholic* reported with regard to the opening of a St. Ignatius novena in 1895. The Jesuit church was also a center of devotion to St. Aloysius. Young people especially were urged to make the "six Sundays of St. Aloysius"—the devotee confessed and received communion for six successive Sundays prior to the saint's feast—in order to receive the graces necessary to preserve innocence and purity. The "novena of grace" to St. Francis Xavier, which became in the Depression a source of consolation for thousands of Detroiters, was first preached by the Jesuits at SS. Peter and Paul's in 1914.[26]

The devotional life was not, of course, attractive to every Catholic. Even in the 1930s, the crowds at devotions were still preponderantly female, and those in middle life and old age almost certainly outnumbered the young. But the devotional life had, nonetheless, an important effect on the whole of the Catholic population, for it helped to define a people and support a distinctive worldview. In this sense it had meaning even for Catholics who never made a novena.

What the devotional life did most fundamentally was to make visible the theological differences that separated Catholics from nearly all Protestants. Other things did this as well: the Mass itself, the practice of confession, a celibate clergy and religious. But if the Mass spoke eloquently to many Catholics of the immanence of God, the various devotions expressed this distinctively Catholic orientation in a way that was even warmer, even more emotive, even more satisfyingly concrete for a considerable segment of the Catholic population. The devotional life gave the most unlettered Catholic the opportunity to imagine God in terms that were close to his own experience—to see himself as an actor in a spiritual

universe peopled with heavenly friends, all of them deeply interested in the affairs of what the world regarded as unimportant lives. It provided the faithful
with a plethora of material testimony to the presence of God in the midst of His
people, for its paraphernalia were everywhere—rosaries, scapulars, medals,
statues. And depending as it did on a world of intercessors, the devotional life
gave enormous support to a hierarchical model of the Church. The devotional
life, in short, emphasized just those aspects of Catholic belief and practice that
have always most offended Protestants—the disposition to express the mysteries
of God in human and material images and to stress the importance of mediators,
both human and supernatural, as the believer approaches God.

In the context of the American Church, the spread of popular devotions also
served to unify a Catholic population badly divided by ethnicity. If the externals
of the devotional life disturbed most Protestants, they served to affirm an elementary solidarity among Catholics, even for those who were not especially devout.
Nearly all Catholics knew the prayers of the Rosary, the uses of the scapular,
and felt at home worshiping amidst baroque statuary. And if the veneration of
saints identified with a particular ethnic group was a means of preserving group
identity, the growing popularity of cults that appealed to many ethnic traditions
did much to integrate ethnic Catholics into an "American" Church. SS. Anne
and Anthony had clients in the Diocese from many ethnic backgrounds, and the
great novenas of the 1920s and 1930s drew Catholics from parishes across the
Diocese to common places of prayer. What had begun as peculiarly French or
German or Irish devotions became, sometimes in the space of a single generation, the property of the entire Catholic community.

Ironically, perhaps—in the light of recent feminist critiques of Catholic theology and practice—traditional devotions gave vivid expression to what are sometimes called the feminine qualities of God. Many of the most popular intercessory figures in Catholic life have been female, the Virgin Mary preeminent
among them. Those male saints who have captured the popular imagination,
moreover, have tended to be conspicuously feminine in their most admired
traits. St. Anthony's purity and gentleness, his tender devotion to the Holy
Child—these were, at least until recently, indisputably female qualities. And in
the brief history of the Diocese of Detroit, no male saint has surpassed St.
Anthony in popular appeal, nor have those saints celebrated for such "masculine" virtues as physical courage or intellectual prowess had a large following.
St. Aloysius seems always to have been more popular than St. Ignatius.

Then, too, most Catholics probably regarded the intercessory role of the
saints as an essentially feminine one. Their experience had taught them that
women generally wielded power indirectly, often by negotiating or interceding
with male authority. Nor were women believed to be as concerned as men with
norms of disinterested justice. Women were moved by pity, women dispensed
mercy. And it was particular mercies that most Catholics sought as they approached a novena or other special devotion. The spiritual world imagined by
the devotee of St. Anne or St. Anthony was, then, a world infused with a very

real sense of female presence and power; if God was Father, His fatherhood partook in good measure of the tender solicitude associated with the Blessed Mother and the more popular saints. (The Gospels, of course, in nowise contradict this. What is significant for us is the naturalness with which our Catholic forebears expressed this vision of God in feminine as well as masculine images.) Indeed the Church implicitly endorsed the feminine associations of the devotional life when it came to liturgical practice. While men were accorded the honorific positions in Eucharistic processions — women were sometimes excluded altogether — girls and women played the leading parts in Marian processions and those which honored female saints. We must not underestimate the importance of this in a Church where a popular pastoral manual could advise the clergy at the turn of the century that "in all Church ceremonies the male sex is considered and treated as the most worthy."[27]

For all its vitality, however, the devotional life had its critics, even in the Foley years. There was always the danger that it would encourage eccentricities of belief, and lead to a more "magical" view of religion than most priests could easily countenance. Father Henry Kaufman wrote to the *Michigan Catholic* in 1902 from his parish in Dearborn to complain about "a superstitious prayer to St. Joseph which is being extensively circulated in this city and elsewhere, and which is used even by people who ought to know that the prayer with the accompanying explanation is a fraud." This prayer, like many others, was circulated in the form of a chain letter. "Is it not a pity that, whenever such a superstitious fraud or some other un-Catholic invention makes its appearance, many of our people offer their services, even at the expense of five stamps and labor, to speed them before they consult their pastor?" The integrity of Catholic doctrine was at stake; so was the reputation of the Church in what was, after all, a mostly Protestant country.[28]

The clergy were increasingly inclined to worry about "superstition" in popular religious practice as their own view of the world was affected by the rationalist mentality that came more and more to dominate American culture after the late nineteenth century. We see this nicely illustrated in the columns of the *Michigan Catholic,* which, as a lay-edited but officially recognized diocesan paper, never deviated seriously from Chancery policy in its news coverage or its editorials. For many years, the paper carried wholly uncritical accounts of miraculous cures and other extraordinary favors gained through the intercession of the saints. The St. Blaise blessing was characteristically commended to the faithful in 1888 by means of a cautionary tale in the guise of an editorial: "In a town in Ohio a few years ago the blessing was given in one parish and it was neglected in an adjoining one. An epidemic of diphtheria visited that town; not one child of the parish in which the blessing of St. Blaise had been given was attacked, while in the other fifteen children died of the disease." As late as 1914, the paper was publishing glowing accounts of miracles worked at Detroit's St. Anne's Church, apparently on the testimony only of the person who claimed to have been miraculously healed. "At the fourth day of her devout exercise and after the fourth application of the precious relic," ran a typical story, "Mrs. Lefebre was delighted to recognize the fact that she was completely cured."[29]

After 1914, however, the *Michigan Catholic* no longer carried accounts of cures and miraculous favors, although the number of such attributed locally to St. Anne and other intercessors continued to grow. The paper's reticence is not surprising. Church authorities have generally been anxious to apply objective criteria to the miracles claimed at shrines — witness the elaborate procedures long in place at Lourdes to verify cures. What is a bit surprising is the *Michigan Catholic*'s having resisted for so long a more skeptical stance. Perhaps this was due to the obvious pleasure that William Hughes, editor from 1882 until his death in 1917, took in asserting the reality of the supernatural against the increasingly limited claims of liberal Protestant theologians. But finally even Mr. Hughes had to accommodate the sensibilities of a world where notions of scientific rigor set the standards for evaluating the mysterious work of the Lord.

St. Anne's shrine had long before 1914 been a magnet for Catholics of many ethnic backgrounds. But this shared experience of the devotional life should not obscure for us the distinctive liturgical world still inhabited by many ethnic Catholics. For the liturgy was different in important ways in the ethnic parishes. Even at Mass, the ethnic congregation generally made liberal use of the vernacular. Congregational singing and the recitation of traditional prayers were a regular part of the liturgy — and evidently the ethnic congregation participated wholeheartedly, although priests in the English-speaking parishes often lamented the reluctance of their parishioners to sing at Mass. Poles in the Diocese were justly admired for the beauty of the carols they sang at the Pasterka, or Shepherds' Mass, in the early hours of Christmas morning. And no one who heard the undulating minor strains of the "Gorzkie Żale" ("Bitter Lamentations") sung by a Polish congregation during Lent ever quite forgot the experience. Devotions, too, had a distinctive quality. Even after the older ethnic parishes had begun to hold devotions in English as well as the language of the parish founders, the children of the parish were taught to venerate the saints especially revered by the group and to honor the Virgin as their grandparents had done. The most indifferent Catholic of French descent understood that the feast of St. John the Baptist was a special day. And the most Americanized Pole was likely to know the story of Our Lady of Częstochowa.

The Catholicism inherited by the child of the ethnic parish, in short, had a flavor distinct in varied and often subtle ways from that of the English-speaking congregation. It was a matter in part of the hymns sung and the prayers learned, the metaphors employed in sermons, the saints especially venerated. It was a matter in part of the way in which religious tradition reinforced a cultural identity, especially at holidays and the great moments of birth, marriage, and death. And often it was a matter of an unusually vivid religious imagery. The German or Polish or Hungarian church interior was generally more elaborate than that in English-speaking parishes: there were more images of the saints, more graphic representations of the life and sufferings of Christ and His mother. Ethnic congregations, moreover, were the more likely to make prominent use of relics in devotions.[30]

The integrity of the various ethnic religious traditions was gradually but surely eroded by the assimilation of the American-born generations. This process was already well underway, by the middle years of the Foley episcopate, among the older ethnic populations. Some contemporary observers feared that assimilation brought in its wake a growing religious indifference, especially among the young. "Theatricals in the midst of Lent; pleasure in the period of fasting and prayer and penance!" a columnist for the *Michigan Catholic* sputtered in 1907. "There is a hoodlum class of young Polacks, Italian and Irish rowdyism in this city—youth born into the Catholic faith—that is a disgrace to the Church and the creed of their ancestors." But in fact the trend among assimilated Catholics was almost certainly toward the highly disciplined sacramental practice that increasingly characterized the American Church. Assimilation had its costs, to be sure. Assimilated Catholics had generally surrendered a vibrant liturgical heritage, one that had made the liturgy for their forebears a genuinely communal experience. But they may well have entered into the sacramental life of the church in a more intimate and immediate way.[31]

DEATH AND THE CATHOLIC RELIGIOUS SENSIBILITY

Catholics in the Foley years inhabited a religious world that was considerably more preoccupied with death—with preparation for death, with the fate of the dead—than American Catholicism is today. This was true in large part because most Catholics then, like their parents and grandparents before them, knew from their own experience that death came often—and early—to the families of the poor. As late as 1900, Poles in Detroit had a life expectancy at birth of only forty years, mostly because mortality among infants and young children in Polish families was very high. More than 17 percent of the children in Detroit's Polish families died in the first year of life, according to the 1900 Census, and another 10 percent died before reaching the age of five. Polish mortality rates were among the highest in the city at the turn of the century, but all Detroiters understood the precariousness of life among the very young. Thirteen percent of the babies born to the wives of blue-collar workers in the city at the turn of the century were likely to die in infancy; a further 7 percent of their children were likely to die by the age of five. Even among the families of white-collar workers in 1900, 15 percent of the children could be expected to die before their fifth birthday.[32]

Although mortality among the young had almost certainly declined in Detroit by 1900, it is unlikely that most Detroiters then were less aware of the precariousness of life than their parents or grandparents had been. If the chances of one's own children surviving to maturity had in fact improved, the death of children—and of young adults—was still very much a part of ordinary experience. The funerals in the parish church were likely to be preponderantly those of children, especially in immigrant parishes, where the death rate was relatively high and the population generally a youthful one. Fully 70 percent of the funerals at Detroit's Sacred Heart (German) parish in the 1880s were those of children under the age of eleven — 31 percent were those of children in the first year of life. Only 10 percent were the funerals of men and women over the age of sixty. Over the next two decades a significant change was evident, as the death rate among children fell and the population of the parish aged. The funerals of children under eleven made up 56 percent of the 801 funerals at the church in the 1890s and 42 percent of the funerals held between 1901 and 1908. The wealthier, and probably older, population at St. Patrick's Church — the cathedral after 1890 — had fewer children's funerals. Of the 527 funerals at St. Patrick's in the 1880s for which the age of the deceased is known, 46 percent were those of children under eleven, while 21 percent were those of persons over sixty. (The figures for the 1890s are 29 and 22 percent, respectively.) But if we can see clearly the dramatic change at Sacred Heart and see at St. Patrick's the extra security enjoyed by the more affluent, the ordinary Catholic in these years was probably less impressed by his own improved chances for longevity — or those of his children — than he was by the sight of bereaved parents, young widows, and — as a well-known mission preacher liked to say — "the short graves in the graveyard."[33]

A world where "short graves" were so numerous was obviously a world in which the young were acquainted with death, and this is nowhere more poignantly conveyed than in the letters to the children's page of the *Michigan Catholic.* The page was inaugurated in 1891, and was at its spontaneous best for the remainder of that decade. The children who regularly wrote for its columns were mainly of Irish descent, and most were the offspring of relatively prosperous families. Their homes were not visited by death nearly as frequently as the homes of the immigrant poor, but many of their letters speak of the deaths of siblings, cousins, schoolmates, and parents — and during the 1890s several of the children who wrote to the page died as well. "Since I wrote you before our city was visited with diphtheria, and two of my little schoolmates died of it, little Frank and Immaculata Houran, she was 10 years old," wrote young Nellie Dunn from Flint in 1892. "There has been another death in our family, auntie, but this time it was a dear little brother. He was 6 years of age, and had long light curls and dark blue eyes. He was sick just about six hours," wrote a youngster from Bay City in 1893. "I will be 10 years old the 4th of next month," wrote another Bay City child. "It will not be a very pleasant birthday for me, for death has just claimed my two brothers and my sister Nellie." There were noticeably fewer accounts of deaths among family and friends in the letters that appeared after the late 1890s, but even then the topic was not rare. "Last week one of our classmates died," Margaret Leahy wrote from Jackson in 1906. "For three days his desk in school was decorated in white and blessed candles burned all day in remembrance of him. My mother will be dead a year the 25th of this month, and we always pray for her."[34]

The children who wrote to the *Michigan Catholic* probably came from fairly devout families — their parents were almost bound to be subscribers to the paper. And they nearly always spoke of death in a conventionally pious way. The younger among them took comfort in having "angel brothers and sisters." "It all most broke our hearts to part with them," wrote one little girl of the deaths of a younger brother and sister in 1896, "but they are better off, for we know they are bright angels in heaven." The older were sometimes troubled by the fear that a loved one might be suffering in purgatory, but were hopeful that the "beautiful death" of the departed and his good life had won him a place in heaven. "It is very hard, dear Aunt, to see those we love pass away from us," wrote a young woman of seventeen about the death of an older brother, "but consoling when we think they are out of this world of sin and misery, and I pray and have cause to believe that my dear brother is in heaven with the blessed. He received the Holy Communion three times during his illness and was anointed and fully prepared for death." Even a quite young child was capable of appropriating the language and logic of her elders when it came to placing death in a religious context. "I am seven years old. . . . I think it would be a nice idea to pray for the repose of the soul of any deceased members of our 'Merry Band,'" suggested a little girl in 1892.[35]

What these youngsters reflected, and made their own, as they struggled to find meaning and consolation in the face of death was an adult piety which at the turn of the century was still very much preoccupied with dying. Preparation for death was an important theme in the preaching of the period and it was a staple of popular religious literature. Catholic authors and editors delighted in the edifying deathbed scene — real or fictional — and few cautionary tales for the young failed to warn, sometimes in improbable detail, that death could come with terrible suddenness for even the most carefree and privileged. Purgatorian or "happy death" societies were increasingly popular in the parishes of the Diocese in the late nineteenth century. The "Bona Mors" Society at Detroit's St. Vincent's parish had 700 members in 1896; they assembled each month for Rosary and Benediction, pledged themselves to monthly confession and communion, cultivated a special devotion to St. Joseph — patron of a happy death — and had a high Mass sung for each member when he died. "The object of the association is to obtain for one's self and fellow members a happy death," the *Michigan Catholic* explained.[36]

Nearly all parish societies, moreover, obliged their members to pray for fellow members who had died, although none in the late nineteenth century seems to have required, as the Catholic Guild of Detroit had done in the 1850s, that they "advise with and read some spiritual work" to any member who was in danger of death. More typical was the Altar Guild at Kalamazoo's St. Augustine's parish, which in the 1890s obliged its members to pray for the dead, to attend the annual Requiem Mass for deceased members of the society, and to "receive holy communion once for each member who dies during the year." Even parish benefit societies, more social and economic than religious in their purposes, normally required that members attend the funeral and pray for fellow members when they died. When forty-year-old James Barry, president of Branch No. 1 of the Catholic Mutual Benefit Association (CMBA) and a member of Detroit's Holy Trinity parish, died in 1901, "over 300 members of the CMBA assembled at the late residence of the deceased . . . and joined in prayer for the repose of the soul of their deceased associate and brother." Prayer for the dead was a good and wholesome thing, or so devout Catholics firmly believed. It was also an excellent stimulus for the living to assess their own spiritual health. The clergy, and the pious laity too, who insisted on prayer for the dead as an obligation of membership in parish societies were almost certainly motivated in part by this latter consideration. The growing popularity of prayer for the dead is of a piece, then, with the increasingly disciplined religious practice that was evident by the late nineteenth century.[37]

What little we know about Catholic funerals in the nineteenth century provides some further insight into popular piety—and evidence for the increase in disciplined religious practice. The nineteenth-century clergy, it seems, were often unhappy with prevailing funeral customs. Before the late nineteenth century their complaints had mostly to do with what looked to be the indifference of many Catholics to the fate of their dead. Bishop Lefevere thought it necessary in 1857 to issue regulations requiring that every Catholic funeral in the city of Detroit include a Requiem Mass. (He extended the regulations to the City of Grand Rapids in 1860.) And in 1858 he announced to the pastors of Detroit that all baptized infants who died, "however young or small they may be," must be buried with a Mass and with all the ceremonials prescribed by the Roman Ritual. The Lefevere regulations were probably directed mainly at the impoverished immigrants who had flooded into the Diocese during and after the mid-1840s. "Most of the two million Irish who emigrated between 1847 and 1860 were part of the pre-famine generation of non-practicing Catholics," according to historian Emmet Larkin, "if indeed they were Catholics at all." How quickly and thoroughly the bishop and his priests were able to reform what they saw as essentially pagan funeral practices we do not know. Certainly by the late nineteenth century, however, one almost never finds the clergy complaining that the laity neglect to make provision for proper Church funerals, at least in those communities with resident priests. But as late as 1890 it was still possible for the Capuchin who tended the mission at L'Anse Creuse—now St. Gertrude's in St. Clair Shores—to note that "the people of L'Anse Creuse sometimes bury little children without notifying the priest."[38]

What most disturbed the clergy by the late nineteenth century was the extravagance of Catholic funerals. "In order to please the souls of your dead, spend less for elaborate funerals and more for alms to the poor in their name; less for monuments of stone and more for contributions to the foreign missions," the *Michigan Catholic* advised in 1896. "One Mass offered to God in their behalf would do them more good than the costliest casket, the richest floral piece, and the use of all the hacks in the city. Let us have Christian funerals, not pagan displays." But despite what became in the 1890s something of a campaign against lavish funerals — in Detroit and other dioceses as well — the Catholics of the Diocese of Detroit seem not to have reformed at all. A lavish funeral was an important measure of family status in all ethnic groups and, in the eyes of ordinary Catholics, a mark of respect for the dead. What a later generation called life insurance the working class in this period called a "death benefit," and it was often spent almost entirely on an elaborate funeral. There were elegant carriages to be hired for the procession, flowers for the wake at home and for the church, food for the mourners, and the handsomest possible casket.[39]

If the deceased had belonged to a parish society or to a trade union, the efforts of his family were likely to be matched by those of his confreres. When a member of the Knights of St. John was buried from St. Boniface parish in 1891, the uniformed Knights of the parish, "headed by a band," marched behind the casket from the home of the deceased to the church, and after Mass accompanied the body to the cemetery. (The promise of a well-attended funeral was an important drawing card for many parish societies in this period.) The members of Branch No. 31 of the Molders' Union sent "a pillow of roses and chrysanthemums" to the funeral of a fellow worker at St. Vincent's Church in Detroit in 1894, and attended the funeral "headed by a band." Parish societies and secular organizations vied with one another in the elaborateness of the flower arrangements sent to funerals. A young Detroit fireman killed on duty in 1893 received "beautiful and appropriate floral offerings" from every engine house in the city when he was buried from Holy Trinity. "Conspicuous among these was a large truck seat in chrysanthemums and mermet roses. The designs also included a badge with the cap number of the deceased . . . and several 'last calls,' the number of the alarm to which he was responding when he met his death being 431. . . . The casket was almost hidden from sight by the flowers piled up around it." Parish societies generally favored more spiritual themes. The young men at St. Mary's parish in Chelsea "presented an exquisite piece, 'Gates Ajar'" for the funeral of a young woman in 1894, while St. Mary's Sodality chose the popular "Broken Wheel," which seems to have symbolized the vagaries of fortune and the unexpectedness of death. Even the funerals of the very young were more and more apt to be elaborate affairs. "He looked as if he were sleeping in his little white casket," a Jackson child recounted in 1897 of the funeral of her infant brother. "We had the grave lined with white." The 1916 funeral of the three-year-old daughter of a prominent Lenox businessman "was the largest ever held here for so young a child. . . . Little girls dressed in white and wearing wreaths of white carnations and smilax were active and honorary pall-bearers."[40]

That the funerals of infants and young children were increasingly likely to be celebrated in church and even, by the close of the century, characterized by a certain lavishness, was due in part to the falling death rate among the young. A community where a large proportion of children die in the first months and years of life is simply less likely than a more fortunate community to make elaborate provision for children's funerals. But the change reflects as well the growing discipline that characterized the religious practice of Catholics in the

Diocese. Just as the most indifferent among them were increasingly likely to make their Easter duty, just as the mass of Catholics were increasingly willing to receive the sacraments more than once a year, so growing numbers of Catholics came to recognize the church funeral—even for the very young—as a religious obligation. When the *Michigan Catholic* criticized the "pagan" customs which the editor believed characterized most Catholic funerals at the turn of the century, its perspective was—to a historian—a peculiarly limited one.

What disturbed the *Michigan Catholic*—and a good many priests—was not simply the hardship that extravagant funerals imposed on poor families. It was also the extent to which purely secular customs were incorporated into what was supposed to be a religious ceremony. Similar criticisms were sometimes made of weddings, although in the nineteenth century it is fair to say that weddings in the working class were generally less lavish than funerals. (Appropriately, the *Michigan Catholic* in the late nineteenth century devoted considerably more space to funerals than it did to weddings, despite the paper's editorial war against extravagant funeral customs.) But the odd mix of the sacred and the secular that characterizes weddings and funerals alike does not necessarily detract from their fundamentally religious character. They were less "pagan" events than religious ceremonies where the laity had more influence on the shape of the ritual than was normally the case in the Church. In the Diocese of Detroit we find that it was funerals which, longer than any other ceremony, retained distinctive ethnic features. And evidently the funeral ritual varied from place to place in the Diocese long after the liturgy in English-speaking parishes had become virtually uniform. Fathers Hugh McCarthy and Clemens Krebs discovered for themselves that this was so when the priests of the Lansing deanery gathered for a conference in 1901. Young Father McCarthy was asked to address his confreres on funeral rubrics, which he cheerfully proceeded to do, being "well-posted on the question, having of late had plenty of experience." He was not long into his narrative, however, when Father Krebs demanded the floor. "He protested against accepting the Williamston rubrics as typical," the conference minutes tell us. "We are to carry out the Roman Ritual and not the Williamston Ritual."

> He drew a volume of Rubrics out of his pocket and pleaded most pathetically with Fr. McCarthy and the Dean for a genuine Roman Ritual. The Dean requested him to remain calm, as each one present undoubtedly meant to do right as far as he saw it, and that the Roman Ritual can be carried out only so far as circumstances here are the same as at Rome.[41]

One final aspect of funeral practice in this period bears attention, for it helps to measure the distance that separates our religious world from that of our forebears. It is the role played at funerals by children. Children were not generally shielded from the reality of death in the years around the turn of the century, for theirs was a world where brothers and sisters and schoolmates died, and where wakes were often held at home. It was also a world where children regularly took a prominent part at funerals, especially those of their peers. Boys and girls as young as six or seven served as pallbearers when schoolmates or siblings died, and the young members of parish sodalities were expected to turn out for funerals just as the older members did. Agnes Landry was twelve in 1895 when she participated in the funeral of a fellow sodalist at Anchorville's Immaculate Conception Church. The deceased was a grown woman — still unmarried — and not well known to young Agnes. But as a member of the junior branch of the Young Ladies' Sodality, Agnes was obliged to take part. Deeply impressed by the somber affair, she wrote in some detail to the children's page of the *Michigan Catholic.* "She had a white coffin," Agnes began, "there were six big girls dressed in white wearing each a wreath, that carried her."

> There was a man that carried the banner of the Blessed Virgin and there were two long white ribbons tied to each tassel, two little girls dressed in white, with each a wreath that held the ribbons, walked on each side of it, and went out of the church to meet the corpse, while all the ladies of the Sodality walked behind them. It was a great sorrow for her parents for she was a girl of about twenty-eight years old. I was one of the girls who held the ribbons.

The little girls from St. Vincent's Orphan Asylum who were taken in 1896 to the wake and funeral of one of the institution's benefactors were probably similarly impressed. Clustered in the bedroom where the body lay in state, the children sang "Nearer my God to Thee." "Again at the grave their plaintive voices were heard in the same hymn, and as the mourners gathered around the casket for the last time, they sang Cardinal Newman's 'Lead Kindly Light,' in a manner that started the tears afresh in the eyes of all."[42]

Over time, of course, the role that children played at wakes and funerals was much diminished. The decline seems to have corresponded with the falling mortality rate among the young, although it may have varied from one ethnic group to another. One still finds very young pallbearers in the 1920s, but the practice appears to be much less common than it had been before the First World War. And while the children at St. Gabriel's parish in Detroit were still in 1931 the mainstay of the annual All Saints' Day pilgrimage to nearby Holy Cross cemetery, there are few accounts, by this time, of very young sodality members participating at funerals. After the turn of the century, moreover, wakes were increasingly likely to be held, not at home, but in the parlors of the neighborhood undertaker. This change too had the effect of protecting the young from the full force of adult grief and mourning.[43]

There were other changes in these years as well. The numbers enrolled in purgatorian or "happy death" societies seem to have declined sharply after about 1914. The societies themselves continued to exist and to sponsor the usual round of devotions, but they were more than ever the province of the old, and especially of elderly women. And while sermons and tracts continued to dwell on the need to be always prepared for death, the sentimentality of an earlier literature on death was slowly eroded. In a world where the death of a child or a young parent was more and more an exceptional event, a literature which dwelt mawkishly on the death of the young was apt to disturb or offend a growing number of

Catholics. Still, the typical Catholic before Vatican II was a good deal more likely than the member of a mainstream Protestant denomination to have been raised on a steady diet of the Four Last Things. He knew the dangers of mortal sin, knew at least in outline the theory of indulgences, had occasionally attended Poor Souls devotions in the parish church. He differed from his grandparents chiefly in the extent to which consciousness of death had been pushed to the margins of his own mind and the mind of the community around him. It had become more and more the territory of the old alone.

RELIGIOUS EDUCATION

Catholics in virtually every generation have worried about their ability to pass the faith on to the young. "Of young Americans we believe that it can be generally taken for granted that they are nothing if not irreligious," the *Michigan Catholic* declared in 1893, "and it is only to be expected that many of our Catholic boys growing up surrounded by non-Catholic influences should be gradually alienated from the Church. . . . Let any one who wishes to test this set quietly to work and by careful inquiry find out how many of the Catholic young men of his acquaintance have anything more than a limited belief in the supernatural." If the editor was certain in 1893 that young women were inclined to more orthodox views, he was no longer so confident a decade later. His paper more and more lamented the growing attraction of a "pagan" society for boys and girls alike. When Father John Gabriels at the cathedral warned parents in 1907 that their children's attendance at Sunday afternoon catechism classes had to be carefully enforced, he referred to daughters as well as sons. "The eyes of some of our good Catholic fathers and mothers would open wide with astonishment and dismay could they see, as we have seen, their innocent little children making regular Sunday afternoon visits from one to another of the degrading and very often nasty and immoral catch-penny picture machine galleries along the main thoroughfares of the downtown districts." Father Gabriels, like many of his contemporaries, was sure that the rising generation was more godless than any that had gone before. He evidently knew very little about the early history of his own Diocese, where, long before the advent of catch-penny picture machines, unhappy pastors had bewailed the failure of Catholic parents to teach the young the fundamentals of the catechism or to send them for religious instruction.[44]

Anxieties of this sort quite naturally led to the early founding of Sunday schools, which, dating at least to the 1830s, are among the oldest Catholic institutions in the Diocese. By the 1870s, most parishes and a good many missions were apparently maintaining fairly regular catechism classes. Father Camillus Maes taught catechism every Sunday at St. Peter's Church in Mt. Clemens in 1870, and there were daily instructions in the parish school as well. "During the summer the children come for preparation to first communion. Three lessons a week and as many in [F]rench lasting an hour are given during 4 months."[45]

The Fourth Diocesan Synod in 1878 mandated weekly catechetical instruction in all parishes and missions, and established Butler's Catechism as the required text. This latter was not a widely popular decision. "Butler's in my opinion is exceedingly hard to learn by heart and harder to remember and children *at their age* learn too little from it—also the questions are often too long," a priest complained in 1876, and he was not alone in his dissatisfaction. The extent to which the various parishes and missions complied with the synod's instructions varied according to locale and, occasionally, with the disposition of the pastor. Rural children who lived some distance from a church were often unable to attend catechism in winter or when spring rains turned primitive roads into channels of mud. Catechism was taught "for about seven months" of the year at St. Alphonsus in Dearborn in 1868. "Our people are living very far from church and it is impossible to have the children regularly for catechism," the pastor at Erie noted in 1890. But the pastor at heavily Catholic Emmett had by the late 1870s solved his problem by having catechism taught, after hours, in the public schools. "The catechism is taught regularly in every school in this district, after 4 o'clock by the respective [C]atholic teachers. That is, all children attending the schools study and recite the catechism, as a daily lesson. And I examine the children on their catechetical knowledge when they come to confession."[46]

By the late nineteenth century, Sunday schools in certain parishes had grown to be very ambitious endeavors. The Sunday school at Detroit's Holy Rosary parish had twenty-four teachers in 1896, while the cathedral in 1898 had 600 students in its Sunday school under the tutelage of an astonishing seventy-five instructors. The Jesuits at SS. Peter and Paul's had organized evening classes in 1889 "for the benefit of working boys and men who have not had the opportunity to receive instruction in their youth"; these continued throughout the 1890s. The "young lady teachers" at St. John the Evangelist parish in Detroit could boast in 1902 of their Sunday school library, "which is one of the best-equipped in the city." And the women of St. Mary's parish in Lansing had by that year established a catechetical program at the State Industrial School in their city. "Of course there are boys under the State's roof who will not study their Catechism," the *Michigan Catholic* told its readers, "but on the whole they recite well and seem greatly interested during the time devoted to their lessons. There are 160 Catholic boys in the school."[47]

Clerical support for the Sunday school was strong in the late nineteenth century, despite the growth in parochial school enrollments. Pastors knew, if they did not like to admit, that there were Catholic children in all city parishes who attended the public schools. And at least some pastors hoped to attract to the Sunday school those boys and girls who had left school in their early teens to go to work. Nearly all priests agreed, moreover, that even youngsters who were attending parochial schools should come for instruction on Sundays as well. They hoped to accustom the young to a properly reverent observance of the Sabbath—Mass in the morning, Sunday school and vespers in the afternoon. And, as a priest at Holy Trinity noted in 1893, "in these days of religious warfare our Catholic youth cannot be too well instructed in their holy religion."[48]

The history of the Catholic Sunday school, however, has to do with more than the clergy. Sunday schools were often initiated and sustained by lay people, especially by women. In those many communities in the nineteenth century that did not yet have a resident priest, it was often the Sunday school that brought Catholics together each week, at least in decent weather, and kept alive a strong sense of Catholic identity. Our Lady of Help parish in Detroit, closed in 1967, could trace its beginnings in the 1860s to the Sunday school run by the women of the Elbert family in what was then a sparsely populated area east of the city proper. It was the senior Mrs. Elbert who eventually persuaded Bishop Lefevere to found a parish there. St. Augustine's parish in Lenox has its roots in the Sunday school begun by Mrs. Mary McCarthy when Lenox was still a mission visited occasionally by priests from St. Clair and New Baltimore. Sacred Heart parish in Yale dates its history from the founding of a Catholic Sunday school and library in the village in 1890.[49]

Yale was located in Michigan's rural and heavily Protestant Thumb, which was even in the 1890s poorly supplied with priests. The Sunday school necessarily loomed large in the life of the region's missions. "We have Mass every fifth Sunday only; there is no Catholic school here," explained a youngster from Port Sanilac in 1892. "Now perhaps I should not tell you this, you might think I was pretty near a 'heathen.' But we have Catechism every Sunday at the church three miles west of here, which helps out some. Nice, pious young men teach us." Just why the men of Port Sanilac were so forthcoming we do not know, but they seem to have had relatively few counterparts in the rest of the Diocese. Contemporary accounts of Catholic Sunday schools in cities and small towns alike make clear that their lay teachers were usually female. The conscientious priest was expected to help teach, or at the very least to supervise, the catechetical classes in his parish and its missions, and apparently most of them did. But they depended heavily in this task on the work of laywomen.[50]

We know very little about how these unsung lay teachers — or the clergy, for that matter — tried to instruct the restless young in the essentials of Catholic doctrine. The much-maligned Butler's Catechism was replaced in 1886 as the mandatory catechism of the Diocese by the recently issued Baltimore Catechism, which was presumably used thereafter in virtually all parishes and missions. But at least some teachers tried to supplement the catechism with a more vivid and imaginative presentation of the faith. When Father Cornelius Kennedy visited the mission at Charlotte in 1897 for his regular monthly Mass and taught the catechism class which met there every week, he read from Cardinal Gibbons' *Faith of Our Fathers* and explained it to the children. A number of Sunday schools included Bible history in the curriculum — a happy narrative respite from the rigors of the catechism. (The prize for excellence in Bible history at the Cathedral Sunday School in 1900 "was a beautifully-bound volume of Cardinal Newman's *Apologia Pro Vita Sua*.") "Bible History must remain the principal object of religion" for younger children, a popular pastoral manual urged, warning against an approach to catechetics that stressed the importance of rote memorization of questions and answers over suitably illustrated explanations of religious truths. "The analytical method seems to be a torture for children, and against the apostological principle, *fides ex auditu*; it is exegesis, not catechetical instruction, dissecting sentences, examining the meaning of words." A fair amount of memorization, however, could not be avoided. "They must know their prayers," Father Cornelius Moutard wrote in 1865 of the children at his Bunkerhill mission who wished to be confirmed, "Our Father; Hail Mary; Confiteor; Apostles' Creed; Acts of Faith, Hope, Love and Contrition. The ten Commandments of God and of the Church. The lesson of Confirmation." And Father Moutard was making concessions for what was, after all, a remote and tiny mission. The IHM Sisters insisted that the children in their schools who were preparing for first communion should not only "learn their prayers" but memorize the catechism, "an easy examen of conscience, the manner of hearing Mass well, what belongs to the sacraments in general . . . and in particular . . . and a simple explanation of indulgences and of the application that can be made of them to the suffering members of the Church."[51]

Few lay teachers, in all likelihood, were able in their weekly classes to instruct children as thoroughly as the IHM Sisters tried to do in their schools. But lay teachers may well have placed a heavy emphasis on memorization of the catechism, in order that instruction be orthodox and as systematic as possible. Certainly the children who wrote to the *Michigan Catholic* in the 1890s complained about the tedium of learning the seemingly endless lessons in the Baltimore Catechism by heart. "Mamma says I am slower than time where catechism lessons are concerned," confided Mikey Hanafin of Lapeer in 1893, "but my teacher said I would soon be up with the big class if I kept on. Mamma thinks I ought to learn it as well as Mary, but boys aren't like girls, you know. When I get out to play, I forget about my catechism lessons, and then mamma makes me study it in the night, and I get awful sleepy and can hardly keep my eyes open." Young Frankie Eardley agreed. He was only ten, he wrote, but "papa makes me work very hard." He had to feed the chickens on the family farm and tend the lambs. "Then, the worst of all is to come yet, and I don't think you could guess what that is unless I tell you—but it is the 'Catechism,' and . . . I would rather take a dozen kicks from the calves than to study that for fifteen minutes." "I am like Frankie Eardley about my catechism," Alice Cody confessed. "I enjoyed his letter and hope he will have better success than I in learning it." The more pious Rosellen Devero of Pinckney, however, had long since got her catechism by heart and was radiantly happy in the recollection of her recent first communion. "We had three weeks of catechism and instruction in our own little church, and I wish it had been twenty," she wrote in 1893. "Our teacher was our own dear Father Considine."[52]

The method to be employed in religious instruction was increasingly a topic of discussion in the early years of the twentieth century, as Sunday schools in Detroit, especially, came more and more to be regarded as essentially missionary enterprises. With growing numbers of children in the parochial schools, and with those children receiving first communion early in their school careers, it was hard for the sternest of pastors to make a persuasive case for attending Sunday school as well. And by the early twentieth century there was evidently a growing disinclination on the part of even quite devout Catholics to center their Sundays wholly on the Church. Father Gabriels at the cathedral was not the only priest in 1914 who "regretted that more people do not attend the Vespers and Benediction." But even as the parish Sunday school seems to have been in decline, the city of Detroit was receiving a vast new — and mostly Catholic — population of immigrants and their children. A number of them had only tenuous ties to a parish, if they had any at all, and were little interested in parochial education. The Sunday school, could it reach such families, might be a means of bringing them into closer contact with the Church. Reaching the marginal Catholic, however, was an almost insuperable problem for the clergy in a city as mobile and ethnically diverse as Detroit. Father James Doherty of St. Vincent's "would be pleased to have parishioners leave the address or addresses of children who are now attending public schools and desire instruction in Catechism," announced the *Michigan Catholic* in 1917. How large a class resulted from his appeal the paper did not say, but we can reasonably guess that many nominally Catholic youngsters in the neighborhood of St. Vincent's continued to be strangers to their pastor.[53]

For all the good intentions of a Father Doherty, it was a laywoman who finally made the Sunday school an effective means of evangelization in Detroit. She was Josephine Van Dyke Brownson, a public school teacher in the city and the daughter of a prominent Catholic family. Miss Brownson began her pioneering catechetical work in 1906, when she organized classes at the Jesuit church for children from Italian and Syrian immigrant families. Her work was distinguished not simply by its scope, although that was impressive. Brownson's Catholic Instruction League, as it came to be called in 1916, had twenty-one centers in Detroit by 1918, when the league was only at the threshold of its growth in the Diocese. But Brownson also developed and publicized an innovative approach to catechetics, one that repudiated the memorization and drill which all too frequently characterized religious instruction. The catechism should be used sparingly, she told the teachers she recruited to the league, as a supplement to stories from Scripture and the lives of the saints. "If the class is composed of foreigners or of children who have difficulty in memorizing, it may be wiser to omit the catechism." Nor should a child ever be placed in a class with younger children because he did not know the rudiments of the catechism; children should always be taught with their peers. For the point of religious instruction was to engage the imagination and affections of the child. "To cause the children to love their class will do more for them than to teach them to define the indefectibility of the Church. If they love their class, they will love their religion." And so the successful teacher was one who spoke in simple but vivid language, who could convey the essentials of doctrine in narrative form, who took a deep and affectionate interest in the lives of her pupils. (The league's teachers were expected to visit their pupils' families, and encourage them to a regular religious practice.) Above all, the successful teacher was one who was willing to prepare assiduously for the hour spent in class. The weekly instruction "should be thought over and studied much as one would prepare to play a part on stage. Posture, gesture, tone of voice, choice of expression, all make a deep impression on the child. If the teacher allows herself to be carried away by her subject, the class will be spellbound. If the teacher has fallen in love with the beauty of God and religion, the children will be entranced."[54]

Brownson's activities were not much publicized in the Foley years, nor did she receive, to the best of our knowledge, any special encouragement from the Chancery. A handful of priests in the Diocese were, to be sure, among her most ardent supporters. But her work was controversial. The catechism, whatever its defects, was a guarantor of orthodoxy, and Brownson's approach was thought by some critics to give too much teaching authority to members of the laity. The Catholic Instruction League, moreover, was widely regarded as a challenge to the parochial school. Since its purpose was to instruct Catholic children who attended the public schools, the critics argued, recognition or encouragement of the league was tantamount to endorsing secular education for Catholics.

That Brownson and nearly all of her associates in the Catholic Instruction League were women may have fueled opposition as well, especially as the scope of her plans for the league became apparent. For Brownson not only envisioned a network of teaching centers in Detroit and the rest of the Diocese, she hoped through her writings to stimulate something like a nationwide movement in the cause of catechetical reform. Brownson had from the first supplied her teachers with a detailed narrative for every lesson they taught — narratives that were published, in 1918, as *To the Heart of a Child,* the first of numerous Brownson volumes. These books gained for Brownson a national, even an international, reputation as an authority in the field of religious education. "I still confess to a lingering backward glance at that 1918 book with its spare and workmanlike simplicity," the English catechist Father Harold Drinkwater acknowledged in the early 1950s. But her status as a laywoman was always a handicap. Neither the Bruce publishing house nor *Our Sunday Visitor* would issue a Brownson title without including the name of at least one priest as a collaborator. She was denied membership in the Catholic Biblical Association in the 1930s. And several years before her death in 1942, Archbishop Edward Mooney brought the Catholic Instruction League under clerical control, incorporating it gradually into the newly established Confraternity of Christian Doctrine.[55]

By Mooney's day, the work of catechetical instruction was increasingly done by women religious, even when that instruction took place outside the parish school. Such had not been the case in the Foley years, for the number of Sisters in the Diocese then was still too small for them to assume so broad an educational role. Even in 1918, religious instruction outside the parochial school was largely in the hands of the laity. There were signs by then, however, of the greatly expanded role that Sisters would eventually come to play in religious education. Father John Gilmary Cook organized a "vacation school" at his parish in Reese in the summer of 1915, where two IHM Sisters taught catechism every day in tents on the church grounds. ("Some of the scholars had never seen Sisters before," according to one of the young participants.) Father Cook's was apparently the first such venture in the history of the Diocese, but his example was increasingly imitated. "Vacation schools," taught by Sisters, were inaugurated in a number of rural parishes in the 1920s. The growing number of Sisters in the Diocese made this new ministry possible. That it was thought necessary reflects the distrust that clerical education bred with regard to the theological literacy of the laity. Priests in the 1920s were living with the legacy of men like Bishop Stang, whose 1896 pastoral manual had no high opinion of the lay catechist. Lay teachers could "help in keeping order and in hearing lessons," Stang acknowledged. But "they should not be permitted to go any further, by changing the places of the children, punishing them, and so forth. . . . The real catechetical instruction must be given by the priest before the close of Sunday-school, and should occupy fifteen minutes."[56]

Catechetical classes and instruction in the schools were not the only ways that Catholics taught children the essentials of the faith. Children absorbed a good deal from their parents. And although the *Michigan Catholic* was certain that many parents neglected the spiritual health of the young, the more disciplined religious practice of many adults in the Foley years probably helped to bind their children firmly to the Church. Children in nearly all parishes, moreover, were incorporated into the round of liturgical events that marked the Church year. They were, to be sure, often restless in church: the best thing about the children's Mass at her Jackson church, according to one youngster, was that "it is not so long." But many children obviously loved the processions and flowers and candles that signified special occasions, and liked the prominent role they were often asked to play. "Sunday night after Vespers there was a procession of the Blessed Sacrament," a child from Pinckney recounted in 1893. "There were four little girls with baskets of flowers, throwing flowers before the Blessed Sacrament. They were dressed in white, wearing wreaths and blue sashes. . . . The girls and boys of the first communion class were in the procession. We marched around the church."[57]

Children who wrote to the *Michigan Catholic* in the years around the turn of the century spoke with enthusiasm too about the parts they played in Marian processions and May crownings and Christmas masses, and even in such "adult" observances as Forty Hours and Sacred Heart devotions. ("I like this month because there are so many beautiful flowers, and we go to the woods and gather them and make a wreath to crown the statue of the Sacred Heart of Jesus during the month of June.") They liked the badges and other paraphernalia that came with membership in a sodality. "We are going to have a society for all the children in the school who made their first communion," a boy from Detroit's St. Joachim parish reported in 1892. "On the first Sunday of January we had two beautiful banners blessed. . . . The girls have white badges and the boys have red ones." And children were often sensitive to what they saw as the beauty of the parish church, hushed and holy, reminiscent of a host of sacred friends and helpers. ("I wish you could see our church; we have so many beautiful statues.") Perhaps the *Michigan Catholic* was right to lament the indifference of many young people to their religious heritage and to the obligations it imposed upon them. There were objective grounds for the editor's discontents. But it was also true that the Catholicism that flourished in the Diocese at the close of the century was remarkably good at catching, and holding, the imagination of the young. There was tedium in church, but there were magic moments too. "The church was trimmed up lovely," wrote a youngster from tiny Yorkville at Christmas in 1894. "The altar was a mass of burning candles and lamps. The tabernacle was crowned with lights and the crib was beautiful."[58]

THE PARISH AS A COMMUNITY: SOCIAL LIFE, PARISH ORGANIZATIONS

On the Fourth of July in 1893, the members of St. Patrick's parish in rural Northfield assembled, with their relatives and friends, for the annual parish picnic. A fund-raising as well as a social event, the picnic must have been profitable that year: "about 1400 sat down at the grove to dinner, which was served on long tables under a canopy of green, with the cooling zephyrs from the lake augmenting the powers of appetite." Sports and dancing followed, Minnis's orchestra having been engaged for the occasion, and in the late afternoon the crowd gathered for an entertainment. Father Edward Kelly from nearby Ann Arbor opened the festivities with a patriotic speech; the orchestra, not to be outdone, played a medley of patriotic airs. Bruno St. James sang "Rose Marie," Northfield's own Father Louis Goldrick sang "Home Rule for Ireland," and "Mr. Riley of Detroit" performed a German dialect sketch. "All in all," the anonymous local reporter concluded, "it was a day which will be long remembered."[59]

It was presumably just such a day which the *Michigan Catholic's* "Rosaleen" had in mind when she complained in 1906 that the modern city parish had none of the sociable atmosphere which had characterized "the old fashioned parishes, with their old fashioned customs and old fashioned festivals." These were "almost of the past" now; what had replaced them, at least in Detroit and the larger towns, were parishes where "the people do not mingle. . . . There is an aloofness amongst them that is positively painful to behold." Her male counterpart at the paper—a columnist known as "The Rambler"—agreed entirely. "I have discovered," he wrote, also in 1906, "that many of the Catholic men and women, strangers to the city, employed in the earning of an honest livelihood, are disgusted with the indifference which the 'parishioners' show them." Both "Rosaleen" and "The Rambler" believed that the problem had to do in part with the rapid growth of Detroit, but that it was caused more fundamentally by the growing tendency of the laity to center their lives on institutions other than the Church. It was the simple faith—and the simple lives—of our parents and grandparents, they argued, that had made those "old fashioned parishes" the warm and sociable places they had been.[60]

This version of recent Catholic history would surely have puzzled Jesuit Father Michael Dowling, president of Detroit College from 1889 until 1893. Shortly after he came to Detroit, Father Dowling took the occasion of a public lecture to deplore the unfriendliness that he believed prevailed in most Catholic parishes. "Generally speaking, church organization among Protestants is more compact and the social element is more closely regarded. Newcomers are welcomed to church membership, an opening is made for them in business life, they are introduced more freely to the congregation. There is far more sociability as a rule than among Catholics." This was especially hard on young men whose work took them regularly from city to city. "They have no way of becoming acquainted with other Catholics. They find themselves strangers wherever they go." The problem, as Father Dowling saw it, was the unwillingness of Catholics of different social classes to be friendly toward one another. Presumably he had in mind his own experience as rector of SS. Peter and Paul's Church in Detroit, which included within its rather narrow parochial boundaries both the wealthiest and some of the poorest streets in the city. The parish in 1890 had about 500 families—a large parish then, but small by today's standards—and supported an impressive number of active church societies. But as a community it was apparently badly divided, if not by class antagonism then by suspicion and resentment. "Among us, those on a higher plane of life hesitate to take part in anything that has the appearance of a social character, lest they might commit themselves to friendly relations with those with whom they are brought in contact in church work. Those of the more moderate station in life look up with jealousy and suspicion and refuse to be under the leadership of a caste." Father Dowling did not look to revolutionary notions of social equality to solve the problem—"I do not mean to say that social condition should be obliterated, for that would be impossible. Such conditions have been established by Almighty God." But Catholics might at least try to promote a greater friendliness—a more welcoming atmosphere—in their parishes.[61]

Father Dowling believed that the conditions he diagnosed were sufficiently widespread to help explain why Catholics in the United States were slow to become socially mobile. His considerable pastoral experience, however, had probably been confined to English-language parishes. Whether the tensions he described were characteristic of ethnic parishes we do not have the evidence to say, nor indeed do we know with any certainty that Father Dowling was right in his observations with regard to English-speaking Catholics. But it is the case that most Catholic parishes in this period had members from several social classes, and that this was less likely to be the case in Protestant congregations. The city of Detroit, as we have seen, was in the 1890s still largely segregated on the basis of ethnicity; the typical city neighborhood—and hence the typical parish—contained prosperous business and professional men, self-consciously "respectable" skilled workers and struggling shopkeepers, as well as a large population of unskilled workers and day laborers. The cultural gulf that separated these groups one from another was very great—greater, in many ways, than it would be three or four generations later. This was true even in the ethnic parishes, and despite the bond that nationality represented in a strange and sometimes hostile world.

To be sure, in those ethnic parishes in the Diocese where the men of the congregation elected the church committee, the working-class majority seem regularly to have voted for the businessmen and lawyers and doctors who made up the parish elite. But this would not preclude a lurking resentment on the part of some men, or even a refusal to participate in parish affairs—"to be under the leadership of a caste," as Father Dowling had it. A detailed reading of the Kolasinski affair, for example, suggests an element of class tension at work in the dispute. Perhaps some of the many Catholics in this period who did not join church societies were kept away by the "jealousy and suspicion" that Father Dowling thought was often a response to the domination of parish life by the well-to-do. Priests in the late nineteenth century sometimes worried that Catholics were more attracted by fraternal orders—militantly egalitarian—than they were by parish societies. "Many members of this parish do not belong to any of the church societies," Pontiac's Father Thomas Ryan chided in 1896, "or if they do they are only dead members, whereas they are most active members in societies not approved by the church." Mrs. Josephine Jones Donovan found it impossible in the 1890s to enlarge the women's reading circle at the cathedral to include a larger constituency than the parish elite. "The unfortunate fact that in this free land of ours, especially in our churches, there exists that bane of the present era—Social distinction," she lamented in 1895, "limits in an enormous degree our possibilities to aid and uplift each other."[62]

In the small town or rural parish, the bane of social distinction was often coupled with the divisive effects of nationality, for many of these parishes, as we have seen, had multiethnic congregations. The pastor might himself be a talented linguist and all things to all men; his parishioners were usually less accommodating. (Father John Gilmary Cook faced a larger task than most in his parish at Reece. He was obliged to import confessors in 1914 for the Forty Hours devotion so that confessions might be heard in German, French, Hungarian, and Polish as well as English.) The rural Catholic, moreover, often lived some distance from the parish church and especially in winter or during a rainy spring might be hard pressed to attend Sunday Mass, much less the meetings or devotions of a parish society. The typical village or rural church in this period had many fewer societies than the most modest city parish. And there were still Catholics in the Foley years who were almost completely isolated from anything like a normal parish life. As late as 1900 the heavily Protestant villages of western Wayne County—in which Detroit is located—were home to Catholics who only rarely saw a priest. They were apparently unable or unwilling to make the journey to the village of Wayne, which, as a mission of St. Mary's, Milford, had mass twice a month. "In the past we had a very creditable church and congregation at Northville," a businessman who knew the area wrote to the *Michigan Catholic*. But this tiny band of Catholics had not survived as a community. "The church at Northville has fallen into decay, and the congregation is dispersed."

In the absence of a priest's regular visits, he warned, many of the Catholics in the vicinity were being absorbed into the Protestant culture that surrounded them.

> There is no church at Plymouth, though there are quite a number of German Catholic families in the village who have not seen Mass these many years, and there are many others who profess to have been Catholics by education and are yet in sympathy, who carry the badges of proscribed secret societies. At Newburg, just east of Plymouth, there are in the neighborhood of twenty Catholic families now endeavoring without any outside assistance, to organize themselves into a congregation, the most that they expect to accomplish being to have their children taught the Catechism by some competent person every Sunday afternoon. In the same neighborhood several German families, formerly Catholic, have been attracted, most strangely of all, to the Christian Scientist services, finding expression therein, no doubt, to their ancestral faith in prayer.[63]

What looks from a distance, then, like a world where the parish was for most Catholics a natural focus of social life may well have been a world where a fair number of practicing Catholics were alienated from, or indifferent to, the parish as a social community. There were surely many Catholics — particularly women in and beyond their middle years — for whom parish organizations and activities provided welcome relief from the tedious round of daily life. There were many more who looked forward to the picnics and entertainments regularly sponsored by even the smaller parishes. And the church was nearly always an important focus of cultural and political life in ethnic communities. But even in the most cohesive ethnic communities, even in the most homogeneous small town parishes, we find pastors in the late nineteenth century distressed at the want of solidarity among the faithful, disturbed that so many Catholics saw the church as a place of worship and nothing more. Perhaps they, like their successors, believed that Catholics in the past had managed to create in their parishes the warm and inclusive community that so stubbornly eluded the present generation of the faithful.[64]

Over the course of the Foley years, and in the decades that followed, the growth of Detroit and its hinterland generated changes that had important effects on the social composition of many parishes. These changes affected parish social life in both positive and negative ways. Parish populations became much larger, something which clergy and laity alike have long deplored as a barrier to sociability. But at the same time, the typical parish in Detroit was becoming increasingly homogeneous with regard to social class. For Detroit by 1920 was a city characterized by a strong and growing degree of class segregation. The effects of this may well have been positive, at least with regard to parish sociability: there is reason to believe that working-class Catholics were more willing to participate in parish organizations and activities once they were no longer "under the leadership of a caste." As for the small towns, where the local church was necessarily home to all Catholics, the assimilation of the immigrant populations — and the end of unrestricted immigration in the 1920s — meant that these parishes were less and less divided by language and culture. These same parishes benefited from those quintessential products of early twentieth-century Detroit — cheap cars and good roads. What Detroit had wrought would eventually transform the face of rural America, but in the mid-1920s the typical rural Catholic knew only that it was considerably easier to get to church than it had ever been before.

The more homogeneous congregations in evidence by the 1920s did not give rise, by all accounts, to a warm and welcoming atmosphere. Catholics continued to complain that their churches were cold and unfriendly, especially when compared to the typical Protestant congregation. "The glacial attitude of the ordinary Catholic to the stranger within his gates has become historic," the *Michigan Catholic* claimed in 1921. "Courtesy to a stranger in a Catholic church to some persons smacks of heresy and to be set down as a case reserved to a Bishop. We have been a resident of this city for six months, and attend a church every Sunday. With but two exceptions, we have been let severely alone and we might continue in that condition till the crack of doom for all our Catholic brethren care." But these same congregations typically supported a wide variety of social activities. The Foley years, indeed, are noteworthy for a dramatic increase in the numbers and variety of parish organizations devoted to boys and young men — organizations that continued to grow and develop during the tenure of Foley's successor. If the typical city parish by the middle decades of the twentieth century was too large to be anything like a cohesive community, it had nonetheless become a contender in the recreation market. Pastors naturally worried about those many Catholics whose involvement in the parish was limited to hearing Mass on Sundays and holy days of obligation. But they were probably wrong to think, as many of them did, that the parish had declined significantly over time as a center of lay sociability. For the male portion of the Catholic population, the opposite may well have been true.[65]

Organizations for Boys and Young Men

The clergy of the Diocese had long been troubled by their young male parishioners, who often seemed indifferent, even resistant, to the claims of religion. But the priests who served in the Diocese during its first half-century were unable to do much about young men except preach and pray: the relatively few young men's sodalities that were organized before the 1880s seem to have been short-lived, for the most part, and poorly supported. By the later 1880s, however, the growing number of clergy in the Diocese made it possible for at least some priests to contemplate a new and imaginative assault on the fortress of young men's indifference. They were inspired in part by similar currents in British and American Protestantism. Such large and well-publicized organizations as Christian Endeavor, the Epworth League and the Student Volunteer Movement date from the 1880s and the 1890s. And in their fondness for military metaphors and military discipline, for team sports and the outdoor life, Protestant and Catholic proponents of "youth work" were remarkably alike, although Catholics lagged well behind when it came to organizational progress. "Especially at this time we are struck with the extent of young people's organization in the so-called evangelical churches," the *Michigan Catholic* admitted in 1898. "In this line of organization we are singularly deficient." This was a painful admission, for Catholic spokesmen at the end of the century were sensitive to charges that the Catholic population in the United States was responsible for a disproportionate share of the nation's crime. "Boy work" was seen as a means to check youthful delinquency, and it was hard to acknowledge that Protestants were far ahead of Catholics when it came to organizing the young.[66]

The boys and young men's organizations that appeared under Catholic auspices in the Foley years were mainly of two kinds. Some were intended for boys in their early and mid-teens, who had made their first communion and perhaps left school, but who did not yet enjoy the freedoms, or run the risks, of their older and more worldly brothers. These younger boys, according to Kalamazoo's Father Frank O'Brien, were drawn to groups with a martial flavor. He recommended uniforms and military drill to catch and hold their interest. The boys should receive communion together once a month, preferably in uniform, O'Brien advised. And they should be taught the importance of disciplined habits. The youngsters whom Father O'Brien had organized in his own parish were pledged to abstain from liquor and tobacco. They ran the risk of a nickel fine for missing meetings or the monthly communion, or coming "late to meetings twice in succession."[67]

Father O'Brien's sentiments were apparently shared by a number of his fellow clergy: military societies for boys became increasingly popular in the 1890s. The Cadets at St. Boniface (German) parish, for example, were accustomed to a round of activity that combined military discipline and outdoor adventure in much the same proportions as the early Boy Scouts. Camping out at Algonac in 1899, "the boys spent the time in drilling, hunting and fishing and having a good time." They regularly received communion in the parish church "in full dress uniform." The interest in things military was characteristic in this period of Protestant as well as Catholic clergy. It probably had primarily to do with a concern in all denominational camps about the visibly dominant role that women played in church affairs. A parish military society, whether for boys or for men, was a way of staking an emphatically masculine claim to a portion of what often looked to be female territory.[68]

It was not the boy in his early teens, however, who was the principal concern of the Catholic clergy. His older brother—the youth in his late teens and early twenties—was generally thought to be more resistant to the guidance of the Church, but in greater need of control. The preponderance of parish "youth" organizations before the First World War were, as a consequence, directed toward this older group. Some of these organizations placed a heavy emphasis on military dress and discipline. The Detroit Catholic Cadets, organized at St. Patrick's Church in 1888, were a case in point, for the members ranged in age from seventeen to twenty-five. "The Cadets have recently been armed," the *Michi-*

gan Catholic informed its readers, "and will meet for drill every Friday evening."
But military trappings were apparently less appealing to young men than to adolescent boys, and a growing number of young men's clubs depended mainly, or
exclusively, on athletics and social events to attract and keep their members. The
young men's society organized at St. Joachim's (French) parish in 1889 "com-
bines religious instruction with physical development and sociability," according
to a parish spokesman. The members "are permitted the use of a very complete
gymnasium." St. Joachim's opened a Young Men's Hall in 1890, where the group
held regular meetings and entertainments. For all its preferential treatment,
however, the group was relatively small. The young men's society at St. Joachim's
had 35 members in 1890, while the Young Ladies' Sodality claimed a membership of 115.[69]

Still, the St. Joachim approach was a popular one. St. Boniface parish in 1893
furnished its new hall with a bowling alley, pool and billiard tables, and a small
gymnasium—all for the express use of the parish young men's society. Other
Detroit parishes made similarly generous provision for this hard-to-hold constituency: St. Joseph's opened a gymnasium, a billiard room, and a reading room
in the basement of the parish school; SS. Peter and Paul's provided a gym for
its "Working Boys' Sodality"; and in 1903 St. Vincent's parish broke ground for
a young men's clubhouse, which was home for a number of years to one of the
largest Catholic youth organizations in the city. Out in Kalamazoo, Father
Frank O'Brien dedicated an entire building to the young men of St. Augustine's
parish in 1894, complete with a gymnasium, a smoking room, and reading and
reception rooms. Detroit's Holy Redeemer parish followed suit in 1911 when it
opened a large and well-equipped recreation facility. The parish had long been
home to the Holy Redeemer Greys, widely known for their precision drill team
and for their prowess in sports. The Grey's track team took national honors in
the Catholic Amateur League in 1912 and again in 1913. "The new man, the
athletic man, is a product of our own time," Bishop Edward Kelly rather porten-
tously announced as he dedicated the recreation building at Holy Redeemer.
"The gymnasium here will give him a chance to work out his superfluous energy
under untainted conditions."[70]

Where a parish young men's club was successful, it was nearly always because
a priest invested considerable time and energy in initiating and sustaining the
activities of the group. Young men, by all accounts, tended to be wary of parish
organizations even when well-equipped facilities were available for their use. By
all means make provision for such activities as debate and dramatics, Father
Frank O'Brien advised his fellow priests in 1896, and build a gymnasium if possible, but never think that this alone will result in a flourishing young men's
organization. "Let the priest visit personally every young man in the parish, and
invite them one after another to come to the meeting." Even a functioning club
must be carefully monitored, lest its members begin to drift away or—and this
was especially likely—to neglect their religious obligations. "Have them receive
the sacraments at least four times a year. Make it your business to go after them

if they miss their Communion Sunday." It was a demanding role that Father O'Brien urged on the clergy, and the frustrations, as he admitted, might well exceed the rewards. But for Father O'Brien, as for many of his confreres, the fear that the Church was losing the allegiance of young men was so great that "youth work" took on the urgency of a crusade. It was less the illusion that young men had once been more pious than the resurgence of anticlericalism in Europe, the appeal of socialism for the young even — it was feared — in the United States, and the obvious preponderance of women in many Protestant congregations that seem to have worried a growing number of priests by the end of the century. That young women were gaining greater social freedom, that the city offered ever more alluring — and unsupervised — places of amusement simply confirmed the necessity of keeping young men under the influence of the Church.[71]

Anxieties like these were almost certainly familiar to Bishop Foley. Still, he made no attempt, in the course of his episcopate, to organize "youth work" on an interparochial basis. As a consequence, the work remained almost wholly a parish affair. There had been, to be sure, a short-lived Diocesan Union of Young Men's Societies in the earliest years of the century. But this was composed exclusively of organizations from the German parishes. A lay-initiated effort to establish a citywide association was more successful: the Young Men's Institute, later called the Young Men's Order (YMO), was founded in Detroit in 1907 and survived until 1928. Originally a branch of a national Catholic fraternity, the YMO had several hundred members at its height, most of them probably in their early twenties. It sponsored social events and, for a time, regular league play for a roster of baseball, basketball, and bowling teams in Detroit. And at least between 1910 and 1914, the group staged an annual Passion Play. "It is hoped by the young men who are charter members to make it the local Catholic YMCA," the *Michigan Catholic* explained in 1907, and the YMO was indeed remarkably similar to the YMCA in its emphasis on sports and manly piety.[72]

For all its achievements, however, the YMO was something less than a genuinely citywide association. Its membership looks to have been disproportionately middle class and, as a consequence, mainly Irish and German in its ethnic origins. The group almost certainly failed to penetrate the newer ethnic parishes. And the YMO was never as large as its organizers had anticipated. The group never managed to build the clubhouse for which it opened a public subscription in 1915. Its demise in 1928 concluded what was apparently a long decline in numbers and vitality.[73]

Like the Young Men's Order, the various parish youth groups that began with such promise in the years around the turn of the century were sooner or later disbanded. Even the flourishing St. Vincent's Young Men's Club, among the longest-lived, succumbed in 1918. But their passing did not necessarily mean that the Church was losing control of ever-greater numbers of boys and young men. Working-class boys after 1914 were increasingly likely to remain in school until their mid-teens. As a consequence, the focus of "youth work" was increasingly shifted from parish clubs to the parish school. As for young men, they did indeed remain a problem. But the lengthening years in school, coupled with a falling age at marriage, were eroding the troublesome period of restless young adulthood. Then too, there were new efforts on the part of the clergy to meet the needs of this elusive group, some of which had modest success.

For evanescent as the youth groups of the Foley years proved to be, they embodied an approach to the "young man problem" that was enduring and popular. It was this approach that informed the work of the Catholic Youth Organization (CYO) after its founding in the mid-1930s, as well as the promotion of Catholic Scouting. (The activities of the Scouts and the various units of the CYO neatly parallel those of the juvenile military societies and parish athletic clubs that were so much the vogue at the turn of the century.) The potential of this new approach was slow to be fully realized, for priests were in short supply in the Diocese in the 'teens and the twenties, and the need to build churches and schools claimed much of their attention. But by the 1920s, there were not many priests who still objected to what many of their number had once regarded as the faddish cult of muscular Christianity.

Organizations for Men

Parish organizations for adult men in the Foley years had something of the flavor that permeated the "youth work" movement. Military trappings were widely popular, organized sport increasingly so. The priests and laymen who led these groups, moreover, were apt to be earnest promoters of a disciplined and manly piety. Other developments were important too. The last quarter of the nineteenth century saw the rise of Catholic fraternal groups that were regional, even national, in scope. These increasingly displaced the modest parish benefit societies that had been so ubiquitous a feature of the ethnic congregation. As fraternal groups grew larger and richer, they came to play a more prominent role in the life of the Church. They played a significant role as well in the evolution of a genuinely American Catholicism.

Of the national fraternal groups born in this period, the best known today is the Knights of Columbus, founded in Connecticut in 1882. But the Knights had no affiliates in the Diocese of Detroit until 1898. The largest of the many Catholic benefit societies in the Diocese in the late nineteenth century was the Catholic Mutual Benefit Association, founded at Niagara Falls in 1879. Open to Catholic men between the ages of eighteen and fifty, the CMBA had fifteen branches in Detroit in 1889, and another thirty-eight in the rest of Michigan, for a statewide membership of some 3,500. Besides the usual sickness and death benefits, the CMBA afforded its members "many moral, mental and social advantages. It aims at the education of its members in integrity, sobriety and frugality," the *Michigan Catholic* explained, "and endeavors to make them contented with their sphere in life."[74]

The avowed political purposes of the CMBA, then, were conservative, and this was true of virtually all the fraternal organizations of the day, church-sponsored and secular alike. But the emphasis on equality and fraternity that characterized these groups was almost certainly a source of confidence, and even a heightened political awareness, for a good many working-class men. It is no accident that the largest trade union movement in the nineteenth century—the remarkable Knights of Labor, which enjoyed considerable strength for a time in Detroit—was modeled on the lines of a fraternal organization. The CMBA locally sponsored the usual round of outings and entertainments and by the early twentieth century was increasingly involved in organized sport. There was a CMBA baseball league in Detroit by 1914, and a bowling league as well. But it also sponsored at least occasional lectures and debates, some of them of a controversial political nature. Detroit's Branch 22 hosted a proponent of Henry George's single tax at a meeting in 1897, when memories of the late depression were fresh in the Catholic mind. "He spoke for an hour and a half and impressed his audience favorably," a member of that audience informed the *Michigan Catholic*. "The writer of these few remarks is almost persuaded to become a single tax man in future. Mr. Bawden gave a very clear explanation of how the single tax, if properly applied, would even things up, and give the poor man a fair show. Great wealth, unless controlled in this way, is dangerous to society."[75]

The CMBA, because it was so large, had a multiethnic membership in the Diocese. It was especially strong in the Irish and the German parishes—a branch had been organized at Holy Trinity as early as 1879—but there were branches in other ethnic parishes as well. A prominent layman in Kalamazoo was of the opinion in 1894 that "the CMBA came pretty nearly to the ideal of what a society should be. There should be no Irish, no Poles, no Germans, but all Americans, no matter what country they come from. The color line should not be drawn." The color line was, of course, nearly always drawn, as it continued to be for many generations. But there were occasional exceptions. A black attorney in Detroit who belonged, oddly enough, to St. Stanislaus (Polish) Church was a member of the parish branch of the CMBA when he died in 1908.[76]

Despite the "catholicity" displayed at St. Stanislaus, the CMBA had only limited success when it came to breaching the ethnic divide. The group did sponsor a wide array of interparochial activities, but these were probably mostly attended by thoroughly assimilated members. Still, groups like the CMBA were of great importance for the polyglot Church in Detroit. For they provided an arena where Catholics could broaden their social contacts and confirm for themselves the reality of a truly American Catholicism.

The most vigorous rival to the CMBA in the late nineteenth century, at least in the Diocese of Detroit, was the Knights of St. John, which had fifteen commanderies in the city of Detroit in 1889. Similar to the CMBA in its insurance provisions and the entertainments it sponsored, the group was distinguished by its military discipline, its elaborate uniforms and compulsory drill. The Knights' membership locally and nationally never approached that of the CMBA, perhaps because its discipline was so strict. But the Knights had great esprit de corps. They were a fixture of local parades, able in their colorful regalia to draw admiring notice even in a city accustomed to a vivid street life.[77]

Like the various parish military societies for boys and young men, the Knights of St. John promoted a self-consciously masculine piety. Loyal Knights battled "with their glittering swords . . . against the temptations and evils of the world, against vice and for virtue," in the words of Father Charles Reilly. The Knights aimed to stimulate in their members a visible pride in their religion and in a devout practice of it, according to J. B. Mueller, who wrote a history of Detroit's St. Boniface parish in 1894. The St. Boniface commandery of the Knights of St. John had been founded in 1887. By 1894 it had forty-five members, who had learned "to show publicly that they do not apologize for their faith, but on the contrary are proud to belong to the church." Like the members of other Catholic societies, the Knights were "required to be punctual in the performance of their religious duties." But they also played an active role in the liturgy, standing at attention in full dress uniform at important moments in the Mass — first communion at Holy Rosary in 1894 featured "the Knights with drawn and uplifted swords, at the Gospel, and again at the Elevation of the Host" — and providing a uniformed guard of honor for Eucharistic vigils and devotions. The Knights of Columbus would later play the same role in the liturgy, the effect of which, for a good many Catholics, was a pleasurable heightening of the pomp and solemnity that normally surrounded a high Mass. And it made for a prominent male presence in church, something much valued by the clergy and presumably by many of the laity.[78]

There were other national fraternal groups that were active in the Diocese in the years around the turn of the century. The Ladies' Catholic Benevolent Association (LCBA) made rapid progress in the Diocese after its founding in Meadville, Pennsylvania, in 1890. The Catholic Order of Foresters, based in Chicago, began a period of respectable growth in the Diocese of Detroit in 1893. The Catholic Benevolent Legion opened a recruiting drive in the Diocese in 1899, although with apparently minimal success. The Catholic Knights and Ladies of America, unusual in its recruitment of both men and women, had branches at the cathedral, in Holy Trinity and St. Vincent's parishes, in St. Josephat (Polish) parish, and in Sacred Heart (German) parish by 1900. (There were almost as many women as men holding elective office in these parish branches in that year.) The Knights and Ladies claimed nearly 2,000 members in Michigan in 1902, when the organization's Supreme President was a Detroiter. Finally, the Knights of Equity were active in the Diocese by the early twentieth century.[79]

The twenty years before the First World War were the great age of the fraternal organization, for commercial insurance firms had not yet cut deeply into the principal business of such groups. Still, competition for members was keen — it occasionally came even from groups explicitly forbidden to Catholics by their bishops — and sometimes assumed nearly comic proportions, although not in the eyes of those who were seriously committed to a particular organization or to the principal of fraternalism more generally. An irate member of St. Mary's parish in the village of Chelsea complained bitterly in 1900 about the damage being wreaked there by the agents of rival societies. "In May, 1890, Mr. John H. Breen, of Detroit, came here and organized a branch of the CMBA with a membership of about twenty, but we are sorry to say that the members did not seem to possess the energy and push exhibited by the ladies of the LCBA," he — or perhaps she — began. "However they got along fairly well until last summer when an organizer of the Modern Woodmen came here and took everything by storm. Some of the members of the CMBA went over to that society and amongst them (strange to relate) the worthy president of the CMBA." The anonymous informant was less disturbed by the incursion of the Woodmen, however, than by an even more recent invasion by the Catholic Knights and Ladies of America. St. Mary's parish could not support three fraternal societies; trying to do so "will only result in the collapse of them all — a result which must be patent to every one and to none more clearly than to the organizers of this rival society. But these organizers usually have a mercenary motive if they have no other, and when their branch is organized and they have the fee in their pockets, it is a matter of but very little concern to them whether the branch survives or whether all fraternal organizations may be destroyed in the parish."[80]

Out of this frenzied competition, the Knights of Columbus emerged in the dominant position shortly after the turn of the century. Although its first branch in the Diocese was not organized until 1898, the order grew rapidly there, outstripping even the CMBA in membership within just a few years. The Knights of Columbus had already had great success in the East, and their large membership enabled them to offer unusually attractive insurance premiums. This was essential to their subsequent rapid growth, but was perhaps not the only explanation for the enduring success of the organization. For the Knights of Columbus had the advantage of entering the Diocese on the eve of an unusually long period of prosperity and rapid population growth. The group's initiations and entertainments, as a consequence, exuded an aura of affluence — a happy contrast to the makeshift arrangements of the ethnic parish hall. By 1908 the Detroit Council was able to buy its first clubhouse, only to replace it in 1911 with a new building, "elegant and commodious," at a fashionable Woodward Avenue address. Cardinal Gibbons and Archbishop John Ireland, in town for the consecration of Auxiliary Bishop Edward Kelly, were among the well-dressed crowd that gathered for the formal opening. The cardinal had probably forgotten his 1891 visit to the ill-fated Catholic Club of Detroit, but others would surely have remembered and perhaps been pleased to realize how much more capable Detroit's Catholics now were of sustaining large interparochial organizations.[81]

The Knights of Columbus claimed some 11,000 members in Michigan by 1914. The order figured prominently by then in the efforts of the clergy to promote among men a more disciplined sacramental practice. The clergy were perhaps especially heartened by the growing popularity of the organization's annual retreat, which drew respectful coverage from the secular as well as the Catholic press. Bishop John Carroll of Helena, Montana, preached the retreat in 1915, when some 1,400 men were in attendance — a splendid demonstration of virile piety, according to the *Michigan Catholic,* and an example to the whole community. The organization's leaders were ready, by this time, to test the political waters. The Michigan State Council of the Knights of Columbus issued, in 1915, what may have been its first resolution on a matter of foreign policy. This concerned the persecution of the Church in Mexico, which the Michigan Council denounced in characteristically American terms as a violation of liberty of conscience: "And be it further resolved, that this State Council records its strong opposition to the recognition of any government which does not grant to the people absolute liberty of conscience."[82]

The Knights of Columbus was indeed regarded—by the bishops and clergy as well as its own leaders—as an important Catholic voice in politics. This was especially true after the First World War, when the Knights gained prominence as dispensers of services and entertainment to American soldiers at home and abroad. But the Knights of Columbus was never large or inclusive enough to satisfy the purposes of the hierarchy and the more militant clergy. It was the Holy Name Society, in the years after 1900, to which the bishops increasingly turned to advance their devotional and political agendas. By 1911, the bishops of New York and Boston as well as Hartford, Newark, Pittsburgh, Covington, and Trenton had decreed that every parish in their jurisdiction should have a Holy Name Society. And at least in the East, massive parades of Holy Name men were by this time a familiar aspect of devotional—and political—life. The organization was relatively slow to develop in the Diocese of Detroit, in part because the necessary episcopal leadership was lacking. But in Detroit as in most other dioceses, the Holy Name Society eventually proved to be a powerful means of promoting male piety, of increasing Catholic influence in local politics, and of bridging the ethnic divisions in the Catholic community.

The Holy Name Society, promoted for centuries by the Dominicans, was represented in the Diocese of Detroit as early as the 1880s. St. Aloysius parish had a Holy Name Society by 1887, St. Augustine's in Kalamazoo had one by the early 1890s, and the pastor at Holy Redeemer parish was able to announce in 1898 that "the Holy Name Society has been established in this parish for the suppression of profane language." These early societies seem to have been purely devotional in nature. A Holy Name Society ought to include every man in the parish, Kalamazoo's Father Frank O'Brien explained in 1896, as he recommended the society to his fellow priests as "the better all-around society for men," and for this reason a pastor should not "exact too much—in terms of money or time—remember that laboring men have small resources and work long hours." A Holy Name man must pledge to abstain from "cursing and improper language," and encourage others to do the same. He should "receive the sacraments . . . six times a year" and attend the funerals of deceased members. But his pastor should not impose on him further, either by way of long meetings or participation in various parish affairs. The Holy Name Society was not a social club, according to Father O'Brien. Its purpose was bringing men regularly to confession and communion, and encouraging reverence for the name of Jesus in a world increasingly inclined to question the divinity of Christ.[83]

By the early twentieth century, however, a growing number of priests and bishops envisioned a political as well as a religious role for a society that had the potential to organize vast numbers of Catholic men. Even in 1899, the Holy Name men in Father O'Brien's parish had seen fit to hold a special meeting for the purpose of protesting the rumored desecration of Catholic churches by American soldiers in the occupied Philippines. The Kalamazoo branch seems thereafter to have regarded as part of its mission the defense of Catholic interests. At a meeting in 1913, for example, the members denounced a local Republican club for sponsoring an anti-Catholic speaker—"Republicans must understand that insulting Catholics will not bring votes to their ranks"—sent a resolution to their state representative with regard to a bill on divorce law reform, and deplored the opening of theaters on Sunday. What was happening locally in Kalamazoo had already assumed diocese-wide proportions in the northeastern states, where more and more bishops saw in a mobilized Holy Name Society the first line of defense against anti-Catholicism and against manifestations of radicalism as diverse as the preaching of socialist doctrine or the public endorsement of birth control.[84]

A well-defined political role for the Holy Name Society evolved only gradually in the Diocese of Detroit, and much more slowly than it had in the East. The number of parish branches increased steadily after 1900: there were thirty of them in 1914, when the Detroit Diocesan Union of Holy Name Societies was formed to foster the growth of the movement. Evidently it succeeded: the Diocesan Union, which had claimed 7,000 members at its founding, had grown to "perhaps 30,000" at the close of 1917. But the astonishing growth in its membership did not persuade the more cautious of its leaders, or the Chancery, that the organization should flex its political muscle in Detroit as it had been accustomed to do in Boston and New York. The union's first public demonstration, a "monster parade" scheduled for the autumn of 1916, was canceled just months before the event for fear that a show of Catholic strength so close to a national election would have anti-Catholic repercussions locally. The Chancery was at least in part responsible; perhaps the aging Bishop Foley himself had ruled against the parade, for he had long favored an accommodating course in local politics. Not every Holy Name man was pleased by the decision. M. J. Tobin, an influential figure in the early days of the Diocesan Union, was bitterly disappointed "that after two years' preparation, our 'procession' must be called off at the very last moment." Why did Catholics have to fear the reactions of "a few unprincipled bigots," he wanted to know. "Have we no spirited men in our ranks who are willing to stand up for our privileges and rights? Are we always to be in the background?" The moderates prevailed, however. It was not until the summer of 1920 that the Holy Name Society in the Diocese of Detroit staged its first mass rally, and then for the clearly defensive purpose of protesting a referendum aimed at closing all parochial schools in the state.[85]

The leaders of the Holy Name Society were not reluctant, however, to promote what they regarded as purely religious interests in an overtly political way. The same men who saw dangers in Catholic parades at election time were warm supporters of a movement to persuade merchants and theater owners to close their establishments from noon to three on Good Friday. The effort dates from 1916, when Holy Name men at Blessed Sacrament parish in Detroit and St. Augustine's in Kalamazoo initiated campaigns to have neighborhood shops and businesses close during "Tre Ore" services on Good Friday. The Diocesan Union made the work its own in 1917, and by 1919 it was said that on Good Friday "more than 16,000 merchants closed their places of business from 12 to 3." By the early 1920s, Good Friday closing was a fact of commercial life in Detroit and in many other places in the Diocese.[86]

Just what non-Catholics thought of this surprisingly successful campaign is not clear. In Kalamazoo, according to a Catholic spokesman in 1916, "the efforts of the Holy Name Society are greatly appreciated by Non-Catholics." And insofar as the divide between churchgoers and the indifferent was greater than the divide between Catholics and Protestants, this may well have been true in Kalamazoo and other towns as well. "Mr. Poole of Ionia" met with widespread support in 1920 when he directed the Holy Name campaign in that small town. "He said that a general committee had waited upon the mayor," the *Michigan Catholic* told its readers, "and that in accordance with the mayor's proclamation every saloon and store of every description would be closed tight on Good Friday." But in Detroit, the Protestant clergy were reluctant for many years to cooperate with the annual Good Friday closing campaign. A few of them were perhaps repelled by the "ritualism" of the Tre Ore observance; most were worried about growing Catholic political strength in the city.[87]

Catholics, of course, did not see the Good Friday campaigns as remotely political. But in a population as religiously diverse as that of Detroit, the movement inevitably had political content and at least the potential for exacerbating ethnic and religious antagonisms. That the leaders of the Holy Name Society could not see this is perhaps indicative of the security they felt as members of the political mainstream, despite the anti-Catholicism about which they often complained. For they saw themselves as part of a majority Christian community, much as those Protestants did who sought to have the state enforce temperance and Sunday observance. The Holy Name Society, needless to say, never sought any but voluntary compliance in its Good Friday campaigns. But the fear of a Catholic boycott could not have been far from the minds of most businessmen. And the methods and strategies of the avowedly apolitical Good Friday movement were those of masterly politicians. The Holy Name Society annually deployed hundreds of men throughout the Diocese to canvass merchants, to distribute "closing cards," to lobby local officials and the press. The Good Friday campaigns schooled Holy Name men in the ways of politics, and paved the way for their organization to assume a more aggressive political stance in the 1920s.

Already by 1918, the society represented a vehicle for Catholic political assertion the likes of which had never been seen in the Diocese of Detroit.[88]

Despite its growing political importance, however, the greatest success of the Holy Name Society was always its ability to bring large numbers of men to the sacraments on a regular basis. "The society has been largely instrumental in promoting frequent Holy Communion among men," the *Michigan Catholic* claimed, looking back in 1931 at nearly two decades of Holy Name work in the Diocese. "Twenty or thirty years ago pastors were gratified if they induced the majority of the men to turn out three or four times a year. Now large numbers approach the Eucharistic Banquet every month and many of them weekly." Open to every man in the parish and having usually the largest membership of any parish organization, the Holy Name Society gave its members the courage they needed to be devout in an unbelieving world. Hundreds of men marching to communion was a fine confirmation of piety as a manly virtue, according to the *Michigan Catholic,* and "an inspiration to those inclined to be indifferent or backward." Indeed, the editor, like a good many priests, preferred that men receive communion with the society rather than with their families.[89]

The Holy Name Society also contributed, albeit in a modest way, to the breaking down of ethnic barriers among Catholics. The Diocesan Union promoted the society in virtually all the ethnic parishes, and by the early 1920s it was well established among them. Holy Name men were urged to the same standards of piety and personal conduct regardless of their ethnic origins or social class, and the union periodically sponsored meetings and rallies where men who ordinarily had no contact with one another were brought together and asked to regard themselves as fellow soldiers in "the bodyguard of Christ." The delegates to the Detroit Diocesan Union who assembled at Holy Trinity school in the summer of 1916 tendered a cordial welcome to new members from St. Maron's (Syrian) parish and St. Peter Claver's parish for blacks. Eight men from St. Peter Claver's attended the meeting, at a time when even nominally integrated assemblies were rare. Six months later the Diocesan Union held a quarterly meeting at St. Peter Claver's parish hall. For a good many delegates, this meeting was surely the first visit in years to what had become a heavily black section of the city. Since the Holy Name Society was primarily a religious organization and since its purposes could be served only by a large and heterogeneous membership, the discrimination that Catholics endorsed for their fraternal groups could not be countenanced within its ranks. And so in a limited way the Holy Name Society contributed to the slow process of delegitimizing racial and ethnic prejudice in the American Church.[90]

Organizations for Women and Girls

If the clergy displayed initiative and imagination in the Foley years when it came to organizing men and boys, the same cannot be said of their work with women and girls. Father Frank O'Brien, full of lively suggestions for attracting boys and young men to parish societies, had nothing to recommend for girls but annual sales of their needlework. "In this way will our real workers for the future be trained." Nearly all the clergy assumed that women were by nature more devout than men, and certainly they did not seem to need special inducements to attach themselves to parish societies. It was the rare parish where the altar or Rosary society for women was not the most active of parish organizations.[91]

Even more heartening to the clergy, perhaps, was the popularity of religious sodalities among adolescent girls and young women in the late nineteenth century. The sodalists at SS. Peter and Paul's parish in Detroit were numerous enough to fill their own pretty chapel when thirty-five new members were inducted in the spring of 1888. An earnest Jesuit praised the sodality on that occasion as "one of the bright links which binds the soul to heaven," and urged the young congregation "to be faithful in their profession as clients of the Immaculate Mother." The Young Ladies' Sodality in the parish had 320 members by 1897. At St. Vincent's parish in Detroit, the Young Ladies' Sodality was large and active enough in the mid-1890s to warrant twenty-eight elected officers. And at Our Lady of Help in Detroit, energetic sodalists raised enough money in 1893 to build a chapel in honor of the Blessed Virgin. "To desire is to do with the young ladies of the congregation," according to the *Michigan Catholic*, "and after it was decided that the chapel should be built, a delegation called on Father Wheeler and told him so. There was nothing left for the genial pastor to do but to locate the site for the proposed edifice." With evidence of success at every hand, most priests concluded that young ladies, unlike their restive brothers, required rather little in the way of clerical time and attention.[92]

In the decade before 1914, however, a growing number of priests began to complain that girls were no longer attracted to parish sodalities as readily as they once had been. The scattered parish reports that survive from these years do indicate that sodalities for girls were not growing nearly as fast as the Catholic population of the Diocese. But the clergy were surely responding in part to changes they saw in the world around them. For a greater sexual freedom seemed quite suddenly to be possible for girls, and this called into question the comfortable assumptions that had guided the clergy in previous generations. It was hard, in short, for priests to see in these embryonic "new women" the naturally pious creatures their mothers were supposed to have been.

Still, the clergy were evidently less alarmed by the rebellious young woman than by the rebellious young man, or perhaps an unmarried clergy is at a particular disadvantage in situations of this nature. For there were no innovations in parish organizations for girls comparable to the military and athletic societies being promoted for boys and young men. A "business woman's club" was formed at Holy Redeemer parish in Detroit in 1914, but apparently on the initiative of a group of young working women in the congregation. The club provided an employment bureau to its members, and offered "opportunities for advancement along educational lines" as well as the usual social activities. It eventually became part of the League of Catholic Women. A handful of pastors did encourage the female graduates of their parish high schools to form alumnae associations, which had as their purpose the continuing education of women, but of the most genteel and politely literary sort. The largest of these groups seem to have been those sponsored at the turn of the century by SS. Peter and Paul's, St. Vincent's and Holy Trinity parishes in Detroit.[93]

Adult women in the Foley years continued to join the usual parish organizations in large numbers. But there were two developments in the late nineteenth century, both of them lay initiated, which indicate that an important minority among Catholic women now envisioned their lives in less limited terms than their mothers and grandmothers had done. Catholic women began in the 1890s to join benefit societies in large numbers, and in that same decade they were instrumental in organizing and sustaining a surprisingly large number of parish groups devoted to adult education. In different ways, these developments in women's church-related organizations reflect the growing sense of their members that women not only possessed a clear individuality apart from the family but that they might in good conscience enlarge the boundaries of "woman's sphere."

That Catholic women should be increasingly anxious to buy their own life insurance does not seem, at first glance, to be especially noteworthy. Life insurance in the nineteenth century often provided little more than the wherewithal for a respectable funeral. But until the end of the nineteenth century, life insurance was widely regarded as something appropriate only for men, on whom, as the principal breadwinners, the welfare of the family depended. The typical working-class family could hardly see the logic of paying insurance premiums for a wife and mother, despite the importance of her labor in the home. Thus when Catholic women rushed to join the several national benefit societies established for their sex in the 1890s, they were asserting their worth as contributing family members. They were no more likely than their mothers had been to be at work for wages—not, at least, if they were married. But their understanding of their own importance had evidently reached a point where they wanted the formal recognition of their place in the family economy that insurance conferred.

The Ladies' Catholic Benevolent Association (LCBA) was far and away the largest of the women's insurance organizations in the Diocese at the close of the nineteenth century. The association was founded in 1890; its longtime national president, Mrs. Elizabeth McGowan, was a former Buffalo teacher who parlayed her administrative abilities into a career in insurance and genteel reform. "She is identified with a number of other societies," the *Michigan Catholic* explained in 1901, "and is a member of the board of women managers of the Pan-American exposition." The LCBA made rapid progress in the Diocese after a first branch was organized in St. Vincent's parish late in 1890. Nearly every Irish and German parish in Detroit had a branch by 1900; there were thirty-five branches in the city by 1915, with a membership of 7,000, and another 5,000 members in the rest of the state. The membership even in 1915 was probably predominantly Irish and German, these being the groups from which the bulk of the more assimilated Catholics in the Diocese came. But after 1901, when Branch 629 of the LCBA was founded at St. Albertus (Polish) Church in Detroit, the order made considerable headway in the newer ethnic parishes. Among the Detroit parishes sending delegates to the 1917 convention were St. Joachim (largely French-Canadian), San Francesco (Italian), Our Lady of Sorrows (Belgian) and five of the city's Polish parishes.[94]

The LCBA was a significant development for Catholic women not simply for the insurance it provided. It was a national, Church-sanctioned organization run exclusively by laywomen — perhaps the first such in the history of the American Church. The sixth biennial convention, held in Detroit in 1901, introduced local delegates and guests to the poised and confident Elizabeth McGowan, presiding with ease over the 600-member assembly; to Miss Alice Blaney, editor of the LCBA's house organ, the *Fraternal Leader;* and to the exciting world of politics. Mrs. McGowan was being challenged that year for the presidency of the organization and, as the *Michigan Catholic* told its readers, "there will be a good-natured fight for the office of supreme medical examiner, many of the ladies wishing to give this office to a lady physician instead of a man as heretofore." The Detroit delegation was promoting the candidacy of Dr. Anna T. Dunn-Roe, a prominent figure in LCBA circles locally. A native of Detroit, Dr. Dunn-Roe had had a career as a music teacher and organist at Holy Rosary Church before taking a medical degree at the University of Michigan in 1894. She had subsequently established a successful city practice, become a bicycling enthusiast (her book *The Wheel for Women and Girls* "earned many commendations from other physicians") and kept up with her music. "She also finds time for recreation and is a member of Rounds Ladies' Orchestra, playing the viola and violin." Dr. Dunn-Roe was not appointed supreme medical examiner of the LCBA — the newly elected board of trustees reappointed the male incumbent — but local feelings were assuaged by the election of Mrs. Felice Giradot of Detroit as supreme treasurer.[95]

Like the LCBA, the reading circle movement in the Diocese of Detroit had its genesis in the 1890s. And like the LCBA, the movement reflected important changes in the mentality of assimilated Catholic women. Some parish reading circles offered their members the opportunity for serious and sustained intellectual work; the best of them functioned essentially as a substitute for the higher education still denied to the vast majority of middle-class girls. And even the less rigorous groups must be seen, in the context of late-nineteenth-century Catholic America, as evidence that a growing number of Catholic women imagined their lives in terms that would have been wholly alien to their immigrant grandmothers.

If the reading circle movement had its origins in the growth of the Catholic middle class, it was also the product of the optimistic liberalism that prevailed in certain segments of the American Church at the end of the nineteenth century. The confidence with which Bishop Foley and his more celebrated episcopal allies looked to the future of the Church in the United States was shared by many of the more assimilated Catholics in the Diocese, a portion of whom were eager not only to claim for themselves a fully American identity but to claim a more active role in the Church as members of an educated laity. The Lay Catholic Congress, convened in Baltimore in 1889, provided a first national forum for this small but growing lay elite, whose aspirations were perhaps best set forth in a sermon preached in the course of the Congress by Archbishop John Ireland. "The world is in throes; we are assisting at the birth of a new age," Ireland told his congregation. "All things which may be changed, will be changed, and nothing will be tomorrow as it was yesterday, save that which emanates directly from God, or which the Eternal decrees to be permanent." Rightly understood, it was a time of great possibilities. "Despite its defects and its mistakes, I love my age. I love its aspirations and its resolves." But there were dangerous intellectual and political currents rising, and the Church was increasingly on the defensive, especially in Europe. "Is there a need of the Church?" Ireland asked bluntly. "Is she not, rather, a barrier to the best ambitions and the progressive march of humanity? A reply is urgent." He did not doubt, of course, that "the Church is divine and belongs to all ages"; needed, however, was an imaginative new approach to an era hostile to traditional authority but hungry for spiritual truth. "Religious action to accord with the age must take new forms and new directions," and the laity might have to be in the vanguard of reform. "Let there be individual action. Laymen need not wait for priest, nor priest for Bishop, nor Bishop for Pope." The entire sermon was indeed "a very uncommon discourse coming from the mouth of a Catholic prelate," as the *Michigan Catholic* noted in an approving editorial, having printed the text of the sermon in full. But uncommon as it was, it caught the spirit of the age, at least as that age was experienced by a small but significant minority in the Catholic population.[96]

Laywomen, of course, found it harder than laymen to translate their Christian principles into action to accord with a revolutionary age. The lay Catholic congresses that met in 1889 and 1893 were open to male delegates only. Some of Detroit's most prominent laymen — notably Major Henry Brownson — were active in planning the 1889 congress, and the image locally of the "new Catholic laity" was very much a male affair. Nor were women able, for the most part, to bring their principles to bear directly on politics, for Michigan women in the 1890s possessed the suffrage only in school elections, and Catholics had an uneasy relationship to the public schools and proposals for their improvement. But women could certainly work to broaden the intellectual horizons of the Catholic community, something that Archbishop Ireland had particularly urged in his celebrated sermon. An educated laity was the best assurance of principled reform in the Church and in the world, according to the archbishop. And a liberally educated laity was essential, in Ireland's view, to the ultimate conversion of America to Catholicism.[97]

The reading circle movement of the 1890s, then, was rooted in the desire of certain laywomen to play an expanded role in the Church. It was rooted too in their wish to be seen as the intellectual equals of their Protestant counterparts. (The growth of the Catholic Study Club of Detroit, in the view of one member, "successfully refutes the charge that Catholic women are not fin de Siecle.") By defining themselves as intellectual leaven, it need hardly be said, "reading circle women" were claiming for their sex a role that Catholic tradition had nearly always assigned to men.[98]

Ironically, the reading circle movement was not initially meant to be a female domain. The founders of the Catholic Education Union (1889) and the Columbian Catholic Summer School (1892) envisioned a nationwide network of parish reading circles that would provide continuing education to men and women alike. But men were apparently not much interested. Most of the students at the Catholic Summer School in its early years were women, as Detroiters learned first-hand in 1900 and again in 1901, when the school was briefly located in the city. The great majority of local registrants in both years were women, and a sizable proportion of the men attending from the Diocese were priests. Of the reading circles founded in the Diocese between 1890 and about 1910, moreover, most were women's organizations. Only two Catholic men's organizations in the Diocese in these years are known to have had a primarily intellectual purpose. The Cathedral Lyceum, founded in 1894 and drawing its membership in part from the students at Detroit College, was for perhaps six years a lively center of discussion and debate. ("The question to be argued is: 'Was the Career of Napolean Bonaparte Productive of More Good than Evil?'" the *Michigan Catholic* informed its readers of the Lyceum's inaugural debate, in which the opponents of the emperor carried the day.) The heavily German Alumni Society of St. Joseph's Commercial College in Detroit was longer-lived. Apparently founded in the 1890s, its members were still gathering in 1907 for monthly debates on such diverse topics as municipal ownership of public utilities and the segregation of Japanese pupils in the public schools. (The critics of segregation won handily.) But on the whole, the middle-class Catholic men of the Diocese seem to have been indifferent to the reading circle movement. Absorbed in the business of getting a living, they were, for the most part, not much impressed by purely academic achievement.[99]

For a fair number of women, however, the parish reading circle proved to be a means of self-discovery and intellectual growth. There were at least twelve women's reading circles in Detroit by 1900, and an unknown number in the rest of the Diocese. Some provided their members with at best a smattering of decorative education—lectures on "The Madonna in Art" or "Shakespeare as a Catholic Writer." But others approached the standards of a first-rate college in the rigor of their course of study. The two most interesting were the Cathedral Reading Circle, founded in 1894, and the St. Leo Reading Circle, founded shortly thereafter. The cathedral group was said to have "80 or 90" members by 1897; the size of the group at St. Leo's is unknown. Both concentrated mainly on historical study, devoting their early years to an extraordinarily detailed examination of Church history. "The programme for the ensuing year embraces a continuation of Church History from the year 590 AD with the additional study of Church Liturgy," the secretary of the St. Leo Circle announced in the fall of 1898. A typical weekly meeting in 1899 featured "an instructive paper on the pontificates of Victor II, Stephen X, and Benedict X" by Mrs. Lareau, as well as a paper on "The Causes of the Crusades" and the usual discussion of current events, "the subject being 'Was Dreyfus Innocent or Guilty?'" The Cathedral Reading Circle took "Church History of the First Seven Centuries" as its principal topic during 1896, having the previous year explored Roman history, as well as pre-history and the theory of evolution. Father Joseph Hallissey provided a lecture on the latter topic, "clearly demonstrating," according to a circle member, "that the Catholic Church in her teachings in no way conflicts with the deepest scientific research." But the usual procedure was to have papers written and read by the members themselves. This surely enhanced the educational value of the weekly sessions, and the members of the more ambitious circles were obviously proud of their achievements. "A continuous course in the history of the Catholic Church has been pursued and the Circle has now reached the time of the Royal Supremacy and Henry VIII," a spokeswoman for the Cathedral Circle informed the *Michigan Catholic*. "Interspersed with these historical papers have been papers on the life and work of classic poets and authors and readings from many of their works. Not content with this, the Circle has also had prepared book reviews of many volumes, both those included in the church history course and those outside of it."[100]

The members of the reading circles were almost certainly from prosperous families and had at least some high school education. Some were married, but probably a majority were young and single — women of college age, whose own daughters would one day be among the first generation of students to attend Catholic women's colleges in large numbers. Whether their hunger for education led some of these women to broader feminist sympathies we do not know, but the reading circles of the period offer occasional evidence to this effect. Members of the Cathedral Reading Circle took part in a debate in 1895 with the Cathedral Lyceum, the women defending female suffrage, the men arguing against it. "No pen could do justice to the earnestness, the gracefulness and eloquence of the brilliant young orators," the *Michigan Catholic* glowed. "We went there with a firm determination to preserve our opinion regarding the subject, but came away thinking perhaps the ladies were maybe right after all." The Catholic Study Club of Detroit, always more eclectic in its curriculum than the Cathedral Circle, sponsored discussions in 1914 on women's suffrage, on the legal status of women, and on the contemporary woman's club movement. The Study Club had given an emotional welcome to Archbishop Ireland in 1899 when he spoke in the club parlors in support of higher education for women. ("Especially did he emphasize the desirability of women taking up the study of history, in order to be able to discuss mooted questions of historical importance," an anonymous reporter noted approvingly, "and he especially called attention to the fact that in the Roman Catholic Church there were no rules prohibiting such work among women, as some people fancied.") Equal access to higher education had long been a rallying cry of the organized women's rights movement, and if that movement was disproportionately Protestant in its leadership and its active ranks, there were obviously Catholic women by the late nineteenth century who shared at least some of its goals.[101]

The reading circle movement in the Diocese—and in other parts of the country as well—lasted little more than a generation. The circles at the cathedral and at St. Leo's disbanded at some point after 1911, and by 1921 the *Michigan Catholic* could identify only the Catholic Study Club of Detroit as a survivor of a movement which had once "blossomed like a green bay tree." And even the Catholic Study Club had by this time departed from the rigorous regime that had characterized the most ambitious circles of the 1890s, sponsoring guest lecturers and various social and charitable events rather than requiring research and writing of its members. The *Michigan Catholic* quite predictably blamed the decline on the younger generation. "Our young people spend altogether too much of their precious time in dancing, card playing and motoring." But a more likely explanation is the growing availability of higher education to Catholic girls. St. Mary's College in Monroe, which became in 1910 the first Catholic college for women in the Diocese of Detroit, might plausibly be regarded as the successor to—and, in part, a consequence of—the reading circle movement.[102]

Parish government

An educated laity, contemporary commentators often say, is almost bound to question the legitimacy of hierarchical authority in the Church. There were those in the late nineteenth century who thought so too. "They do not like this usage and do not see the sense of that; this idea is behind the times and that impracticable," complained Father Michael Dowling in 1893, having in mind, apparently, the better-educated members of the laity as he had encountered them in Detroit and in the pages of the Catholic press. "One objects to certain kinds of music in the church or thinks there is too much millinery in the sanctuary; another thinks that fasting is obsolete and that clerical celibacy should be abolished, together with all religious orders." The editor of the *Michigan Catholic,* himself an advocate of a wider lay role in the Church, nonetheless worried on occasion that there were educated Catholics who were too anxious to usurp clerical prerogatives as they campaigned for an "updated" Church. He was particularly outraged at the liturgical reforms advocated by the pseudononymous "Layman" in an 1888 *Catholic World.* "'Layman' . . . looks upon the Sanctuary railing as a 'barrier' which should be removed as quick as possible," the astonished editor reported, "so as to permit 'the people' to run in and take part in the *performance* of the sacred functions, if not in the *administration* of the Sacraments." The last fifteen years of the century were a yeasty time in American Catholicism, when an educated elite among the laity argued reform with a freedom reminiscent in some ways of the 1960s. But however annoying they may have been to the clergy and the more conservative laity, these fin de siècle reformers were too few and spoke to too small an audience to have much effect on the

Church in the United States. And this would have been true, in all likelihood, even without that stifling of dissent which came in the wake of the condemnation of modernism in 1907.[103]

The real challenge to clerical authority in these years, ironically enough, came not from the educated laity but from the immigrant working class. Their concerns were not doctrinal or disciplinary or even liturgical, save where they wished to defend traditional liturgical practices against "reform." They wanted, rather, to preserve the greatest possible autonomy for the laity in the governance and administration of the parish. And here they had considerable success. Apparently a substantial number of parishes in the Foley years continued to elect their committeemen, rather than have them nominated by the pastor and appointed by the bishop, as diocesan regulations required. Most pastors, it seems, did not object to this. Since committeemen normally collected the pew rents and handled parish finances, it was essential that their authority be seen by the congregation as wholly legitimate. That the parish often functioned better as a limited democracy than the monarchy which diocesan regulations imagined it to be was a fact almost never commented on, but one that was recognized even at the Chancery. Save for prohibiting saloonkeepers to serve as committeemen — a reform that apparently dates from 1912 and was probably a concession to rising prohibitionist sentiment in Michigan — Bishop Foley did little to interfere with democratic modes of parish government where these existed in his Diocese.[104]

There were, however, occasions when democratic norms led to conflict between the pastor and his congregation, or at least a portion of it. This happened most frequently in new immigrant parishes, for reasons that have already been discussed. (It was largely due to heavy immigration in the Foley years that interest in lay government of the parish remained as high as it did.) "He induced a committee of two to wait on me last Sunday and tell me that as they (people) paid for the church it was theirs by right," wrote Father Henry McManus in 1908 of the "ring-leader of the malcontents" in his heavily French-Canadian mission at St. Clair, "and if they could not do what they pleased with it in the matter of making the repairs to the furnace they would quit coming to church or supporting the church, and as they bluntly put it 'as the Bishop and I got our bread and butter from the people it behooved us to try and please them.'" The problem for Father McManus, as for other priests in his situation, was not that most parishioners were anxious to do battle with their pastor, but that the appeal to democratic norms was hard for the clergy to argue against. That the Church as universal institution was a monarchy was easy for most Catholics to accept, for it had little meaning in the context of their daily lives. (Contraception, to all appearances, was not yet a major source of division between Rome and the mass of the laity.) But it was often difficult for the ordinary Catholic to see why the parish he supported with his hard-earned wages should not be governed to some extent by "the people." "This is the idea of many of them in regard to obedience, honesty and decorum," the unhappy Father McManus admitted, for his "ring-leader" had an apparently substantial following. "It actually seems as if the poor priest was there only to say Mass and preach the Gospel," an irate partisan of the pastor at St. Wenceslaus (Bohemian) informed Bishop Foley in 1890. The priest in question had only recently assumed charge of the parish, which was governed by a strong lay committee. "The Priest can do nothing without their consent. If he wants anything he must ask them if he may get it. They even hold sway over the Sisters in charge of the parish school. . . . Why they even appoint the women and men who are to do the washing for the Priest and the cleaning of the church they even go in after both Masses and count the collections."[105]

No group, however, was more tenacious in its defense of lay authority in the parish than the Poles, who came to the Diocese in enormous numbers during the Foley episcopate. The very enthusiasm they brought to parish-founding and church-building contributed to their determination to protect a strong role for the laity in parish affairs. Bishop Foley, chastened by the denouement of the Kolasinski crisis, must have been a bit uneasy when he received in 1899 a second importunate petition from a lay committee anxious to establish a Polish church in Wyandotte. "We are not accorded the same privileges as our German and Irish brethren," they had explained in their first appeal, referring to what they saw as discriminatory treatment of Poles in the city's existing parishes. Their first request for permission to found a parish had not been granted, but the petitioners were not discouraged. "In that comparatively short space of time we have not been idle," they told the Bishop in their second appeal.

> We have secured one [of the] most beautiful and desirable church sites in this Diocese, free of charge. We have in our possession the signatures of 125 of the most wealthy and influential [P]olish citizens of Wyandotte, who are ready at any time, to contribute the necessary sum for the purpose of erecting an edifice. We have chosen a name for our proposed church — it is to be "The Church of Our Lady of the Scapular" but we leave that to the consideration of your excellency. We also wish to submit to you the name of the priest whom we desire appointed as our pastor.[106]

Bishop Foley shortly thereafter granted permission for a Polish parish in Wyandotte — one might say that he had little choice but to do so — and he was willing to have the parish named in honor of Our Lady of Mt. Carmel. But he was not willing to allow the parishioners to choose their own priest, something all too reminiscent of the Kolasinski affair. The Wyandotte Poles, however, were willing to concede this point, and were ready by Christmas to lay the cornerstone for their new church and school. "Nearly every Polish society in Detroit was in attendance," the *Michigan Catholic* noted of the gala event, "and the Lake Shore road ran four special trains to accommodate the crowd."[107]

Differences between the Chancery and the Polish congregations were not, unfortunately, always so amicably resolved. Throughout the years of heavy immigration, there were conflicts between the Chancery and the Polish laity over the extent to which elected committees might exercise authority in the parish. Tensions on this point were sufficiently great that two congregations of the Polish National Catholic Church were established in Detroit during the Foley episcopate. (The Polish National Catholic Church differed from its Roman parent chiefly in matters of church governance; its parishes enjoyed considerable autonomy.) Resurrection parish in Detroit was initially organized in 1917 as an "American-Polish Catholic Church," very much on the model of a Polish National Catholic congregation. During its "independent" days, the parish was governed according to by-laws that called for the election of the church committee by the men and women of the congregation, who were also the legal owners of all church property. The pastor, who "must be a Pole," was to be elected by the church committee and might be dismissed, in the event of his having committed a "punishable violation or crime," by a two-thirds vote of the congregation.[108]

The Chancery generally responded to parish conflict in a cautious way, supporting the beleaguered priest but slow to intervene directly. For all that his critics had to say about his arrogance, Bishop Foley was much less precipitous than Bishop Borgess in his dealings with angry members of the laity. And his essentially passive strategy was usually successful, although the priest involved might well sustain some damage to his ego before the trouble had run its course. "I am tired of all this; I have done enough for them," Father Clemens Krebs complained of his parishioners at St. Agatha's parish in Gagetown in 1895, a minority of whom had been campaigning for Krebs's removal in extraordinarily aggressive language — but for reasons that are not apparent from the documents that have survived. "If possible, procure me a place far away from here," he pleaded, a request that Bishop Foley did not grant until 1901. But when the dissident parishioners were numerous and well organized, they sometimes brought the Chancery to heel. This happened at St. Albertus parish in 1891, when many parishioners withheld their pew rents to force the removal of a pastor who, they claimed, was "a Pole by name only, but by nationality a German." No compromise was possible, the parishioners maintained, for "as an old Polish proverb says: So long [as] the world will stand no true Pole will become a true brother of a German." Bishop Foley, appalled at the intolerance that fueled the affair, refused at first to remove the priest, but in the end acceded to the demands of the angry parishioners. The parish could not function without funds, nor could the bishop close it with Father Kolasinski's "schismatic" congregation just blocks away. Members of St. Mary's (German) parish in Detroit withheld their pew rents in 1893 with similar results. They were protesting the appointment of a diocesan priest to their parish, which had for most of its history been in the charge of religious orders. Bishop Foley's determination to support the pastor at St. Mary's, who was a conscientious priest in excellent standing, eventually gave way to economic realities, and St. Mary's was assigned to the Holy Ghost Fathers, in whose care it has remained to this day.[109]

The strangest of the many parish disputes that troubled the Foley years took place not in Detroit but in the village of North Dorr. Like the Kolasinski affair, the conflict at North Dorr reveals radically different understandings on the part of the laity and the Chancery as to what constituted the legitimate exercise of authority in the Church, although in North Dorr the bishop was at least formally the victor in the case. Organized in 1864, St. Mary's parish in North Dorr served a mostly German farming population that lived in both Kent and Allegan Counties. In 1882, the Catholics of Kent County became part of the newly established Diocese of Grand Rapids, and the parish at North Dorr found itself divided by the new diocesan boundary, which followed county lines. This had little practical meaning, however, until 1896, when the church at North Dorr burned to the ground and the Bishop of Grand Rapids decided that the moment was right to establish a new parish only a few miles from North Dorr. All communicants of St. Mary's who lived in the Grand Rapids Diocese were directed to become members of this new parish.

There was immediate resistance, however. Many of the longtime members of St. Mary's refused to attend any other church, arguing that "we have acquired an inviolable right as Catholics to remain members of St. Mary's Church North Dorr, on account of the money invested with a great sacrifice to ourselves and to our families" in the parish church and school. The North Dorr pastor, worried about the loss of nearly half his congregation, seems to have encouraged their intransigence, and he himself appealed to the Apostolic Delegate for restoration of the original parish boundaries. The appeal was rejected, and the pastor was subsequently transferred, apparently at his own request. Bishop Foley declined to replace him, and ordered St. Mary's parishioners to attend the church at New Salem, a village about two miles distant from North Dorr.[110]

If Bishop Foley had hoped that removing the priest would eliminate resistance at North Dorr, he was much mistaken. Like Father Kolasinski's supporters, a number of St. Mary's parishioners from both sides of the diocesan boundary formed themselves into a lay-led congregation. The teacher at St. Mary's school served as the principal leader of the group, conducting Rosary services on Sunday and even an occasional novena. At least some of the members of this congregation were convinced that the teacher enjoyed the tacit approval of Bishop Foley and that the bishop would soon send a priest to rebuild the North Dorr church. But as the months passed, doubts began to grow. "I hant heard a mass since Father Buchsenmann is gone and a good many more like myself," wrote a troubled parishioner late in 1897. Evidently concerned about the state of his soul, he urged the bishop to make clear to the people that the teacher had no ecclesiastical authority. "If we people will see the Bishop['s] signature what to do they will give in an[d] do there duty."[111]

Bishop Foley seems to have dealt with the dissident parishioners with remarkable patience, even after "a riot equalled only by the rioting Polanders of Bay City" occurred at North Dorr in March 1898. A former parishioner of St. Mary's had attempted to have the body of her husband removed from the parish cemetery and tranferred to the Catholic cemetery in Grand Rapids, where she now lived. "A drunken mob stopped the proceedings," according to a horrified priest who lived in a neighboring village. "Swearing at you, the Bishop, at me and all authorities, they opposed even the Health Officer Dr. Coburn of Dorr." (The dead, as well as the living, apparently, were expected to be loyal to St. Mary's.) Despite the violence, a few days after the riot Bishop Foley decided to send a new pastor to North Dorr. His assignment was to rebuild the church there, but only after the people had agreed to honor the duly established parish boundaries.[112]

But by this time, the resistance had acquired a legitimacy of its own. A large majority of the congregation refused either to recognize the new parish boundaries or to approve the dismissal of their former leader as teacher of the parish school. Both were conditions on which Bishop Foley insisted. The hapless pastor quickly lost what little moral authority he had possessed in the community. "Mr. J. Fetz of Jamestown died the day before yesterday and they buried him today under my eyes in this cemetery," he informed Foley late in June, having reference to the funeral of a man who had lived in the Grand Rapids Diocese. "Mr. Quirin Thomas of Byron had to conduct the funeral services. He received the corps at the church door sprinkling holy water on it and taking it into the church. After singing and praying there he (Mr. Quirin Thomas) blessed the grave in the cemetry in the presence of a great multitude." Lay-led services had recently resumed, moreover, and the parishioners had begun the construction of a new church, despite Bishop Foley's having forbidden them to do so.[113]

At this point, Foley withdrew his priest and initiated proceedings to establish legal title to the church and the land on which it stood. The Michigan Supreme Court in 1900 granted him the victory he sought, but by this time what was left of the dissident congregation at North Dorr was functioning as an independent entity. There were Catholics in the Grand Rapids Diocese still refusing in 1903 to attend what had long been designated as their rightful church. They "will never be led to do anything else," admitted a priest who served in the vicinity, "they will rather sell their farms to Hollanders." The schoolteacher who had been so influential during the early years of the dispute was as late as 1905 conducting what he called a Catholic school at North Dorr and leading devotions there. The members of his congregation apparently still regarded themselves as Catholics, for they received the sacraments at least on occasion with a Polish congregation in the village of Hilliards. "It's the people who go to Hilliards for baptisms, weddings and first Communion that you find participating in the schismatic services the Sunday after," according to a local priest. But here the record ends. The parish at North Dorr was never reestablished; how long a remnant of its former members remained in open defiance of their bishop is simply not known.[114]

The resistance at North Dorr was initially inspired by practical as well as philosophical considerations. A divided congregation would be too small to maintain a school, the parishioners argued, nor could their reduced number easily finance the rebuilding of the parish church. But more fundamentally at issue were conflicting visions of the parish, and by extension, conflicting visions of authority in the Church. The bishops of Detroit and Grand Rapids, supported by the Apostolic Delegate, assumed that the parish was a creation of the local ordinary, who might fix its boundaries at will, providing, of course, that he ensured that his people were able to receive the sacraments. That the creation of a new diocese had divided a parish was unfortunate, but since the Vatican had refused in 1888 to enlarge the Grand Rapids Diocese to include the entire parish of North Dorr, there was nothing to be done but to enforce the new parish boundaries, now that the Bishop of Grand Rapids had quite legitimately decided to establish a parish in the area. It was simply a matter of obedience to Church law.

The parishioners at North Dorr, however, believed that a parish was more than a legal creation. The parish was a living community, and its boundaries were dictated, not by episcopal fiat, but by the loyalties and memories shared by members of the congregation. The parish community, moreover, included the dead as well as the living. Those members of St. Mary's who lived in the Diocese of Grand Rapids could not sever their ties to the parish, a trustee of the North Dorr church explained to Bishop Foley in 1899, because "they have their dear beloved relatives slumbering here. How would I feel, for instance, if I where living on that side. I have my GrandFather, my Father, my Mother, my three Sisters are resting here. Now in case I were living on that side, Would I not long to go to the Church where my dear ones are slumbering and where my forefathers has offered up so many Lords prayers." To insist that a diocesan boundary be honored at the expense of these sensibilities was plainly wrong, as it was wrong to forbid a priest to administer the sacraments to persons who lived outside his diocese. "Did Christ speak so to his Apostles. No, he said unto them, go ye in all lands and preach the gospel to all nations." The resistance at North Dorr was inspired by profoundly religious sentiments, according to Trustee Schneider. These were not men and women in rebellion, but good Catholics who had been wronged by episcopal authority and who were bound in conscience to resist the directives coming out of Detroit and Grand Rapids. "There is no Sunday to[o] stormy we meet in the Schoolroom and pray The Rosary. . . . We pray for our Holy Father the Pope, for the Bishops, for all pastors of souls, for the living and the dead we pray to the Almighty God to enlighten the heart of our Bishop, that he may some day greet us with a good pastor that will remain with us a long time." Indeed, as far as Schneider was concerned, the rebuilding of the North Dorr church, in defiance of Bishop Foley's orders, was but additional testimony to the lively faith and true Catholicity of the congregation.[115]

CHARITY AND SOCIAL SERVICE

The Foley years saw significant progress in the development of lay-initiated charities. This was due in part to growth in the Catholic middle class. It was also due to the heady political climate that prevailed between the turn of the century and the First World War. National political discourse in these years was increasingly dominated by demands for reform, and was at the same time suffused by a buoyant optimism. That educated men, and women too, could provide the leadership necessary for humane reform within the confines of the existing political system was a conviction widely shared by middle-class Americans, and one that spurred the more idealistic among them to work for change through avenues as diverse as party politics and neighborhood community centers. Women figured prominently among these active idealists, especially at the local level. Certainly in Catholic Detroit it was women who played most of the principal roles in lay-run charitable activities.

The modest scope of lay Catholic charities in the 1890s provides a useful benchmark for measuring progress in the years after 1900. A number of parishes in that decade did support societies devoted to assisting the poor. But these groups were typically short-lived, and had only the most limited financial resources. Most seem to have been women's groups, like the society that met regularly at Holy Trinity parish to sew clothes for the deserving poor. "They investigate all cases," the *Michigan Catholic* assured its readers, "and never misplace their charity." The St. Vincent de Paul Society, the principal charitable organization for Catholic men, apparently had only two parish conferences in Detroit in 1890, one at St. Joachim's and one at SS. Peter and Paul's. The latter conference, large and active by the standards of the day, spent $187.21 for the relief of 126 persons during 1890, as well as providing clothes for first communion to children of the parish poor. "It likewise performs the very desirable work of preventing imposition, by professional beggars, on the members of the parish," according to the conference report for that same year. At nearby St. Mary's parish, and perhaps at other German parishes as well, there was a men's society of some years' standing "for the relief of the sick, poor and orphans" of the parish. The tradition of parish charity was strong among German Catholics in the Diocese, and the men in German parishes were more likely than most to be active in parish organizations.[116]

The devastating depression of the mid-1890s does not seem to have caused much increase in the number of parish charitable societies, not even in Detroit, where Catholic institutional life was more fully developed than elsewhere in the Diocese. Detroit's Catholics were mostly working-class, and at the depths of the depression as many as one-third of the city's labor force may have been unemployed. The burden of even token relief was simply too great for most parishes to bear. Detroit, moreover, had by the late nineteenth century developed an unusually generous system of municipal poor relief, and many Catholics were accustomed to turn to the city rather than the parish in times of need. Indeed, it seems that Catholics looked with particular favor on municipal relief, for the Protestant-dominated Detroit Association of Charities was the major source of private assistance in the city. Perhaps the preference among Catholics for municipal over private relief retarded the development of Catholic charity locally, although this is only speculation.[117]

If the depression did not immediately spawn new charitable organizations, it may well have shaken the complacency of many middle-class Catholics and thus prepared the ground for a more vital interest in charity and social reform. The depression of the 1890s was the most severe in living memory, and the appalling destitution it created could not be dismissed as the consequence of intemperance or improvidence among the poor. Those active in Catholic charities did not cease to believe that it was possible, and necessary, to distinguish the deserving from the undeserving poor. But Catholic charity after the turn of the century was increasingly characterized by an awareness that poverty was caused by social injustice as well as personal weakness, and that its alleviation required more than token assistance and good advice. The growing scope and sophistication of Catholic charity in these years was the fruit of this new point of view.

An early sign of the vigor that increasingly marked charitable work after 1900 was the appearance in 1906 of the St. Mary's Aid Society, which seems to have been the first truly interparochial charitable group to have been organized in Detroit. "The society has as its object the relieving of distress among the poor and aged of the city, irrespective of creed or past condition," the *Michigan Catholic* informed its readers, and women and men from any parish in the city were invited to join. Men, however, were permitted to be honorary members only, which meant that they paid dues but left the work of "friendly visiting" to women, and left the organization's leadership in female hands as well. The society claimed 125 members late in 1907, coming "from almost every parish in the city," and in the spring of 1908 the ranks had grown to more than 200. The society's resources were probably modest, based as they were on small monthly dues and the proceeds of card parties, but the organization had at least succeeded in demonstrating the possibility of conducting lay charity on a citywide scale. And this was important, for as Detroit's parishes became more segregated by class, the burden of parish charity fell ever more disproportionately on those least able to bear it.[118]

More ambitious in its purposes than the St. Mary's Aid Society, if not at the outset an interparochial organization, was the Weinman Settlement Association, also founded in 1906. It was named in honor of Jesuit Father Ferdinand Weinman, an assistant at SS. Peter and Paul's Church from 1898 until his death in 1906, and a tireless evangelist to the city's immigrant poor. During his years at SS. Peter and Paul's, Father Weinman enjoyed the assistance of a remarkable group of parish women. (Among them was Josephine Van Dyke Brownson, whose Catholic Instruction League grew from her work as a catechist at the Jesuit church.) Affluent and socially prominent, for the most part, this small band of women was also alert to reforming currents in the world around it. They succeeded, in 1908, in opening the first Catholic settlement house in Detroit's long history. The Weinman Settlement, as it was known, served a mainly Italian and Syrian neighborhood on the city's near east side, providing its families with clubs and classes, and eventually with a playground, a modest gymnasium, and a free clinic. The success of the settlement led the members of the Weinman Association to expand their membership beyond the confines of the Jesuit parish, in the hopes of eventually establishing a network of Catholic settlements in the rapidly expanding industrial slums of Detroit. Accordingly, they rechristened themselves the Catholic Settlement Association in 1911.[119]

The first major undertaking of the rebaptized association, however, was not a second settlement house but a boarding home for single working women. The Barat Club was opened early in 1913, a response in part to the critical shortage of housing in Detroit. But the project was also a product of the "white slave panic," as contemporaries called the near-hysteria that prevailed in American cities in this period with regard to prostitution. A woman alone in a city, it was widely believed, was a woman in danger, and the members of the Catholic Settlement Association wished to do what they could to provide such women with protection. "During the summer of 1913," an association report tells us, "a resident from the Weinman Settlement met three trains daily and was able to render much valuable assistance to women and girls travelling alone." Later that same year, the Catholic Settlement Association opened a downtown center for working women, where inexpensive meals could be had, and where classes were offered in subjects as diverse as English and "esthetic dancing." By 1915, the association was conducting employment and lodging bureaus at this downtown site, and had "secured a delightful cottage near Orchard Lake, where a large number of young ladies expect to spend their vacation."[120]

Presumably because their work could no longer be adequately described as settlement activity, and perhaps because of some nascent feminist consciousness, the Catholic Settlement Association at its annual meeting in 1915 became the League of Catholic Women, by which name the organization is still known. It was a genuinely interparochial group by 1915, and the largest Catholic charitable organization in the history of the Diocese. It did not remain an exclusively charitable organization, to be sure; by the mid-1920s the League of Catholic Women was heavily involved in activities of a social and cultural nature. But in its earliest years, the league reflected the most humane impulses of the Progressive era, and was passionately committed to social amelioration. An appeal for new members in 1918 addressed itself to women who were not afraid to confront the hard realities of city life, and pleaded especially for members willing to work with the juvenile court as probation officers and to oversee the placement of children in foster homes. "We are now co-operating with the St. Vincent de Paul Society in the care of homeless children and find that for this work we are in absolute need of more paid workers and additional accommodations . . . also we would like to take care of delinquent girls when released from the Detention Home and House of the Good Shepherd until a good permanent home can be found for them." At least some Catholic women, it seems, were responsive to liberal currents in the larger society, and quite capable of appropriating for themselves an active role as citizens.[121]

The growth of the League of Catholic Women in Detroit was paralleled — albeit on a more modest scale — by the growth of the St. Vincent de Paul Society after the turn of the century. There were at least six parish conferences of the society in Detroit in 1899, when a Particular Council was organized in the city to coordinate the work of the society locally and encourage its expansion. That expansion was slow to come about, but by 1913 there were eighteen parish conferences in the city, with an active membership of about 200 men. It was the brief but severe recession of 1914, however, that seems to have been the critical stimulus to the growth of the society in Detroit. By the close of 1915, there were thirty parish conferences in the Diocese, all but a few of them in Detroit. Many of the 1,100 men whom the society claimed as members in that year had apparently been recruited into new and existing parish conferences to help relieve the misery that came in the wake of widespread unemployment in the auto industry.[122]

The growth in membership—and the greater revenue it represented—had allowed the Particular Council in 1912 to inaugurate a "child caring department," whose purpose it was to provide probationary supervision and foster care for delinquent youths from Catholic families. Working closely with the juvenile court and various public and private agencies, the child caring department quickly became the most visible and the most generously funded work of the society locally, in large part due to the growing problem of delinquency in what was now a large and disorderly city. The department represented a departure from the Vincentian tradition of friendly visiting in the parish, for it was under the direction of a trained social worker—the first appointee was a woman, as were subsequent additions to the staff—and its conduct was as much affected by the canons of that nascent profession as it was by Vincentian ideals. The expansion of the paid staff, moreover, had the effect of giving women an unprecedented leadership role in an organization long the exclusive province of Catholic men.[123]

The Society of St. Vincent de Paul, like the League of Catholic Women, drew its members mainly from the ranks of the Catholic middle and upper-middle classes—a population that had grown substantially in Detroit by the early twentieth century. Conditions peculiar to the Diocese made it possible then for an educated lay elite to exercise considerable authority in organizations of this sort. (We have already noted the administrative drift that characterized the latter part of the Foley episcopate.) Both the League of Catholic Women and the Vincentians were the products of lay initiative; an overburdened clergy seems to have played mainly honorific roles in these organizations, and the Chancery followed a policy of benign neglect in their regard. It was laity too who established, in 1917, the first central body to coordinate the work of the various Catholic charitable groups in Detroit. The Federation of Catholic Charities, later the Bureau of Catholic Welfare, was initially organized under the auspices of the Knights of Columbus. Responsibility for its administration, however, soon passed into the hands of its longtime director, Elizabeth Kelley Frase. By this time it no longer seemed in the least remarkable that a lay woman should hold what was in effect a policy-making position in a major Catholic charitable organization.[124]

The vitality of Catholic organizational life in Detroit in 1918 is one measure of the changes that had taken place in the course of the Foley episcopate. The Catholic middle class had grown considerably in size and confidence, its members more and more likely to be thoroughly assimilated, belonging to parishes where social class rather than ethnicity defined the boundaries of the community. If the city continued to receive large numbers of immigrants from abroad, its Catholic population nonetheless achieved in the Foley years a greater degree of respect and acceptance than ever before, and gained a greater political influence. Outside Detroit, especially in the larger towns, we see a similar growth in the size and sophistication of Catholic organizations, and in the confidence with which the Catholic middle class moved in the larger society.

There were other significant developments too. Nearly all Catholics were introduced in the Foley years to a new standard of piety. And a surprisingly large number of them changed their religious behavior because of this: they went more frequently to confession and communion, and made the devotional life of the Church in the Diocese more lively than ever before. Their more disciplined religious practice made possible the distinctive Catholicism that came to fruition in the middle decades of the twentieth century—a Catholicism characterized by its intensely sacramental focus, its clericalism, its scrupulosity. The Foley years, then, were a transitional time in the history of Catholic spirituality in the United States, and a chapter of immense importance in the history of the American Church.

9

CATHOLIC SISTERS, CATHOLIC SCHOOLS

When the bishops who gathered in Baltimore in 1884 for the Third Plenary Council of the American Church affirmed their commitment to a separate system of parochial schools, they ensured that American women religious would be primarily a teaching population. And they perhaps unwittingly ensured that Sisters would play a major role in the shaping of the American Catholic community. This was especially true in those dioceses where, as in the Diocese of Detroit, the Chancery was slow to bring the schools under effective control. Without that control, and without a clergy trained in pedagogy, it was Sisters who made the principal decisions with regard to the contents of Catholic education and the methods employed in Catholic schools. This was a decision-making power of no small consequence, for Catholic schools have had, historically, a profound effect on Catholic spirituality and on the worldview of believers, especially the more devout. Indeed, it is not too much to say that no population has had a more decisive impact on the history of the American Church than that of its many teaching orders.[1]

The growth of those orders, so essential to the expansion of parochial education, had various causes. Foremost among them was the conviction, shared by many Catholics and certainly by the more devout, that the religious life was truly the "better part," worthy of respect and admiration in this world and a long step toward salvation in the next. That the clergy and religious were for many years a better-educated population than the mass of the laity helped to perpetuate this mentality, which has its origins in Catholic sacramental theology, and which the Tridentine liturgy itself did much to bolster. The increasingly disciplined character of American Catholicism, evident in most parts of the country by the late nineteenth century, was an additional support, as indeed was the growing ability of Catholics to separate themselves—in their own schools and colleges and service institutions—from the larger society. Until quite recently, then, the realities of American Catholic life served to legitimize the consecrated life as something fundamentally nobler than the life of the laity. And the idealism and enthusiasm of their numerous young recruits gave the religious orders an élan that carried them safely through the 1950s, despite the better-educated and perhaps more restive laity coming of age in that decade.

But the religious life was not only the nobler choice. It was also a decision for extended education and professional work—opportunities, both of them, that were closed to the vast majority of Catholic girls in the years before the Second World War. Educational standards varied from one religious order to the next, but it was nearly always true that teaching Sisters were among the best-educated people in the parish. The Polish Felician Sisters in the late nineteenth century provided probably a less extensive training to their recruits than any order in the Diocese, sending young Sisters out to teach with as little as a year or two of high school education. But even this modest preparation marked the Sisters as part of an elite, for they served an immigrant community where the fourth grade was often the limit of children's schooling, and where many adults, especially women, were illiterate. In 1907, it has been estimated, teaching Sisters made up fully two-thirds of the professional workers in Detroit's Polish community. And as that community grew richer, the Sisters were able to raise their own educational standards. The first high school in a Detroit Polish parish was begun in 1915; in 1917, the Felicians sent the first of many contingents of Sisters to take degrees at the Teachers' College of the Catholic University.[2]

Those orders that drew their members from the more affluent reaches of the Catholic population provided a more extensive education than the struggling Felician community. The young woman who entered the convent of the Immaculate Heart of Mary Sisters, the largest teaching order in the Diocese, would even in the nineteenth century have received the equivalent of some college training and been thoroughly grounded in the order's distinctive approach to pedagogy. In 1906, moreover, the IHMs began sending one postulant a year to the University of Michigan to take an undergraduate degree—this despite the school's reputation among Catholics as an outpost of radicalism and free thought. (By sending postulants rather than professed religious, the order was able to thwart the Chancery's clear desire to bring an end to the practice.) The "Michigan connection," which continued for some twenty-five years, was a sign of the order's commitment to rigorous training for at least the ablest of its members. And at a time when the more prestigious Catholic colleges would not permit women to matriculate, it was a provocative affirmation of women's intellectual capacities and their claims to higher education.[3]

When the Catholic University opened its summer school for teaching Sisters in 1911, it was thus a vindication of sorts for the IHMs. Five members of the order attended the first session, and when the program was expanded soon after into a full-year curriculum at the university, the IHMs regularly sent sisters to study there. Most IHMs, however, continued to receive their training at the motherhouse in Monroe, where a summer school had long served to supplement the academic work done in the novitiate. Over the years, the scope and content of the courses at this school became broader and more sophisticated; the school had evolved, by 1915, into a respectable substitute for college training. By this time, of course, the IHMs had opened a college for women, and the order was granting degrees of its own.[4]

When a young woman considered the religious life, then, she did not necessarily think in terms of narrowed horizons or suppressed individuality, despite the convent's rigid discipline. A bright, ambitious girl might easily endow the religious life with an aura of romance and adventure. The convent meant study and travel, it meant an admired professional role, it meant the heroic spiritual life. It was the domain of powerful female personalities, and a sphere where women held positions of authority. Perhaps the world by contrast sometimes seemed the narrow place, for few Catholic girls before the 1920s could look forward to college and fewer still could reasonably expect to have careers. A working-class girl was lucky if she entered high school, and unusual even in 1920 if she stayed there long enough to earn a diploma. The years around the turn of the century, moreover, were a time when the advances made by a handful of American women in higher education and the professions had captured the attention of a broad national audience. Even the daughter of immigrant parents might sense that her own life need not be patterned on her mother's, although her vision of independent womanhood was probably a limited one — confined, quite possibly, to the example of the Sisters in the parish school.

And so there was a steady increase, especially after 1900, in the numbers of young women who sought admission to religious orders in the Diocese. The Felicians, who accepted girls as young as sixteen years of age, admitted 314 candidates to the novitiate at their Detroit motherhouse between 1901 and 1909. The IHMs added 84 professed members between 1895 and 1905, and another 160 over the next ten years. Other orders grew as well: the number of teaching Sisters employed in the Diocese increased in the course of the Foley episcopate from 236 in 1889 to 901 in 1917. This growth made possible the founding of forty-two parish schools between 1891 and 1917, and the expansion of many existing parochial schools to include some or all of the secondary grades. Detroit and the larger towns in the Diocese could lay claim by 1917 to something like a comprehensive system of Catholic schools, nearly all of them taught by religious. But there were still seventy parishes in 1917 — most of them rural or village congregations — that did not have schools of their own. Indeed, the proportion of parishes maintaining schools had not changed appreciably since 1891, when 59 percent of the parishes in the Diocese had done so.[5]

The Foley years saw real progress, nonetheless, in the availability and quality of parochial education in the more populous parts of the Diocese. And if this was due in good measure to growth in the ranks of the teaching Sisters, it was also due to the increased willingness of Catholic parents to support parochial schools. This willingness was in part a result of Chancery policy. Bishop Borgess, as we have seen, had as early as 1877 instructed his priests to deny the sacraments to parents who sent their children to public schools "without good and sufficient reasons." Disturbed, apparently, by the reluctance of some priests to enforce this regime, Borgess had subsequently made attendance at the public schools a reserved sin, absolution for which could be secured only upon application to the bishop.[6]

When Bishop Foley took charge of the Diocese late in 1888, he was evidently reluctant to break with the unyielding stand of his predecessor. Father James Savage told his congregation at Detroit's Holy Trinity church in 1890 that "the Bishop at a meeting of his consultors held last week decided to reserve absolution to himself in the case of any Catholic sending his child to the public schools." Since Father Savage was a diocesan consultor, he was presumably rightly informed, although the archival record is otherwise silent on the question. Late in 1892, however, Archbishop Francesco Satolli, acting as the Pope's representative, issued a controversial statement on Catholic education, which forbade the American bishops to deny the sacraments to parents simply because they had used a public school. If Bishop Foley had indeed embraced his predecessor's stern policy, he was now—and quite suddenly—obliged to revise it.[7]

The Satolli statement aroused anxiety among many priests and bishops, for they feared that parents would read it as permission to abandon the Catholic schools. Detroit's Father James Doherty, for one, thought the priests of the Diocese should respond to the statement by adopting a uniform—and unbending—policy on school attendance. But the priests who assembled in Detroit for a deanery conference in the fall of 1893 were unable to agree on a common course of action, some being more lenient than others when it came to defining acceptable reasons for attending a public school. Father Doherty and other "strict constructionists," however, had by this time been preaching for months on the necessity of Catholic school attendance. Father James Wheeler, firing a last salvo before the advent of a new school year, denounced as a dangerous fallacy "the impression that Catholic parents need not send their children to schools conducted under the auspices of the Church."[8]

But by the 1890s, there were substantial numbers of Catholics who were prepared to support sectarian schools without the threat of ecclesiastical censure. Bishop Borgess had done his work well, and most of the priests who served under him had come to accept his views on the need for Catholic schools. They in turn had urged their parishioners to regard parochial education as something essential to the life of faith—to see support of the parish school as an obligation no less binding in conscience than attendance at Sunday Mass. Not all Catholics were persuaded, but a goodly number of the more devout seem to have embraced this view. By the late nineteenth century, the more disciplined religious practice that was apparent in a growing portion of the Catholic population was accompanied by—had indeed largely given rise to—a growing moral commitment to parochial schooling. And this was evident among even those assimilated Catholics who had no need to look to the parish school as the means by which a particular language and set of cultural loyalties might be passed to the next generation.

The growing commitment to parochial education was presumably the reason that Col. John Atkinson, Detroit attorney and prominent layman, was unable to rally his coreligionists to what he had hoped would be a popular campaign against the Catholic school. Atkinson had apparently been encouraged to act by the publication in 1891 of a controversial pamphlet on education by Father Thomas Bouquillon. Bouquillon, professor of moral theology at the Catholic University, argued that the state possessed a legitimate responsibility for education and had rights in this regard that were equal, in most circumstances, to the rights of parents and the Church, and that might, on occasion, enjoy priority. His was by no means an attack on the parochial school. But his willingness to broaden the area in which the state might properly determine education policy alarmed many defenders of parochial schooling and gave heart to those who, for various reasons, doubted the wisdom of a separate system of Catholic schools. Colonel Atkinson, for his part, read Father Bouquillon as endorsing a parent's "inalienable right" to choose freely between parochial and public schools, and he was ready to argue that Catholics had compelling reasons to prefer state education. Accordingly, he arranged for his views to be made known in a lengthy interview that appeared in the spring of 1892 on the front page of the *Detroit Evening News.*[9]

Atkinson emphasized primarily the social and economic disadvantages that Catholics suffered, in his view, because of the very existence of parochial schools. Separate schools increased prejudice against Catholics and made it hard for them to be elected or appointed to public office. "The alleged opposition of his church to public schools is used as an argument against him," Atkinson noted of the Catholic candidate, "and is often decisive in close contests." Children in the parochial schools, separated from non-Catholics, were prevented "from becoming acquainted with those with whom they must do business and associate in later years. Many of the most valuable friendships of our lives are formed in the school-room." The mass of the Catholic population, moreover, was condemned to poverty because of the financial burden of school support. And the cost of maintaining schools imposed a nearly insuperable burden of anxiety on American priests. "They become chronic beggars. Overwork often makes them almost unfit for the sacred duties of office." Far better, Atkinson believed, to devote the resources of the Church in America to the work of evangelization, and let the public schools produce Catholic men "well prepared to win material dividends in this life."[10]

Atkinson, himself a figure in local Democratic politics, was articulating what he took to be the concerns of more affluent Catholics in the Diocese, who were anxious at this point about a resurgence of anti-Catholicism in local and national politics. And he apparently assumed that these same Catholics shared his confidence that their children's faith and morals would not be compromised by attendance at the public schools. He, like most Catholics of his generation, had attended the public schools and his recollections were happy ones. "I look back to my own youth and memory recalls from among my schoolmates pure hearted boys and girls who belonged alike to all denominations. I cannot now say that any one denomination had anything to boast of over the others." And it was absurd, in any case, to imagine that the survival of Catholicism depended on parochial schooling. "I assume that catholicity is reasonable, that it is supported by unanswerable arguments, that Christ is with his church and will remain with it to the end of the world." The time was right, then, for articulate members of the laity to voice their objections to parochial education, especially since priests "are by their very position doomed to silence. But if laymen express themselves freely and the great men who adorn the American hierarchy find an intelligent, strong public sentiment behind them, they will remove the hindrances which confront catholics in the race of life." The Colonel assured the *News* that many Catholics in the Diocese shared his views. Indeed, he counted Pope Leo himself as a friend of the public school.[11]

The public response to Atkinson's rallying cry, however, was curiously limited and almost entirely hostile. Of the five "leading laymen" and two priests subsequently interviewed by the *News,* only Michael Brennan, a Detroit attorney, was at all sympathetic, although each of the respondents acknowledged that parochial schools imposed certain hardships on the Catholic population. Brennan was an admirer of Archbishop John Ireland, and hoped that his tolerant views on schooling might one day prevail throughout the country. Catholics, Brennan thought, would be well advised to place their schools under full state supervision and limit religious instruction to the afterschool hours, in exchange for which they might reasonably claim state financial support. But even Brennan was not prepared to call for the abolition of separate schools for Catholics.[12]

As for the *Michigan Catholic,* which presumably spoke for Bishop Foley as well as its lay editor, Atkinson's challenge to the parochial school was nothing less than an assault on the Church. The paper's editorial campaign against the Atkinson position was brief but exceptionally bitter—a warning, perhaps, of what local laymen might expect if they joined the Colonel in public criticism of parochial education. Atkinson was pilloried for what could most charitably be regarded as his ignorance. Abolishing the parochial schools would not end the assaults of what the paper called "the devil, in the form of Protestant prejudice." On the contrary: his Protestant minions "would insist that the celibacy of the clergy be abolished; and auricular confession would follow; and then the Mass." The editor, however, suspected that Atkinson's real motives had to do with his own political ambitions; these, the editor believed, had so distorted the Colonel's moral sensibilities that he was unable to see his arguments for the sheer opportunism they were. "The chief duty of man is to put money in his purse and to so fix things that Protestants will never refuse to vote for a Catholic when he wants to go to Congress. In other words, Catholics, from the Pope down to Col. Atkinson, should avoid the prejudices of non-Catholics by abolishing the Catholic Church." The anonymous priest whose attack on Atkinson appeared in the *Michigan Catholic* was less inclined to dismiss him as a venal politician than as an unprincipled "liberalizing" Catholic, typically eager to gain acceptance for Catholics "by making Catholics as like to Protestants and unbelievers as possible." But those Catholics who understood their faith and valued it rightly knew that the "chief merit" of the parochial school "is that in religious principles and practice it makes Catholics as unlike as possible to Protestants, infidels and in-differentists." And in any event the issue of parochial school attendance had al-ready been decided by the hierarchy. "On this subject the stage of discussion is past and the stage of obedience has been reached." If the bishops were still con-sidering what relationship Catholic schools might bear to the state, this was a discussion to which the laity had nothing to contribute. "As it is eminently a re-ligious question, pertaining to faith and morals, it cannot belong to the laity to decide."[13]

Whether Atkinson had expected a groundswell of lay support for his stand against the parochial school we simply do not know. He was, by all accounts, a pragmatic politician, skilled at reading the public mood. Even if he sought mainly to ingratiate himself with Protestants as a friend of the public school, he must have assumed that his stand would not offend Catholics, on whom local Democrats depended heavily at election time. Whatever his initial expectations, however, Atkinson was apparently chastened by the actual response to the *News* interview, and he refrained thereafter from public pronouncements on the school question. When he died in 1898, the *Michigan Catholic* noted approvingly that despite his views, the Colonel had sent each of his children to Catholic schools. The schools of the Diocese had by this time weathered the most devastating de-pression of the century. Their survival was eloquent testimony to the willingness of many Catholics to bear the burden of school support, Colonel Atkinson's ob-jections notwithstanding.[14]

But if a substantial portion of the Catholic population had embraced the pa-rochial school by the end of the century, there were still Catholics who chose state schools for their offspring. Colonel Atkinson claimed in 1892 that only 40 percent of Detroit's Catholic children attended parochial schools. This figure is almost certainly too low: parochial school pupils made up about 23 percent of the total school enrollment in Detroit in 1887, which indicates that well over half of the city's Catholic youngsters were attending a Catholic school in that year. Still, contemporary testimony in the late nineteenth century points to many chil-dren who were schooled outside the parochial system. Some of them had no pa-rochial school to go to. Parishes like Holy Rosary and St. John the Evangelist, located in the early 1890s on the thinly populated fringes of the city, were not yet able to support schools. Other parishes had schools that were too small for their large and growing populations. This was especially true after 1905, when Detroit began its years of unprecedented growth. "There is scarcely a Catholic church in the city that is not crowded to overflowing at nearly all Masses on Sundays," the *Michigan Catholic* noted in 1917, calling for more churches and schools to be "erected at once," but prudently declining to criticize a Chancery that had for some years now failed to take action to meet the needs of this enor-mous population.[15]

The limited capacity of the parochial schools, however, accounts for only a portion of the Catholic children who attended the public schools in the 1890s and after. Many parents objected to the cost of parochial schooling, which was indeed a burden for working-class families. Bishop Foley apparently did what he could to maintain "free schools," where the entire congregation, rather than the parents alone, bore the cost of school support, and for a time this policy met with some success. Of the fifty-eight schools in the Diocese in 1892, thirty were said to be "free," although this would not rule out the solicitation of "voluntary" contributions of "school money" from the parents. The many schools taught by the IHMs were partially supported by revenues from private instruction in music, which by the 1890s was usually provided by at least one Sister in each school. But by 1914, when the rising cost of educating Sisters caused the IHMs to request that a more generous portion of the "music money" be returned to the order, there were few schools in the Diocese where tuition was not required. And no matter how nominal it was—teaching Sisters in the Foley years were paid only $200 a year—tuition was a burden that some Catholic parents simply refused to bear.[16]

That these parents were generally less attached to the Church than the parents of children in parochial schools is not an unreasonable supposition. Some were partners in mixed marriages. (An obstinate Protestant husband was sufficient reason to absolve a woman whose children attended the public schools, according to Bishop Foley in 1911, by which time a papal decree had once again made public school attendance a reserved sin in American dioceses.) Others were little more than nominal Catholics. Still others were Catholics who, although believing Christians, were unwilling to adopt a perspective that set Catholics against the rest of the world and made the Church, in the persons of its clergy and religious, the primary agent of discipline in the lives of the faithful. This latter group surely included certain ethnic Catholics whose ambivalence about the institutional Church derived from the troubled history of church-state relations in Europe. Italians in the Diocese of Detroit, like Italians in other American dioceses, were for many years less likely to use the parochial schools than Catholics of any other ethnic group. Detroit's first Italian parish dates from 1898, when San Francesco Church was built by a mostly northern Italian congregation. But not until 1912 did the parish open even a modest school, and that in space rented from the now-declining Sacred Heart (German) parish. San Francesco's parishioners did not build a school of their own until 1923.[17]

There were some Catholics, even in the nineteenth century, who declined to use the parochial schools on the grounds that they were academically inferior. This concern could hardly have been widespread in a mostly working-class population, but it was nonetheless the cause of a certain defensiveness on the part of the clergy. "The standard of our parochial schools is quite equal to that of the public," Father Savage told his Holy Trinity parishoners in 1890, "and there is no reason why Catholic parents should not send their children to the parochial schools." He was probably not far wrong, at least with regard to the quality of Catholic education, which did indeed improve over the course of the Foley episcopate. The decentralized system of the Foley years was, it is true, characterized by wide variation in the quality of schooling offered: the Sisters of one teaching order might be far better trained than those who taught in a neighboring parish, and physical facilities varied according to the size and wealth of the congregation. "We have 93 children, litterally packed into one schoolroom," the pastor at St. Clement's parish in Centerline told the Chancery in 1897. "That this hampers the efficiency of the teachers you will readily understand." The larger city parishes, on the other hand, had by this time invested in stoutly built facilities that were fully the equal of those in the public system. St. Vincent's School, the pride of Catholic Detroit in the 1890s, "has fourteen commodious rooms for the students in regular studies and four rooms are devoted to the cultivation of music and art," according to the *Michigan Catholic*. "Any . . . sorehead who thinks Catholic schools not up to the standard of public schools, might be convinced to the contrary by a visit to Rev. Father Doherty's school." Classes were large, however, even in the wealthier parishes. Only four of the nineteen parochial schools in Detroit in 1889 had one teacher for every forty-nine pupils. (The situation had improved by 1917, when half of the forty-one parish schools in the city had a student-teacher ratio of less than 1:50.) The Polish schools nearly always had the largest classes, for Poles, despite their poverty, used the Catholic schools more heavily than any other group. St. Casimir's School in Detroit had one teacher for every seventy-five pupils in 1889. And in 1917, Hamtramck's St. Florian's School had only nine Sisters for a student population of 750—a ratio of one teacher for every eighty-three children.[18]

Parishes outside Detroit were likely to have smaller classes, at least in the late nineteenth century. Nearly half of the thirty-nine schools in what the Chancery liked to call "the country" had at least one teacher for every fifty children in 1889. But in the rural and village schools, attendance was often irregular. Fifteen of the thirty-nine pupils at Dearborn's St. Alphonsus school missed at least half the 166 days taught in 1895, and the school was almost certainly not unusual in this regard. (Eleven-year-old Lizzie Sullivan, who walked four miles to the parish school in the village of Hubbardston, was sometimes obliged to go instead to the more convenient district school, "when the roads are bad and the weather is cold," as she explained in 1892.) The village school was also unlikely to have enough children to permit the school to be organized according to grades. "There are two rooms in the school," young Julia Beauvais wrote from her home in Anchorville in 1894, "one for the junior class and one for the senior." But in these respects the public schools in rural districts were not much different, nor indeed were the public schools in the immigrant neighborhoods of Detroit likely to be significantly less congested than their parochial counterparts. And if the public school teacher was apt to be more extensively educated than the members of many teaching orders, there was no guarantee that she could speak, as the Sisters often did, the language that her pupils spoke at home.[19]

Public and parochial schools alike, then, varied in quality according to the wealth of the population they served, and sometimes according to the size of that population and its proximity to the school. But the academic curriculum was remarkably similar in both systems. Parochial schools were generally founded later than the public schools in the same vicinity, and seem to have modeled their curriculum largely on what was taught in the public system. Father James Burns, surveying conditions in parochial education nationally, attributed this imitative impulse in 1912 to "the desire of the pastor and Catholic teachers to have the parish school recognized as fully abreast of the public schools, so that parents may not have cause to complain." (Father Frank O'Brien had introduced manual training and home economics courses at Kalamazoo's St. Augustine's School in 1900 "to keep pace with the more progressive work in this line in the public schools.") And Father Burns was astute enough to recognize that the Catholic schools were affected by "the same general causes that have operated to bring about changes in the public school curriculum." Parochial schools mirrored the larger culture, then, however much they were designed to ensure that Catholics remained the inhabitants of a distinct and separate world.[20]

The curriculum in the primary schools of the Diocese seems everywhere to have centered on the same basic subjects. "I am in the fourth grade," wrote John Conroy from Ionia in 1894. "My studies are Catechism, Bible history, arithmetic, grammar, geography, reading, spelling and United States history." His testimony was echoed by children throughout the Diocese, the only notable variations coming from those parishes where a foreign language was regularly taught, together with the history and the literature of the nation from which the parish founders had come. "I go to St. Joseph's German school, which is taught by the Dominican Sisters," observed Adrian's Launie Conley in 1892 — notwithstanding his Celtic name. "I love my teacher, but you can imagine it is hard for a little boy like me to learn from four books, two in English and two in German." A passion for geography characterized the curriculum of ethnic and English-speaking schools alike, as well as that of the public schools — evocative of the period's penchant for rote learning and its conviction that the acquisition of objective knowledge was the essence of education. "I know all the counties in Michigan, all the principal railroads and principal rivers and cities," wrote eleven-year-old Grace Quirk, a public school pupil whose Imlay City mission church could not support a school of its own. "We were trying to beat the girls in geography and did so," according to George McDace, a student at Detroit's St. Vincent's School in 1892, where the girls could evidently have used the likes of Grace Quirk in their ranks.[21]

American history was also a favored subject, and lent itself nicely to instruction in patriotism. Even the ethnic schools were fervent Americanizers when it came to commemorating national holidays and venerating national heroes. "We are going to celebrate Washington's birthday in our school," Fanny Hogan told the *Michigan Catholic* in 1892, "and many of my companions and I have pieces of poetry to declaim for the occasion." Eleven-year-old Fanny attended school in St. Joachim's (French) parish in Detroit. Her classmate, Rosa Daigneault, looked forward as well to the birthday event, and — like Fanny — had no difficulty seeing herself as a full-fledged daughter of the Republic. "We are preparing a Washington's birthday," she wrote, "and all my cousins are as anxious as I myself to do honor to our great President and father." Rosa's very notions of eloquence were thoroughly American. "Every Friday we have composition, and I do wish I were a little Longfellow to speak to you about all the nice things in my classroom." Her contemporaries at nearby St. Mary's (German) School likewise imbibed a healthy draught of Americanism along with their training in German language and literature. An evening's entertainment featured the boys in the German drama "Das Wiedersehen," followed by tableaux from the American Civil War and "The Boys of 1861," in which "the chief characters engaged in the Civil War were represented and in turn described their successes or their failures." As for Annie Nolan of Holy Redeemer School, she was one of 10,000 parochial school youngsters in Detroit to march in the city's "Catholic" Columbus Day parade in 1892, when the nation marked the 500th anniversary of the historic voyage. Annie and her female classmates "wore white dresses, blue sashes and red caps. The parade was a grand sight. I am sure we will never forget it."[22]

The competitive ethos of the Catholic classroom in this period also gave it a thoroughly American cast, although the origins of the competitive mode may have been as much Catholic as they were American. Like their public school counterparts, parochial school teachers tried to maintain discipline in their large classes by emphasizing rote memorization and encouraging keen competition between individuals and groups of students with regard to learning and deportment. "Each class has a gold cross to compete for and the one who knows their studies best gets it," wrote a pupil from SS. Peter and Paul's School in Ionia in 1894. "My little brother had it last week. I always try to have my lessons good. I did not speak during school hours since commencement." "We have two sides in school," according to Katie McGoldrick from Detroit's Holy Trinity parish, "one called the 'A.A.' and the other the 'B.B.' and every day the side that has the fewest mistakes gets an 'X' and the side that has the most 'X's' each week gets a star, and at the end of the month the side that has the most stars draws for a religious picture." The children at Detroit's Holy Redeemer School were seated in class each month "according to points, and I have been the first for three months," explained ten-year-old Alice Rattenbury. Little Gussie Cook, a pupil at SS. Peter and Paul's School in Detroit, was delighted in 1893 when "he got his name in the church calendar and he got one of the three medals a Jesuit Father gave to Sister for the boys that got the most head marks." Gussie had a counterpart at St. John's School in Jackson, in the person of nine-year-old J. Leo Harrington: "I am in the fourth grade and am wearing the silver medal this month for having the highest average in the class."[23]

Competition between the sexes seems to have been a particularly effective means of encouraging pupil achievement, and one to which the Sisters often turned. "I go to school every day, and the boys are trying to get more stars than the girls but the girls have more stars than the boys," according to Katie Cassidy, a pupil in 1896 at Leo Harrington's Jackson school. Girls would seem to have had an advantage in contests of this sort, being, on the whole, the more readily disciplined sex and the more amenable to female authority. Perhaps the stronger-minded of the teaching sisters enjoyed displays of female achievement. Certainly there were girls who did. Loretta McPherson, in the fifth grade at Our Lady of Help School in Detroit, had even drawn a feminist lesson from her own experience of classroom competition. "This time I will tell you of a great contest that has taken place between the boys and girls of our class," she wrote to the *Michigan Catholic* in 1893:

> A picture of the ship in which Columbus sailed, was drawn on the blackboard and under the ship was written the quotation: "Don't give up the ship, boys." The boys were to take one mast and the girls another. A star was to represent a sailor climbing the mast. The side that won the greater number of stars for perfect recitations, order, and deportment would reach the top first, and, of course, gain the contest. The boys had chosen the green flag, while the girls had taken the red. The contest ended on the eve of St. Patrick's day, and, what do you think? Why the boys lost their flag, and the next day the girls wore the green ribbon and were proud of their victory. It was too bad to think that the poor boys had to "give up the ship." Still the contest was fair, and there is such a thing as "girls' rights" as well as "boys' rights," although all do not think so.

Loretta's belief in "girls' rights" could only have been strengthened over the course of the following year. "We have a contest or monthly review, and the girls have their average added together and the boys theirs together," she reported in the winter of 1894, "and the girls have won since the beginning of the term."[24]

The "contest or monthly review" to which Loretta referred was apparently a fixture of the curriculum in many parishes. Father James Doherty of Detroit's St. Vincent's parish was one of a number of pastors in the 1890s who personally administered monthly oral examinations to the youngsters in their schools. Those children at St. Vincent's who performed up to standard had their names recorded in the St. Vincent's *Monthly Calendar*. "About 150 names appeared in last month's number," the *Michigan Catholic* reported in 1895, when the practice had just begun, "but as each pupil seems desirous of leading in his or her class, a far greater number is anticipated in the coming months." Whatever ambitions were centered on the monthly review, however, and whatever anxieties were attendant on it, could hardly have matched the emotions attached to the public examinations that were a tradition in certain parishes. The children at Detroit's St. Boniface School, for example, were examined twice a year by the pastor and the parish trustees, the examinations typically absorbing the better part of three days. Every school in the Diocese, moreover, was visited once a year by a priest-examiner, who was delegated for this purpose by the regional school boards that had been created by Bishop Foley in 1889. Almost none of the examiners' reports have survived, but we do have a record of the 1895 visit of Father John Schreiber to St. Alphonsus School, then in a rural area west of Detroit. The performance of the children there was mixed: the younger children read well in English, according to Father Schreiber, although their German reading was "middling" at best. Their copy books were only "fair," but their work in spelling and arithmetic was "good." The older children — the school went only through the fourth grade — were good spellers too, and some of them read well in German and in English. But their performance in arithmetic and geography was no better than "fair." All of the pupils, however, recited fluently from the catechism.[25]

It is nearly impossible to judge how effectively the competitive mode of the Catholic classroom encouraged learning and good order. The children at St. Alphonsus School were apparently making decent progress toward acquiring the basic skills of literacy and computation, despite the high rate of absenteeism that plagued the school in its rural setting. Father Schreiber was not trained in pedagogy, but he was surely capable of determining how well a child could read and perform simple sums. The children who wrote to the *Michigan Catholic* in the years around the turn of the century, moreover, spoke happily of their own schools as cheerful, orderly places, where students were eager to learn and teachers liked to teach. Thirteen-year-old Francis Ford of Owosso came the closest to even an implied criticism of the parish school when he intimated in a 1914 letter that his pastor was better able than "Sister" to maintain order in the classroom. "Our teacher was sick last week and our reverend pastor taught our room for a few days," Francis reported. "We were very sorry Sister was sick, but we like Father to teach us. I don't think he missed anything. It was so quiet you could hear a pin drop."[26]

The balance of the fragmentary evidence that remains to us, then, suggests that the parochial school performed reasonably well when it came to imparting at least the basic academic skills. But there is occasional evidence to the contrary. A Polish-born Felician Sister, for example, was deeply distressed by her experience in one of Detroit's congested Polish schools, where conditions were such that some of the pupils may have failed to acquire even the rudiments of literacy. "This past year I had 130 of the younger children," she wrote in 1896. "Very often I just did not have the stamina or physical strength to carry on and experienced difficulty. One has to be like a sentinel in the classroom; every moment must be planned." Whether the Sister was of different social origins than her young charges we do not know, but she seems to have regarded them as an alien brood. "These children are different from those in Europe, and one needs more strength to control them. Parents don't register any concern. They want their children to study and become wise, but you can't find any such traces of parental concern or influence in the children." Many of the parents, of course, had themselves had little formal schooling, and most expected that their children would leave school and go to work early in adolescence. St. Albertus School in Detroit did not add the seventh and the eighth grades until 1907 and 1908, and even at this late date it was the first of the local Polish schools to do so.[27]

Polish schools were not the only schools in the Diocese where discipline and academic achievement failed to meet the expectations of the Sisters. A refreshingly unsentimental recollection of the early days at Holy Cross (Hungarian)

School evokes a world where the boys, at least, were at war with the disciplinary and academic standards of their hapless teachers. "The Sisters sent to civilize and educate us led a most turbulent and tempestuous existence," according to Andrew Untener in 1936. (He had attended the school from its opening in 1907 until 1910.) "Our natural inclination to mischief was a source of great annoyance and vexation to the Sisters, and it was not uncommon to see Sister chasing someone around the room with a ruler, trying to catch him and administer some promised punishment. Incidents such as these were not very conducive to tranquillity and serenity in the classroom." Nor were the pupils at Holy Cross much disposed to see the point of academic achievement. "In fact, few of the older children completed even their grade-school education, but were withdrawn by their parents when reaching the fifth or sixth grade, given their working papers and sent out to help the family exchequer." Not that most youngsters objected, at least as Untener remembered it. "You know how tedious and irksome school work can become, and it seems a most humdrum life compared to work at the Michigan Sprocket Chain or driving some grocer's delivery wagon, and getting paid for it, to boot!"[28]

For at least some Catholic parents, then, the academic quality of the parish school was of little practical importance. And even those who looked to the school as a means of upward mobility for the young were not invariably inclined to think that academic excellence was more important than, or even as important as, the religious and cultural functions of Catholic education — functions that nearly all parochial schools performed remarkably well, considering the attractions of the secular culture in which the American Church made its uneasy home. The ethnic schools did what they could to teach a foreign language. "Our mother tongue is most intimately interwoven with our religious convictions," the annual convention of the German Catholic Societies of Michigan proclaimed in 1908, and the sentiment was shared by conservatives in every ethnic camp. But even more important was the cultivation of a religious loyalty that could, if need be, withstand the erosion of a particular ethnic identity. Not every ethnic Catholic was anxious to have his children be more European than American in their linguistic and cultural allegiances. There were no supporters of parochial schooling, however, who did not want their children to be good Catholics.[29]

The parochial school developed such Catholics mainly by giving religion a prominent place in the curriculum. The day began with morning prayers and sometimes with Mass. There was daily instruction in the catechism too, and in such a way that the children knew, even the most restless among them, just how important the subject was. The religion class should be given "if convenient at the beginning of the class in the forenoon," advised the manual of pedagogy used by the IHM Sisters, "commanding a more rigid silence as treating a subject far above the common things — avoiding as much as possible to punish during that time — or if punishment is necessary not inflicting it but with discretion and as with reluctance." The parish priest generally made regular visits to the school to hear the children recite from the catechism, and his presence confirmed the special status of religion in the curriculum. Father William Considine "examines in catechism every Tuesday and in Bible history every Friday," according to one of the pupils at St. Mary's School in Chelsea in 1908, and he was no more diligent than many of his contemporaries. Priests sometimes assumed full responsibility for the religious instruction of students in the secondary grades, indicating, perhaps, in what low regard they held the theological competence of the Sisters in the parish school. "Father Taylor teaches us Catechism and Church History and is very fine," explained a high school girl from St. Thomas parish in Ann Arbor, who seemed to be learning, in the course of this instruction, more about her Church than simply the history of its dogmatic pronouncements. "He instructs the boys' choir and takes great interest in them. Of course the girls would be much more pleased if he liked them as well as he does the boys."[30]

Formal religious instruction, however, was not the only way in which a Catholic identity was formed in the parish school. "Remember, in a real Catholic school the Catholic religion is *always* present," the *Michigan Catholic* cautioned its readers in 1890, as the debate on the parochial school and its relationship to the state was approaching its height. That presence was manifested "in the teacher's manner and garb, in the child's conception of the very purpose of the teacher, in the crucifix on the wall, in the statue of the Blessed Virgin or of the patron saint in the niche or on the bracket over the teacher's desk — not to speak of the prayer said at certain hours during the day — the Hail Mary when the clock strikes, the Angelus when the noon hour sounds, etc, etc." By 1890 this exemplary classroom could be found throughout the Diocese. More than 80 percent of the teachers then were members of religious orders. (That figure had climbed to 96 percent by 1917.) And it was the rare classroom that did not, in its various appointments, make the school appear to be an extension of the church. "Our schoolroom is very pleasant and we have many beautiful holy pictures in it," wrote a youngster from Detroit's Holy Rosary School in 1907. "I am going to tell you about the May Altar[s] we have in our school. Every room has one, and every one likes ours," confided a little girl from St. Leo's School in Detroit. "The name of our room is St. John Berchmans, as each room has a name," wrote eleven-year-old Philomena Holden from her school in Jackson. The omnipresence of the sacred in the classroom had an undeniable power: if it did not transform the behavior of the all-too-human "average student," it still communicated to him the emotional content of a rich devotional tradition.[31]

We have already seen that the parochial school played an important role in habituating young Catholics to a more disciplined sacramental practice. It played an equally important role in popularizing the florid devotional style that was more and more common to Catholics in the Diocese during and after the late nineteenth century. Parochial school children were introduced over the course of the school year to a variety of special devotions, and encouraged to make these a part of their own religious lives. Devotion to St. Joseph was taught in the month of March; May was given over to Marian observances; June was the month of the Sacred Heart. "As we are now in the beautiful month of June . . .

our May altar has disappeared, and in its place we have erected another, in honor of the sweet Sacred Heart of Jesus," wrote a youngster from Ionia. "We have no statue, however, so Sister placed a beautiful picture of the Sacred Heart of Jesus on the same, which rests on an easel." October meant Rosary devotions, and November brought devotions in aid of the Poor Souls in Purgatory.[32]

November, especially, was a time when death and judgment loomed large in religious instruction, when fear and guilt-producing aspects of the Catholic tradition came to the fore. "The wailing winds of the Fall remind us that the poor souls are crying, many of them in deep distress," the editor of the *Michigan Catholic*'s children's page advised her young readers in 1901, aware that her columns were a popular teaching device in many of the local parochial schools, "and they depend upon us to remember them in our prayers and entreat our dear Lord to release them from their sufferings." But the emphasis in religious instruction seems to have been more fundamentally on the tender and consoling elements in the tradition. The unseen world was peopled by friendly protectors: the IHM Sisters were urged to "accustom" their pupils "often to have recourse to their guardian angel and their holy Patron." Christ was portrayed as a loving and forgiving friend far more often than He was presented as the Just Judge. Sisters throughout the Diocese, moreover, were zealous in their promotion of Eucharistic piety, and especially stressed the intimate union with Christ that the Eucharist represented. The IHMs worked hard to inspire their pupils "with a tender love towards our Lord, present in the tabernacle and to inspire . . . affection for all that regards His adorable person." (Their efforts had borne fruit in the heart of young Margaret Shay of Detroit, whose letter to the *Michigan Catholic* at Christmas in 1912 was a model of devotional piety: "Then I thought how thankful we ought to be to our dear Savior, who came into the world and suffered death on the Cross for our sake, and how He still lives on our altars that we may eat His flesh and drink His blood. I thought of all these things with a grateful heart and promised to serve more faithfully the Jesus Who had done so much for me.") The Sisters were equally intent on encouraging devotion to Mary, "and a childlike confidence in Her intercession." The children at St. Boniface School in Detroit, who in 1894 staged "Bernadette, or the Wonderful Providence of God," were being introduced to Mariology in all its high-Victorian fervor. "It relates how a young shepherdess who dwells near the Grotto of Lourdes procures the restoration of sight to a little blind girl. . . . The scenery throughout was very fine, but the Grotto scene deserves especial mention. . . . A fountain of real water was employed, representing the water flowing from the feet of our Blessed Lady, producing a charming effect."[33]

If its religious preoccupations distinguished the Catholic school from the neighboring public institution, so too did the emphasis on bilingual instruction in those Catholic schools that were supported by an ethnic congregation. In the absence of a central school board with the power to prescribe texts and curriculum, the schools in the Foley years were shaped in good part by the expectations of parents and the pedagogic traditions of particular religious orders. And in the ethnic parish, this often meant that second- and even third-generation Americans were taught the language of their forebears. Most of the pupils in the German parish schools by the 1890s were American-born, and many came from homes where English was spoken. But they learned the German language in their schools, and some of them, apparently, learned it well. "The Germanic script is equal to the English," an admirer of Detroit's St. Mary's School informed the *Michigan Catholic* in 1894. "All the children are bi-lingual." The young men's dramatic clubs at St. Mary's and St. Boniface parishes were still producing plays in German in the 1890s. Indeed the reputation of the German schools was such that Father James Doherty, inspecting the schools in the Detroit deanery in 1891, hastened to assure the city's Catholics that youngsters in the German schools acquired facility in English. "Father Doherty is well satisfied that the work of the pupils in the lower grades in our German parochial schools is up to the standard," the *Michigan Catholic* reported, "and there is no reason why the German Catholics of this city should send their children to the public schools to learn the English language."[34]

Poles were as tenacious as Germans when it came to preserving their language and traditions. Polish parish schools in the Diocese were taught at least partly in Polish throughout the Foley years, when many of the Sisters who staffed those schools spoke very uncertain English. Sisters belonging to the Felician order were not allowed to use the English language except in the classroom from 1894 until 1900, years when an especially zealous guardian of Polish culture served as the mother superior. A looser regime prevailed thereafter, but the Sisters continued to see their mission in terms of preserving the language and culture of a people in exile. "Generally speaking . . . from one-fourth to one-half of the school-time is given to teaching Polish," according to Father James Burns in 1912, and this was apparently the case in Detroit, where the Felicians were accustomed to teach some eight separate subjects in Polish in the early grades of the grammar school. Father Burns was worried that many Polish-American youngsters were, as a consequence, failing to acquire facility in English reading and spelling. But most Polish parents were not troubled by this, not, at least, in the Foley years. Many Polish adults in the Diocese then were themselves unable to speak or read English, and they lived in a world whose horizons were bounded by the institutions and mores of their heavily Polish neighborhoods, and by the factories where they labored. (Only 5 percent of Detroit's Poles were employed in white-collar occupations in 1900, while 65 percent were unskilled workers.) Under the circumstances, it is hardly surprising that the schools should be seen primarily as the guardians of language and culture, and only secondarily as the means by which an exceptional child might become socially mobile.[35]

Not every ethnic group in the Diocese, however, looked to the parish school to preserve its language and culture. We have already seen that the Italians were little interested in parochial education. Other groups were too small or too dispersed to support an ethnic parish school. Detroit's only Lithuanian parish was without a school in 1917, as was the city's westside Bohemian parish; the Syrian parish did not yet have a school, and the city's growing Croatian community had not yet organized itself into a congregation. The Hungarian Catholics at Holy Cross parish in extreme southwestern Detroit had opened a school in 1907, but those Hungarians who lived in other parts of the city could hardly make use of it. Their children attended the public schools or, at least on the city's near east side, a nearby parochial institution. "The school is in full swing again," the *Michigan Catholic* reported in 1914 with regard to St. Mary's parish, still nominally German, "and especially striking is the large percentage of Italian and Hungarian children in attendance." The school had by this time largely abandoned its German-language curriculum, but the Sisters were in no position to replace it with instruction in Magyar or Italian.[36]

Even those groups that were able and willing to support ethnic schools eventually found that those schools were less and less effective at keeping the ancestral language alive. The German parish schools in the Diocese provided daily instruction in German throughout the primary and secondary grades, and did so at least through the first decade of the twentieth century. But even in the late nineteenth century, growing numbers of German-Americans preferred English to German not simply for business and social purposes, but for devotional purposes as well. Sermons were preached in English as well as German at Detroit's German parishes in the 1890s, and missions and devotions were conducted in both languages. The end of heavy German immigration, moreover — something that had occurred in Detroit by 1900 — meant that the historically German parishes became more and more heterogeneous in their ethnic composition, both because of intermarriage and the changing character of neighborhoods. St. Mary's Church by 1914 was already a monument to a vanished German past, looming above the tenements and shops and factories of a district now peopled principally by Greeks and Italians and Eastern European Jews. Germans were still a majority of the parishioners at St. Joseph's parish, but the neighborhood now included large numbers of Italians, Hungarians, and Syrians. Even St. Elizabeth's parish, located well to the east of the city core, counted "many Irish families" in its congregation by 1914. The changing population of the parish did not necessarily mean that the teaching of German was abandoned in the parish school: St. Joseph's school kept its German language courses until 1918, when wartime hysteria caused the teaching of German to be curtailed in public and sectarian schools alike. But the changing composition of the once-German parish meant that the Sisters there could no longer expect that their pupils would master what was for many of them a wholly alien tongue.[37]

Polish parishes were slower than those of other groups to lose their distinctive ethnic identity. Poles in the Diocese were relatively slow to be socially mobile, and Detroit's Polish neighborhoods have historically been more homogeneous and more stable residentially than any others. But if the American-born youngster of Polish descent was likely to raise his own children in a mostly Polish neighborhood and send them to a Polish parish school, he was more and more likely, especially after 1914, to speak English at home and to regard a command of English as an essential goal of his children's education. "Even now, more time is given to English in Polish schools than was given ten years ago," noted Father John Burns in 1912, surveying the parochial school scene nationally. He was pleased to quote the anonymous Polish priest who wrote in the *Catholic Standard and Times* in 1910 that the children in his own parish, particularly the boys, rarely used Polish among themselves. Their older brothers and sisters, moreover, had quickly forgotten much of the Polish they had learned while in the parish school. "It is a growing difficulty to find a young man or young woman equipped with a sufficient knowledge of Polish to assume the duties of recording secretary in our parish and national societies." How closely the Polish experience in the Diocese approximated that of this anonymous pastor's community is difficult to say, given the dearth of evidence in the Chancery archives about the Polish schools. Certainly those schools continued to teach the catechism in Polish and to teach compulsory courses in Polish language and history into the 1930s. But even in the 1920s, there were growing numbers of Polish-American parents who wanted instruction in Polish removed from the primary school curriculum. Like the critics in an earlier generation, they feared that Polish instruction would hinder their children in the hard struggle for academic achievement.[38]

The indifference to foreign-language study that eventually afflicted the great majority of ethnic Catholics in the American-born generations is accounted for most fully by the seductiveness of the secular culture that found its way into the most cohesive immigrant neighborhoods. The use of English in street games; the lure of popular music and popular entertainment; the appeal of the English-language tabloid with its fill of sports and scandal — these worked far more effectively than any Chancery directive to ensure that the immigrant young learned to speak and read in English. Whether Bishop Foley instinctively knew this to be true we have not the evidence to say, but there were no serious efforts in the course of his episcopate to legislate standards with regard to the teaching of English in the parochial schools. What directives there were came from the state. Michigan was by 1909 one of nineteen states that required an ability to read and write in English before an employment certificate could be granted to a child who was below the legal school-leaving age — legislation that was probably of mostly symbolic importance. A more formidable challenge to ethnic school autonomy came with American entry into the First World War. As anti-German sentiment mounted throughout the nation, so too did pressure on all schools to purge the curriculum of "Germanic" elements. Apparently worried that the Michigan legislature might seize the moment to expand its control of sectarian schools, Auxiliary Bishop Edward Kelly, administrator of the Diocese for some ten months in 1918, appointed a diocesan superintendent of schools. He was Father Frank Kennedy, onetime antagonist of the late Bishop Foley.

Father Kennedy was an active superintendent for less than a year. But during his brief tenure, he did what he could to allay public fears about the "foreign" content and inferior quality of parochial school instruction. He had already mandated uniform textbooks for the schools of the Diocese, Father Kennedy told the *Detroit News* in the summer of 1918, and he may indeed have done so, although pastors and the various teaching orders paid no heed whatsoever. (Uniform texts were an achievement of the 1930s.) He had also taken steps to ensure that the Sisters in the Polish schools attained "complete mastery of the English language," but he denied that there were teachers in the parochial schools of Detroit who were unable to speak English at all. "The main trouble that I have found with the Polish schools is that the devoted sisterhoods that have charge of them are trying to accomplish too much with the means at their command," Father Kennedy explained. "Some of the schools are badly congested. There is need of increased equipment." As for the teaching of German, Father Kennedy told the *News* that it had been "put under the ban" in all the schools of the Diocese. This directive had in fact been unnecessary, he noted, for "after this order went into effect, I found that German had already been dropped from the curriculum of the schools by voluntary action of the teachers." This may well have been true, given the intensity of popular resentment against things German and the by then mostly ceremonial content of German-language instruction in the historically German schools. Father Kennedy, however, was in no position to enforce even limited changes in the curriculum that had not been approved or initiated at the parish level. The first effective sanction against "excessive" foreign-language instruction came in 1919, in the form of a Michigan law that required all schools to be conducted in English from the first through the eighth grades. The law did indeed bring changes to the ethnic parish schools, although its provisions were sometimes ignored. As late as 1944, it was possible for a parent in Transfiguration parish to complain that "the Sisters speak only in broken English. . . . The sister insisted the pupil study from a Polish book which was impossible and against the wishes of the parents."[39]

SECONDARY EDUCATION

The Foley years were the seed-time of Catholic secondary education in the Diocese of Detroit. Nearly all of the oldest parish high schools in the Diocese date from the 1890s — only St. Vincent's and Holy Trinity schools in Detroit are known to have offered a regular secondary curriculum before that time. By 1918, most of the larger parish schools had made at least some provision for education beyond the eighth grade, with the notable exception of the Polish schools. (St. Josaphat's was the first of these to offer a ninth grade curriculum, in 1915.) Opportunities for what Catholics sometimes called "private" secondary schooling grew as well: the Dominican Sisters opened St. Joseph's Academy for girls at Adrian in 1896, the Sisters of St. Joseph opened Nazareth Academy for girls near Kalamazoo in 1897, and the Christian Brothers came to staff the new St. Joseph's Commercial College in Detroit in 1889. (This latter, although nominally a parish high school for boys, was an institution that drew its students from many parts of the city.) These schools joined the select educational ranks already defined by St. Mary's Academy in Monroe, the Academies of the Sacred Heart in Detroit and in Grosse Pointe, the Felician Academy in Detroit, and Detroit College — still in the 1890s an institution whose curriculum spanned the high school and college years in the centuries-old mode of Jesuit educational organization.

Secondary schooling in the Foley years was something of a luxury, however, and it was a distinct minority of Catholic children whose education continued beyond the grammar school. It was a heavily female minority as well. The great majority of the graduates of Catholic secondary schools in the Diocese in the years before 1914 were girls, and they probably continued to outnumber male graduates well into the 1920s. Many Catholic parents, evidently, regarded the secondary school as a sheltered and socially acceptable place for a girl to pass her adolescent years. What she learned there could only enhance her prospects for happiness as a wife and mother, at least according to the nation's leading educators. Early wage-earning, moreover, was widely thought to be more dangerous for girls than boys. The young girl at work, ran the popular logic, was exposed to a welter of dangers, which ranged from sexual precocity to a vulgarization of speech and manners. Boys, however, learned at work to be independent and self-disciplined, qualities thought to be more important than a high school degree for success in business and the trades. And girls were generally happier and more successful in school — more likely to beg for "one more year." Small wonder, then, that even reasonably affluent parents in the years before 1914 were more apt to keep their daughters than their sons in school for the full twelve years. (The pattern was not peculiarly Catholic; the graduates of American public high schools before 1914 were mostly female.) "There is not room for more than one respectable college or academy for boys in Detroit," warned Jesuit Father Michael Dowling in 1891, alarmed at a *Michigan Catholic* editorial in support of a central Catholic high school for boys. He naturally feared that such a school would erode the constituency on which his own Detroit College depended. But he was essentially correct in his assessment of the limited local demand for boys' secondary schooling. The situation had changed by 1918, but not so much that high school education was not still associated, in many Catholic minds, mainly with the female sex.[40]

The history of secondary schooling in the Diocese of Detroit differs from that in most other large dioceses in one important respect, and it is one that bears on the popular association of extended schooling with girls. Bishop Foley failed during his long episcopate to establish a single central high school. This meant that what secondary schools were established were, nearly all of them, parochial high schools, many of which were too small to provide separate classrooms for the sexes, much less separate facilities. Some parishes simply excluded boys from the high school grades: Holy Trinity and St. Anne's parish high schools in Detroit, for example, were open to girls alone. But most were at least nominally coeducational, at least after 1900, despite strong opposition to coeducation in adolescence on the part of most Catholic authorities.

Coeducation in a world where girls were the great majority of students meant, naturally enough, that the males among them were resident in formidably female territory. St. Vincent's Academy, established as the parish high school in 1884 and opened to boys in about 1900, did not have its first male graduate until 1908. Whether female domination of the parish high school discouraged boys who would otherwise have continued their education is something that can hardly be proved. But we can say that the failure to establish central high schools in Detroit in the Foley years had a lasting impact on the shape of Catholic education in the city. "The Diocese of Detroit reported by far the largest number of co-educational Catholic secondary schools—63," according to a national survey of parochial education in 1928. Even in that year, girls still outnumbered boys in the secondary schools of the Diocese. But by 1928, a growing population of male students had begun to have an effect on the curriculum of the secondary school, and on its ambiance as well.[41]

This was not the case, however, in the years before the First World War, when the parish secondary school had a palpably feminine aura. The faculty in these schools was almost entirely female: the number of male religious teaching in the parish schools of the Diocese declined from twelve in 1889 to eleven in 1917. The curriculum was generally centered on literature and the arts, subjects in which Sisters were most likely to be trained and which did not require the expensive facilities needed for industrial arts and the laboratory sciences. The curriculum was affected too by the standards set at such "private" institutions as St. Mary's in Monroe and the Academies of the Sacred Heart. Schools like these did indeed become more ambitious academically in the 1890s and after. But they never wholly abandoned their emphasis on decorative accomplishments. The excellence of its courses in music and painting, including painting on china, was a feature of which St. Aloysius parish high school was proud, even as late as the First World War. The 1899 commencement exercises, which took as their theme "an evening with Mozart," presented the school to the public in the polite guise it cherished. The St. Aloysius orchestra—composed of four guitars, three mandolins, three violins, and a piano—played various selections, after which Bishop Foley crowned the four "young lady graduates" with floral wreaths. The school's chorus performed next, followed by the reading of the graduates' essays, all of which had to do with Mozart's life and times or his place in the history of music. (Miss Grace Seymour presented what was presumably an expurgated version of "Mozart's Social Life.") The whole affair was doubtless quite respectable in an academic sense. But it partook of the cloying gentility that the era associated with women of a certain social class. It was hardly an environment in which a young man was likely to feel welcome or at home.[42]

Not all parish high schools were as self-consciously genteel as St. Aloysius. The Immaculate Heart of Mary Sisters, who were teaching at nine parish high schools in Detroit by 1917, were justly proud of the rigorous academic standards they brought to those schools, and anxious to offer as thorough a course of study as possible. St. Vincent's Academy in the late 1890s taught not only literature, history, composition, algebra, geography, and Christian doctrine, but "natural philosophy, geometry, chemistry, minerology, geology, zoology, botany, anatomy [and] physiology," not to mention bookkeeping, stenography and typewriting, and the usual courses in vocal and instrumental music. This extraordinary range of subjects was, it is true, the responsibility of a mere handful of teachers. Most parish high schools in the Foley years were too small to permit the kind of specialized instruction that later generations regarded as essential to educational excellence. Still, the IHM high schools enjoyed a solid reputation in the Diocese for educational rigor. For all their reputation, however, those schools did not attract male students in the Foley years in any significant numbers. Only at the Cathedral School, where the graduating classes were very small, were boys at all equitably represented in the secondary grades. The *Michigan Catholic* was delighted to see that the Cathedral graduating class in 1902 consisted of "a young lady and a young gentleman. . . . It is an excellent beginning, and parents should endeavor to allow their sons the same years in the schoolroom as their daughters, so that annually the graduating classes at our academies may be able to boast as many names of boys as of girls."[43]

The feminine associations of the high school may well have had effects that extended far beyond the Foley years. For, coupled with the growing emphasis on an emotional style of devotionalism, these associations served to define the female sex as the guardians of Catholic culture and Catholic intellectual life. "That the sons of wealthy parents should be satisfied with a merely commercial course must be a great misfortune for the nation at large," a Sister at the Grosse Pointe Convent of the Sacred Heart wrote to Henry Brownson in 1901. "As far as our limited sphere of action allows, we try to counteract this evil by trying to make young girls under our charge desire learning 'for learning's sake,' and not on account of the purely material advantages to be expected later on." The Immaculate Heart of Mary Sisters had a similar sense of mission. The pedagogic system in which they were trained had always emphasized the particular importance of educating girls because of the influence they would one day possess as wives and mothers. But by the late nineteenth century, the ambitious scope of the order's secondary schools suggests that the Sisters now envisioned for women an intellectual influence that extended far beyond the family. "Learning for learning's sake" was promoted not only in the classroom but in the "study clubs" that encouraged both students and alumnae to broaden their intellectual horizons. (The Study Club at St. Vincent's Academy met in December 1898 to hear original papers by members—"Religion in Literature" and "The Holy Grail"—followed by a debate on the resolution "That Longfellow was a greater poet than Tennyson." The judges were gratifyingly patriotic in their support of the affirmative side.) Education for boys and young men, however, continued to be seen by nearly all Catholics in largely instrumental terms, necessary only insofar as specific careers required it—a point of view that was probably strengthened by the growing association of women and girls with literary training and pursuits. What critics in a later generation saw as the aversion of many Catholic men to anything resembling the intellectual life may well have a part of its origins in this turn-of-the-century chapter in the history of Catholic education.[44]

HIGHER EDUCATION

If girls enjoyed an advantage when it came to secondary schooling, it was boys who were favored when it came to higher education. Despite impressive growth in the ranks of the nation's college students during and after the 1880s, those students were still very much an elite, even as late as the First World War. This was particularly true among Catholics, largely because of their poverty. Catholic parents were, for this reason, especially inclined to associate college training with males, and with preparation for the higher professions. Catholic women's colleges in the United States developed mainly after 1920, although women's colleges under secular and Protestant auspices had been flourishing since at least the 1870s.

The national boom in college enrollments was eventually reflected on Catholic campuses. Enrollment at American Catholic colleges quickened perceptibly after 1900, although women's colleges lagged in their growth and development about a generation behind those for men. The national trend was readily apparent in the Diocese of Detroit. It was in the early years of the century that Detroit College evolved into something like a modern university: the College of Engineering dates from 1911, the College of Law from 1912, and the School of Commerce and Finance from 1916. During this same period the Diocese gained its first Catholic college for women. What had begun in 1899 as a postgraduate tutorial for one young alumna of St. Mary's Academy in Monroe had become by 1905 a two-year college for women, and by 1910 a four-year college chartered to grant degrees. There were fourteen students at St. Mary's College in 1914, the year the school bestowed its first Bachelor of Arts degree on Teresa Lorraine Cahn. The college was still housed in the academy from which it had grown, and was still very much an extension of the academy both intellectually and pedagogically. In the 1920s, however, its increasing enrollment and the norms of the various national accrediting agencies achieved for the college a growing autonomy and an intellectual identity of its own. The transformation was complete with the transfer of the college to Detroit, where classes were opened in 1927 under the new name of Marygrove College.[45]

The growth of the college population in the Foley years is explained in good part by the growth of the Catholic middle class. The mostly Irish- and German-surnamed students who enrolled at Detroit College—the University of Detroit by 1911—or at St. Mary's College were the offspring, for the most part, of assimilated and reasonably prosperous parents. Important too were the rising educational standards that were increasingly enforced in the various professions after the late nineteenth century. These standards were generated, at least in part, by the better secular universities, which were moving, in the latter decades of the century, toward greater curricular specialization and away from the training in classical texts that was still in 1900 the staple of the Catholic college. With growing enrollments, then, came new pressure on the Catholic colleges to adapt their curricula to what was essentially a secular standard. The effects were especially visible at an institution like Detroit College, which evolved, in little more than a generation, from a traditional Jesuit academy to a university where the liberal arts were but one focus of the increasingly specialized faculty.

But if the Catholic college had necessarily to adapt itself to a changing world— to become more like the institutions that set national standards for excellence in university training—the Catholic educator did not cease to believe that the mission of his institution was unique. Only in the Catholic college would the rising professional be thoroughly schooled in apologetics. Only in the Catholic college could he develop the friendships that would keep him loyal to his Church as he moved among the Protestants and "infidels" who numbered so mightily in the ranks of the higher professions. Only in the Catholic college would he see, in the persons of learned but devout religious, the examples he so badly needed of fidelity to ancient dogmas in a world increasingly inclined to moral relativism. Indeed, as the larger society became more and more openly secular in its preoccupations and as the liberal Protestant denominations began to jettison portions of their own theological heritage, the mission of the Catholic college seemed the more urgent to a growing body in the Catholic population.

A decided shift in attitudes toward the secular college—and, by extension, toward the necessity of Catholic college training—can be traced in the editorial columns of the *Michigan Catholic* over the course of the Foley years. Until about 1900, the paper maintained a tolerant, even an admiring, stance toward the state's principal institution of higher learning, the University of Michigan in Ann Arbor. Catholics were known to be in attendance there, although estimates of their numbers varied considerably. An 1886 survey, admittedly incomplete, by the Students' Christian Association at the university put the number of Catholic students at 58, well behind the Methodists (at 264), the Presbyterians (at 188), and the Baptists (at 136) but ahead of the Lutherans (at 35) and ahead of Jews, of whom there were only 9. But an 1889 letter to the *Michigan Catholic* from an anonymous Ann Arbor resident claimed that the student body included "about 150 practical Catholics." Father Edward Kelly, pastor of St. Thomas Church in Ann Arbor, placed the number of Catholic students at the university in 1898 at "over 200"; his assistant, Father Michael Bourke, who worked closely with the university's Catholics, believed that the Catholic enrollment in 1914 was "about 600." By 1919 he was claiming that Catholics made up about 10 percent of the university's student body, placing their number at about 700. A survey conducted among Michigan students in the fall of 1917, however, had placed the number of Catholics at 349.[46]

It was understandably tempting for Catholic spokesmen to inflate the number of Catholic students in Ann Arbor, for they understood in what high regard the university was held throughout the state. "All positions are open to the gradu-

ate of Michigan University," admitted a Catholic critic in 1889, who feared nonetheless that "this great school" was thoroughly anti-Catholic in its ethos. For
Catholics to number among those graduates was a sign of Catholic progress socially, whatever it might signal about loyalty to the Church among the upwardly
mobile. Signs of such progress were bound to be valued by assimilated Catholics, perhaps especially in times of rising intolerance. During the 1890s, when
bitter anti-Catholicism infected politics, the editor of the *Michigan Catholic* was
inclined to think that the risk of attending the better secular colleges was out-
weighed by the social and economic advantages that such colleges brought to
their Catholic graduates and, indirectly, to the community that they represented.
"We should not like to see Yale and Harvard without Catholic students," William
Hughes wrote in 1899, "any more than we should care to see Oxford and Cambridge boycotted by the students who profess our religious faith, because we believe their presence there will have a good effect during school days, and later
on in life their membership in the alumni associations of these great schools cannot fail to reflect credit upon the Church." Indeed, Hughes was not persuaded
that these schools posed significant threat to the faith of their Catholic students.
Save perhaps for Presbyterian Princeton, he argued, "we do not believe that any
of the great schools of this country is today purposely antagonistic to Roman
Catholicity."[47]

Among these "great schools" the editor numbered the University of Michigan, which he had treated warmly in his columns for a good many years. Virtually the only criticism of the university to have appeared in the paper for at
least a decade had come from an anonymous Ann Arbor correspondent, whose
indictment of the school was published in 1889. The fears he expressed prefigure
those of a later generation of critics; missing, however, is the conviction — common to those later critics — that the secular university encourages sexual immorality. The Michigan faculty "cultivates skepticism in the heart if not the head
of the Catholic student," the anonymous correspondent warned, and Ann Arbor's Protestant clergy "seem to be in league to destroy any spark of Catholicity
that may appear in the ranks of the students." The ambitious young Catholic,
aware that his religion is a social handicap, was peculiarly vulnerable to Protestant proselytizing, at least according to this observer. Home again after four
years in Ann Arbor, the Catholic graduate was well prepared for success in the
world. But he might be lost to the Church. Only then do his parents understand
the true cost of the schooling they have labored to give him:

> The good and proud mother hastens to have his diploma framed and placed on the
> parlor wall — it is to her eyes the most beautiful picture in the house — and then she
> looks at her learned son and discovers — what? That the cross she had given him is
> not visible, and that the compass and square of Free Masonry are *very* visible on
> the lapel of his coat. She asks to see the prayer-beads which he had always carried
> in his pocket from the time of his early youth; but they too are gone — he has for-
> gotten when or where he lost them, or when he last used them.
> These souls, lost to God, laugh at the remonstrances of parents — sometimes they

sneer at them — and the mother's reproof is met with an answer like this: "Oh, mother, those notions of yours are very old-fogyish; they will not do for the 19th century."

But even this anonymous critic was not ready to say that Catholics should boycott the state's only university. The answer, rather, was to establish a "Catholic hall" on the campus where carefully chosen clergy might offer the lectures and personal counseling necessary to keep young Catholics in the Church and bring converts into the fold. "If the good seed of the One and Only True Church could have an equal chance on this fertile soil," he concluded, "it would germinate and take root and spread in this great home of talent — I might say one of the greatest in the world."[48]

By the early twentieth century, however, even the "Catholic hall" had come to seem, to the editor of the *Michigan Catholic,* an unconscionable compromise with the mammon of secularity. William Hughes had by this time joined the growing number of Catholic spokesmen who decried the secular college as dangerous to the faith and morals of the Catholic young. "The modern college is making thousands of unbelievers in the existence of God," he warned his readers in 1906. "Better for a Catholic young man or young woman to remain in ignorance than to acquire an education which entails a loss of faith and disbelief in God." Nor was the University of Michigan above reproach in this regard: there were "some Ann Arbor professors," he remarked in 1907, whose skepticism with regard to revealed religion "is dangerous to the faith of Catholic students." Where right belief was undermined, moreover, the standards that ensured right conduct were bound to be weakened as well. "For the past six months the *Michigan Catholic* has published many instances of non-Catholic colleges being made the scene of wild orgies and disgraceful conduct of pupils," Hughes reminded his public in 1906. "Send your son or daughter to a Catholic institution." He did not exempt the University of Michigan from his general indictment, advising his readers in 1907 that "one-half of the students at Ann Arbor are addicted to the use of intoxicating liquors." ("Thank God it cannot be said of youth undergoing instruction in Catholic Colleges that they are lovers of intoxicants," he observed just one year later.) The presence of a Socialist Club at the university inspired an angry editorial in 1911. "Socialistic clubs are not for Catholic young men," Hughes pointed out. "We would ask . . . if it is not time for Catholic parents to wake up and look after the welfare of their sons enrolled in these institutions." In vain, apparently, had an Ann Arbor resident appealed to the editor in 1908 to judge the university more fairly. "Townspeople unanimously declare that the behavior of the students is a cause for edification," he wrote. "The Catholic students are always well represented at devotions on the 'First Friday,' besides on Sunday at Mass and Vespers. The boys themselves say that they pay more attention to these matters than they did at home."[49]

What had happened to the editor of the *Michigan Catholic* is explained in good part by changes in his Church and in the world he saw around him. The ascendency of conservative ideas, and of conservative bishops, that followed the election of Pius X in 1903 discouraged even a cautiously tolerant view of non-Catholics and their institutions. It reinforced for Catholics a sense of their immense vulnerability to the forces of secularism, and strengthened the most defensive impulses in Catholic thought. This was particularly true after the publication of the antimodernist encyclical, *Pascendi Dominici Gregis*, in 1907.

The rightward turn within the Church, moreover, came at a time when religious orthodoxy generally seemed to be under concerted attack. This made the resurgent conservatism emanating from Rome all the more appealing to a conscientious layman like William Hughes. We have already seen that he, like many of his clerical contemporaries, was deeply disturbed, in the early years of the century, by what he believed to be a growing obsession in the larger society with sexuality and materialism. The university, as he saw it, was part of that society, and his altered view of the secular college was a measure of his disenchantment with the cultural shifts that defined the age.

Other Catholics clearly shared these fears: the growing enrollment in Catholic colleges after 1900 can be read in part as evidence of this. But the number of Catholics in secular colleges continued to grow as well. A 1907 survey of Catholic college students nationally had fully two-thirds of them enrolled at secular institutions. How to provide for such students spiritually, without appearing to condone their presence on a secular campus, was an increasingly vexing problem for American bishops. Some of them, indeed, had not come to terms with it even in the 1950s.[50]

What most bishops finally embraced as the best approach to the problem was the campus "Newman Club," where Catholic students could meet their fellows and receive religious instruction. Detroit's Bishop Foley was apparently among the very early supporters of the concept, for the "Foley Guild" at the University of Michigan, founded in 1889, is thought to have been one of the first Catholic student organizations at a secular American college. (Intended "to promote the spiritual, intellectual and social advancement" of Catholic students at Michigan, the Guild's initial membership was said to number 122.) The fledgling guild had taken Foley's name out of admiration and gratitude: they believed that he sympathized with their situation as Catholics on a secular campus. And the members identified closely with their new bishop's liberalism. "The boys are anxious to have as lecturers for the season — first Bishop Foley, to be followed by Cardinal Gibbons, Archbishop Ireland, Father Dowling, SJ, and others of like eminence," a "Catholic Citizen" of Ann Arbor informed the *Michigan Catholic* in the fall of 1889. Bishop Foley did indeed address the guild in December of that year, and encouraged them warmly in their purposes. "He dwelt upon the fact that fidelity to the faith they professed and its faithful practice could in no manner restrict their cultivation of scientific pursuits," the *Michigan Catholic* noted approvingly, "for there could be no conflict between faith and true science, since the one God was author of both. He exhorted them to the consistent fulfillment of their religious duties while pursuing higher studies under the guidance of the eminent professors of the celebrated University of which they were so proud."[51]

Foley's active support of the "Foley Guild" seems to have continued throughout the 1890s, and that support was seen by many Catholics as at least tacit approval of Catholic attendance at the University of Michigan. The president of
Detroit College, the respected Father Michael Dowling, SJ, addressed the guild
in 1890 and again in 1891, taking as his subject the scandal of widespread poverty in a purportedly Christian nation. He urged his audience to do all that they
could to relieve the sufferings of the poor—"It is ever Lazarus that beseeches
you"—but rejected the "nostrums" of the "agitator." ("Socialism supposes virtues
man has not.") He had nothing to say, however, about the propriety of Catholic
attendance at a secular college. Foley's close friend Bishop John Keane, president of the Catholic University of America, spoke to the guild in 1891 on "The
American of the Future," and apparently assured his young audience that as educated Christians they had much to contribute to the nation's destiny. And the
diocesan newspaper to which Foley had given his approval was, as we have seen,
warm in its support of the Foley Guild and of the university itself at least through
1900. In 1898 the paper commended those Catholics throughout Michigan who
had contributed to the fund that helped Ann Arbor's Catholics build a fine new
church. "The plain old frame church erected many years ago . . . has had to
stand comparison with the churches of the Methodists, the Episcopalians and
the Universalists," the paper pointed out. "There has been no definite attempt
heretofore made to present the church to the eyes of this great body of students
as well as to their minds, and it is this presentation which Father Kelly is now
seeking to make." The editor urged his readers to direct their charity next to
the building of "an social home for Catholic students"—a spacious clubhouse for
the members of the Foley Guild.[52]

The growing conservatism in the American hierarchy with regard to secular
education, however, caused Bishop Foley to withdraw his active support from
the Foley Guild soon after the turn of the century. The group began to call itself
the "Catholic Club" at some point between 1900 and 1906, presumably so as to
relieve the bishop of any public association with the organization. But the rechristened club did not suffer the eclipse it might otherwise have done, for
it had the strong support of Ann Arbor's Father Edward Kelly, who became
Auxiliary Bishop of Detroit in 1911, while remaining pastor at St. Thomas
Church in Ann Arbor until he went to Grand Rapids as bishop in 1918. Father
Kelly helped to keep alive the vision of a "Catholic clubhouse" on the campus—
a fund for this purpose was opened under his auspices in 1900—and the Catholic
Club continued to meet regularly in St. Thomas parish hall, sponsoring an annual round of lectures, study groups, and social events. (These were carefully
monitored: Bishop Kelly himself had proscribed the tango at Catholic student
parties, the *Michigan Daily* reported in 1914.) The busy Kelly made it a practice
to assign one of his assistant priests to serve as unofficial "Catholic chaplain" to
the university, and students there benefited from the longstanding Foley policy—a policy continued by his successors—of assigning only the brightest and
best-trained priests to serve in Ann Arbor. Father William Murphy, the first

Bishop of Saginaw, was an assistant at St. Thomas from 1910 until 1912; Father Michael P. Bourke, trained as a lawyer before his ordination in 1914, received St. Thomas parish as his first assignment, and while there he developed the Catholic Students' Club, as it was now called, into a larger and more active organization than it had ever been before. It was Bourke who, with Bishop Kelly, was instrumental in buying property on the Michigan campus for a chapel and a "Catholic clubhouse"; and it was Bourke whom Bishop Michael Gallagher appointed in 1919 as the first official Catholic chaplain to the University of Michigan and who, in 1925, brought the plans for a permanent campus chapel to fruition.[53]

Bishop Kelly's unwavering support of the Catholic students at the University of Michigan probably had more to do with his long residence in Ann Arbor than with his vaguely liberal views. Like other prominent Ann Arbor citizens, he was proud of the university, and found it hard to see that institution as the outpost of unbelief and immorality that its critics believed it to be. And the growing numbers of Catholic students on the campus were for Kelly an ever-present pastoral problem. Their spiritual needs could hardly be ignored because a campus "Catholic club" might be seen by some as sanctioning Catholic attendance at a secular institution. Kelly was certainly an advocate of Catholic education. His own parish school in Ann Arbor had long been admired as one of the best in the state. But he was apparently willing to recognize that a separate Catholic educational system could not, in the absence of direct state support, be so comprehensive as to serve every Catholic child and young adult.

Over the course of the Foley episcopate, there were two significant developments with regard to the history of Catholic schooling. The first was a growing consensus in the Diocese as to the need for parochial education. By 1918, most younger Catholics were probably unaware that quite respectable laymen, even the occasional priest, had once questioned the wisdom of separate Catholic schools. Even more important was the development of a true system of Catholic education, at least in the more populous parts of the Diocese. The Foley years saw a significant increase in parochial school attendance, saw the birth of secondary schools in many parishes, and a distinct improvement in the quality of schooling offered. This was hardly the consequence of a more centralized school administration, for the regional boards of the Foley years had only very limited powers to set and enforce academic standards. But the rising educational attainments of many teaching sisters and the smaller classes made possible by the growing number of sisters in the Diocese meant that instruction did indeed improve. Finally, the Foley years saw the establishment of an accredited Catholic college for women and the transformation of the Jesuit academy into a recognizably modern university.

During the Foley years, in short, the Catholics of the Diocese were more and more committed to a policy of institutional separatism, at least with regard to education. This commitment matured at a time when the Catholic middle class was growing, and when more Catholics than ever before were thoroughly American in their speech and habits. The choice for parochial schooling, then, entailed more than the impulse of immigrant Catholics to preserve their language and their culture. It was also a manifestation of the more disciplined religious practice that increasingly characterized American Catholicism. Appropriately, it was not until the sea change of the 1960s that the need for Catholic schools was again the "open question" that Col. John Atkinson had believed it to be in 1892.

10

CATHOLICS AND THE LARGER SOCIETY

When Bishop John Foley came to Detroit in 1888, he came to a city where Catholics had long been divided, politically and socially, from most of their Protestant brethren. The same was true, to a greater or lesser extent, of Catholics in the rest of the state. Foley hoped that his own charm and his impeccably "American" credentials would help to ease these tensions, and we have seen that he achieved a substantial popularity among non-Catholics locally. That popularity, however, did not prevent the rise of a virulent anti-Catholicism in politics in the early 1890s, or its recrudescence in the years after 1914. Indeed, when Bishop Foley died, early in 1918, the Church in Michigan was on the eve of the most serious political challenge it had ever faced.

But despite the anti-Catholic sentiment that flourished in the Foley years, the gulf between religious camps was narrowing perceptibly. Anti-Catholicism, for all the rancor it caused, ceased in this period to be the ideology of a major political party and was identified instead with an increasingly marginal protest vote. The incidence of marriage between Catholics and Protestants rose sharply in the Foley years, the result, for the most part, of assimilation and Catholic social mobility. Neither Catholic nor conservative Protestant leaders were pleased by this latter development. Still, they were more and more able to find common ground when it came to marriage and the family. For what they called Christian standards of sexual conduct were under a growing assault in the Foley years. Thus conservatives in every church were increasingly likely to see one another as allies.

There was additional progress on the political front. Catholics in the 1890s and after demonstrated a greater independence in political behavior than they had previously done, and the politics of Detroit and Michigan were the less polarized between a "Catholic" and a "Protestant" party as a result. Catholics flocked to the colors in 1898, with the declaration of war against Spain and again in 1917, with the declaration of war against the Central Powers. The rapidity with which Catholics were integrated into these twin crusades is a measure of how thoroughly most Catholics identified themselves as Americans and how willing most non-Catholics were to accept them as fellow citizens. (The experience of war, at home and abroad, was itself an important cause of rapprochement between Catholics and the rest of the population.) Finally, it appears that Catholics and Protestants in Michigan's towns and smaller cities enjoyed surprisingly amicable relations in the Foley years, at least insofar as the Catholic residents of those towns were relatively well assimilated. This era of small town good feeling had unexpected political consequences on occasion, as we will later see.

INTERMARRIAGE, DIVORCE, AND CONTRACEPTION

We have already seen that Bishop Caspar Borgess, worried by a growing incidence of mixed marriage, had probably revised diocesan policy with regard to granting dispensations for such marriages, making them extremely hard to get. Such a policy would explain the small number of mixed marriages performed by priests in the Diocese in the mid-1880s. Bishop Foley, on the other hand, seems to have issued dispensations willingly, probably assuming that most "mixed" couples would otherwise marry outside the Church. He was no more pleased than his predecessor would have been, however, by the substantial increase in mixed marriage that took place during his episcopate. Diocesan figures in this regard, it should be noted, are not wholly reliable: the number of dispensations issued in any given year will almost certainly be accurately recorded, but this is not true of the number of marriages. The Chancery relied on pastors for information of this sort, and some were more conscientious reporters than others. And the Chancery itself often seemed uninterested in accurate accounting, despite its professed concern about the rising incidence of mixed marriage. (The *Catholic Directory* lists the same number of marriages for the Diocese of Detroit in each year between 1903 and 1906.) Still, the trend in the Foley years was decidedly upward. The number of dispensations issued annually grew by more than nine times between 1890 and 1917, a rate of increase that was considerably larger than the growth in the Catholic population.[1]

The best estimates for the 1890s place the incidence of mixed marriage in the Diocese at between 14 and 19 percent. Between 1900 and 1910 the figures generally range between 19 and 22 percent, with a high of 25 percent occurring in 1909. The reported rate does not drop below 20 percent between 1911 and 1916, save for the 18 percent recorded in 1915. (A 30 percent figure for 1911 — startlingly high, under the circumstances — is almost certainly the result of an underreporting of marriages.) Mixed marriage appears to have been largely a phenomenon of the English-speaking parishes. Seven of the twenty-one marriages performed at St. Augustine's Church in Kalamazoo in 1905 involved a non-Catholic. "In common with the bishops and priests of the Church, we must deplore the increasing numbers of these marriages," the pastor lamented, worried that his mostly Irish-American parishioners had adapted all too well to the social world of heavily Protestant Kalamazoo. "One dreads to look ahead 25 years, and forecast how many of the descendants of these couples will go to swell the ever-increasing tide that sweeps thousands into indifferentism." At Wyandotte's Our Lady of Mt. Carmel (Polish) parish, on the other hand, mixed marriages were not a problem. "Do you preach every year on the Sunday prescribed upon Marriage and caution the people about the danger of contracting mixed marriages?" asked the printed form on which all pastors submitted their annual reports to the Chancery in the Foley years. "Have no mixed marriages at all," the Mt. Carmel pastor responded in 1913—a situation apparently typical of many immigrant parishes.[2]

For clergy in the English-speaking parishes, the rise in mixed marriage was cause for alarm. They worried especially that the children of such marriages would be lost to the Church. Few priests, it seems, had much faith in the promises required of the non-Catholic party with regard to the religious training of offspring, and little confidence that he would eventually embrace Catholicism. "Three families, to the pastor's certain knowledge who have been married in the last few years, have children who are not baptized," the St. Augustine's parish paper warned in 1906. "In another family where the mother belonged to no church, he met children from 10 to 14 years of age, who did not know how to make the sign of the cross, nor say a prayer of any kind, not even the Our Father, and hadn't the slightest idea of God or His Commandments." The obduracy which the clergy assumed in the non-Catholic party was perhaps the cause of the surprisingly minimal requirements for religious instruction before the wedding. "At least one month of instructions once a week," was stipulated by the Chancery, although pastors were apparently free to waive the requirement. "When possible yes," the pastor at Holy Cross parish in Marine City answered, when asked in 1914 if he provided the necessary instruction to non-Catholics who were about to be married in his church, "but scarcely ever possible." Bishop Michael Gallagher eventually issued more stringent regulations: "a minimum of ten instructions in the Faith" was required after 1934, and pastors were no longer permitted to decide on their own initiative to waive or alter the law. But this reform came late, fully thirty-five years after the incidence of mixed marriage in the Diocese had risen to what nearly all good Catholics regarded as worrisome proportions.[3]

Mixed marriage was also seen by the clergy as a principal means by which individual Catholics were led to tolerate divorce and contraception. Both were subjects of growing concern by the turn of the century. The divorce rate nationally more than doubled between 1880 and 1910, and contraceptive practice rose substantially in this same period. By the time of the First World War, moreover, the United States was home to a militant "birth control movement," led by the flamboyant Margaret Sanger.[4]

Catholic spokesmen were inclined to blame this doleful state of affairs at least in part on Protestantism. It was the Reformation, after all, that had reduced marriage to a civil contract and had abolished confession, the principal means by which so private a sin as birth control might be detected and admonished against. "Who is it that fosters conjugal infidelity under the sacred sanction of law, who sweeps away the bulwark of society by legalizing divorce, practices the sin which threatens the extinction of the race that was once dominant in New England?" demanded the Jesuit Michael Dowling in an 1890 speech before an audience of Catholics and Protestants in Detroit. "Is it not the Catholic Church alone which applies any effective remedy to the most dangerous diseases of modern society?"[5]

But it was not possible for even the most triumphalist Catholic to blame the sins of the marital world wholly on Protestants, for many Protestant clergy and laymen were outspoken in their opposition to divorce and birth control. The *Michigan Catholic* in the Foley years was increasingly willing to acknowledge this. "Outside of the Catholic Church, thank God, there are to be found honest men who are noble and patriotic enough to cry out against one of the great evils of this century, an evil which is fast sapping the family life of America," the editor wrote in 1916, with regard to an appearance in Detroit by the infamous Margaret Sanger. The warmth which the editor felt for his Protestant allies was only increased by the worries he nursed about certain elements in the Catholic population. Despite clerical opposition, birth control was rapidly acquiring something like legitimacy in the eyes of many Americans, and it was no longer possible to assume, as Catholic leaders had long been accustomed to do, that it was an exclusively Protestant practice. "In Philadelphia, last week, a speaker was almost crushed by an ignorant mob, in their desperation to get Birth-Control literature, which was freely circulated," the *Michigan Catholic* reported uneasily in 1916. Evidently it was a more thoroughly secular world than many of the clergy had hitherto believed, and an astonishingly large proportion of the population was either "without religion" or ignorant "of the reason as to why God's commandments were spoken." The Catholic population would bear watching, then, and Catholic reticence on the topic of contraception — in the confessional as well as the pulpit — would have to give way to more frank and vigorous teaching. This was also the conclusion of Father John A. Ryan, who warned, in an influential article in 1916, that many Catholics were practicing birth control under the illusion that it was not a mortal sin. Perhaps partly in response to Father Ryan, the American bishops made their first collective statement in opposition to contraception in 1919. It was contained in the pastoral letter issued by the hierarchy to mark the return of peace to a ravaged Europe.[6]

Were there priests in the Diocese of Detroit who believed, as Father Ryan did, that some of their parishioners practiced birth control? There is very little evidence that bears on the question, and what there is bears on it only indirectly. Were the members of St. Joseph's parish in Erie, who were angry with their pastor in 1899 because he "interferes with peoples private affairs and troubles," upset about close questioning in the confessional with regard to contraception? (Whatever the "interference" entailed, it was sufficiently resented that "many" were "declining to attend Church[,] refusing to contributing toward Extra Collections and in their ordinary conversation refer to [the priest] with the omision of the title justly due him.") Were anxieties about birth control a cause of the greater hostility to women that characterized some of the sermons reported in the *Michi-*

gan Catholic after about 1905? The paper's editor had apparently come to believe that women were often the initiators of contraceptive practice—he did not indicate whether or not he had reference to Catholic women—and in 1907 he gave front-page play to an unusually frank interview in which Baltimore's Cardinal Gibbons made the same point. "No doubt many women thoughtlessly discuss this subject among each other," Gibbons told a correspondent from the New York *World:* "It is not unusual, in all probability, for older women to advise their younger sisters, who are about to assume the relations of wifehood, not to bring children into the world for a few years, but to 'have a good time and travel.' This instruction that has been given the young wife is probably without the knowledge of the husband."[7]

Like Cardinal Gibbons, certain priests in the Diocese were inclined to believe that the "new woman" was notably less modest, less passive, less domesticated than her mother and grandmother had been. And their pronouncments on women were considerably more alarmist than anything that the *Michigan Catholic* had carried in the 1890s. The changing fashions of the prewar years seemed to Father Henri Blanchot, C.S.Sp., assistant at St. Joachim's parish in Detroit, to signal a new aggressiveness in female sexuality. "The outrageously immodest dress of modern women has broken down the line of demarcation between the pure Christian lady and the harlot," he told a Lenten congregation in 1913. The cathedral's Father John Dempsey saw ominous meaning in the growing acceptability of women's drinking in public. "To speak mildly," he told a local reporter in 1908, "any woman who, either alone, or attended, enters a café and drinks intoxicants, is utterly devoid of self-respect." Bishop Foley himself told a crowd at Holy Redeemer parish in 1913 that "no greater danger to the young exists than cheap theaters with representations of bad women." And Father Michael Esper made the national press wire in 1907 with a sermon against the newly popular teddy bear, which was, according to the priest, promoting a contraceptive mentality in a dangerously vulnerable female population. "The very instincts of motherhood in a growing girl are blunted and oftentimes destroyed if the child is allowed to lavish upon an unnatural toy of this character the loving care which is so beautiful when bestowed upon a doll representing a helpless infant," he informed his congregation in the town of St. Joseph. "No more disgusting sight has ever come to my eyes than is presented by the spectacle of a little girl fondling, caressing, and even kissing these pseudo-animals."[8]

Father Esper's belief in a veritable conspiracy against the procreative instinct was hardly typical of his fellow priests. Most of them seem to have maintained a more balanced view of the larger culture, whatever worries they may have harbored about the laity and birth control. But there is little doubt that many priests, and many of the laity as well, were deeply disturbed by the more aggressive sexual content of popular culture in the decade or so before 1914. The rapid growth of Detroit in this same period only exacerbated these anxieties, at least for that majority of Catholics in the Diocese who lived in the city and its environs. As new factories were built and the city's population swelled, so too

did the numbers of saloons, dance halls, pool rooms, and burlesque houses —
not to mention the newly minted "moving picture show." "For the past two years
the *Michigan Catholic* has waged war on the obscene picture shows and cautioned
its readers against the evil of allowing their children to patronize these places
of iniquity," the paper reminded its readers in 1910, when there were "over a hundred of these places of entertainment" in Detroit. The city's population was
changing as well, becoming more diverse ethnically and more and more disproportionately male. Detroit in 1900 was still a city of families, with children
under ten forming the single largest age group and with a small surplus of
women in the population. By 1920, however, adults between twenty and thirty-
five made up the single largest age group, and males outnumbered females by
a sizable margin. The surplus of young adult men was a source of considerable
social disorder, and a principal reason why commercialized vice — prostitution,
gambling, illegal saloons — prospered so mightily and so openly. "Detroit is in
a stage of shocking, horrid, abominable life," wrote an agitated columnist in the
Michigan Catholic as early as 1906, "and monstrous evils are encouraged by the
indifference of the police department."[9]

Not all Catholics, of course, were troubled by the changing urban scene, or
even by the altered values it apparently expressed. "Sorry to relate there are any
number of so-called Catholics who make it a point to attend these performances,"
the *Michigan Catholic*'s "Rosaleen" commented bitterly in 1908, in an attack on
what she called "salacious plays." "They do not care a bit for Church rules or
priestly admonition." The more ambitious of these "independent" Catholics, according to "Rosaleen," moved in "decidedly Protestant" circles, but she took care
to distinguish between nominal Protestants and those who were devout. "Good
Protestants, like decent Catholics, taboo all that is vile and despise the lukewarm
Catholic." These sentiments were not new to readers of the *Michigan Catholic*;
they had been told before that Catholics and Protestants shared a common
moral agenda. "There is no denominationalism in protecting young women
from looseness of morals and the curse of drink," the editor had pointed out,
in a characteristic editorial in 1898. "We can all be Catholics, Methodists or Baptists together on that score."[10]

The frequency with which the paper invoked "good Protestants" as allies in
moral reform, however, does seem to have increased in the years around the turn
of the century. In part this reflected the growth of the Catholic middle class locally, moral reform being — at least in its political dimensions — a largely middle-
class preoccupation. But the sense of solidarity with "good Protestants" also grew
because editor William Hughes, and many Catholics like him, believed by the
early twentieth century that Christian beliefs and values were under an attack
unprecedented in the United States in its scope and ferocity. The religious foundations of the culture were fast eroding, Hughes believed, and this could not
help but stimulate rapprochement among the churches. "The new condition
which makes the strange bed-fellows is the attack upon the fabric of Christianity
itself," he explained in 1901, with reference to manifestations at a recent Presby-

terian General Assembly of "a kindlier feeling toward the Catholic body than heretofore prevailed." "Presbyterianism is not menaced today by other forms of Christianity as it is by the attack on Christianity itself." Hughes spoke here of the dangers posed by "liberal doctrine, which is modified infidelity," but modified doctrine, in his view, was directly responsible for the widespread erosion of standards for right behavior. And it was in defense of those standards, which included most prominently an uncompromising opposition to divorce and contraception, that Catholics like William Hughes found common ground with many conservative Protestants. That this common ground was increasingly seen by its occupants as a besieged position served to make their "kindlier feeling" for one another all the stronger. This is likely a principal reason that anti-Catholic sentiment nationally declined in the early twentieth century.[11]

Politics

For much of the nineteenth century, the politics of Detroit and Michigan was essentially a politics of religious divison. The dominant Republican party was widely regarded as the party of evangelical Protestantism, and it championed such "Protestant" reforms as prohibition — or, at the least, a stringent regulation of the liquor trade — and Sabbatarian laws. And the party was generally assumed to be hostile to the parochial school and to any increase in Catholic political power. The Democrats, on the other hand, were prominently identified with Catholics and with the ethnic population of the state, and with that tradition of "personal liberty" which, in Catholic eyes at least, mandated tolerance for the saloon and Sunday amusements and the further expansion of the parochial schools. Most state and local elections turned on these evocative issues, which simply reinforced the religious divisions within the electorate.[12]

Bishop Foley had hardly settled himself in his see city when that divided electorate threatened to become even more polarized. A resurgence of organized anti-Catholicism was evident in the Midwest by 1889, orchestrated mainly by the American Protective Association (APA), founded two years earlier at Clinton, Iowa. Alarmed by heavy immigration in the 1880s and by the increasingly Catholic composition of the immigrant population, members of the APA pledged themselves never to vote for a Catholic or to employ one when a Protestant was available or to join with Catholic workers in a strike. The organization found Michigan to be especially fertile ground: there may have been more members of the APA in Michigan by 1894 than in any other state. Its principal organ, the *Patriotic American,* was published in Detroit, and its chief spokesman nationally was a congressman from Saginaw, who had been elected with APA support in 1892. The strength of evangelical Protestantism in Michigan's towns and cities and the bitterness locally over Catholic efforts to expand the parochial schools help to explain the steady growth of the APA in the state. But what caused the membership to balloon — in Michigan and much of the rest of the nation — was the depression that began in 1893 and continued, nearly unabated, until 1897. The severity of the depression in Detroit and its hinterland, coupled with a strong political tradition of anti-Catholicism, made many voters susceptible to a logic that blamed their considerable troubles on the Papacy and its immigrant agents.[13]

The APA was strong enough in Detroit in 1891 to be a major factor in politics. Its sympathies naturally lay with the Republican party, where local members of the APA enjoyed a wide influence. "The Republican ticket this year is Protestant from governor to coroner," an APA circular boasted in 1892. "Briefly, we have compelled it to fall into line." A Republican majority, sympathetic to the APA, had the previous year been elected to the school board in Detroit, and in the fall of 1892 that majority prohibited the hiring of teachers who had not received the whole of their education in the public schools. This regulation did not long survive: by the fall of 1893 the *Michigan Catholic* could tell its readers that a recent St. Vincent's Academy graduate had "passed a splendid examination and was admitted to the force of public school teachers." But the board in 1896 revived a religious issue that had lain dormant for many years when it ordered compulsory Bible reading to be introduced into the public schools.[14]

The APA enjoyed considerable success as well in Detroit's police department. "Many of the prominent officers, and probably half the patrolmen on the force, have identified themselves with the Sons," the Detroit *News* reported in 1892 with regard to the Patriotic Sons of America, a fraternal organization that worked closely with the APA in Detroit, "and it is said that the more zealous members of the order hold periodical meetings in the central station." A Detroit police sergeant was elected treasurer of the APA organization in Michigan in 1894, when he was known as "one of its most prominent and active promoters." Police departments in the United States have, or course, traditionally been contested terrain: newly assertive ethnic and racial groups nearly always demand recognition in the form of appointments to, and promotions within, the ranks of the local police. Detroit's Protestant policemen had good cause to worry in the 1890s: they knew that the Catholic population of the city was growing, and that its political power was bound to increase. As a consequence, they were unusually vulnerable to the alarmist rhetoric of the APA.[15]

The strength of the APA in the ranks of the city's police did decline after 1896, when the organization all but disintegrated locally and nationally. But the department remained something of a Protestant fiefdom. Even the election of a Democratic mayor in 1897 and again in 1899 did not result in the appointment of a Catholic to the Metropolitan Police Commission, a gesture that had been pointedly requested in the editorial columns of the *Michigan Catholic*. Nor did it result in an end to discrimination against Catholics within the department itself. "Since the formation of the commission in 1865, there has never been a Roman Catholic citizen in its membership," the *Michigan Catholic* pointed out in 1900, noting that Mayor William Maybury, elected with strong Catholic support, had appointed four Protestants as police commissioners since 1898. "There are very many Catholic officers in the police force," the paper continued. "They are doing hard work. When the time for advancement comes these men generally find themselves passed over in favor of the men who wear Masonic charms on their waistcoat fronts." Indeed, the highest ranks in the Detroit department remained closed to Catholics until the 1930s.[16]

The APA wielded a good deal of influence in the Michigan legislature, especially between 1892 and 1896. Both legislative houses were heavily Protestant, and a substantial minority in each was openly sympathetic to militant anti-Catholicism. A bill to tax churches, church schools, and charitable institutions — something opposed by the leaders of nearly every denomination in the state — was defeated in the House of Representatives in 1892 by the surprisingly narrow margin of 35 to 32. (Its supporters had intended it principally to undermine the growing network of Catholic schools.) An even more serious threat, from the Chancery's point of view, surfaced in 1895, with the introduction of a measure to repeal the 1867 law that gave the Catholic bishops of the state the right to hold Church property in their own names. Catholics could look for no Protestant allies in their efforts to defeat the Jamison Bill, as it was known. Nor were the Catholic laity or even the clergy unanimous in their opposition to it. "I feel free to say to you that I believe the bill relating to ownership of church property will surely pass the House and Senate this winter," John Donovan, himself a state legislator, told Bishop Foley early in 1895. "A good many of our own people near as I can learn from Grand Rapids were instrumental in bringing the matter to the attention of Sen. Jamison." The indomitable Father Peter Baart was apparently an influential lobbiest in support of the bill, a stand that was consistent with his longtime opposition to growing episcopal power.[17]

The Chancery mounted a major campaign against the Jamison Bill shortly after its introduction. But in order to do so, Bishop Foley himself had to overcome what was, given the times, an astonishing degree of political ignorance. "I would ask you the name of any Catholics in the Senate or House or of those you judge likely to be friendly toward us," he wrote to John Donovan in January 1895, asking as well that copies of the legislature's daily journal be sent to the Chancery. Donovan had discouraging news for his bishop: "At present I know of but one other of our faith in the present membership," he wrote, and he could name only a single additional member who might readily be persuaded to the Chancery's point of view. Pessimistic as to the outcome, Foley nonetheless contacted the bishops of Grand Rapids and Marquette, and the three of them orchestrated an apparently formidable lobby against the Jamison Bill. "It cost $3000 to kill the bill in lawyer expenses and etc.," the chancellor of the Detroit Diocese subsequently recorded. "I paid said sum to parties who fought the bill." Crucial to the campaign, evidently, were the wide social contacts that many Catholics had established as longtime residents of the state. "I have done as much as I could with regard to defeating the bill at Lansing to which your Lordship called my attention," Father Anthony Ternes reported from Adrian.

I had several interviews with Mr. A. W. Smith, one of the most prominent and influential Republicans in Southern Michigan. He has written to some of his friends in the legislature, and if his health will allow it, he will be at Lansing on Tuesday evening next.

Today I went to Hudson, the home of the State Senator of this district, and through Father Nacy's influence, prevailed upon several friends of the Senator, to write him and request him to oppose the bill.

Mr. Smith thinks that perhaps the best plan would be to see the governor and have him veto the bill, if it passes.

Not all of Michigan's Catholics were the impoverished immigrants on which anti-Catholic propagandists liked to dwell, and in the end the Catholic lobby had its way. The Jamison Bill was defeated in the spring of 1895.[18]

The defeat of that bill, at what was probably the height of APA influence in the state, suggests that the appeal of anti-Catholicism as a political ideology was not as great as alarmists on either side of the religious divide were inclined to believe. The behavior of Michigan's leading Republicans in the 1890s indicates that this was the case. Unwilling to repudiate the APA, most party leaders were also unwilling to risk their political futures on its program. The Republicans succeeded in drawing significant Catholic support in the Detroit mayoral elections in 1889, 1891, and 1893 by abandoning their traditional anti-saloon rhetoric and soliciting votes for the Pingree ticket in the German and Polish areas of the city. Mayor Hazen Pingree proved to be an effective apostle of municipal reform, and his Catholic support was only enhanced by his campaigns on behalf of the three-cent streetcar fare and lower prices for gas, electric, and water service. During the six years of Pingree's mayoralty, indeed, the politics of Detroit were focused more sharply than ever before on substantive rather than symbolic issues, as Pingree sought to bring a portion of Detroit's traditionally Democratic voting blocs into a new Republican coalition. His success led in 1896 to his nomination and subsequent election as Republican governor of Michigan. By this time it was clear to even the convinced anti-Catholics in the party's councils that Pingree's pragmatic orientation was essential to continued Republican domination of a rapidly changing state.[19]

The triumph of pragmatism over ideology among Michigan's Republicans was matched by a similar shift in the national Republican party after 1892. The party made substantial gains in the congressional elections of 1894, due almost entirely to the devastating depression that had begun, under a Democratic president, in the course of the previous year. Detroit's Catholics voted more heavily than usual for Republicans in 1894, notwithstanding the clear links between that party and the APA—links that even Mayor Pingree's popularity among Catholics could not obscure. Anxious to exploit the depression for all its political worth, the Republicans in 1896 campaigned largely on economic issues, choosing as their standard bearer Ohio's Senator William McKinley, who was prominently identified with the protective tariff. McKinley's own political history identified him as a supremely pragmatic Republican, inclined to ignore, as excessively divisive, such traditionally Protestant preoccupations as regulation of the saloon and Sunday amusements. The Democrats, on the other hand, nominated William Jennings Bryan, a devout Presbyterian and an active temperance man, whose political vision and political style were shaped almost wholly by his religious convictions.[20]

The 1896 election was a decisive one in American political history, and nowhere more so than in Michigan. Catholic voters in the state — and in the city of Detroit — cast a majority of their votes for McKinley, although they had been a mainly Democratic population even in 1894. Bryan, however, attracted unusually strong support among certain segments of the normally Republican Protestant population. This abrupt realignment was caused by what was essentially a reversal of political images: Bryan looked and sounded, to a good many Democrats, much like those Republicans who had historically threatened the "personal liberties" of men who liked to drink and to enjoy themselves on Sunday afternoons. (Those enemies of personal liberty had often been enemies of the parochial school as well.) McKinley, on the other hand, appeared to stand for what Democrats regarded as their own tradition of tolerance for ethnic and religious diversity.[21]

The political realignment of 1896 proved to be an enduring one. The Republican party was widely seen thereafter not as the party of evangelical Protestantism but as the party of prosperity. It was the dominant party nationally, on the strength of this image, until 1932. Catholics in Detroit and Michigan did not, to be sure, become a mostly Republican population. But they were never again as heavily Democratic in their allegiances as they had been before the 1890s. Nor were the politics of the city or the state ever again as polarized on the basis of religion.[22]

What happened politically in Michigan in the 1890s happened in part because the Catholic population of the state had changed considerably since the religious wars of the 1850s. Its growing middle class was now able to enlist the support of influential Protestants in the fight against anti-Catholicism. "It is a matter of satisfaction to witness the stand taken by respectable Protestants against the vile APA organization," the *Michigan Catholic* commented in 1893. "Clergymen have denounced it from their pulpits as un-American, un-Christian and villainously bestial; the public press has scored it unmercifully, and public officials have ignored the pleadings of its howling officials." The utility of religious toleration had also become more apparent to many members of what was an increasingly diverse society. The introduction of the Bible into Detroit's public schools in 1896 was challenged, and eventually thwarted, almost entirely without Catholic assistance. "The teaching of the Bible, in the most innocuous form, could not possibly be accomplished without sectarianism," the *Michigan Catholic* pointed out, "and this became apparent at once upon the motion of the Jewish and free-thinking citizens of the city, who took steps to have the proceedings stopped and the selected readings eliminated from the school course."

> The matter went to the courts and Circuit Judge Carpenter, himself a Protestant, decided, in a most masterly piece of legal writing, that the law against the teaching

of religion in the schools was being violated and enjoined the school board from continuing this part of the curriculum. The school board, still obstinate, carried the case
to the Supreme Court, where it still rests.

Meantime, the non-Catholics who opposed the introduction of sectarian teaching
in the schools, had had their influence on the election of new inspectors, and the
Board which had just taken office has done so on the platform that the Bible readings
must go.

The force of public opinion in this matter has been wholly exercised without
Catholic intervention, and the wholesome lesson has been given in the whole matter
that the Catholic position was the right one years ago, as it is the right one now.
The fact that no Catholic voice has been raised in the matter has enabled the difficulty to be settled without the injection of prejudice.

The election of a Catholic as Detroit city treasurer in 1897 seemed to confirm
that at least a portion of the city's non-Catholic majority preferred tolerance to
religious controversy. William B. Thompson, a lifelong member of St. Vincent's
parish, served as treasurer until 1906, when he was elected mayor of Detroit —
the first Catholic to hold the position.[23]

The politics of Detroit and Michigan were relatively free of overt religious
bigotry between the late 1890s and about 1910. This was indeed the case in much
of the United States. After 1910, however, a resurgent anti-Catholicism was increasingly evident throughout the nation, as the general political mood became
progressively more apocalyptic. A weak economy in 1913 and a short but sharp
depression in 1914 helped to broaden the audience for anti-Catholic — and anti-
immigrant — propaganda, which now emanated primarily from small-town and
rural America. From the Missouri hamlet of Aurora came the *Menace,* a vitriolic
anti-Catholic paper that claimed a circulation of 1,000,000 by 1914, just three
years after its founding. It was regularly sold on the streets of Detroit and apparently circulated widely, even among Catholics. "A good Catholic cannot be
stirred through the 'rot' published in this vile sheet," a worried factory foreman
told the *Michigan Catholic* in 1913, "but I am convinced that there are some lukewarm Catholics who fully believe all they read in this paper. In the factory in
which I work — one of the largest auto factories in the city — there are many
Catholics and in the department in which I am employed, a number of these
men take the *Menace* and try to corrupt their companions." His "know-it-all ignorant" fellow workers were attracted to the *Menace,* he believed, by the paper's
progressive stand on economic issues and its cautiously cordial attitude toward
the growing socialist movement in the United States. "I only regret that Catholics do not work for the Church equally as hard as these men are hustling for
the *Menace* and Socialism."[24]

The resurgence of anti-Catholicism also brought in its wake the usual company
of itinerant lecturers. A few of them claimed to be former priests and nuns —
a venerable tradition on the anti-Catholic circuit; nearly all of them scented
vast Roman conspiracies behind most of the nation's troubles, including some
from the past. "A Boston evangelist . . . has taken up quarters at the Patriotic
Church, corner Fourth and Howard Streets, for the purpose of 'enlightening'

his friends and hearers of the part the Catholic Church had in the assassination of President Lincoln," the pastor at Holy Trinity Church reported in 1915. The more typical anti-Catholic diatribe focused on the threat to political liberties posed by the parochial schools and by the growing network of Catholic charitable institutions. "The parochial school is the foundation of their great power," the Methodist Bishop Albert Ryerson told a purportedly "secret meeting" to which the Protestant clergy of Detroit were invited in 1915. "More than 1,000,000 of Catholic children are isolated from all that makes for good citizenship." Bishop Ryerson looked to the state as the best hope for curbing Catholic power. "Not only would I advocate the government control of parochial or private schools, but every institution, private or ecclesiastical, should be regularly inspected. Sweatshop conditions, which are known to exist in many Roman institutions would then be made impossible." He did not see these proposals as themselves a violation of individual liberties; on the contrary, they were meant to enable Catholics to claim their inalienable rights to independent thought and action. "We fought a bitter war to liberate a few millions of slaves," he told his audience. "I would gladly give my life to help in the emancipation of 14,000,000 slaves of the Roman church, who are in greater bondage than any southern negro ever was."[25]

Bishop Ryerson was hardly alone in his militance. "At present Detroit has a number of anti-Catholic lecturers holding meetings in this city," the *Michigan Catholic* noted in 1916, "and the House of the Good Shepherd is being regularly attacked for its work of reformation. . . . A number of meddling bigots have called at the House and tried to force their way into the private apartments, which house unfortunate girls sent up from the juvenile courts to be cared for." The Sisters at the house were variously accused of employing their residents under illegal conditions, of holding girls against their will without any authorization from the courts, and of forcing young women to enter the cloistered sisterhood which had its convent on the property. The campaign against the House of the Good Shepherd had attained such proportions by 1916 that Bishop Foley asked the Michigan State Board of Corrections and Charities to visit the house and issue a formal report with regard to their investigation. They did so in the spring of that year, assuring the public that the Sisters ran a model institution. "The spirit of the place is remarkable. There is nothing that would indicate to a stranger a reformatory."[26]

Attacks on the House of the Good Shepherd diminished thereafter, but the fears that had fueled them were not much allayed. These found subsequent expression in a growing agitation against the parochial schools. This led eventually to two statewide referenda — the first in 1920, the second in 1924 — in which Michigan's voters were asked to approve legislation that would have closed nearly every parochial school in the state. Both referenda were soundly defeated, as we will later see, but at considerable cost to Catholics in terms of money and political energy.

The anti-Catholicism that emerged in the decade after 1910 was essentially reactionary—a fear-ridden response to a world that had become progressively more secular in its orientation and in its values. But it sometimes wore a liberal guise. The Church was frequently attacked for its purported opposition to intellectual freedom and to democracy. "Why do the papists want to steal from us our God-given rights, life and liberty?" a woman from Galesburg (Michigan) asked Father Frank O'Brien in 1914. "Why are the Priests so wicked, and why do they lie to their poor dupes, as they do to get their hard-earned money? You all know there is no such thing as purgatory. I truly pity the poor ignorant creatures, but why are they such fools as not to think for themselves?" The *Menace* repeatedly denounced the Church as an enemy of social welfare legislation and of trade unions. *Watson's Magazine,* a former Populist party organ that converted to anti-Catholicism in 1910, identified the Church as a primary ally of corporate tyranny in the United States. These accusations had, in the main, little basis in fact. Those Catholic clergy and editors who spoke at all about social issues in this period were likely to be sympathetic to moderate trade unionism and to social welfare laws that did not appear to threaten the independence of the parochial schools. The *Michigan Catholic*'s William Hughes defended the right to strike, denounced anti-Semitism in Europe and America, and argued against efforts to restrict immigration. (Like many trade-unionists of his day, however, he was an ardent proponent of the Chinese Exclusion Act.) And if he remained neutral on the issue of women's suffrage until his death in 1918, his paper still carried occasional features that argued in favor of the woman's vote.[27]

Catholic spokesmen were certainly vocal in their opposition to socialism, and this may have looked, to the jaundiced eyes of some anti-Catholics, like confirmation of their hostility to social progressivism. A Catholic "cannot be a Socialist, when Socialism is antagonistic to religious truth, and be a Catholic at the same time," the *Michigan Catholic* warned in 1908. "The Socialism which Catholics should keep far-removed from, starts with the untrue postulate that all men are equal, though they evidently are not and never were and never can be, whether physically, mentally, or morally." The paper gave more space, in the years between 1905 and 1914, to denunciations of socialism than it did to criticisms of existing social inequities, mainly because of the growing size and popularity of the recently founded Socialist party. The appeal of that party among Catholics was never very great—at its height it was no more than a minor third party—but men like William Hughes and his clerical allies in Detroit were fearful nonetheless that the recent history of Europe might be reenacted in the United States. Given their fears, the occasional socialist in the Catholic community was a threatening creature indeed, to be opposed no less resolutely than the advocates of birth control.[28]

The Catholic socialist, on the other hand, might well be puzzled by their opposition. Such was the case with one M. Sullivan, a Detroiter who undertook in 1902 to persuade Father Peter Baart of the desirability—and the inevitability—of a socialist America. He was "an old CMBA man and above all a zealous Catholic," but could not agree with the priest that "no Catholic may be a social democrat," as Father Baart had recently told an audience at Marshall. "As to socialism or the Co-operative Commonwealth," Sullivan wrote, "I think it is coming, as sure as the abolition of slavery came, and I for one do not want to see the Catholic Church obstructing it as they did slavery. . . . Truth must prevail you might try to stop the Detroit river as stop it. I believe ⅔ of the thinking people of the world are Socialists." As far as Sullivan was concerned, the socialist movement was not hostile to Christianity but was, on the contrary, its fuller realization. "When Socialists come," he concluded, "the gospel will be preached to the poor."[29]

In wartime

During the years that Bishop Foley served in Detroit, the United States twice declared war against a foreign enemy. On both occasions the response of local Catholic leaders was intensely patriotic, and the mass of Catholics seemed willing, even eager, to offer their services in the nation's cause. These wartime experiences worked to integrate Catholics more fully into the larger society, and to make overt anti-Catholicism a less and less respectable preoccupation. In the short term, it is true, wars nearly always take their toll of civil liberties and tolerance for unpopular minorities. But for American Catholics, war has historically made for greater toleration.

War with Spain in 1898 provided an especially effective backdrop for manifestations of American Catholic patriotism, for Spain was associated in the popular mind with ultramontane Catholicism and an implacable hostility to liberal political values. Catholic spokesmen, aware of this sentiment, took care as war approached to assure the public that Catholic loyalties lay with the United States. (Their job was made easier by the negligible numbers of Spanish immigrants resident in the country.) When the battleship *Maine* was sunk in Havana harbor, kindling indignation among Americans, the *Michigan Catholic* was quick to point out that Catholics not only shared in the anger but were actually the more ardent patriots. The many Masses offered for the victims of the *Maine* disaster showed "how far Catholic patriotism goes," the paper noted. "It follows them who are the strong arms of the country through their battles and it remembers them after they are gone by the prayers of the Church. We have not noticed that any of our separated brethren have devoted themselves to the holding of services in memory of these dead." Bishop Foley spoke publicly, in March of 1898, in support of Cuban independence, and assured a rally in Detroit that "in the event of war, the nation would have upholding her hands, every Catholic Bishop, priest and layman in the United States." A declaration of war came just one month later, and with it the opportunity for Catholics to show the nation how firm their commitment to America was. Bishop Foley reminded Detroiters that Catholics had a special stake in this war when he spoke to a public reception for the men of the Michigan National Guard who were sent late in April to train for an invasion of Cuba. "Defend that flag," he told the troops, "and spread its folds over Cuba until there is the same liberty there that we enjoy. . . . To the Catholic soldiers, let me say: Remember your duty. Fight as soldiers should fight, and show yourselves the better soldiers that you belong to our Church."[30]

Nearly every member of the American Catholic hierarchy stood with Bishop Foley in strong support of the war. "Whatever may have been the individual opinions of Americans prior to the declaration of war, there can now be no two opinions as to the duty of every loyal American citizen," according to the pastoral letter issued by the archbishops of the United States early in May. "We, the members of the Catholic Church, are true Americans, and as such are loyal to our country and our flag and obedient to the highest decrees and the authority of the nation." The Catholic laity, or at least the English-speaking among them, were as much infected by war fever as other Americans. "I suppose that it is all war talk in Detroit as well as here," young Mary Loftus wrote from Ionia. "My little brother Johnny is always talking about what mamma is going to do with this and that of papa's if he goes to war." The Detroit Catholic Cadets convened after war was declared and offered their services as combat troops to Governor Pingree. A soldier already in uniform wrote to the *Michigan Catholic* on May 3 to exult in the number of Catholic volunteers with him at camp near Brighton. "As you are aware the Spanish nation is a Catholic nation," he began, "and for that reason there is a certain class of the American people so bigoted as to believe that we American Catholics would sympathize with Spain in the contest."

> But I am proud to say, Mr. Editor, that I belong to one of the military companies encampted here, namely, the Montgomery Rifles, seven-eighths of whom are Catholics, and from Capt. Considine, Jr., down, every man of them would give up his life in defense of the Stars and Stripes.
>
> We have in our company at camp 86 men and out of that number only three declined to volunteer their services, and they had good reason for doing so. The boys are anxiously waiting to be called to the front to help expel from this Western Continent the cruel Spaniards. So you can see the position of the Catholic soldiers in our company and the same feeling exists among all our co-religionists in camp.[31]

Those Catholics too young or too old to fight were warm in their demonstrations of support for those who could. "The soldiers here went to Island Lake April 26," Edwin Sanscrainte wrote from his school in Monroe. "All the schoolchildren, the band, the Knights of St. John and the old soldiers accompanied them to the train." Patriotic themes dominated parochial school closing exercises in June. The pupils at St. Anne's school in Detroit presented a "patriotic operetta 'Old Glory,'" which "closed with a glorious tableau, 'Liberty,' in which 'Cuba,' represented by Miss Irene Cotton, stretched out her shackled arms toward the Goddess of Liberty, represented by Miss L. Patton." Among the children in the "soldier's chorus," one G. Paré — the future historian of the Diocese — "carried off the honors for singing and dancing."[32]

The actual fighting in the Spanish-American War lasted less than ten weeks, far too brief a time to engender the weariness and cynicism in the civilian population that have come in the wake of other American wars. Rejoicing in the liberation of Cuba and in the relatively small number of American battle deaths (fewer than 400), most Americans agreed that, in the words of Secretary of State John Hay, it had been a "spendid little war." Its aftermath, however, was more sobering. Deaths among the American troops in Cuba and the Philippines mounted rapidly after the armistice, mostly because of disease. The nation was deeply divided by President McKinley's decision to annex the Philippine Islands and to use American troops to quell a popular rebellion there. The eagerness with which certain Protestant organs had pressed for annexation had made many Catholics uneasy, nor were their fears allayed when McKinley explained to an assembly of Methodist ministers that he had had no choice but to annex the Islands and "to educate the Filipinos and to uplift and civilize and Christianize them." "We . . . protest most energetically against the forcible setting aside of a Catholic civilization that has endured far beyond a hundred years, and against the proselytizing efforts which are being made under the banner of imperialism by a band of sectarian fanatics and of unscrupulous hypocrites in the islands of the Southern Sea," the German-American Catholic Association of Michigan resolved at its annual convention in 1900. "We condemn as unnecessary, imprudent and brutal the imposition of our godless Public School system in the islands of Cuba, Puerto Rico and the Philippines." The *Michigan Catholic*'s William Hughes was by this time so embittered by the course of American foreign policy that he could not bring himself to speak of the recently reelected McKinley with the respect he nearly always gave to duly constituted authority. "In St. Mary's hospital, this city, lies a soldier, Willis Hausner, whose young life is fast ebbing away," he told his readers in an impassioned editorial.

> He is another victim of imperialism, and after serving his country well both in Cuba and the Philippines has been sent home to die—absolutely penniless. . . . Think of it. Some poor mother's son, junketed thousands of miles over land and sea to his home city, absolutely starving for want of proper nourishment, without a penny in his pocket, while Emperor William of Canton is spending thousands of dollars paying for the feasting at his coronation. Like Nero of old this Washington imperialist chuckles over his splendid conquests, while the life of this boy, as well as that of hundreds of others, is being offered up to satisfy his greed for pomp and power.[33]

Most Catholics in the Diocese probably knew little about events in the Philippines, for all the emotion spent by William Hughes on his anti-imperialist editorials. McKinley won broad support when he was reelected in 1900, most Americans apparently content now to ignore the war that still went on in those remote Pacific islands. Press censorship kept some of the more brutal aspects of the Philippines campaign from the public, and the return of prosperity after 1897 had the effect of muting dissent generally. But however great their indifference to overarching questions of foreign policy, most Catholics must been aware of the dramatic decline in anti-Catholic activity after 1898. "Anti-Catholicism broke down even more completely than other forms of nativism during the war with Catholic Spain," historian John Higham has noted. "The shattered ranks of the American Protective Association shrank entirely out of sight." A revived economy contributed to the era of denominational good feeling that followed the war, but the war itself had clearly been a primary cause of rapprochement between Catholics and their fellow citizens. It had given a polyglot nation the experience of unity, and reassured all but the most recalcitrant nativists that the children of Catholic Europe were indeed becoming good Americans.[34]

The war that began in Europe in August 1914 did not initially appear to challenge the American loyalties of the Catholic population. German-Americans, in the Diocese of Detroit and elsewhere, were openly sympathetic to the Central Powers, but did not believe — as they had no reason to do — that their sympathies were inconsistent with their allegiance to the United States. The delegates who assembled in Detroit in 1914 for the annual convention of Michigan's German Catholic Societies unself-consciously endorsed a collection for those victims of the war whom they identified as "our countrymen." The German-born pastor of St. Anthony's parish in Detroit had been traveling in Germany when war broke out. He remained there for some months, serving as a chaplain in the German army. Certain Irish-Americans in the Diocese too were supporters of the Central Powers, mainly because of their undying enmity toward England. Probably a majority of the Irish, however, were in the early stages of the conflict disposed to a genuine neutrality.[35]

French and Belgian Catholics, on the other hand, were partisans of the Allies, as were most Poles. The members of Our Lady of Sorrows (Belgian) parish solicited funds in 1914 "in the interests of their distressed brethren in Europe," and even dispatched their pastor to Belgium, from whence he returned with more than 100 refugees. The French-surnamed residents of Detroit's East Side, many of whom had left the precincts of St. Joachim's (French) parish, were moved to return in "very large" numbers in 1915 for "Peace Sunday," when Catholics in the United States and other countries too assembled, at the behest of Pope Benedict, to pray for an end to the European war. "In Detroit . . . . the churches were thronged to capacity at all of the Masses," the *Michigan Catholic* noted of the occasion, "and the number of communions was unprecedented in the history of many of the parishes."[36]

It was still possible in 1915 for Americans to believe that the war menaced only the unhappy nations of Europe. Catholics had particular reason to cling to this illusion, for the Catholic community was more divided by nationality than any other religious group. "Our American people, during the coming months, will have to be on their guard," the *Michigan Catholic* warned in the summer of 1915, "and will have to make it plain to their legislators and statesmen that no propaganda, financed from abroad or by the selfish interests of this country, will avail to involve us in this old-world insanity." The paper had been scrupulously neutral in its own editorial stance and in its coverage of the war itself. Editor Hughes had declined to publish the first reports of German atrocities that came out of Belgium in 1914 — reports that had been hotly disputed by German-Americans, Catholic and Protestant alike. "If there are atrocities perpetrated other than the privileged acts of war, in the awful conflict now raging in Europe," he finally brought himself to say, "these acts are not committed by Catholic soldiers."[37]

As tensions increased between Washington and Berlin, Hughes maintained his neutral stance. "The newspapers dish up lurid stories, highly colored," he complained in 1916, "until the sound of martial music sets the minds of men distraught and unsettled, and untrained they are ready to leap into the fray, with no knowledge or little preparation for the awful scenes they will become a part of." The large German population of the Diocese was doubtless on his mind as he looked with apprehension to the future. For that population had sustained, over four generations, what looked to be a vibrant sense of German identity. Even in 1917, German-American Catholics supported a network of social and religious organizations that was unrivaled in the Diocese. The aggressiveness with which German-American spokesmen defended the Central Powers during the years of nominal American neutrality had roused deep resentments against that community long before the United States entered the war, and Hughes may well have feared that the loyalty of many German-Americans was dangerously divided. But in fact that population was more thoroughly assimilated than most observers believed.[38]

The United States entered the First World War in April 1917. Uncertain as to the depth of popular support for this decision, the Wilson administration, aided by a compliant press, immediately undertook an intensive propaganda campaign. The Allied cause was presented as a veritable crusade for liberty, while Germany was depicted as a brutal, almost diabolical nation, bent on destroying the very foundations of Christian society. Catholic spokesmen appropriated these themes for their own pronouncements on the war, aware that certain of their ethnic constituencies were suspected of divided loyalties. Bishop Foley was too old and feeble to rally his people to the colors, but most of his clergy were ardent patriots. Those young men who had been conscripted into the army, the pastor at Belding told his congregation, had "won a new heritage of honor."

> Soon the best young men of our country will be in training—a few more months and they will be fighting for humanity, for the world—suffering and dying to rescue the Sacrament of liberty from those who would despoil it and deny it to humanity. The call comes to Uncle Sam's boys like the call to the Crusaders of old, to fight a system—not a nation, to rescue liberty . . . that people shall have a right to live.

Father John McClory, SJ, was no less eloquent in a September 1917 sermon preached to newly conscripted soldiers at Detroit's Holy Rosary Church. "A military death is not a calamity, but a triumph," he told the crowd, which filled the church to its doors, "not a slaughter, but an apotheosis." Those who died on the field of battle, he assured his hearers, would be numbered "among the heroes of the Civil and the Revolutionary wars and indeed the wars of all time. But best of all, with your life's blood streaming from you, you will realize that you have done God's will; that He will welcome you: that you will hear those sweet words from His lips: 'Well done, good and faithful servant. Because thou hast been faithful over few things, I will place thee over many; enter thou into the joy of thy Lord!'"[39]

Perhaps inspired by Father McClory's vision of the war, the students at the University of Detroit, where he was on the faculty, enlisted in large numbers in the spring of 1917, as did students at colleges across the country. The Polish parishes were fruitful sources of recruits as well, for an Allied victory was widely assumed to mean restoration of the Polish nation. A contingent of young Polish-Americans, some 300 strong and "Catholic to a man," marched to Detroit's City Hall on Memorial Day to offer their services in the cause of liberty. "The Poles of Detroit stand behind President Wilson," their spokesman told Mayor Marx, himself a German-American. "The fathers and mothers of these Polish boys love them as devotedly as parents can, yet they are willing to spill Polish blood for independence." Those young men who were not moved to volunteer for the armed forces were, after May 1917, subject to conscription. Father John Vismara gave an especially emphatic seal of approval to the draft when he agreed to serve as chairman of Kalamazoo's board of registration. Other clergy made the same point in more conventional ways. "When the president of the United States sends out the call to arms the Catholic church teaches obedience to the voice of God," Father Peter Slane told the graduates of SS. Peter and Paul's school in Owosso. "It may mean sacrifice, but the Catholic has never been known to be a slacker in the cause."[40]

There was little opposition to conscription among Americans generally during the war, and almost none within the Catholic community. Catholics nationally made up a larger proportion of the armed forces than they did of the general population, and local spokesmen claimed that this was true in the Diocese of Detroit as well. Parishes throughout the Diocese proudly displayed the "service flags" that indicated, by their variously colored stars, the numbers of young men from the parish who were in uniform, or had been wounded or killed. "The service flag for St. Vincent's Church was blessed Sunday, June 9, at the 12 o'clock Mass," the *Michigan Catholic* reported in 1918:

> The services were carried out in a very patriotic manner. The flag was carried by the boys from the parish school, some of whom were dressed as sailors, others as soldiers. Before the blessing of the flag a very fine sermon was delivered by Rev. Father Chawke. In the sermon our beloved assistant laid before the people the necessity of assisting the president, laying before the congregation innumerable instances in which the Catholic element of the US showed particular courage and undaunted bravery. All in all, there are about two hundred stars on the flag, each denoting some member of the parish who is in the service. On the flag also are three golden stars to call to mind the three young men, Leo McIlkenny, Leo O' Grady and William Frank, who have already sacrificed their prospects and life itself in order that democracy might remain untrampled by the heel of Kaiserism.

Holy Redeemer parish, to the west of St. Vincent's, had 675 young men in the armed forces by September 1918, five of whom had died. (Our Lady of Help parish, on Detroit's East Side, had in March 1918 had "the honor of giving the first hero, from this city, to fall on the firing line of France in the cause of Liberty and Democracy.") If there were those who wondered, as the war ground on, whether the prize was worth the mounting cost in lives, the state of public opinion did not encourage them to voice their doubts. "The man who cries for peace today is either a traitor to his country or crazy," Father John Zindler told his congregation in the town of St. Joseph. "Plato said 'Carthage must be destroyed,' and the time has come when we must say 'The Kaiser Must Be Destroyed. . . . There will be no peace until there is victory. It may take one, two, or thirty years, but when it does come the stars and stripes will be floating over the fields of France and Flanders and liberty will be proclaimed throughout the world."[41]

Buoyed, perhaps, by the passionate rhetoric of their clergy, Catholics were notably active, for a heavily working-class population, in war work on the home front. Pastors and lay committees solicited funds for the various war bond drives, with the parochial schools in Detroit vying to see which could sell the most subscriptions. (Bishop Foley had declared, in an October 1917 pastoral letter, that buying war bonds was a "moral duty.") Catholic women locally were active in Red Cross work. "A little army of volunteers" could be found in Holy Redeemer parish at the biweekly meetings of its Red Cross unit, and similar scenes were evident at other churches too. The Knights of Columbus distinguished themselves by establishing soldiers' recreation centers at Camp Custer near Battle Creek, in Detroit, and in Ann Arbor. Like all of the Knights' facilities for soldiers in the United States and abroad, these were open to any man in uniform. "The non-Catholic soldier is meeting with our priests, many of them for the first time, and are finding that they are men's men, and they like them," a delighted observer reported from Camp Custer. And by the spring of 1918, Catholics in Detroit had joined the rest of the populace in support of the Detroit Patriotic Fund. "Future campaigns to raise money for war relief and public welfare work in Wayne County will be combined in one great drive, staged once a year," the *Michigan Catholic* noted, explaining what was in fact the first of the annual "united fund" drives by which Catholic charities in Detroit were largely supported between 1918 and 1944. Catholics were well represented among the fund's directors in 1918, and among the thousands of workers who solicited contributions that year.[42]

The loyalty that Catholics displayed during the war did not go unrewarded. The strength of organized anti-Catholicism, both locally and nationally, declined precipitously after 1915, as the fears and resentments of the mass of Americans were more and more directed toward Germany. Circulation of the *Menace,* which peaked in the spring of 1915, declined by more than a million copies in little better than a year. The paper continued to be hawked in the streets of Detroit, however, until the summer of 1918, when the City Council prohibited its public sale or distribution. There was widespread support in Detroit for the council's action, which was generally seen as a wartime bid for unity. "The Detroit Board of Aldermen is to be commended for its courageous decision to prohibit the sale of that contemptible sheet *The Menace,* upon the streets of Detroit," the Detroit *Jewish Chronicle* commented. "This action should have been taken long ago. Moreover, similar action should be taken in every city of the country."

Never before had local opposition to anti-Catholicism been so broad or so strong, and Catholic spokemen were obviously gratified by the turn of events. It is not too much to say, in fact, that the war gave many Catholics a greater sense of belonging to the larger society than they had ever known before.[43]

For Catholics of German descent, however, the war was an experience of a wholly different order, as it was for German-American Protestants. The anti-German sentiment that had been building nationally since 1915 erupted, after the American declaration of war, into a veritable hysteria. German-Americans were widely suspected not simply of divided loyalties, but of working as domestic agents for the Kaiser. German-American institutions were therefore the targets of enormous hostility, and their leaders sometimes the objects of real persecution. We have already seen that the German-language curriculum in the parochial schools of the Diocese was either eliminated or greatly curtailed during the war, out of deference to a hostile public. Detroit's German Catholic weekly, *Stimme der Wahrheit,* first published in 1875, ceased publication in 1918, due largely to a precipitous drop in advertising revenue. And while most of the German Catholic organizations in the Diocese survived the war, they never again possessed the élan and the clear sense of purpose that had characterized them in the days when Germans were perhaps the most admired and confident of the nation's many ethnic groups. The war, no doubt, simply hastened the end of German cultural nationalism, which was probably doomed to extinction by the progress of assimilation and intermarriage. But it was a bitter chapter nonetheless in the annals of the local German community. And it was a signal that the United States, now a world power, was almost bound in the future to be less and less tolerant of those who clung to the language and culture of their forebears, even as the country was becoming more tolerant of those Catholics whose cultural and political loyalties were demonstrably American.

Catholics and protestants in michigan's small towns

Catholics in the Diocese of Detroit, as in most American dioceses, were a mainly urban population in the years around the turn of the century. Much of what we know about Catholic life in this period, including the relationship of Catholics to other Americans, reflects the experience of this urban majority. We know rather little about those Catholics who lived on farms and in small towns, and even less about their relations with their Protestant neighbors. At first glance, they would seem to have been a more embattled population than their urban cousins, at least in the Diocese of Detroit, where most small towns were predominantly Protestant and were said to give organized anti-Catholicism much of its support. But the pages of the *Michigan Catholic* in the Foley years convey a different story. The local correspondents on whom the paper depended for its small town news nearly always described the relations between Catholics and Protestants in their own communities as tranquil and cooperative, whatever the appeal of anti-Catholic propaganda might be elsewhere. "We have none of this in Mt. Morris," an anonymous correspondent assured the *Michigan Catholic* in 1914, with reference to resurgent anti-Catholicism. "*The Menace* is hardly known, because the Mt. Morris people do not want it." He had impressive grounds for his optimism: "every elector in the village" had recently signed a petition asking the Catholic pastor at Mt. Morris to run for mayor, although Catholics were a tiny minority in the town's population. (Father Thomas Luby had declined the nomination.) And Catholic religious practice seems to have enjoyed a surprising measure of tolerance, even of respect. "In the village public schools there are nearly three hundred children — thirty of these are Catholics; yet on every holy day and during missions, Forty Hours' devotions and Holy Week they are sent in a body from the school to attend Mass. Whenever the priest needs servers for funerals or weddings, he simply telephones the superintendent of the High School and servers are on hand."[44]

Father Luby's experience in Mt. Morris was perhaps not typical. Priests were not normally asked to run for public office, although Father Patrick Dunigan was elected mayor of heavily Protestant Lapeer in 1912 and Father Charles Koenig was elected president of the village of New Baltimore in 1914. But priests were often highly respected figures in the small towns of the Diocese, enjoying much the same status as the local Protestant clergy, particularly where the priest took care to cultivate good relations with the Protestant majority. "Everyone likes him," wrote young Ella Lynch in 1894 of Father J. A. VanHoomissen, pastor at Mt. Clemens, "not only Catholics, but people of every race, sect, and religion, on account of his friendly ways." Numerous reports from across the Diocese in the Foley years tell the same story. Priests were asked to speak at patriotic celebrations and high school graduations, to lend their support to various efforts at civic improvement, and they were sometimes the recipients of affectionate tributes from their non-Catholic fellow citizens. Protestants and Catholics in the village of Durand came together in 1906 at a farewell reception for Father Dennis Hayes, about to leave for a new pastorate at Coldwater. The local Baptist minister graced the occasion and "made a very felicitous speech of commendation and praise of Father Hayes, ending by wishing him God speed and good wishes for his success in his new field of labor." The citizens of St. Joseph turned out in force in 1917 to say goodbye to Father Michael Esper, for he had belonged to the Chamber of Commerce and been a charter member of the Civic Improvement Association, which achievements were duly noted by the mayor and other dignitaries in their addresses. Father Joseph Hallissey, pastor in mostly Protestant Hudson, was the guest in 1918 at a surprise reception to mark the twenty-fifth anniversary of his ordination. "The opera house was decorated patriotically," a local correspondent reported. "Every denomination was represented in the assemblage." Over 2,000 people attended the funeral of Battle Creek's Father Michael Sadlier in 1908, including the mayor and the city council — which had "adopted a resolution . . . to attend the funeral in a body" — and the members of the local Protestant clergy. "His Protestant fellow citizens are saddened by his passing, and mourn his death as the loss of an honest, upright citizen, one who had always stood for righteousness and justice and whose charity was unbounded," an anonymous parishioner wrote.[45]

No priest in the Diocese, however, received a more touching demonstration of non-Catholic affection than Father Cornelius Korst, who served as pastor of St. Charles parish in Coldwater from 1866 until his retirement in 1900. In that latter year, the Coldwater Odd Fellows sponsored a contest to choose the most popular man in town, who stood to win a trip to Paris. Citizens might vote as often as they liked, the cost of each vote being just one penny. "The four leading candidates were Rev. C. Korst, of St. Charles Catholic Church; Rev. French of the Methodist [church]; Rev. Dr. Wilson, of the Seven[th] Day Adventists, and Mr. Sydney Champion, book-keeper at the Cement Factory," explained a local correspondent, who proceeded to describe the unexpected denouement of the affair:

> It was evident from the start that Father Korst was the favorite of most of the city people, but the Cement people made a great bustle at their plant for their man, with lots of money behind them, and Mr. Champion won by less than 100 votes, Father Korst having about 3,000 votes when counted, Mr. Champion about 3095; but still the leading business and professional men of the city claimed Father Korst was the most popular and had ought to go, and would go, and the next morning a committee from the Odd Fellows and business men started out and in one hour and forty minutes they collected $221 for the Rev. Father, and the most surprising part of all was they would not accept a cent from a Catholic, claiming they had done their part, and furthermore, they wished to show the Rev. Father in what high esteem the non-Catholics of this place hold him.[46]

Just why the Catholic clergy should be so widely accepted in a state where anti-Catholicism has historically been strong is not entirely clear. Certainly they benefited from the respect that was generally accorded the clergy in Michigan's small towns and from the tradition of tolerance that was necessitated by the wide variety of Protestant denominations that flourished in the state. Father Walter Elliott, preaching a mission in Freedom Township in 1894, found that this rural hamlet supported no less than seven Protestant churches, as well as a Free-Will Baptist College. "This denomination has a good church building also, and so have respectively the Calvinistic or Hardshell Baptists, the Methodists, the Congregationalists, the Episcopalians, and the Seventh-Day Adventists, the Free or Howling Methodists having a nascent society which meets in a little hall." As the Catholic clergy were increasingly a native-born population, moreover, they were able to dispel some of the fears that linked Catholicism with foreign ideologies. And many of them discovered that the rigidities of their seminary training had prepared them rather well for the religious and social climate of the typical small town. Their Protestant neighbors might harbor grave doubts about certain Catholic doctrines, but they stood with the Catholic clergy on the literal interpretation of scripture and on an unrelenting opposition to the sins of the flesh. "A man must be an outright and aggressive total abstainer to succeed in this work," Walter Elliott warned in 1893, with regard to his recently inaugurated missions to non-Catholics in the small towns of the Diocese.[47]

Many of the small town pastors who got on well with their Protestant neighbors were, in fact, ardent proponents of temperance. Father Joseph Cullinane, pastor at Niles, was surely a force for ecumenism when he gave "his celebrated lecture on 'Intemperance'" in the various towns of the Diocese. "The hall was crowded, and the eloquent young lecturer created a favorable impression on his listeners," an observer at St. Joseph reported in 1897. "Father Cullinane also presented his stereopticon views of 'Ten Nights in a Bar-Room.'" The diocesan clergy in the Foley years were almost certainly more favorably disposed to the temperance cause than were the mass of the laity, and a few of them shared the near-apocalyptic vision of its more extreme Protestant proponents. "It did not require a political clairvoyant to see that a conflict was coming in this country between the saloon and the temperance elements," Father Charles Reilly told a temperance meeting at Hudson, "and the Catholic Church was taking steps to determine the faithful on the position they should occupy in the strife." Most Catholic temperance advocates did stop short of endorsing prohibition, preferring moral suasion and such limited legal reforms as the closing of saloons on Sunday. But there were priests in the Diocese who advocated prohibition. Fathers Dennis Hayes and Patrick Dunigan campaigned in 1916 on behalf of the "drys" in Michigan's prohibition referendum — the prohibition forces carried the day, despite losing badly in heavily Catholic Detroit — and Father John O'Rafferty was known in rural Shiawassee County for his efforts in an earlier "dry" campaign there.[48]

The small town priest also had the advantage of representing a modest population of Catholics, who were usually a distinct minority in the local population. Whatever fears the small town Protestant might entertain about the political designs of the Pope, he did not have to worry, for the most part, that Catholics locally were about to assume political power. (Protestants in the city of Detroit, on the other hand, had every reason to fear this.) And as a growing number of his parishioners became assimilated and reasonably prosperous, the small town priest was able to present Catholicism to his Protestant neighbors as a potent force for Americanization and sound morality. Catholics, after all, went regularly to church, eschewed theological liberalism, and were taught the virtues of obedience, thrift, and temperance. Certainly by the late nineteenth century there seem to have been many small towns where the gulf between the churched and the unchurched was considerably greater than the gulf between Catholics and Protestants, a state of affairs from which priests could only benefit. "He is everywhere known as a great-hearted, brave, patriotic American gentleman, a true servant of the Master," the Protestant editor of the St. Joseph *Evening Press* informed Bishop Foley in 1899 with regard to Father James Gore, who was prominent as a St. Joseph civic leader. Ironically, the editor wrote to defend Father Gore against the complaints of an unhappy faction in his congregation.[49]

Small town priests themselves appear to have been increasingly disposed to appreciate the virtues of Protestants and especially the Protestant clergy, with whom they were likely to have much more contact than would have been the case in a heavily Catholic city like Detroit. Msgr. Francis Kelley, who founded the Catholic Church Extension Society in 1905 when he was pastor at Lapeer, recalled in 1916 that during his years in Lapeer he had "learned to love everyone in the city, finding that the line of religion was observed only on Sunday and that the same friendship existed for him among Protestants as among his own parishioners." Seated with Msgr. Kelley at the speakers' table at this 1916 reception were Dr. and Mrs. S. G. Livingston of Lapeer, he the longtime Presbyterian minister there. Kalamazoo's Father Frank O'Brien seemed to think it quite natural, in 1895, that some of the young Catholics in his parish Sunday school should be students at the local Baptist College, where he evidently trusted that no untoward proselytyzing would take place. Father O'Brien had apparently amicable relations with most of his city's Protestant clergy, and indeed with influential Protestants throughout the state. "He was appointed a member of the State Board of Charities some years ago by the Governor of Michigan," the *Michigan Catholic* noted in 1896, "and later on, was commissioned as one of the examiners of West Point by President Harrison. The degree of Doctor of Laws has been conferred on him both by the University of Michigan, and Notre Dame University. He is thoroughly wide-awake and up to the times, and it would be a good thing for every diocese if they had a few more Father O'Briens."[50]

If the small town was often surprisingly hospitable to "wide-awake" priests like Father O'Brien, it was apparently no less so for assimilated members of the Catholic laity. Such, at least, is the picture that emerges from the *Michigan Catholic* in the years around the turn of the century. Catholics and Protestants were surely aware that they differed theologically and in their mode of worship and probably in political allegiance as well. They almost certainly did not want their children to marry across the religious divide. But the intimacies of small town life seem to have made, at least on some occasions, for a startling degree of interfaith cooperation. Respectable social life in the small town generally centered on the churches, and by the late nineteenth century Catholics and Protestants were evidently accustomed to frequent one another's bazaars and entertainments. "The ladies of the Episcopal church gave an entertainment at the opera house last week in which I took part," young Florence Dwyer wrote from the village of Hudson in 1895. "It was quite a decided success." The women at Dearborn's Sacred Heart parish, for their part, had no trouble drawing an ecumenical crowd to the Thanksgiving Day supper they served in 1891 to benefit the parish treasury. "The tables were set in the Town Hall and they were surrounded by a very happy company, including people of all the Protestant denominations as well as the Catholics." Not every Catholic social event, to be sure, enjoyed the same degree of Protestant support that Father Stephen Witliffe found when he assumed the pastorate at tiny Pewamo in 1906. The parish picnic that year was immensely successful, raising $800 for the church building fund. "The day was an ideal one and fully two thousand people, many of them coming a distance of ten or twelve miles, participated in the festivities. The townspeople turned out en masse, non-Catholics vieing with their Catholic neighbors in contributing to the success of the event, and the Protestant merchants of the town closed their places of business to give the new pastor . . . a helping hand."[51]

The merchants of Pewamo were understandably eager to see a new St. Joseph's Church rise in their village, for the number and grandeur of a small town's churches bore witness to its growth and prosperity. An imposing Catholic church, by this logic, was more to be desired than feared, and small town Protestants in the Foley years seem often to have contributed to Catholic building funds in their communities. The Protestants of Dowagiac, according to a local correspondent, were nearly as delighted as the Catholics by the completion of Holy Maternity Church in 1893, "because through their generous contributions they have assisted a good work and have added another ornament to their beautiful little city." Protestants at Swartz Creek not only contributed to the church fund but took a leading part in the 1913 celebration that surrounded the dedication of the new St. Mary's Church there. It was the "Methodist ladies . . . who entertained the visiting clergy and the large crowd in attendance at the dedicatory services, at dinner in the Odd Fellows' hall. Mrs. Passmore, the estimable wife of the resident Methodist minister, was chairman in charge of the arrangements. All of the stores were closed and in the afternoon the businessmen played baseball and devoted the receipts of the gate to the church fund."[52]

Patriotic holidays in the small town were apparently often marked by an earnest ecumenism, as Catholics and Protestants came together to pay tribute to those myths and symbols that defined their common American identity. Fin-de-siècle nationalism, as John Higham has noted, was an increasingly secular ideology, still employing religious imagery but, happily for Catholics, an imagery that was more and more vague and inclusive. The "fully 1000" persons who gathered in St. Mary's Church in Chelsea on Memorial Day in 1898 were bound more firmly together by the patriotic myths they celebrated than they were divided by their various religious allegiances — such was the case, at least, for the duration of the day's festivities. "The ministers of the different churches, the members of the local post of the G.A.R. [Grand Army of the Republic] and of the W.R.C. [Women's Relief Corps], with all the prominent non-Catholic citizens of Chelsea occupied the place just in front of the Sanctuary," an observer explained, noting that Father William Considine's "magnificent address" was the highlight of the occasion. "It is the simple truth to state that never was such a patriotic, impressive, and eloquent address given in Chelsea. . . . You should have heard the grand rendition of 'Columbia' by the entire audience, which so deeply stirred the patriotic souls of all." The Chelsea correspondent thought that this occasion marked the first time "that memorial services under the auspices of the G.A.R. were ever held in a Catholic church in our State," but such services had in fact been held at St. John's Church in Monroe in 1894, when Father James Hally had distinguished himself "in a patriotic address of over an hour's duration."[53]

Catholic devotion to the Constitution and to the separation of Church and State was generally a major theme when priests addressed patriotic assemblies, as was the willingness of Catholics to lay down their lives in defense of their country. Father Joseph Hallissey, addressing the citizens of Wyandotte on Memorial Day in 1895, invoked the martyrs of the Civil War to protest the activities of anti-Catholics in the vicinity. "In the days of the rebellion the man who fought and bled for his country was not asked his religion. Catholics and Protestants fought together side by side, died together, and were consigned to the same grave." And he assured his audience that Catholics posed no threat to republican liberties. "In glowing words he showed there was no hostility between Church and State, quoting Archbishop Satolli's undying words to the Catholics of this grand Republic: 'Go forth with the Bible, the light of God's truth in one hand, and in the other the Constitution of the United States.'" Archbishop Satolli was not in fact the champion of religious liberty that Father Hallissey believed him to be, and Roman authorities were seldom invoked, especially after 1900, to make the case for religious pluralism. But a Roman imprimatur was hardly necessary, for religious tolerance was more and more an article of the prevailing national faith, for Protestants and Catholics alike. "You do not belong to the same branch of the Christian Church that I do," Father Timothy Murphy told the members of the G.A.R. and the W.R.C who had assembled in 1907 for memorial services at his church in Flint, "but you all belong to the brotherhood of man and the fatherhood of God, and that to me is a union of Church and State in which every intelligent man ought to take a just pride. Duty to God and loyalty to country are attributes that know no fine lines of demarcation between religions and creeds."[54]

The easing of tensions between Catholics and Protestants in the small towns of the Diocese was presumably a gradual thing, accomplished as Catholics became a more and more assimilated population. But there is some evidence that Catholic-Protestant relations in many small towns improved significantly during the later 1880s and the 1890s, as the "Americanizing" bishops and a newly assertive lay elite drew favorable comment in the secular press. Convinced that American Catholicism was finally being purged of its "autocratic" and "superstitious" elements, a growing number of Protestant clergy were ready to mute the polemics with which they were accustomed to greet all things Catholic. The Rev. W. K. Spencer, a Presbyterian minister at Adrian, was apparently among their number, or so it seemed when he introduced Bishop Foley to a heavily Protestant audience in that city in 1890. "It is a very felicitous circumstance that we as Protestants can gather here and look back to a few months past, when at Baltimore the council of perhaps the wisest and best at least among the laity of the Roman Catholic Church assembled," he told the crowd, referring to the Lay Catholic Congress held in 1889. "It was with the deepest interest that I read the verbatim reports of those very able addresses . . . made at that time, and I hailed it as amongst auspicious omens that there was in the church which our brother, the one to whom we all do honor tonight, represents, that growing spirit of charity and that breadth of liberality." Liberality in the Catholic ranks was evidently seen by many Protestants as a harbinger of true ecumenism. "It is said by Protestants that the Catholic people of America, as they become Americanized, are imbibing the principles of Protestantism, and will soon join hands with Protestants in one common faith," the Paulist Walter Elliott was told in the course of one of his missions to non-Catholics in the Diocese. "Is this so?" Father Elliott also looked toward an ecumenical future, but of a different sort. "American political principles, based on the dignity of man and the need of a strong central government to secure human liberty and equality, are to the political order what Catholic principles are to the religious order," he told his questioner. "Enlightened Catholics believe that the providence of God in establishing this Republic has prepared the way for the return of the northern races to Christian unity in the Catholic Church."[55]

Father Peter Baart, himself a small town pastor, believed that Catholic-Protestant relations were undergoing significant change in the 1890s. Writing pseudononymously in the *St. Louis Review* in 1898, Baart claimed that Catholics in the Diocese of Detroit had, since the Parliament of Religions at Chicago in 1893, become much less reluctant to join with Protestants in what were essentially religious endeavors. (Catholic representation at that famous ecumenical assembly was regularly criticized by conservatives in the 1890s, and on ecumenical questions Father Baart was very much the conservative.) What specifically troubled Father Baart was the willingness of Catholics in certain unnamed communities to participate in the annual Sunday school picnics that were sponsored jointly by the local Protestant churches. "First they march in procession through the streets," he explained of these affairs, "each school headed by its banner, and accompanied by its teachers. They proceed to a chosen ground where prayer is offered, hymns sung and addresses made on Sunday school topics. Then all the children, and the old folks, have their picnic." Catholic children in many communities had been asked to participate in these picnics in recent years, according to Father Baart, "and in quite a number of places, not only did the Catholic children march in procession with the Protestant schools, but their priests participated with them in all the religious exercises. In fact, the Sisters who taught the children also assisted. On one occasion it rained — all, ministers and priests, Protestant and Catholic children went to a Protestant church for the exercises and the picnic." Father Baart clearly hoped to embarass Bishop Foley by these revelations — "a certain practice which is known to exist in the Diocese of Detroit may prove interesting to some of the foreign subscribers to *The Review*" — and he may have exaggerated the extent of Catholic participation in such Protestant-sponsored activities. But this participation was almost certainly not the product of his imagination. The *Michigan Catholic* in the 1890s bears ample witness to the ease with which Catholics and Protestants were able to cooperate in those many activities of small town life that were both civic and religious in nature.[56]

Still, the 1890s were also a decade of virulent anti-Catholicism, and particularly so in Michigan. How can we reconcile this fact with the abundant anecdotal evidence that seems to indicate a perceptible thaw in Protestant-Catholic relations in the same decade? There were, of course, many Michigan Protestants who had almost no contact with Catholics, for Catholics were only sparsely represented in certain areas of the state. Anti-Catholicism may well have flourished in such settings. There was undoubtedly an unreconstructed anti-Catholic minority in those many small towns where the majority of Protestants got on amicably with their Catholic neighbors. And it is certainly possible that many individuals were capable of feeling real affection for those Catholics whom they knew, while at the same time crediting the most outlandish claims of anti-Catholic propagandists. Anti-Catholicism served to express the discontents of many small town dwellers with a world they never made—an economically precarious world for much of the 1890s—and with the disorders of the distant big city. Local Catholics, however, were not necessarily seen as one with the superstitious foreigners whose growing numbers were believed to be the cause of unemployment and corruption and political unrest.

No Catholic made a more concerted effort in the 1890s to fathom the mysteries of the Protestant mind than Paulist Father Walter Elliott. The Detroit-born Elliott returned to the Diocese of Detroit in 1893 to preach a series of missions to non-Catholics, confining his work to the small towns. "He will hire halls, speak in churches, distribute books, pamphlets, leaflets, go into villages and country districts, and there expound and explain the doctrines and practices of his Church in plain and simple language that cannot be misunderstood," the *New York Sun* reported. This Michigan tour was the first time that Elliott had set out to preach primarily to non-Catholics, and it marked a shift in his own career and in the work of the Paulist Order, which, after the mid-1890s, turned more and more to mission work of this distinctly ecumenical nature. The conversion of Protestants was the "remote object" of the missions he preached in the Diocese in 1893, according to Elliott; "my immediate object was to dispel prejudice." Prejudice certainly existed, as Father Elliott's experience confirmed. But he also found in the Diocese a gratifying store of Protestant good will.[57]

Elliott drew substantial crowds wherever he preached in the Diocese, and nearly always enjoyed a warm reception. "The spacious opera house was densely crowded each evening, many being unable to gain admission," Joseph Leszczynski wrote from Sand Beach—now Harbor Beach—where Elliott inaugurated his mission series in September. "Every seat was occupied and many remained standing in the rear of the hall, whilst hundreds returned to their homes not being able to gain admission into the building," came the report from St. Joseph, where the stage in the Academy of Music had been "decorated with the national colors, while a portrait of Columbus in a frame 8×6 was most conspicuous upon the platform." Elliott's reputation as an orator helped to swell the crowds, good preaching ranking high as entertainment among the church-going population in Michigan's small towns. (Protestants often attended Catholic parish missions in the Diocese in the years around the turn of the century. "Many who attended came a distance of twenty miles, and our separated brethren were present in large numbers at nearly all of the exercises," ran a typical report, this one concerning a mission preached in Sebewaing in 1900.) Father Elliott benefited too from the evident curiosity of many Protestants about Catholic doctrine and practice. "My hearers inundated me with inquiries concerning the confessional, the Sacraments, the Communion, the power of the priesthood, the danger to the civil authority of the Papacy, purgatory and the intercession of the saints. Purgatory appeared to be a difficult point with many of them."[58]

The warmth with which Elliott was generally received had to do in part with his own appealing personality, but was also the effect of his reputation as a temperance man. "His lecture on temperance and total abstinence was a masterpiece and one that will never be forgotten by those who heard it," a correspondent reported from Milford. "On the 13th his subject was 'Intemperance as a Vice and as a Disease,'" a Vermontville resident wrote. "A number of the leading Prohibitionists told me it was the best lecture they ever heard on temperance." The temperance sermon was always among the four to six sermons that Father Elliott preached at each stop on this tour, for his audiences were composed, as he described them, of "the best and most religious elements in the population . . . . church members and adherents of churches." Few of these in the 1890s looked with equanimity on the saloon. Father Elliott found favor too because of his theological conservatism. The Protestants in his audience might question the scriptural basis for purgatory or auricular confession, but they were pleased to learn that Father Elliott had no quarrel, as certain liberal Protestant theologians did, with such hard doctrines as eternal damnation. "I found, I am happy to say, that in the masses of the people agnosticism and religious doubt had made little headway," he reported in December, although he cautioned that this could not be said of the masses who lived in big cities. The church-going population of the small towns was still convinced "that Christ in God is the actual deity; that the Scriptures were God's Book, and that men need Christ as a Savior." Theirs was a strictly Biblical faith, and while they were not unaffected by liberal religious currents, their allegiances were conservative:

> It is an instructive fact that the awful truth of eternal punishment still holds its place in the vast majority of Protestant minds, in spite of the tendency to pick and choose doctrines at will which their notion of private interpretation so inevitably fosters. It is easy, indeed, to find Protestant men and women who will doubt the terrible dogma, who like to say both no and yes to it; but a settled conviction of universal salvation is rare to find — rare to find a flourishing or even small-sized Universalist church society outside large cities.[59]

But if Father Elliott found large and cordial crowds on his circuit of the Diocese, he also discovered that a significant minority in his audiences shared many of the prejudices, even the paranoia, of the more extreme anti-Catholic propagandists. This was apparently especially true in those areas where few Catholics lived. Rural Freedom Township, heavily Protestant, was "neck-deep in bigotry," Elliott recalled. And in Vermontville, where "a Catholic priest was never before heard to speak in a public meeting," the questions submitted to Father Elliott via the "query box" that was a feature of his missions revealed, in the words of a local correspondent, "that those who propounded them had read and credited the calumnies of the contemptible APA." The Vermontville audience was curious about confession and about the celibacy of the clergy, as were the members of virtually every audience before whom Elliott spoke. But they also wanted to know why "Catholics were Placing Firearms in Their Churches" and "Why were Catholics all Democrats?" "Did the Catholics elect Grover Cleveland?" one man wondered, presumably because the hapless Cleveland was being widely blamed for the hard times that were already evident in the state. "Why is Mexico, a Catholic Country, so far Behind the United States in Knowledge?" another listener asked. Elliott encountered many of these same questions in other towns as well, although the majority of queries seem always to have had to do with dogma and ritual and the extent of papal authority. "The questions put in the question box betrayed a great deal of misapprehension and ignorance of Catholic doctrines, beliefs and ceremonies," a correspondent wrote from Ypsilanti. "An intelligent person, not a Catholic by any means, sitting near us one evening, expressed the fear that many of the questions would give Mr. Elliott a low opinion of the people of Ypsilanti, but there need be no fear of that. All the questions were just such as the lecturer meets whereever he goes."[60]

The contents of the question box must have assured Father Elliott that his new work was a needed one, for when he completed his missions in the Diocese of Detroit in May 1894, he anounced plans for a similar series of missions in the Diocese of Cleveland. Two of his Paulist brethren preached a series of missions to non-Catholics in the Diocese of Grand Rapids in 1897, and for a number of years thereafter the Paulists periodically visited the Diocese of Detroit to preach such missions there. (The first Paulist mission to non-Catholics in the city of Detroit was given at St. Aloysius Church in 1899.) The Holy Ghost Fathers preached a mission to non-Catholics at Wayne in 1907, and the Redemptorists followed suit in the heavily Protestant towns of the Michigan Thumb in 1908. Two diocesan priests, Fathers James Cahalan of Hillsdale and Edwin Fisher of Clinton, began, probably in 1907, to give lecture series on Catholicism in the small towns of the Diocese, "their aim being," according to the *Milan Leader* in 1908, "to remove misunderstanding in these matters and promote the interests of truth and charity. We have nothing but kind words for these consecrated men who have been in our midst for some short time in the interests of their chosen religion." The mission to non-Catholics had in fact become so familiar a part of the small town religious landscape by 1908 that Father Henry DeGryse, pastor at Anchorville, was moved to tell his congregation that "in this beloved country of ours the strictly Catholic missions have ceased to exist. Henceforth they should be considered and properly called Christian missions, because all Christians are welcome to our churches, without any distinction whatsoever in regard to nationality or religious denomination." The Redemptorist Fathers were about to open a "Christian mission" in the Catholic church at Anchorville to which "the well-meaning public in general" was invited. "If therefore you are so fortunate as to find time to attend this mission," Father DeGryse concluded, "you will hear that the different topics of their great evening sermons . . . are taken from religious points of Faith, generally admitted, and believed in by all Christians of good will."[61]

There was still division between Catholics and Protestants in the Diocese by the time of Bishop Foley's death, the ecumenism of men like Father DeGryse notwithstanding. Nor was organized anti-Catholicism yet eliminated as a factor in Detroit and Michigan politics: the Ku Klux Klan enjoyed strong support in both the city and the state in the early 1920s on a largely anti-Catholic platform. But the Foley years are still best seen as a time of transition from a situation of religious polarization to one of relative amity, where confessional frictions were notably muted, and where Catholics were more at home than they had ever been before. When Bishop Michael Gallagher came to Detroit in the fall of 1918, he found a Catholic population that was better organized than it had ever been, wealthier, more numerous, and more confident politically. And he found a see city that suddenly ranked among the largest and richest in the nation. The future of Detroit looked wonderfully bright, and so, despite ominous rumblings from a vocal anti-Catholic minority, did the future of Catholics in that city and in its rapidly developing hinterland.

PART III

1919–1958

11

MATURITY: *THE GALLAGHER AND MOONEY EPISCOPATES*

With the close of the First World War, the Catholic Church in the United States entered a period of unprecedented confidence and prosperity. This vigorous period can be said to have lasted into the 1960s. The Catholic population grew substantially in these decades, and, despite the ravages of the Great Depression, became increasingly affluent. It was a more homogeneous population too, for federal legislation in the 1920s sharply reduced the numbers of immigrants entering the United States and especially limited the numbers coming from Southern and Eastern Europe. Catholics were generous in their support of the Church in these decades, and dioceses throughout the country saw a steady increase in the number and scope of their Catholic institutions. Catholic secondary schools multiplied rapidly, and so did the number, and the enrollments, of Catholic colleges. The size and vitality of Catholic lay organizations grew as well. And the laity were generally more disciplined in their religious practice than they had ever been before. Catholics were more and more likely to attend Mass at least weekly, to receive the sacraments frequently, to send their children to parochial schools, and to support Catholic organizations. It is fitting indeed that the American Church should cease in this period to be a church to which missionaries were sent, and begin itself to send a growing corps of priests and sisters to far parts of the earth.

The decades after 1920 were also a time of administrative reform. The reach of episcopal authority was extended in nearly every diocese as administrative functions were more and more centralized in the local Chancery. The bishops themselves were a more effective political presence than they had previously been, for they met annually after the First World War and had a standing secretariat—the National Catholic Welfare Council, founded in 1919—through which they might orchestrate action in support of particular Catholic concerns. (These ranged, in the decades after 1920, from the alleged immorality of many popular films to matters of foreign policy.) Despite their growing national cohesion, however, many—perhaps most—American bishops in this period were more thoroughly identified with Rome, in their training and in their mentality, than their predecessors had generally been. "None of us today can go as far as

Gibbons went," Detroit's Cardinal Edward Mooney is reported to have said to the Jesuit John Courtney Murray, with regard to the question of religious liberty. This was so not simply because the American Church in 1950 was of greater interest to the Vatican than it had been in the nineteenth century, but because the principal bishops themselves were more self-consciously Roman than had once been the case.[1]

The decades of growth and vitality opened nowhere more auspiciously than in the Diocese of Detroit, whose Catholic population swelled from 386,000 in 1919 to 725,000 in 1929. Much of this growth occurred within the city of Detroit. Already a boom town in 1918, Detroit's population more than doubled in the 1920s, and its geographic area increased by nearly 75 percent. (The city's population stood at more than 1.5 million in 1930.) Detroit was still a heavily immigrant city in the 1920s—many of its newest residents had come from abroad—and it was a heavily Catholic one. Perhaps as many as 40 percent of its inhabitants were at least nominal members of the Church.

The growth of the city's Catholic population, and the growing prosperity of that population, led in the 1920s to a new political assertiveness among Catholics. Detroit elected a Catholic mayor in 1924, despite vigorous opposition from the Ku Klux Klan, and reelected him in 1925. The ascendancy of the Democratic party after 1930 meant enhanced political leverage for Catholics nationally, and in many cities and states as well. This was especially welcome in those places, like Detroit, where Catholics had not previously wielded great political power. Catholics were an integral part of Detroit's political establishment after 1930, and they dominated the city's political life in the 1950s and the 1960s.

The size and the variety of diocesan institutions increased after 1918, and the administrative reforms that were occurring in many dioceses were particularly striking in Detroit. For Detroit in 1918 was a diocese that was notably loosely governed. It had no seminary of its own, no effective means of regulating the conduct of its schools, and no reliable way of generating adequate revenues for its charities. Its ethnic parishes were remote, for the most part, from the broader Catholic community, and often resistant to Chancery control in matters ranging from education to liturgical practice.

By the late 1940s, however, the Church in the (now) Archdiocese of Detroit looked very different. A much-expanded Chancery governed the conduct of parochial schools and Catholic charities. A number of Catholic activities that were initially lay-directed had been brought under Chancery, and hence clerical, control. There had been since 1943 an annual campaign to raise money for the various archdiocesan institutions, and the success of these campaigns had lent new vigor to Catholic education and Catholic charities. A major seminary was opened near Detroit in 1949—a provincial seminary for all the dioceses in Michigan—and this, coupled with the minor seminary that had been opened in 1919, meant that the priests of the Archdiocese of Detroit could at last be trained "at home."

A greater sense of solidarity among the diocesan clergy was quite reasonably anticipated with the opening of the major seminary, and a greater uniformity in their worldview, their values, and their conduct. And this seemed appropriate, for the laity were now a more homogeneous population than ever before. Save for a small population of recent immigrants — from Mexico and Puerto Rico, the Middle East, and Eastern Europe — the Catholics of the Archdiocese were now a mostly English-speaking population. The typical ethnic parish was less isolated from the larger community than it had previously been, and it was more and more the domain of the old. Younger Catholics, working-class and middle-class alike, were by the late 1940s moving in large numbers to Detroit's outer ring and even beyond — to subdivisions and suburbs that had no particular ethnic identity, although they often had a religious one. Like their immigrant forebears, these mobile Catholics were church and school builders, and what had been an urban church began to replicate itself in a suburban landscape.

The vigor of Catholic life in these years was hardly the creation of administrative reformers in the Chancery. It had most fundamentally to do with the changing character of the Catholic population. But it is still right to credit Bishop Michael Gallagher (1918–1937) and Archbishop — later Cardinal — Edward Mooney (1937–1958) with critical roles in the history of the Archdiocese of Detroit. Both men were builders and consolidators, Mooney expanding on Gallagher's considerable achievements and initiating many reforms of his own. Together they were responsible for something akin to an administrative revolution, shifting power away from the parish to the Chancery and, in some areas, from lay to clerical hands. What Gallagher and Mooney achieved had been anticipated in the various administrative reforms of their predecessors, for every bishop of Detroit had tried to enhance his own power with respect to his clergy and the laity. But it was only after the First World War that the growing size and wealth of the Catholic population and the easing of ethnic tensions made far-reaching administrative reform a feasible proposition.

That reform would not have occurred, however, without the initiative and drive of reform-minded bishops, which is what Michael Gallagher and Edward Mooney so evidently were. In the most general sense, the two men shared a vision of the Church and the reforms they wished to accomplish. Both looked to a future where Catholics might live in an institutionally complete community of their own, served not only by Catholic schools and hospitals and orphanages but by Catholic colleges and universitites, social service agencies of every variety, and trade and professional organizations. Both measured the health of the Church primarily by the discipline that characterized it, and worked for the day when even the details of Catholic institutional life would be governed by a smoothly running Chancery. Both were certain that clerical leadership was essential in all aspects of Church life, and both worked hard to cast their growing corps of priests in a disciplined and uniform mold. Each man regarded the seminary he built as his single greatest achievement, and the key to all of the other reforms he hoped to bring to fruition.

Despite the vision they shared as administrative reformers, however, Bishop Gallagher and Cardinal Mooney differed greatly in personality and administrative style, and in their orientation to the world. Michael Gallagher was an abrasive and impetuous man, and inclined to conspiratorial, even apocalyptic, views on history and politics. His strength as an administrator lay in the breadth of his vision. He built generously, even extravagantly, in the 1920s, when Catholic Detroit was richer than ever before, and he bequeathed to later generations a legacy of splendid buildings. But he was apparently little interested in the details of financial planning, and can be fairly charged with having overextended his Diocese in the palmy days of the 1920s, and failing to cope with the financial chaos that came in the wake of the Great Depression. When he died, early in 1937, his many achievements were overshadowed by the virtual bankruptcy of his Diocese and by the controversy that surrounded the career of Father Charles Coughlin, whose patron Gallagher had been.

Edward Mooney, by contrast, was a meticulous administrator, abreast of the financial particulars of his Archdiocese even in those years when national activities absorbed much of his time. His administrative style reflected his judicious temperament: he was as incapable of fiscal imprudence as he was of intemperate pronouncements on politics, although he had deep political interests and concerns. His predecessor had been a vocal Irish nationalist and a bitter isolationist, and—like his protégé, Father Coughlin—inclined to idiosyncratic positions on monetary policy and the need for industrial reorganization. Mooney, however, is best described as a sophisticated internationalist. Sympathetic to industrial unionism and to most New Deal reforms, he had cordial relations with the Roosevelt administration during and after the late 1930s, when he served repeatedly as chairman of the Administrative Board of the National Catholic Welfare Conference. His refined intellect, his understated political skills, his modesty, and his integrity won him vast respect among his fellow bishops. When he died, late in 1958, he was mourned far beyond the boundaries of his Archdiocese, and his career was almost universally judged to have been an exemplary one.

For all the differences in their personalities, however, and in the extent to which their careers were judged to have been successful, Michael Gallagher and Edward Mooney can be said to have collaborated in the writing of a single critical chapter in the administrative history of the Archdiocese of Detroit. Bishop Gallagher's achievements were essential to the triumphs of Cardinal Mooney, although this was not always evident to Mooney's contemporaries. It was widely believed in 1937 that he had inherited a Diocese in organizational as well as financial disarray. But Gallagher had in fact accomplished a good deal in the way of administrative reform, effectively laying the foundation for Mooney's eventual centralization of control over virtually every aspect of Catholic institutional life. From a distance, the Gallagher episcopate takes on a more successful hue than it appeared to possess in the darker hours of the 1930s.

THE GALLAGHER YEARS

The history of the Gallagher episcopate is more difficult to reconstruct than that of any other of Detroit's ordinaries, save for the enigmatic Bishop Frederick Rese (1833-1840). This is because relatively few documents from the Gallagher administration are deposited in the Detroit Chancery archives. Just how the Gallagher papers came to be so sparse is something of a mystery, but it certainly has to do with Gallagher's close connections to Father Charles Coughlin. There are relatively few documents in the archives today that bear on Father Coughlin's career, and almost none that bear on his relationship to Bishop Gallagher. The Gallagher papers were obviously edited at some point in the past, and material relating to Coughlin—and perhaps other sensitive material as well—was removed and presumably destroyed. Any account of the Gallagher episcopate, then, and particularly of Gallagher's association with the controversial Father Coughlin, must be disturbingly incomplete. And the Gallagher personality, a key to much in his clouded career, must remain fundamentally an enigma.

We do know that the future bishop was born late in 1866 in Auburn, Michigan, a farming hamlet in the vicinity of Bay City. His parents were Irish immigrants, the father a boilermaker before he took to the rural life, and the mother a hotel cook in the years before her marriage. The couple apparently met in Detroit, where they were married, in the Jesuit church, in 1862. They eventually had three children—daughters Kate and Fanny, and son Michael.[2]

As the only boy and a promising student, young Michael was apparently made aware at an early age that his family's hopes for success in this life rested largely on him. It is not clear, however, at what point he decided to become a priest. He was sent at the age of twelve to live with relatives in Bay City so that he could attend a Catholic school, and completed high school in St. James parish at the age of seventeen. He then taught briefly in the public school at Pinconning, a village north of Bay City, but evidently only to earn money for his further education. He subsequently attended the Basilians' Assumption College in Windsor (Ontario), presumably as a seminarian from the Diocese of Grand Rapids. His academic achievements were impressive enough that his bishop sent him abroad for the rest of his seminary training. Gallagher received a degree in philosophy from Mungret College in Limerick in 1889, and took his theology courses at Innsbruck, where he was ordained in 1893.[3]

The life of the Gallagher family by this time turned almost wholly on the needs and prospects of the young seminarian. "Your Degree and the Pope's picture are hanging at home for Ma," Fanny wrote to Michael in the fall of 1890. "When you send your picture, try to have a good one, for if I don't do it in crayon Ma will certainly have it enlarged life size." Fanny was now a teacher, and putting a portion of each month's salary into an account for her brother's benefit. "I hope you will not need this money badly and can go to some places of interest," she wrote in 1891, enclosing a generous twenty dollars. Fanny could surely have used the money herself, for she was engaged to be married. But she seems to have accepted with only muted protest the precedence her adored older brother enjoyed in the family. "If ma sees you come back ordained she will have nothing left to wish for," she told Michael in 1891. "If anything happened to you it would kill her." Both Fanny and her sister Kate were apparently worried about the well-being of their aging parents, who still lived at the family home in Auburn. "They are both getting very old looking living up there all alone," Kate had written to Michael in 1890. "I think it is very lonesome for them." But Kate, like Fanny, looked to Michael's career to redeem their parents' hard and lonely lives. "Joe and Eleanor never go to bed without saying 'God bless Uncle Mike, and make him a priest someday, Thy will be done,'" she told her brother with reference to her own small children. "I suppose we won't know you, you'll be so changed in every way."[4]

Father Michael Gallagher did not return to Michigan until 1895, nearly two years after his ordination. His parents were still living, but both his sisters had died, Kate leaving four young children. Fanny, the closer of the two to Michael, died of typhoid fever late in 1891, the news of her death reaching Gallagher at Innsbruck in a letter from a Bay City priest whom he had never met. "The news will be indeed hard for you to bear," Father Thomas Whalen wrote to the young seminarian, "but I feel that you know enough of this world's crosses to make this one meritorious by bearing it in the proper spirit and in the depths of your sorrow to exclaim 'O Father Thy will be done on Earth as it is in heaven.'" Kate wrote soon after to confirm the sad news. "I can't realize she [is] gone from this world forever; living with me for the last five years she was one of the family and [it] seems awful without her but when I think of her lovely death I feel a little consoled." Kate went on to provide a disconcerting glimpse into the world that she inhabited as a carpenter's wife. "She is better off than if she lived," she wrote bluntly of her sister, who had been about to marry. "'There's to[o] much work is there not Kate' was one of the things she said to me before she died." Kate herself was dead of typhoid fever less than two years later.[5]

The distance between the world of a Bay City working man's family and the world of an Innsbruck seminarian was vast indeed in the 1890s. Perhaps this was the reason that Gallagher wrote only infrequently to his sisters while he was abroad but kept up an apparently lively correspondence with friends at other European seminaries. "I wonder if Matt has forgotten the feast we had," a friend from Mungret College wrote in 1894. He was now a seminarian at Aix-en-Provence, but had vivid memories of the days when he and Gallagher were students together in Limerick. "You remember the big bucket of current jam that was in the middle of the table when [F]ather Farrelly came into the room. You remember how astonished Farrelly was to see Matt and myself in our nightshirts. Since that night (unfortunate) no philosopher [has] occupied those rooms but must sleep with the kids in the dormitory, and suffer the cold breeze which enters the dormitory when they jump out of their warm nest in the morning." The regulated life at Mungret College had apparently been irksome to Gallagher, for he chose to reside outside the seminary when he went to Innsbruck, living a life there that was not unlike the life of a secular university student. His friend in Aix was astonished at the liberty enjoyed by the seminarians and young priests studying in the Austrian city. "Are you not obliged, like us, to wear the soutane in the streets and everywhere you go?" he wondered. "What kind of priests do these fellows turn out to be? Down here, with the Sulpicians, we have no liberty whatever. We are always under their eyes and can[']t turn our head without being noticed. We are rarely allowed to go out alone in the city and when we do, if we enter a cafe, it is immediate expulsion." As far as he was concerned, however, the rigors of the Sulpician regime were all to the good. "I don't think that if I were there at Innsbruck, I would associate with those high-livers as I would be afraid of losing my head."[6]

The stubborn independence that Gallagher periodically displayed as a bishop may have had something to do with his experience at Innsbruck. His naturally pugnacious personality seems not to have been much subdued during his years as a major seminarian. Innsbruck may also have introduced Gallagher to certain of the political ideas that led to his support of Father Charles Coughlin. Austrian Catholic social thought in the 1890s was dominated by the romantic corporatist theory that permeates *Rerum Novarum,* and Gallagher was exposed there to a view of the world that saw interest and credit as the twin supports of a rapacious economic order, and a clerically dominated state as the best hope for economic justice. (It was an anti-Semitic view of the world as well, but nothing in Gallagher's surviving papers indicates any anti-Semitism on his part.) How much he absorbed at Innsbruck in the way of ideology is unknown, but he claimed in later years to have been interested in politics as a seminarian. Certainly it is evident from the letters of his friends that he was already an ardent Irish nationalist, although it is not clear whether these sentiments had been developed at home or during his time in Limerick. "The city is pretty nearly crowded at present with English people, coming to see the sights of Rome during this week," a friend wrote to Gallagher from the American College at Easter in 1890. "Is it not horrible to think of such a thing? And I assure you it is still worse to be here and see it."[7]

When Gallagher finally returned to his home diocese he served briefly in two rural parishes and then, in 1896, became an assistant at St. Andrew's Cathedral in Grand Rapids, where he also served as secretary to Bishop Henry Richter. Richter had long had ambitions for this bright young priest. "Piety coupled with learning can achieve great things," he had counseled Gallagher in 1891. "Protestantism is fast crumbling to pieces in this country. Just now the [P]resbyterians are making themselves the laughing stock of the people by their wrangling over the revision of their creed." If the future of religion in the United States lay with the Catholic Church, it behooved a conscientious bishop to groom his most talented priests to be confident and articulate leaders. Gallagher was made Chancellor of the Diocese of Grand Rapids in 1900, and was subsequently named Vicar General. He was consecrated an auxiliary bishop there in 1915, and succeeded Henry Richter as Bishop of Grand Rapids when Richter died in 1916. Bishop Gallagher's ascendant star was sufficiently bright that he was chosen, in 1918, to head the rapidly growing Diocese of Detroit. Detroit's then Auxiliary Bishop Edward Kelly, who had himself hoped to succeed Bishop Foley in Detroit, was sent to Grand Rapids as Gallagher's successor.[8]

Bishop Gallagher's arrival in his new see city was attended by less than auspicious omens. His coming was postponed for several weeks because of the severe influenza epidemic that raged throughout the United States in the fall of 1918. A massive parade of welcome was finally scheduled for November 17, but the day was rainy and cold, and only about half of an anticipated crowd of 50,000 Catholic men was on hand to escort the new bishop from the Michigan Central depot to his residence on Washington Boulevard. That modest dwelling, incongruously located in what was now a busy commercial district, was something of a disappointment to its new proprietor. "It was reported that the furniture in the episcopal residence was shabby and insufficient," the notes of Gallagher's first meeting with his consultors remarked, "and that there were not even sufficient dishes and tableware for the dining room." The political climate locally was hardly more welcoming than the inadequately furnished episcopal residence, for Detroit was the center of a movement to make attendance at the public schools mandatory for all children in the state. As Bishop of Detroit, Gallagher was expected to lead the opposition to this proposed law, should its supporters succeed, as they were expected to do, in having the measure placed on a statewide ballot.[9]

However disappointing his welcome might have been, Gallagher began his years in Detroit with a characteristic burst of energy. And it was well that he did, for the Diocese had suffered badly, over the previous decade, from a want of leadership at the Chancery. Many of Detroit's churches and schools could no longer accommodate the Catholics who lived within their parochial boundaries. "Every mass is crowded, standing room," complained a member of Holy Rosary parish in 1920, "and it certainly isn't pleasant to stand an hour or more[.] [O]ne's mind wanders and half of the people can't hear a word that the priest says." The Diocese had long been large enough to warrant its own seminary, and most Catholics would probably have agreed that "dynamic Detroit" deserved a cathedral of more impressive proportions than the modest SS. Peter and Paul's, which was no longer surrounded by the homes of prosperous families but by "rooming houses and a transient class of people who do not make desirable neighbors." The loosely regulated parochial schools were a particular problem, for it was imperative now to assure the electorate that Catholic schools were no less rigorous, or less American, than their public counterparts. And Catholic charities were still under a mostly decentralized lay control. Largely because of this, the charitable and social service institutions of the Diocese were of a more limited scope than might have been expected, given the size of its Catholic population.[10]

Gallagher turned his attention first to the acute shortage of priests that had plagued the Diocese for at least a decade. He began to recruit clergy and seminarians from other dioceses and from abroad, and partly by these means he increased the number of priests in his Diocese from 318 in 1918 to 496 by 1925. Recruitment from outside the Diocese, however, was in Gallagher's eyes little better than a necessary evil; like virtually all of his episcopal confreres, he preferred that his clergy be locally born and raised. For this reason, the bishop had come to Detroit with plans to open a minor seminary as soon as possible, a prospect that delighted, among others, the editor of the *Michigan Catholic.* (This was now Josephine Byrne Sullivan-Conlon, a longtime associate editor under the late William Hughes.) "The scarcity of vocations in this great city of Detroit alone is deplorable," she lamented at the close of 1918, "and is another evidence that too many amusements and too much license is a bar to growing piety." A "Junior Seminary," which boys would attend from about the age of fourteen, would "be the means of fostering vocations, of keeping young boys away from evil amusements and of inculcating in these lads religious thoughts at the formative period." Mrs. Sullivan-Conlon's thinking was very much that of her bishop and his closest clerical advisors. When Sacred Heart Seminary opened its doors in September 1919, its curriculum encompassed only the ninth and tenth grades. The course of study was thereafter to be expanded annually, until in six year's time a complete high school and college curriculum would be available.[11]

The new seminary was housed in manifestly temporary quarters when it opened in 1919. The need for a permanent facility was urgent, especially as enrollments swelled far beyond initial expectations. (There were 85 students in the fall of 1919; 212 were enrolled just two years later.) Accordingly, Bishop Gallagher made plans for a fund-raising campaign that would not only provide for a vast new seminary but underwrite tuition for its students. The campaign was inaugurated in the spring of 1920, under the sponsorship of what the *Michigan Catholic* described as "a committee of the most prominent laymen in the city."

The seminary campaign proved to be a model of efficiency and so successful that it seemed to many Catholics to bear out the motto which its organizers had adopted: "It Is God's Work; God Wills It." Every pastor was required to organize a committee in his parish for the purpose of soliciting contributions door-to-door, and every parish was expected to raise a certain sum of money. More than one hundred of Gallagher's priests were assigned, in the summer of 1920, to carry the seminary campaign to the pulpits of those churches that were located beyond Detroit and its suburbs, and certain of these priests were also deployed to call on well-to-do Catholics in search of donations of at least $500. Bishop Gallagher had set his sights on pledges totaling $4,000,000, a very nearly audacious expectation even in a diocese as prosperous as Detroit. But when the campaign had come to a close, the bishop was able to announce that more than $9,000,000 had been subscribed, one-third of which had already been paid. The stunning success of the campaign not only assured Detroit of its splendid new seminary but made it possible to endow a fund to defray the costs of sending students on to major seminaries outside the Diocese. "The results of our Seminary Campaign have aroused the wonder and admiration of the Catholic world," a jubilant Bishop Gallagher told his people in the spring of 1921.[12]

Ground was broken for the new Sacred Heart Seminary late in the winter of 1923. Built on what was then farmland beyond the western fringes of Detroit, the seminary at its completion in 1924 was one of the largest and most lavish facilities of its kind. Its "collegiate Gothic" architecture was at once airy and massive; it spoke simultaneously of power and of the contemplative life. Its size bespoke great expectations: the Seminary was built to accommodate 500 students, 350 of them as boarders. Its generous athletic facilities reflected the ebullient masculine style that had since the late nineteenth century come more and more to characterize American priests. "We aim to make real boys, masculine boys, spiritual boys, boys of self-control, boys who think," the seminary's first rector had announced in 1919. The seminary, in short, was a monument to a clergy—and to a Catholic community—in the full flush of confidence. And as such it was an especially gratifying achievement for a bishop to claim as his own.[13]

If Gallagher regarded the seminary as the single greatest triumph of his years in Detroit, it was only one of a multitude of ambitious building projects that were accomplished in the 1920s. Fully 222 parish buildings were constructed in the Diocese of Detroit between 1919 and 1929, including 86 churches and 77 schools. (The number of parishes with resident priests increased in these same years from 174 to 298.) In order to ensure that the myriad parish construction projects were financially prudent and at least inoffensive aesthetically, Gallagher in 1920 established a Diocesan Building Committee, whose task it was to "pass on locations, estimates, plans and specifications proposed by the pastor and reported to the Bishop." Gallagher's predecessors had handled this task themselves, with only the aid of a secretary.[14]

The Chancery also began, in the 1920s, to play a more aggressive role in determining the location of new parishes. Gallagher was anxious to establish parishes in advance of population growth, and he worked closely with former mayor William Thompson to acquire property in those areas of Detroit that were just beginning to be settled. Father John Koelzer, asked in 1920 to organize a parish in one such sparsely populated zone, was a bit puzzled by his bishop's interest in so unpromising a piece of suburban terrain. "Soon the sidewalk stopped and the mud began," he remembered of his initial encounter with what became St. Margaret Mary's parish on Detroit's East Side. "I turned west on Warren and that was only a mud road. . . . I then walked west on Warren to McClellan. More mud. Some wooden sidewalks. Some old houses on side streets, some just under construction." The growth of Detroit was so precipitous in the 1920s, however, that St. Margaret Mary's was soon a thriving parish, peopled mainly by a newly prosperous working class. (The decline of Detroit's East Side as a populous Catholic district was nearly as precipitous: St. Margaret Mary's Church was closed in 1982, its congregation numbering only about fifty persons. The surrounding neighborhood, long since poor and mostly black, was by this time in an advanced state of decay.)[15]

The growth of Detroit in the 1920s brought an even more diverse population to the city than it had previously known. The foreign-born accounted for most of the city's population increase between 1920 and 1925, and this last great stream of immigration included Catholic groups that had not hitherto been represented in the Diocese. Like his predecessors, Bishop Gallagher was generous in his provision for foreign-language parishes. Thirty-two of the ninety-eight parishes established in the Diocese between 1918 and 1929 were foreign-language parishes, including the first to be founded for Mexicans (Our Lady of Guadalupe, 1920); for Maltese (St. Paul, 1920); for Russians of the Slavonic Rite (St. Nicholas, 1920); for Croatians (St. Jerome, 1920) and for Slovenians (St. John Vianney, 1927). A second parish was established for Romanians of the Byzantine Rite. Two parishes were opened for Slovak Catholics and two for Lithuanian Catholics, as well as nine additional parishes for the rapidly growing Polish population of Detroit. (Three Italian-language parishes were established between 1919 and 1927, but two of these served an English-speaking population as well. Italians were still the group least likely to give strong support to an ethnic parish.) And Bishop Gallagher gave permission in 1927 for the establishment of a second parish for Detroit's black Catholics, the first, St. Peter Claver's, having been founded in 1911. It was not that the numbers of black Catholics in the city warranted a second parish — their numbers were in fact very small — but that Bishop Gallagher had adopted a black seminarian for his Diocese. When Father Norman Dukette was ordained in 1926 — the first black priest to serve in the Diocese — he was asked to undertake what was essentially missionary work among Detroit's growing population of southern black migrants. The young priest could not be assigned to St. Peter Claver's parish — it had been from the first in the care of the Holy Ghost Fathers — and Bishop Gallagher was unwilling, as virtually all of his episcopal contemporaries would have been, to assign a black priest to a white congregation. St. Benedict the Moor parish was the first fruits of Father Dukette's long career, of which we will hear more in a later chapter.

Bishop Gallagher quickly discovered that he needed formidable administrative and diplomatic skills to govern his heterogenous Diocese. The recruitment of clergy from abroad was always a risky business — at least from the Chancery's point of view — and Gallagher had the same disciplinary problems with certain of his foreign-born clergy that his predecessors had encountered. There were still European bishops who disposed of their "problem priests" by sending them to the United States, and even a docile priest understood that he had more leverage with his bishop, when that bishop needed his language skills, than priests from ethnic groups where the supply of priests was reasonably adequate. Many ethnic congregations, moreover, still insisted that the laity play a major role in the government of the parish, and Gallagher, like his predecessors, found the Poles to be particularly aggressive in their defense of this prerogative. His view of his numerous Polish constituency seems to have been that of bishops Borgess and Foley before him: for all their evident devotion to the Church, Poles were a troublesome lot, easily offended and forever demanding unwarranted concessions from episcopal authority. "Hamtramck is the easiest place in the world to get any desired number of signatures, when there is a question of fighting somebody," Gallagher told the Apostolic Delegate in 1925, with reference to a petition protesting the removal of a priest from a parish in that predominantly Polish industrial enclave.[16]

Unlike his predecessors, however, Gallagher understood the importance of having at the Chancery a reliable liason to the local Polish community. He appointed Father Stephen Woznicki, American-born but fluent in Polish, to serve as his secretary in 1919, a position that Woznicki held until shortly before Gallagher died. The bishop evidently counted on his secretary to take responsibility for nearly all Chancery dealings with the Polish clergy and the Polish laity. "The Polish problem in Detroit, insofar as it was a problem, was solved from the beginning by my appointment of a Polish Secretary, who ably handled any question that arose," he wrote in 1925. Gallagher was assigned a Polish-born auxiliary bishop in 1924, which further enhanced his authority in the local Polish community, but he seems rather to have resented the appointment. There was "no great need of a Polish Auxiliary in Detroit", he asserted in 1925, attributing the 1924 appointment to "pressure that was brought to bear on the Holy See in favor of Polish episcopal aspirations in America." For his auxiliary personally, however, Gallagher apparently had great respect, having recommended him, when he was still a parish priest, to head the Diocese of Fort Wayne. Bishop Joseph Plagens had "ability, energy, zeal and tact," according to Gallagher, and "he stood out among the Polish priests of America as one who was not clannish." Plagens had been raised in Detroit and had served as a priest in the Diocese since his ordination in 1903. His tenure as Auxiliary Bishop of Detroit was by all accounts a successful one, and he was of inestimable help to his Ordinary in maintaining good relations between the Chancery and the various Polish parishes. He could hardly ward off all conflict, however. The women who staged mass pickets of Our Lady Queen of Apostles rectory in 1925 to protest the removal of their pastor—and to prevent a new priest from taking his place—were no more inclined to listen to episcopal authority than Father Kolasinski's supporters had been forty years before.[17]

The rapid growth of Detroit created certain problems that could not be solved by Chancery diplomacy and an episcopal enthusiasm for building. The expansion of the downtown and of the factory districts that had once defined the city's perimeter had as early as 1914 begun to change its residential patterns. Once-prosperous parishes in the city core now found themselves with dwindling and significantly poorer congregations. The problem was exacerbated by the ethnic diversity of the Catholic population, and by the tenacity with which a minority in that population clung to their ethnic identities. The enormous German churches on the city's near east side, for example, maintained their German traditions long after the bulk of the German population had moved away. The Greeks and Italians and Hungarians and Syrians who colonized the district after 1905 were understandably reluctant to be an unwelcome minority in a "German" church, and anxious to have parishes of their own. "It is enough to see the ruins of once glorious parishes like St. Mary, Sts. Peter and Paul Jesuit, St. Joachim, St. Joseph, to convince one of what may occur in the near future," Father John Vismara wrote gloomily in 1923, troubled about the fate of his own Holy Family Church, located on the edge of the downtown, whose South Italian parishioners had begun to move toward the eastern fringes of the city. One reason for their flight was the growing black population of Detroit's near east side, for the city sustained, after 1915, its first great wave of migration from the American South. There had been fewer than 6,000 blacks in Detroit in 1910; there were 120,000 living there by 1930, and tensions between the black population and the mostly Catholic ethnics with whom they competed for housing were growing more and more severe. [18]

Bishop Gallagher never spoke publicly about the worsening racial tension in Detroit — in this respect he was no different from other bishops in similar situations — nor did he move to close any parishes on the increasingly derelict fringes of the expanding downtown. Nearly all of the declining parishes had long since paid for their buildings and virtually all of them retained enough members to meet ordinary expenses. Unlike his successors in more troubled urban times, Gallagher presided over a see city that was growing at a healthy rate, however much its residential patterns might be changing. He could well afford to ignore the problem of the center city parishes.

The view from the Chancery throughout the 1920s, indeed, was one of manifest optimism in Detroit's future as a major metropolis and as a center of Catholicism. Bishop Gallagher moved quickly to provide the city with buildings that spoke to his faith in its Catholic future. He sold the modest episcopal residence where bishops Borgess and Foley had lived before him, and replaced it with a lavish mansion in a fashionable district on Detroit's northwest side. For like many, probably most, of his episcopal contemporaries, Gallagher thought that a bishop ought to live splendidly; a near-baronial style of life was a satisfying rejoinder to those many Protestants who associated the Church with immigrant poverty. Bishop Foley had administered the Diocese from offices attached to his residence, and Gallagher replaced these with a handsome Chancery Building that rose eight stories above an ever-more-elegant Washington Boulevard. Construction of the Chancery Building required the razing of St. Aloysius Church, itself of proportions more in keeping with ninteenth-century Detroit than with the city of the 1920s. A new St. Aloysius was built in 1930, with a handsomely carved facade and an ingenious design that made possible a commodious church on what was a very small site. (The interior arrangement of the new church, with seating for the congregation in three tiers, bears a marked and rather startling resemblance to that of the era's movie palaces). St. Aloysius was thus able to continue its work as Detroit's "downtown" church, a symbol, in its new incarnation, of Catholic Detroit's unprecedented prosperity.

No building speaks more eloquently of the wealth and prestige of the Church than a great cathedral, and Bishop Gallagher was determined to build a cathedral worthy of his populous Diocese. Early in 1922, he bought two city blocks in what was then developing as an exclusive residential neighborhood—bounded by Webb and Burlingame avenues, the site lies in the former Visitation parish on Detroit's west side. Intending this generous parcel for his new cathedral, Gallagher commissioned the Boston architectural firm of Maginnis and Walsh to draw plans for a church of imposing proportions. "The building . . . will have a nave of 70 feet span; the entire width of the church . . . being 125 feet," the architects informed the bishop in the summer of 1922. "The total length of the building is 350 feet; seating capacity is provided at least 3500." The architects had striven for a massiveness and simplicity in the facade that gave the plans a certain originality. The proposed Cathedral had a stately rather than a devotional mien; it spoke of dignity and power, as Bishop Gallagher, pleased by the preliminary drawings, had presumably wished it to do.[19]

Gallagher had apparently not intended to break ground for his cathedral before 1927, at the earliest. The building of Sacred Heart Seminary, new Chancery offices, and an episcopal residence were each of greater priority. In fact the bishop soon concluded that it would be necessary, given the cost of the proposed cathedral, to proceed with its building in stages, commencing with a Lady Chapel. Just when he expected the chapel, and the cathedral itself, to be completed is not clear from the correspondence that has survived. Certainly he hoped that the centenary of the Diocese in 1933 would be marked by the dedication of at least a portion of the building. But by 1933 the Diocese of Detroit was effectively bankrupt. "All the Cathedral funds on hand were invested in the property and now the Bishop finds it impossible to borrow a single cent from any bank or insurance company," a harried Chancellor John Doyle explained to the architects, to whom the Diocese still owed a considerable sum. "A Diocesan Tax is impossible, for the reason that the parishes are having terrible struggles in making ends meet within their own little spheres." The cathedral project had only been postponed and not abandoned, Doyle hastened to assure the Boston firm, although ground had not yet been broken even for the Lady Chapel. Bishop Gallagher "is hopeful that the day is not far distant when he will be able to raise the necessary funds to proceed."[20]

That day never arrived. When Bishop Gallagher died, in January 1937, the Diocese was still burdened by an enormous debt, and the Chancery had not yet found an institution willing to lend it money. Gallagher's successor, Archbishop Edward Mooney, succeeded in refinancing the debt in 1941—the wartime boom in Detroit solved all the financial problems of the Archdiocese shortly thereafter—but Mooney had by this time abandoned his predecessor's plans for a new cathedral. (He had designated Blessed Sacrament church as his cathedral in 1938. A handsome neo-Gothic structure and one of the largest churches in Detroit, it serves as the cathedral today.) Like Bishop Foley before him, Bishop Gallagher was buried from the modest SS. Peter and Paul's Cathedral on a now nearly derelict Adelaide Street, the old church a symbol, or so it seemed to many, of what had been a flawed career. For it was hard to remember, after more than seven years of financial and political crises at the Chancery, that Bishop

Gallagher had also presided over a decade of building and expansion more impressive than any the Diocese had previously known.

It was, of course, the onset of the Great Depression and its particularly disastrous effects in Detroit that undermined the Gallagher episcopate, the final chapter of which is a sorry tale of political incompetence and administrative drift. But before we turn to the Depression years, it is right to note, if only in passing, the many achievements of the Gallagher episcopate that have not yet been mentioned. These were especially impressive in the realms of social service and education. No fewer than nine hospitals were opened in the Diocese between 1919 and 1929, nearly all of them, it seems, the fruit of Gallagher's intensely personal interest in the expansion of his diocesan institutions. The Catholic hospital at Lansing, opened in 1919, was — according to Gallagher — the consequence of his own aggressive leadership and the docility of the Sisters of Mercy in Jackson, whom he had ordered to undertake the Lansing project. "From their limited ranks they assumed the task, though it meant doubling the burden on the whole community, in order that they might correspond with the desire of the Bishop," Gallagher told the Superior of the Sisters of St. Joseph in 1920. "I now ask the Sisters of St. Joseph to imitate the spirit of obedience and sacrifice shown by the Sisters of Mercy and spare four Sisters to open a hospital in Flint. A place in which to begin will be ready next week." The Sisters of St. Joseph did indeed open a hospital in Flint — and shortly thereafter.[21]

Gallagher also had success when it came to dealing with the rich and powerful. It was the Fisher fortune, one of the few Catholic fortunes made in the auto industry, that endowed the Burtha M. Fisher Home for the Aged. Opened in 1928 in then rural Southfield, the Fisher Home replaced the Detroit facility maintained for nearly sixty years by the Little Sisters of the Poor. Fisher money also underwrote a new nurses' residence at Providence Hospital and the Sarah Fisher Home for Children. The growing number of well-to-do Catholics in the Diocese meant prosperity for its larger lay organizations, many of which were active in charitable work. The various lay-initiated and lay-run charities in the Diocese were brought under formal Chancery control in 1934, when Bishop Gallagher named Msgr. Michael Grupa the first diocesan director of charities. The extent of Msgr. Grupa's effective authority is not clear, but the appointment signals a commitment at the Chancery not simply to consolidating episcopal authority but to bringing system and efficiency to what was at best a loosely coordinated assortment of Catholic charitable organizations.

The educational achievements of the Gallagher years were most vividly memorialized in the new campuses built in the 1920s by the University of Detroit and St. Mary's College, both of them in sylvan settings on Detroit's northwestern frontier. It was apparently at Gallagher's insistence that the principal operations of St. Mary's College were moved to Detroit, where it could serve a much larger Catholic population than it had done in Monroe. The growth in Catholic college enrollments in the 1920s was a consequence in part of the expansion of Catholic secondary schools in that same decade, and Bishop Gallagher moved to make secondary education in his Diocese more respectable academically and more cost-efficient than it had hitherto been. A central high school for girls was opened in 1927 and one for boys in 1928, the first such schools in the history of the Diocese. The appointment of a diocesan superintendent of schools in 1921 was intended to achieve a greater quality and efficiency in Catholic education at both the primary and secondary levels, but Gallagher discovered, as his predecessors had done, that it was not easy to extend his authority over the parish schools. It was not until the appointment of Father Carroll Deady as superintendent in 1934 that the schools of the Diocese came for the first time under effective Chancery control. The Deady appointment, and the multifarious reforms to which it led, were among the most enduring legacies of the Gallagher episcopate.

There were other initiatives in the Gallagher years from which his successor benefited. The *Michigan Catholic* was bought by Bishop Gallagher in 1920, a purchase that quickly led to important changes in the content and function of the paper. The *Michigan Catholic* had been a conservative organ in its lay-owned years, and had rarely strayed far, in its editorial columns, from the political and theological views that were current at the episcopal residence. But for all this, it had a certain vitality—a lively eccentricity that came with its function as a social and political notice-board for the Irish-American community. Under diocesan auspices the paper was directed to a broader audience, and its circulation increased substantially between 1920 and 1940, the years when Father Francis Pokriefka served as managing editor. But it lost much of the personality that had once marked its pages, for it no longer carried its former wealth of parish news, most of which had been written by lay correspondents. The paper after 1920 was mainly devoted to stories that emanated from the Chancery and the larger lay organizations and to the activities of the American hierarchy and the Pope. As such it served to promote particular episcopal objectives and to convey a view of the Church in which the laity occupied a subordinate and largely passive role. But it may also have encouraged an emerging sense of unity and purpose among more assimilated Catholics, as it directed their attention away from the parish and towards diocesan, national, and even international issues that affected large Catholic populations. Besides the advantages of a diocesan newspaper, Gallagher bequeathed to his successor an embryonic Catholic Youth Organization — essentially a network of parish athletic teams — and the foundations of what became a fairly active Catholic Scouting movement, as well as an array of large and vigorous lay organizations as various as the Holy Name Society and the Catholic Instruction League.[22]

It is even possible to credit Bishop Gallagher, at least indirectly, with a quickening of devotional life in the Diocese, for he brought into the Diocese no fewer than nine men's religious orders, each of which sponsored — and sometimes aggresively publicized — particular religious devotions. He also invited into the Diocese two orders of contemplative nuns: the Discalced Carmelites and the Sisters of Mary Reparatrix, whose Detroit convent was a center of the women's retreat movement locally. Gallagher himself was instrumental in popularizing the cult of the recently canonized St. Theresa of Lisieux, erecting a shrine in her honor in his cathedral in 1925 and authorizing the construction in the following year of a chapel on Parsons Street in Detroit that became a center of devotion to the saint for Catholics throughout the Diocese. Gallagher's seems to have been a more emotional piety than Bishop Foley had ever betrayed, and in this respect he was at one with the prevailing religious mood. It was probably during the 1930s that devotional Catholicism had its widest appeal, at least in the Diocese of Detroit.

The anguish spawned by the Depression was a powerful stimulus to devotion. And that anguish came early to Detroit, dependent as it was on a single, and highly cyclical, industry. Automotive employment fell sharply in the final quarter of 1929: "Many families are in real misery, these last months of the year," the chronicles of Santa Maria parish in Detroit recorded. The smaller cities of the Diocese were part, by now, of a regional economy whose health depended on a strong Detroit. "For St. Peter's the depression began in August 1929 with the closing of the Detroit Automobile Factories," Father Dennis Hayes reported from his parish in Mt. Clemens in 1933. "Scores and scores of families have been without employment all these years, from that month on business conditions grew worse and worse; a constant decline in employment in every line of endeavor within and without Mt. Clemens; a continual widening and deepening area of poverty and suffering, until today things are worse than ever experienced by men now living." Poverty and suffering were sufficiently evident on Detroit's East Side by the autumn of 1929 that the Capuchins at St. Bonaventure's Monastery opened a soup kitchen early in November. Supported and staffed by lay members of the Franciscan Third Order, the kitchen was soon feeding 1,500 to 2,000 men a day.[23]

By the early months of 1930, the desperation of thousands of families in Detroit had become visible in the long lines that stretched through the corridors of the Department of Public Welfare, and in the crowds that thronged its seven district offices. Detroit was one of the few American cities in 1930 with a strong tradition of public relief, and its citizens turned to the city for assistance in this time of crisis as they had done in previous periods of economic decline. But by the spring of 1930, Detroit had the highest unemployment rate of any major city in the country, and the city's modest resources were soon overwhelmed by the needs of its destitute inhabitants. It could not make adequate provision for even the most desperate families, and there were growing numbers it could not help at all. The Department of Public Welfare investigated 897 families in the fall of 1931, all of whom had been dropped from the city's welfare rolls, and found that only 25 percent were living on income that a family member had earned. The rest were dependent, to a greater or lesser degree, on relatives and friends and private charity, and on the sufferance of the landlord and the grocer. "The poor were helping the poor," as Mayor Frank Murphy noted, but their resources were limited. Forty of the families whom the Welfare Department was investigating had been reduced to begging for food.[24]

By late 1932, when it was estimated that more than half of Detroit's wage-earners were unemployed and that many more were working only part-time, signs of collapse were everywhere. Vacant factories, stores, and houses blighted what had recently been a buoyant and expanding city. The population had fallen, since 1930, by more than 137,000, as immigrants returned to Europe and other Detroiters sought work elsewhere. ("On account of the great depression a number of the children returned to Malta, this lessening the number of our pupils," the chronicle kept by the Sisters at Holy Trinity School reported.) The numbers of homeless men in the city's streets grew steadily, and so did the numbers of mortgage foreclosures and evictions. The Welfare Department was reduced in July 1932 to housing families in a city park. As churches and other organizations increased their efforts to help the unemployed, reports of widespread suffering gained currency in the more affluent reaches of the community. The Madonna Guild, a Catholic women's group founded in 1919 to provide layettes to the families of the poor, turned late in 1930 to the more demanding work of feeding women and children. The guild's free kitchen provided lunch to "several hundred" schoolchildren on Detroit's near east side. "Many of these school boys and girls have no substantial food in their homes," a spokeswoman told the *Michigan Catholic*. "It has been found out by teachers that a large number of children receive no breakfast at all." It was rumored that Detroiters were actually dying of starvation. The *New Republic* had run a story to this effect in October 1931, and despite denials from the mayor and the Public Welfare Commission, the rumors persisted. They were grimly credible in the world of hunger and despair that untold numbers of the unemployed inhabited.[25]

The immensity of Detroit's economic problems made the city a magnet for leftists of every sectarian bent, and a fertile field for a vigorous politics of reform. Mayor Frank Murphy, who served from 1930 until 1934, was an eloquent advocate of public assistance to the unemployed and their families. During his administration, the city made what can only be regarded as heroic efforts to aid the destitute; certainly no other major city equaled its record. But the city's resources, as we have seen, were not equal to the task, and the situation only worsened when one of Detroit's largest banks collapsed early in 1933. The city's banks were effectively controlled by two great holding companies, whose fiscal management had been irresponsible even by the lax standards of the day. The demise of the Union Guardian Trust Company threatened nearly every financial institution in Detroit, few of which had anything like adequate reserves. The governor of Michigan, alerted to the crisis, declared a statewide bank holiday in mid-February, which continued into March and into the nationwide moratorium on banking proclaimed by Franklin Roosevelt when he assumed the presidency. The effect was to increase the already insuperable burden of want in Detroit and other Michigan towns and cities. Many of those lucky enough to have jobs went without their wages; private agencies found themselves without funds; and the Murphy administration abandoned its last desperate efforts to avoid defaulting on the city's massive debt. Detroit, which had been subsisting for more than a year on loans from the Reconstruction Finance Corporation, was now utterly bankrupt. A more dramatic demonstration of capitalism's death-throes could hardly have been scripted by the left, or a more urgent argument for federal relief been provided to the Roosevelt administration.[26]

The virtual collapse of Detroit's banks undermined an already precarious financial situation at the Chancery, where Bishop Gallagher was consumed with worry not only about the impending bankruptcy of his Diocese but about the political future of his see city and of the nation itself. The mostly working-class Catholic population had been badly hurt by the Depression, and reports that came regularly from many parishes bore witness to the spread of an alarming destitution and despair. "Of the 286 families who are represented in our school, 150 are in the 'bread line,'" the pastor at Our Lady of Help reported late in 1931. "Many of the children are miserably clothed and underfed, some even are given breakfast by the good sisters before the children begin the day's studies." How long it might be before Catholics like these were drawn to extreme political movements was an open question, and certainly the sectarian left was active and visible in Detroit, staging frequent demonstrations and drawing crowds all out of proportion to its small numbers. Bishop Gallagher repeatedly warned more affluent Catholics to be unstinting in their charity for the duration of the crisis, and he warmly supported Mayor Murphy's efforts to expand municipal relief. (The devoutly Catholic Murphy had been "a God send to Detroit . . . and to the Catholic Church during these troubled times," the bishop told Father Charles Coughlin in 1932.) But the unemployment crisis was simply too great to be countered by local initiatives, as Gallagher himself pointed out in a 1932 call for federal bank deposit insurance and for "public works on a vast scale." During the twilight of the Hoover administration, however, there was little sympathy in Washington for such views, and Gallagher, like many others, looked with apprehension to the economic and political future. "In 1931 we were told we were at the bottom," Father Dennis Hayes reminded his bishop, "and therefore business had to become better. In 1932 we were told exactly the same thing. However in 1933 we find ourselves a great deal lower than ever, and whether we are now at the bottom or not God alone knows. Homes in town and country continue to be lost and evictions are becoming more and more numerous on account of months and years of unpaid rent. Our people are drained dry; yes, bled white."[27]

Bishop Gallagher had as early as 1930 found an outlet for his political anxieties in Father Charles Coughlin, about whom we will hear more shortly. But he could not depend on Father Coughlin to bear the burden of anxiety that came with the mounting fiscal crisis of the Diocese. The unemployed and the underemployed could hardly give generously to the Church, and although most parishes reported a notable increase in church attendance and religious devotion in the early 1930s, their income plummeted sharply. The poorer parishes were affected first and most dramatically: St. Boniface Church, now in a declining area of the central city, saw its annual revenues fall from more than $24,000 in 1928 to $11,600 in 1930. But the financial crises that came with the Depression were most acute in those parishes that carried a heavy debt, and many of these were among the newer and hitherto more prosperous parishes in the Diocese. St. Peter Claver's parish, with its small black congregation, was in better fiscal health in the 1930s than St. Paul's parish in wealthy Grosse Pointe. For St. Peter Claver's had entered the Depression free of debt, while St. Paul's had borrowed heavily in 1927 to build a new school.[28]

Bishop Gallagher, as we have seen, had throughout the 1920s established parishes in advance of Detroit's population movement, and he had encouraged pastors to build on a generous scale in order to accommodate future population growth. But with the decline in the city's population that occurred after 1930, those parishes that had borrowed extensively in anticipation of future growth found themselves in serious trouble. St. Veronica's parish, for example, which had been founded in East Detroit in 1925, was unable in the early 1930s to pay even the interest on its considerable debt. "The parish [was] started to take care of the phenomenal growth directed toward East Detroit," a 1935 inventory of parish indebtedness noted. "The depression arrested everything. The buildings, erected for a much larger parish of the future, cost more than the present number of parishioners are able to take care of." Those parishioners were mostly the "families of men who formerly worked in Detroit factories and are purchasing their homes in the suburb on time payments," the *Michigan Catholic* explained early in 1931. "Since last September only 13 families have paid tuition for their children attending the parish school, which has an attendance of 260 pupils." St. Veronica's pastor had by this time opened a free food depot in the rectory garage, as well as a storefront on nearby Gratiot Avenue where bread was distributed to needy families.[29]

Bishop Gallagher can reasonably be faulted for having encouraged the rapid expansion of a diocese whose prosperity depended so heavily on the health of a volatile industry. He apparently assumed that the frenetic pace of population growth in and around Detroit would continue indefinitely, although this was hardly a sensible conclusion. (The pace of new construction had declined in the city after 1925.) Perhaps he was too impressed by the inactivity that had marked the latter part of the Foley episcopate, too determined that his own career would not be flawed in this particular way. Whatever the reason, Gallagher paid dearly after 1930 for the bold expansionist policies he had pursued, and so did many of his clergy. At least seventy-one parishes in the Diocese failed to meet even the interest payments on their mortgages in the first six years of the Depression. "At the present time it is rather gratifying to feel that a pastor is not delinquent in payment of at least the interest," Chancellor John Doyle told a local banker in 1933, not a little surprised that the man expected payment on the principal as well.[30]

Those pastors who had contracted or inherited large debts labored after 1929 under a grievous burden. It was they who were responsible, in the eyes of the Chancery, for the financial health of their parishes, although the bishop was legally liable for all debts on Catholic Church properties. Not every man was equal to the pressure. "I am tired of paying or rather trying to pay interest and debts," Father John Koelzer told the Chancery in 1934. "I can no longer get money out of my people. I am a dismal failure." He was more than ready to be moved from St. Margaret Mary's parish in Detroit, which he had founded in 1920. "Some of the priests who are anxious for a city parish might be able to succeed where I have failed." Father Koelzer was not in fact moved—he remained at St. Margaret Mary's until 1938—but the Chancery did transfer pastors whom the bishop believed were not working aggressively enough to pay their debts. And sometimes, despite the severity of the unemployment crisis, a new pastor was able to raise more money than his predecessor had done. "The late Most Reverend Bishop Gallagher did a fine piece of work as Diocesan Executive in asking me to step aside and allow you to take over a Pastorate which was utterly beyond me," Father Dennis Hayes told his successor at St. Peter's Church in Mt. Clemens, who had between 1934 and 1940 not only liquidated the parish debt but improved the property as well.[31]

Pastors who managed to survive financially against almost insuperable odds seem often to have turned to bingo and dances and bazaars as major sources of revenue. St. Rose parish on Detroit's East Side found that bingo with groceries for prizes was a popular attraction in a neighborhood hard hit by unemployment. (Still, the pastor was obliged, in the spring of 1931, to send the children from the parish school to solicit door-to-door for contributions from parishioners.) A number of parishes depended on donated labor to maintain and even improve their properties. The pastor at Detroit's St. Monica's Church, which had only a modest debt, sought permission in 1930 "to erect a small temporary hall—of the ready-cut variety. The men of the parish who are out of work will gladly supply the labor. . . . The cost of such a hall could easily be paid off by means of weekly card parties, dinners, dances, etc., and by means of annual bazaars." St. Martin's parish in Detroit was even able, in the summer of 1932, to pay subsistence wages to a number of its unemployed members in exchange for their work in building an addition to the parish school. The pastor, Father William Hennigan, had borrowed from a friend to cover the cost of materials, and those in the parish who still had jobs "are giving money to provide compensation for the workers on the basis of need." But Father Hennigan's imaginative leadership could not stave off an eventual financial crisis. St. Martin's parish, with its commodious school, was listed in 1935 among the many parishes that had been unable to meet the interest on their debts.[32]

The parish school generally proved in the Depression to be a serious financial liability. Revenue from tuition fell in nearly every parish, and parishes with heavy debts were in no position to subsidize their pupils. The pastor at tiny St. Bartholemew's parish on Detroit's far east side was borrowing heavily by late 1931, not only to pay the interest on his mortgage but to pay "for coal, Sisters' salaries, and repairs in the school." The enrollment at St. Bartholemew's school was only about sixty children, but neither the congregation nor the Chancery were disposed to close it. St. Bartholemew's was a Polish-language parish, and its members were apparently determined to keep their children in a "Polish" school. Bishop Gallagher, for his part, was committed to keeping all of the schools in the Diocese open, no matter how heavy the cost. ("My impression is that the alternative of closing the schools is something you will not think of for a moment," an overburdened pastor remarked to his bishop in 1933.) The bishop nearly realized his ambition: only two parochial schools were closed in the 1930s, one of them briefly. They were the school in St. Maron's (Syrian) parish, badly factionalized after the death of its longtime pastor in 1933, and the school in St. Joseph's parish in the village of Dexter. St. Joseph's School reopened in the fall of 1936, just as three additional parochial schools were opening their doors for the first time. Among them was a school for St. Peter Claver's parish, the first parish for black Catholics to have been established in the Diocese.[33]

The survival of the parochial schools in the 1930s was due not only to the sacrifices made by hard-pressed parents and their fellow parishioners, but to the charity of the various teaching orders. A good many parishes in the Depression failed to pay their teaching Sisters anything like their full salaries, although, at $40 a month, these were hardly generous. The Felician Sisters, for example, were owed more than $70,000 in 1937 by sixteen of the parishes where they maintained schools. Archbishop Mooney, initially of the opinion that the Sisters should forgive the debt, eventually agreed to require the delinquent parishes to pay the order half of what they owed.[34]

Parishes that could not pay their teachers or meet the interest on a mortgage were in no position to pay any but nominal taxes to the Chancery, and Bishop Gallagher was soon hard put to support the various diocesan institutions. Especially affected was Sacred Heart Seminary, whose endowment was exhausted as many donors failed, after 1929, to redeem their still-outstanding pledges of financial support. The collapse of Detroit's banks early in 1933 brought matters to crisis proportions, for the Diocese had its funds frozen in those insolvent institutions. Seminarians were asked for the first time to pay tuition — this caused enrollments to decline from 414 in the fall of 1932 to 288 one year later — and plans to add a theology course to the curriculum were abandoned. But the financial crisis was not thereby resolved. "Different creditors are constantly calling on the phone, or sending collectors to the building, looking for payment of accounts," the seminary's rector told Bishop Gallagher late in 1933. "While the list of employees has been cut away down from other years we have not been able to pay the wages of our present crew. . . . The priests who are teaching here have had no salary for the year 1933, and some of them have had few Mass stipends." Matters had not improved very much by 1935, when Gallagher told his consultors that the seminary had "an indebtedness for salaries, food etc of about $100,000 with practically no income."[35]

The financial crisis of the Diocese could not be remedied unless the Chancery was able to borrow heavily, and by 1935 the bishop was anxious to find a lender willing to refinance the entire diocesan debt. Money was cheap in the mid-1930s, and Gallagher hoped to ease the burden of interest carried by many parishes.

Then too, economic conditions had improved modestly: revenue in nearly every parish was higher than it had been in 1933. There was reason to hope that re-financing would lead to eventual fiscal health. Gallagher's agent in the search for a massive loan was George L. LeBlanc, a New York financier and one-time gold trader who had been, since 1932, an advisor to Father Charles Coughlin. The surviving evidence does not indicate whether LeBlanc's close association with Coughlin handicapped him in his dealings with the various banks and in-surance companies he tried to interest in refinancing the Detroit debt, although bankers especially had little love for the "radio priest." In any event, LeBlanc's efforts were fruitless. At his death early in 1937, Detroit's once-celebrated "builder bishop" bequeathed to his successor a diocese in financial chaos.[36]

It was not the financial troubles of his Diocese, however, that was the major cause of Bishop Gallagher's clouded reputation among his fellow bishops at the time of his death. What overshadowed the considerable accomplishments of the Gallagher episcopate was the bishop's relationship with Father Charles Cough-lin, who had long since passed from impassioned pleas for social justice to vi-tuperative attacks on the Roosevelt administration and on the president person-ally. (He had not yet, however, embarked on the openly anti-Semitic phase of his career.) By 1936, when Coughlin sponsored a third-party candidate for the presidency in hopes of throwing the election into the House of Representatives, even Bishop Gallagher seems to have been wavering in his staunch support of his longtime friend. But apart from his own backhanded endorsement of Roose-velt's reelection, Gallagher did nothing publicly to indicate that Father Coughlin no longer enjoyed his bishop's confidence. On the contrary, he denied rumors that he would silence Coughlin after the 1936 election, and praised the man whose protector he had been from the opening of Coughlin's controversial ca-reer. "I consider you a national institution," he wired the priest in November 1936, "invaluable to the safeguarding of genuine Americanism and true Chris-tianity. And I hope you will live long to carry out this sublime vocation."[37]

Gallagher's support of Coughlin can be understood only in the context of his own political history and that of Depression-ravaged Detroit. We have seen that Gallagher had been exposed, as a student at Innsbruck, to political theories that bear some resemblance to certain of Coughlin's own pronouncements, although Coughlin's could hardly be described as a theoretical or even a consistent politi-cal mind. Gallagher had apparently maintained an interest in corporatist social doctrine as it was enunciated by leading Austrian Catholics, for he was a friend of that country's Chancellor Engelbert Dollfuss, whom he visited in the early 1930s and whose funeral he attended in 1934. (The *Michigan Catholic* never in-timated that Gallagher's was more than a distant acquaintance with the Aus-trian head of state.) Gallagher's Austrian connections may have inspired his near-obsession with what he called "the morals of money", which for him—as for Father Coughlin—centered especially on interest and credit. Austria may have strengthened, or even given rise to, his apparent belief that the clergy might legitimately exercise political leadership. And it is possible that Gallagher's

failure to be alarmed at the authoritarian implications of certain Coughlin proposals stemmed from his sympathy for a worldview that placed order and economic justice above concern for individual political rights. No one, however, has
found evidence to link Gallagher with the anti-Semitism and the antidemocratic
values that were a part of Austrian Catholic political thought. (Nor indeed was
Coughlin's undoubted anti-Semitism a theme of significance in his sermons and
writings while Gallagher was alive.) And it is only right to note that, for all the
controversy surrounding his political opinions, Michael Gallagher showed more
concern for social justice over the course of his career than many—possibly
most—of his fellow bishops. Perhaps his Austrian years were responsible in part
for Gallagher's eloquent endorsement of collective bargaining in 1920, a statement that hardly pleased employers in the notoriously anti-union auto industry.
"The working man has a right to bargain for his wage," he told a crowd in Kalamazoo, "for to take what is offered or starve is not liberty but oppression and
slavery. Therefore the living wage and share of profits is the cure for unrest, for
Socialism, Bolshevism and IWWism."[38]

Gallagher's enduring alliance with Coughlin, however, may have had more
fundamentally to do with certain similarities of temperament between the two
men than with Gallagher's interest in Catholic social doctrine. Both were impulsive and stubborn and extremely sensitive to criticism, and both were resentful
of the ambiguous social position assigned even to affluent Catholics in a country
where the social elite had historically been Protestant. (Coughlin's fame in the
early 1930s and his apparent political influence were balm indeed to wounded
Catholic sensibilities.) And both were inclined to an almost paranoid view of history and politics, an inclination that was nutured, if not born, in a passionate
commitment to Irish nationalism. Gallagher had been a partisan of Irish independence since at least his student days, and he, like Coughlin, had embraced
a view of the world that blamed the English ruling class not only for Ireland's
manifold troubles but for much of the world's injustice.

The struggle for Irish independence had reached a critical phase when Gallagher was appointed Bishop of Detroit, and despite the burdens of his new position he found time to campaign for the Irish cause. He was active in the Friends
of Irish Freedom in the years immediately following the First World War, serving as national president of that Irish-American organization in 1920 and 1921.
He apparently saw no impropriety in a bishop's playing such a role—the Irish
hierarchy, after all, had been political leaders for generations—nor did he seem
much concerned about the violence sponsored by the Irish republican forces.
Gallagher himself celebrated a Requiem Mass in Detroit for Terence McSweeney,
the late Lord Mayor of Cork, whose death in 1920 was the consequence of a
politically motivated hunger strike. A crowd that overflowed the spacious sanctuary of St. Mary's Church turned out to support Ireland and their bishop on
that occasion. "The outer portal was draped in American flags," the *Michigan
Catholic* reported, "and the sanctuary shone with the national colors and with the

green, white and orange flag of the Sinn Fein government. . . . The catafalque, representing the bier of the dead, was draped simply in the Sinn Fein colors."[39]

The establishment of the Irish Republic in 1922 spelled an end to Gallagher's activities in behalf of Irish freedom, but not to his conviction that British power was the primary factor in world events, and a major influence on American politics. He had been a vocal opponent of American entry into the First World War, urging Americans as late as March of 1917 to petition Congress against intervention. He believed then—and continued to believe—that British domination of the American press had led to American intervention on the Allied side. Gallagher remained an isolationist for the rest of his life, always ready to see, in any argument in favor of an international role for the United States, a nefarious British hand. In this respect he and Father Coughlin were of one mind. It was Coughlin's bitter isolationist diatribes—and their considerable appeal among Irish-Americans—that made the priest, in the eyes of the Roosevelt administration, such a dangerous figure in the late 1930s.[40]

Gallagher and Coughlin shared as well a distinctive perspective on domestic politics. Both thought mainly in terms of conspiracy: politics was simply the manifestation of an eternal struggle between an unscrupulous monied elite and the mass of humanity. That struggle had been dominated by the forces of wealth since at least the eighteenth century, for the Reformation had eventually meant, in Gallagher's words, that "the Church was superseded by the State as the protector of rights, and the individual began to struggle through life under a new system of cut-throat competition accompanied by unrestrained freedom in industry." (There were apparently few events of note that Gallagher could not place in an economic context. "Even the contest over the marriage of the English king and Mrs. Simpson is really a capital and labor issue," he told a meeting in Detroit in 1936. "Premier Baldwin represents the old aristocracy and established wealth. The king is a friend of the common people. His opponents fear that during the next 20 or 25 years legislation to benefit the laboring classes will be introduced.") Both Gallagher and Coughlin, moreover, endowed monetary policy with an almost mystical significance in the struggle for social justice, much as the Populists of the 1890s had done. "The battle was lost in every generation from Alexander Hamilton down to Henry Morgenthau, from the immortal Father of the Country to the present incumbent in the White House," Gallagher explained in a 1935 broadcast from Coughlin's Royal Oak church, with reference to the priest's proposals to "nationalize" money and credit.

> I know the power that, in the past, won this battle for the banking interests. It is a power that today would gladly endow, if it could, a majority of the members of this Congress with five million dollars each to keep the control of money and the allotment of credit in private hands. Nor would these money lords and robber barons stop with the defilement of the majesty of the State, but willingly would they go into the very ranks of the Church, there to find anew a Judas willing to sell his soul for thirty pieces of silver.

However embarrassing Coughlin's rhetoric might become on occasion and however confusing and inconsistent his political nostrums might be, Gallagher was in sympathy with the rage that moved the man. He could never see Coughlin's critics as anything but agents — unwitting, in some cases — of the shadowy powers that oppressed small nations and condemned the working man to want in the midst of plenty.[41]

For all the controversy he eventually generated, Coughlin began his radio career as a homilist of the most conventional sort. Born in Canada in 1891 and educated by the Basilians in Toronto, Coughlin was ordained in 1916. He was closely associated with the Basilians in the early years of his priesthood when he taught at the order's Assumption College in Windsor, Ontario. Detroit lay just across the river from this small Canadian city, and Coughlin was soon volunteering as a weekend assistant in the priest-poor Diocese of Detroit. He quickly gained a modest reputation as an orator: "A rare treat was to hear the eloquent address of Rev. Chas. Coughlin, C.S.B.," a local women's organization informed the *Michigan Catholic* in 1918, "beautiful thoughts, cleverly expressed, a golden tribute to Our Blessed Lady." Parish work was apparently more congenial to Coughlin than the quiet life of a teacher, and in 1923 he severed his Basilian ties and was adopted as a diocesan priest by Bishop Michael Gallagher. Coughlin served as an assistant at St. Augustine's parish in Kalamazoo and then at St. Leo's parish in Detroit, both of them longtime training grounds for more promising members of the junior clergy. He was made pastor of SS. Peter and Paul's Church in rural North Branch in 1926. Just six months later, he was sent by Bishop Gallagher to found a parish in Royal Oak, then a mostly Protestant village, but soon to be a suburb of Detroit.[42]

Royal Oak and its environs had long been a stronghold of anti-Catholicism, and in the 1920s the Ku Klux Klan was active there. A cross was burned on the lawn of Coughlin's church not long after its completion in 1926. A more serious problem, however, was the small size of his congregation, for the Shrine of the Little Flower — Coughlin had named his church in honor of St. Theresa of Lisieux — was one of many parishes founded in the Gallagher years in advance of Detroit's population growth. Coughlin had borrowed heavily to build his Royal Oak church, and the mortgage was more than its congregation could carry. The Chancery assumed that Catholic migration into Royal Oak would soon alleviate the problem. But Coughlin had reason to fear that Klan activity in the vicinity might deter many Catholics from settling there.[43]

It was to solve his financial problems that Coughlin took to the air, delivering his first radio sermon from the pulpit of his church in the fall of 1926. The audience was initially very small, but it grew quickly. Within a year, the modest Royal Oak church could not contain the crowds that were drawn by Coughlin's Sunday sermons. His finances by now well in hand and the local Klan quiescent, Coughlin turned to the business of building a new church — one that would bear vivid witness to the vigor of Catholicism in hitherto-hostile Royal Oak. Its first and most dramatic component was begun in 1929. This was a massive granite tower, lavishly adorned with statuary—the figure of the Archangel Michael bearing the unmistakable features of Bishop Michael Gallagher.[44]

Coughlin's sermons in the late 1920s were hardly controversial. He rarely mentioned politics, save for occasional attacks on the Ku Klux Klan and the proponents of birth control. His themes were mostly religious, not fundamentally different from the Sunday sermon in any number of parishes, and he devoted many broadcasts to catechising children. What attracted his ardent and growing following was evidently less the content of his broadcasts than the almost hypnotic qualities of his voice. That voice, and Coughlin's knack for fusing his florid oratory with simple, homely anecdotes, made for a radio presence unlike any other in the early days of the medium. By the summer of 1930, he had signed an agreement to broadcast over the Columbia network. His potential audience was now as large as 40 million people.[45]

Coughlin had already ventured into political waters by the summer of 1930. But the content of his sermons was not yet particularly divisive. The early political sermons spoke in general, but indignant, terms about the suffering of the poor, and warned that the poor might eventually turn to Communism. Coughlin had as yet no well-developed theories as to the origins of the Depression, other than the "greed" and "corruption" he regularly assailed, and no well-defined proposals to end it. He urged employers to pay their workers a "just and living wage," and to do what they could to make steady work available. He praised contributory pension schemes. And he urged Christians of every denomination to give generously to the poor: "If there ever was a time in the history of this generation when there was demand for duplication of the multiplication of the loaves," he warned, "that moment has arrived."[46]

Coughlin's vague but increasingly insistent radicalism came to dominate his broadcasts in the latter part of 1930 and in 1931. And his audience continued to grow, fed by rising unemployment and by the inactivity of the Congress and the bland official optimism of the White House. "Contrary to the opinion of those who soothe us with the sophistry that depressions are cyclic happenings in the history of nations," Coughlin declared in 1930, "there never was such an occurrence as the one which at present we are experiencing. It is unique in the history of Christian civilization that such widespread starvation has existed when our granaries are choking with wheat; that such noticeable privation has existed when our banks are bursting with gold." His growing popularity, and the increasingly apocalyptic political mood, made Coughlin a controversial figure, at least in the eyes of the national networks. CBS refused to renew his contract when it expired in the spring of 1931, and NBC refused to negotiate with him at all. But Coughlin was by this time a sufficient power in the radio world that he was able to assemble a network of his own, based mainly though not exclusively in the northeast and the Midwest.[47]

Coughlin's sermons were characterized by a more developed ideology in 1932 and 1933. He acquired several influential advisors in this period, among them the financier George LeBlanc, and his radio sermons increasingly reflected their tutelage. Coughlin was more and more obsessed with monetary policy after 1932, convinced that the Depression had been caused, and was being sustained, mainly by a shortage of currency, which he attributed to the unscrupulous manipulations of bankers and financiers. An end to the Depression, then, could be accomplished only by a reinflation of the currency—this was his principal economic theme in 1932 and 1933—and by a restructuring of the nation's banking system, a topic to which Coughlin turned with particular vigor after 1934. Coughlin's economic prescriptions were hardly sophisticated—a part of his appeal lay in the simplicity of the remedies he offered—nor was his a consistent economic program. One could never be certain that the doctrine enunciated one week would not be changed, even contradicted, in the next. But that was apparently of little importance to his audiences. What mattered to them was Coughlin's impassioned defense of the poor against the rich, of the weak against the heartless and the powerful. For Coughlin's various economic proposals were always cast in terms of a struggle between the forces of greed and privilege and the mass of poor but honest Americans. And however vague and inconsistent those proposals might be, the moral drama did not change.[48]

Coughlin's broadcasts in 1933 were also noteworthy for their fervid adulation of Franklin Roosevelt and of his various New Deal measures. Coughlin had been introduced to Roosevelt by Detroit's Mayor Frank Murphy early in 1932, and had become an enthusiastic partisan of the Roosevelt candidacy. (He attended the Democratic national convention in 1932, where he apparently worked informally in Roosevelt's behalf.) But he did not campaign for Roosevelt, although his radio sermons in 1932 fairly bristled with attacks on the Hoover administration. As a priest, Coughlin told the Democratic standardbearer, he was obliged to refrain from explicit political endorsements. Once Roosevelt assumed office, however, Coughlin abandoned all pretense to neutrality, lavishing fulsome praise on the president and his advisors, and even on administration proposals that contradicted his own prescriptions for economic recovery. "The New Deal is Christ's Deal!" he told his audiences, and—at least in 1933—Coughlin seems to have believed his own extravagant rhetoric. Top officials in the administration, and Roosevelt himself, were careful to nourish Coughlin's illusion that he was a valued advisor, and Coughlin surely knew that his own popularity was strengthened by his association with an immensely popular president. Never a consistent political thinker, Coughlin chose to ignore the disparities between his own increasingly eccentric views on monetary policy and Roosevelt's pragmatic legislative program.[49]

But Coughlin could not maintain this precarious balance over the long term. His was too large an ego to labor in the shadow of another man, and he seems genuinely to have believed that his conspiratorial views on money and banking described the whole of political reality. More and more it looked to Coughlin as if the president's advisors, even Roosevelt himself, served the interests of the very financial powers that Coughlin believed had caused the Depression. Still, for the duration of 1934, Coughlin refrained from attacks on Roosevelt personally, although he was more and more critical of the president's program. Toward the end of the year he announced the formation of the National Union for Social Justice, which he described as "an articulate, organized lobby of the people to bring united pressure upon the representatives in Washington for the purpose of securing the passage of those laws which we want passed." Coughlin clearly hoped that the union would enhance his own political influence, and enable him to survive an open break with Roosevelt.[50]

The National Union for Social Justice, however, was never much more than a paper organization — hardly a means, for Coughlin, of enhanced political leverage. And by the end of 1935, an increasingly frustrated Coughlin was attacking the president as well as his policies. As those attacks became more frequent and more bitter, Coughlin's popular support began to wane and the composition of his audience to change. By the summer of 1936, when Coughlin's plans for a third-party challenge to Roosevelt had been announced, there is considerable evidence that the priest's once-enormous and disproportionately lower-middle-class following had been eroded, leaving him with a poorer, less articulate, and more heavily Catholic constituency. Whatever claims Coughlin might once have had to national political stature had been eroded as well. By 1936, Coughlin was the leader of a socially marginal and politically extremist constituency, and his own views increasingly reflected this.[51]

Coughlin had become a source of controversy among Catholics long before 1936, and a cause of bitterness and division within the American hierarchy. But open criticism of the priest was slow to come from Catholic sources. A principal reason for this was Bishop Michael Gallagher, whose warm support of Coughlin's activities made the job of Coughlin's Catholic critics an exceedingly delicate one. No one knew this better than Archbishop John McNicholas, who was Gallagher's Metropolitan in the Province of Cincinnati. It was McNicholas whom two successive Apostolic Delegates employed as an intermediary when they wished to communicate with Gallagher on the subject of Father Coughlin, both delegates having learned from experience that dealing directly with Detroit was frustrating and unproductive. "There was much of the American boy in Bishop Gallagher," Archbishop McNicholas remarked at the time of Gallagher's death. "The former Delegate could not understand him at all."[52]

McNicholas had reference here to Archbishop Pietro Fumasoni-Biondi, whose tenure as delegate came to an end in 1933. Fumasoni-Biondi had complained in the summer of 1930 about Gallagher's public criticism of the Hoover administration. "I am sure that it is as painful to you, as it is to me," he told McNicholas, "to hear one of our bishops so express himself on a purely political question . . . . and particularly because his Lordship's utterances have turned to a personal attack on the president of the United States." Would McNicholas "say a kind word of advice" to Gallagher, the delegate asked, "in order to prevent further interference in political matters." Fumasoni-Biondi wrote directly to Gallagher in the fall of 1932, this time with regard to Father Coughlin. Gallagher was "obligated," the delegate warned, to see that the priest's future radio addresses were limited to religious matters. This utterly ineffective instruction was followed by at least one further admonition, which was relayed by the hapless Archbishop McNicholas. McNicholas told Gallagher early in 1935 that the delegate "wishes Your Excellency to direct Father Coughlin to give up his practice of mentioning names in his broadcasts as something contrary to priestly charity." It was perhaps on this occasion that Bishop Gallagher turned to scripture to defend his priest. "It is true that [Coughlin] seems to violate charity in denouncing people by name," McNicholas told Archbishop Edward Mooney in 1936, "and I have said this to his bishop. Bishop Gallagher says, 'Well, St. John the Baptist denounced Herod and his wife because of their adulterous union!'"[53]

Archbishop Fumasoni-Biondi was succeeded as delegate by Archbishop Amleto Cicognani. He too looked to Archbishop McNicholas for help in dealing with Detroit. But McNicholas was by this time exceedingly reluctant to play the intermediary. Bishop Gallagher "is marvelously clever in turning a thing into a joke," he explained to Cicognani in the spring of 1935. "He is indeed good-hearted beyond any doubt, and he loves the Church, but his *criteria judicandi* are not those of a Bishop having a fine, balanced judgment." Nor did Gallagher bother with even a semblance of obedience. "I do not think the Bishop will answer my letter," McNicholas warned, Cicognani evidently having asked him to relay a message to Gallagher with regard to Father Coughlin. Archbishop Cicognani subsequently asked McNicholas to bring the Coughlin matter before the Administrative Board of the National Catholic Welfare Conference (NCWC), which the delegate hoped would issue a statement on the growing Coughlin controversy. But the board's jurisdiction in the matter was far from certain, as Archbishop Edward Mooney pointed out. (Mooney was then Archbishop-Bishop of Rochester.) "I am wondering whether, when all concerned, including the Delegate, see the only kind of statement which they feel can be made, they will not conclude that it is not worth making," Mooney cautioned McNicholas in March of 1936. "After all, there are just two authorities who can, with clear right, step into this affair, his own Bishop and the Holy See. . . . I very much fear that any statement which stops short of condemnation—and it must do that—will almost inevitably be taken as some sort of approbation."[54]

Presumably for these reasons, the Administrative Board of the NCWC never issued a statement on Father Coughlin. And individual bishops were slow to speak against him, perhaps out of deference to Bishop Gallagher, but also because they feared to alienate the Coughlin supporters in their own dioceses. For Coughlin's more fanatical followers shared the paranoid views of their champion, and were quick to see evil in high places, even in the Church—a tendency that was the more pronounced as the Coughlin movement became a more extremist one. Archbishop McNicholas was keenly aware of the problem. "I am sure if Father Coughlin comes to Cincinnati one hundred and fifty or more thousands will turn out to hail him as the only fearless leader in the country," he told the Auditor of the Apostolic Delegation in August 1936. "Many of our best priests are convinced absolutely of Father Coughlin's sincerity. They believe that substantially he is doing a great work against radicalism in our country, which they feel is making greater progress in secret than in the open." McNicholas was afraid by now that the mercurial Coughlin might leave the Church, were he silenced by ecclesiastical authority. "Some time ago I personally heard Cardinal Hayes say something to the following effect, when speaking about Father Coughlin, to about twenty of us Bishops — that we who have gone through the McGlynn case know that today hundreds of souls are dying outside the Church because of McGlynn. And yet the McGlynn case would be as a drop of water to the bucket in comparison with Father Coughlin's, if the worst should come to him!" As far as McNicholas was concerned, the situation warranted the greatest caution on the part of Church authorities: "In considering Father Coughlin and all the questions connected with him we must have one thing in view — the supreme interests of religion."[55]

Father Coughlin's increasingly strident rhetoric, however, caused Archbishop McNicholas to issue a reluctant public criticism of the priest in the fall of 1936. Several other bishops, Chicago's Cardinal Mundelein most prominent among them, had by this time already made public statements in opposition to Coughlin. What made the priest vulnerable to Catholic criticism was his open break with Roosevelt in 1936. (Boston's conservative Cardinal O'Connell, in 1932 the earliest of Coughlin's episcopal critics, was obviously moved by other considerations.) But the rising tide of Catholic criticism had no apparent effect on Bishop Gallagher, although Coughlin's vitriolic attacks on Roosevelt — he called the President a "liar" and a "double-crosser" in an infamous speech at Cleveland — were causing the bishop great embarrassment. Gallagher did publicly chastise Coughlin for the Cleveland remarks, reportedly at the behest of the Apostolic Delegate, and he put clear distance between himself and Coughlin's activities on behalf of the Union party presidential bid of Congressman William Lemke. But he continued to insist that Coughlin's ideas and his manifold activities were in full accord with Catholic social teaching.[56]

Those activities, however, had clearly raised anxieties at the Vatican. Gallagher went to Rome in the summer of 1936, at the behest of the Pope, or so it was widely assumed. (The bishop insisted that the trip was his own initiative.) What transpired in Rome is still not known, although the secular press at the time was rife with rumors that Gallagher would be removed as Bishop of Detroit. A principal cause of the rumors was an attack on Coughlin in the *Osservatore Romano,* an attack that coincided with Gallagher's return to the United States in early September, and that criticized Gallagher directly for his alleged claim that Coughlin's activities enjoyed the "full approval" of the Pope. The bishop knew that "this did not correspond to the truth," the paper asserted. The *Osservatore* was not then — and is not today — an official voice of the Holy See, and newspaper speculation that the paper spoke in this instance for the Pope was merely educated guesswork. Gallagher, however, knew the facts. The *Osservatore* piece "accurately represents the mind of the Holy See with regard to the matter it discusses," the Apostolic Delegate warned Gallagher at the end of September.

Presumably Gallagher had been told in Rome that his priest's abuse of Roosevelt was embarrassing to the Church, and could not be tolerated in a time of ominous international tensions.[57]

Still, Gallagher did not succeed in moderating Coughlin's rhetoric. Perhaps he did not even try. Coughlin's speeches on behalf of William Lemke in the 1936 campaign were almost wholly devoted to strident attacks on Roosevelt. Gallagher himself, of course, was far more damaged by Coughlin's assaults than Roosevelt could possibly be, poised as he was on the verge of an overwhelming electoral triumph. Gallagher was by now almost wholly isolated from his fellow bishops, the object of their pity if not their outright contempt. Coughlin later claimed that Cardinal Eugenio Pacelli, Secretary of State to Pius XI and shortly to become Pope, had refused to receive Gallagher when Pacelli visited the United States in the fall of 1936, although Gallagher had traveled to Cincinnati to seek an audience with him.[58]

Why Gallagher persisted in his support for Coughlin is one of the many enigmas to which the now-depleted Gallagher papers may once have held the key. Certainly more was involved than Gallagher's commitment to Coughlin's political and economic theories. The bishop's open preference for Roosevelt in 1936 meant a tacit rejection of Coughlin's economic program, at least as a workable solution to the nation's problems. But Father Coughlin was a phenomenon greater than his programs, and Gallagher was perhaps unwilling to repudiate the man whom he had long regarded as a powerful force for social justice. Perhaps too he feared the inevitably savage reaction of Coughlin's still-numerous followers, although Detroit was not nearly so staunch a Coughlin city by 1936 as Boston or Cincinnati, both of whose ordinaries had spoken against the priest. But the explanation seems most likely to lie, as it was earlier suggested, in Gallagher's personality and in his tendency, so much like Coughlin's, to see the world in simplistic, almost paranoid, terms. His advancing age and deteriorating health seem only to have strengthened the more abrasive aspects of his personality.

It was death that rescued Bishop Gallagher from the Coughlin inbroglio: the bishop died, quite unexpectedly, on January 20, 1937. Father Coughlin was at this point in an apparently self-imposed exile from the airwaves, a response, or so he said, to the devastating defeat of his candidate in the November elections. Coughlin soon resumed broadcasting, however, announcing on January 24 that he was resurrecting his weekly program in obedience to Bishop Gallagher's dying request. "From this great bishop I gained my inspiration," he told his listeners. "By virtue of his encouragement I pursued the path that he had blazed for me." Under the circumstances, it was an ambiguous eulogy. But Gallagher's achievement was so mixed, his vision so quixotic, that the ambiguity seems oddly appropriate. Still, the much-respected Archbishop McNicholas was inclined to a more charitable judgment. "He was one of nature's princes," he told Archbishop Cantwell of Los Angeles not long after Gallagher died. "One might not agree with him in many things of administration, but he was utterly incapable of taking a small view of things. He was generous to a fault. He was so guileless that he simply could not understand deceit or double-dealing. . . . He has left a great diocese behind him. . . . We shall never see his like again."[59]

THE MOONEY EPISCOPATE

Gallagher's successor as Bishop of Detroit was not a man from whom Father Coughlin could expect either "inspiration" or "encouragement." Indeed it was widely assumed that Archbishop Edward Mooney was sent to Detroit in part to solve the Coughlin problem. Mooney was expected to be a strong leader — something Gallagher had not been since the outset of the Depression — and there were those who thought that he would move quickly to silence the radio priest. (Others, perhaps more realistic, looked for Mooney to moderate the tone and limit the content of future Coughlin broadcasts.) Whatever their expectations with regard to Coughlin, however, knowledgeable observers agreed that Mooney possessed — if any man did — the skills and the political acumen necessary to govern a diocese as troubled as Detroit was thought to be. Gallagher, as we have seen, had left his successor a massive debt. The administrative efficiency of the Chancery had been badly eroded since 1930. And Detroit was still in 1937 the nation's most politically volatile city. The great sit-down strikes at General Motors and Chrysler had ended by the time the Mooney appointment was announced in May 1937, but labor relations in the auto industry were extremely tense. The campaign to organize the Ford Motor Company, moreover, promised to be a violent one. The priest whom Mooney named as his chancellor in 1938 was blunt when he met his new archbishop for the first time. "On that occasion he said, 'Father Ed, what are my problems?'" Bishop Joseph Hurley reminded Msgr. Edward Hickey many years later. "Without hesitation, you said, 'There are four–first, Organization; second, Finances; third, Labor, and fourth, Father Coughlin.'"[60]

The man to whom these daunting problems fell was born in 1882 to a Maryland family in apparently comfortable circumstances. (Mooney's paternal grandfather had come to the United States from Ireland in 1836.) The Mooney family moved to Youngstown, Ohio, when Edward was four, and it was there that he attended school. His seminary training, however, was taken in Maryland, at St. Charles College and at St. Mary's Seminary in Baltimore, and at the North American College in Rome. He was ordained in Rome in 1904 as a priest for the Diocese of Cleveland.[61]

Mooney's was a distinguished academic career, both in Baltimore and in Rome. "In the Seminary Mooney was always looked up to as a brilliant student, one who applied himself very earnestly to his work," a classmate at the North American College remembered. Accordingly, his bishop appointed him to the faculty of the Cathedral Latin School in Cleveland when he returned to the United States. He remained at the school until 1922, serving as headmaster after 1915. In 1922, however, the school was put in the charge of the Marist Fathers, and Headmaster Mooney was sent to St. Patrick's parish in Youngstown. The year he spent there was the only stint of parish work in his career.[62]

Father Mooney was by this time out of favor with Bishop Joseph Schrembs, who was a good friend, ironically enough, of Bishop Michael Gallagher. Mooney had been closely associated, according to Schrembs, with what his bishop called "a bad crowd in the Diocese"—apparently a faction of priests who were critical of the Schrembs administration. It seems unlikely, however, that Father Mooney was much of a clerical Young Turk. Certainly he was known in Rome as a deferential and prudent man, qualities that his many Roman friends may have cited when they pressed for his appointment as spiritual director of the North American College. That appointment was made in 1923, evidently over the objections of Bishop Schrembs, and Mooney spent the next three years in Rome. His performance there simply enhanced his already considerable reputation. Mooney was named Apostolic Delegate to India in 1926—he was the first American to be appointed a delegate—and consecrated the titular Archbishop of Irenopolis.[63]

Archbishop Mooney's nearly six years of service in India was followed by a two-year stint as Apostolic Delegate to Japan. Evidently he served in both posts with characteristic grace and distinction. Bishop Lawrence Casey, a longtime Mooney intimate, later claimed that Mooney was the first delegate in India "to visit every Catholic mission in that vast country. Where he went, there were no trains, and he rode the native horses bareback for hours on end. He rode on the backs of elephants through the jungle. He travelled on insect-ridden boats with no sleeping accommodations save for the hard, uneven boards of the boat-bottom." Bishop Casey was speaking shortly after Mooney died in 1958, and his recollections may well have been colored by the years and by his desire to honor the memory of his friend. But during his time in Detroit, Mooney received numerous letters from priests and religious whom he had met in India and Japan, and who invariably remembered him with admiration. His had been a gracious presence, they agreed, and a tireless devotion to duty.[64]

Mooney was apparently deeply moved, during these years of service in the East, by the fervor of the Catholic minority in India and Japan. And his service there may well have helped to shape his relatively liberal views on Church-State relations. Still, he returned from the East with his Roman loyalties firmly intact. He evidently saw no need for the Church to adapt its worship or its discipline to the cultures of the East. The strength and beauty of the Church, in Mooney's eyes, lay principally in its doctrinal and liturgical unity, and Rome was for him both the symbol of that unity and its source. Then too, his career had progressed largely under Roman auspices. This only strengthened the Roman loyalty that was so much a part of his training and of his religious sensibilities.

The years abroad came to an end in 1933, when Mooney was appointed Archbishop-Bishop of Rochester. The Rochester see was not a major one, and it was widely assumed that Mooney would shortly move to a diocese of greater size and importance. Detroit was occasionally mentioned as a post that Mooney might eventually fill, and it was indeed Detroit to which he was assigned in the spring of 1937. Soon after his appointment, the Diocese of Detroit was raised to an Archdiocese, and its archbishop made head of a newly created Detroit Province, to which all the dioceses in Michigan belonged. (A fourth Michigan diocese was created by this same decree. It was the Diocese of Lansing, which incorporated fifteen counties in the western and central portion of the state, and which removed forty-six parishes and seventy-one priests from the jurisdiction of the Bishop of Detroit.) Archbishop Mooney was already a major figure in the American hierarchy by the time he went to Detroit. He served as chairman of the Administrative Committee of the NCWC from 1936 until 1939, and held the post again from 1941 to 1945.[65]

The man who became Detroit's first archbishop bequeathed to posterity a more voluminous set of papers than any of his predecessors had done. Few of these papers, however, are of a purely personal nature, and a majority of them deal with Mooney's national activities rather than with his work in the Archdiocese of Detroit. The archival record of his Detroit years, then, is probably not complete, nor is the personality that emerges from this record necessarily an adequate representation of the man himself. Still, that personality is an attractive one. Mooney's correspondence reveals a fine and nuanced intelligence, and a man who was temperate, tolerant, and unaffectedly gracious. He was a generous man, one who gave freely to charity and lived as simply as the trappings of his office would allow. He had a wonderfully wry and understated sense of humor, and an apparently genuine modesty about his own achievements. (He was "constitutionally a bit allergic to decorations," he told Bishop Edwin O'Hara in 1946, declining a proffered award.) Evidently rather shy, he played only the most limited role on Detroit's social stage, and in his later years, especially, seemed to be "a personage distinguished and capable but somewhat distant and retiring." To his friends, however — and these were mostly fellow clerics — he "had a warm and human personality," as Bishop Lawrence Casey said in 1958. "You had the feeling that you could talk to him, that he respected you as a person and was interested in what you had to say."[66]

Mooney was naturally not without his critics, but the faults with which he was occasionally charged were in keeping with his judicious temperament. His was a view of the world that saw complexities rather than clear moral choices, at least when it came to politics. The politically engaged among his priests and people sometimes thought he was too reluctant to take public stands on controversial issues. (He was especially slow to speak publicly on race relations, although he was generous in his support of the black Catholic parishes in Detroit.) He was perhaps too much concerned with discipline and good order in the Church and too little attentive to signs of intellectual and spiritual restlessness among the better-educated laity. He seemed curiously unaware, moreover, of the serious pastoral problems that were rapidly developing around the issue of contraception. But each of these shortcomings, if such they can fairly be called, was characteristic of nearly all the bishops of Mooney's generation, and many in the next as well.

Father Coughlin

Mooney's cautious temperament is surely a key to his dealings with Father Coughlin. Despite Coughlin's increasingly provocative behavior, Mooney permitted the priest to continue with many of his political activities, and was remarkably restrained in his response to Coughlin's repeated testing of Chancery authority. It was only the prospect of federal sedition charges against the priest in 1942 that caused the archbishop to bring full ecclesiastical sanctions to bear against the fractious Father Coughlin. Whether Mooney was wise to have pursued so circumspect a course is still a matter of debate. Certainly his decisions in the Coughlin affair were the most controversial of his career. But Mooney himself seems never to have doubted that the course he chose was the only prudent one, although it had damaged his own prestige and that of the American Church. His first round of conflict with Father Coughlin had convinced the archbishop "that the situation cannot be cleared up without some injury to the Church one way or another"—or so he told New York's Archbishop Spellman in 1942. Under the circumstances, Mooney was inclined to be grateful that the harm to the Church was no greater than it was.[67]

Mooney apparently came to Detroit with every intention of restraining the irresponsible Father Coughlin. Not long after he took office, Mooney appointed an ecclesiastical censor for Coughlin's radio speeches and for his weekly column in *Social Justice,* the news magazine that the priest had founded in 1936. (Coughlin had hitherto functioned without any Chancery censorship at all.) And the archbishop pointedly refused his imprimatur for a trio of *Social Justice* articles that Coughlin planned to publish in pamphlet form as "Can Christians Join the CIO?" (the Congress of Industrial Organizations). "To the censors and to me it seemed that the articles in question were such as to stir up unnecessary and unduly bitter strife among Catholics in a matter of critical importance to our workingmen," Mooney explained to Cardinal Eugenio Pacelli, to whom Coughlin had informally appealed the matter, "and above all that the articles in question contained inaccurate quotations from the Encyclicals of Our Holy Father, gave distorted interpretations to these documents and, by clear implication, invoked the authority of the Holy Father for certain theories of Father Coughlin which should be discussed on their own objective terms." Coughlin at this point had not yet begun his regular autumn broadcasts. But he was deeply alarmed by the policies of his new archbishop, who was clearly intent on restricting the content of the priest's political speeches and writings.[68]

The uneasy Coughlin was quick to counterattack. He gave a provocative press interview on October 4, 1938, in which he referred to the "personal stupidity" of President Roosevelt, and asserted that no Catholic could in conscience be a member of the CIO. Mooney promptly issued a public rejoinder: he chastised Coughlin for failing to avail himself of "the prudent counsel of a friendly critic, which it is the aim of Church legislation to provide," and defended the right of Catholics to be members of CIO-affiliated unions. "No Catholic Church authority has ever asserted that the CIO is incompatible with Catholicity on the basis of its publicly-stated principles." As for the reference to Roosevelt, Mooney reminded Coughlin that priests were always and everywhere required "to impose upon themselves a fine sense of restraint in the language they use." Mooney had shown this statement to Coughlin before it was published in the *Michigan Catholic,* and Coughlin had assured his archbishop that he accepted what was, after all, a gently worded reproof. But shortly thereafter, the priest announced publicly that he was preparing a statement of his own. The Coughlin rebuttal, in typically rambling fashion, "evaded the points at issue and went into a long disquisition on matters that were irrelevant and would only confuse the whole situation," Mooney subsequently told the Apostolic Delegate. "I advised him earnestly against publishing it." Coughlin then informed the press that Mooney had refused to allow the rebuttal to be made public. He announced at the same time that he was canceling his radio broadcasts for the 1937–1938 season. "It was quite apparent that Father Coughlin would be permitted only to talk platitudes," Coughlin's lawyer told the press on October 9, "that he could not say what he thinks, but only what the Archbishop thinks."[69]

Coughlin's followers reacted with predictable bitterness to what they saw as the silencing of their champion. Angry letters flooded the Chancery in Detroit, and on October 19 a Toledo businessman launched a nationwide campaign to restore Father Coughlin to the air. (It was to this man, one Walter Baertschi, that Coughlin had just transferred ownership of *Social Justice.* Baertschi pledged to return control of the publication to Coughlin when "his voice is freed from restrictions; when his pen, likewise, is free to write as it did in the past.") Baertschi's campaign, largely orchestrated through the pages of *Social Justice,* seems to have generated an impressive response. Coughlin's supporters in New York announced that they were soliciting letters on the priest's behalf in every county in the state. Enthusiasts in Cleveland set a goal of 100,000 signatures on a petition to the Pope. Baertschi himself spoke to large pro-Coughlin rallies in Chicago and Detroit. The volume and the tenor of the protest were such that Archbishop Mooney asked for help from Rome. "One word from the Holy See now will count for a great deal," he told the Apostolic Delegate on October 29. "If the matter is allowed to drag and the agitation based on suppressions of facts among undiscerning Catholics and exploitations of ignorance and prejudice among Protestants is allowed to gain momentum, much more may be required later on—and poor Father Coughlin may be so deeply committed that it will be much harder for him to submit."[70]

The Apostolic Delegate was immediately sympathetic, asking Mooney himself to compose a statement that might be issued by the Holy See. Mooney proceeded to do so. The statement was made public on November 20 by the Apostolic Delegate, who told the press that Archbishop Mooney's criticisms of Coughlin's early October remarks had been "just and timely" in the eyes of the Holy Father. "Every bishop has not only the right but the duty to supervise Catholic teaching in his own Diocese," Archbishop Cicognani pointed out. An aggrieved priest, moreover, although he might appeal a superior's actions to the Holy See, "has the duty of using his influence to keep the matter from becoming the occasion of public agitation." Coughlin responded to Cicognani's statement with a public appeal for an end to all efforts on his behalf. Walter Baertschi announced on the same day, however, that he would continue his fight to return an uncensored Coughlin to the air.[71]

Even before the Cicognani statement was published, Coughlin had initiated negotiations with the Chancery in Detroit about a return to the air. (Msgr. William Murphy, whom Mooney had appointed as Couglin's censor in August, served as intermediary in these negotiations.) The principal issue was censorship: what rules would govern future broadcasts, and who would act as censor? Mooney seems to have yielded nothing in these discussions, almost certainly hoping that Coughlin would decide to give up his radio career. But Coughlin had no intention of doing so. He twice visited the Apostolic Delegate in Washington, on November 26 and on November 30, the purpose of the visits being to secure the delegate's support for a return to the air and for the replacement of Msgr. Murphy as censor. Characteristically brazen, Coughlin proposed that three of his assistant priests at the Shrine of the Little Flower serve as his censors instead.[72]

Coughlin did not succeed in displacing Msgr. Murphy as censor, but he did use his visits to the delegate as a weapon in the war of nerves in which he and his archbishop were engaged. "The Apostolic Delegate graciously granted me the interview I requested," he wrote to Mooney on Nov. 30. "As a result of our conference His Excellency expressed the opinion that the confusion resulting from my withdrawal from broadcasting and the circumstances which attended it could best be dissipated by my return to the air." (Cicognani's was a rather different version of the conversation.) Mooney was probably not prepared at this point to forbid the priest to resume his broadcasts, although in retrospect this would seem to have been the opportune moment to have done so. Having finally acceded to Mooney's requirements with regard to a Chancery censor, Coughlin was able to announce, on December 4, that he would return to the air in January 1938.[73]

Mooney by now had a vivid sense of the manner of man he was dealing with. Father Coughlin had enormous charm; even his detractors admitted as much. But he was a duplicitous and manipulative man, uncannily alert to the vulnerabilities of those around him. Coupled with his essentially paranoid view of the world and his penchant for impulsive action, these qualities made him a formidable opponent. Coughlin seems indeed to have gained the upper hand psychologically with his archbishop as early as December 1937, although it was widely assumed that Mooney had won their just-completed battle. The hitherto-unmuzzled Coughlin, after all, was returning to the air under firm ecclesiastical supervision. But Coughlin had succeeded by December 10 in forcing his archbishop to allow him to resume control of *Social Justice* magazine, something that Mooney had been loath to do. (Censorship of a weekly magazine would be a good deal more burdensome for the Chancery than policing a weekly radio address.) Coughlin had simply outmaneuvered Mooney, announcing to the press on December 7 that he would become "Editorial Counsel" to *Social Justice*, "provided this met with the approval of his Superior." An astonished Mooney hurriedly conferred with Msgr. Murphy, "and we decided," as Mooney told the Apostolic Delegate,

> that it was better, in the circumstances, to disregard the evident lack of courtesy and make the best of the situation by giving formal approval to his re-association with Social Justice, in such a way, however, as to make him responsible for the "content and policy" of the whole paper as well as for making it such as the name of a priest might properly be associated with. In answer, therefore, to a call from me Fr. Coughlin came over and wrote a formal request for the permission in question to which I gave an affirmative answer under the condition outlined above. . . . The whole procedure had in it a good deal of the character of a "sanation" or a rather naive effort to make the best of a fait accompli. But I thought it best not to provoke a situation in a petty affair with one who from day to day becomes for me a more mysterious combination of self-willed impetuosity and strategic cleverness in putting "one on the spot."

Mooney's subsequent dealings with Coughlin were very much in this mode, with the Archbishop reacting to the successive faits accomplis of his unpredictable priest. And the note of bemusement that is evident here became more and more pronounced in Mooney's letters about "Royal Oak," the archbishop's shorthand for Coughlin and his multifarious activities.[74]

Coughlin's initial broadcasts in 1938 were relatively noncontroversial. In March, however, he presented a proposal for a corporate form of government in the United States that revealed what can only be called an alarming indifference to democratic values. *Social Justice* by this time was preoccupied with maintaining American neutrality in the likely event of a European war, and was more and more inclined to apologize for the excesses of fascist regimes in Germany and Italy, while excoriating Great Britain as a major culprit in the looming conflict. The magazine assumed an overtly anti-Semitic editorial stance in the summer of 1938, when it began the serial publication of the "Protocols of the Elders of Zion," which appeared under Father Coughlin's byline in his weekly column, "From the Tower." Coughlin's prefatory remarks to each of the "Protocols" were deeply anti-Semitic in tone, although he always included some strategically placed disclaimers. He was critical only of antireligious Jews, Coughlin repeatedly pointed out, and firmly opposed to hatred of the Jews as a people. He readily admitted that the "Protocols" were probably a forgery. But their authenticity was not important, according to Coughlin. What mattered was their "factuality"—the remarkable correspondence between the plans of the perhaps-fictitious "elders" and events that currently menaced the future of Christian civilization. It was this menace that preoccupied Coughlin in the first of his openly anti-Semitic broadcasts, that of November 10, 1938—a broadcast that was ostensibly devoted to the evils of religious persecution. Jews had been principally responsible for the Russian revolution, he told his audience, and they bore the major responsibility for the spread of Communism throughout the world. Nazism, however deplorable it might be, could only be understood "as a defense mechanism against the incursions of Communism."[75]

There is little doubt that Coughlin had long held anti-Semitic views. But the virulent anti-Semitism that appeared in his writings and in his broadcasts in 1938 was something with which the late Bishop Gallagher had never had to deal. The change had partly to do with Coughlin's growing fears about the international scene: he was more and more obsessed with what he saw as a transnational conspiracy of Jews and bankers and British imperialists to involve the United States in a second European war. And he found in the writings of Father Denis Fahey, an Irish priest with whom he began to correspond in the fall of 1938, a theological context in which to place his anti-Jewish paranoia. Couglin's attacks on Roosevelt became more extreme after 1938 as well, for Roosevelt, in his view, was a principal agent in the plot to take America to war. (The President was "the world's chief war-monger," *Social Justice* told the nation in the fall of 1940.) But at least in retrospect, the attacks on Roosevelt pale in comparison with Coughlin's attacks on Jews and his periodic defenses of European fascism.[76]

Archbishop Mooney, it goes without saying, was neither an anti-Semite nor an apologist for fascism. In his own utterances and through the pages of the *Michigan Catholic*—which gave only perfunctory coverage to Coughlin's radio talks—he made clear his deep disagreement with nearly everything that Coughlin had to say. "Totally out of harmony with the Holy Father's leadership are Catholics who indulge in speeches or writings which in fact tend to arouse feelings against the Jews as a race," the *Michigan Catholic* warned in the summer of 1938. "For safe guidance on such issues loyal and thoughtful Catholics look to the official spokesmen of the Church." And yet each of Coughlin's most notorious anti-Semitic broadcasts had been approved by a Chancery censor, who apparently made only minor changes in the text. (Archbishop Mooney himself effected substantial changes in the broadcast of December 11, 1938, but was unable to persuade Coughlin to alter the subject of the address.) Each of Coughlin's *Social Justice* columns in 1938, moreover, also had Chancery approval, including the infamous columns devoted to the "Protocols." Indeed, Coughlin had been permitted to assume the presidency of the Social Justice Publishing Company in October of that year. The principal censor for Coughlin's work in 1938 was Father Sebastian Erbacher, a Franciscan who was widely known for his generous support of the labor movement and of the Catholic Worker movement in Detroit. He was no more likely an anti-Semite than his archbishop.[77]

What, then, explains Mooney's apparent tolerance of Couglin's increasingly extremist rhetoric? For it was widely seen as tolerance, if not outright approval. Archbishop Mooney received congratulatory letters from Coughlin sympathizers in the wake of the November 20 broadcast, once it was clear that Mooney was not about to order Coughlin off the air. He received a good many angry and bewildered letters too, especially from Jews but also from Catholics. "Perhaps you have hesitated to actually silence Father Coughlin," Margaret Mary

Gillan wrote from New York on November 21, "but I think you would be justified on the ground that to incite racial and religious intolerance is downright cruelty just now—and cruelty is a sin." To letters like these—provided that they were not abusive—the Chancery sent a standard reply. The Archbishop had already made clear that "permission" for Father Coughlin to speak and write did not imply "approval" of what he said. "Those who request more decisive action in such matters by Church superiors are evidently not fully informed on the absolute character of ecclesiastical authority in situations of this kind."[78]

Archbishop Mooney did indeed believe that there were no clear grounds in canon law on which he might act against Coughlin, or so he said to the NCWC's Msgr. Michael Ready late in 1938. But the real problem was political: there was "no little danger," he told Ready, "of a disturbing reaction in certain Catholic strata against anything that looks like 'muzzling' under outside pressure." Mooney had in mind especially the increasingly violent "Christian Front" in New York and Boston, whose angry anti-Semitism was regularly fueled by editorials in the pro-Coughlin *Brooklyn Tablet*. (The Jesuits' *America* was also supporting Coughlin in 1938, much to Mooney's annoyance.) Mooney may well have feared that silencing Coughlin would lead to anti-Jewish violence in a place like Brooklyn, although his own see city was virtually free of "Christian Front" activity. Certainly he feared that silencing Coughlin meant risking the defection of many Catholics, for Mooney believed that the priest was fully capable of inaugurating a schismatic movement.[79]

But if Mooney could not silence Coughlin, why did he not more effectively govern the contents of his writings and broadcasts? A principal reason, according to Mooney, was Coughlin's extraordinary verbal facility. "Father Coughlin's own articles on Jewish matters are, as you no doubt noticed, so cleverly gotten up and so contrived to say and unsay a thing in almost the same breath that it is impossible for a censor to do much deleting," Mooney explained to Msgr. Ready. Nearly as important was Coughlin's refusal to give any but token cooperation to the Chancery. He habitually submitted copy to the censors at the very last minute, threatening on occasion to broadcast a half-hour's silence should his script be severely edited. Nor was Coughlin amenable to friendly suggestions from his archbishop. "I have no advisory influence with Fr. Coughlin," Mooney told Msgr. Ready. And Coughlin had been "clever enough" to have chosen an issue about which many Catholics felt deeply. It was true that Jews were active in the cause of Communism "out of all proportion to their number in the population," Mooney told the Apostolic Delegate at the close of 1938. The persecution of Christians in Spain and Mexico had indeed been downplayed in the liberal press, just as Father Coughlin had charged. Jews had been instrumental, moreover, in much of the publicity that Coughlin was currently enjoying. "They could simply have ignored Father Couglin," Mooney pointed out in a private letter. "Or they could have accepted the offer of equal time on the same chain of stations to refute calmly and factually what they considered to be mistakes in his statements and to overcome the wrong impressions he might have left in the minds of the indiscriminating. Unfortunately, they did neither. On the contrary, they set up a terrific howl and then ran."[80]

Looking back at the late 1930s, it is difficult not to fault the archbishop's moral judgment. How could he have failed to see that Coughlin's disclaimers did not make his writings any less anti-Semitic in purpose and effect? How could he have found only "covert" anti-Semitism in Coughlin's columns on the "Protocols"? (He had used the word in a letter to the Apostolic Delegate.) How could he have thought that the anti-Semitism in Coughlin's speeches and writings was not "manifestly wrong"— Mooney's own words for the kind of thing a bishop was obliged to censure, no matter what the cost? Perhaps a part of the answer lies in the cultural isolation not only of Catholics but of Protestants and Jews as well. Despite his sophistication and his international experience, Mooney's was still a thoroughly Catholic world. His contacts with Protestants and Jews were infrequent and always formal. And Protestants and Jews were not, on the whole, notably more ecumenical in their vision of the world. American society in the 1930s, for all its apparent secularity, was a good deal more tribal than it is today. It took the horrors of the Second World War to breach the walls that kept the tribes apart.[81]

For his own part, Mooney believed that he had acted as quickly and as effectively as possible to mute Father Coughlin's anti-Semitism. He argued the matter with Coughlin on at least two occasions in December 1938, and wrote to the Apostolic Delegate to ask for a letter from the Pope that explicitly criticized the "general tenor" of Coughlin's recent broadcasts and his commentaries on the "Protocols"—as well as the publication of the "Protocols" themselves. Mooney had in mind to use such a letter in private negotiations with Coughlin. (The archbishop still clung to a probably exaggerated notion of the priest's respect for papal authority.) Should Coughlin continue in an anti-Semitic vein, however, Mooney would want to make the papal letter public. But no such help was forthcoming. Pius XI, very near death, was reluctant to become embroiled in what he regarded as a purely American—indeed, diocesan—affair. Help from Rome was limited to a message from Archbishop Cicognani, in which Coughlin was told, in the name of the Holy See, to follow "the suggestions and directions" of his bishop "in a spirit of priestly docility."[82]

This indirect word from a higher authority does seem to have had some limited effects. Coughlin did not abandon his anti-Semitic themes, but he did temper his rhetoric. The broadcasts of late 1938 are generally thought to have been the worst of his career. And the Chancery's censors gradually grew bolder: when Coughlin submitted an openly anti-Semitic text early in February 1940, Father John Vismara and Auxiliary Bishop Stephen Woznicki refused to give it their approval. Coughlin responded with his infamous "silent broadcast" of February 5, where music was interspersed with tense-voiced announcements urging a record audience for the next Sunday's program. Coughlin then resubmitted the offending text to the censors, who passed it on to Archbishop Mooney. "We went over it carefully," Mooney told the Apostolic Delegate, "and made deletions amounting to possibly seven pages. I sent back the manuscript thus marked up with a letter . . . in which I strongly and officially advised him not to touch on the main topic of the address and forbade him, in any case, to use the parts deleted. Really, with the deletions, the address would have constituted almost an apology to the great body of Jews." The archbishop's firmness worked: Coughlin spoke on another topic altogether.[83]

Mooney was increasingly resolute too in a second critical area, that of Father Coughlin's partisan political activities. A new diocesan regulation, published late in 1938, forbade priests in the archdiocese "to enter into political contests by giving public expression to their endorsement or disapproval of candidates for political office except in cases where the expressed judgment of the Ordinary has authorized them to do so in defense of the essential interests of religion." Had Coughlin been inclined to test his archbishop's mettle on this score, he had fewer than his accustomed opportunities to do so. For most of the stations that had previously carried his program were unwilling to renew their contracts with him, and he was obliged to cancel his 1940–1941 broadcast season. Coughlin's career as the "radio priest" had finally reached its end.[84]

The end of his radio days, however, did not completely silence Father Coughlin. There was still *Social Justice* magazine, bitterly anti-Roosevelt in 1940, and openly anti-Semitic. Father Coughlin had no official link to the magazine by the fall of 1940 — he had formally severed his ties to *Social Justice* in the spring of that year — but the Chancery was convinced, and rightly, that Coughlin was still its guiding influence, for *Social Justice* was published in Royal Oak by a group of Shrine parishioners. The problem lay in the apparently informal nature of that influence: it would be hard to prove that Coughlin had violated the letter of his spring 1940 agreement with Mooney. And Mooney could certainly not interfere with the activities of the magazine's lay staff, who made no claim that theirs was a Catholic publication. It took the threat of federal sedition charges against its publishers to bring an end to the *Social Justice* dilemma.

The Mooney-Coughlin struggle over *Social Justice* had begun in the spring of 1939. It was then that Mooney formally reproved Father Coughlin for the magazine's anti-Semitic tone and its "abusive language." The reproof had little real effect: Mooney wrote twice to Coughlin in June 1939 with specific complaints about recent issues. Then, on August 18, Mooney told Coughlin that *Social Justice* must either be declared a Catholic publication and placed under Mooney's authority, or that Coughlin must sever his connection with the magazine. Coughlin chose the latter course, at least to all appearances. Archbishop Mooney, however, had serious doubts in this regard. "In my heart I fear that the dissociation is more formal than real," he told former governor Al Smith in December 1939. "The magazine is largely a promotional sheet for his activities. He contributes occasional supervised articles — under a permission which was given in order to avoid the danger of even greater scandal." But Mooney did not see how he could muzzle Coughlin further.

In confidence I can tell you that the situation as I see it sums up to this: if a priest lacks the spirit which would make him follow the guidance of his ecclesiastical superiors and is, at the same time, devious and resourceful, outside of the field of faith and morals there is simply not enough Canon Law in effect in this country to handle the case on a legal basis. You have had experience enough to realize that Church control is much more a matter of spirit than of law — and I know of no more striking instance of this truth than the one in question.[85]

The increasingly scurrilous content of *Social Justice*, however, and the magazine's obvious connections with Father Coughlin caused Mooney to try a second time to put a clear distance between his priest and that offensive periodical. In February 1940 he ordered Coughlin to sever his *Social Justice* ties completely or to bring the paper under full ecclesiastical supervision. This time Coughlin chose to make *Social Justice* a Catholic publication, thereby admitting — if indirectly — that he had never really surrendered control of the magazine. *Social Justice* lasted from March 25 until May 27 in its "Catholic" incarnation, blander than heretofore, but hardly a conventional Catholic periodical. (Its new status was never made public, Archbishop Mooney having wisely insisted on that.) Then Coughlin abruptly abandoned the project, apparently frustrated by his lack of editorial freedom. Accordingly, the Chancery ordered Coughlin to disassociate himself completely from *Social Justice* and from all activities in its behalf.[86]

Mooney had not expected that Coughlin would carry out the spirit of this instruction. But he did expect conformity to its letter. And this he apparently got, for as he told the delegate in September 1940, *Social Justice* "has not since May 27th carried an article signed by him or directly attributed to him." Mooney knew that Coughlin was still the principal influence on the paper's staff. His disappearance from its pages, however, coupled with the cancellation of his broadcasts, meant that Coughlin himself had been effectively silenced. "I would say that the situation in regard to Father Coughlin is far more satisfactory at this moment than it has been at any time since I came to Detroit," Mooney confided to Cicognani. "There is no question now of his activity; what is surprising to most people is his inactivity." There had evidently been inquiries from Rome as to the possibility of harsher action than heretofore against the mostly quiescent Coughlin. But Mooney thought that escalation now would be "little less than calamitous. . . . Such action would, in my judgment, be particularly inadvisable during the heat of a political campaign, and if taken at the insistence of those who, in all charity, seem not so much concerned with keeping clerics out of partisan politics (which is our purpose) as with keeping them out of the ranks of their political opponents — if they cannot get them on their own side."[87]

It was the war that finally made a harsher action necessary. *Social Justice* was unfazed by the attack on Pearl Harbor: it continued to be bitterly critical of Roosevelt and his advisors, of the British and their war aims, even of the conduct and the purposes of the war as these were enunciated in Washington. Archbishop Mooney learned in March 1942 that the federal government planned to bring sedition charges against the magazine's editors and its publisher. "Father

Coughlin, rightly or wrongly, is closely identified with *Social Justice* in the public mind," Archbishop Spellman warned Mooney on March 25, "and in any action taken against *Social Justice,* he is certain to be involved, at least so I am informed." Rumors to this effect were already circulating, and on April 2 the *Michigan Catholic* reminded its readers that Father Coughlin had broken his ties to *Social Justice* nearly two years earlier. Since that time "no priest of this diocese has asked or received permission to contribute to 'Social Justice' and no priest of this diocese has been authorized to associate himself in any capacity with its publication or circulation — or, to the knowledge of this office, has actually done so." On April 20, however, Father Coughlin announced that he alone was responsible for the contents of *Social Justice* by virtue of his "effective moral and spiritual influence and direction over the editor, publisher and owners" of the magazine. He all but invited Attorney General Biddle to indict him.[88]

Mooney moved decisively after this, albeit in the measured way that was his hallmark. He ordered Coughlin to make a public admission of his disobedience and to announce publicly that he was finally surrendering all responsibility for *Social Justice.* Should he fail to do so, Mooney warned, "I shall be obliged to proceed, however reluctantly, to canonical measures designed to enforce clerical obedience." Coughlin assumed that this meant suspension from the priesthood, and this was almost certainly what Mooney had in mind, although he planned to submit the case to his Diocesan Court for a recommendation. The two men had a long and sometimes heated meeting at the Chancery on April 28. Coughlin argued that an ecclesiastical punishment would prejudice his case in the likely event of an indictment. (Coughlin did not want to "appear for trial under the handicap of having been previously condemned by his ecclesiastical superior as disobedient and deceitful," Mooney subsequently explained to the delegate.) Mooney was not unsympathetic to this argument, and agreed to delay any disciplinary proceedings until he spoke with Coughlin's attorney, a man whom Mooney knew and trusted.[89]

Mooney met with Coughlin's lawyer on April 30. Both men agreed that the priest was in serious legal trouble, and that his best chance to avoid indictment was for *Social Justice* to cease publication immediately. Mooney knew by this time that high officials in Washington were anxious to settle the *Social Justice* case without the embarrassment of a trial. (The principal intermediary in the matter was Leo Crowley, who was then serving as chairman of the Federal Deposit Insurance Corporation.) Negotiations in early May brought the hoped-for result: the case against the now-defunct *Social Justice* was quietly dropped, and with it the likelihood of a Coughlin indictment. On May 9 a grateful Mooney wrote his thanks to Roosevelt himself. "It is, of course, evident to me that no such happy solution of a problem embarrassing alike to civil and ecclesiastical authority would have been possible but for your own magnanimous attitude." As for Father Coughlin, he was pledged to refrain from involvement with *Social Justice* or any other publication. Failure to honor his pledge meant automatic suspension of his priestly faculties. "Thus we can write 'finis' to this sorry chapter in the life of a misguided priest," a much-relieved Mooney told Archbishop Cicognani. "It is significant, too, that in this instance I have received only an almost neg-ligible number of letters on the subject and those from people who are evidently fanatics—and for the most part abusive fanatics. Apparently he has alienated the major portion of the simple Catholics who followed him so blindly. For that, at least, it may have been worthwhile to be patient."[90]

Coughlin's wartime silencing was the effective end of his political career. The Chancery kept a watchful eye on his activities throughout the war, intervening promptly in 1942 when Coughlin began to solicit memberships and money through the mail for his League of the Little Flower. He did remain pastor of his Royal Oak church until he retired in 1966, and from his own pulpit, after the war, he gave at least occasional vent to his extreme views on domestic and international politics. But there his influence ended. He was denied permission to speak outside his parish in the years immediately following the war. Even in the 1950s he was generally required to submit the text of his public addresses to the Chancery for approval. He gave relatively few public speeches in the 1950s, however—the Chancery saw to that.[91]

Father Coughlin retained a following in the Archdiocese of Detroit, and else-where too, in the postwar years. (Indeed, he has loyal defenders to this day.) Many of his diehard followers became partisans of Senator Joseph McCarthy, whose political strength appears to have come from the same geographic areas and the same social groups that had given support to Father Coughlin. Senator McCarthy was a layman, however, and responsibility for his conduct could not fairly be laid at the doors of his Church, although there were those who tried. It was not until the 1960s that the vexing question of priests in politics was again raised in a substantive way, as the nation became increasingly polarized and po-litical styles and rhetoric grew more and more provocative.

Labor

Archbishop Mooney's "labor problem" was not unrelated to his "Coughlin problem," for Coughlin was a vocal opponent of the CIO unions that by 1937 were enjoying their first victories in such industries as automobiles, rubber, and steel. The CIO was Communist-dominated, Coughlin insisted, and Catholics were therefore obliged to oppose it. There were certainly Communists in the ranks of virtually every CIO union in the 1930s, including the United Auto Workers (UAW), which was, by mid-1937, the single most important union in Michigan. Relatively few unions, however, were under the firm control of a Com-munist faction. And whatever their political complexion, the militant unions that made up the early CIO were the best hope for organizing the mass of in-dustrial workers.

Archbishop Mooney was obviously worried about the dominant role played by Communists and other members of the sectarian left in a number of CIO unions. But he was convinced that overt opposition to those unions by the Church would only strengthen the hand of the left. Coughlin's assaults on the

CIO were dangerous, Mooney believed, because they created the impression that the Church was an ally of the employer. The numerous Catholic workers in Detroit and other industrial cities were, in Mooney's view, a potentially powerful force for moderation in the labor movement. That force would remain inert, however, unless substantial numbers of those workers could be persuaded to become active trade unionists.

It was with this ambitious goal in mind that Archbishop Mooney launched the Archdiocesan Labor Institute early in 1939. The purpose of the institute was worker education, and to this end it sponsored parish "labor schools" where Catholic trade unionists were offered a short course in Catholic social doctrine and the essentials of parliamentary procedure. Eight such schools were inaugurated in February 1939, and they met weekly, for two-hour sessions, until the end of May. By 1940, the program had been expanded to include thirty-four parish labor schools with an enrollment of nearly 1,200 men and more than 50 women. Each school had its own "priest-director," who was expected to lecture on the social encyclicals and to keep discussion within orthodox bounds. (The Chancery naturally worried about subversive influences, and not only from the left. "Because of an unfortunate experience in one of the schools, where literature condemning the CIO was distributed," the institute's board of directors noted in 1939, "it was decided that no literature is to be distributed at meetings except by known and approved Catholic authors, unless it had been OKed by the Board.") The priest-directors seem, on the whole, to have had things well in hand. "The Democratic or conference form of imparting knowledge of the right principles of Labor problems is not dangerous," the pastor at St. Leo's parish assured the Chancery in the spring of 1939. "The conclusions arrived at after discussion were in every instance the conclusions that those who arranged the program intended that the group should reach."[92]

The success of the parish labor schools is not easy to measure. No diocese had a larger program of this nature than Detroit's in 1940, but even at its height that program was a modest one. Many, perhaps most, of the students attended class irregularly, at least in part because of their own indifference. The social encyclicals, it was quickly discovered, were hard to translate into terms that were immediately relevant to contemporary politics. Instruction in parliamentary procedure, however, was of considerable value to those students who came regularly to classes, for it gave them a skill essential to participation in local union meetings. "I now understand what men talk about and I can talk to them and make myself understood," a worker who had attended the labor school at St. Leo's parish explained. Still, the director of that school was not at all certain that his efforts had borne visible fruit. "As far as training for actual leadership very little was done by this method," he told the Chancery in 1939. "Perhaps the greatest value was that the point was driven home that the Church was interested in their problems and helping them solve them."[93]

The parish labor schools were at their most numerous in 1940. Only a handful survived the war, and there was virtually nothing left of the program by the early 1950s. ("Too much depended on the priest-director," Father Karl Hubble later concluded. "Too much was expected of him in view of his rather superficial training.") But the schools were only one of the means by which Archbishop Mooney sought to give a Catholic blessing to, and exert a Catholic influence over, the industrial union movement. He was a strong supporter of the Association of Catholic Trade Unionists (ACTU), whose Detroit chapter was an unusually active one, at least in the decade when founder Paul Weber was its president. That chapter was organized in 1938, its purpose being, in the words of its constitution, "to foster sound trade unionism along Christian lines, so that the Labor movement may be effective toward the establishment of a Christian social order as set forth in the Papal Encyclicals." In the context of the late 1930s, this meant a generous ACTU contribution to local organizing drives and strike support campaigns. "We have helped to organize a number of plants in this area," ACTU secretary Thomas Doherty reported in 1941. It meant educational work as well. Detroit ACTU inaugurated a weekly—later monthly—labor paper in 1938, one that quickly gained a reputation for intelligence and integrity, although its circulation was always small. (The *Wage-Earner* counted for a number of years on a subsidy from the Chancery.) ACTU members worked closely too with the various parish labor schools, eventually developing a training program of their own. And they were active in the "right wing" caucuses of many unions, most notably in the UAW, where "ACTists" were a small but vocal minority in the anti-Communist coalition led by Walter Reuther. The ACTU was never a large organization, although the Detroit chapter was larger than most. Its membership apparently peaked in 1940 at about 1,500, a majority of whom took no active part in the group. Still the ACTU was important, for it helped to assure many Catholics that industrial unions were a legitimate means to social change.[94]

The legitimacy of industrial unions was the message conveyed as well by the growing number of "labor priests" in the Archdiocese. Archbishop Mooney encouraged his clergy to take an active interest in unions, and a minority among them responded with infectious enthusiasm. "Catholics! get in the labor parade. Don't just stand on the sidelines and find fault," a 1939 issue of St. Vincent's *News* urged the members of that large Detroit parish, where Father Harold Markey was pastor. "If Christ Who 'had compassion on the multitudes' were to walk in our midst today, we would find Him in the march with Labor, and He would ask you: 'Why are you not in my ranks.'" Probably the most notable of the priests who were identified with the trade union cause was Father Raymond Clancy, who served as secretary of the Archdiocesan Labor Institute when it was founded in 1939 and was later appointed director of the Archdiocesan Social Action Department. It was Father Clancy who took to the airwaves during the 1939 Chrysler strike to rebut an attack that Father Coughlin had made on the UAW. Clancy delivered a detailed defense of the union—the broadcast was paid for by the UAW—and bluntly accused Father Coughlin of having misrepresented the points at issue in the strike. "According to this morning's 'New York Times' you certainly made the best of Fr. Charlie's fumble," a clerical friend wrote admiringly from New York state. "It looks to me as if you had scored at least three times, and there is considerable joy here in consequence."[95]

Few priests in the Archdiocese had anything like the extensive ties to local and national labor leaders that Father Clancy enjoyed; indeed, only a handful were directly involved in the labor movement. But there seems to have been among the priests of the Archdiocese in the late 1930s a widespread sense that labor's was a moral cause. The respectability that a sympathetic clergy conferred on the movement was a source of annoyance to at least one Catholic industrialist in Detroit. "It has been a matter of concern to me to find so much support given by the Church in Detroit to the Union movement — Invocations at mass meetings; articles in the *Michigan Catholic;* Sermons on Sunday in all the Catholic Churches and the intense efforts put forth by the Study Clubs," the president of the Chevrolet Division of the General Motors Corporation wrote to Archbishop Mooney early in 1940. "I cannot believe it is constructive to have the Catholic Clergy take the position that Labor has been wilfully abused and imposed upon by Management."[96]

For all his interest in unions, Archbishop Mooney apparently had few personal friends in the ranks of the trade union leadership. He did have a cordial relationship with Philip Murray of the Steelworkers' Union, who succeeded John L. Lewis as president of the CIO in 1940. Murray was a Catholic, however, and the principal leaders of the UAW were not. This may have been why Mooney had so few labor contacts in his own see city, where his lay friends were mostly professionals and well-to-do businessmen. Mooney evidently believed that he had a responsibility to introduce this conservative group to Catholic social teaching. "I dream of the day when leaders of management who hold Christian principles will sit down with us and study the impact of those principles on the so-called liberalism or individualism of the Manchester School, which in theory represents the extreme anti-thesis of communism and in practice acts as one of its inciting causes," Mooney wrote to GM executive Semon Knudsen in 1939, responding to a Knudsen letter that had evidently complained about an editorial in the *Michigan Catholic.* "We believe there is a middle way of organized cooperation which will serve best the long-range interests of capital and labor alike." Mooney had spoken eloquently of this "middle way" before the Economic Club of Detroit in 1938, when the city was in the still-tense aftermath of the greatest "strike wave" in its history. "I think we will all agree that we are in the grip of an economic system that is cruel, hard, and relentless," Mooney told his affluent audience, at least some of whom would have dissented vigorously. Nor was that audience entirely pleased to hear that the principles guiding contemporary economic life "are in flat contradiction with the ethics of historic Christianity, and historic Judaism as well." Collective bargaining was a necessary if not sufficient means to the realization of an ethical economic system, Mooney argued, and he urged employers to negotiate willingly and equitably with their workers. ("Men want to be treated *with* even more than to be treated *well.*") Refusal to do so would lead not only to violence on the picket line but to an eventual collapse of democracy. "Who that loves America and all that America stands for can fail to be deeply disturbed at the sight of preparations to fight out differences rather than to talk them out?" he asked. "Is it too much to say that the fate of our country in a critical day depends chiefly on our finding *moderate men* on the side of capital and labor who are willing to sit down together in patient and considerate good will to talk out their differences and difficulties in an effort to further interests which are essentially in harmony and not in conflict?"⁹⁷

Mooney's fears of labor violence in Detroit were fortunately not realized. Even the unionization of the Ford Motor Company was accomplished without loss of life. But industrial relations in the auto industry remained tense, despite the formal moratorium on strikes and the "maintenance of membership" protections that prevailed during the war. These tensions came to a head late in 1945, when the UAW embarked on what was to be a 113-day strike against General Motors. Archbishop Mooney was privately of the opinion that the strike was almost entirely the fault of the corporation. "The unions are pressing for an advance in employer-employee relations which the industrialists term 'socialistic' but which, in fact, fall[s] far short of what the Social Encyclicals call for," he told Bishop Walter Foery of Syracuse, who had written to ask his views on the strike. "General Motors has been particularly backward in its outlook in this regard as even during the war it set itself definitely against having management-labor committees to promote better relation[s] in the interest of the war effort, while many other large concerns set them up and found them very useful." He himself had tried on many occasions to persuade his friends in the corporation to adopt a more ethical view of labor relations and of corporate behavior generally, but without success. "In confidence I can say that friends of mine in high circles in General Motors who are excellent Catholics in a sacramental sense are utterly allergic to Catholic social doctrine," he confessed to Foery. "Whether it is their own background or their present environment, it is hard to say. We get on together in mutual patience and personal respect, but to date I cannot boast of having converted them to the views of Pius XI or even Leo XIII."⁹⁸

Mooney continued to give strong support to the Association of Catholic Trade Unionists in the years immediately following the war, and to the work of "labor priests" like Father Raymond Clancy. And he continued to make plain his personal support for unions and collective bargaining. The postwar years saw a growing conservatism in the national political mood, and a mounting preoccupation with the influence of Communists in American life. The trade union movement quite naturally reflected this: Communists were formally expelled from CIO-affiliated unions in the late 1940s. Catholics were prominently associated with the anti-Communist factions in a wide variety of unions, and largely for this reason, it has sometimes been argued that the prolabor posture of bishops like Mooney was motivated primarily by anti-Communism. But Mooney's view of the world was more complex and more generous than that of a man whose only concern is to defeat the left. He had his own vision of the just society, the realization of which was hampered as much by the reactionary element at General Motors as by Communist domination of the industrial unions. His prolabor stance can be fully understood only in terms of his progressive social views.

That prolabor stance, moreover, may well have contributed to the maintenance of an uneasy peace in Detroit during and after the bitter strikes of 1945 and 1946, and to the survival of a vigorous union movement in the city. For the very existence of unions in the mass production industries was at issue in those strikes. "The unions feel that many big industrialists, and signally those in General Motors, would like to sabotage the Wagner Act and are not willing to carry on collective bargaining in the real sense of the word," Mooney explained to Bishop Foery late in 1945. "They know, too, that the present congress is not 'forward-looking' and could easily be led to enact labor legislation which they would consider penalizing them." In such a political climate, Church support for unions and for collective bargaining was a not-unimportant source of legitimacy for industrial unions as they battled to win a permanent place in American life.[99]

Finances

Archbishop Mooney arrived in Detroit in 1937 to find that the parishes of his new diocese were $22 million in debt, a debt for which he, in his episcopal capacity, was ultimately responsible. Like Bishop Gallagher before him, Mooney soon discovered that lenders were not eager to involve themselves with what looked to be a highly decentralized institution, certain components of which were carrying debts too great for their present or their foreseeable future resources to bear. "We hacked away at it until 1941," the Archbishop later remembered of the debt, "trying to sell ourselves to bankers and insurance executives in a way to inspire their confidence." The appointment of Father Edward Hickey as chancellor of the Archdiocese in 1938 was one important source of confidence, for Hickey, who held a degree from the Harvard Business School, was the son of an old and respected merchant family in Detroit. His advent at the Chancery seemed to signal a new era of fiscal competence there, and it was through Hickey that Archbishop Mooney made the acquaintance of certain local bankers who were instrumental in negotiating the agreements that ultimately led to refinancing. Those negotiations were time-consuming, however, and it was not until early in 1941 that the Archdiocese of Detroit was able to borrow $18 million from a consortium of banks and insurance companies.[100]

The 1941 refinancing immediately lowered the rate of interest that most parishes were obliged to pay on their mortgages, and this alone improved their financial standing. By 1941, moreover, the unemployment rate in Detroit and its environs had begun to decline sharply; by 1942 there was a shortage of workers in the now-booming metropolitan area. Earning higher wages than ever before and with little in the way of consumer goods to tempt them, Catholics were generous to the Church throughout the war. Holy Cross (Hungarian) parish in southwest Detroit was typical of many when it announced in 1945 that it had liquidated a debt that only three years before had stood at nearly $126,000. Archbishop Mooney saw the total Archdiocesan debt decline to $7.5 million in 1944 — at which point he refinanced the loan at a still-lower rate of interest — and the entire debt repaid, "except $25,000 which I have left on the bank loan to keep the contract alive," by the middle of 1945.[101]

The agreement negotiated with the various banks in 1941 is particularly interesting for the financial relationship it established between the Chancery and the parishes. Each pastor pledged to pay an annual "commitment" to the Chancery — greater in some cases than the amount actually owed on his mortgage and less in others — and the Chancery used these funds to make payments on the refinanced debt and to accumulate a surplus against future hard times. Even those parishes that were free of debt were required to contribute, the Chancery — in its capacity as "banker" — promising to pay interest on all such "deposits." These arrangements, as Archbishop Mooney explained, marshaled "the financial power of all the parishes to build up credit and thus obtain the same low rate of interest for all." They also gave the Chancery a greater leverage over parish finances than it had ever had before. The "banker Chancery" was able to spot financial trouble in a parish almost as soon as it developed, and it was able to use the resources of the wealthier parishes to aid the weaker ones. Nothing approaching a major redistribution of resources was accomplished during the Mooney years, but Mooney (by then a Cardinal) did use his power as archdiocesan "banker" in the late 1940s and the 1950s to make "gifts" — occasionally over the objections of a pastor — from established parishes to neighboring parishes that were just being organized.[102]

Organization

When Father Hickey told Archbishop Mooney in 1937 that "organization" was a major problem in the Diocese of Detroit, he presumably had reference to the still quite decentralized character of diocesan administration. The educational reforms of Superintendent Carroll Deady had only just begun, and the Chancery seems to have had only nominal control over the various Catholic charities. The principal program by which Catholic children in the public schools were given religious instruction was wholly under lay control, and taught mainly by laywomen. (Ambitious as that program was, it was much too small to serve the many thousands of Catholic children who were enrolled in Detroit's public schools, much less those who lived in other parts of the Diocese, where the program was weak or did not exist at all.) The Chancery, moreover, was without the funds it needed to maintain existing diocesan institutions and establish new ones. This was principally due to the Depression, but it was also true that there was no regular means by which to raise money for specifically Catholic charities and educational endeavors. Bishop Gallagher had chosen to continue Catholic participation in the annual United Fund appeals that had begun in Detroit in 1918. This appeal was providing funds to fifteen Catholic organizations in the

Diocese by 1934, and it is likely that Catholic participation in what had become an annual community ritual had helped to ease religious tensions in Detroit. But by depending on the United Fund to support his major charitable institutions, Bishop Gallagher had surrendered a certain control over social services in the Diocese to a mostly Protestant organization. It was ultimately not the Bishop but the executives of the fund who determined which Catholic institutions would be supported and how generously, and it was not easy to include new projects in a budget that was perennially overtaxed by demands from a religiously diverse constituency.

Archbishop Mooney was quick to demonstrate his commitment to a centralized mode of diocesan administration when he came to Detroit. He lent his strong support to the Deady school reforms, and these proceeded rapidly in the late 1930s and early 1940s. He assigned Father John C. Ryan to head the newly founded Confraternity for Christian Doctrine (CCD) early in 1938, and this organization — under firm clerical control — absorbed the lay-run Catholic Instruction League. Under Ryan's direction and with Mooney's support, the CCD grew rapidly, nearly doubling its enrollment between 1938 and 1940. And the composition of its teacher corps changed rapidly: by the fall of 1938 there were more priests and Sisters serving as teachers than members of the laity. Lay teachers would not again outnumber priests and religious in the archdiocesan CCD until 1960.[103]

The rapidly growing CCD was financed in good part, after 1943, by the Archdiocesan Development Fund, which Mooney inaugurated in that year "to provide for outstanding diocesan needs." Chief among these were completion of the still-unfinished Blessed Sacrament Cathedral, the expansion of Sacred Heart Seminary to include a school of theology, the extension of youth work through the CYO and a broadened social welfare program, as well as "the promotion of urgently necessary home mission work" — under which heading the archbishop included the work of the CCD. The fund was planned as an annual appeal — yearly quotas were set at a sensible $500,000 throughout the mid-1940s — and from the first it was conducted with the thoroughness that had marked the spectacularly successful Seminary Campaign of 1920. Every pastor was expected to deploy a committee to solicit contributions door-to-door, and to urge his parishioners to contribute as generously as they could — a day's pay was suggested as a "minimum contribution" from wage-earners.[104]

The results of the annual campaigns were quietly gratifying. Nearly $714,000 was raised in 1943; just under $693,000 in 1945. And totals rose steadily in the mostly prosperous postwar years: the 1957 appeal raised more than $1.6 million. (The per capita contribution, however, was lower in 1957 than it had been in 1943.) The Archdiocesan Development Fund was never intended to supplant the United Fund in Detroit and other Michigan cities as a source of support for Catholic charities. Catholics continued to participate in these community-wide appeals, as Archbishop Mooney regularly urged them to do. What the Development Fund was meant to do — and what it in fact accomplished — was to provide a regular flow of revenue that the Chancery was free to expend as it wished for charitable, educational, and religious purposes. It was not only a source of the much-expanded institutional network in the Archdiocese after 1945, but a source of independence for an increasingly powerful Chancery.[105]

A consolidation of episcopal power will almost inevitably affect the circumstances under which the clergy live and work. And it was not long before Archbishop Mooney moved to strengthen his authority over what was an already well-disciplined corps of priests. Every parish in the Archdiocese was visited by a representative of the Chancery in 1940, visits that were repeated in 1943 and again in 1954. These "canonical visitations" entailed a close inquiry into details of parish life ranging from the number and condition of the sacred vessels to the size of the various lay organizations. Included in the extensive list of questions — which was sometimes filled out by the "canonical visitor" and sometimes by the pastor — were several that bore particularly on social and devotional life in the ethnic parishes. The Chancery wished to know, for example, whether "Archdiocesan rules regarding the sale of intoxicants on church property [are] observed." ("Yes, but it is considered damaging insofar as it does not permit serving beer and wine at parish banquets," the forthright pastor of Detroit's Holy Cross parish responded in 1940. "These Hungarian Catholics who cannot mix with Americans should have their own social occasions. However, to drink soft drinks after some Hungarian dishes is plain sickness.") The form asked as well whether "singing in the vernacular [is] tolerated during High Mass," papal decrees in 1903 and in 1928 having prohibited vernacular hymns during solemn liturgical functions. Congregational singing in the vernacular, however, was even in the 1940s a part of the liturgy in many ethnic parishes. Polish hymns were sung at High Mass in St. Francis Church in Detroit, the pastor admitted in 1948, "and church is packed to capacity."[106]

Archbishop Mooney was not an unreasonable man; the purpose of the canonical visits was not to punish those pastors whose parishioners clung stubbornly to traditional liturgical ways. But the visits were clearly meant to confirm for all priests the importance of diocesan regulations, even those that seemed alien to their parishioners. The synod that Archbishop Mooney convened in 1944 was similarly intended to underscore the importance of diocesan discipline and the need for the clergy to stand in solidarity with their bishop. The regulations of the Archdiocese were amended and updated at this gathering, which was the first synod to be held in Detroit since 1886, and the Archbishop's plans for postwar expansion were explained to the enthusiastic assembly. The generous scope of those plans and the aura of success that surrounded their well-respected Archbishop almost certainly generated a lively esprit de corps among the priests who were there. Nothing, of course, could have been more conducive to the legitimization of a strict diocesan discipline than this stirring sense of membership in a priestly caste.[107]

By 1944, Archbishop Mooney had already taken steps to bring the various Catholic charities under Chancery direction. The Federation of Catholic Charitable Agencies had been established in 1943, its purpose "to coordinate the activities of the charitable agencies and institutions conducted under Catholic auspices in the Archdiocese of Detroit." The federation's various committees were also charged with assessing the future social service needs of the Archdiocese, and it was through the recommendation of one of these committees that the Catholic Family Center was opened in Detroit in 1946. The center, which specialized in casework with troubled families and adolescents, was a measure both of the growing professionalization of Catholic charities and of the alarm, widespread among Americans generally, over what was seen as a wartime erosion of Christian family values. ("Strains on family responsibility are indicated by startling increases in the past five years in truancy, divorce, venereal disease, illegitimate births, and delinquency complaints," the federation's Family Committee reported in 1945.) The Federation of Catholic Charities continued to grow in size and scope as the institutions under its jurisdiction multiplied. There were thirty-two "constituent" and "affiliated" social service organizations under the aegis of the federation by 1958, including family casework agencies in five of the eight counties that made up the Archdiocese. The Federation was by this time looking forward to membership in a statewide organization, the Catholic Charities of Michigan, which was intended to enable the bishops of the province to conduct their various charities in efficient concert. Cardinal Mooney had been instrumental in initiating the negotiations that had led to the creation of this statewide body, which was incorporated late in 1956, but he did not live to see it begin operations late in 1959.[108]

Mooney cared deeply about the charitable work that was carried out under Catholic auspices, and he looked to centralized control of those charities to enhance their efficiency and their responsiveness to emerging social problems. "You said once, when your life was written you hoped they would be able to write that you were the one who really organized Catholic Charities in Detroit," a Sister from St. Vincent's Orphanage reminded the Cardinal in 1948. Mooney did indeed earn this distinction, despite a 1960 claim by Msgr. Wilbur Suedekamp — secretary for charities to Cardinal Mooney and to his successor — that "Catholic charities in Detroit is still in the formative stage." Msgr. Suedekamp's discontents simply indicated how high the standards of the Church now were with regard to the scope and the efficiency of its charities. For the Monsignor was essentially a social work professional, and he judged the performance of Catholic charities by professional standards.[109]

Msgr. Suedekamp's specialized ministry was emblematic not only of Cardinal Mooney's approach to charities but of the Mooney administration generally. For Mooney almost instinctively preferred clerical to lay control of Catholic enterprises. It was not that he had contempt for the laity: he gave generous encouragement to a variety of Catholic action groups in the Archdiocese, at least some of which were out of favor with more conservative members of the clergy. But his vision of the Church was a thoroughly clerical one: priests represented the Church in a way that the laity could never do, and in a well-run diocese they ought to assume leadership in virtually every area of Catholic life. Accordingly, Catholic charities, like Catholic education and even Catholic social action, were brought firmly under clerical supervision in the Mooney years. But for all this, Mooney was apparently able to respect the competence of those laypersons and Sisters on whom the success of charities and education and social action depended. "I shall never forget all you did for us at Vista Maria and for your wise counsels which helped me so often," a Good Shepherd Sister wrote to Mooney in 1945, shortly after she had been transferred from Detroit. "How fortunate the Sisters in Detroit are to have you for their Archbishop. . . . The whole spirit in Cleveland seems so different from Detroit. Everything is so centralized, so organized that it is almost impossible to make a move without consulting someone or other."[110]

The various charitable institutions that were founded or expanded in the Mooney years are too numerous to mention individually. The care of troubled adolescents was a major concern in these years — the consequence, mainly, of a fairly high rate of delinquency among the more marginal elements in the Catholic population. Cardinal Mooney himself was a major force behind the creation of a residential school for "boys in trouble" that was opened near the village of Clinton in 1948. "Boysville," in the charge of the Holy Cross Brothers, was an early beneficiary of the Archdiocesan Development Fund. Social services for the elderly were increasingly in demand in the postwar years, and Msgr. Wilbur Suedekamp was especially proud of the Kundig Center, an innovative recreation and healthcare center for the elderly that was opened in Detroit in 1954. And efforts were made — the first since the late nineteenth century — to provide education under Catholic auspices to mentally impaired children. A residential day school for retarded girls was established at Northville in 1957, an undertaking in which Cardinal Mooney apparently took a considerable personal interest. A day school for retarded children was opened in Detroit just one year later, occupying classrooms in the now-underenrolled school of St. John the Evangelist parish. "Since requests for admittance to the new school will far exceed its capacity, His Eminence . . . hopes to utilize in the years to come vacant classrooms in other parochial school buildings in Detroit with the idea of establishing two or three more schools of this nature," the chancellor of the Archdiocese noted in the summer of 1958. Mooney did not live to see these hopes realized, but under the aegis of his successor, Cardinal John Dearden, five additional day schools for mentally impaired youngsters were opened in and around Detroit.[111]

Mooney's achievements with regard to financial and organizational reform are particularly remarkable in light of his extensive national activities in the decade after 1938. (It was these national activities that were the principal reason he was named a Cardinal late in 1945.) As we have seen, the Archbishop served as chairman of the Administrative Board of the NCWC from 1936 to 1939, and again from 1941 to 1945. He remained a member of the board, moreover, during the later 1940s and was, in company with Cincinnati's Archbishop John Mc-

Nicholas and Chicago's Cardinal Samuel Stritch, a dominant influence in the NCWC throughout the decade. Mooney was not, in his "national years," the American bishop who was closest to the White House. Chicago's Cardinal Mundelein had been Roosevelt's principal contact in the hierarchy before his death in 1939, and New York's Archbishop, later Cardinal, Francis Spellman assumed this role thereafter. (President Harry Truman was apparently not on close terms with any of the American bishops.) But Mooney had a greater influence over his fellow bishops than the abrasive Spellman ever achieved, and his views carried special weight in their councils during the troubled years of the war and in its clouded aftermath.[112]

Mooney's preoccupations as chairman of the Administrative Board had largely to do with foreign policy, although he was more and more concerned, especially after 1943, with the circumstances under which Catholics might formally cooperate with non-Catholics and with the larger question of the Catholic position on religious liberty. He resumed the chairmanship in 1941 as the debate over American intervention in the Second World War was reaching its zenith. Isolationist sentiment was strong among American Catholics, especially those of Irish and German descent, and Catholic champions of neutrality were arguing that even limited material aid to the Soviet Union violated the papal ban on Catholic cooperation with Communists. Mooney was not the ardent advocate of American intervention that Bishop Joseph Hurley was. "I know that I have said some things of which you would not approve," Hurley wrote to his friend Mooney in the wake of a controversial speech in the summer of 1941 in which Hurley had vigorously defended the extension of Lend-Lease to the Soviet Union. "More and more I am convinced that someone had to correct the notion that the Church in some way was out of harmony entirely with the policy of the Government; that we were tinged with the color of the dictatorships." But Mooney, like Hurley, was deeply worried about the menace of Nazism, and he too saw the war in terms of a struggle between democracy and totalitarianism. In this sense he had embraced the necessity of eventual American participation, and it was Mooney who suggested to the Apostolic Delegate in the fall of 1941 that the Pope make clear that aid to the Russian people was different from cooperation with Communism. This was indeed the interpretation of the encyclical *Divini Redemptoris* that was shortly after communicated by the delegate to the American bishops. And it was this understanding of American aid to the Soviet Union that the Administrative Board of the NCWC employed in November 1941 when it issued a judiciously worded statement that gave a cautious episcopal blessing to Roosevelt's policies vis-à-vis the European conflict. (The statement was less vigorous in its support of Roosevelt, however, than Mooney was disposed to be in his private communications. "Whether one likes Mr. Roosevelt or not," he had told the Apostolic Delegate in March, "it seems clear that no president was ever closer to a pope in broad principle.") Less than a month after the November statement, the bombing of Pearl Harbor brought an end to the debate over neutrality.

On December 23 Archbishop Mooney wrote to the president in the name of the American bishops to assure him of their "whole-hearted cooperation" in the prosecution of the war.[113]

For Mooney personally, this pledge reflected more than the patriotism that he, like nearly every Catholic, had been taught was a fundamentally religious virtue. Despite his anxieties over Soviet designs on the postwar world, he never ceased to regard the war as a conflict between Christian culture and the diabolism of modern totalitarianism. "I pray for the President incessantly," he wrote in 1943 to Myron Taylor, who was then completing his fourth year as Roosevelt's personal representative to the Holy See. "What a load he has to bear—the burden of the hopes of the weak and the oppressed throughout the world are centered on him. His optimistic temperament will naturally lead him to make much of the real accomplishments of Moscow and Teheran—the well-founded promise of international cooperation throughout the war and into the peace. Surely he is too wise to fail to see the shadows which the still unresolved Russian enigma throws across the picture."[114]

Mooney's letter to Taylor was written, interestingly enough, at a time of growing tension between the American bishops and the president over Allied policy with regard to the bombing of Rome. That city had been bombed by Allied planes in July 1943, when the basilica of San Lorenzo was badly damaged, and bombed again in August. At the urging of the Apostolic Delegate, archbishops Mooney, Stritch, and Spellman met with Roosevelt on September 15 and delivered to him a formal appeal to respect the recent declaration of the new Italian government that made Rome an open city. The occupation of Rome by German forces, however, soon robbed this declaration of all but symbolic content, and fears were strong at the close of 1943 that Rome would soon be bombed again. Mooney wrote personally to Roosevelt in February 1944, pleading with him to do all that he could to spare the city. "The record would stand that we destroyed Rome. In that record the circumstances of Nazi provocation would serve only to highlight our lack of cleverness or our failure to rise above Nazi standards of cultural appreciation and religious reverence." But despite Mooney's concern for the fate of Rome, his view of the Allied cause as a moral crusade was not diminished by his realization that military logic might result in the further bombing of the city. For the American bishops to make a public issue of the bombing of Rome, Mooney had told the Apostolic Delegate late in August, would be a serious error, for "such an agitation would be taken up most vociferously by that relatively small but very noisome sector of our Catholic population which has been outstanding in its political opposition to the domestic and foreign policies of President Roosevelt, and at the same time most recalcitrant to the leadership of the Holy Father and the American Hierarchy in regard to the moral issues of the present global struggle."[115]

By 1945, however, clouds had gathered on the moral horizon, for the specter of Soviet control over Eastern Europe already haunted the American bishops. "If the moral conscience of the West does not succeed in getting written into the charter of the World Organization an international guarantee of fundamental human rights . . . we may well fear that disillusioned democracies may turn isolationist almost overnight," Mooney wrote to the Archbishop of Westminster (London) in March 1945. "That spells the ruin of our high hopes for an organized world. . . . We were strong when almost without armaments we stood on the firm ground of principle; we are weak when armed as never before we shift on the sands of expediency. Let us pray that San Francisco sees an assertion of principle. What a tragic anticlimax it will be if a free Poland is not represented there!" Archbishops Mooney, Stritch, and Spellman had by this time communicated to Roosevelt their worries over Stalin's intentions in Eastern Europe: "He is seeking to establish domination of the Soviet Union over other nations by promoting, subsidizing and directing Communistic minority groups in other countries which aim at full political control," they wrote to the president in December 1944. Their fears were far from groundless, and Mooney himself may well have been grateful that the constitution of the NCWC required that he step down as chairman of the Administrative Board after five consecutive years of service. For the postwar world seemed in many ways to belie the moral grandeur of the Allied crusade. (Significantly, perhaps, there are no references in the Mooney papers to the moral dilemmas created by atomic weapons.) Mooney did not abandon his interest in international affairs after 1945, nor did he cease to be a major voice in the councils of the NCWC. But his attention was more and more drawn to the peculiarly domestic question of what role the Catholic Church should play in a multiconfessional but increasingly secular society.[116]

When Mooney came to Detroit in 1938, he came to a diocese where the tradition of Catholic cooperation with non-Catholics in civic affairs was relatively strong. The various "home front" activities of the war years simply strengthened that tradition. And Mooney, like many of his episcopal contemporaries, was deeply worried by what he saw as the thoroughgoing secularization of American society. (It was Mooney and his close friend Cardinal Stritch who were the principal authors of a 1947 letter from the American hierarchy that decried the excessive secularity of contemporary culture.) This conjunction of experiences and concerns was apparently the cause of Mooney's growing interest in the problem of "intercreedal cooperation" and the closely related problem of the formal Catholic position on religious liberty. During and after the late 1940s, Mooney's was a voice for moderation and flexibility on these questions, and a voice of some importance, since he still had considerable influence among his fellow bishops and even in Rome. The circumstances and traditions of individual nations ought to be taken into account when the Holy See issued directives on the delicate question of cooperation with Protestants and Jews, he advised the Apostolic Delegate in 1952, in a letter that suggested—with characteristic diplomacy—that conditions in the United States were so different from those in Europe that prohibitions from Rome might well do harm to the American Church. It was best to leave matters in the hands of the bishops. For his own part, Mooney was ready to tolerate cautious Catholic participation even in such self-consciously ecumenical groups as the National Council of Christians and Jews. (This was not the case with many of his fellow bishops.) The danger that such participation would promote indifferentism among Catholics was, he thought, fairly remote, and the Church stood to gain allies not just in its struggle against a newly respectable anti-Catholicism but in the more fundamental, if related, struggle against the forces of secularism.[117]

Mooney's growing interest in problems of this nature had led by the mid-1940s to an interest in the work and the career of John Courtney Murray, the Jesuit theologian whose writings on religious liberty recast the terms of the Catholic debate on that topic in the 1940s and the 1950s. Murray was principally concerned to find persuasive theological grounds on which to argue that the religious neutrality of the American government was, from a Catholic point of view, a wholly legitimate solution to the problem of Church-State relations. (Accepting the "Murray thesis," of course, meant abandoning the position that Catholics, when they constituted a majority in a nation's population, should demand that the Church be established or at the very least given a privileged status.) Murray's work was highly controversial, exciting opposition especially in Rome, and few American bishops in the 1940s were willing to be known as his partisans. Still, Mooney was open in his support for Murray, and he eventually persuaded Cardinal Samuel Stritch to join him in the Murray camp. Influential friends like these did not save Murray from a virtual silencing by his Jesuit superiors in the latter half of the 1950s. He was finally vindicated, however, serving as a *peritus* at the Second Vatican Council, where he was a major force behind the Declaration on Religious Liberty, that singular American contribution to the council's achievements. Cardinal Mooney had been dead for nearly four years by the time the council opened in 1962. But his quiet support for Murray had helped prepare the ground that bore this distinctively American fruit.[118]

Despite his continued national and even international interests, the last decade of Mooney's life was devoted primarily to the business of running his own Archdiocese. He was especially absorbed in the building of a major seminary for the Province of Michigan. St. John's Seminary, the first stage of which was opened in the fall of 1949, was located in a rural area near the village of Plymouth, some twenty-five miles west of downtown Detroit. Like Sacred Heart Seminary before it, St. John's reflected the Tridentine ideal of a secluded clerical training, although the once-rural precincts of Sacred Heart Seminary had long since been engulfed by the city of Detroit. St. John's, however, was an altogether more austere facility than Sacred Heart, for Mooney believed that the clergy—and their bishops as well—ought to be noted for simplicity of life. ("He was always on the defensive," Msgr. Edward Hickey remembered of Mooney's emotions about the lavish episcopal residence in Detroit, "lest the lay people should be scandalized or the working people become hostile and feel more inclined to communism because of the size and costliness of his residence.") The government of the new seminary was formally shared by all the bishops of the Michigan

Province. But it was Mooney who was most intimately involved in its planning, and whose stamp the completed facility bore.[119]

Mooney was also the bishop most deeply involved in the life of the seminary after 1949. He spent at least two months of every summer in residence there, and lectured on pastoral theology every spring to those students who were nearing ordination. (He had given similar lectures at St. Bernard's Seminary in Rochester when he was bishop there.) "The training of priests has ever been the first duty of the Bishop," Mooney reminded the crowd that assembled for the dedication of the still-incomplete St. John's facility in the fall of 1949, and he cherished his new seminary in part because it bore witness to the fidelity with which he had fulfilled his obligations. "The building of a Major Seminary, its organization as a canonically provincial institution and the assumption of its direction by the Sulpician Fathers represents the achievement of my highest ambition as Archbishop of Detroit," Mooney wrote in 1954, "and I am confident that down through the years it will mean more than anything else which the Bishops of this generation have done for the Church in Michigan." St. John's was also dear to Mooney because it represented the essence of the priesthood as he understood it. No other environment so fully expressed the discipline, the solidarity, the spiritual vigor that Mooney believed ought to characterize the clergy. And he seems to have drawn emotional sustenance from his contacts with young men who stood, filled with anticipation and hope, on the brink of their priestly careers. "It is surprising and disappointing that routine should wear the edge off devotion even in so sublime a work as ours," he told the senior seminarians in the spring of 1956. "If only we could freeze our ideals on Ordination Day!"[120]

The prosperity of the postwar years, which had made the new seminary possible, also made possible the completion of Blessed Sacrament Cathedral, which had been dedicated as a parish church in 1930. The Depression had prevented its congregation from constructing the massive twin towers that were meant to be the dominant feature of its imposing facade. Those towers were finished late in 1951, in time for the celebration of the twenty-fifth anniversary of Cardinal Mooney's consecration as a bishop. The consecration of the completed cathedral and the commemoration of Mooney's Silver Jubilee took place on November 17, and—according to Msgr., later Bishop, Lawrence Casey—the ceremony was a memorable one. "Louis Edelson who has traveled much in Europe and witnessed many church celebrations said he never saw anything to equal it," Casey wrote to Mooney. "As the hundred bishops filed by, I thought what other prelate in the country could command enough respect and affection to get a turnout like that. Damn few came from a sense of duty." Casey had liked nearly everything about the service: "The precision of the boys on ceremonies, the complicated bows. . . . The music of the choir was superb." Bishop Stephen Woznicki, Mooney's auxiliary from 1938 until 1950 and now Bishop of Saginaw, had delivered an admirably "workmanlike" sermon. It had been fun to watch Cardinals Stritch and Spellman, between whom little love was lost, exchanging the ritual kiss of

peace. ("Spelly tiptoed along like a sublimated Buddha," Casey remembered of
the hierarchy's procession into the cathedral, "eyes on his breviary and not missing a trick.") But Casey had been particularly moved by Mooney himself, who
had celebrated the Mass and who delivered a characteristically modest speech
at its conclusion. "In looking back over the two hundred and fifty years of organized Catholic life in Detroit . . . I am struck by the thought of how truly it
is said of a bishop that he enters into the labors of others," Mooney had told
the vast congregation. How like Mooney it was, Casey observed, to be "hon-
estly shoving off the credit to predecessors and the common people when the
audience knew that one man was primarily responsible for bringing order out
of chaos, and there he stood like Simeon with his Nunc Dimittis, the diocese
well organized, the debt liquidated, the Seminary a reality and the Cathedral
completed."[121]

For all these achievements, however, a good deal of work remained to the
Cardinal in the last seven years of his life. The Catholic population of the Archdiocese grew substantially in the postwar years, from an estimated 800,000 in
1945 to 1.3 million in 1960. That population, moreover, was an increasingly
suburban one. The population of Detroit proper reached its peak in 1953, after
which the city entered a long period of population decline, becoming, in the process, more and more heavily black. (Blacks made up 16 percent of Detroit's population in 1950, and almost 29 percent in 1960.) The growth of the Catholic
population and its rapid relocation to the edges of Detroit and to its suburbs
required that parishes be founded at a pace second only to the record of the
1920s. There were 209 churches with resident priests in the Archdiocese in 1945,
a figure that rose to 243 by 1950 and to 291 by 1958. The growth in the number
of parochial schools was even more dramatic: from 169 elementary schools in
1945 to 257 in 1960; from 78 high schools in the former year to 100 in the latter.
And two more Catholic women's colleges were opened under Mooney's auspices.
The day-to-day supervision of this ecclesiastical building boom was largely the
work of the various pastors and of Mooney's auxiliary bishops. (He had three
of these by 1955.) But Mooney remained in the 1950s a bishop very much in
touch with the financial and administrative details of his Archdiocese.[122]

The final decade of the Mooney episcopate is considered by many in the Archdiocese today to have been something of a "golden age." Never before, and certainly not since, had the Church been so disciplined or so prosperous, they
argue. There is abundant evidence for this position. The 1950s saw probably
the greatest proportion of Catholics in the history of the Archdiocese attending
Mass at least once a week. The typical Catholic almost certainly received the
sacraments more frequently than he had ever done before. More Catholic parents chose parochial schooling for their children than had ever been the case,
despite the sharply rising cost of parochial education. And lay organizations
throughout the Archdiocese were large and vigorous and nearly as varied as the
Catholic population itself. The theological certainties of the Church, moreover,
were attracting converts in record numbers. No longer a "foreign" institution,

the Church in the Archdiocese — and in much of the nation — enjoyed respect as a source of conservative social values and as a counter to the excessively specula- tive and relativizing tendencies of liberal Protestant theology. The American Church, indeed, was a model for much of the Catholic world. In no other coun- try could the Church claim such disciplined religious behavior among the laity or such generosity when it came to financial support. One might almost say that the reforms of the Council of Trent, legislated four centuries earlier, came to their fullest fruition in the American Church of the 1950s.

Still, there were shadows on this sunny landscape. The economic troubles that eventually undermined the parochial school system in the Archdiocese were already evident in the 1950s. The number of priests ordained for the Archdio- cese in that decade was smaller than it had been in the 1930s, and only slightly higher than the total for the 1940s. And conscientious priests sometimes worried that the spiritual life of the laity was not what it should be. Attendance at Mass was impressive, but many Catholics seemed to have a purely passive relationship to what was supposed to be a communal rite. Had the fervor and devotion gone out of American Catholicism, it was occasionally wondered, as the Church had become more homogeneous and more disciplined? The strength of the liturgical movement locally among a well-educated elite suggests that these discontents were shared by a portion of the laity, for if the liturgical movement was a sign of health in the American Church, it was also a protest. Perhaps most ominous, however, was the growing division between the clergy and the laity over the ques- tion of birth control. A majority of Catholic couples did not yet use contracep- tives — or they did not admit to using contraceptives — but there is good evidence that by the 1950s the moral grounds for the prohibition on birth control had ceased to be convincing for a goodly number of younger Catholic adults. A crisis in clerical authority, then, was already in the making in those placid preconciliar years, although it would not become evident until the 1960s.

Another crisis, this one of purely local dimensions, was also developing in the 1950s. It was no longer just the parishes in Detroit's core that were in finan- cial trouble, but parishes in a wide swath of the city's midsection, from which whites were moving at an ever-increasing pace. This was especially true of De- troit's heavily Catholic East Side, which was losing its industrial base by the mid-1950s. Cardinal Mooney, however, was loath to close any of his churches, no matter how small or how poor their congregations had become. He simply bequeathed the problem to his successor. That problem, like many others, grew markedly worse in the following decade.[123]

The Mooney episcopate came to an end on October 25, 1958, when the Cardinal died of a heart attack at the North American College in Rome. It was perhaps fitting that this most Roman of Detroit's bishops should die in the city that he loved above all others. And it seems in retrospect that his death came at a peculiarly appropriate symbolic moment, for Mooney was in Rome to par- ticipate in the conclave that was to choose a successor to Pius XII. Mooney would almost certainly have approved of the compromise that the conclave eventually reached when it elected Cardinal Angelo Roncalli as Pope. A theological conservative, Roncalli was also known for his interest in social questions and—at least in the rigid context of the Italian hierarchy—for his openness to ideas. Whether Mooney would have approved of the liturgical and theological changes that were set in motion over the course of this pontificate, however, is more problematic. We have seen that Mooney was fully in sympathy with the John Courtney Murray position on religious liberty. Had he lived, he would surely have been a force for its acceptance at the Second Vatican Council. But Mooney might well have been slow to embrace the various liturgical reforms of the council, and deeply concerned that these reforms would undermine the Tridentine sacramental theology to which he was committed. Nor would his fears have been without foundation. For the Church in the Archdiocese by the late 1960s was in many ways an institution quite unlike the Church that Mooney had known. If the changes had much to do with changes in the social composition of the American Catholic population—changes that were underway long before the council convened—they also had to do with the council itself. The reform of the liturgy and the popularization of a new theological language were critical in altering for many Catholics their understanding of the Church and of their place in it.[124]

The council, however, and the revolution that came in its wake were hardly imaginable in 1958. Catholic Detroit was unaware that in burying its Cardinal it was marking the end of an era. Still, the farewell was worthy of a historic moment. Mooney was widely admired for his work in Detroit, and his funeral was one of the largest that the city had ever witnessed. Particularly moving was the role played by children from the parish schools. "When his body was brought to the Cathedral our children joined in the Guard of Honor which lined Woodward Avenue," the chronicles of St. George's school recorded. "On the following day, October 30, the children walked over to view the Cardinal's remains, along with students from all over the archdiocese. We waited in slowly moving lines for about three hours. On the day of the Funeral Mass, our children again joined others of the archdiocese to form a Guard of Honor as his remains were transported to their final resting place at St. John's Seminary in Plymouth." The St. George's children were nearly all from poor black families. Their presence in the honor guard would have deeply touched their Cardinal, bearing witness as it did to a Church that was disciplined and yet extraordinarily diverse, wedded to tradition but able to hold the allegiance of the young. This was the Church as Mooney longed for it to be.[125]

ILLUSTRATIONS

Bishop Michael Gallagher.

Students and faculty at Sacred Heart Seminary, Detroit, in 1919, the Seminary's inaugural year.

The blessing of the cornerstone of the first church of St. Rose parish, in September 1920.

Sacred Heart Seminary, Detroit, under construction in 1924.

Father Charles Coughlin.

Bishop Gallagher and some of his priests at the Diamond Jubilee of St. Joseph's Retreat, Dearborn, in January 1935.

Cardinal Edward Mooney, center, with New York's Cardinal Francis Spellman, left, and Chicago's Cardinal Samuel Stritch at the dedication banquet for St. John's Provincial Seminary in 1949.

St. John's Provincial Seminary, Plymouth, under construction in 1949.

12

THE DIOCESAN CLERGY

The Gallagher-Mooney years were, on the whole, a serene and successful period for the priests in the Archdiocese. Their numbers more than trebled between 1918 and 1958, rising from 318 to 1,119. And the growing clerical ranks were marked by an apparently greater solidarity than ever before. Circumstances made it possible now for the great majority of priests to inhabit a world of their own, for their lives to be governed by the norms of that world— by its traditions and patterns of sociability. The values that informed the clerical world were shared, to be sure, by the more devout among the laity. (The evident devotion of a large and growing portion of the Catholic population in these years was an important source of clerical élan.) But there was a clear division nonetheless between the world of the clergy and the various worlds of the laity, and that division was maintained, indeed in some ways made more evident, even as the Catholic population was losing its heavily immigrant cast.

One major source of priestly solidarity was the increasingly assimilated status of the diocesan clergy, who had in fact been a more assimilated group than the larger Catholic population even in the days of Bishop Foley. And so they continued to be for the greater part of the Gallagher-Mooney years, as the ethnic divisions that persisted among them were steadily diminished. The vast majority of the priests who were ordained in these years had been born in the United States. Of the priests ordained for the Diocese between 1918 and 1926, only 20 percent had been born abroad, most of them in Poland, although the Catholic population of the Diocese was still a heavily immigrant one. Between 1927 and 1936, fewer than 7 percent of the *ordinandi* were foreign-born. And over the course of the Mooney episcopate, the numbers of foreign-born *ordinandi* declined even further. It is true that Bishop Gallagher had been obliged to recruit clergy from Europe during the 1920s. Of the sixty priests who are known to have been incardinated into the Diocese during his episcopate, thirty-two were born abroad. But their numbers were not sufficient to dilute the now thoroughly American cast of the clerical ranks.[1]

The clergy were bound together, however, by more than the American birth that most of them could claim. The founding of a minor seminary in the Diocese in 1919 meant that more and more of them spent the equivalent of their college years together, and a growing number their high school years as well. The opening of a major seminary in 1949 made it possible for the seminarians of the Archdiocese to complete their training as a group. By the late 1920s, moreover, the young *ordinandi* looked forward to a markedly longer service as assistant priests than any preceeding generation had done. (Priests ordained in the 1930s and 1940s generally waited eighteen to twenty years before they had parishes of their own.) The long years of apprenticeship brought special hardships — mainly of a psychological order — but they had the effect of placing young priests firmly within the bounds of a disciplined clerical world.

That world had a more self-consciously masculine flavor than had been the case in the nineteenth century, and the boyish vitality that seemed to characterize many of the younger clergy gave the clerical world in these years an appealing aura of certainty and vigor. The priest seemed less and less a man marooned in a mostly female sea of piety; more and more a man who managed to be "separated from the mass of men" yet very much at home among them. (The spate of priest-heroes in Hollywood films in the 1940s and the 1950s reflects this altered image, albeit in an exaggerated way.) No doubt the hearty masculine style was a cover, in certain cases, for loneliness and frustration. But it was nonetheless important as a source of solidarity among the clergy, and of the vitality that drew record numbers of recruits to the clerical ranks.

The clergy were also affected by the growing identification with Rome that characterized the American bishops after the turn of the century. For it was during the Gallagher-Mooney years that seminarians from Detroit were first sent abroad for study in any significant numbers. A majority of them studied in Rome, and it was from this group that candidates were especially likely to be drawn for positions of prestige and responsibility in the Archdiocese. The diocesan leadership, then, became more and more consciously Roman in its outlook, particularly during the Mooney years, when seminarians were sent to Rome in larger numbers than ever before. Young men who studied abroad generally found it an exhilarating experience, despite the rigors of seminary discipline, and they returned to Detroit with a quickened sense of loyalty to the Holy See and to a priesthood that they had witnessed in all its international variety. Naturally they shared their enthusiasm with their friends. The prestige that Roman training brought with it, moreover, confirmed for all priests'the growing importance of Rome in the life of the American Church. The lengthening Roman shadow had a number of consequences, one of which was to bolster the prestige of the clergy and to shield them from uncertainties about their role among an increasingly well-educated laity. The least-gifted parish priest was, by virtue of his ordination, linked to the grandeur of distant Rome, and a member of a priestly fraternity that included the Holy Father himself. As long as he and at least the more devout among the laity were convinced of this, the priest's sense of otherness — of standing apart from and above the world he served — was likely to be strong.

Solidarity in the priestly ranks seems to have grown steadily stronger through-out the Gallagher-Mooney years. This does not mean, of course, that genera-tional tensions and personal animosities were unknown among the clergy. That could hardly have been the case. Nor did ethnic divisions disappear entirely, even in the 1950s. The large contingent of Polish-American priests, many of them destined to serve only in the Polish parishes, still had their own social world, although the younger inhabitants of that world, especially, were likely to have connections to a larger clerical world as well. But whatever divisions re-mained, it is fair to say that the Mooney years saw a greater unity among the clergy than had ever prevailed before — or than has prevailed since. As a conse-quence, the integrity of the clerical world was protected against the erosion that might otherwise have come with the growth of an assimilated and well-educated laity. When Cardinal Mooney addressed the deacons at St. John's Seminary, something that he was accustomed to do every spring, he simply assumed that these young men were destined for a world of their own, however enticing the territory of the laity might look to them on occasion. "Your best friends are priests," he told them bluntly. "'He has only lay friends' is a terrible indictment against any priest." In one's own parish, indeed, even casual friendships with the laity were to be avoided. "Make pastoral visits, fine! Social visits, no! Don't ac-cept dinner invitations in the parish." A priest should never appear in public, moreover, in other than clerical dress. "We ought never to go where we can't take a Roman collar. . . . Wear your collar and black when you go out for a walk with another assistant after the last convert has left. Even strolling around in a jacket then could do harm." The Cardinal did acknowledge that the life of the priest was sometimes lonely. (Women were a source of temptation for younger priests, in his view, less for sexual than for emotional reasons: "Don't let any of them exert their gift of sympathy over you.") But even an unhappy priest belonged ir-revocably to the clerical world.[2]

Solidarity in the clerical ranks, whatever else it accomplished, did not in the post-Depression years guarantee an adequate supply of priests. The Archdiocese had a serious clergy shortage by the late 1940s, the combined effect of a rapid rise in the Catholic population and a modest decline in the number of ordina-tions. The 228 priests ordained for the Diocese of Detroit between 1930 and 1939 was a record never equaled again: about 200 men were ordained in the 1940s and probably not more than 205 over the course of the 1950s. These latter figures are still quite large, especially by today's standards, and they do not in-dicate any widespread uncertainty as to the meaning of the sacramental priest-hood. The ideal was sufficiently clear and firm to fill the classrooms of two spa-cious local seminaries, although the rate of attrition at Sacred Heart was a source of growing worry at the Chancery. The decline in ordinations was caused at least in part by the rapid growth of educational and professional opportunities in the later 1940s and the 1950s, a period of sustained prosperity for a substantial majority of Catholics in the Archdiocese. For more and more Catholic boys, the priesthood was only one of many possible routes to community leadership and community service. And despite the comfort in which most priests lived, they were no longer members of a tiny economic elite, as they had been in the days when their rectories were commodious landmarks in the immigrant districts of Detroit. In a world where Catholic youngsters increasingly looked forward to college as a matter of course, the priesthood was no longer the evident choice for social mobility that it once had been.[3]

The clergy shortage of the postwar years had an effect on every priest in the Archdiocese and on the laity as well, although it is much more difficult to demonstrate the consequences among this latter group. The burden of work increased for almost every priest, particularly those assigned to parishes. There was one priest for every 1,111 Catholics in the Archdiocese in 1950, up from 1 for every 689 in 1940, but even this substantial increase obscured the full dimensions of the problem, for a growing number of priests by 1950 were unavailable for parish work, having been sent for graduate training or assigned to educational work or to a position in the burgeoning Chancery bureaucracy. The regularity with which many of the Catholic laity now approached the sacraments simply increased the already considerable demands on the clergy. Some priests seem to have thrived on what looks to have been a strenuous round of sacramental and administrative duties. But for others the growing burden of work was a source of discontent, and there is evidence too that a minority among the laity were increasingly unhappy with the necessarily impersonal life of the larger parishes. Nor did matters improve during the final years of the Mooney episcopate. The ratio of clergy to laity in the Archdiocese had risen to 1:1,218 by 1960.

The shortage of diocesan clergy also led to a growing dependence on religious order priests. We have seen that Bishop Gallagher had invited a number of men's religious orders to establish foundations in the Diocese. Still, even in 1930 the priests of the various religious orders in the Diocese made up only 15 percent of the total number of priests who were active there. (That figure had been 18 percent in 1920.) During the Depression, however, the number of religious order clergy in the Diocese increased dramatically—the consequence mainly of growth in the religious order population nationally—and by 1940 fully 30 percent of the clergy in the Archdiocese were members of religious orders. Archbishop Mooney was uneasy about the situation, apparently worried that his authority over the diocesan clergy was almost bound to be compromised by the presence of so large a group of priests who owed loyalty to a religious superior as well as to their bishop. (He worried too that the various orders would attract recruits in their parishes who might otherwise have joined the diocesan priesthood.) But rapid growth in the Catholic population of the Archdiocese after 1940 left him no choice but to make even more extensive use of religious order priests. They made up 36 percent of the clergy in the Archdiocese by 1945, and 40 percent by 1960.[4]

The religious order clergy in the Archdiocese did not in fact pose any notable disciplinary problems for Cardinal Mooney, nor did their presence in such large numbers weaken the authority he was able to exert over his own diocesan priests.

Religious orders were no longer the ethnic strongholds that many of them had been in an earlier generation, when ethnic animosities had contributed powerfully to the difficulties they often encountered with bishops. Nor does it appear that the religious orders drew recruits at the expense of the diocesan clergy, for if Detroit had a shortage of diocesan priests in the postwar years, those same years saw the diocesan preparatory seminary well supplied with students. (The graduating class of 1952 was, at fifty-two students, the largest to date in the history of Sacred Heart Seminary.) The problem lay not in a shortage of seminarians, but in the growing number of students who were leaving seminary before ordination. And this was a problem with which the religious orders had very little to do. Indeed it might be argued that the example of the ever more numerous religious order clergy had helped to enrich the spiritual lives of many diocesan priests, which worked in turn to strengthen the diocesan clergy generally. For a growing number of diocesan priests do seem to have been attracted to a quasi-monastic spirituality. Bishop Gallagher and seventy-two of his diocesan clergy were "priest-members" of the Third Order of St. Francis in the mid-1930s, having pledged themselves to a rule of life that centered on a regular round of prayer and meditation and fasting. Their ardent piety presumably gave a deeper meaning to their lives as priests. And priests who were at peace with themselves and filled with enthusiasm for their work could only enhance the reputation of the clergy and bolster its morale.[5]

The extent to which the clergy were able — and willing — to inhabit a distinctive world of their own is a question whose importance is made evident by the course of Church history since Vatican II. The seemingly solid clerical world was one of the early casualities of the post-conciliar years, as younger priests rebelled against the restraints of rectory life and the inhibitions of clerical garb. "The unity of God's people is best served by reducing to a minimum the differentiation between layman and minister," Father Robert Begin told the members of St. Margaret Mary parish in 1970, and he spoke for many of his restless contemporaries. With the erosion of a distinctive clerical way of life, however, came a growing uncertainty among many priests about the function and meaning of the priesthood itself. To what extent the latter phenomenon was caused by the former and to what extent the reverse was true is almost impossible to determine. But the two phenomena were intimately related. For that clerical world had sheltered priests from the intellectual and cultural changes that had transformed the larger society over the course of the century. It had helped to keep at bay a world whose very assumptions about the human person — his origins, his nature, his requirements for happiness — were sharply at variance with those upon which Catholic seminary training rested. As the younger clergy fled the restrictions of the clerical world, they left behind its protections as well and found themselves in the midst of a culture for which the certainties of their seminary years had not prepared them. The resultant confusions and anxieties had profound effects on their lives as priests and on a laity for whom the priest was almost inevitably an evocative symbol of the Church.[6]

The pages that follow, however, are less concerned with the erosion of clerical solidarity than with its apparent health, less with doubt than with the certitude that appears to have characterized the American priesthood on the eve of the Second Vatican Council. A goodly portion of the chapter, then, will be given over to the local seminaries, those "cradles of the priesthood" that were the proudest achievements of Bishop Gallagher and Cardinal Mooney. It was those seminaries, filled to capacity and utterly traditional in their curricula and their discipline, that seemed even in the late 1950s to ensure that the next generation of priests would be very much like their predecessors and very much at home in their world. We will look too at the experience of that "elite-in-training" who studied in European seminaries during the Gallagher-Mooney years. We will examine the ways in which the careers of priests in the Archdiocese changed over the course of those same years, and consider the satisfactions and the discontents that seem to have been attendant on these changes. Finally, we will look briefly at two unrelated but important episodes in the recent history of the diocesan clergy: the experience of those who served as chaplains in the Second World War, and the establishment in the Archdiocese of Guest House, that innovative center for the treatment of alcoholic priests to which reference has already been made.

"AWAY AND RETIRED FROM THE WORLD": THE SEMINARIES

Sacred Heart Seminary opened in the fall of 1919 in thoroughly makeshift quarters. A pair of houses had recently been bought on Martin Place in a neighborhood less than a mile north of Detroit's downtown, but these were not yet ready to serve as classrooms or as living quarters for those students who came from outside the city. The eighty-five boys who made up the inaugural class had their lessons at Holy Rosary school—the four members of the seminary faculty lived there as well—and the would-be boarding students were evidently placed temporarily with families in the vicinity. The students were nearly all between the ages of thirteen and sixteen, and enrolled in either the ninth or the tenth grades, which were as yet the only grades taught. Subjects in "first high" that year included Latin, English, Ancient History, Algebra, Plain Chant, and Etiquette, and the student received marks as well for "Piety," "Application," "Politeness," and "Conduct." It was his introduction to twelve years of an ever more rigorous classical education—philosophy classes would be taught in Latin beginning in "third college"—and his introduction as well to the norms of disciplined piety and conduct that the seminarian was expected to make his own.[7]

The enrollment at Sacred Heart grew rapidly after its first year. There were 148 students enrolled in the fall of 1920; 212 in the fall of 1921. Two additional buildings were bought to accommodate the increasing number of boarding students. (There were 119 of these by 1921.) Quarters were crowded, and classes were held not only at Martin Place but at the Cathedral School and at Sacred Heart parish school, which was located in an increasingly derelict section of Detroit's near east side, just over a mile away from the seminary. The youngsters who marched in pairs to classes there probably saw a good deal more of city life than their priest-instructors would have liked. Indeed, the seminary itself was surrounded by the sights and scents and noises of a rapidly expanding city. The alley that ran between the buildings, where seminarians and faculty members liked to read and say the Rosary, was shared with "a parade of ice cream vendors, junk dealers, vegetable peddlars and fishmongers," Father Albert Hutting remembered. "Often a junk peddlar's shrill horn would shriek forth suddenly and stop all prayers and conversations, or shouts of 'Ice cream! Ice cream!' would send seminarians hurrying after the vendor." Neighborhood children were naturally attracted to the vacant lot and driveway that served the seminarians as a playing field. "After supper a gang of small Jews were around the basketball court and the Midgets played them," thirteen-year-old Clement Kern noted in his diary in the spring of 1921. "We won but by a small score [because] of all the razzing we were getting." Slightly older residents of the area had other recreations that impinged on seminary life. "Just now a bowling alley on Alexandrine Ave. keeps the boys awake all night," Rector Dennis Hayes complained in 1921, "and the noise of the streets and the autos destroy[s] that silence and quiet which should characterize the study hall." Father Hayes was of the opinion that the permanent seminary facility should be located beyond the city limits of Detroit: "the general idea of the Church is to have the boy away and retired from the world." And he looked forward to the day when all the boys would be boarding students, even those who lived within easy commuting distance of the school. Only then would the true seminary spirit be fully realized, and students enabled to live the life of prayer and detachment from the world that was essential to the formation of true priestly ideals.[8]

The transfer of the seminary to its permanent quarters in the fall of 1924 gave Father Hayes the seclusion he longed for. The spacious facility was surrounded by farmland; the distractions of the city were several miles away. (Large as it was, however, Sacred Heart was never exclusively a boarding school. High school students who were able to ride the streetcars to and from classes every day did so from the beginning. Only in the college years were students required to live on the premises.) Father Hayes had of course done his best to keep the city and its lures at bay even in the crowded confines of noisy Martin Place. Students were forbidden to leave the seminary grounds without permission, and never allowed to go on errands in the city alone. They were liable to expulsion for smoking, drinking, dancing, and "attending moving picture shows or any other commercial amusement unless the faculty of the Seminary has made the necessary arrangements." Boarding students were allowed visitors only once a month — for two hours on a Sunday afternoon — and only those visitors who had been approved by the rector. They were not permitted to use the telephone, and their mail was subject to faculty "supervision." The faculty also supervised the four hours a day that boarders spent in the study hall — time that was evidently essential if a student was to master a curriculum that placed a premium on memorization and drill. The piety required of even the younger students, more-over, was a highly disciplined one. Daily Mass and weekly confession were man-datory, as were regular visits to the Blessed Sacrament and a weekly Holy Hour. Boarding students, even those in high school, were obliged to maintain silence from a certain hour after dinner each evening until the following morning. This "Grand Silence," common to nearly all seminaries in the preconciliar era, was meant to encourage self-discipline, a deep interior piety, and detachment from the pleasures and distractions of social life.[9]

It was no easy matter to impose such discipline on a mass of adolescent boys, even boys who came, for the most part, from strict and pious families. (Father Hayes had occasion in 1921 to complain of "a continual spirit of rowdyism" in one of the Martin Place dormitories.) Rules were broken with some frequency, although not with impunity. Students were indeed expelled on occasion for single violations of seminary regulations. "The faculty had a meeting last night. They decided to run the Seminary like a real one and canned the three fellows who were caught [smoking]," an awed Clement Kern confided to his diary in 1921. Whether an offender was expelled or disciplined in a less drastic way seems to have depended on what the faculty thought of his general performance at the seminary and on the likelihood that his was a genuine priestly vocation. Sixteen-year-old Howard, for example, was in seemingly perennial trouble during "second high." Caught smoking not once but several times, he was also among a group who had sneaked away from the annual seminary outing to Belle Isle Park and been apprehended at a nearby amusement arcade. He was not expelled from the seminary, however, and went on to have a blameless career as a priest in the Archdiocese.[10]

More senior students were rarely dealt with so leniently, for the closer a young man came to ordination the more necessary it was that he manifest a will-ing submission to authority. Seminarians in the last two years of college wore cassocks and Roman collars, a constant reminder—to themselves and others—of their allegiance to the clerical world, its mores and its values. They were not only expected to have internalized the discipline of the seminary at this point in their careers, but to help keep order among the younger students. Even in the college, however, there was palpable tension over discipline. The most ardent piety could not entirely subdue a young man's natural resentment of authority, and authority at the seminary was often wielded—on principle—in what looked to be arbitrary ways. "Went out Thursday with Fr. Hannick's permission," a dis-gruntled collegian wrote to a friend in 1929. "When I came back he called me in the showers and told me he wished to see me after I'd dressed. After dressing, I went up to see [him] only to discover that he wanted to know where I'd been and with whose permission? (Crude humor or asininity?)" By writing so freely to his friend, who happened to be an ex-seminarian, the young man found him-self—as he perhaps wished to do—in trouble with seminary authorities. (His letter was read and confiscated.) The incident was a minor one, and had no ef-fect on the course of the student's career: he went on to ordination and to eventual honors as a monsignor. Still, it hints at the generational tensions that simmered beneath the well-regulated surface of seminary life. The "priestly ideal" demanded great sacrifice of young men whose sexual drive could hardly be willed away and whose curiosity about the world and its manifold attractions was rarely diminished by sermons and cautionary tales. "Am reading a book, 'Happy Mountain,' with a hero who feels exactly like I do upon the arrival of spring," the above-mentioned student had written in the letter that was confiscated by the seminary censor. "All soft and fuzzy within, restless, eager to travel (but he only wants to go as far as the ocean—Atlantic or Pacific—I'd rather see Spain, southern France and Italy, Switzerland and parts of Africa.) How's that for a bill of fare?"[11]

The seminarian had few outlets—other than sports and furtive gossip—for his restlessness and his resentments. He was not much encouraged to dwell on the emotions that sometimes disturbed his peace of soul, to explore his ambivalent feelings about authority or his sexual anxieties. He was expected rather to overcome these difficulties by prayer and acts of will, and by hewing closely to seminary regulations. Some seminarians, resilient and emotionally secure, were able to come to something like maturity in this unusually restrictive environment. But others entered the priesthood with a burden of unresolved conflicts and anxieties, the origins of which, to be fair, were probably located in childhood. "We have missed the seasoning process that most young men living in the world have gone through," Father Leo Trese wrote in 1955. "As a consequence (and let us be honest enough to admit it), often we come from the seminary still emotionally immature. Many of the normal conflicts of adolescence are still ahead of us—the conflicts that result from youth's urge for independence, on the one hand, and an unrecognized desire for security on the other." Father Trese was mainly concerned, as he wrote, with the causes of conflict between pastors and their young assistants. But priests had to deal with the laity as well as with each other, and some priests, at least, were not well prepared by their seminary years for this emotionally demanding role.[12]

Seminary discipline was meant to be a winnowing process, and a good many students did find it too much to bear. Most boys who entered Sacred Heart in the ninth grade did not go on to become priests. The freshman class of 1925 had lost more than half its members by the fall of 1929, and it seems to have been typical in this respect. (The preparatory seminary was an expensive way to recruit and train one's clergy, but Bishop Gallagher apparently thought it a necessary one, for he announced a free-tuition policy for Sacred Heart in the summer of 1920.) Still, the seminary retained a greater portion of its students in the high school years than most Catholic high schools in the Diocese were able to do in the 1920s and the 1930s. This was mostly the result of the seminary's relatively selective admissions policy. Its students were almost bound to be more motivated—and perhaps more talented academically—than the mass of boys in the parish secondary schools. (The seminary was more concerned with an applicant's "character" than with his academic ability: a boy was required to have "at least average talent.") But the seminary also had a vitality about it that made it, for all its rules, an attractive place for many of its students, even those who did not go on to ordination. A group of former seminarians organized themselves in 1945 as the "Gallagher Club of Sacred Heart Seminary," and managed in fairly short order to attract more than 300 members.[13]

Athletics was one obviously important source of morale at the seminary, and a valuable means of defusing the tensions bred by close and highly restricted living. Sacred Heart boys played baseball, basketball, football, and handball from the very beginning, despite the limited facilities at the Martin Place location. (There was no greater treat in those days, apparently, than a swim at the Knights of Columbus Clubhouse pool.) The permanent seminary buildings, opened in the fall of 1924, included generous athletic facilities: a large gym and spacious playing fields, handball courts and gleaming ranks of showers. These splendid facilities were in keeping with the emphasis on "manliness" that was so prominent in seminary publications in the early years especially, and in the rhetoric of the seminary faculty. The "real boys, masculine boys" whom Rector Dennis Hayes had vowed to produce were expected to take an interest in sports and to make them a principal focus of seminary life. And they did so, with typical adolescent enthusiasm.[14]

Sports were not the only focus of seminary social life, although they were surely the most important. The seminary supported a number of student organizations — most with a decidedly literary flavor — as well as a choir, an orchestra, a band, and a monthly magazine, later converted to a much-expanded quarterly. The senior play, where boys of necessity took the female roles, was one of the year's most eagerly anticipated events. And although the faculty and the student prefects kept close watch against the development of intense or exclusive friendships, the sheer number of boys under a single roof inevitably made for a certain amount of horseplay and hilarity. (The enrollment had risen to more than 450 students by 1928.) Theirs was a world with its own distinctive rituals and traditions, and the friendships that blossomed there were often enduring ones, if they were not exactly intimate. It had been "pretty hard to leave" his family at the close of the Easter holidays, young Clement Kern admitted in 1921, when he was a boarding student in "first high." Life at home had been "one round of fun." Still, the return to the seminary had not been without its compensations: "Arrived about 5:30. Saw all the fellows. It ain't so bad after all."[15]

The disciplined piety required of seminarians was often burdensome to them — especially to the younger students — but it too contributed to the peculiar vitality of seminary life. Their parish schools had accustomed most boys to daily Mass and regular confession. The seminary, however, demanded more: periods of prayer and meditation daily, the Grand Silence for boarding students, an annual retreat where every student was expected to keep "absolute silence" for three long days of prayer and instruction. ("All he is to do at your house during the Retreat is eat and sleep," the Rector advised the parents of the day students in 1925. "Make him keep to himself with no talking to anyone in the house during

the dinner and supper hours if he goes home for these meals.") And students
were encouraged to embrace an even more strenuous religious discipline than
seminary regulations required: to receive Communion every day; to become
members of the Third Order of St. Francis, which had a large and active fraternity at the seminary by the mid-1920s.[16]

What this stern regime meant to individual seminarians is something to
which the historical record rarely speaks. The pious essays produced by generations of Sacred Heart students have a curiously stilted quality: ponderously di-
dactic or sentimental, they are largely formulaic. One would not expect much
else from adolescent boys, particularly those who had inherited a religious vocabulary heavily weighted with scholastic terminology. And it would be wrong
to conclude that their seemingly inauthentic prose reflects a lack of religious feeling. Seminary piety, after all, was simply an intensification of a piety absorbed
from early childhood on, both at home and in the parochial school. Religion
was for nearly every seminarian so entwined with family and neighborhood that
it could hardly be a matter of the head alone. And seminary piety had a heroic
quality that seems to have appealed to many students. High Mass in the seminary's handsome chapel, accompanied by a well-trained Gregorian choir, had
a dignity and a masculine aura that parish masses rarely possessed, and such
"majestic and inspiring" events as the annual Forty Hours devotion — students
kept vigil in the Chapel in cassock and surplice, lighted candles in their hands —
confirmed for many seminarians their sense of membership in a spiritual elite.
The priesthood itself was held up as the most heroic of all ideals, requiring enormous sacrifice and marked by a dignity that was "great and incomprehensible,"
as one student essayist explained. "The priest is a man set apart from thousands,
with a divine power, enriched with graces, in keeping with his heavenly calling,"
this student wrote in 1927, shortly after three young men had been ordained in
the seminary chapel. "He is stamped with a heavenly character that will distinguish him from other men for all eternity. He is an 'alter Christus,' since he has
received the power to do precisely the work which Our Divine Lord Himself
did while He was on earth."[17]

The missionary priest was for generations of Sacred Heart students the most
compelling embodiment of priestly heroism. The seminary's founding coincided
with a rising interest among American Catholics in foreign missions, and devout
young Catholics especially were stirred by the vision of a world won for Christ
and for His Church. That vision was at the heart of the Catholic Students' Mission Crusade, which was founded in 1918 as a national federation of student
societies with an interest in the foreign missions. A unit of the crusade was organized at Sacred Heart Seminary in 1920, and throughout the decade the seminary
unit was the largest and most active of the many that were founded at schools
and colleges in and around Detroit. Its members worked at fund-raising and,
according to the seminary *Register* for 1929, "the members of the Unit visit the
Catholic High Schools of the city during the year to address the students on
the subject of the Missions." Fellow seminarians too had to be reminded that the

missions needed prayers and financial support. The seminary's student magazine, christened the *Gothic* in 1925, regularly carried a column devoted to "Mission Notes." "Tuesday is Mission day!" the editor alerted his fellow students in the fall of 1927. "It's Seminary tradition to offer prayers, aspirations and money on this day for the salvation of the unfortunate pagan." The seminary by this time had its own representative in the mission fields, for Father Sylvester Healy had left the Sacred Heart faculty in 1923 for service with the Benedictines at the Catholic University in Peking. He was a young and attractive man, the son of a prominent merchant family in Detroit, and his departure for the missions seems to have fired the imagination of many of the seminary's students. Father Healy was a seminary hero for many years thereafter, his example often invoked to illustrate the heroic self-sacrifice that defined the priesthood at its best. Later generations had a wider array of heroes to choose from, as the American Church sent growing numbers of its sons and daughters to the missions. War and revolution, indeed, provided them with a pantheon of missionary martyrs. But Father Healy was quite sufficient in his day as a symbol of youthful aspirations.[18]

The "mission consciousness" of the idealistic seminarian seems to have given way, to some extent, to a preoccupation with social reform during the turbulent 1930s. The number of socially conscious essays in the *Gothic* increased notably in that decade, although the magazine retained its largely literary focus. Student authors took the Church to task for failing to champion the rights of labor, supported Gandhi's movement for Indian independence, and denounced racism in the American South and even within the ranks of the Catholic community. More predictably, perhaps, they defended the beleaguered Church in Mexico and in war-ravaged Spain, and worried about the growing strength of Communism at home and abroad. But students worried too about the evident brutality of German fascism and about the slow pace — as they saw it — of necessary reforms in the United States. (Interestingly enough, Father Coughlin is mentioned only once in these various *Gothic* essays, and that reference was merely incidental.) A handful of seminarians, moreover, discovered the Catholic Worker movement and the various forms of radical Catholic Action with which it was generally associated, thereby providing themselves with models of heroic virtue who were laymen and -women rather than priests. "That is the one thing emphasized over and over again — the idea of daily Mass and communion, of leading the liturgical life, the life of the Church, the life of voluntary poverty," a seminarian wrote in 1938 of his visits to the recently founded Catholic Worker house in Detroit. "Special stress is placed on corporate prayer. They have spiritual reading at their meals, round table discussions and Compline in the evening, in which everyone joins. And these people, we must not forget, are lay people." Like many others who had contact with the Catholic Worker in its early years, he was certain that the movement was of utmost importance for the Church and for the world, despite that movement's negligible size and its notorious lack of organization. "It is almost too immense to grasp its entire significance," Henry Offer told his fellow seminarians. "It is far greater than anything the world has seen in many a day."[19]

Piety and idealism saw Henry Offer safely through the seminary and on to ordination as a priest in the Josephite Order. He later served in Detroit as the widely admired pastor of a small black parish. He was certainly not a typical seminarian: most of his classmates were far less socially aware, despite the political ferment of the 1930s. The tide of social consciousness, moreover, seems to have receded somewhat with the coming of the war and the years of domestic conservatism that followed. Still, a minority among Sacred Heart's students continued to be interested in social issues. A number of the older collegians were members of a labor discussion group that met in the early 1950s under the direction of Father Karl Hubble, whose ties to organized labor and Catholic Action groups locally kept his students abreast of developments on these still-lively fronts. The Blessed Martin League, founded at the seminary in the mid-1940s, had more than 100 members there by 1952. The organization was devoted primarily to the betterment of race relations, and under its auspices seminarians absorbed the theology—and the sociology—that informed the work of a small but influential minority of socially active laity. "The groups chose their own texts," the *Gothic* noted of the twenty discussion groups that made up the league in 1952. "Fourth high, for example, used the current 'Inter-racial Review.' One first college group studied the Mystical Body. The philosophers on the whole used Fr. O'Leary's dissertation *A Psychological Approach to Prejudice*." The *Gothic* was ready by this time to endorse a Fair Employment Practices Act for the city of Detroit ("discrimination is immoral, unscientific, unethical and illogical") and to reprove those "selfish Catholics" who regarded religion as a private affair, without implication for the life of the Christian in the world. And it had nothing but admiration for those priests and seminarians who were actually engaged in the social apostolate. The recently suppressed Worker-Priest movement in France was the subject of a sympathetic article in 1954, albeit one that carefully avoided criticism of Church authorities. There were admiring articles too about various domestic varieties of Catholic Action: the Association of Catholic Trade Unionists, the Catholic Interracial Council, the Jocist Movement in the United States, The Grail, the Christian Family Movement, as well as local efforts to minister to a growing population of Spanish-speaking Catholics. That many of these activities were lay-initiated and lay-led seems not to have diminished their appeal; they seemed to stand, for at least a minority of seminarians, as models of the disciplined piety and compassionate social action that ought to characterize the priest.[20]

The seminary itself was hardly a center of social action in the postwar years: students were kept to a rigorous round of prayer and study, and permitted to read only carefully selected—and carefully censored—periodicals. And there were certainly faculty and students who were indifferent, even hostile, to the very notion of Catholic social action, at least in any but a defensive mode. But the seminary was in fact less isolated than it seemed. Many of its students were affected by the mounting assault on racism that was perhaps the most significant political development in the decade after 1945, and sympathetic—sons of the

New Deal that they were—to visions of liberal reform. The moral appeal that the Civil Rights movement held for a number of Catholic clergy in the 1960s—something that surprised many people, by no means all of them non-Catholics—could perhaps have been foreseen by a perceptive observer in the 1950s. He might even have foreseen that the issue of race would be especially divisive for Catholics, with the clergy tending to a greater sympathy than the laity for the demands of civil rights activists.

The curriculum at Sacred Heart Seminary was never expanded to include the theology course that normally encompassed the last four years of preparation for the priesthood. Those years were often spent outside the Archdiocese, at least until 1949 and the opening of St. John's Seminary near Plymouth. The single largest number of theology students from Detroit in the years between 1918 and 1949 attended Mt. St. Mary's Seminary in Norwood, Ohio—the seminary of the Archdiocese of Cincinnati. Bishop Gallagher did not seem to share his predecessor's enthusiasm for St. Paul's Seminary in Minnesota or even for St. Mary's in Baltimore, long regarded as one of the more distinguished in the nation. Like Archbishop Mooney, Bishop Gallagher wanted as many of his priests as possible to be trained together, something he thought to be good for morale and for the maintenance of discipline. (He had hoped that Sacred Heart Seminary would eventually include a school of theology.) He made exceptions, it is true, for the fortunate few whose talents seemed to merit European training, as Archbishop Mooney would later do. And the growing Polish population of the Diocese caused Gallagher to send nearly all his students of Polish descent to SS. Cyril and Methodius Seminary in Orchard Lake, where their sometimes faltering Polish became fluent and their often limited knowledge of Polish history and literature was expanded and refined. A number of these students spent the whole of their seminary years at Orchard Lake.

SS. Cyril and Methodius Seminary drew its students from many dioceses, for Poles were arriving in the United States in large numbers as late as the early 1920s, and they were, on the whole, a population that was relatively slow to acquire facility in English. Theirs was a community that would need its own clergy for a long time to come, as many bishops recognized. Archbishop Mooney thought that this was true even in the 1940s, when he required all his students of Polish descent to attend the Orchard Lake Seminary for either their preparatory course or for theology. (The policy was in fact continued into the 1950s.) Had the Orchard Lake schools not been close at hand, however, and staffed mainly with priests from the Archdiocese of Detroit, Mooney might not have depended so heavily on them. For the practice surely helped to perpetuate the division that had long existed between the Polish-American clergy and the rest of the priests in the Archdiocese. That division did narrow considerably after the 1920s, as Poles became a more assimilated group and Polish-American seminarians were more and more likely to spend a portion of their training at a seminary other than Orchard Lake. (There was a Polish Literary Society at Sacred Heart Seminary by 1929.) But it was nonetheless a real division, even in the 1950s.[21]

The Archdiocese, as we have seen, acquired its own major seminary in 1949. Staffed by the Sulpicians, St. John's Provincial Seminary was opened in the fall of that year with a student body drawn from all the dioceses of Michigan. Rector Lyman Fenn was cautiously pleased with the young men who had been placed in his charge. "Their spiritual life seems fervent," he noted in the spring of 1950. "They are interested in mental prayer, and are faithful to their spiritual exercises. . . . Obedience to the rule is generally good and there is a docile spirit among the students." His principal worries had to do with academics: "some of them were not working well at the beginning. The results of the first quarterly examinations produced a salutary shock." Those students who had previously been enrolled at other major seminaries had perhaps been surprised by the intellectual demands quite suddenly placed upon them. For the Sulpicians were justly proud of the rigorous standards they set for their seminaries. "The Course of Studies at St. John's Seminary will be based on the course which obtains in the Catholic University of America," the bishops of the Michigan Province had been assured. "It will also be such as will meet the requirements necessary to obtain the status of a Pontifical Seminary."[22]

That course of study was not particularly innovative. Dogmatic and moral theology and canon law—all subjects that were taught in Latin—formed the core of the curriculum. These were thoroughly traditional courses. The approach to Scripture, however, was more than usually rigorous. Students were formally required to study Hebrew and Biblical Greek, although in practice the weaker students were exempted. There was, moreover, an effort to include at least a modicum of instruction in the social sciences and in "Christian social principles." Seminarians were introduced to the work of Father Clement Kern, whose extraordinary leadership at Holy Trinity parish had made the Church an important source of social services in what was now one of the poorest sections of Detroit. ("Seminarians from St. John's came to visit school and to study the social problems of the neighborhood," the chronicles of Holy Trinity school recorded in 1951. "A dinner was served in the cafeteria and Father Kern conducted their meetings.") Father Kern was also among the lecturers who participated in a "two-year cycle course" in Christian social doctrine, which was inaugurated at St. John's in the fall of 1954.[23]

The gentle emphasis on Christian social doctrine seems to have borne fruit. Seminarians regularly contributed their services as instructors in religious education programs, as counselors in Catholic boys' summer camps, as parish census-takers. (Work of this sort was necessary, in Father Fenn's opinion, "to keep their spirituality from getting too personal and monastic.") Forty-five students at St. John's were studying Spanish on an extracurricular basis by 1955, with an eye to working eventually among the growing Hispanic population of the Archdiocese. But the students at St. John's were apparently not given to intellectuality, something that distressed the scholarly Father Fenn. "One problem which is of concern to the fathers of the faculty is a general lack of intellectual interests on the part of many students," he reported in the spring of 1955. "The students do work hard at their required tasks and assignments; they do what they have to do. But that impulse to self-activity arising out of an interest in intellectual pursuits is rather rare among them and perhaps is growing rarer every year."[24]

Cardinal Mooney was wholly in sympathy with Fr. Fenn's desire to produce intellectual priests. "Most of us don't do enough reading," he cautioned the deacons at the seminary in 1956, urging them to "be up on current literature in a church way." The students, however, may well have been puzzled by the emphasis on intellectual achievement for men who looked forward to parish work. The parishes from which they came had not been marked by any particular interest in the intellectual life. Nor had their own training been the sort that is usually associated with the development of intellectual curiosity. The good seminarian was the obedient seminarian, properly detached from the world and well defended against contemporary intellectual currents. (Cardinal Mooney might want his priests to "be generally well-informed," but he was uneasy about most contemporary books and magazines. "Probably the further back in time we go, the better," a seminarian recorded in his notes from one of the Cardinal's lectures. "So much tripe is coming out.") Few American seminarians in the 1950s were aware of Catholic theological developments in Europe; if names like Congar, Chenu, and de Lubac meant anything to them at all, they probably stood for the suspicion, even hostility, with which venturesome theology was regarded in Rome.[25]

The seminarians of the 1950s were not much different in this respect from their predecessors: American seminary training had never been noted for its intellectual liveliness. But the seminarians of the 1950s began their careers as priests on the eve of a veritable revolution in Catholic theology, one for which they were utterly unprepared. That lack of preparation must account in part for the precipitous decline in morale among the younger clergy that came in the wake of the Second Vatican Council—a widespread uncertainty, hitherto noted, about the very meaning of the priesthood. Older priests, similarly unprepared, were by no means immune in these difficult years to painful doubts of their own. But it was inevitably the younger clergy who were the more affected.

If they were not prepared for a theological revolution, however, the seminarians of the 1950s seem for the most part to have been ready—indeed eager—for the priesthood as they understood it. His students might not be intellectuals, but Father Fenn was proud of their "vigorous" spiritual life: "the students seem very serious in developing their spirit of prayer and priestliness," he assured the Michigan bishops in 1955. He was proud too of the enthusiasm with which they offered their services to groups like the Confraternity for Christian Doctrine, and of the energy and cheerfulness with which they performed the janitorial duties that were part of the seminary's regime from the very beginning. (St. John's might have its own golf course, but the students could not use it unless they worked a certain number of hours—fifty per year in 1950—on the crew in charge of the seminary grounds.) St. John's was evidently turning out a generation of pious and hard-working priests, and Father Fenn was justly pleased by the achievement. He wished, it is true, that the seminary were producing more of them. He was sensitive to the growing clergy shortage in Detroit, and aware that large enrollments at Sacred Heart were not resulting in a bumper crop of *ordinandi*. Still, St. John's was able to supply its governing bishops with a steady supply of priests into the mid-1960s. That twenty-eight men were ordained in 1960 — up from nineteen and seventeen in the previous two years — seemed to be an auspicious beginning to the decade.[26]

Americans Abroad: European Seminary Training

Not every theologian from the Archdiocese attended an American seminary — a handful were trained abroad. Cardinal Mooney, himself an alumnus of the American College in Rome and its onetime spiritual director, liked to send at least two students to that institution every year. (During the Second World War, of course, this was not possible.) Bishop Gallagher was similarly enthusiastic about European training for his brightest students, although he sent them to a wider array of European schools — to the American College at Louvain, to his own alma mater at Innsbruck, even to Oxford and Fribourg. But Gallagher too was partial to the North American College in Rome: he sent more students there than to any other European seminary.[27]

The decision to send a student abroad for training was, in the Gallagher years, occasionally motivated by the student's need to master a particular language. Andrew Jacobs had grown up in Detroit's Hungarian parish, but he apparently spoke only English when he enrolled at Sacred Heart Seminary in 1929. His pastor, however, was of the opinion that the young man should be prepared to serve among Detroit's Hungarians, and Bishop Gallagher obliged by sending Jacobs to a seminary in Hungary for four years of training. It was not an altogether happy time for the young Detroiter. During the early years of the Depression, the Diocese gave no travel money to its seminarians in Europe. As a consequence, Jacobs spent his summers alone at the Kalocsa seminary, where he was the only foreign student. "I try to amuse myself in reading and walking to the Danube," he wrote to the Chancery in 1934. "It's a very nice way to spend the summer but tiresome and of course very lonesome. True, there is a public bathing beach about ten minutes from the seminary but that's 'severissime prohibetur.' Forbidden even to go near the grounds." The years in exile, fortunately, won him fluency in his ancestral tongue: by 1934 he was able to work as a catechist in a Hungarian primary school. A visit to the North American College that same year — the gift of an anonymous benefactor — even caused him to worry that he was losing his facility in English. "My tongue has completely turned Hungarian. Jack Donovan and Jim Shannon smiled at my terrible pronunciation. Merwin Lenk said Jake you've gone Hungarian entirely. Do all the boys studying abroad undergo this change?" Those "boys" did not normally study in such remote locations or in such isolation from other English speakers. But Jacobs was hardly unique in his failure to have learned his parents' mother tongue.

Bishop Gallagher sent Robert Pomponi to an Italian seminary in 1935 so that this son of Italian immigrants could learn to speak Italian. He, like Jacobs, spoke only English when he arrived, and was wholly unaware that what scraps of Italian he knew were actually bits and pieces of a South Italian dialect.[28]

Most seminarians who were sent abroad, however, were not destined for ethnic parishes but for seminary faculties or an eventual position in the Chancery. European training, and Roman training in particular, was widely believed to be more rigorous than that in most American seminaries, and that rigor — coupled with the ambiance of Catholic Europe — was thought to be a virtual guarantee of orthodoxy. Certainly Roman training was untainted by contact with contemporary ideas; the seminarian was inducted into a closed and legalistic world, the intricacies of which were hard to master. "These professors speak [L]atin more rapidly than I speak English," John Donovan complained in 1932, when he was a student at the North American College and finding the lectures "very difficult to understand." The seminarian was almost bound to acquire an exemplary self-discipline as he struggled to cope with this unfamiliar regime. But European training was effective mainly because it engaged the heart as well as the head. Seminarians who studied abroad nearly always returned with an intensely personal loyalty to the Pope and with a lively sense of membership in a universal Church. This derived less from their study of conservative theological manuals than from their experience of European Catholicism.[29]

That experience was a circumscribed one, to be sure. "We have been allowed to travel under the usual seminary conditions, that is, avoiding certain cities such as Paris and Brussels and traveling with at least one seminarian," John Finnegan told the Chancery in 1924. The usual itinerary ran from one famous shrine to the next. Francis Flynn and a classmate, for example, set off from the North American College at Easter in 1928 to wander a bit in Italy. "The little itinerary included Assisi (St. Francis and St. Clara), Perugia, Orvieto (the miraculous corporal), Bolzena where the miracle occurred, and Viterbo (St. Rose)," he wrote to the chancellor in Detroit, hastening to assure him that "we travelled in cassocks." Students enrolled at other than Roman seminaries were sure to make at least one trip to Rome during their time in Europe, and it was conservative Catholic Rome that they visited. "The greatest thing for all of us was to see the Holy Father and kiss his ring," Gerald LeVasseur wrote in the spring of 1933, shortly after he and a group of classmates from Louvain had visited the city. "Then we heard Mass in the catacomb of St. Callistus." Fascist Rome was indeed a more visibly Catholic city than it had been under the Republic, despite persistent tensions between the Vatican and Mussolini. For the strident anticlericalism of the Republican years had been muted. (The future Bishop Gallagher had learned from a friend in Rome in 1889 that European seminarians in the city were taunted whenever they appeared on the streets, "and occasionally rotten eggs, dead cats and tomatoes are lavished with an unsparing hand on the unfortunate students . . . but on the Yankees never. They use their boots and fists, and the Roman rag-tag know that they do.") The young

Detroiters who studied in Rome in the 1920s and the 1930s seem to have had little knowledge of, or interest in, European politics. But they were able to move undisturbed in a deceptively tranquil world, one whose Catholicity appeared to be ardent and deep-rooted. "Rome has been celebrating in grand style and in a religious way the great feast of today," Russell Pacquette wrote on the Feast of the Immaculate Conception in 1929. "The statue of Mary Immaculate in the Piazza di Spagna was illuminated and banked with flowers and with the surrounding buildings decked in damasks and tapestries the whole affair was a grand spectacle."[30]

"Grand spectacles" such as this help to explain why Europe was so moving an experience for nearly all American seminarians. It meant a liberation of the senses for many of them, despite the formidable sexual discipline that was integral to their lives. They came, for the most part, from a raw industrial landscape, and found themselves amid the mellow beauty of baroque cities and an ancient countryside. The change in diet alone was a revelation to Gerald LeVasseur, the son of an auto worker from Flint, who spent the summer of 1933 with a curé in the Haute Savoie: "The food here is really the most excellent I have ever had. I never was much of a vegetarian but the vegetables here are prepared so deliciously that I eat them like ice-cream." And the manifold shrines of Europe spoke eloquently of a Catholic history that had hitherto been confined to seminary textbooks. "I said my First Mass on the tomb of St. Peter," the newly ordained Father Merwin Lenk told the Chancery in 1934. "My second Mass was read at the shrine of Our Lady of Perpetual Help in St. Alphonsus Church and the third at the Sacred Heart shrine in the Gesu. I also said Mass in the Catacombs about a week ago." It was a Mass in the Catacombs of Domatilla that had been a high point of 1929 for young Frank Flynn: "The ruins of the old subterranean Basilica paid silent tribute to the Faith of those early Christians, and we all felt thrilled to actually be on the hallowed spot about which we had so often read. Now and then I have to pinch myself to realize that I really am in Europe and have not fallen asleep over the pictures in some history book."[31]

The emotions stirred by the encounter with Catholic Europe often came to focus with particular intensity on the person of the Pope. The students at the North American College had annual audiences with both Pius XI and Pius XII, and were often in St. Peter's for the celebration of major Church feasts. "The occasion that impressed me above all others was the Eucharistic procession of Corpus Christi at St. Peter's," Merwin Lenk wrote in the summer of 1933. "The Holy Father was carrying the Blessed Sacrament and the entire College walked in line with a multitude of priests and seminarians that only Rome could furnish." Neither Pius XI nor his successor was a notably charismatic figure, but the seminarians from Detroit seem to have been genuinely moved by even fleeting glimpses of their Pope. "We never tire of seeing His Holiness in St. Peters, especially as he enters that huge basilica or leaves it riding in his Sedia Gestatoria and blessing everybody on the right and left," John Donovan told the Chancery in 1934. "The novelty of hearing the clamorous shouts of the Italians in the Church has worn away and even we now join them in welcoming the supreme pontiff. It's funny how an atmosphere will influence one." Loyalty to the Pope, in such an atmosphere, almost inevitably took on more than an abstract and carefully qualified meaning. It became something deeply personal, bound up with memories of sunny days and splendid occasions and a warm and spontaneous Catholicism.[32]

The European seminary also seems to have made the sense of "priestly otherness" unusually vivid for its American students. They were far more isolated from their families than they would have been had they studied at home, their Christmases and their summers too being spent in the company of other seminarians. They were ordained abroad and said their first Masses there, entering the priesthood not in the context of family and parish but of a self-contained clerical world. "Perhaps the 'del Nord' spirit at this time is unique," Father Frank Flynn wrote early in 1931, shortly after the ordination of twenty-eight of his North American College classmates. "At home the men are ordained in their various dioceses, or if they are ordained at the Seminary, immediately scatter. Here all of them come back to share their joy with the other students who are anxiously looking forward to their own happy day." The bonds forged with classmates under these conditions were likely to be especially strong, and so was the sense of membership in a clerical elite. Frank Flynn, at least, had come to see his college—and the priesthood that it served—as a spiritual family, not simply a surrogate for the family at home but one with even greater claims on its members' loyalties. Grieved by the death in 1930 of a classmate from Detroit, he took comfort in the knowledge that the young man was buried in Rome, at the North American College crypt-chapel in Campo Verano Cemetery. "It was much better to have him buried here than at home, I think, for he will always be remembered by the students, whereas at home except for his family he would probably be forgotten after a short while." Young Father Flynn, it seems, had accomplished that transfer of loyalties which seminary education, Roman or otherwise, was designed to produce.[33]

PRIESTLY LIFE AND WORK

The work that a parish priest was expected to do did not change much over the course of the Gallagher-Mooney episcopates, nor was it greatly different from what was expected of his late-nineteenth-century counterpart. What did change significantly were the conditions under which he labored. The growing size of most parishes required ever more assistant priests, and fewer and fewer of the clergy lived and worked alone. Of those diocesan priests assigned to parishes, 48 percent worked alone in 1925, as compared to only 14 percent in 1955. Fewer and fewer of the clergy, moreover, lived in the kind of isolation and poverty that had been the lot of many rural pastors even in the early years of the twentieth century. Variations in clerical standards of living became gradually less pronounced after 1918, something that helped to ease—although not to end—the jealousies and resentments that were part of the darker side of clerical life. The single most important change, however, was an abrupt and dramatic increase in the number of years spent as an assistant priest. Priests ordained in the 1930s and the 1940s could expect to wait eighteen to twenty years before they became pastors. Some waited even longer, and a few men died without ever having had parishes of their own. The situation constituted "something of a tragedy," Father Leo Trese wrote in 1955, seeing in the long years of apprenticeship a powerful cause of apathy and depression. "Little by little the drive and energy of youth languish, without the spur of responsibility to replace them. Unless a man has developed a very deep spiritual life for himself, he is in danger of becoming a mere timeserver in his later years as an assistant."[34]

Priests who were ordained between 1918 and the mid-1920s largely escaped this danger. Bishop Gallagher, like Bishop Foley before him, did not keep to a strict seniority system for pastoral appointments. Talented young men often found themselves in charge of parishes after only four or five years' "seasoning" as an assistant. Indeed, Gallagher preferred younger priests for the difficult but prestigious work of establishing new parishes in and around Detroit. Gallagher's policies naturally roused resentment among the less favored clergy, much as Foley's had done, but an acute shortage of priests in the early years of the Gallagher episcopate meant that nearly every man, regardless of his standing at the Chancery, became a pastor within ten years of ordination. And while this was a lengthy apprenticeship by the standards of previous generations, it meant that a priest had achieved a position of relative independence by his midthirties, and that his career in this respect was not notably different from the careers of men in the secular professions.[35]

The years of apprenticeship had begun to lengthen, however, by 1925, largely due to rapid growth in the clerical ranks. Nearly every priest ordained in the mid-to-late 1920s served as an assistant for at least ten years, and some served considerably longer. Men in this latter category might reasonably have numbered themselves among the victims of the Great Depression, for it was the virtual cessation of parish-founding in the 1930s that, coupled with the ever-growing number of priests in the Diocese, made the long years of assistantship necessary. Wartime restrictions on building simply lengthened the period when few new parishes were opened—only six were established in the Archdiocese between 1940 and 1946. The effect, as we have seen, was to extend the years spent as an assistant to eighteen, nineteen, twenty, and even beyond. Only a handful of diocesan priests—those picked for jobs at the Chancery or at the seminaries—escaped this fate. Cardinal Mooney kept to a rigid seniority system when it came to promotions; he had "followed seniority so closely in the appointment of assistants," a longtime pastor remembered in 1960, "that they almost got to think of themselves as numbers."[36]

The long years of assistantship meant real emotional hardship for many priests. Conflict between pastors and assistants was hardly a new phenomenon, but it assumed more serious proportions after the mid-1920s. The number of complaints that came to the Chancery from unhappy assistants and disgruntled pastors increased substantially, although the contents of these complaints were generally not much different from the contents of earlier ones. Pastors were accused of being arbitrary and dictatorial, of treating their assistants like children. "The pastor insists that the assistant has no rights in canon law," a Chancery investigation of one notably unhappy rectory reported, "and if he does not do what he is told or what he wants the pastor will deprive him of privileges." Pastors, for their part, complained about the arrogance and rudeness of their young — and sometimes not-so-young — assistants, about their neglect of parish duties and penchant for late nights. The growing number of older assistants seems to have given the natural tension between a pastor and his subordinates an especially bitter tinge, at least where the pastor failed to delegate authority and deal with his assistants in a thoroughly tactful way. Some pastors were particularly threatened by the older assistant, whose years and experience made him look to be a plausible rival as a parish leader. And the older assistant, approaching his middle years but still a dependent and a subordinate, did sometimes openly resent his pastor's authority and work to undermine it. "I trace most of the trouble to the fact that all assistants remained here when I was appointed pastor," a German-born priest in Detroit reported in 1943. "This gave them the upper hand and they have maintained it ever since." One of the three assistants — a man of thirty-seven — had previously served as administrator of the parish. "This went to his head and he resented my appointment from the beginning." The pastor could see no solution to his problem but the transfer and replacement of his whole recalcitrant crew. "I am also waiting for the day when some definite rules will be drawn up for assistants."[37]

The Chancery did occasionally intervene in rectory disputes, although there was little that could be done to a pastor who had not violated canon law. (In the case just mentioned, one of the assistants was transferred. Another took matters into his own hands and volunteered as an army chaplain.) And at least in the Mooney years, assistants could count on being moved with some regularity: it was unusual for any of the junior clergy to remain longer than five years in a particular parish. If Mooney had sympathy for the priest who faced as many as twenty years of apprenticeship, however, he still expected his junior clergy to master their resentments and learn to live with even notoriously difficult pastors. "Your first appointment (in the Archdiocese, at least) is largely chance," he told the deacons at St. John's Seminary, urging them to "go to your appointment with no prejudice." Pastors who were reputed to be aloof and difficult men were often just "excessively timid"; patience and tact on the assistant's part might well succeed in winning their confidence. "Ease your way in! Study the man and the situation. . . . Get along if it is humanly possible." Above all, Mooney cautioned his deacons, "never let anything interfere with the work." A priest's happiness lay principally in the conscientious performance of his pastoral duties and in a disciplined life of prayer. It was not a happiness that was rooted in intimate personal relations, however desirable it was for priests to be friends and companions to one another. Mooney himself seems to have thrived on a steady diet of work and prayer, and in circumstances that made close personal relationships difficult to sustain. He had, of course, been in positions of authority from an early point in his career. And he had been raised in a world whose prevailing values were a good deal closer to the disciplined priestly ideal he espoused than was the case in the 1950s.[38]

We have already seen that more men were ordained for Detroit in the 1930s than in any other decade. No single cause can account for this, but it was surely no coincidence that this record crop was harvested during the Great Depression. Seminarians who might otherwise have been tempted by life in the world saw few opportunities there in business or the professions, and they could not help but be aware of the appalling insecurity that haunted countless families, even many who had hitherto been comfortably middle-class. The generation that came of age in the 1930s looked to a future where mobility would evidently be very limited, and it is hardly surprising that the priesthood should look more attractive as a consequence. For whatever burdens the priesthood might bring, it also carried a virtual guarantee of economic security.

The priests of the Diocese enjoyed a perceptible rise in their standards of living during the 1920s. The salary of a pastor had been raised in 1919 to $1,000 a year — this was the first increase since 1873 — and that of his assistants to $700, "out of which they are to pay $300 for board." These were not notably generous salaries; there were other dioceses that paid far more handsomely. But they were certainly sufficient to support a single man in modest comfort, particularly one whose housing was provided. Most priests, however, earned more — often considerably more — than the prescribed salary, which had come over the years to be regarded as something of a minimum wage. (This was probably the reason that Bishop Foley had never bothered to raise the salaries of his clergy.) Priests were entitled to the various fees and offerings that were attached to baptisms, weddings, funerals, and masses for the dead, and entitled as well to the usually generous collections taken up in their parishes at Christmas and Easter. These collections alone might easily treble a pastor's salary, at least in prosperous years. (He was expected in turn to be generous to his assistants.) The prosperity of the 1920s seems to have made for generosity all around. Parish income rose steadily, and so did the income of the diocesan clergy. The 1930s, of course, brought economic troubles to nearly every parish, and a heavy burden of anxiety to many priests. But they were protected from the poverty and insecurity that was the lot of many families in their congregations.[39]

Not all priests lived equally well, despite what was a general rise in clerical standards of living. The smaller the parish, as a rule, the smaller its pastor's income. And even in the 1920s there were country parishes in the Diocese that could barely support a priest. "I cannot afford a decent meal like other priests," the pastor at tiny Swartz Creek complained in 1919. "I cannot afford a decent suit, my last cassock was purchased in 1910." His parish had "scarcely 30" families who attended church regularly; it was only his practice of saying Mass in the nearby city of Flint that allowed his meager ends to meet. ("Truly, Dear Bishop, if I did not have the Flint service on Sunday I could not live, but would have to starve.") His congregation was so small, indeed, that he found himself with "nothing to do," a startling contrast to the situation in most parishes in 1919, when the Diocese was acutely short of priests. "All week I have to sit idle . . . and when Sunday comes, and I see those few in Church, I feel entirely discouraged." Frustrated and resentful, he implored his bishop to send him to a larger parish, although some unidentified troubles in an earlier assignment apparently ensured that he would not be sent to Detroit. "I do not expect Heaven, but forgive my expression, it is a hell at Swartz Creek," he wrote. "Swartz Creek is not a place for any priest to stay, it should be a mission only. . . . A priest that could stay at Swartz Creek for so many years, said one priest, can be considered a hero."[40]

Swartz Creek did not revert to a mission, although it had a new pastor by 1920. (Its former pastor spent the last few years of his career in rural parishes that were only marginally more prosperous than Swartz Creek. He died at forty-five, an aggrieved and disappointed man.) His former parish fared rather better. Swartz Creek, like most rural places in the Diocese, became progressively less isolated in the 1920s. Vastly improved rural roads enabled more families to come regularly to church, and enabled rural priests to move more easily around their usually extensive parishes. It was in the mid-1920s that the Michigan Thumb — long the most neglected part of the Diocese — was made the site of an experiment in rural evangelization by the Catholic Church Extension Society. The four priests who were assigned to this work regularly visited parishioners who were scattered over an area of some 2,000 square miles, something that was possible only because of "good gravel" roads and sturdy Fords. The work of the Extension Society in the Thumb bore abundant fruit and bore it quickly, as the various missions reported dramatic increases in attendance at Mass and in reception of the sacraments.[41]

Other rural parishes too showed signs of growing spiritual vigor as more and more parishioners had ready access to a church, and that vigor generally resulted in more regular and more generous church support. It was not poverty that made work in the Thumb so difficult, at least according to Bishop Francis Kelley, who pointed out in 1928 that all the priests who participated in the Extension Society experiment there had been able to collect their full salaries. It was rather the loneliness of the work and the stamina it required. "The work should be confided to young men," Bishop Kelley wrote of such rural undertakings. The mission superior had necessarily to be a man of some maturity. "But the assistants should come fresh from the Seminary without any experience in the city." Father Albert George, who was pastor in the village of Palms from 1926 until 1937, seemed to agree that the rural parish was properly a young man's domain, and he was ready, even at the age of forty-two, to make way for a more vigorous successor. "During all these years I have been pastor, janitor and gard[e]ner of a far off country parish," he told the recently installed Archbishop Mooney. "I am not discontented, but I could stand 'transplanting.' My good parishioners will support my contention that I am still doing fairly well as pastor, but I am weakening a little on the other two jobs."[42]

There were certainly priests in the Archdiocese who preferred rural parishes, attracted perhaps by the intimacy of a small congregation or—for a man of different temperament—by the independence that relative isolation afforded. But most priests seem to have agreed that a large parish in or near Detroit was the most desirable of all assignments. Detroit priests were widely believed to be the most prosperous in the Archdiocese, although this was not invariably true. "A priest is spoiled for assistantship in a place like Battle Creek if he ever served in Detroit," Father David Dillon told the Chancery in 1924, echoing the sentiments of many small town pastors. "The reason is he is always thinking of his income." The putative prosperity of the city's parishes and their proximity to the administrative heart of the Archdiocese gave those parishes an undeniable glamor in the eyes of many priests, and a Detroit appointment enhanced a man's reputation in a way that no small town or rural pastorate could do. The Jackson pastor who asked in 1931 for a transfer to Detroit had no complaints about his standard of living, nor was he mired in rural isolation. (Jackson was large enough by then to support four parishes.) But he was distressed at the Chancery's failure to grant him what he called a "decent promotion," which could only mean, apparently, an assignment in Detroit. The Detroit parish that he frankly coveted was carrying a heavy debt in 1931, and hardly seems, at least in retrospect, to have been much of a prize. But the Jackson priest was by no means the only man to hanker after it: "The air is filled with rumors with regard to the appointment . . . we hear that so many are striving for that parish, most of whom have had a number of changes and promotions."[43]

Whatever else a Detroit appointment meant, it generally brought with it a heavy burden of work. The largest parishes in the Archdiocese were concentrated there, and those parishes supported a generous array of devotional and social activities. The pastor at Holy Name parish wrote in some detail to the Chancery in 1947 about the duties that devolved on him and his three assistants, one of whom—a Precious Blood priest—had just been transferred by his superiors. ("We are therefore appealing to you in this emergency to help us acquire the services of another priest who is badly needed here.") There were seven masses said at Holy Name on Sundays and holy days, and "our confession schedule is very heavy"—as indeed it must have been in a parish of some 2,000 families. "We have the usual number of sick calls, baptisms, funerals, weddings and instructions. . . . Moreover, we receive many calls each week for commitments in Mt. Olivet Cemetery, which means that a priest must be available for this purpose every morning." The parish school and the catechetical program absorbed a good deal of time: "Besides teaching each day in the school, the priests also have some three hundred Public School children under religious instruction here, and also supervise the catechetical instructions at the Emerson Project which employs six lay teachers from the parish." The various parish clubs and sodalities required at least the nominal supervision of a priest, and sometimes required a good deal more. The Junior and Senior Young People's Clubs, some 500 strong, "require the services of a priest two full evenings a week, besides the extra outings, trips and entertainments which are also under the personal supervision of a priest and take place monthly." The parish had an active Boy Scout troop, and participated "as far as our facilities warrant" in the athletic program of the Catholic Youth Organization. "One priest bowls weekly with the parish Bowling League. . . . We also have teams in baseball and basketball for both the boys and the girls. Each team is under the supervision of a priest." The Holy Name Society had a membership of over 600, nearly half of whom received communion at a special monthly Mass. "Five times a year we arrange a breakfast and program for the members." The women of the parish were even better organized: the Christian Mothers had almost 700 members, there was a "very active" branch of the Ladies' Catholic Benevolent Association, and junior and senior units of a Young Ladies' Sodality. These groups required rather little in the way of clerical supervision, but a priest was expected to appear at least briefly at their meetings and to keep his eye on their progress and their projects. The altar boys, on the other hand, required intensive care. "One priest . . . trains the altar boys and has an enthusiastic Ad Altare Dei Society organized." And there was the usual round of administrative tasks—bound to be heavy in so large a parish—as well as such incidental demands on a priest's time as devotions three evenings a week—nightly in May and October—and the editing of a weekly parish paper.[44]

Holy Name was a well-run and active parish, but it was not greatly different from many others. Nor were its priests more burdened than many of their contemporaries, although the ratio of priests to people was higher at Holy Name than it was for the Archdiocese as a whole. There was an acute and growing shortage of priests in 1947, when the ratio of parish clergy to the Catholic population was slightly greater than 1:1,400. (Nearly 170 priests in the Archdiocese were engaged in other than parish work by 1947.) That ratio had been exceeded only once before—at least since the early days of the Diocese—and then only briefly, during the period of rapid population growth that followed the First World War. Even priests in the smaller parishes found themselves with a growing burden of work by the mid-1940s, and it grew progressively heavier in a good many cases. There is, indeed, an increasingly desperate edge to the letters that flooded the Chancery in the postwar years, begging for an additional assistant or—in lieu of that obviously unlikely relief—for extra weekend help. "I may console myself that it is not my doing that there is a shortage of priests," one overburdened pastor wrote in 1955, "and that if God does not want the school and mission in preference to other more needful activities, He will make it impossible to carry on, and thus relieve the situation. But all of us have not this perfect faith which casts out fear and worry."[45]

The extent to which priestly morale was affected by the growing burden of work is virtually impossible to ascertain. There is no survey data that bears on the problem, and relatively little archival material that speaks directly to it. What there is seems to indicate a varied response. Some priests apparently thrived under this more demanding regime, deriving a sense of competence and purpose from their numerous and varied tasks. Men like these might well have suffered had there been less to do, had time weighed heavy on their hands. But there were others who found their work emotionally draining, even under optimal conditions, and for whom the increased workload was a source of resentment and anxiety. Priests were in many ways not well trained for the fragmented round of work that was characteristic of the parish, or for the frequent contact with the laity that parish life entailed. Their seminary days had been orderly to an almost unnatural extent — minutely regulated by an omnipresent authority and shielded from the world. Under the circumstances, it is perhaps remarkable that so many priests adapted well to parish life and responded generously to its many emotional demands. But there were those who did not, as the parish files at the Chancery archives make painfully clear. The "nervous" priest, the pathologically timid priest, the perennially angry priest, the priest who is terrified of women — they are all there. Such men lived in perpetual psychological distress; they were hardly equipped to handle the increased pressures of the postwar years. Father Leo Trese, ordained in 1927, thought that the number of such deeply unhappy priests was small. But he feared that many priests in the postwar years were too overburdened to maintain disciplined spiritual lives, and that they were, as a consequence, vaguely but disturbingly discontented. "How many priests do we not know, who are hard working and duty-minded, and yet seem to find their work a drudgery and their duty a burden?" he asked his fellow clergy in 1955. "I do think that there are many heavy-spirited priests; I do think that too many of us, too often, are moody and depressed — too often with an urge to 'get away from it all.'" Moodiness and depression have many causes, and what Father Trese reported may have had little to do with the growing burden of work. Trese himself, however, was inclined to think that it did.[46]

Father Trese was not unduly worried, as he wrote, about the future of the priesthood. He saw plentiful signs of health around him. And he was right to do so. There were some remarkable men ordained in the 1950s, men who helped to make the Church a force for social justice in an increasingly troubled and racially divided Detroit. Trese's own generation of priests, moreover, had produced its share of men whose ministry was carried out with such grace and such compassion that they strengthened the Church in ways that a historian can never fully know. Some of them spent their careers in obscurity, obviously held in affection by their congregations and a small circle of fellow priests but not otherwise obtruding on the public consciousness. They appear — at least a few of them do — in the letters that the Chancery sometimes received when it transferred clergy. "We all like Father Lahey very much and would feel lost without him in our Parish so please do not have him taken away," ran a typical specimen, this one from the western Michigan village of Watervliet. "I think it would be very unjust to move him away after he had labored so hard amonge the People and a good many people that did not go to mass for years are going to mass nearly every Sunday now." Other exemplary priests were drawn to more visibly heroic roles, modeling their lives in some small way on the missionary priests who loomed so large in the popular mind. Father Hubert Roberge, for example, left Detroit in the early years of his career to serve for at time in the Diocese of Mobile, at a small and penurious mission for the city's blacks. "Since my arrival in October I have been trying to make a canvass of the local situation and find that the Negroes here are wretchedly poor and pitiably neglected," he wrote to his fellow priests back home in 1935, optimistic nonetheless that Mobile's black citizens presented "a wide-open opportunity for a great in-gathering of converts to the Church." Roberge returned to the Archdiocese in 1943, and was one of the first diocesan priests to work in Detroit's black community. He did a great deal to alert his fellow clergy to the festering problem of racial injustice in the city, and as he did so, he helped them toward a more generous vision of the priesthood.[47]

No priest, however, captured the hearts of his fellows — or the imagination of a large and varied public — like Father (later Monsignor) Clement Kern. The engaging seminarian whom we have briefly encountered matured into a priest whose spirituality and playful charm and seemingly boundless compassion made him, as Msgr. George Higgins wrote at Kern's death in 1983, "the most beloved clergyman in Detroit for more than half a century." He was best known for his work at Holy Trinity parish, where he served as administrator and then pastor from 1945 until his retirement in 1977. Holy Trinity by the 1940s was one of the poorest parishes in the Archdiocese. It served a heavily immigrant community, one that included large numbers of Hispanic Catholics and a population of Maltese, and encompassed within its boundaries a generous slice of Detroit's Skid Row. Father Kern set about to minister to every constituency in this generally troubled territory. "We run 'wide open' and have priests in the Church for many services and the Rectory is open to everyone and at all hours," he explained in 1950. "We have tried to make the school available to all elements in the community at all hours with a view to make the parish influence first in the minds of all in the neighborhood." This he surely succeeded in doing. Holy Trinity parish by the mid-1950s had given rise to a medical and a dental clinic, an adult education program in English and Spanish, two cooperative residences for the elderly, and a legal services program, as well as the "Corktown Coop," a parish-sponsored salvage business, that gave employment to at least a few of the area's unskilled men. And its perpetually open rectory continued to be a source of solace for an endless stream of troubled humanity. That rectory "was frequently a madhouse," Msgr. Higgins remembered, "a magnet-like haven for people from all walks of life with problems they thought only Father Clem could help them solve."[48]

For it was "Father Clem" himself, even more than the social services his parish offered, that made Holy Trinity the symbol it was of a vibrant and compassionate Catholicism. He was a man of immense good cheer, but infinitely capable, or so it seemed, of empathy with even his most troubled parishioners. He was a welcome guest in some of the wealthiest households in Detroit, but he lived in unassuming poverty. "As far as personal money is concerned we are poorer than many of the poorest in our midst," he assured Cardinal Mooney in 1950, writing to ask for financial assistance to keep his parish afloat. (Father Kern's "first official act," according to the chronicle kept by the Sisters at the parish school, had been to give up his claim to the Christmas and Easter collections.) He had extraordinary stores of patience, and a serenity that was rarely disturbed by the chaos that often surrounded him. Not that the chaos was wholly unrelated to Father Kern himself, and his firm conviction that charity—and not good order— was the first priority of the Church. "About 50 exploited Puerto Ricans from the beet fields were taken in by Father Kern and allowed to sleep in the school," the Sisters' chronicle recorded in September 1950. "As a result we could not get the school ready. The Birmingham Sisters came to help us clean. Without their kind help we could never have opened school on time."[49]

Father Kern's eminently gracious influence was widely felt. He was something of a hero to many of his fellow priests, and to several generations of seminarians. (He spent the final years of his life on the faculty at St. John's Seminary.) He was certainly a favorite of Cardinal Mooney, who was more than generous over the years in his financial support of Holy Trinity parish. "I realize . . . that this may seem like a lot of crust to be begging you in this fashion, yet I confess that we do not feel ashamed, because all five of the priests living here feel very deeply that you understand this kind of work and that we have your confidence," Kern wrote to Mooney in 1950, confessing in a letter the following year that "if it was to anyone else we would not have the nerve to even approach them." He was held in affection by many of Detroit's Hispanic Catholics, for whom Holy Trinity was something verging on an ethnic parish. Father Kern had been among the first priests in the Archdiocese to learn Spanish—he made regular trips to Mexico after the mid-1940s, characteristically grateful for these opportunities to "see the Faith of the priests and people, truly very inspiring." His example—and his active encouragement—caused a number of his fellow priests to acquire at least a rudimentary Spanish, easing what had been a critical shortage of priests who could minister to the Hispanic minority in the Archdiocese. He was an active supporter of the labor movement locally, especially close to the United Auto Workers, whose progressive politics he frankly admired. (It was on behalf of the Hotel, Motel and Restaurant Employees, however, that Father Kern made his most memorable pro-union gesture, walking a picket line in 1963 at the Detroit Playboy Club, to demand a minimum wage for the "bunnies" who worked there.) He was well known too for his work with prisoners and exconvicts, something that he continued until the end of his life. And he moved with ease among the rich and influential. He was perhaps more successful than any of his contemporaries in keeping alive for affluent Catholics a vision of the social Catholicism that had had such appeal in the 1930s.[50]

Priests in military service

Few priests from the Archdiocese served in the military before the 1940s. The Spanish-American war had stirred deep patriotic emotions locally, but only Father Francis Kelley, pastor at Lapeer, was moved to volunteer his services as a military chaplain. World War I attracted a larger number of clerical volunteers: nine priests from the Diocese of Detroit were among those attached as chaplains to the Army and the Navy. Among them was Father Patrick Dunigan, four times decorated for his service with the American infantry in France. Father Dunigan was unusual in that his military connections preceded American entry into the war. He was a long-time member of the Michigan National Guard, and had been attached to the American Expeditionary Force that pursued Pancho Villa in the Mexican border regions in 1916 and 1917. Most American dioceses were still short of priests in the early decades of the century, and the peacetime army was small. The spiritual health of the Catholics in its ranks was of necessity a low priority for nearly all American bishops.[51]

Circumstances changed fundamentally, however, with the coming of the Second World War. More than thirty priests from the Archdiocese served as chaplains in that war, and a number of them saw combat. Most had returned to the Archdiocese by 1946, but a handful chose to remain in the armed forces, recognizing, presumably, that those forces were destined to be a large and permanent presence in American life. Cardinal Mooney was in no position to encourage his younger priests to volunteer for peacetime military service — the shortage of clergy in the Archdiocese was too acute — but he was genuinely regretful that he could not provide the Military Ordinariate with "the number of priests that I would like to give." (He had, however, promised that he "would never recall any of our priests from service and would replace any of them who of their own volition returned to the diocese.") The spiritual well-being of Catholics in the military was of great concern to him, as it almost had to be, considering the size of the postwar armed forces and the continuation of the draft.[52]

The priests who volunteered as military chaplains during the Second World War seem to have been largely motivated by patriotism, although there may have been some who were also looking for a greater independence in their lives as priests. Those young enough to be considered for chaplaincies, after all, were members of a generation that could anticipate as many as twenty years of assistantship. The evident shortage of chaplains was the decisive factor for at least a few. Father Leo Trese had been "willing" to serve as a chaplain when the war began, he told his Archbishop in the fall of 1942, but "now I have got to the point where I actually want to go." It was the shortage of priests in the battle zones that had made him decide that he belonged in the military rather than in the Archdiocese, for all its own acute shortage of clergy. "It's only a few months ago that I was asking for another priest here myself," he acknowledged. "But if the folks of this parish, or any parish, lose their souls, it won't be because they couldn't have gone to confession if they had wanted to, or heard the Gospel preached if they would come to listen. And that's more than we can say for a lot of the boys in the service." Father Trese was gently told that he was needed at home, and that it was the Archbishop's policy to select his chaplains from among the men who had been ordained in the past ten years. (Trese was forty, and already a pastor.) Besides, the Chancery had a larger number of volunteers than it needed to fill its quota of chaplains.[53]

Those priests who served as chaplains during the war seem to have valued the experience, and to have found it, on the whole, an ennobling one. This, at least, is the message conveyed in the letters they sent periodically to Archbishop Mooney. Those letters, of course, may not have told the entire story: had a man's faith been shaken by the carnage he witnessed and his worldview undermined, he would probably not have confided these things to his Archbishop. But the letters have a candor and an informality about them that one seldom encounters in correspondence between priests and the Chancery. If their authors were trying to conceal their real emotions, they did an unusually skillful job. Certainly it is possible that some of them were deceiving themselves and hence their Archbishop, that unacknowledged doubts and fears were eating at their souls. But here we trespass on something other than the territory of the historian.

What moved and gratified the chaplains most was their sense of being vitally needed. They generally reported a quickened interest in religion among the Catholics in their charge. "This is a staging area for troops who are embarking and naturally they are much concerned about their spiritual condition before stepping into the danger zone," Father Michael Collins wrote from California in 1943. "You would be surprised how many come back to the sacraments after years, when face to face with sailing forth to the battle areas." Not every Catholic soldier, unfortunately, was properly anxious about his soul, nor was every correspondent impressed by the religious fervor of the troops. "After more than a year in the field with a combat outfit," Father Joseph Dion wrote from North Africa, "I'm afraid I can't feel as optimistic as some of our writers back home over the big hunks of religion that our boys are supposed to be getting. There are still quite a few atheists in the foxholes over here. The good boys are getting better, the bad ones worse, and we are still battling for the large middle class." More typical of the letter-writers, however, were the sentiments of Father Stephen Dzienis, who accompanied the 126th Infantry on its bloody march across New Guinea in 1943. "I am enjoying my work," he told his archbishop, explaining that the experience of combat had only strengthened his own faith and that of the men in his care. "The state of grace gave them calmness under fire, and a peaceful death. For myself, I may say, at no time in my priestly life have I been so conscious of my priestly powers than at the front. Oftimes the men would come just to receive a blessing, or call for it when they saw me at a distance. Other instances are beyond description."[54]

Even the less sanguine correspondents were willing to admit that the typical American Catholic recruit was much more devout than his European counterpart. "Our soldiers are really showing these so-called Catholics up over here — and not merely in the collection basket," Father Vincent Myrick wrote from Sicily. "Native priests and people have been edified by the way our men attend Mass and receive the Sacraments. As you know, the men here don't bother too much about attending church. They leave that to the women." Father Myrick was proud of the American Catholic chaplains too — "most of them are courageous, zealous and virile men" — and not much impressed by what he had seen of clerical life in Europe. "The French and Italian priests whom I have met, with few exceptions, seem to be weak, lacking in courage and zeal." Northern Europeans were generally conceded to be more devout than their southern coreligionists, but Father Hubert Maino was not much impressed by Catholics in the north of France. "As church-goers they appear to me to be only so-so, the women doing the greater share. Several have told me that their own soldiers never received the Sacraments in such numbers as ours do, during the campaign of '39 and '40." Father John Downing, for his part, was rather unnerved by his 1945 visit to a Czech village whose inhabitants were "supposed to be Catholics. I say 'supposed' because they had a parade yesterday in honor of John Huss who was born not far away. . . . During the parade they sang songs about the Bishops who burned poor John at the stake about 1415 (I think). They are trying to make him a martyr. All of which confuses me and makes me wish I could talk Czech." This confirmation of American superiority in matters of religion seems to have strengthened the essentially religious patriotism with which all the chaplains were imbued — and had been, in all probability, since they were boys. "Good, great good, is bound to come out of this war," Father Myrick declared, envisioning not only the defeat of fascism but a spiritual revival in Europe — and all of this due to American power and will and example.[55]

The American liberators of Catholic Europe included a good many Protestants and Jews, a fact that had its effects on many of the chaplains. Their vision of the war was shared by their Protestant and Jewish counterparts, and this alone helped to narrow the confessional divide. For some of them, moreover, the war provided the first real contact with other-than-Catholic clergy. "This is . . . the first time in my life that I came in contact with [P]rotestant ministers," Father Boguslaus Poznanski wrote from North Carolina in 1944. "Some of them are very nice chaps, sincere and zealous." Father Joseph McElgunn reported generally amicable relations among the various chaplains at his base in North Carolina, and looked forward to continued good feeling after the war. "I'll say this for the Protestants," he told his archbishop. "With but few exceptions they are very good about putting us in touch with the things that involve our boys. I think when it is all over we will owe them a lot more than they will owe us. Now I don't want anyone to think that I am going heretical but I do think that when the war is over there is going to be a huge number of ministers who saw service upon whom we can count for a friendly cooperation in such few things as we can cooperate with them." Contact with Jews was considerably less frequent than contact with Protestants, and burdened with considerably greater fears and misconceptions — on both sides of the divide. But there were occasional moments of recognition, when the shared experience of war made for a sense of a common spiritual patrimony. Father Hubert Maino had his "closest call" on the front in northern France in some rather unlikely company and under rather unlikely circumstances. He had inadvertently been issued obsolete route instructions and found himself driving through a town behind the German lines. "They must have been eating breakfast, or something, as one mortar shell was all that I got in the way of greeting. It was only when I arrived at my destination that I learned that I had passed through unfriendly territory. The odd part is that at the time I was returning with a vehicle full of Jews whom I had taken to a nearby city for Yom Kippur services. Abraham, Isaac and Jacob must have been the patron saints on duty that day." Neither Father Maino nor his fellow chaplains were converted to ecumenism during the war. But their world was made larger and more complicated—a necessary precondition to the ecumenical impulse.[56]

GUEST HOUSE

Alcoholism continued to afflict a small minority of clergy during the Gallagher-Mooney years. For much of this period, these priests were dealt with essentially as they had been in the nineteenth century. Chronic offenders were usually sent for treatment to a Church-sponsored institution, where the therapeutic regime consisted mainly of prayer and penitent meditation. For the alcoholic priest was still regarded as a weak and sinful man. It was his weakness, indeed, that was generally invoked to explain the failure of the various Church-sponsored institutions to rehabilitate more than a tiny fraction of the priests assigned to their care.

It was a layman, himself a recovered alcoholic, who was the first to offer an alternative to what he called these "disciplinary jails." That alternative was Guest House, which opened early in 1951 in the Diocese of LaCrosse. Guest House was intended only for priests, but it differed greatly from the ecclesiastical institutions that treated alcoholic clergy. Austin Ripley, the founder of Guest House, had won his own battle against alcoholism with the help of Alcoholics Anonymous, and his work at Guest House reflected this. Alcoholism was a "disease of the whole man," Ripley insisted. The patient needed physical and psychological as well as spiritual care. Above all, the patient had to be prepared for lifelong therapy: "the only hope for *permanent* recovery for any alcoholic lies in continuing therapy until he dies," as Ripley wrote in 1954. Accordingly, patients at Guest House were introduced to the work of Alcoholics Anonymous, and arrangements were made for them to meet regularly with an AA group when they returned to their home dioceses.[57]

Ripley's approach was controversial in part because he insisted that alcoholism was a disease. The American bishops, like most of their countrymen, were uneasy with the notion that what looked to be manifestly sinful behavior had physical and psychological causes over which the individual had little control. But Ripley was also controversial because he insisted that Guest House be administered and staffed only by laypersons. The alcoholic priest was deeply resentful of ecclesiastical authority, Ripley argued, and the presence of clerical authority in the institution where he was being treated made it difficult for him to assume responsibility for his condition and his future. Few bishops, however, were prepared to cede even temporary authority over their priests to a layman, and it was Ripley's insistence on lay control that spelled the end of Guest House in the Diocese of LaCrosse. Bishop John Treacy apparently demanded that the Guest House chaplain act as Ripley's codirector. Ripley's refusal to accede to this demand caused Treacy to withdraw his support from Guest House just four months after it had opened.[58]

It was at this juncture that the first efforts were made to interest Cardinal Edward Mooney in the future of Guest House. Ripley had a number of friends in the Archdiocese of Detroit, and they hoped to win Mooney's support for a transfer of Guest House from Wisconsin to his own archdiocese. Ripley had by this time appealed to Rome for relief from Bishop Treacy's "unlawful" interference in the operation of Guest House. Mooney refused even to discuss the future of the institution until the Roman case was decided, something that did not happen until late in 1952. Ripley lost his appeal, which was hardly surprising, but the decision commended him for his work, and he was encouraged by knowledgeable friends in Rome to transfer that work to a different diocese and the jurisdiction of a sympathetic bishop. Mooney heard much the same thing when he traveled to Rome in 1953, and later that year he invited Ripley to establish Guest House "on a site deemed suitable by you and me within the confines of the Archdiocese of Detroit."[59]

It was generous, even courageous, for Mooney to lend his patronage to Ripley's work. He knew how controversial that work was, and knew that raising money for its support was likely to be difficult. (Milwaukee's Archbishop Meyer refused to approve any fund-raising efforts in his archdiocese when he was approached by Ripley in 1954.) Mooney's decision stemmed mainly from his longstanding worry about alcoholism among the clergy—his seminarians had to pledge to abstain from hard liquor for ten years after ordination—and from some happy, if limited, local evidence as to the soundness of Ripley's approach. A priest from Detroit had been among the first patients at the Wisconsin Guest House, and his stay there, in Mooney's words, "did more for him than any of the other institutions I had tried over a period of years." Mooney's considerable psychological sophistication was a factor as well, and so was his not-unrelated respect for professional competence. The Cardinal held Austin Ripley "in deep esteem," according to Chancellor John Donovan, and he gave Ripley the autonomy that Bishop Treacy had denied him. Other than a nonresident chaplain, who visited only at a patient's request, Guest House in the Archdiocese of Detroit was run and staffed by members of the laity.[60]

There were many Catholics in the Archdiocese, apparently, who were less sophisticated and a good deal less tolerant than their Cardinal, at least when it came to the vexing problem of the alcoholic priest. "We encountered many obstacles and set-backs," remembered Frank McGinnis, who with his wife Mary had been active in early efforts to raise money for Guest House in Detroit. "Individuals who were too deeply shocked, who could not believe that there were such men as alcoholic priests; others who said they thought the problem called for sterner disciplinary measures by the church. We encountered one group of Catholic clubmen who said flatly that we should not have such a thing as Guest House in Detroit, because it would be a scandal to the community." Reactions of this sort were not peculiar to Detroit. Cardinal Mooney was warned by a Milwaukee layman in 1954 that his own work on behalf of Guest House had convinced him that it was "a singularly difficult cause for which to raise money." Catholics had been taught to regard the priest as "another Christ," and it was often hard for them to make the distinction between the sacramental powers of the priest — wherein lay his likeness to Christ — and his personality and conduct. (That distinction was often blurred in popular writing about the priesthood.) And devout Catholics, especially, had been deeply affected by the rigorous moralism that formed the larger part of their religious education. Temptation, they were repeatedly told, could be overcome by acts of will and by prayer. Theirs had not been a training that made much allowance for psychological disorders, and some of them, at least, had encountered the same unyielding moralism in the confessional. Small wonder, then, that many Catholics even in the 1950s were disturbed by a therapeutic approach to alcoholism, and particularly to alcoholism among the clergy. And small wonder that many priests, including many alcoholic priests, shared their basic assumptions.[61]

Cardinal Mooney's personal interest in the project helped to overcome some of the initial resistance. Austin Ripley was able to buy a former country estate near the village of Lake Orion in 1955, and Guest House opened on this site in 1956. The Catholics of the Archdiocese, moreover, rather quickly came to be an important source of support for the institution. Auxiliary Bishop John Donovan hosted the first in a series of annual "Bishop's Dinners" to benefit Guest House in 1956. (Successful as that first dinner was — the principal speaker was television's Ed Sullivan — the publicity that preceded it was deliberately vague with regard to the project that was to be benefited.) Cardinal Mooney had also given permission to his clergy to contribute up to $300 a year to Guest House from parish funds, something that his successor encouraged as well. Contributions from this source came to almost $26,000 in 1960, when it was estimated that various individuals and groups in the Archdiocese were providing Guest House with more than $100,000 a year. No other diocese came close to this kind of generosity, although Guest House treated priests from every part of the nation. Aside from perhaps five bishops, Austin Ripley complained in 1967, "we receive very little help indeed from the Hierarchy. And our yearly appeal to the priests of the country produce[s] minimal results." The support that Guest House received in the Archdiocese had largely to do with the willingness of many affluent Catholics to follow their archbishop's lead in charitable matters. Both Mooney and his successor were popular men, and open in their own support of Guest House and its work. But it seems likely too that a growing number of Catholics were coming to an essentially therapeutic understanding of what their parents had called sin.[62]

Guest House rewarded Cardinal Mooney's faith and generosity by being a remarkable success. (A second Guest House was opened in Rochester, Minnesota, in 1969.) A study done in the mid-1970s, which questioned some 400 priests who had attended the Lake Orion and the Rochester facilities, reported that nearly 75 percent of these Guest House "alumni" were abstaining from alcohol. Another 14.6 percent were no longer drinking regularly, but still suffered occasional lapses. Just under 11 percent reported no significant change in their drinking habits despite the Guest House stay. "Guest House offers the most solid and the most hopeful program for the rehabilitation of such priests as can be found anywhere in the United States," Detroit's Archbishop John Dearden wrote in 1962. This was, it seems, indisputably true.[63]

Cardinal Mooney had reason to be proud and hopeful when he lectured to the deacons at St. John's Seminary. If the numbers of the soon-to-be-ordained were not as large as he would have liked, his seminarians were, to all appearances, devout and idealistic. Virtually all of them had come of age in a world that offered them a variety of educational and professional opportunities. Their choice of the priesthood was likely, then, to have been a carefully considered one, and one that entailed a generous vision of the priestly calling. Cardinal Mooney, for his part, was eager to pass on to them his own highly disciplined vision of the priestly life, one that had indeed been embraced by the great majority of priests in the Archdiocese. Their lives ought to be grounded in a regular round of prayer and meditation, he told the deacons. They must be utterly devoted to their work. And they must never forget that they were priests; all their conduct should be guided accordingly. "We are never private characters," he reminded them. "Wherever we are, we stand for the Church."[64]

If the Cardinal was aware that the life he urged on his seminarians was one that a growing number of Americans regarded as narrow and unhealthily repressed, it did not greatly worry him. The priestly life, after all, was meant to be a sign of contradiction. Overt criticism of that life, moreover, came almost exclusively from non-Catholics and generally from a wholly secular perspective. But more and more Catholics, in point of fact, belonged to an affluent world that valued self-expression and fullness of experience a good deal more than it valued the Cardinal's vision of duty and self-denial. The growing rate of attrition at the seminaries of the Archdiocese was almost certainly a reflection of this. At least in retrospect, in short, there looks to have been a worrisome gulf between the values of the seminary and those of many educated Catholics, whose own experience, in turn, reflected important cultural shifts in the world around them. The rapidity and extent of change in the postconciliar American Church surely suggests that this was the case. And the erosion of priestly morale in the 1960s — pervasive as it was — cries out for an explanation that goes beyond vague references to the Second Vatican Council.

13

THE LAITY

The confidence and vitality that marked the American Church in the decades after 1920 were nowhere more apparent than among the laity. More and more Catholics in these years were drawn to a highly disciplined religious practice, with growing numbers of men among the throngs that now went regularly to confession and communion. Interest in nonsacramental devotions increased as well. Here too a growing male presence was apparent, although women continued to dominate this aspect of Catholic religious life. Women were also prominent in the various Catholic organizations that were established or expanded in the years between the First World War and the Second Vatican Council. Those organizations were more numerous and more varied than ever before, making the Church — at least in the more populous dioceses — an important force in the social and political life of many communities. This happened in good part because a growing minority in the Catholic population was well educated and reasonably affluent, able to move with ease in the world beyond the parish. That the Church was able to hold the loyalties and employ the energies of this rising constituency was an apparent sign of health, particularly as it continued to serve the needs of its working-class — and largely ethnic — majority. Only in retrospect is it clear that serious divisons were opening between working-class Catholics and an educated lay elite, between a celibate male clergy and an increasingly restive minority of Catholic women.

Those divisions proved to be of great significance for the American Church: the course of its history since Vatican II has been shaped in important ways by an activist — and disproportionately female — lay minority, educated, articulate, open to change. We will naturally be concerned to trace the evolution of this reform-minded group, which has its principal roots in the Catholic Action movements that were born in the 1930s. But reform-mindedness is not the whole of the story, for the numbers drawn to the more radical forms of Catholic Action were small. We must look too at the essentially conservative devotional life that flourished in these years, at the disciplined sacramental practice of the mass of Catholics, at the many Catholic organizations that reinforced for the laity a hierarchical view of the Church. And we must look at the ethnic parishes, despite the dwindling and aging congregations that were characteristic of most, for a majority of Catholics even in the 1950s were close to the immigrant past. It was a reality known to them through parents and grandparents, and incorporated to some extent in their own beliefs and religious practice. We must, in short, be aware of the diversity that characterized the seemingly monolithic Church in the decades after World War I. And we must avoid examining that Church from an exclusively post-conciliar perspective. For although that Church was in fact a divided one by the 1950s, with an elite among the laity ready for reform, it still possessed a genuine vitality. It was a disciplined and surprisingly cohesive institution whose people appeared to possess a certitude in religious matters that was rare in the Western world by the middle of the twentieth century.

SACRAMENTAL PRACTICE

We have seen that many Catholics in the Diocese had become accustomed to a regular sacramental practice in the early years of the twentieth century. Younger and more assimilated Catholics, especially, were more and more likely to receive communion at least once a month and to go to confession nearly as often. Their example was increasingly emulated in the decades after the First World War, as the mass of Catholics made frequent confession and communion the center of their religious lives. Father Peter Ternes was delighted by the progress he saw in his parish at Marine City, where he and an assistant heard an average of 2,580 confessions per month in 1921 and administered a monthly average of 6,021 communions. (The parish had perhaps 3,000 members in 1921, although its summer population was larger, Marine City being a popular resort.) The happy trend continued in the following year, as Ternes reported in the summer of 1922. "For the past six months we have averaged 2911 confessions and 7144 communions." The growing numbers in the confessional and at the communion rail included a good many men, something that most observers attributed to the work of the Holy Name Society. That society had 270 branches in the Diocese by 1928 — one in nearly every parish and in several of the missions as well — and its monthly "corporate communions" were generally well attended. Men were still the notably less devout sex, however. Men had "souls to save," the St. John Evangelist parish *News* pointed out in 1930, "yet at the communion rail many more women are found than men." But the anonymous author of this hortatory piece had no patience with the pastoral "double standard" that had prevailed in the nineteenth century. "The Church recognizes no distinctions in inviting all Christians to the Sacraments. If a distinction is made in practice, it is unauthorized and harmful."[1]

If the 1920s saw a sizable increase in the number of Catholics going regularly to confession and communion, the Depression years were widely reported to have accelerated the trend. "During the past few months, there has been a great spiritual reawakening amongst the Holy Name men in the city," the *Michigan Catholic* reported in March 1930. "Some parishes are confronted with the prob-

lem of finding accommodations for the large number of men and boys present-
ing themselves for the Holy Name Communion." This reawakening was evidently most visible in the English-speaking parishes, where there had generally
been the least resistance to a reformed sacramental practice. It was English-
speaking parishes that the *Michigan Catholic* singled out for special notice, particularly Visitation and Gesu parishes in Detroit, the former with 950 Holy
Name communions in March of 1930, the latter with standing room only on
the most recent Holy Name Communion Sunday. But the ethnic parishes were
affected too, albeit more gradually. The pastor at Santa Maria (Italian) parish
had found it difficult in the 1920s to get certain of his parishioners into church,
much less to frequent the sacraments. Things were different, however, with the
coming of hard times. "On the spiritual side we noted quite a progress during
the year," he recorded in 1931. "Church attendance has been much better, and
we reached 20,000 Holy Communions." Progress continued throughout the
decade: 25,000 communions were distributed in the parish in 1934, when attendance at Mass was estimated at 1,500 every Sunday. Communions reached
30,000 a year in 1938.[2]

The habits established during the Depression proved to be enduring: all the
evidence indicates that Catholics in the 1940s and the 1950s were more disciplined than ever before when it came to attending Mass and receiving the
sacraments. Not all Catholics were equally disciplined, to be sure. A small minority were extremely devout—daily communicants, many of them—while a
somewhat larger minority received the sacraments infrequently or not at all.
Some were indifferent, others—an unknown number—stayed away from the sacraments because of difficulties with Church teaching on birth control or marriage. And some had been raised in ethnic traditions that placed little emphasis
on frequent reception of the sacraments. When Father Bernard Jarzembowski
arrived in Pontiac in 1939 to take charge of its small Polish parish, he was told
by a neighboring pastor that "the Polish people here are known for not going
to the Sacraments. He was right—they went only twice a year, at Christmas and
Easter. It took me quite a while to change that habit." Father Clement Kern
reported in 1954 that fewer than half of his parishioners at Holy Trinity Church
had made their Easter duty. Those parishioners were poor, many of them recent
immigrants, and the Spanish-speaking among them, especially, were not accustomed to go regularly to Mass. Still, Father Kern did not doubt their fundamentally religious disposition. (There was great enthusiasm in the parish for the
cult of Our Lady of Guadalupe.) And he counted among his parishioners some
notably devout men and women. Father Kern had been able in 1949 to establish
a Nocturnal Adoration Society in his parish, something that presupposed at least
fourteen men willing to devote one night a month to prayer before the Blessed
Sacrament.[3]

The popularity of Nocturnal Adoration Societies in the 1940s and the 1950s
suggests that the clergy had been remarkably successful in their long campaign
to make piety appealing to men. Women might participate in Eucharistic vigils,

but it was traditionally the men of the parish who kept watch during the late night and early morning hours. It was during the 1940s too that the Holy Name Society inaugurated its annual Holy Hour at the University of Detroit Stadium. Women were encouraged to attend, but it was men who took the lead in this public display of Eucharistic devotion. The First Friday Club, organized in the Archdiocese in 1941, was yet another sign that growing numbers of men were willing, even eager, to make a public profession of their faith. Intended primarily for business and professional men, the club asked its members to receive communion on the first Friday of every month, and meet on that same day for lunch and a talk on a Church-related topic. The Detroit group had more than 700 members by 1946. Four additional First Friday Clubs were organized in the Archdiocese between 1948 and 1958.[4]

First Friday Clubs had their roots in the men's retreat movement of the 1920s and the 1930s, a movement promoted by a number of religious orders—the Jesuits chief among them—and one that had important effects on the religious life of many middle-class men. The Jesuits opened their Manresa Retreat House in the Diocese of Detroit in 1926; by 1930 more than 2,300 men were said to have participated in the Ignatian retreats held there each weekend. It was with respect to retreats, indeed, that the clergy had the rare pleasure of commending to Catholic women the example of their men. "Father Cogley urged the women of the city and the diocese to avail themselves of the newly established retreat house for women, Mt. Mary, conducted by the Sisters of Mary Reparatrix," the *Michigan Catholic* reported early in 1930. "He said he hoped to see the women form an organization like the Manresa Retreat League." It did not take the women long to do so: a Laywomen's Retreat League had been organized in the city by the following April. And women quickly proved to be more enthusiastic retreatants than men, at least in the Diocese of Detroit, where more women than men by the early 1930s were making retreats and days of recollection. But the interest in retreats among middle-class men remained strong, and seems to have grown stronger in the years after World War II. "Our Laymen's Retreat work, thank God, has expanded beyond our accommodations at Manresa," a delighted Jesuit told Cardinal Mooney in the spring of 1946. "Each week since January, 1946, we have been blessed with a capacity crowd. And we have not been able to take care of all that apply." It was a rigorous piety that the Jesuits preached at Manresa, and one firmly centered on Eucharistic devotion. As such it seemed reassuringly masculine, and a good many men were apparently grateful for it.[5]

The success that the clergy enjoyed in these years—and the disciplined standards they held up for both men and women—are nicely illustrated by the work of the Catholic Church Extension Society in the Michigan Thumb. This experiment in rural evangelization was launched late in 1923, when Father Thomas Carey, a priest of the Diocese, was sent as pastor to Lapeer. Lapeer was the principal town in what was a heavily rural and mostly Protestant region. Carey's predecessor had been responsible for two mission churches, one of which had Mass twice a month, the other only once. A third mission in the vicinity was visited once a month by a priest from the town of Rochester; two other villages had Mass only in the summer. As for the mostly Hungarian community of Allenton, it was visited "every now and then" by a priest from Detroit. The Church Extension Society plan provided for three assistant priests to be attached to the parish at Lapeer, men who would spend the better part of every week in the various outlying missions. ("They roomed with one of their families," Father Carey reported late in 1924, "and took their meals wherever they happened to be.") Pastor and assistants met once a week at the "mission house" in Lapeer to report on their work and to give each other the encouragement they needed to persevere in this unusually demanding assignment.[6]

For Father Carey and his assistants quickly discovered that the Catholics in and around Lapeer were a thoroughly undisciplined lot, at least when it came to religious practice. A good many failed to attend Mass on Sunday. Attendance in the early months of the experiment had led the priests to conclude that there were about 200 Catholic families in the mission territory; a subsequent census revealed more than 500 families who identified themselves as Catholics. Attendance at Mass on holy days was negligible, and there were no devotions in any of the churches. Nor were those Catholics who came regularly to Mass accustomed to receive the sacraments more than two or three times a year. "The faith of Lapeer seems very cold and unresponsive," Father Carey complained. "I have been informed that it is not uncommon to have no Communions in Lapeer on Sunday." His first Christmas in the parish, however, brought a gratifying crowd to the communion rail. "I suppose Lapeer is a Christmas and Easter parish," he concluded. Father Carey's parishioners knew by then that their pastor held to different standards. "On Sunday Dec. 9," he recorded, "we began the practice of saying a Pater and Ave for the spread of frequent Communion among us."[7]

Carey's assistants were kept busy that first year visiting their parishioners and taking a census in each of the missions. They were inexperienced young priests — one, at least, had just been ordained — and they were shocked by the extent of the religious laxity that they encountered. "Visited Millington[,] the northern frontier[,] in search of stray sheep," Father Rupert Dakoske recorded in a typical weekly report. "Found a family of ten children, not one of whom had received first communion. Terrible! Dragged the Lapeer field again this week — listing 7 more families. The work is endless. Children by the dozens have been without instruction." Father Thomas Gorman, "on loan" from the Diocese of Wichita, discovered "scores" of Catholic families in a mission whose records listed only twenty-four. "Many had so fallen into indifference that they were sending their children to Protestant Sunday schools." And there proved to be a larger immigrant population in the region than anyone had anticipated. The neglected Hungarians at Allenton were known to be a problem, but Father James Grady, from the Diocese of Boise, was startled to find "a number of [P]olish families . . . who have not been to the sacraments for some time due to the fact that they cannot go to confession in [E]nglish." The difficulties uncovered in the various missions seemed at times to be overwhelming. "The early days of the experiment had many discouragements," Father Carey admitted. "It is not easy to arouse people from spiritual torpor and undo the neglect of many years standing."[8]

For all the discouragements, however, the Lapeer experiment proved eventually to be a fine success. But that success was accomplished only through hard work. The priests visited lukewarm families again and again, organized and taught catechism classes in each of the missions, encouraged "First Friday" Mass and communion, and inaugurated weekly devotions. They organized Holy Name Societies in their missions, and urged the women to join the Order of Martha. And they preached doggedly on the need for a disciplined religious practice: the good Catholic not only went regularly to Mass, he attended devotions and received the sacraments frequently. "After all the Communion Table is the test of faith," according to Father Carey, who was especially insistent in his advocacy of frequent communion. "I read the riot act on attending evening services, with good results," he recorded in 1925. "The number of Communions on an 'off' Sunday was increased by the same method. . . . I took the high Mass in Imlay [City] Sunday, and exhorted them to renewed fervor."[9]

Progress toward a more disciplined practice was slow at first, and it was uneven. It was hard to get people to weekday masses, even on holy days of obligation, and farmers were not easily persuaded that religion came before their crops. "Attendance at Mass very small due to the fact that the cold and rain we have had held them back from their farm work," a discouraged Father Grady reported from Allenton. "Do what you may these people consider their farm first and Mass and church second. They keep their children home from instructions for the same purpose." In every congregation, moreover, the men were less willing than the women to come regularly to Mass and the sacraments. It was the women on whom the missions depended for much of their financial support, a substantial portion of which came from bazaars and dinners and picnics. This led to trouble in at least one mission. "The Marthas of Imlay City are becoming busybodies," Father Carey complained late in 1925. "They think they hold the pastor's place and regard the priest in charge as their assistant. To remedy this condition, I am going to pay all bills from parish revenue instead of asking them to assume the bills."[10]

But despite disappointments and setbacks, the success of the work in Lapeer became more and more apparent. The various missions were able to support their priests by 1925, when the Church Extension Society withdrew its subsidy. Attendance at Sunday masses increased from about 46,000 in 1924 to more than 83,000 in 1927. Attendance at Sunday evening devotions nearly trebled in this same period, rising to more than 21,000 annually. The number of communions increased even more dramatically. Lapeer and its missions had never had more than 3,000 communions a year, Father Carey estimated late in 1923. The total for 1924, however, was nearly 9,000. And that number rose to more than 14,000 in 1925, to more than 22,000 in 1926, to just over 31,000 in 1927. (The Lapeer experiment came to an end in 1928, when the three assistants were made pastors of the principal missions, all of which had long since built rectories.) Father

Rupert Dakoske, who replaced Father Carey in Lapeer in 1928, was still not satisfied with the spiritual condition of the parish. "Lapeer has little devotion to the Sacred Heart," he complained in December, when only seventeen parishioners attended the first Friday Mass. Nor was he pleased by the showing on the feast of the Immaculate Conception, when 214 people were in church. "The big stick must be wielded again. Lapeer's attitude on attending holyday Masses is most discouraging." But in fact the progress at Lapeer had been little short of remarkable. Father Dakoske and his companions had accomplished in four years what some nineteenth-century priests had not been able to achieve in a lifetime.[11]

DEVOTIONAL LIFE

The emphasis on frequent communion, so much a part of Catholic life after about 1910, helped to make Eucharistic devotion widely popular among the laity. We have seen that a quickening of Eucharistic devotion was evident in the Diocese by the end of the nineteenth century, as Catholics in ever-growing numbers were attracted to Forty Hours devotions, to Holy Hours, and to Eucharistic processions. Devotions of this sort became even more widespread in the years after World War I, and among the devout there was growing interest in what might be called ascetic variations on the Eucharistic theme. "Perpetual adoration"—a devotion normally practiced only among the enclosed religious orders—was more and more appealing to an elite among the laity. Students at St. Mary's College, for example, inaugurated a daily Eucharistic vigil at the school in the spring of 1925. Nearly 250 students were involved by the autumn of that year, many more than were needed to ensure that there would be at least two "adorers" in the chapel throughout the daylight hours. St. Aloysius Church in downtown Detroit began daily exposition of the Eucharist in 1932. "For some time . . . we have had exposition every Thursday," the pastor explained, "and this has drawn a large number of worshippers to the church throughout the day. In every large city there is some downtown church where our Divine Lord in the Eucharist is enthroned publicly throughout the day on every week day to receive the homage and petitions of the faithful and we felt that Detroit should not lag in this respect." The popularity of "nocturnal adoration" societies during and after the Second World War has already been noted. Some of these were begun in response to the war. The pastor at St. Patrick's parish in Wyandotte requested permission in 1945 "to have the Blessed Sacrament exposed for the veneration of all of us one day a week, as is done in St. Gregory Church, Detroit, to invoke divine protection upon our boys." But the popularity of Eucharistic vigils was even greater in the postwar decade.[12]

Marian devotion has traditionally been integral to Catholic religious life, but it too seems to have acquired a new fervor—and certainly a greater visibility—in the decades after World War I. A perpetual novena to Our Lady of Lourdes at Detroit's St. Mary's Church was drawing large crowds by the early 1920s, as re-

ports of miraculous cures at the grotto in the church began to circulate locally.
The Redemptorist Fathers announced a perpetual novena to Our Lady of Perpetual Help at Holy Redeemer Church in 1922, a devotion that was soon attracting "clients" from all parts of Detroit and even beyond. "Thirteen separate
services are held every Tuesday," the *Michigan Catholic* reported in 1933, "and,
according to the Very Rev. Joseph A. Elenz, C.SS.R., the average attendance
is 18,000 men, women and children." Perpetual Help devotions had by this time
been inaugurated in at least forty other churches in the Diocese, and were proving to be immensely popular. "More than 4000 downtown workers" attended
the first Perpetual Help novena at St. Aloysius Church in 1933. Reports from
other parishes too indicate an intense and growing interest in the devotion.[13]

Marian devotions were widely popular in the 1920s, but the Depression saw
the advent of an even more fervent Marian piety. It was a piety that was, for
the most part, explicitly promoted as an antidote to hard times. The Jesuits, for
example, announced a novena to Our Lady of Victory "for relief of the unemployed," a novena that proved to be so successful that it was repeated less than
four months later. (The first novena, held in the summer of 1931, had, according
to the *Michigan Catholic,* "attracted large numbers of non-Catholics.") Other religious orders and many diocesan clergy too offered devotions for the relief of
the needy, and as a consequence the number and variety of Marian devotions
increased markedly. New to the Diocese were devotion to Our Lady of LaSalette,
to Our Lady of the Miraculous Medal, and to Our Lady of Sorrows. This last
devotion, inaugurated by the Servite Fathers in Chicago in 1937, was drawing
nearly 70,000 people a week to Our Lady of Sorrows Church in that city by
1938. The novena never attained such proportions in Detroit, where it was begun at St. John Berchman's Church in the spring of 1938, but the crowds were
still impressive. "More than 4000 persons are attending weekly," the *Michigan
Catholic* reported early in 1939. The Miraculous Medal novena at St. Aloysius
Church drew considerably larger crowds, perhaps because the novena was introduced there at the depths of the Depression, in 1933. "Over 30,000 followers"
had been enrolled in the Miraculous Medal Confraternity attached to the Church
by 1934. The devotion was sufficiently popular that the Dominicans announced
a perpetual novena to Our Lady of the Miraculous Medal at St. Dominic's
Church in Detroit in 1936.[14]

Marian devotion can hardly be said to have brought a speedy end to the Depression. But Bishop Gallagher was not alone in his conviction that such devotion "greatly assisted large numbers of people in bearing the trials of the panic."
It also seems to have provided a powerful symbol of Catholic identity in what
was in many ways a militantly secular decade. It was in 1931 that the Sodality
Union of the Diocese held the first of many annual Marian days at the University of Detroit Stadium, promoting it — in fine contemporary fashion — as a
"May Day rally." "Prayers were offered for the persecuted youth of Russia,"
the *Michigan Catholic* reported, "and for American youth threatened by neo-
paganism." That first rally was attended by some 10,000 students from various

Catholic high schools and colleges, and the crowd at the rally in 1932 was apparently just as large. Attendance did decline over the rest of the decade, although an Assumption Day rally in honor of Mary, Queen of Peace, was inaugurated in 1935 and reportedly drew 15,000 persons in 1939. (Held at Detroit's Belle Isle Park, this was a more public display of Marian devotion than the University of Detroit rally.) The Marian Day was revived, however, in 1946, and for twenty years thereafter was a major event in the life of Catholic Detroit. "There will be the living Rosary, public singing, bands, floats and the crowning of Our Blessed Mother," the St. Margaret Mary parish *News* announced in 1952, urging "all Catholics" to attend the forthcoming rally. "And also there will be brought the miraculous Statue of Our Lady from Cap de la Madelain in Canada."[15]

Marian piety was a dominant feature of Catholic life in the Archdiocese throughout the 1950s. The great novenas of the 1930s were a thing of the past, to be sure, but this is explained in good part by the rapid suburbanization of Detroit. Those massive novenas were very much the product of a densely populated city. The suburban parish, however, generally offered regular Marian devotions, and there was a new emphasis in the postwar years on the importance of Marian piety for family life. Families and even groups of neighbors were urged to say the Rosary together, and the example of Mary, the self-effacing servant of God, was held up to Catholic women as the means to personal fulfillment and family harmony. And Marian devotion was still possessed of its traditional antiradicalism. Marian prayer was widely presented as the only effective antidote to Communist subversion. Devotion to Our Lady of Fatima—a cult approved by the papacy in 1942—spread throughout the Archdiocese in the postwar years, and prayers for the "conversion of Russia" were said in many parishes after Mass, in accordance with the instructions purportedly given at Fatima in 1917. (There was a Eucharistic as well as a Marian dimension to the Fatima cult, with devotees urged to receive communion on the first Saturday of the month and to spend at least an hour a week adoring the Blessed Sacrament.) "The strong arm of Communism will wither and die before the prayers of healthy souls," a typical Holy Name Society announcement ran in 1948, asking members to offer their monthly communion "in honor of Our Lady of the conversion of Russia. The just will grow in Grace, RUSSIA WILL BE CONVERTED, and there will be peace."[16]

The popularity of Marian devotion in the 1940s and the 1950s was so extensive that it is hard—at first glance, at least—to understand why Marian piety declined so precipitously after Vatican II. But there are several plausible reasons. The council itself was of critical importance: Mary was honored there, and in most subsequent theological writing, in the context of Christ and the Church and as a preeminent model of the Christian life. Her mediatory role, while not denied, was nonetheless deemphasized. Marian piety, moreover, was doubtless hurt in the 1960s by its conservative political overtones. These were hardly congruent with the mood of the decade, nor with the rise of Catholic feminism. And the excesses of Marian devotion in the immediate pre-conciliar decades very nearly ensured that it would cease to be an authentic expression of faith for an ever-larger number of educated Catholics. For a time it seemed that many of these Catholics delighted in the extravagant sentimentality of Marian piety and even in the more extreme pronouncements of Mary's most devoted clients. There was a certain satisfaction in offending Protestant sensibilities; Catholics, at least, had kept alive a vivid sense of the supernatural. But this essentially defensive mentality had, in the nature of things, a limited life.

The cults of several major saints were well established in the Diocese by the turn of the century, as we have already seen. St. Anne's Church in Detroit was an important local shrine by 1900 — it became something of a regional shrine after 1910 — and numerous cures were attributed over the years to the St. Anne relic that was venerated there. In the 1920s, however, and especially during the Depression, a number of new cults were popularized in the Diocese, and interest in devotion of this sort seems to have intensified, at least as that interest can be measured by attendance at novenas and other public devotions. This happened in part because of the growing number of religious orders in the Diocese. Each of these orders promoted devotion at least to its own saints, and often to other saints as well. The Servite Fathers, for example, introduced the cult of St. Philip Benizi to the Diocese in 1928, with a novena at St. John Berchman's Church. ("He has been invoked successfully throughout the world since his death for relief of those afflicted with spiritual, mental or physical ills," the pastor told Detroiters, aware that this major figure in the history of the Servite Order was virtually unknown to them.) But the religious orders were successful in their efforts mainly because a large and responsive audience already existed. Devotion to the saints, like devotion to the Virgin, was a mode of religious expression cherished by many Catholics, both for its emotionalism and its overt instrumentalism. And it was a traditionally female mode of piety, drawing now on a population of women who moved with greater ease about the city than their mothers and grandmothers had done.[17]

Interest in such well-established local cults as those of St. Anne and St. Anthony remained strong in the 1920s. Miraculous cures were attributed as well to the St. Maurus devotion inaugurated at St. Bonaventure's monastery in the early part of the decade. Here, however, the object of devotion was not only this rather obscure saint, but the Capuchin priest who preached at the services and performed the blessing of the sick. Father Solanus Casey, the porter at St. Bonaventure's from 1924 until 1945, was believed by many Detroiters to possess extraordinary powers as an intercessor, even as a healer, and his prayers were credited with scores of cures and other near-miraculous favors. "So large is the attendance" at the St. Maurus devotions, the *Michigan Catholic* reported in 1933, "that special cars are run on the Charlevoix line of the D[etroit] S[treet] R[ailway]."[18]

The single most popular cult of the 1920s, however, was probably that of St. Theresa of Lisieux, canonized in 1925. Bishop Gallagher inaugurated a novena in her honor at the cathedral in that same year, declaring that "God in His Infinite Wisdom has undoubtedly raised up St. Therese to be our guiding star through the dangers with which the social order of our present day surrounds us." The devotions drew unprecedented crowds. Ten thousand persons were said to have attended the first of the Cathedral novenas in 1926; as many as twenty thousand were reported at the final novena of the year. A St. Theresa chapel, affiliated with the cathedral, was opened on Parsons Street in 1928, and was thereafter the principal site in the Diocese of devotion to the Little Flower, as St. Theresa was generally known. But parish devotions to the saint spread rapidly as well, not only in the Diocese of Detroit but throughout the country, for St. Theresa proved to be an evocative symbol of a Catholicism that was at once militant and tenderly sentimental. Father Coughlin, as alert to the public mood as any man alive, began his radio career as the priest of the "Little Flower."[19]

The Depression simply intensified an already lively interest in the cult of the saints. Novena services throughout Detroit in the early 1930s were reported to be more widely attended than ever before, and new cults too gained favor among the laity. Devotion to St. Jude, for example, was inaugurated in 1930 at St. Mary Magdalen Church in the industrial suburb of Melvindale, evidently in response to popular demand. The Dominican Fathers were the next to offer regular devotions to this "saint of the impossible," whose popularity in the Diocese seemed to wax as economic conditions grew more desperate. The Dominicans were the most enterprising of the various orders in the 1930s when it came to initiating and promoting devotions. Aside from St. Jude novenas, St. Dominic's Church in Detroit offered regular novenas to Our Lady of Perpetual Help, Our Lady of the Miraculous Medal, St. Anne, and Blessed Martin de Porres and, periodically, devotions to St. Christopher, in conjunction with which Detroit was introduced to the practice of blessing automobiles. This latter practice proved to be extremely popular. It was adopted in 1934 by the Benedictines at St. Scholastica's Church in Detroit, and eventually spread throughout the Diocese.[20]

The other religious orders were not far behind the Dominicans when it came to promoting devotions, often referring in their appeals to the economic tragedy that was unfolding around them. The Capuchins, for example, were offering their St. Anthony novena in the fall of 1931 "for relief from the present industrial depression." (The Domincans were more detailed in a 1935 announcement of a novena to the Souls in Purgatory, which was to be "offered up especially to obtain employment, for financial assistance, for help in paying debts and for sale of property.") The various orders apparently had great success with their devotional offerings, at least for the duration of hard times. The Jesuits' annual novena to St. Francis Xavier was so popular in the early 1930s that extra services were added both at the downtown Jesuit church and at Gesu Church in fashionable northwest Detroit.[21]

Many of the diocesan clergy too were actively promoting novenas in these years, resentful, perhaps, of the highly public role that the religious orders had come to play in Catholic devotional life. St. John Evangelist parish offered three novenas a week in 1935: one in honor of Our Lady of Perpetual Help, one in honor of St. Jude, one in honor of the Little Flower. And at St. John's, as at so many other churches, "large crowds" were said to be in attendance. A bewildered and increasingly desperate Catholic population was peculiarly susceptible in these years to the appeal of the novena, hoping not only for special favors from God but for relief from the oppressive burden of guilt and shame that so often came with unemployment. (The presence of larger-than-usual numbers of men at the various novenas was repeatedly noted.) There was an apocalyptic feel to Detroit in the early 1930s, and it was manifested in religion more immediately and more intensely than it was in politics, at least among a sizable portion of the Catholic population. The editor of the *Michigan Catholic* was disturbed to discover, late in 1932, that "repeated rumors" were circulating in Detroit about mysterious appearances in and near the city of a figure said to resemble St. Joseph. "These rumors state in general that the man predicts the end of the depression and suddenly disappears." It was "foolish to spread such rumors," the editor advised his readers, "as they do no good. It is better to spend the time in praying to St. Joseph for his assistance in this crisis."[22]

The cult of the saints continued to be an integral part of Catholic devotional life in the 1940s and the 1950s. But attendance at the various novenas declined sharply after the late 1930s, as devotion to the saints became more and more the property of an older—and mostly female—minority. Certain of the cults, indeed, acquired a formidable clerical opposition, for devotion to the more obscure saints, especially, was widely believed to encourage essentially superstitious practices. "At different times we have found in the church mimeographed explanations of the Novena to St. Martha," Father Emmet Hannick told his parishioners at St. Rose Church in 1956. "Now we have nothing against this good and holy woman but I do not think that the emphasis is placed on the prayers but on the days, the lighting of the candle and the leaving of a copy in the church." Such novenas were "not to be recommended," Father Hannick told his flock. "Let your prayer be more Christocentric."[23]

At the Chancery too there was growing concern after the late 1930s about the proliferation of cults and devotions. Archbishop Mooney advised his clergy during a 1939 retreat that he did not want them to advertise novenas, and over the course of his episcopate he took other steps to make devotion to the saints a less public part of Catholic religious life. Novenas and masses at outdoor shrines were prohibited, as were devotional processions in the streets, although these had occasionally been allowed in the Gallagher years. The Chancery in 1940 requested pastors to provide authenticating documents for the various relics belonging to their churches, and this caused at least a few of these hallowed objects to be retired from devotional duty. Nor was Mooney personally associated with any particular saint's cult, although his predecessor, as we have seen, was prominently identified with devotion to St. Theresa of Lisieux. It was Marian devotion that Mooney was known to favor—provided, of course, that this devotion remained within proper theological bounds. And it was with respect to Marian devotion—and Eucharistic devotion too—that Mooney endorsed an occasional public manifestation of Catholic piety.[24]

LITURGICAL REFORM

The sentimentality of Catholic devotionalism and its often excessively instrumental emphasis had critics among the laity as well as the clergy. By the 1930s, a small but growing minority of Catholics in the Diocese were identified with what is usually called the "liturgical movement," the primary goal of which was the education of the laity to a deeper understanding of the Mass and a more active participation in it. The movement's adherents came mainly from the various Catholic Action groups that proliferated in the 1930s — from groups like the Catholic Evidence Guild, the Catholic Worker, the revitalized sodalities. It won converts too in the burgeoning ranks of the Catholic colleges, where courses on the liturgy were increasingly popular in the 1930s and after. (St. Mary's College — Marygrove College after 1927 — inaugurated its first course on the liturgy in the early 1920s.) It was a Christocentric piety that the liturgical movement preached, and one centered firmly on the sacraments. As such it was a logical extension of the movement to promote frequent communion — a movement, it will be remembered, that was initiated in Rome. And in the 1940s, the liturgical movement received what was in effect a papal blessing. Encyclicals issued by Pius XII in 1943 and 1947 endorsed a vision of the Church and its public prayer that was very much the vision on which the liturgical movement was founded. The Church was preeminently the Mystical Body of Christ, the Pope wrote, and the faithful, as members of the Mystical Body, should participate actively in its corporate worship. Especially should they be educated to take a knowledgeable part in the celebration of the Mass.[25]

The liturgical movement made only the most limited progress in the Archdiocese of Detroit before the 1950s. The various Catholic Action groups that were active there were indeed a force for liturgical reform, but their numbers were small and their efforts confined to a handful of parishes. And the priests of the Archdiocese were, on the whole, indifferent to the reforming impulse. Only two or three parishes are known to have experimented in the 1930s with what was called the "dialogue Mass," where the congregation recited the responses normally assigned to the altar boys or the choir. (Because it increased the laity's participation in the liturgy, the dialogue Mass was a reform much favored by the liturgical movement.) Cardinal Mooney, moreover, proved to be exceedingly cautious when it came to liturgical reform. Chancery rules in the 1940s confined dialogue masses to weekdays; only in 1951 did Mooney approve a Sunday dialogue Mass — at the request of the Young Ladies' Sodality at Sacred Heart parish in Dearborn — and that was a Mass that began at 6:00 A.M. "If you find that there is any complaint from others attending the Mass," the pastor was told, "then the practice should be discontinued."[26]

Mooney was even reluctant to permit his priests to say Mass in the evening, a reform that was increasingly urged in the 1950s as a means of bringing Catholics more frequently to Mass and the sacraments. (The evening Mass was also envisioned as a properly Christocentric alternative to the usual evening devotions.) Mooney did grant permission in the early 1950s for evening masses on holy days of obligation, and in 1956 he told his clergy that they might say a weekly evening Mass in Lent. These latter were apparently popular. "It has been the source of untold good to the people," the pastor at Holy Redeemer parish told the Cardinal, "and the increase in the number of Confessions and Holy Communions is amazing." But Mooney was never willing to go beyond these limited concessions.[27]

By the 1950s, however, the balance was shifting in favor of reform. As conservative a pope as Pius XII saw the need for limited changes in liturgical practice. The regulations governing the precommunion fast were liberalized by Roman decree in 1955, and further liberalized in 1957. The liturgy of Holy Week was substantially revised in 1956, with the principal services of the week now held in the late afternoon or evening. It was pastoral concern that motivated these changes, each of which was intended to make it easier for the laity to go to Mass and receive communion. But these limited changes inevitably intensified pressure for more far-reaching reform. "This major reform should cause both clergy and laity to realize that the liturgy is not rigid, is not set for all time, but is always 'becoming,'" *Commonweal* editorialized late in 1955 with regard to the Holy Week reforms. "Perennially vital itself, the outward forms of gesture, rite and ceremony are subject to constant revision."[28]

By the 1950s the liturgical movement had gained a good many converts among the clergy and — no less important — among the various women's teaching orders. The principal texts of the movement were more and more likely to be taught in Catholic colleges and in all but the most conservative seminaries, and its tenets to be incorporated into high school religion classes. The movement had a thoroughly legitimate aura by the 1950s; its clerical proponents, indeed, were widely admired as model priests — fervent, articulate, socially aware. Father Leo Trese was a local case in point. An early convert to the liturgical movement, he used his persuasive pen to promote that movement among the clergy and an educated lay elite, frequently drawing their attention to what he saw as the parlous spiritual state of American Catholicism. (Good reformer that he was, his gloomy assessments were entirely sincere.) "Any pastor who has made a conscientious census of his parish is aware of the appalling leakage in the Church," he wrote in *Commonweal* in 1945. "In almost any city parish, the absent brethren (baptized Catholics) amount to 50% of those present at Mass on Sunday."

The principal causes of this "appalling leakage" — and of the "sterility" that Trese thought afflicted parish life — were the "over-large parish" and the passive role assigned to the laity at Mass. Those enormous parishes would clearly be a fact of life for a long time to come, although, Trese argued, "as new parishes are established the mistakes of the past can be avoided." But reform of the liturgy was eminently possible, and Trese urged not only the introduction of the dialogue Mass in every parish, but the dialogue Mass with all but the canon in the vernacular. "Even though he use a Missal and follow the English translation," he wrote of the layman, "he still feels a looker-on, as though a restrictive circle had been drawn about the altar. . . . It was not so in the early Church." Trese's was hardly the typical view; probably a majority of his fellow priests in the Archdiocese were indifferent to the debate over liturgical reform. But voices like his helped to generate a sense that the Church, for all its evident prosperity, was lacking in spiritual vitality, that pastoral concern required a major reform of the liturgy.[29]

Lay adherents of the litugical movement were nearly always well educated and thoroughly assimilated Catholics, and the number of such Catholics grew apace in the 1950s. The potential constituency for liturgical reform was growing then, although the number of lay people who were active in the liturgical movement was still quite small. But there were signs of quickening interest. St. Leo's parish in Detroit was a model of liturgical reform in the mid-1950s, when members of The Grail—an international Catholic women's organization—worked with the pastor to acclimate parishioners to the dialogue Mass. The nearby Grail center "designed cards for the people to use for sung and recited Mass containing the prayers, music and explanations," a contemporary account recorded. "About ten parishes throughout the city have begun to use the same cards as St. Leo's with good response."[30]

The Grail was the most active lay organization locally in the 1950s when it came to liturgical reform, something that was central to its vision of a revivified Catholic culture. Aside from the work at St. Leo's, the group sponsored workshops on "living with the Church in the home," where mothers were taught to celebrate Church feasts in a properly liturgical way. The enthusiastic response to these workshops reflected in part the self-conscious domesticity of the decade. But it suggests too that Grail women were not alone in their hunger for a less anonymous, more active experience of worship. That hunger characterized a large and articulate and extremely influential lay minority in the years after Vatican II. It is post-conciliar developments, of course, that have caused the work of The Grail, and of the liturgical movement as a whole, to loom so large in the history of the American Church.[31]

"MISSION CONSCIOUSNESS"

The American Church was a mission church in the eyes of Rome until 1908, and subject to the governance of the Sacred Congregation for the Propagation of the Faith. By the early twentieth century, of course, the Church in much of the nation was well developed institutionally and producing priests and Sisters of its own, usually in numbers adequate to care for all but the most recent immigrants. But the Church in the United States was still preoccupied with its own internal development. Efforts to interest American Catholics in the foreign missions were, for the most part, limited and sporadic. Certainly this was true in the Diocese of Detroit, where the IHM Sisters were very nearly alone, in the early twentieth century, in their tradition of support for the missions. Most local Catholics imagined the Church in largely, if not exclusively, parochial terms.

With the close of the First World War, however, came a surge of interest in the foreign missions that affected Catholics in all but the most sparsely settled portions of the country. This was caused in part by the war itself, which widened the world for Catholics as it did for other Americans. But the growth of what contemporaries liked to call "mission consciousness" was more fundamentally a product of the size and wealth of the postwar Church, and of assimilation. It was a product too of the ebullient idealism that characterized the confident Catholicism of the era at its best. It did not seem preposterous then to anticipate the conversion of the world, or to assume that the agency of that conversion would be a relative handful of missionary priests and Sisters.[32]

"Mission consciousness" in the Diocese of Detroit was assiduously cultivated, in the decades after World War I, in the parochial schools, in the Catholic colleges, and at Sacred Heart Seminary—and generally with gratifying results. Young Catholics, especially those from devout families, were peculiarly susceptible to the appeal of the missions, with their intimations of the exotic and their associations with self-sacrificing heroism. "The missionary effort has colored all the school enterprises," the *Michigan Catholic* reported of St. Mary's Academy in Monroe in the fall of 1920, when various activities had raised some $500 for the foreign missions. "Besides these class activities much has been done by individual effort. One pupil in St. Mary's Hall earned enough to buy [i.e., sponsor the baptism of] two Chinese babies. Another pupil counted and packed six thousand cancelled stamps besides a large quantity of tinfoil. Nearly all of the girls have kept self-denial banks." St. Mary's Academy was in the charge of the IHM Sisters, who were well known locally for their "mission consciousness." Virtually all of their schools in the 1920s were engaged in mission support activities, with the younger pupils especially showing great enthusiasm for the "ransoming" of "pagan babies." (A baptized infant was a ransomed soul in the world of mission support.) It was the IHM schools that the Chancery had in mind as models when in 1930 it urged the various teaching orders to enroll all of their pupils in the Society for the Propagation of the Faith. "The prayers of the society will become a daily custom in our classrooms," the *Michigan Catholic* assured its readers.[33]

The appeal of the missions for young Catholics is nicely demonstrated by the growth of the Catholic Students' Mission Crusade in the 1920s. Organized in 1918 as a federation of student mission-support societies, the Crusade had grown by 1931 to "at least" 500,000 members, representing "over 25,000 schools and colleges." Some sixty-five schools and colleges in the Diocese of Detroit had active Crusade units in that same year, the largest and most vigorous apparently being those at Sacred Heart Seminary, at Marygrove College, and at the University of Detroit. Their principal work was raising money for the missions. (The seminary unit was sending $1,000 a year by the mid-1920s to Father Sylvester Healy in Peking.) But the more active "Crusaders" undertook as well to convert their fellow students to an ardent "mission consciousness." They spoke regularly at the various parochial schools, organized "sectional meetings" and an annual mission rally, and attended national conventions.[34]

Many of the more active Crusaders were girls and young women; in this respect the Mission Crusade was similar to other Catholic Action movements of
the day. And in the Crusade, as in many of those other movements, young
women found themselves in decidedly unorthodox roles: speaking publicly before mixed audiences, exercising leadership in an organization that included
males as well as females, interpreting the Gospel—and in ways that few priests
had thought, or dared, to do. A growing interest in the "Negro apostolate" led
the Mission Crusade in the 1930s to progressively bolder stands against racial
prejudice, particularly as it was manifested in Catholic institutions. "The problem is not what to do with the Black man, so much as what to do with the white
man," Margaret Murray of All Saints School in Detroit told her fellow Crusaders in 1935. "Remember, 100,000 Detroit Negroes look to us for a demonstration
of the charity of Christ." A brave voice of conscience, she typified a growing elite
of devout and outspoken laywomen, whose spiritual progeny are today a major
force for change in the American Church.[35]

Mission support work was not, of course, confined to the schools and colleges
of the Diocese. Many parish societies too were deeply interested in the missions,
and contributed generously to their support. So did a growing number of individuals. It was in the 1920s that the annual "Mission Sunday" collection was first
taken up in the Diocese, and that the Society for the Propagation of the Faith
was organized locally. The society reported receipts of just under $9,500 in 1927,
its first full year of existence; these had risen to nearly $80,000 by 1929. The
Depression naturally led to a steep decline in financial support for the missions,
but the Society was surprisingly successful nonetheless in spreading the gospel
of mission consciousness. The nearly $44,500 that was collected for the missions
in 1935 was testimony to this, and so was the $75,500 that was collected in 1938.
The return of prosperity in the 1940s meant steadily increasing contributions
to the society from throughout the Archdiocese. (More than $500,000 was col-
lected in 1947; more than $1,000,000 in 1955.) The parochial schools too were
inspired to a reinvigorated program of mission support in the early 1940s. The
IHM Sisters were delighted to report that the students in their various schools
had in 1943 "ransomed" no fewer than 2,580 pagan babies.[36]

The ransoming of pagan babies is today the stuff of Catholic nostalgia; the
practice did not long survive the Second Vatican Council. The great age of the
missions has come to an end as well, the consequence, in good part, of the end
of the Western colonial empires and the rise of Third World nationalism. But
more than these political realities are involved. The waning "mission consciousness" of the post-conciliar Church is a measure of how distant many Catholics
are today from the easy confidence of the immediate pre-conciliar decades. They
inhabit a less innocent world, one that no longer seems ripe for the Christian
harvest. And that has meant, at least for many educated Catholics, that the dogmatic certainties of the pre-conciliar decades have been critically undermined.
Such Catholics are unable to imagine the Church in the triumphalist terms that
came naturally to their parents and grandparents. Nor do conditions today per-

mit the unself-conscious emphasis on proselytization that was once the hallmark of missionary activity. The "language of example"—to borrow from Dietrich Bonhoeffer—has necessarily come to play a significantly greater role in the work of evangelization. This too has had its effects on the educated laity, reinforcing for many of them a view of the Church that is more communitarian than hierarchical, that accords greater weight to right conduct than to doctrine.

RELIGIOUS EDUCATION

The Gallagher-Mooney years saw a significant expansion in the work of religious education. A larger proportion of Catholic children than ever before were enrolled in the parochial schools; these had the benefit of daily religious instruction. And there were more and more catechetical classes available to those Catholic children whose parents had, despite repeated warnings from the pulpit, sent them to the public schools. By the close of the Mooney years, nearly 100,000 children in the Archdiocese were enrolled in the weekly classes sponsored by the Confraternity of Christian Doctrine. No organization in the Archdiocese had a more remarkable record of growth.

The religious training of children from the public schools was, in the Gallagher years, largely conducted by the laity. (As we have already seen, it was priests and religious who dominated the work under Cardinal Mooney.) The Catholic Instruction League (CIL), whose early history has previously been discussed, expanded at an impressive rate in the Gallagher years, when it was the principal source of teachers—and of initiative and direction—in the task of educating the offspring of what were generally agreed to be indifferent Catholic parents. There were thirty-eight CIL centers in the Diocese by 1931, where some 200 teachers taught weekly classes for more than 4,300 youngsters. The number of centers had grown to seventy by 1937—these were located mainly in and around Detroit—and the number of teachers to nearly 400. Most gratifying of all, the number of children under instruction by 1937 exceeded 13,500—more than treble the number enrolled just six years earlier.[37]

The expansion of the CIL in the 1930s was evidently spurred by the militant Catholicism that characterized this troubled decade. (The CIL had grown slowly in the 1920s.) More and more Catholics, it seems, were drawn to the missionary fervor that had always characterized the group's leadership, and particularly its director, Josephine Brownson. For in Miss Brownson's eyes, the work of the CIL entailed far more than the religious training of children; it meant the spiritual reclamation of entire families through a program of regular home visits. Mrs. Helen Collum was a model of what Miss Brownson hoped for from her teachers: she opened a catechetical center on her own initiative in 1934, and inaugurated a sewing class for the mothers of her pupils. (Mrs. Collum worked out of an abandoned house on Detroit's northwest side, which she had christened "St. Martin's of the Wilderness.") Her achievements were hardly typical; the work of the CIL was attended by at least as much discouragement as success, and many of its teachers were too uncertain of their own abilities to undertake projects on their own. But Mrs. Collum's evident desire to respond in a direct and personal way to the crisis of the age was characteristic of many women who joined the CIL in the 1930s. And it was very much a woman's organization, both in its leadership and in its ranks. It was cause for pleased public comment in 1936 that "several male teachers" had recently joined the group.[38]

Bishop Gallagher was throughout his episcopate a supporter of the CIL, although his interest in the group appears to have grown with the coming of the Depression. It had long been evident that the parochial schools of the Diocese could not accommodate every Catholic youngster, and evident too that many Catholic parents would not send their children to parochial schools. The CIL was necessary, then, if a substantial minority of Catholic children were not to be lost to the faith. Its evident necessity, coupled with Bishop Gallagher's public gestures of approval, eventually won for the CIL a substantial base of clerical support. "The majority of the clergy of the Detroit area" had endorsed the work of the group by 1930, at least according to the *Michigan Catholic*. Bishop Gallagher was even willing to endorse the work of the lay catechist as a good thing in itself, and not merely an expedient required by a shortage of priests and teaching Sisters. "The lay catechist performs a service particularly fitted for him and him alone," he assured the Diocese in 1933, announcing the formation of a fund-raising auxiliary to the CIL. "Enjoying a more intimate association with his fellow man in the world, he can bring the Gospel message to many whom it would otherwise never reach."[39]

What lay catechists could not do, however, at least in the Diocese of Detroit, was marshal a sufficient number of willing workers. "It is conservatively estimated that some 40,000 children of Catholic parents in the metropolitan area are without religious instruction of any kind," the *Michigan Catholic* reported in 1935, when, after several years of rapid expansion, some 12,000 youngsters were enrolled in CIL classes. Further expansion of the CIL, moreover, was likely to be slow: both funds and volunteers were in critically short supply, according to Josephine Brownson, who was still administering the program without benefit of an office or a secretary. To be sure, the CIL was no longer alone in its pioneering work. Several of the larger teaching orders in the Diocese were also engaged by the 1930s in the religious education of children from the public schools. Theirs had initially been a rural apostolate: a growing number of country pastors, unable to establish parish schools, turned in the 1920s and the 1930s to summer catechetical programs taught by women religious. The Diocese of Detroit had been in the forefront of this development, which eventually affected dioceses nationwide. This rural ministry ultimately led, for many teaching orders, to an involvement in urban catechetical work. The Felician Sisters of the Livonia (formerly Detroit) Province, for example, were teaching in eight after-school catechetical centers by 1937, with an enrollment of more than 600 pupils.[40]

It was the advent of Archbishop Edward Mooney in Detroit, however, that brought the teaching orders into after-school catechetics in a major way. Mooney was troubled by the large number of Catholic children who were without any religious instruction, and troubled too that the CIL was under only the most nominal clerical supervision. His response to these problems was characteristically vigorous: he announced the formation of the Confraternity of Christian Doctrine (CCD) in the Archdiocese early in 1938, appointed Father—later Monsignor—John Ryan as its director, and channeled generous sums of money into the infant program. As a consequence, the program grew rapidly: more than 37,000 children were enrolled by the early months of 1940, more than 53,000 by 1945. There were 1,356 teachers in the program in that latter year, the majority of whom were Sisters. (Only 26 percent of the teachers in 1945 were members of the laity. Not until 1960 were lay teachers again in the majority.) "Each of the teaching Communities of the Archdiocese contributed their services to the work of the Confraternity," Father Ryan was able to boast in 1944, and a growing number of priests and seminarians were working as teachers as well. By the late 1950s, theology students from the Archdiocese were expected to devote at least two summers to CCD work. The Archdiocese even produced its own catechetical texts after 1940, these based on the course of study that was followed in the parochial schools. The new texts signified perhaps more poignantly than any other development just how completely the Catholic Instruction League had been superceded by the CCD. For Josephine Brownsons's texts, on which CIL classes had been based, were widely recognized for their narrative flair and acute pedagogical insight. The new Detroit texts did borrow liberally from Brownson's various books, but they were less vivid, less imaginative, more starkly focused on doctrine.[41]

The CCD in the Archdiocese continued its remarkable growth in the years after World War II, notwithstanding the upsurge in parochial school enrollments that occurred in the same period. More than 65,000 children were enrolled in CCD classes in the fall of 1955; nearly 110,000 were enrolled in the fall of 1960. A portion of this growth must be credited to Cardinal Mooney, who ensured that the CCD was well funded and well publicized throughout the Archdiocese. Credit rests as well with the various religious orders, whose members assumed the burden of CCD work at a time when they were under greater pressure than ever before to upgrade their own academic training. Those orders included, by the late 1940s, three that were exclusively devoted to home visiting and catechetical work. The Victory Noll Sisters entered the Archdiocese for this purpose in 1941, the Mission Helpers of the Sacred Heart in 1943. And in 1949, Msgr. John Ryan helped to found the Home Visitors of Mary, an order devoted primarily to catechetical and convert work among Detroit's black population.[42]

Even the much-maligned parents of Catholic children in the public schools deserve some credit for growth in the ranks of the CCD. For they were more willing than ever before to send their children regularly for religious instruction. The growth of the CCD, then, is yet another indication of the remarkable discipline that prevailed, at least in religious matters, among the Catholic laity of the 1950s. Ironically, however, the flourishing CCD was widely regarded in these years as a sign of growing religious indifference. The various diocesan directors of the CCD in Michigan agreed in 1965 that the "attitude in Michigan toward CCD among the Catholic community is poor." Raised to believe "that every Catholic child should be in a Catholic school," many of the laity—and many priests and religious too—were convinced that "those who were not were in some way 'poor' Catholics. CCD for them has always been a second-rate program."[43]

To a historian, of course, the number of "poor" Catholics in the postwar years is almost bound to look astonishingly small, at least insofar as attendance at Mass is a measure of religious devotion. "It is not our people who miss Mass on Sunday, refuse the sacraments and vote the Communist ticket," San Antonio's Auxiliary Bishop Stephen Leven reminded his European confreres at Vatican II. "We have not lost the working class. They are the foundation and support of the Church." Certainly this was true in Detroit, where 74 percent of working-class Catholics, according to a 1961 study, claimed to attend Mass every Sunday. Their affluent coreligionists were even more devout: 82 percent of the middle-class Catholic sample in this same study reported weekly Mass attendance. And the study seemed to indicate a bright future for the Church: third-generation Catholics were more devout than their parents and grandparents had been. (Some 82 percent of working-class Catholics in the third generation reported weekly attendance at Mass.) Assimilation and prosperity evidently led to a more disciplined religious practice, at least in the American context.[44]

Few persons look at the world around them through the eyes of the historian or, for that matter, through the eyes of the sociologist. And there were many Catholics in the postwar years who believed that their grandparents' generation had possessed a more ardent faith than their own, and a greater loyalty to the Church and its teachings. There were those, indeed, who saw a growing spiritual malaise in the 1950s—a looming crisis of faith and discipline. The issue of contraception had become by then a major pastoral problem, and one that promised to grow progressively more severe. The expansion of the Catholic middle class in the postwar years, moreover, swelled the number of critical voices in the Church. (About one-third of Detroit's Catholic population in 1958 was occupationally middle class.) The products of Catholic colleges, many of them, these loyal and idealistic critics looked to the Church not only for the spiritual succor that their grandparents had found, but for a degree of aesthetic and intellectual refinement that had never characterized the Church in America. Talk of reform in the Church—of its liturgy, its art, its intellectual life—was perhaps more widespread in the 1950s than had been the case since the end of the nineteenth century. This was a sign of health, to be sure. But it was also a harbinger of change.

ETHNICITY AND PARISH GOVERNMENT

Reformers were a small minority in the Catholic population, however much it seems today that the future has belonged to them. They were substantially outnumbered in the 1950s by self-consciously ethnic Catholics, most of them working-class, whose vision of the church was largely defined by the boundaries of the ethnic parish. Not that the Catholic population as a whole by the 1950s could be described as anything but assimilated: the vast majority of Catholics in the Archdiocese had been born and raised in the United States. And there were few ethnic parishes that had not passed the peak of their numbers and vitality. But the ethnics were still a formidable presence in Detroit, and one that the Chancery typically accommodated with considerable generosity. They stood, moreover, for the world from which nearly every Catholic had come, even those who seemed to be most thoroughly American.

Of the older ethnic populations in the Archdiocese, there was relatively little evidence by the 1950s. The German parishes had largely abandoned their distinctive liturgies in the 1920s, if not before. St. Elizabeth's parish on Detroit's East Side was apparently the last of them to give up the weekly German sermon, a change announced in 1925. "Only about one-quarter of our people have a sufficient knowledge of the German language to follow the sermon intelligently," the pastor explained "and of these only about one-quarter attend that Mass." The Irish parishes lost their ethnic character at an even earlier date, for Irish identity in Detroit proved, on the whole, to be remarkably transitory. "We have not here a single parish where the people are distinctively of Irish descent," Cardinal Mooney pointed out in 1948. Catholics of French descent were a largely assimilated population too by the 1920s. When St. Joachim's Church was destroyed by fire in 1934, its pastor doubted the wisdom of rebuilding this monument to the French-Canadian presence in Detroit. "It is evident most of the French people prefer to attend their nearest church," he told the Chancery. "They take little interest in their national church, as well as their national societies. They even change their names to be identified as American and not Canadian." (The church was rebuilt, however. Its pastor estimated in 1948 that some 165 families were still contributing to its support.) Even the Poles, probably the most cohesive of Detroit's ethnic populations, had spawned a sizable American contingent by the 1920s. More and more of them were members of "mixed" territorial parishes. And even in the Polish parishes, the American-born generations were generally more fluent in English than in Polish, and looked at the world and at the Church with other than immigrant eyes. "The Michigan Catholic would like a live correspondent for the Polish parishes," the paper announced in 1920. "We have several thousand readers of the younger generation of Poles and we want to give them special notes."[45]

Immigration from Poland did continue into the 1920s; there were nine Polish-language parishes established in the Diocese in that decade. And there were flourishing Polish parishes in the Archdiocese even in the 1950s. "Every high mass . . . is sung in Polish," an unhappy new member of SS. Peter and Paul's (west side) parish complained in 1947. "When the priest intones the Gloria, the choir responds with a Polish hymn, etc. . . . In eight months I have not heard the schedule of masses read once . . . in English." Among the older ethnic populations too a tiny but tenacious minority kept alive the language and at least remnants of the tradition. Our Lady of Sorrows parish, founded in 1884 to serve the Belgians of Detroit, still needed a Flemish-speaking priest in the 1950s. Cardinal Mooney assigned the parish to the Congregation of the Immaculate Heart of Mary in 1953, for this largely Belgian order had the added advantage of an interest in convert work among American blacks. The Belgian church in Detroit was by this time surrounded by a large and growing black community.[46]

It was principally the more recent arrivals, however, that the Chancery had in mind in the Gallagher-Mooney years when it gave thought to the ethnics. We have already seen that Detroit sustained an unusually heavy influx of foreign immigrants in the 1920s, and that the Diocese became more ethnically diverse in that decade than it had ever been before. By far the largest immigrant population in the 1920s was the Poles (They had been the single largest foreign-language group in Detroit even in 1910.) There was a sizable Italian colony as well, although Detroit's Italian population was, by the standards of eastern industrial cities, relatively small. And there were surprisingly large numbers of Lithuanians and Hungarian Catholics of the Latin rite. It was the smaller ethnic groups, however, that gave Catholic Detroit its extraordinary diversity. By 1930 parishes had been founded for Slovenians, Croatians, and Slovaks—the last must be distinguished from the two Czech parishes in Detroit—as well as for Oriental rite Catholics from Russia, from the Ukraine, from Romania and Hungary. There was a Latin rite parish for Syrians, and a parish for Syrians of the Melchite rite. There was a Maltese parish, and one for Mexicans. (Detroit's Maltese population was the largest of any American city by the early 1920s.) A parish for the handful of Armenian Catholics in the Archdiocese was established in 1947, and one for the somewhat larger population of Chaldeans was founded in 1948.[47]

Many of these parishes existed on the margins of the local Church: isolated by language from the larger Catholic community, their more conservative members clung to an intensely parochial, almost tribal, view of the world. Father Michael Cefai, longtime pastor of the Maltese parish in Detroit, often warned his congregation against mixed marriages, by which he meant marriages to Catholics who were not of Maltese birth or descent. (This according to one of his parishioners in 1938.) Father Cefai was waging a losing battle: "I know quite a number of [M]altese that they are happily married and their wives are [P]olish," the disgruntled parishioner reported. By 1938, indeed, a good many Maltese in Detroit had joined English-language parishes. The local Maltese population had assimilated relatively quickly, and many of its members lived far away from St. Paul's (Maltese) Church. But more than distance was involved, at least for a portion of those members, who left St. Paul's because it was a badly factionalized congregation. The tribal quality of the immigrant parish gave it an admirable vitality, but it also led to conflict.[48]

There were, in fact, few new ethnic parishes in the Gallagher-Mooney years that were not divided into warring factions. The causes of division had sometimes to do with political or regional animosities imported from the homeland: the Croatian congregation in Detroit had always been small, according to long-time members in 1953, because the more assimilated element did not want "to listen to Balkan politics. . . . The Archdiocese may even look around and find that in Detroit [are] sprung up two Croatian Churches one a Bapitist and the other a Pentecostal. They are former [C]atholic members driven away by the continuous bellowing of Balkan leaders in our church." A more fundamental cause of conflict, however, was the determination of many parish members to control the financial and administrative aspects of parish life, something that almost invariably led to difficulties with the pastor and often led to rivalries within the congregation. Only in the Italian parishes and in the Mexican parish were there apparently no conflicts over matters of this sort. (At least there is no archival evidence of such conflict.) Both Italians and Mexicans, it is worth noting, were widely reported to have a fairly tenuous connection to the institutional Church.[49]

The newest immigrants in the Archdiocese, then, kept alive the tradition of lay control that had once prevailed in large numbers of parishes. They often elected their church committeemen, although diocesan regulations forbade this (The Chancery under both Gallagher and Mooney generally ignored these breaches of the rules, but Bishop Gallagher was moved, in 1927, to reprove a Lithuanian pastor whose parishioners assembled four times a year for parish meetings. "It is hard to understand just for what purpose these meetings are called. Certainly in a parish like . . . St. George's such great and important matters do not come up every three months that would necessitate a parish meeting to settle them.") The Oriental rite congregations, which were largely independent of Chancery control, all seem to have had a democratic mode of parish government, at least in their early years. The by-laws of St. John the Baptist Ukrainian Church of the Byzantine rite, drawn up in 1918, gave women the right to vote in parish elections. And when the members of the Romanian parish of the Byzantine rite assembled in 1924 for their annual meeting, they elected not only committeemen but a cantor as well. Electing the cantor, who was paid a small salary, was apparently seen as a logical extension of the congregation's control over parish finances. They had for some years been accustomed to vote on the amount of their pastor's salary.[50]

The elected church committee was generally a powerful one, both in the Oriental rite parishes and those of the Latin rite. In some cases, indeed, the pastor had no authority at all over parish finances. The pastor at St. Anthony's (Lithuanian) parish, according to Cardinal Mooney in 1955, "is the meekest of men and is entirely dominated by the church committee—even to the extent that he cannot sign or counter sign a check. Years ago I tried to encourage him to face up to the situation and really take charge of the parish, but he begged off on the plea that it would only cause serious trouble and alienate some of his stiff-necked parishioners from the Church." The committee at Holy Cross (Hungarian) parish would not allow the pastor there to claim the Christmas and

Easter collections as his own, although this was the custom in virtually every other parish in the Diocese. It was not until 1938, apparently, that the committee relented on the matter. Anxious to assert their right to unimpeded control of parish finances and perhaps determined that their pastor should not live sumptuously among his working-class constituents, the committee had held out against some notably strong-willed priests "When naturally I prepared to take over the Christmas and Easter Collections," Father Louis Kovacs recalled in 1927, "such a vehement protest arose in its wake, which took the proportions of a veritable revolution, so rather than create a scandal, I abandoned it, and have not made another effort even at this Easter." Father Kovacs, who served in the parish from 1921 until his death in 1927, was not a timid or retiring man; he seems, on the contrary, to have been a forceful personality. But neither he nor his bishop were prepared to do battle with the committee.[51]

Conflicts such as these were less frequent by the 1920s than they had been earlier. And by the 1940s, only a handful of ethnic parishes continued to elect their committees — committees that were generally less powerful than they once had been. With assimilation, it seems, the world grew larger, and passions were less intensely focused on the parish. Even the once-turbulent Polish parishes were by the 1940s relatively easy to manage. The only difficulty he experienced with his committeemen, the pastor at St. Hyacinth Church told the Chancery in 1948, "is to have them attend the meetings." By the late 1940s, indeed, there were priests who thought that the laity might profitably be encouraged to take a greater interest in parish affairs. St. John the Evangelist parish in Detroit experimented in 1947 and 1948 with what was called a "parish council": its twenty members, ten men and ten women, were chosen by the various church societies and seem to have worked mainly at organizing social events. Father Leo Trese, gentle reformer that he was, encouraged his fellow priests in 1955 to give their people an occasional advisory voice in parish matters. "The Church by its nature is hierarchical, and there is no place in its government for what we commonly term democracy," he wrote. "Yet there seems no good reason why the people of the parish should not be given some voice in the expenditure of their own money." Father Trese had in mind the distribution of questionnaires when a "major improvement" was contemplated or a "notable change in parish policy" was in the offing. "Many successful parish administrators have tried this very thing and have discovered that people who have some small voice in the administration of their parish will in the end take a much greater interest in the physical as well as the spiritual welfare of their parish." It was logic like this that led, in the years after Vatican II, to widespread support, among reform-minded bishops and priests, for the notion of elected parish councils.[52]

LAY ORGANIZATIONS

Catholic organizations flourished mightily in the Gallagher-Mooney years. Established groups like the Holy Name Society and the League of Catholic

Women grew substantially, and achieved an impressive degree of organizational sophistication. New groups appeared too, some of them the products of a politically conscious and theologically literate lay elite — an elite that proved, over the long term, to have an influence on the Catholic community all out of proportion to its numbers. In the shorter term, the thriving organizational life of these years helped to strengthen, in a multiethnic population, a common sense of Catholic identity. And it helped to make Catholics a formidable political presence in Detroit.

The growth of men's organizations was perhaps the most impressive aspect of the period, given the traditional reluctance of men to take an active part in parish life. Nearly all of the fraternal societies that had thrived in the late nineteenth century were in decline by the 1920s — the Knights of Columbus was the single exception — but other men's organizations had by then embarked on a period of unprecedented growth and vigor. The St. Vincent de Paul Society, for example, had 72 parish conferences in the Diocese by 1929 — up from 30 in 1915 — and 101 parish conferences by 1935. The work of the society, moreover, had been considerably expanded. Its members continued their "friendly visiting" among the poor, and its Child Caring Department continued to provide surrogate care, and occasionally to arrange adoptions, for children from troubled Catholic families. But by the 1930s the society was also responsible for two children's camps, for an extensive program of children's medical care — this through the good offices of the Child Caring Department — and for a Mission School Fund, by means of which more than 2,000 children annually were supported in the parochial schools. By the 1930s, it is true, the work of the society was increasingly dwarfed by the growing resources of public welfare programs. And as early as the 1940s, the Chancery was troubled by a lack of social welfare expertise in the administration of the Child Caring Department. (That department was absorbed by the children's division of a reorganized Catholic Charities in 1957.) Still, for all its modest resources, the St. Vincent de Paul Society in the Gallagher-Mooney years must be accounted a success. Largely under lay auspices, it had inaugurated and sustained a variety of needed social services for children, and brought a surprisingly large number of men into a demanding lay apostolate.[53]

The St. Vincent de Paul Society was not a mass organization; its much-expanded work in the 1930s was carried out by a membership that never exceeded one thousand. It was the Holy Name Society, as we have seen, that was meant to incorporate the mass of Catholic men, and in the decades after 1920 it had remarkable success in doing so. The Holy Name Society was said to have had a membership in the Diocese of "approximately 100,000 men and youths" by 1928. Not all of these were active members, of course. But in the winter of 1932, it was "conservatively estimated" that 75,000 men and boys had received communion on the society's annual "Father and Son Sunday." Holy Name membership apparently declined during the Second World War, at the close of which Archbishop Mooney announced a campaign to bring more than 100,000 new members into the society. Membership is said to have trebled under the aggressive leadership of Father Joseph Dion, who was archdiocesan director of the society from 1948 until his death in 1956. It was under Father Dion's auspices that a national convention of the Holy Name Society was held in Detroit in 1951. That convention was the occasion of a massive Holy Name parade — these had been rare events in Detroit — and a Holy Hour at Briggs' Stadium that was attended by a crowd of nearly 90,000.[54]

The growing size of the Holy Name Society and its increasingly well articulated organization made it a natural vehicle for Catholic political action. The Detroit Diocesan Union of Holy Name Societies made its first appearance on an explicitly political stage in 1920, sponsoring three huge rallies against a proposed state law that would have closed every private grammar school in the state of Michigan. The cause of the private schools was easily sustained at the polls in November, but the Holy Name leadership locally seems to have acquired an enduring taste for politics. The final quarterly meeting of the Diocesan Union in 1920 went on record as opposing even limited federal aid to education — this in response to the ill-fated Smith-Towner bill then being debated in the Congress. The annual convention of the Diocesan Union in 1926, attended by some 5,000 delegates, "voiced vociferous approval of attacks on birth control" and protested religious persecution in Mexico. It was the Diocesan Union that in 1933 orchestrated a campaign in Detroit against diplomatic recognition of the Soviet Union, although to no avail. Recognition was announced later that same year by President Franklin Roosevelt. The Holy Name leadership was unhappy too with Roosevelt's Mexican policy, urging the president in 1935 to break diplomatic ties with that country unless religious persecution there ceased "forthwith." And the Holy Name Society was among the groups on which the local chapter of the "Keep the Spanish Embargo Committee" depended in 1939 for its petition campaign against revision of the Neutrality Act. The society's fervent anti-Communism was perhaps even more pronounced in the decade after 1945. Its militant rhetoric in these years reflected, and perhaps contributed to, a general Catholic drift to the right.[55]

The Holy Name Society was not explicitly a political organization; its principal purposes were religious. Indeed, Cardinal Mooney increasingly looked to the Archdiocesan Council of Catholic Men, reorganized in the early 1940s, when he wished to bring Catholic pressure to bear on issues like birth control legislation and federal aid to education. Nor is it clear how fully the society's pronouncements reflected Catholic opinion. Catholic voters generally seem to have been more concerned about economic issues than issues of foreign policy, however much the latter might affect the fortunes of the Church. But groups like the Holy Name Society surely helped to create at least the appearance of Catholic political solidarity. (That Mayor, later Governor, Frank Murphy had begun his career in Detroit by working closely with the Holy Name Society may have enhanced the group's political credibility locally.) Catholics were not, in point of fact, as politically homogeneous a group as they once had been. But a good many Americans in the Gallagher-Mooney years thought otherwise.

Despite its many achievements, the Holy Name Society never quite fulfilled the hopes of its leaders, who were, on the whole, a dedicated and extraordinarily devout group of laymen. Young men were apparently hard to recruit to the group, although a diocesan organization of Junior Holy Name Societies was formed in 1921. And it was always difficult to bring a majority of parish men to the monthly corporate communion. Significantly, perhaps, complaints on this score seem to have grown after 1945. Father Norbert Chateau was typical of many priests in the Archdiocese when he chided the men of St. Rose parish in 1953 for preferring to receive communion on their own rather than with the Holy Name Society. There was apparently considerable resistance to the clerically monitored piety that the society sponsored. And there seems to have been a growing resistance, coming perhaps in part from wives, to the society's idealization of sex-segregated worship. That idealization fit neatly with the values of a celibate clergy, and it had made practical sense when men were a mostly marginal population in the Church. But conditions had changed by the 1950s. The very success of the Holy Name Society in bringing men to a more disciplined religious practice might be said to have been critical to its ultimate demise.[56]

If young men were not much drawn to the Holy Name Society, they were found in unprecedented numbers by the 1930s in Church-sponsored social and athletic organizations. For it was in the 1930s that fears about delinquency and youthful radicalism caused the Chancery to make "youth work" a priority for the clergy. Many parishes, of course, were already sponsoring athletic and social programs for their young men, programs that dated, in some cases, from the late nineteenth century. But there were still many pastors who had not been converted to the gospel of "muscular Christianity." "Less than 50% of the parishes [in Detroit] are carrying on recreational activity among their young people," the Bureau of Catholic Welfare pointed out in 1930. "It is the director's thought that this may account for the vast number of Catholic children who come to the attention of the court in their desire to seek recreational outlets."[57]

Worries about delinquency in the Catholic population had caused the Holy Name Society in 1921 to embark on a "Big Brother" program in Detroit. (The Holy Name "Big Brothers" worked individually with young offenders in their parishes.) The program was evidently a modest one in the 1920s, and by its nature incapable of reaching large numbers of boys. Partly to supplement that program, and certainly in response to the devastating rise in unemployment among the young, the Holy Name Society in 1933 inaugurated the Catholic Men's Athletic Association of Detroit (CMAA). Sport was widely thought to be a powerful antidote to delinquency, and Church-sponsored sport to be a means of ensuring that young men were not lost to religion. Every participant in the CMAA was required to belong to a parish organization, and to receive communion at least nine times a year.[58]

Detroit's Holy Name men were by no means alone in their efforts to combat delinquency and incipient radicalism by means of sport and religion. Chicago's Auxiliary Bishop Bernard Sheil drew admiring comment nationwide when he launched a Catholic Youth Organization (CYO) in his Archdiocese in 1930. The Chicago CYO was soon sponsoring a variety of athletic and social events for young men in their late teens and early twenties, depending especially on boxing to bring working-class boys off the streets and into the various parish centers. Certain Detroit priests had apparently been thinking very much like Bishop Sheil: Annunciation and Holy Redeemer parishes had large boxing programs in the early 1930s. And Bishop Gallagher, like many of his confreres, eventually followed Shiel's example. He announced the formation of a Catholic Youth Organization in Detroit in 1935. Detroit's CYO, the bishop directed, was to absorb the programs of the Big Brothers and of the Catholic Men's Athletic Association. And it was to expand the work of these admirable organizations: to promote additional social and athletic activities for youths between the ages of eighteen and twenty-five, and to extend the work of Catholic Scouting among their younger brothers. "If we don't take care of the Catholic boys they will drift into indifferentism or even communism," Gallagher warned his Diocese in 1936. "We find the communists especially eager to interest the youth, and the revolutions in Russia, Spain and even Mexico were led by youths."[59]

The CYO in Detroit developed much as it had done in Chicago, although a good deal more slowly. (A financially troubled Chancery largely accounts for this.) Boxing quickly proved to be the most popular — and the most profitable — of CYO sports. It was the annual boxing tourney, in Detroit as in Chicago, that did more than anything else to publicize the CYO. Ninety-eight parishes sponsored CYO boxing programs in 1937; softball, the next most popular sport, was played by teams from forty-eight parishes. (Basketball, tennis, and bowling were the other CYO offerings that year.) More than 12,000 boys and young men were involved in CYO activities in 1937, a number that increased in the following year, when the first CYO sports teams for girls were begun. By 1939 the program was sufficiently well established that its leaders were willing to make certain religious demands of participants. "Membership in a parish society that encourages reception of the sacraments, has been set down as a prerequisite for eligibility for CYO softball this season," the *Michigan Catholic* announced in the spring.[60]

The CYO also gave impetus to the Catholic Scouting movement in Detroit. Bishop Gallagher had given his blessing to that movement in 1919 — "on the condition that the boys belong to the Junior Holy Name Society and that the Scoutmaster be a Catholic" — and precisely because he was worried about delinquency among the young. Even with Chancery approval, however, the Catholic Scouting movement grew slowly: "there are (in metropolitan Detroit) 350 non-Catholic troops and only 25 Catholic troops," the Holy Name Society announced in 1930. "Many Catholic boys belong to troops sponsored by non-Catholic churches and organizations." The Depression had prompted the Holy Name leadership to a quickened interest in Catholic Scouting, and they were instrumental in the early 1930s in promoting the movement in Detroit. Bishop Gallagher apparently shared their view, for he made Scouting a major program of the CYO in 1935, when there were said to be forty-one Catholic Boy Scout troops in and around Detroit. By 1939, that number had risen to sixty-seven.[61]

The CYO expanded enormously after the early 1940s. Well-equipped community centers were built to supplement the work of the parish-based programs, and young priests came to their first assignments expecting to be much involved in CYO activities. The importance of sports in securing the loyalty of young men to the Church was seldom questioned in these years, nor would the most conservative Catholics have challenged the legitimacy of Catholic Scouting. (The movement still had many critics in the 1920s, who believed that the Scouts were so thoroughly imbued with Protestant values that no troop could ever be a truly Catholic organization. Scouting placed excessive emphasis on the "natural virtues," one critic wrote to the *Michigan Catholic,* and ignored "the spiritual virtues — faith, humility, piety, penance, etc." It made for too much independence in the young, and removed them at too early an age from the influence of the home.) Episcopal support of the CYO had helped to silence any lingering critics; perhaps the program's evident success had this effect as well. It was hard to quarrel with an organization that kept young men by the tens of thousands within the orbit of the Church. By the standards of the late nineteenth century, indeed, the achievements of the CYO were nothing short of remarkable. Boys and young men had been integrated into parish life to an extent that only the most optimistic fin de siècle reformers had thought possible.[62]

For all the greater presence of boys and men in parish life, however, it was the exceptional parish where women were not a majority of the most active members. The Altar Guild, the Christian Mothers, the Rosary Society — these were still, in most parishes, the principal sources of extra revenue and volunteer labor. On the diocesan level too, laywomen continued to outnumber men as active members of Catholic organizations. The League of Catholic Women, for example, had a much smaller membership than the Holy Name Society, but a much larger corps of members willing and able to devote themselves to the work of the organization.

That work was especially impressive in the prosperous 1920s. The league continued to offer a variety of social and educational services at its Weinman Settlement on Detroit's near east side. (There were Mexicans as well as Syrians in the Weinman English classes by 1920.) It opened a second settlement house, St. Anne's Community House in Hamtramck, in the spring of 1920, and a third in the spring of 1921. This was St. Rita's Community House, located in Detroit's St. Augustine's parish, a section of the city housing "26 different nationalities . . . with large families, the major portion with no social or religious life" — at least according to league investigators. Like St. Anne's Community House, St. Rita's sponsored a variety of classes and athletic activities, regular social events, and a flourishing Sunday school. It was, in addition, the site of a public clinic for mothers and young children.[63]

The league also expanded its services for young working women, who were drawn to Detroit in record numbers by the employment boom of the 1920s. There was a dormitory at St. Anne's Community House for "young women employed in the factory district," and by 1921 a "League Home" had been opened in Pontiac for this same constituency. "Rowena House" and "Watson Club," intended for young women employed in stores and offices, were opened in Detroit not long thereafter. And the league's eight-story Activities Building, completed in 1928, housed a Residence Club for working women. The league's leaders had long regarded working women on their own as an especially vulnerable population. This was perhaps an indication of a nascent feminism on their part, for it suggests a tendency to see the world in terms of male power and female victims. In any event, the league's concerns on this score had led by 1926 to a new kind of "woman-serving" venture—the establishment of the Madeleine Sophie Barat Home, "a protectorate for girls," where adolescents with a history of delinquency were given academic, vocational, and religious training.[64]

A nascent feminism was surely evident in the league's many educational activities. The advent of full suffrage for women occasioned a reinvigorated program of political education early in 1920. This effort was partly aimed at mobilizing the Catholic women's vote for the upcoming referendum on the status of private schools in Michigan. But it was aimed too at making league members informed and active citizens. "A grave responsibility rests on women," a league spokeswoman pointed out in 1920, "and they should make it a matter of conscience to use the means placed in their hands to bring about a better political condition in our city and country." To this end, the league had organized a civics class for women at its downtown clubhouse, one meant to supplement the forums it regularly sponsored on issues of the day. A class in "social service" had been organized under league auspices by 1921. "This course will consist of practical talks and discussions calculated to be of profit to the volunteers in social service and will serve as a preparation to any one who may wish to take it up as a profession."[65]

Many league members, of course, were indifferent to the political concerns that animated their leaders. Parish units of the league were often more devoted to cards and sociability than to politics and social service. Partly because of this, league membership was badly eroded in the early years of the Depression: the league had only about 2,500 members in 1935—down from some 12,500—and had been unable to pay the interest on its Activities Building mortgage since 1933. But the importance of the league was always greater than its numbers. Its committed members were a talented and articulate group, and their much-publicized example had helped to legitimate an expanded role in politics and social welfare work for Catholic women. (The organization of the Polish Activities League in 1923 brought a similar influence to bear on Detroit's Polish-American community. Largely the creation of Clara Swieczkowska, the Polish Activities League founded St. Elizabeth Community House in 1923, and eventually assumed responsibility for St. Anne's Community House in Hamtramck.)

And the League of Catholic Women did indeed recover from its mid-Depression doldrums. It opened a fourth settlement house early in 1939, this one located in the heart of Detroit's black community. St. Peter Claver Community Center meant that the league had joined that handful of Catholics in the late 1930s who believed that the Church had a role to play in the troubled realm of race relations.[66]

The establishment in 1939 of the Archdiocesan Council of Catholic Women was meant to provide a means by which every member of a Catholic women's organization could turn her hand to social reform and to public defense of the Church. (Diocesan councils of Catholic women and of Catholic men had been urged on the American bishops by the National Catholic Welfare Conference since 1920. They were federations of existing parish organizations, and intended both for educational and for political purposes.) The women's council in Detroit, like its male counterpart, was not well organized until the late 1940s, despite Cardinal Mooney's interest in the enterprise. But by 1950, both councils were playing an active role in Catholic religious life and, increasingly, in politics. The men's council was probably the better known, for it sponsored several radio programs locally and had inaugurated a "May Day Demonstration of Faith" in 1947. The work of the women's council was less conspicuous: it promoted programs in "family life education," was active in a series of local campaigns against "indecent literature," and tried—via speakers and a newsletter—to alert Catholic women to political developments that bore on the Church. (These concerned issues as diverse as contraception and the fate of displaced persons after World War II.) Both councils had been essentially the creation of the Chancery, and both seem, at least through the 1950s, to have operated under a more than usually vigilant clerical supervision. But neither group could have accomplished the work that it did without skilled and devoted lay leadership. The councils were a measure of the increasing sophistication of Catholic organizational life, and of growth in the ranks of the educated laity.[67]

The work of the archdiocesan councils in the 1940s and the 1950s was regarded at the Chancery as the most exemplary sort of "Catholic Action," a term first heard by many Americans in the early years of the Depression. Catholic Action was generally understood to call for a more fervent religious practice on the part of the laity, for careful study of Catholic doctrine and Catholic social principles, and for a deeper involvement of the laity in Catholic organizations and in defense of the Church. (All of this was to be carried out, according to Pius XI, under strict episcopal supervision.) The papal call to Catholic Action had been elicited primarily by the beleaguered state of the Church in Europe, and did not initially cause much stir in the United States. But the Depression brought a sense of beleaguerment to the American Church as well. Fearful of Communism and troubled by a growing public sentiment in favor of contraception, many bishops and priests in the early 1930s urged a more militant Catholicism on the laity. And there were many Catholics, most of them young and relatively well educated, who saw in the crisis of the 1930s a summons to Christian social action. Eager to do battle for Catholic truth, they responded generously to clerical initiatives and, increasingly, embarked on campaigns of their own.

The call to Catholic Action in the 1930s gave rise to a number of new organizations in Detroit, and in many other dioceses as well. It also led to a more aggressive stance on the part of many existing Catholic organizations. In Detroit, at least, it was students who were drawn in the largest numbers to the various Catholic Action movements. High school and college sodalities enjoyed a widespread revival in the Diocese, the consequence, in part, of a nationwide sodality revival led by Father Daniel Lord, SJ. These reinvigorated sodalities were just as devoted to the sanctification of their members as sodalities had always been, but Father Lord preached Catholic Action too, particularly after the onset of the Depression. (It was in 1931 that Father Lord inaugurated his Summer Schools of Catholic Action.) Father Lord's sodalists were especially encouraged to study the liturgy of the Church and its social doctrines, for true Catholic Action, as every sodalist knew, was the fruit of a deep spirituality and a clear understanding of papal teaching. Indeed the "study club" was a staple of Catholic Action movements in every part of the country. A Federation of Catholic Study Clubs had been formed in the Diocese of Detroit by 1935, and the "study club movement," as it was known locally, enjoyed a further surge of growth in the late 1930s under the patronage of Archbishop Mooney. It was under Mooney's auspices too that a more overtly political phase of Catholic Action was inaugurated in Detroit. A Catholic Worker House was opened in the city late in 1937, the Detroit chapter of the Association of Catholic Trade Unionists was organized in 1938, and a chapter of the Catholic Interracial Council was formed in Detroit in 1942, after an apparently abortive attempt at organization in 1934.[68]

In Detroit, as in most large dioceses, Catholic Action in the 1930s included an enormous range of activities. The most visible, at least in the first half of the decade, was a highly publicized campaign against "obscene movies," a campaign led by the *Michigan Catholic* and given strong support by the newly formed Detroit Council of Catholic Organizations. Detroit was not unusual in this regard. The American bishops had long complained about the sexual content of many films and their seeming celebration of criminality and violence. Nor was this an exclusively Catholic issue. The Detroit Federation of Women's Clubs, overwhelmingly Protestant, launched a "campaign against salacious motion pictures" in 1933, one that encouraged Detroiters to boycott offensive movies. The boycott was also the weapon most favored by the Catholic bishops, and in 1934 they agreed to establish a nationwide "Legion of Decency," by means of which the laity could be mobilized to boycott films that failed to conform to Catholic standards. Catholics in the Diocese of Detroit were introduced to the legion in the spring of 1934, when "all adults and children of movie age" were asked to sign a statement promising to boycott "objectionable films." (It was initially up to the Detroit Council of Catholic Organizations to determine which movies were offensive.) By the close of 1934, the bishops had agreed to observe an annual Legion of Decency Sunday, when Catholics would recite the legion pledge at Mass. They had also taken steps to establish a single national list of films, rated according to their acceptability for Catholic audiences.[69]

The Legion of Decency was greeted locally by a good deal of Protestant praise. "The Roman Catholic Church is setting a noble example by organizing a 'Legion of Decency,'" a Baptist congregation in Ann Arbor resolved, hoping that their own denomination would "take an equally aggressive stand." Catholic lay leaders were enthusiastic too: the legion was a long step toward needed reform, they believed, and one that, happily, avoided government censorship. But Catholic Action in Detroit was not much distinguished in the 1930s by a concern for civil liberties. The Detroit Council of Catholic Organizations commended the Detroit police in 1935 for their recent banning of a Soviet film. "The effect of this film upon workers and unemployed would be radical, subversive and destructive," the council's statement claimed. "It glorifies the theories of Lenin and Marx, neither of whom has any place in our American democracy." A film sympathetic to the Spanish Republicans was withdrawn from a downtown theater in 1938 after a campaign against it had been mounted by Catholic organizations and by the American Legion. The Detroit Public Library too was periodically a target of Catholic reformers, who believed that its holdings included numerous books that were "a menace to Christian morals and to public welfare," in the words of the *Michigan Catholic*. (The Detroit Council of Catholic Organizations succeeded in 1938 in having Hemingway's *To Have and Have Not* removed from the general circulation shelves.) Fortunately, however, the efforts of certain Catholic organizations and their Protestant allies did not result in the destruction of Diego Rivera's controversial murals at the Detroit Institute of Arts. "It was a fine piece of Catholic Action" nonetheless, the *Michigan Catholic* editorialized in 1933, of the opinion that the murals "would be more proper for a machine shop in Soviet Russia than for an art institute."[70]

Catholic Action involved far more than policing the arts and popular amusements, as even the *Michigan Catholic* was willing to recognize. The paper gave generous coverage in the early 1930s to the many works of charity carried out in the parishes. And it often commended Catholic reformers for their efforts to make the social encyclicals better known, and to champion the cause of a devastated working class. A 1936 meeting of the Detroit Catholic Students' Conference, a federation of high school sodalities, seemed to the editor to represent an exemplary catholicity in the breadth of its concerns. The 500 delegates voted not only to inaugurate a campaign against "Class B" movies (offensive in part, by the standards of the Legion of Decency), but "to learn and publicize the wage scale paid many students and young people in stores and where possible to buy in neighborhood stores even at a higher price if it is proven that another store is paying low wages."[71]

The *Michigan Catholic* was also pleased by a growing lay interest in catechetics and the work of evangelization. The Catholic Instruction League, which expanded rapidly in the early 1930s, was often commended to readers as a splendid example of Catholic Action. The organization of a Catholic Evidence Guild in

Detroit drew admiring comment too, although the guild planned eventually to deploy both women and men as speakers in the streets and parks of Detroit. The Detroit guild inaugurated its outdoor meetings in the spring of 1934; before that summer had drawn to a close, some sixty outdoor forums had been sponsored by the guild, most of them in Detroit's Clark Park. The Catholic Action Club at St. Matthew's parish took up the work in 1935 and, in concert with the Evidence Guild, staged regular meetings in Chandler and Pingree parks, where speakers discussed social and economic questions as well as Catholic doctrine. (The Clark Park meetings continued too, featuring, among others, Miss Dorothy Broeder on "Confession" and Miss Nina Greening on "Why we have an unmarried priesthood and sisterhood.") By 1938, the work of the Evidence Guild had expanded to include "interracial meetings" in Detroit, where lay speakers and members of the Passionist Order tried "to promote friendship between the races and to stimulate interest in Catholic teachings." Not all the talks at these meetings were devoted to religion, however. Marius Risley spoke in June on "Uncle Tom's Cabin—Firebrand of Emancipation."[72]

An interest in race relations was evident among a number of Catholic Action groups by the late 1930s, although Catholic reformers had not hitherto been much concerned with racial issues. Detroit's third annual Convention of Catholic Action, sponsored in 1937 by the Federation of Study Clubs, was addressed by a Paulist priest on "Catholic Action among the Colored." (Other speakers included Dorothy Day of the Catholic Worker and Fathers Charles Owen Rice and Carl Hensler, well known in Catholic Action circles for their work with the labor movement.) The Catholic Students' Mission Crusade, as we have already seen, was marked in the 1930s by a growing interest in the "Negro apostolate." The Catholic Worker in Detroit was from its founding in 1937 an eloquent voice for racial justice. As for the Association of Catholic Trade Unionists (ACTU), which had close ties to the Catholic Worker, it had necessarily to speak directly to the issue of racial intolerance. Enmity between black and white workers was a formidable barrier to organization in certain Detroit plants, most notably at the Ford Motor Company's River Rouge complex. Racial animosities ate away at solidarity in existing local unions too: "Paul Weber and myself had some very disquieting and authentic information a few days ago," an ACTU leader confided to a colleague in 1940. "It appears that the KKK is becoming very strong in the various auto plants." Both the ACTU leadership and that of the Catholic Worker had warm relations with the Catholic Interracial Council in Detroit, which was, at its founding in 1942, the first enduring Catholic organization locally to be exclusively devoted to the betterment of race relations. As such, its advent was particularly significant, despite the group's small size and its resolutely apolitical posture.[73]

Racial attitudes among Catholics changed slowly, for all the eloquence of Detroit's more radical apostles of Catholic Action. But their preaching and example with regard to race were still of great importance: over the course of the 1940s, as we will later see, both the Chancery and many priests were converted to a more egalitarian stand on racial issues. The power of example was, indeed, a principal tenet of Catholic Action. It was not the size or wealth of an organization that mattered, but the willingness of its members to lead genuinely Christian lives. Even a handful of committed believers could transform an institution, a community, perhaps ultimately the world. This "personalist" philosophy was carried to its extreme in the Catholic Worker movement, which was everywhere distinguished by an uncompromising evangelical poverty and a deep suspicion of organizational structures. But it permeated all the more radical Catholic Action groups, and helps to explain the vitality of those small and often inefficient organizations. It helps to explain their laicism as well. For if the world was to be transformed by the power of Christian example, the laity had as important a role to play as the clergy. In fact the laity had certain advantages: they were more numerous and, often, more knowledgeable and more at ease in secular surroundings.

The Catholic Worker was the most doggedly independent of the left-leaning Catholic Action groups. The lay apostolate, as the Worker saw it, meant lay leadership, and it meant a laity free to act on the basis of an informed conscience. This did not mean that the laity should ignore the clergy or the bishops; the Worker was utterly orthodox in its understanding of Church authority. But the Worker did insist that its radical apostolate be as free as possible from clerical control. It insisted too that the laity might in conscience disagree with the hierarchy on other than doctrinal matters. Rightly educated, the Worker maintained, the laity were capable of judging the world according to Christian principles and of acting on those judgments. They were capable, indeed, of offering the clergy some needed lessons in Christian social action.[74]

The Catholic Worker in Detroit was largely the creation of Louis J. Murphy, a 1931 graduate of the city's Jesuit university. It was he who, along with a handful of coworkers, opened St. Francis House of Hospitality late in 1937. Like other Catholic Worker houses, St. Francis House was principally devoted to the "corporal works of mercy." Its small staff did what it could to shelter the homeless, and maintained a soup kitchen for what quickly became a sizable clientele. "As many as 900 hungry men" were being fed daily at St. Francis House by the spring of 1938. The house was also a gathering place for Catholics interested in the labor movement. Classes in parliamentary law and economics had been organized there within days of its opening; over the next few months a lecture series on the social encyclicals was inaugurated and plans were laid for a "Catholic Action conference," one that was to focus especially on the industrial worker. There were occasional forays into the turbulent politics of Detroit: a Catholic Worker contingent was part of a UAW-sponsored march against unemployment in 1938. And it was St. Francis House that served as the headquarters for the Association of Catholic Trade Unionists when that group was formed in Detroit in the summer of 1938.[75]

The Worker made remarkable progress in Detroit in its early years, given the small number of its active members. A "communal farm" was established near South Lyon in 1938, and it eventually supplied eggs and vegetables and even meat to the houses of hospitality in Detroit. (A second house, St. Martha House for women, was opened in the early 1940s.) St. Benedict Farm was also a place of retreat for Catholic activists, and something of a center for the liturgical movement locally, the Catholic Worker being very much identified with the cause of liturgical reform. St. Anthony House, devoted to classes and neighborhood social activities, was opened in Detroit in 1940, the result of an unexpected gift to the Worker community—much as St. Benedict Farm had been. "We were able to get out of debt," Lou Murphy explained, "which is a most unhealthy state for the Catholic Worker and then we got a call from the Chancery Building. We went down to see what was up, and Father John Donovan, the Archbishop's secretary, gave us fifty dollars which the Archbishop told him to give us. We could think of nothing better to do with this money than start a new house. The rent on the new house is twenty-five dollars. I don't know how we will be able to maintain this place, but we will trust in God, and if He doesn't want us to have this place, He will soon let us know."[76]

Money proved to be a less serious problem than a shortage of personnel. Lou Murphy was of draft age in 1942, although he, like many other Catholic Workers, was a pacifist. He was eventually allowed to register as a conscientious objector, and subsequently served with an ambulance corps in North Africa and Italy. (The Chancery was of little assistance when it came to Murphy's dealings with his draft board. "The most that can be said for Mr. Murphy's claim," Msgr. Edward Hickey wrote, "is that there is no sound Catholic doctrine forbidding a civilian from bearing arms.") Murphy's absence from Detroit placed a heavy burden on the Worker staff he left behind. But they were apparently equal to it, for the various houses and the farm survived the war. It was during this period too that the Worker gained the full-time services of Justine L'Esperance, a 1940 graduate of Marygrove College and a woman with strong interest, and a good deal of experience, in the labor movement. She and Lou Murphy were married early in 1947.[77]

The Detroit Worker was very much a Murphy family enterprise over the next two decades. (There were eventually six Murphy children.) The growing family lived at St. Martha House, where they continued, for a time, to provide shelter for destitute women and their offspring. But the expanding population of Murphys finally filled the house to capacity, and the work of hospitality was thereafter confined to nearby St. Francis House. Here the clientele had changed considerably since the late 1930s. "It has become a home for the unemployable mostly," Father Clement Kern had noted in 1946. Neither Kern nor the Murphys, however, seem to have been daunted by the change. They collaborated in 1946 in the founding of St. John Vianney House, a cooperative residence for elderly men. And in 1949 the St. Thomas Aquinas Reading Room was opened under Catholic Worker auspices. It served as a "club" of sorts for the many unemployed—and the many unemployables—who, like the Catholic Worker, called Holy Trinity parish their home.[78]

The Murphys also presided over a gradual expansion in the educational mission of the Worker. A "Lay Apostolate Library" was opened in 1950, the same year that the Murphys assumed management of a rural retreat house near Monroe. And there was the usual round of lectures and discussion groups that normally characterized a Worker community. There were visits from Catholic luminaries too, most notably from Dorothy Day, whose annual speaking tours in the 1950s did much to make the Worker known among a new generation of Catholics. The Murphys did their share of this as well. St. Francis House welcomed many young visitors in the postwar years, including a good many seminarians, and the Murphys often spoke to student audiences. They were, in fact, unusually attractive ambassadors, warmer and more accessible than the redoubtable Dorothy Day, and the Worker enterprise in Detroit bore the marks of their appealing personalities. "The kindly atmosphere of the Catholic Worker house here," a visitor wrote in 1952, "and the cheerfulness of Lou and Justine Murphy and their happy children is outstanding." Families were something of a rarity in Catholic Worker circles; as Dorothy Day envisioned it, the Worker was essentially a celibate's apostolate. The Murphys' commitment to the Catholic Worker, then, exemplified a generosity of spirit that was remarkable even by that movement's high standards, and a "holy foolishness" that troubled and moved a good many Catholics locally. "Life in the Detroit Worker has been precarious to say the least," the Murphys wrote in 1957, "but somehow each day's problems seem to resolve themselves. Needless to say we have seen daily, and gratefully, the hand of God in all things, to the point of making us ashamed of our spiritual and physical indolence." Their example was always the Murphys' most effective teaching tool. And they had an effect on the life of the Church in Detroit.[79]

That Church was home to an increasingly affluent population by the 1950s, and one that was increasingly conservative in its political views and behavior. Catholic Action locally reflected this, although to a lesser extent than might have been expected. Interest in the labor movement did indeed decline after the mid-1940s: the ACTU was "a very inactive organization," its leaders admitted in 1951. As for the Catholic Worker, it was celebrated mainly for the faith and heroic charity of people like the Murphys. The movement's critiques of industrial capitalism were largely ignored. But Catholic Action was still a vehicle for social criticism and, on occasion, for social reform. The Christian Family Movement, which was brought to Detroit in 1950, saw social reform as essential to the strengthening of family life. The Grail, which came to the city in 1952, included on its ambitious agenda the betterment of race relations in the inner-city parishes. The group had particular success in St. Leo's parish, where Grail members helped to organize a cooperative buying plan and a credit union. Race relations were also of concern to Convert Making Our Apostolate, which established its national headquarters in Pontiac in 1949. (One of the group's cofounders was a Pontiac laywoman, Margaret Lynch Gibson.) The CMOA, as it was known, devoted considerable energy to convert work in Pontiac's black neighborhoods and to the peaceable integration of St. Vincent's parish in that city. And there were numerous Catholic activists who hoped to transform the larger culture by a Catholic revival in the arts. The Grail was an especially prolific source of contemporary Christian art and handcrafted religious articles, most of which were produced at the group's headquarters in Loveland, Ohio, and sold in various Grail-run shops. The Detroit Grail opened an "art-book center" in the early 1950s and, for a time, maintained a "Workshop of Arts" for would-be local craftsmen. There was even a Catholic Theater in Detroit, founded in 1940, whose members believed their work to be a "powerful instrument for the dissemination of Catholic Doctrine, Catholic Thought and Catholic Ideals."[80]

The most enduring legacy of Catholic Action, however, was not the social reforms it spawned or supported, but the mentality it encouraged among an influential portion of the laity. For it was by means of Catholic Action that an educated lay elite was able to challenge the pervasive clericalism of the American Church. Catholic Action, after all, celebrated lay participation in the life of the Church — in its liturgy, its organizations, its forays into politics. Catholic Action gave rise to several generations of talented lay leaders, some of whom were models of piety and courage not only for the laity but for the clergy too. His experience of the Catholic Worker in Detroit, Father Clement Kern confessed, left him "humbled, chastened, inspired by the sacrifices of these Catholic laypeople." And Catholic Action accomplished what might be called a confusion of boundaries between the lay and the clerical worlds. Catholic activists were urged, often by their lay leaders, to cultivate a highly disciplined, almost monastic, spirituality. The Federation of Catholic Study Clubs, according to its president in 1936, "has promoted lay retreats; frequent, even daily, Holy Communion, spiritual and otherwise inspiring reading and daily meditation." Lay activists assumed roles on occasion that were widely regarded as the exclusive property of the clergy. The men and women of the Catholic Evidence Guild, who took to the streets and parks of Detroit to defend their faith and win converts to it, looked to most Catholics very much like preachers. (This was undoubtedly why Archbishop Mooney was unhappy about women's participation in the guild.) Both The Grail and Convert Making Our Apostolate were involved in the instruction as well as the recruiting of prospective converts, although this was often assumed to be a priest's particular responsibility. Grail members were active too as liturgical instructors and as advocates of liturgical reform. This seemed to many Catholics to be an incursion into clerical territory, an incursion all the more disconcerting for its having been conducted by women.[81]

Catholic Action was in fact a disproportionately female enterprise, and not only in the Archdiocese of Detroit. The sodality movement, for example, which introduced the language and logic of Catholic Action to thousands of high school and college students, was overwhelmingly female in its membership. And in the sodalities, as in other Catholic Action groups, women often assumed positions of leadership. Even the ACTU in Detroit, whose membership was mostly male, was headed by a woman from 1949 until 1952. They very rhetoric of Catholic Action encouraged women to take on unaccustomed roles. Catholic Action flowed from faith, its advocates argued; the courage and militance of its practitioners was simply a measure of their spiritual vitality. It was not easy, under the circumstances, to insist that women be less militant than men, no matter how wedded most Catholics were to a conservative view of the female role. (The "Marygrove girl" should be trained "as an angel and an apostle," according to a Catholic Action Crusade held at the college in 1931. One could hardly phrase the ambivalence more succinctly.) The example of women in pioneering roles was a force for change as well. And there were many such examples, not only on the local scene but nationally too. A girl who admired the likes of Dorothy Day and Maisie Ward and Catherine de Hueck Doherty was almost bound to imagine her own role as a laywoman in terms that went beyond the confines of the parish altar society.[82]

Catholic Action, in short, was something of a "forcing house" for the aspirations of an educated lay elite. It gave voice to, and legitimized, the perhaps inevitable desire of that elite for a greater autonomy in the Church and for a more responsible role in its liturgical and organizational life. Theirs was not, in the main, a call for lay participation in the governance of the parish: middle-class Catholic reformers generally saw the Church in larger than parochial terms. But they did want recognition of their competence as educated men and women who moved with ease—and with authority—in the worlds of education, the professions, social reform. This meant, at the least, a wider field of action for the laity, and a greater independence for lay leaders. And, for many, it meant a more communitarian view of the Church, one where the laity shared equally in the task of bringing Christ to a sinful world. It was this vision that came to fruition in the years after Vatican II, although the Council itself had spoken in ambiguous terms about the role and authority of the laity. In Detroit, however, as in most American dioceses, many Catholics understood those reforms to endorse an essential equality between the clergy and the laity. And a growing number of Catholic women were prepared to insist that their sex be accorded full equality in the Church.

It would have been difficult, in the late 1950s, for even a prescient observer to have predicted the turmoil that came in the wake of the council. For the Church in Detroit seemed less divided and more disciplined than ever before. Ethnic tensions in particular had eased enormously, and there were signs that racial animosities were ebbing too. Assimilation, moreover, had made for notably less conflict in the various parishes, especially with regard to their administration. And the largely assimilated Catholic population was remarkably devout. This was true of men as well as women, for the divide between the sexes in matters of religion had narrowed considerably. Men, even young men, were well integrated into the life of nearly every parish, a development that helps to account for the unprecedented size and visibility of Catholic organizations in these years. As for women, they were seemingly pleased to share the territory that they had dominated for generations. A minority of younger women were apparently eager to see an expanded role for their sex in the helping professions and in the various lay apostolates. But theirs were not overtly feminist sympathies. On the contrary, they celebrated motherhood and regarded employment as the domain of the unmarried woman. Cardinal Mooney gave a cheerful blessing in 1957 to a Grail-sponsored program on careers for single women, evidently unperturbed by The Grail's growing interest in professional work as a female vocation. For neither he nor the program's sponsors imagined that The Grail would one day be a channel of feminist protest in the Church.[83]

But that is what The Grail became, and not only because of changes in the larger culture. The Catholic community had changed as well. That community was in fact a divided one in the 1950s, for all its apparent unity. It was divided most fundamentally by social class, a division that became more evident, and more consequential, as the affluent minority within the community attained critically large proportions. This division accounts for much of the polarization and bitterness that came with reform, the effects of which still haunt the Church. And it helps to explain why the cautious reforms of the council gave rise to a veritable revolution, at least in the American context. If this much is clear in retrospect, however, we dare not forget how unexpected these developments were. The most ardent pre-conciliar reformers were startled by the Pope's decision to convene an ecumenical council, and astonished by the eventual scope of its agenda. Largely unaware of their own historical development, American Catholics could not know that the pressures for change had been building for at least a generation.

14

CATHOLIC EDUCATION

When Bishop Michael Gallagher came to Detroit in the fall of 1918, he found that many of his immediate problems had to do with schools. The 102 parochial schools in his new diocese were too few and too small to accommodate the rapidly growing Catholic population. The quality of those schools, moreover, varied enormously, due in part to the veritable immunity of the schools to effective diocesan control. Most disturbing, however, was a growing opposition to the very existence of parochial schools—something spawned by a recrudescence of organized anti-Catholicism. Michigan's voters were asked in 1920 and again in 1924 to amend the state's constitution for the purpose of outlawing any but public schooling for children in grades one through eight. These were costly referenda: the Catholic bishops of Michigan spent heavily on both campaigns, although Catholic schools throughout the state were critically short of funds. (The leaders of Michigan's Lutheran and Dutch Reformed communities had schools to defend as well; they too spent generously on the school campaigns.) And there were psychological costs, perhaps especially for Catholics, against whom the school campaigns were principally directed. Coming as it did in the wake of the First World War, the assault on the parochial school seemed to say that even an ardent and amply demonstrated patriotism could not win for Catholics an unassailable American identity.

For all the bitterness it caused, however, the campaign against parochial education worked in the long term to strengthen the Catholic schools of the Diocese. That campaign enabled both state and diocesan authorities to bring the parochial schools under stricter regulation, particularly with regard to the qualifications of teachers. And it strengthened the hand of educational reformers, especially those who favored a highly centralized mode of administration. By the mid-1930s, the Diocese of Detroit had begun to implement a uniform curriculum in its schools, and to monitor the quality of instruction in its classrooms in a systematic way. These reforms appear to have accomplished a genuine improvement in the quality of Catholic education locally, particularly in the weaker schools. They were a spur as well to a nascent professionalism on the part of many teaching Sisters. And because these reforms reflected much-publicized trends in Michigan's public schools, they helped to assure the laity that Catholic schools were in no way inferior to their state-run counterparts. Partly for this reason, lay support for Catholic education grew substantially in the Gallagher-Mooney years. Nearly 80 percent of the parishes in the Archdiocese of Detroit had schools in 1940, compared to 59 percent in 1918. Catholic school enrollments more than doubled between 1918 and 1940, although the Archdiocese had lost a portion of its territory to the newly created dioceses of Lansing and Saginaw. And by 1940 there had been a dramatic increase in the number of Catholic secondary schools in the Archdiocese.

The growth of the system and its reform did mask certain critical weaknesses. Some teaching orders were slow to meet the educational requirements laid down for their members by state law. And the Diocese was perennially short of teaching Sisters. The shortage was especially acute in the 1920s and in the 1950s, times of rapid population growth for the Archdiocese. The "Sister shortage" of the 1920s caused severe overcrowding in many schools, and frustrated efforts at curricular and administrative reform. The shortage of the 1950s led to an increasing dependence on lay teachers, who made up nearly 25 percent of the parochial school teaching force in 1959. (About 9 percent of the system's teachers in 1945 were members of the laity.) The growing numbers of lay teachers "do pose a special problem," Msgr. Vincent Horkan admitted in 1959, when he was in his third year as archdiocesan superintendent of schools. "Fundamentally it is an economic problem." That problem worsened substantially over the next ten years, as the women's teaching orders nationally entered a period of precipitous decline in membership. By the early 1970s, the parochial system locally was in crisis.[1]

The Gallagher-Mooney era, then, was preeminently a time of growth and reform in the field of education. The principal achievements of these years, indeed, were little short of remarkable. But the period was also one of recurrent crises with regard to the schools, crises caused by the limited resources that Catholics brought to the increasingly costly business of education. "Should we continue to expand?" Msgr. Horkan asked bluntly in 1958, when, despite a prodigious growth in parochial school enrollments, only 56 percent of the Catholic children in the Archdiocese were enrolled in Catholic schools. "Perhaps we should drastically curtail or declare a moratorium on school-building for a period of time." The "baby boom" of the postwar years was the immediate cause of Msgr. Horkan's troubles, which centered on the growing shortage of teaching Sisters. But a rising birthrate was not the whole story. The baby boom simply made clear to a large lay audience what prescient observers had known for decades: without state aid — and that in substantial amounts — Catholics could not expand their schools indefinitely. This realization contributed in no small way to the reappraisal of parochial schooling that came in the wake of Vatican II. And that reappraisal had incalculable effects on the teaching orders, whose sense of identity and purpose was badly eroded in the 1960s. In this respect, as indeed in many others, the post-conciliar crisis in parochial education had roots in the years of the system's greatest triumphs.[2]

"Bigotry is not dead": the school amendment

The campaign to outlaw private grammar schools in Michigan was apparently begun in 1917. Its principal leader was one James Hamilton, a Republican of vast political ambition and a man who wore his anti-Catholicism with a distinctly progressive flair. The public school, as Hamilton saw it, was the culture's principal means of promoting unity and intellectual freedom; religious schools — and Catholic schools in particular — were not only sources of division and disloyalty but of reactionary political values as well. "Never since the first document of liberty [was] won from King John in 1215," Hamilton wrote in a typically florid passage, "has the Hierarchy done anything but oppose every vestige of progress toward human liberty throughout the world." Hamilton and a handful of colleagues had tried without success to have a bill introduced into the Michigan legislature to abolish the private grammar schools. They turned subsequently to efforts to force a statewide referendum on the issue, and apparently found considerable support among the electorate. (Hamilton's proposed amendment to the Michigan constitution provided that all children between the ages of five and sixteen "shall attend the public school in their respective districts until they have graduated from the eighth grade.") It was widely reported by the spring of 1918 that Hamilton's petition campaign was on the verge of success, although he had needed to secure the signatures of more than 40,000 registered voters.[3]

The Catholic response to Hamilton's 1918 campaign was surprisingly muted, apparently because the Diocese of Detroit was then without a permanent bishop. A lay committee was established under Detroit Chancery auspices to generate publicity against the campaign — the "Association for Educational Freedom" had at least two staff members in 1918, both of them on the Chancery payroll — but its lobbying efforts were notably subdued. Auxiliary Bishop Edward Kelly also appointed a diocesan superintendent of schools in 1918, a move that was meant to allay public fears about the quality and patriotic content of Catholic education. (Michigan's Lutheran synod named its first "school inspectors" at about the same time.) Kelly was surely comforted — and perhaps confirmed in his quiet approach — by the storm of protest that greeted the school amendment in 1918, most of it from non-Catholic and eminently respectable sources. Editors, businessmen, public school officials, and not a few Protestant clergy denounced the proposed amendment as a violation of religious liberty, a veiled attack on the overburdened public schools — and on the overburdened taxpayer — and as a subversion of wartime unity. Catholics found this last line of argument especially congenial. "The league has 'Made in Germany' written on its brow," Jesuit Father John McClory declared in June, with reference to the Wayne County Civic League, as James Hamilton's organization was called. "The kaiser himself could not have thought of a better scheme of social disruption just now. It is trying to spoil the present harmony between Protestants and Catholics who have been standing shoulder to shoulder in the war."[4]

The patriotic argument proved to be an effective one, but in the short term only. The Wayne County Civic League announced in July that, "for patriotic reasons," it would not file its petitions until the war was over. That moment came soon enough: the Hamilton forces submitted their petitions to the state in December 1918. Those petitions, however, were found to be lacking the required number of valid signatures, and the Civic League was obliged to begin its campaign anew. This it did, assisted by an apparently substantial number of dedicated workers. "On street car and on boat these agents of the devil's work are to be met with," the *Michigan Catholic* noted bitterly in the summer of 1919, "and last week a number of men working at Ford's Highland Park factory (one a foreman) were detected going about among the employees asking for signatures to the petition." The petition was not invariably presented as anti-Catholic in its purposes, at least according to Catholic sources. Some signers evidently thought that the proposed amendment provided for compulsory education through age sixteen. Still, "bigotry is not dead," as the *Michigan Catholic* pointed out: anti-Catholic rhetoric was prominent in the campaign, and was apparently the principal source of its fervor. That fervor produced the expected results by the close of 1919: sufficient signatures had been collected to ensure that the "school amendment" would appear on the Michigan ballot in November 1920.[5]

The Catholic response to the school amendment in 1919 and 1920 was far more aggressive than it had been in 1918. Detroit had a new bishop by 1919, and Michael Gallagher was not much given, at least in times of crisis, to quiet persuasion and measured speech. The proposed amendment was unjust, he told a gathering at Kalamazoo in the spring of 1919, "and if the law is an unjust law we are not bound to obey. We will not sacrifice the souls of our children, we will all go to jail to protect them, for we cannot in conscience obey any such law." The bishops of Grand Rapids and Marquette were a good deal more guarded in their public comments on the issue, and the Catholic campaign against the amendment in those dioceses was more subdued than it was in Detroit. But it was Detroit's campaign that commanded statewide coverage in 1920, and Bishop Gallagher who was widely regarded as the spokesman for all of Michigan's Catholics. This worried some of those Catholics, who feared that an aggressive and highly visible campaign might simply intensify anti-Catholicism, especially in rural areas. Catholics, after all, were only about 20 percent of Michigan's voters. But Bishop Gallagher was apparently confident that anti-Catholicism, at least as a political issue, appealed to a distinct minority in the population.[6]

The Gallagher-led crusade against the school amendment was formally inaugurated in Detroit in the spring of 1920. The early months were largely directed at Catholics, who were urged to register in good time for the state's late-August primary. (James Hamilton was one in a crowded field for the Republican gubernatorial nomination.) Michigan's women had been granted the full suffrage in 1919, and Catholic women were especially encouraged to register and vote. Bishop Gallagher wrote at least two pastoral letters to this effect in 1919 and 1920 — he had endorsed women's suffrage in 1918 — and the *Michigan Catholic* repeatedly reminded women of "their duty to vote," as did the leaders of the League of Catholic Women. This duty obligated Sisters, too: "every Religious in the Diocese of Detroit must be registered on or before October 16th," Bishop Gallagher instructed the superiors who were under his jurisdiction. Gallagher feared, and with good reason, that Catholic women were less likely to vote than their generally more affluent Protestant sisters, to whom he gave credit for the success of Hamilton's efforts thus far. "Women are far more bigoted than men," the bishop told a Catholic rally in the spring of 1920. "Of the 120,000 names signed to the petition of the Wayne County Civic association to virtually ban all private schools, 75 per cent were those of women." How the Bishop had come to this conclusion is something of a puzzle. A sampling of names from the 1919 petitions shows that fewer than 40 percent of the signers were women. A mostly female opposition, however, whether real or imagined, had its rhetorical uses. "I . . . ask all right-minded women to work for the defeat of the movement," Gallagher urged, "and so clear the name of their sex."[7]

Catholic activity against the amendment reached its height in the fall of 1920. Every parish was expected by then to have a "school amendment committee," whose job it was to see that Catholics locally were registered to vote and that non-Catholics were well supplied with anti-amendment literature. And nearly every parish seems to have complied, although some committees were much more active than others. (The parish committees were units of the Chancery-sponsored "Educational Liberty League.") The Holy Name Society, which had already staged a midsummer rally against the amendment, held two more "monster demonstrations," one at Lansing and one at Flint. The Lansing rally was addressed by Bishop Gallagher and by University of Michigan Regent James O. Murfin, a prominent Methodist, who represented the considerable body of Protestant opinion that had rallied to the cause of the religious schools.[8]

By the time of the Lansing rally—it was held in mid-September—there seemed to be ample grounds for Catholic confidence. The Hamilton forces had been denounced from every respectable quarter, and Hamilton himself had placed a distant seventh in his primary bid for the gubernatorial nomination. Still, there was no cause for complacency, not, at least, in the eyes of Bishop Gallagher. September and October were months of intense political activity in the parishes: a special collection was taken up to defray the costs of the campaign, prayers for victory were said at every Mass and the Rosary recited daily for this intention in the schools, and priests were instructed to preach regularly on the issue and to distribute sample ballots to their parishioners, many of whom had never voted before. Then, on the final Sunday of October, Catholics staged a massive parade in Detroit, one that included most of the parochial school children from the city and its environs. "For more than three hours, Rt. Rev. Michael J. Gallagher . . . surrounded by ten priests of the diocese who served as chaplains in the recent world war, stood on the steps of his residence, reviewing the parade," the *Michigan Catholic* reported. That parade was climaxed by an open-air Mass at Navin Field, home to the Detroit Tigers and the city's largest stadium.

The Mass was celebrated, amidst a sea of patriotic symbols, by Father Patrick Dunigan, thrice-decorated for his valor in the recent war. Bishop Gallagher addressed the crowd at the conclusion of the Mass, commending Catholics for their splendid record in the military defense of the nation and for their steadfast support of religious liberty. More than 100,000 were said to have been in attendance.[9]

The "school amendment" was defeated in November by a margin of nearly two to one. (The Diocese of Marquette, in Michigan's upper peninsula, was more solidly against the amendment — with "no" votes at 70.7 percent of the total — than were the dioceses of Grand Rapids and Detroit, where 62.7 percent of the votes were opposed.) Bishop Gallagher was publicly jubilant, and generous in his praise of the many non-Catholics who had voted against the amendment. But he was in fact disturbed, and apparently surprised, by the size of the vote in its favor. "Our majority was not very encouraging," the diocesan consultors agreed when they met in mid-November. "This means therefore that our enemies are not beaten and our work remains. We must begin immediately to build up and strengthen our forces for a repeated fight." Since the Chancery was in debt for the campaign just ended, a "repeated fight" was a most unwelcome prospect. "The Reverend Bishop," the consultors were told, "suggests the passage of a bill which would require the Supreme Court to pass on all proposed amendments before they are placed on the ballot."[10]

As feared, the Hamilton forces did regroup in the wake of their defeat. They succeeded in placing the "school amendment" on the ballot for a second time in 1924. How best to respond to this turn of events was a matter of debate at the Chancery. Michigan politics were a good deal more polarized in 1924 than they had been in 1920. The Ku Klux Klan was active in many areas of the state, with Detroit alone thought to have more than 20,000 members. Anti-Catholicism was more open and bitter and apparently more widespread in 1924 than had been the case in 1920. This was true across the nation: a referendum in Oregon in 1922 had resulted in the passage of a school amendment similar to that proposed for Michigan, and bills of this nature had been introduced into other state legislatures. Under the circumstances, many Catholics worried that an aggressive campaign in defense of their schools might inadvertently strengthen the Klan, and further fuel anti-Catholicism. (There were fears, indeed, that the 1920 campaign in Detroit had done just that.) It might be prudent, certain of Gallagher's advisors contended, to mount no campaign at all and depend on the courts to strike down the "school amendment," should it become law. For by the summer of 1924 the Oregon law had already been declared unconstitutional by a federal court.[11]

There was in fact a Catholic campaign against the amendment in 1924, but it was a quiet one, aimed almost exclusively at the Catholic population. There were no mass rallies, no parades, no provocative speeches by the bishop. Committees were again established in the parishes and their work coordinated by the Educational Liberty League, but that work was largely confined to registering Catholic voters. This did not mean, however, that non-Catholics were deprived of anti-amendment propaganda. Lutheran and Dutch Reformed and Seventh Day Adventist committees distributed anti-amendment literature, and the Diocesan School Committee, as the Educational Liberty League was sometimes called, sent a letter in October to every signer of the Hamilton petition, most of whom, the committee professed to think, had either given the amendment "little thought, or have been misinformed as to what it proposes to accomplish." The secular press, moreover, was nearly unanimous in its opposition to the amendment, as it had been in 1920.[12]

The 1924 campaign was an exceptionally bitter one, despite the inconspicuous part that Catholics generally played, and it looked for a time to be going badly. "Authentic reports from different parts of the State disclose a hostility to Catholics far in excess of anything encountered in the last school fight of 1920," Bishop Gallagher warned in October. The results of the election, however, were not appreciably different from those in 1920. The "school amendment," in what proved to be its final appearance, was defeated by a margin of slightly less than two to one.[13]

The school campaigns were costly for the Diocese of Detroit, and not only financially. (The state's three dioceses were said to have spent nearly $2 million to defeat the amendment in 1920 and 1924.) Despite the considerable support that their cause had received from non-Catholics, many Catholics were shocked by the extent and the bitterness of popular opposition to their schools. The school campaigns left a residue of resentment in the Catholic community that had its effects on political life for the better part of a generation. The campaigns gave impetus to certain reforms as well, and these too were resented by many Catholics, who saw in them an erosion of what they called their educational rights. A state law, passed in 1919, required that all schools in Michigan be conducted in English, save for instruction in the catechism. Bishops Gallagher and Kelly had both opposed this bill, regarding it as unduly restrictive. But the climate of opinion in the wake of war—and in the midst of charges that Catholic and Lutheran schools were essentially foreign in their curricula and allegiances— caused the great majority of legislators to support it.[14]

There was strong support as well for a move to bring the parochial schools under state supervision. The Dacey law, passed in 1921, placed every private school in the state under the jurisdiction of the state superintendent of public instruction. And it required that teachers in the private schools meet the same educational standards as those in the public schools, and hold the same certification. The state's bishops supported the Dacey bill, evidently afraid that opposition would strengthen the school amendment forces. But the Dacey law was the kind of legislation that the bishops had long sought to avoid. Its advent, however, did give the bishops an additional incentive to promote reform in their schools, and an increased leverage over the clergy and the teaching orders, which had generally opposed attempts at rationalization and centralization of the Catholic systems. Bishop Gallagher, at least, seems to have recognized that in this respect the law was potentially a beneficial one.[15]

SCHOOL REFORM

Despite the provisions of the Dacey law, reform came slowly to the Catholic schools. Local authorities were generally reluctant to police those schools closely and seemingly content to let all but the most egregious violations of state law pass unchecked. Diocesan authorities, for their part, were very nearly overwhelmed by the rapid expansion of the system, and by the consequent shortage of teaching Sisters. Bishop Gallagher did appoint a superintendent of schools for the Diocese in 1921, who succeeded a man whose functions in the post had been almost wholly ceremonial. The new superintendent was Father Charles Linskey, trained in pedagogy at the Catholic University and, at least for the first five years of his tenure, a full-time school administrator. He seems to have begun his new job with laudable zeal, visiting schools and promoting academic competitions. But he apparently attempted no serious administrative reforms, and left the system in as decentralized a state as he had found it. Perhaps this was partly a result of his temperament: reform of so sprawling a system could hardly be achieved by other than a forceful personality. But the failure had more fundamentally to do with the rapid growth of the system and its want of resources. Bishop Gallagher, presumably discouraged by the many obstacles to reform, assigned Father Linskey to a parish in 1926. He was both a pastor and superintendent of schools until 1930, whereupon the superintendency fell vacant, and remained so until 1934.[16]

The system over which Father Linskey had at least nominal jurisdiction was characterized, as it had been for decades, by wide variations in quality and resources. Some teaching orders, most notably the Immaculate Heart of Mary Sisters, had long maintained high standards for the training of teachers. (One hundred and seventy IHMs had college degrees in the mid-1920s.) These orders had no difficulty meeting the rather limited certification requirements of the Dacey law. That law required all teachers to have at least one year of college training, which warranted a "limited certificate." The limited certificate was valid for three years only, but might be exchanged for a grade school certificate, provided that the applicant had completed another sixteen hours of college credit. A "life certificate" was given after four years of college training. The great majority of teachers in the Diocese were certified by the late 1920s, although only a small minority had completed four years of college. But there were certainly teachers who did not meet the standards of the Dacey law. Of the five Sisters teaching at Patronage of St. Joseph School in 1934, for example, only one had Michigan certification. Nearly every order, it is true, made notable educational progress in the 1920s, and most Sisters spent their summers laboriously accumulating college credit. But the disparities in teacher training within the parochial system were still pronounced, and were almost certainly greater than those in the public schools.[17]

Class size too varied enormously, although nearly every Catholic school in Detroit was overcrowded in the 1920s. "For years the Archdiocese of Detroit has had more pupils per classroom than most public or private systems in the country," a Chancery report conceded as late as 1941. Even in 1935, when the teacher shortage had eased considerably, fully two-thirds of the Catholic grammar schools in Detroit had an average of at least fifty pupils per classroom. Three schools still averaged between seventy and seventy-nine pupils per room. It was nearly always the primary grades that were most overcrowded, for even in the 1930s the majority of pupils in the Catholic schools were enrolled in grades one through four. Many parents were apparently still accustomed to remove their children from the parish school once they had been confirmed. (Confirmation was generally conferred, in the Gallagher-Mooney years, at about the age of nine.) The skills that are taught in the early grades are, of course, essential to a child's intellectual development, and it may be that many children were permanently handicapped by their school's overcrowded conditions. But we lack the evidence to determine whether this was in fact the case.[18]

We do know, however, that the most serious crowding occurred in the Polish schools. "New Polish schools in Detroit cannot get Sisters anywhere in America," Bishop Gallagher complained in 1924, "yet it is imperative that they be gotten for the good of religion in some cases. One I have in mind especially, the new school in the Help of Christians parish, [was] founded recently to combat the pernicious activities of an Independent Church." Our Lady Help of Christians School did indeed get Sisters. (The bishop may have requisitioned them from the older Polish schools, as he had done in a similar case in 1922.) But the school was terribly congested: "From the I to the VI grade each classrooms has over 100 children," the pastor told the Chancery. His school, however, was in happier straits than the school at SS. Peter and Paul (Polish) parish, founded in 1923 on the western fringes of Detroit. "Our 242 children are still being taught in the church building, by 2 lay teachers, separated by a canvas curtain," the pastor reported in 1925, not a little annoyed that "the Detroit School Board and the Board of Health are giving us all kinds of trouble." Even the long-established Polish schools were badly crowded. "In many of the rooms seats designed for the occupancy of only two pupils are being used to accommodate three children," a Board of Health inspector noted in 1925 of St. Stanislaus School in Detroit, where he had found as many as 122 children in a single classroom. In the neighboring public schools, on the other hand, even the most populous rooms were only "slightly overcrowded." Conditions there were "not as alarming as those found at St. Stanislaus School."[19]

The Board of Health did accomplish a limited reform at St. Stanislaus—the pupil-teacher ratio declined by some 14 percent between 1925 and 1928, when six new classrooms were added to the school. But it was still overcrowded by contemporary standards. What relieved the crowding at St. Stanislaus, as at many other schools, was the end of mass immigration in the mid-1920s and the plummeting birthrate of the early 1930s. These, coupled with growth in the ranks of the teaching orders, set the stage for major school reform.

Still, there were certain schools in the Diocese that even in the 1920s were at least the equal of the better public schools. Catholic schools were often praised for their exemplary discipline, and many Sisters came to their work with an admirable intensity of purpose. The academies maintained by the various teaching orders were especially respected, by Catholics and non-Catholics alike. He had "found no poor or mediocre work whatever," one W. H. Higbie reported from St. Mary's Academy in 1921, which he had visited on behalf of the University of Michigan. "I would be glad of an opportunity to place my own daughter under such instruction." The "intellectual and moral tone" of St. Joseph's Academy in Adrian was "excellent," according to the University's G. M. Whipple in 1927. A colleague confirmed that judgment in 1931: "I can recommend very highly the instruction you are carrying on," one Dr. Wray told the superior at St. Joseph's Academy, adding that he was especially impressed "by the fine spirit I found on the part of both teachers and pupils." The academies were not parish schools, and they drew their students, in the main, from affluent Catholic families. But many parish schools as well enjoyed respectable reputations. The Immaculate Heart of Mary Sisters had decided as early as 1915 to seek accreditation for all the high schools in their care. By 1935, 64 of the 104 high schools in the Diocese of Detroit had been accredited by the University of Michigan.[20]

The high schools of the Diocese in 1935 were nearly all of them parish schools, something that distinguished Detroit from other large and long-established dioceses. For Detroit, as we have seen, was unusually slow to establish central high schools. The parish high schools throughout the Diocese were generally small, especially in the 1920s, when many of them had fewer than 100 pupils. (As late as 1935, twenty-one of the high schools in the Diocese were not yet four-year institutions.) Some of the schools were too small even to support the minimum of three teachers required for accreditation. "With but one teacher for the four grades of high school," the superior at the Nazareth (Michigan) convent told the Anchorville pastor in 1934, "it is really impossible to accomplish the teaching task in the right way. . . . Your school was at its best when the eight grades only were taught and the children took the County Examinations and passed most successfully."[21]

The small parish high school was usually coeducational, and this too made the Diocese of Detroit unusual. About 78 percent of the high schools in the Diocese were coeducational in 1928, a figure far higher than that reported by any other large diocese. The pastor at Holy Rosary parish in Detroit was among those who deeply regretted this state of affairs, which was, indeed, a trifle embarrassing, given repeated papal pronouncements against coeducation. "Due to the Monsignor's orders, many of the high school boys left us this year to attend schools taught by men," the chronicles of Holy Rosary Commercial High School noted in 1938. "Those who could not afford these schools were enrolled in the different public schools. About sixty courageous souls walked back to us as if nothing had been said, and tried to hide behind their more fortunate feminine companions. No doubt they felt that once settled, they would not be disturbed, and thus it has been." Boys outnumbered girls in the tenth grade at Holy Rosary by the fall of 1943.[22]

High school enrollment in the Diocese grew substantially in the 1920s, as it did elsewhere, although the growth was inhibited to some extent in Detroit by the pressures of rapid development. (The Diocese of Detroit was fifth in the nation in elementary school enrollment in 1928, but sixth when it came to high school enrollment.) And enrollment continued to grow throughout the 1930s. The population of the Catholic secondary schools more than trebled between 1928 and 1941, when there were in excess of 19,000 students in the high schools of the Diocese. This had important effects on many schools: more students meant more teachers, which meant in turn a more specialized instruction and, often, a more diverse curriculum. The growing enrollment also gave Bishop Gallagher a welcome justification for the establishment of central high schools. A central high for girls was opened in 1927 in the former Cathedral School in Detroit, and a similar school for boys, taught by the Basilian Fathers, was opened in 1928. The need for such schools was evident, Gallagher told his clergy. "From every angle, be it of economy or efficiency, its wisdom cannot be called in question." Still, he apparently anticipated opposition, and was quick to assure his priests that the central high schools were not the start of major change in the decentralized parochial system. Those schools were "not intended to interfere in any way with the larger parochial high schools already functioning, but to provide higher educational facilities for grammar school graduates of those parishes where the maintenance of a high school is not practicable."[23]

The growing enrollments of the 1920s and the 1930s included unprecedented numbers of boys, who made up about 50 percent of the Catholic high school population locally by 1935. Their growing presence in the schools made for major changes, both curricular and atmospheric. Athletics assumed a new importance in many schools in the 1920s—a Catholic Schools' Athletic League was organized in Detroit in 1921—and competitive sport was more and more a principal focus of student life. This alone made the high school a palpably different place than it had been in the years before the First World War, when extracurricular activities had been mostly of a literary nature, and genteel standards had prevailed among the largely female ranks. The curriculum too came under scrutiny, and was more and more criticized as excessively academic, too little connected to the work-a-day world for which most boys were destined. The enormously high attrition rates that afflicted most Catholic high schools in these years only gave point to such criticism. "Startling as it may seem," the *Michigan Catholic* reported in 1935, with particular reference to the situation in the Diocese, "over 50% of the pupils who start in Catholic high schools never finish there." It was the boys who failed to finish school that mainly worried Catholic opinion-makers: they were more numerous than their female counterparts, and the social consequences of their undereducation were thought to be the more alarming. Worries of this sort did much to shape the school reforms that were finally inaugurated in the 1930s. For those reforms embodied a more utilitarian view of secondary schooling than had generally been characteristic of the principal teaching orders, whose proudest achievements, even in the 1930s, were likely to be their young ladies' academies — and, of course, the women's colleges that had developed from them.[24]

The reforms of the 1930s are generally credited to the work of a single man. He was Father, later Monsignor, Carroll Deady, who served as diocesan superintendent of schools from 1934 until 1957. Deady was a young man when he came to the job — he was still some months shy of his thirty-third birthday — and not well known in the Diocese of Detroit, at least among the clergy. (Born and raised in Massachusetts, he had degrees from Boston College and the Catholic University, and had taught for a time at Notre Dame.) His youth and his want of local connections were widely assumed to be serious handicaps in his new position. So too was the apparently limited support that he received from the Chancery in the early stages of his career. Father Deady may have been appointed a full-time superintendent of schools, but he had difficulty, at least initially, acquiring even a modest office at the Chancery Building. For the Diocese was in financial crisis in 1934, and Bishop Gallagher was not much interested at this point in the historically nettlesome problem of school reform.[25]

Still, Father Deady brought some formidable strengths to his new job. He was an aggressive and energetic man and a notably adept administrator, who was not without a certain ingratiating charm. His credentials as a pedagogue were genuinely impressive, and this did much to win the confidence of an increasingly well-educated corps of teaching Sisters. He had the good fortune, moreover, to come to the superintendency from a year devoted to teacher-training in the Diocese, during which he seems to have made important friends in the larger teaching orders. (Father Deady was not quite the outsider that his fellow clergy believed him to be.) Perhaps most important, he was passionately devoted to the cause of school reform: his tenure was marked by a singleness of purpose that is seldom encountered in the administrative annals of the Archdiocese. And he had the confidence of a man who knows that his reforms are overdue. Changes of the sort that Deady had in mind had already been achieved in many of the larger dioceses, and had long since been implemented in the larger public systems of the state.

What Father Deady had in mind was nothing less than an administrative revolution. He wanted a uniform curriculum and a uniform approach to pedagogy, as well as a more stringent regulation of teacher education. This meant, of necessity, a highly centralized administration, for the teaching orders varied widely in each of these regards. And there were thirty-two orders at work in the schools of the Diocese by the mid-1930s. Deady knew, however, that he shared a vocabulary and certain major goals with at least the larger teaching orders, whose approach to their work was affected by current pedagogical trends as well as by their own traditions. When he announced that he intended to implement a modified version of the "Hoosic Plan" in the schools of the Diocese, there were Sisters who understood what he meant and were eager to assist him. Women like these were often among the best educated and most influential members of their orders, and they were of inestimable help to Deady in allaying fears about his plans and minimizing resistance to his work among their fellow religious.[26]

Certain of Deady's reforms, moreover, were welcomed by the great majority of teaching Sisters. He announced in the spring of 1934 that teachers in the Diocese would be required, by the fall of 1935, to have at least two years of college training before they began their careers. "It is no longer possible," he maintained, "to prepare a teacher during a summer and assign her a classroom in the fall in which to practice." Deady himself conducted "a course in the supervision and improvement of teaching" at Marygrove College in the summer of 1934, and at his instigation the number of courses available to teaching Sisters in the Diocese increased substantially. Among the most influential was a summer "demonstration school" at the University of Detroit, where "the best teachers from both the parochial and the city systems" taught master classes for the benefit of nearly 500 Sisters. The new emphasis on teacher training—and the generous publicity given to it—did much to enhance the status of the teaching orders locally, and their members were obviously grateful. They were pleased as well by Deady's appointment, in the fall of 1934, of an "elementary school council," which was composed of representatives from each of the twenty-seven orders that taught in the elementary schools. Deady saw the council primarily as a means by which his reforms might be explained to the various teaching orders. But it was at least potentially an advisory body, and, as such, an affirmation of the heightened professional status of the teaching Sister.[27]

The elementary school council had a number of reforms to explain to its constituents even in 1934. Work was begun on a uniform curriculum for the elementary grades in spelling, handwriting, and arithmetic, and a "systematic testing program" was inaugurated in many schools. A textbook rental system was introduced into a handful of schools; this was understood to be a step toward the adoption of uniform texts throughout the parochial system. And the larger teaching orders were obliged to appoint at least one teaching supervisor from among their ranks, who was to be engaged full-time in the work of instructional improvement. (There were ten supervisors in the Diocese in the spring of 1935.) These women functioned too as Deady's agents in the work of reform, explaining his policies and overseeing their implementation.[28]

The Deady reforms were substantially implemented in the grammar schools by 1940. Those reforms had meant extensive changes: children throughout the system now rented their books from the Archdiocese and followed the same course of study. Once they had finished the second grade, moreover, they spent their days with more than one teacher. Third and fourth graders moved between at least two classrooms daily, and children in the higher grades had three or four instructors every day, depending on the size of the school. This sytem was meant to improve the quality of teaching: an instructor was, at least ideally, given only her strongest subjects to teach, and various classrooms were supplied with the books and maps and equipment necessary for thorough instruction in a single subject or subject group. There were "history rooms" and "mathematics rooms" in the schools of the Archdiocese by 1940, as well as the long familiar rooms devoted to music and art. Meant to improve instruction too was the "unit system" that prevailed in grades five through eight. The various curricular units, which were published by the Archdiocese, were detailed course outlines, and these were expected to be followed exactly by every teacher in the system. A uniform approach to pedagogy was thus achieved, at least in theory, and a minimum level of instructional competence all but guaranteed. As for the rigidities inherent in the unit system, these were modified to some extent by regular revision of the units, which had been drawn up initially by committees of teaching Sisters. And every unit included an individual testing program, by means of which the pupil was enabled to move through the work at a pace commensurate with his abilities.[29]

The unit system had been introduced in the high schools too by 1940, and it came eventually to incorporate most of the secondary curriculum. That curriculum was altered in other ways as well. Deady was eager to make the high schools less academic in their orientation, and more responsive to the vocational needs of those many students who did not go on to college. It was under his auspices that shop courses were made widely available to parochial high school students in Detroit, by means of a program of "Saturday schools" that were taught by men from the public system. And Deady encouraged the growing emphasis on sports. "During the past year high school athletics has received more publicity than [at] any other time in its history," he reported in 1935. "This was of inestimable value to the schools." Deady's efforts, of course, simply hastened developments that were caused fundamentally by the emergence of even parochial high schools as instruments of mass education. But he did a great deal to legitimize, for many teaching Sisters, a less traditional understanding of secondary schooling.[30]

The Deady reforms were widely applauded. He had strong support, as we have seen, among the various teaching orders, and his work was much admired by Archbishop Edward Mooney, something that helped to silence any lingering clerical criticism of Deady's centralizing policies. Public school authorities admired his work as well. "I have found that both teachers and pupils have been highly stimulated by the techniques, methods and underlying philosophy which the Diocesan Superintendent is recommending," a school inspector from the University of Michigan wrote with typical enthusiasm in 1938. Deady's reforms did indeed make the Catholic schools more like the public schools, both in terms of curriculum and methodology, although the English-speaking orders had long been accustomed to pattern their curricula at least in part on that of the local public system. Appropriately enough, the high school curricular units in literature, drawn up in the late 1930s by a committee of Sisters, included as mandatory reading not a single specifically Catholic novel.[31]

That the Catholic schools were similar to the public schools in many respects was generally reassuring to parents, at least to those who looked to the schools as a means to social mobility. They did, of course, expect a certain "Catholic content" in their schools. But this was provided by daily instruction in religion, which ranked in every grade as a major academic subject, by daily Mass and classroom prayers, and by the presence of the Sisters. Parents had particular reason to be grateful, moreover, for the economies accomplished by the Deady reforms. The textbook rental system was a popular one, and of real utility in a mobile population. Those who moved house from one parish to another were similarly grateful for a uniform curriculum.

Deady was not without his critics, however, particularly within the ranks of the teaching orders. Some Sisters were never wholly reconciled to his reforms; others came eventually to believe that his reformed system was too rigid, that it failed to tap the full pedagogical expertise of the experienced teacher. This was the case with the women who served on the Educational Policy Board of the Immaculate Heart of Mary Sisters, still the largest of the teaching orders locally. The board was established in 1945, the occasion of the order's centenary, and it quickly became a rival of sorts to the superintendent's office, although this rivalry was never acknowledged and was perhaps not fully recognized by the Sisters themselves. (The board published a regular *Bulletin* for teachers and one for principals, just as Deady's office did.) The board's members were frank, however, about their unhappiness with many of the Deady reforms. They especially disliked the rotation of pupils in the grammar school among several teachers every day. "In our sectionalized system the pupil becomes everyone's responsibility and consequently no one's," it was noted late in 1945. The IHMs' own tradition of pedagogy, known as the St. Andre system, had placed an extremely high value on the moral example of the teacher, and on her intuitive understanding of the children in her care. The intimacy between teacher and pupil, the almost maternal role that the teacher was assigned — these were seriously undermined, in the view of the board, by the rotation system. An intuitive approach to teaching was hampered too by the rigidities of the unit system, at least in the board's opinion. This was especially troubling with regard to the teaching of religion, but here the board looked forward to "more pliable procedures" that were evidently under consideration at the Chancery. As to the teaching of prayers, the members regretted the passing of a program that had once been standard in every IHM school. "It was generally felt that the inability of children to say the Acts, etc., is the result of not saying them regularly in school."[32]

The Educational Policy Board was unhappy too with conditions in the parish secondary schools. These had lost their academic rigor, many members believed, and too much attention was given to vocational courses and to sports and other extracurricular activities. Most students, moreover, were not serious about their work, and the quality of that work was disturbingly low. There were apparently objective grounds for concerns of this sort: Deady's office began, probably in the 1940s, to publish a booklet for high school seniors that reviewed the basics of spelling, grammar, and simple computation. ("Considerable comment is caused by the fact that high school graduates apply for positions and are found deficient in spelling, grammar, arithmetic and similar items that are considered essential knowledge," the parochial schools' *Manual* explained.) But the changes that the board deplored had much more to do with the explosion in high school enrollments than with any deficiencies in the Deady approach to education. High schools were no longer the elite academic institutions they had once been. As for the large classes that the Sisters quite rightly thought made for inadequate teaching, these had long been opposed by Deady himself. The superintendent in the late 1930s had placed a limit of fifty pupils on classroom enrollment. But even in the 1950s, this limit was sometimes ignored.[33]

The discontents that surfaced in the Educational Policy Board may well have been those of a particularly well educated and ambitious elite. Many IHMs, like the members of other orders and like many Catholic parents, seem in the 1940s and the 1950s to have looked on the Catholic schools with enormous pride. The postwar years, indeed, were widely regarded in the Archdiocese as something of a golden age in Catholic education. Enrollments boomed: there were more than 175,000 children in the system by 1959, an increase of some 69,000 over 1947. The number of schools grew rapidly too, as Catholics began their exodus toward and into the suburbs. These new schools included twenty-two high schools built between 1945 and 1960, nearly all of them larger and better equipped than the parish high schools that still made up the great majority of secondary schools in the Archdiocese. (These new high schools were either "private" institutions, run independently by a religious order, or they were interparochial high schools that served a cluster of parishes.) Schools like these helped to bolster the academic reputation of Catholic education, and this, in turn, helped to strengthen the already remarkable support that parochial schools enjoyed among the laity. The demand for Catholic schooling locally exceeded the supply of classrooms well into the 1960s, and there were many parents for whom the teacher shortage of the postwar years was a personal tragedy. "I am disappointed and very unhappy because I wanted so much for my son to attend a Catholic Institution," one distressed father wrote to Cardinal Mooney in 1955. "Our children certainly need the guiding instructions of OUR NUNS in order for them to some-day take their places in this Great World of Ours as respectfull and true servants of Our Almighty Lord."[34]

"Our nuns," however, were in increasingly short supply in the 1950s. And in many orders there were changes underway that seem, at least in retrospect, to foreshadow the vocations crisis of the post-conciliar era. These changes had much to do with the reforming currents of the Deady years. They are, in consequence, best examined in this context.

Msgr. Deady's vision of a thoroughly professional corps of teaching Sisters was shared by many women religious. Certain orders, it is true, did not lengthen the training normally given to their members until they were obliged to do so by state law and diocesan regulation. But others had long been ahead of the law with regard to the education of teachers. Nearly half of the professed members of the IHM Sisters had bachelor's degrees in 1944, although the law required no more than two years of college for what was in practice a permanent certification. And the community's leaders were already looking toward the day when every school principal and high school teacher in the order would hold a graduate degree. There were pressures at work, however, against ambitions of this nature: teaching Sisters were in chronically short supply, and many pastors opposed reforms that limited their availability. Msgr. Deady's gospel of an adequate teacher training was thus of great importance, for it gave an imprimatur of sorts to the educational policies of the more ambitious orders, even when those policies went beyond the standards that Deady himself had immediately in mind.[35]

That gospel also helped to legitimize the growing concern with professional status that was evident in a number of orders by the late 1940s. The IHMs announced in 1950 that their members would henceforth have a full four years of college training before they began to teach. "They arrived at this conclusion from a study of the breakdowns that are caused by the pressure of summer school work and Saturday classes," Msgr. Deady explained to Cardinal Mooney. That the IHMs were no longer willing to endure the grueling round of summer school and Saturday classes is worth noting: it is, at the least, a mark of growing independence in an already independent-minded order. But it also suggests that the Sisters had come to regard themselves as genuine professionals, and to see their loyalty to professional standards as sometimes taking precedence over their role as servants of the Church. For the IHMs' decision was taken in the midst of an acute and worsening teacher shortage, and was greeted with less than enthusiasm at the Chancery. By 1950, however, the IHMs had a wider community of reference than simply the Archdiocese of Detroit. They knew that many teaching Sisters not only supported their stand, but saw it as essential to the future of Catholic education and even of religious life.[36]

This wider community of reference had been quietly forming throughout the 1940s. It was animated by a shared concern for the professional and personal development of the teaching Sister, who, it was increasingly argued, was sent into the classroom both unprepared intellectually and inadequately grounded in a spiritual tradition. These concerns were given legitimacy and force by the various pronouncements of Pius XII on the religious life. The Pope was anxious that the teaching orders be unassailably professional in their work, that the excellence of Catholic schools be evident even to their harshest critics. It was under his auspices that the first International Congress of Teaching Sisters was convened at Rome in 1951, and at his behest that the first National Congress of U.S. Religious was held at the University of Notre Dame in 1952. (Appropriately, the speakers there included Sister Mary Patrick, IHM, who urged a greater reliance on lay teachers in the parochial schools so as to permit a lengthened period of religious and professional training for Sisters.) The National Congress gave rise to immediate reforms in many orders. And it helped to prepare the way for the Sister Formation Conference, which was, for more than a decade after its founding in 1953, the principal forum for American Sisters who wished to explore the possibilities of reform in the religious life. Sister Mary Emil, IHM, was among the founders of the conference and served from 1954 until 1960 as its executive secretary.[37]

The Sister Formation Conference was a force for change in nearly every religious order locally. The *Sister Formation Bulletin* was widely read, even in conservative communities like the Polish-American Felician Sisters. For it spoke to a widespread desire among Sisters for a fuller recognition of their needs as professionals, a desire that was the perhaps inevitable consequence of their rising levels of education. The Felician Sisters, for example, decided in 1953 to increase the preservice training of their members from two years of college to three; this was extended to four years in 1960. Like the IHMs, the Felicians were weary of the interminable summers spent in school, and eager to be as well credentialed as other members of their field. An emerging sense of professional identity was evident too in a 1952 reform that redefined the obligations of the teaching Sister. Felicians were henceforth forbidden to "perform or supervise the children in any janitorial service in the school" or in the church, they were no longer to supervise after-school games or to oversee the collection of money in the schools on any but "*very rare* occasions." Nor would they be allowed any longer to perform such tasks as counting the Sunday collection or writing Sunday bulletins and parish reports. Reforms like these were common to many religious orders in the early 1950s. They were the fruit, in good part, of the First National Congress of Religious and of the various papal directives that urged a more professional approach to teaching on the part of the religious orders. (The Felicians regarded their 1952 reform as a response to "the injunctions and wishes of the Holy Father," according to their Mother General.) But reforms like these are best understood as part of a larger shift in mentality among women religious, a shift that was well underway before the Second Vatican Council.[38]

It was a long step, to be sure, from the heightened professional aspirations of the 1950s to the revolution in religious life that came in the wake of the council. That revolution had many causes, some of which had to do with secular political developments. But the heightened aspirations of the 1950s were almost certainly a precondition for the post-conciliar changes. It was their strong sense of identity as credentialed professionals that enabled many Sisters to demand a greater autonomy as religious, and to carry the work of "updating" their orders beyond the bounds of modest reform. It was this same sense that enabled many women to leave their orders, something that growing numbers of Sisters were doing even before the close of the council. And it was the demoralization of many orders, caused by defections and by the divisions that were born of reform, that explains in part—although only in part—the dramatic decline in new vocations to the religious life. (The number of women religious nationally has declined steadily since 1966.) This is not to say that the crisis of the religious orders was inevitable, or that it could have been predicted with any certainty from the vantage point of the 1950s. But that crisis did indeed have roots in the preconciliar years and in the remarkable work of reform that was the hallmark of the Deady era.

HIGHER EDUCATION

The number of students enrolled in Catholic colleges nationally more than trebled in the 1920s, and very nearly trebled again between 1930 and 1950, largely, in this latter case, the result of the GI Bill. The rate of increase slowed after the late 1940s, but postwar prosperity meant continued health for even the smaller institutions: Catholic college enrollments continued to grow, and many schools moved in the postwar years to strengthen the qualifications of their faculties and to broaden their curricula. These national patterns were closely approximated in the Archdiocese of Detroit. Both St. Mary's—later Marygrove—College and the University of Detroit saw substantial growth in their enrollments after 1920; with the larger enrollment came a greater curricular breadth and an enhanced academic reputation. And Marygrove acquired some local competition: four Catholic colleges for women were founded in the Archdiocese between 1919 and 1947. Two of these developed, as Marygrove itself had done, from long-established female academies. They were the Adrian Dominicans' St. Joseph College, incorporated in 1919, and Nazareth College near Kalamazoo, opened in 1924 by the Sisters of St. Joseph at Nazareth. Madonna College and Mercy College, however, were outgrowths of the training institutes maintained by the Felician Sisters and the Sisters of Mercy for their own young members. These were more frankly vocational in their purposes than the older women's colleges—the genteel tradition of the female academy had been greatly weakened by the 1940s—and their prosperity in the 1950s was due in good part to this practical orientation. But every Catholic college locally was prosperous in that decade. Enrollments did not begin their precipitous decline until the early 1970s.[39]

Support for the Catholic college in the decades after 1920 reflected more than the growing wealth of the Catholic population and the general rise in college attendance among the middle class. It had much to do with a growing Catholic commitment to institutional separatism. The very existence of parochial schools was evidence of that commitment, although there were still many Catholics who regarded these schools as necessary only for the very young. But more and more Catholics by the 1920s were willing to support a broad range of Catholic institutions, including colleges and universities. (Both Marygrove and the University of Detroit received generous local support when they built their new campuses in the 1920s.) And an increasing number of Catholics were pleased to think that they were distinguished, as a people, by what a leading layman in Detroit described as a "proud and glorious isolation" from the larger culture. Catholics in this camp were likely to be assimilated members of the middle class, and more than usually devout. They had particular reason to promote the cause of the Catholic college: theirs was a world where college training was rapidly becoming the norm, but where that training was popularly linked to a decline in religious orthodoxy. Only the Catholic college seemed to offer a means to social mobility that did not threaten the integrity of the religious group.[40]

The Catholic college, then, was widely understood to have more than academic and vocational goals: it was meant to preserve a worldview and a way of life. And this was a task for which the Catholic college was well adapted. For that college, whatever its academic deficiencies, was heir to a coherent philosophical tradition and to the spiritual discipline of its governing religious order. Its curriculum had a unity that had long been absent from the secular college, and its faculty had the confidence peculiar to those who operate within the bounds of a closed theological system. Every Marygrove student was taught that "Civilization is the Faith — the Faith is Civilization," according to President George Hermann Derry in 1927, who was certain as well that contemporary social problems could all be analyzed and solved "in the light of our established Catholic standards of the past." This closed intellectual world was not necessarily a stultifying one, even for the brightest students. Marygrove was a vibrant place in the decades after World War I, and an important local center of Catholic social action. Only the best-educated members of the IHM order were assigned to its faculty, and these included, over the years, a number of women whose intelligence, strength of character, and depth of faith made them formidably influential figures in the lives of the young.[41]

Marygrove was indeed a liberating place for many of its students, and not only intellectually. For they were encouraged by the faculty to expand their horizons to encompass more than an eventual marriage. The "Marygrove girl," according to President Derry, should be "rich in intellectual interests. . . . She should be capable, too, of doing her part in the world's work in whatever sphere of life she may be placed, either as a means of self-support or as an aid to others less fortunate than herself." By 1936, the college catalog was speaking of female independence in language that was less genteel: "OUR PURPOSE . . . is the production of personal POWER; DRIVING POWER, or ambition, the indomitable desire to succeed, to excel, to rise above the ranks; all college activities lead the student to an early determination of a lofty aim in life, and to a career motivated by the ideals of Catholic Action and by the crusading spirit of the Lay Apostle." The school had emphasized careers in social service well before the 1930s: a course in "social science" had been inaugurated at St. Mary's College in Monroe in 1921, and had included a generous provision for fieldwork and research in areas such as "labor, trade, employment and public health." And the life of the college had from the first been geared to producing leaders: students were trained as public speakers in weekly assemblies, and urged to model their own lives on those of the notable Catholics who were regularly brought to the campus. The Sisters too were important models. It was a moment of no small significance when Sister Honora Jack became Marygrove's first woman president in 1937.[42]

Some students, of course, were indifferent to the emphasis on leadership and social service. They betrayed no sign of the intellectuality or the reforming zeal that the faculty aimed to cultivate. But others took the lessons very much to heart. Marygrove students were prominent locally in a number of Catholic Ac-

tion movements, and the school's alumnae have since the 1930s been disproportionately represented in the ranks of Detroit's lay leaders.

The rapid growth in Catholic college enrollments in the decades after 1920
did not mean a decline in the number of Catholic students at secular colleges
and universities. Their numbers too continued to grow. State schools were generally cheaper than their Catholic counterparts, and their academic reputations
were usually stronger. And there were many Catholic parents — and would-be
students too — who were not much worried about the purportedly deleterious
spiritual effects of secular education. Some of them were probably marginal
Catholics, but others were at least ordinarily devout. The Students' Holy Name
Society at the University of Michigan, for example, had some 300 members at
its birth in 1920, when Catholic enrollment at the school was probably around
500.[43]

The Catholic student at Michigan in 1920 had a Catholic chapel on the campus and a thriving Catholic student society to which he might belong. Perhaps
this looked to him like an indirect episcopal blessing on the university, although
it was hardly intended as such. Both Bishop Gallagher and Cardinal Mooney
were ardent supporters of Catholic higher education, and Mooney especially
was convinced that the secular college and the Catholic college were wholly at
odds in their conduct and purposes. He "pointed out the wide variance there
is between the Catholic mind and the non-Catholic mind," the *Michigan Catholic*
reported of a 1938 Mooney address to the Newman Club in Ann Arbor. As to
Wayne University, the former City College of Detroit, it was "a rival secular (and
secularist) institution," according to the Cardinal in 1952, "whose influence on
the cultural life of the city has to be countered as much as possible."[44]

Still, Mooney gave quiet support to Catholic student activities at the University of Michigan, as Bishop Gallagher had done before him. A Catholic chaplain
was regularly assigned to the university after 1919, and these chaplains were, on
the whole, an unusually able and articulate lot. And Gallagher and Mooney
both encouraged lay financial support of St. Mary's Student Chapel in Ann Arbor, which opened in temporary quarters in 1919. (The permanent facility was
completed early in 1925.) St. Mary's apparently drew a substantial majority of
Catholic students to Mass on a fairly regular basis, although it was always a distinct minority who were active in the Catholic students' society, which was
known as the Newman Club after 1929. The club's membership stood at only
282 in 1940, after several years of unusually ambitious activity. The university
had any number of rival attractions, of course, and Catholic students were apparently as eager as most to demonstrate their independence in religious matters. Not that this was easy, at least in the days of Father Michael Bourke, who
had charge of St. Mary's from 1919 until his death in 1928. Father Bourke kept
an evidently careful record of the number of times his student parishioners failed
to attend Sunday Mass, convinced, as he often told his flock, that "the curse of
the U. student is not loss of faith but indifference as to Mass and the Sacra-

ments." "I feel it a bounden duty to write to some parents in this matter," he told his congregation in 1926. "They look to me to keep an account and notify them."[45]

Father Bourke was also careful to prepare his flock for the attacks on revealed religion that they were almost bound to encounter in the classroom. They would be told that "man is a material development from a lower order," that "science and the Bible will not square," that miracles are impossible, that "dogma shackles independent thought." But the students should not be upset by this. "Evolution is only a *theory* after all," Father Bourke pointed out. "What would happen to the lawyer or theologian who used the so-called proofs of the scientist?" A properly circumscribed view of evolution, he hastened to add, was quite consistent with Catholic orthodoxy. Father Bourke cited St. George Mivart to prove this point, although perhaps to dubious effect, for certain of Mivart's writings on science and religion had long since been placed on the *Index expurgatorious,* and the man himself was excommunicated in 1900. But Father Bourke had other, happier examples of intellectual converts with which to reassure his students: it was men like Newman and Orestes Brownson in the last century and Chesterton and Msgr. Robert Benson in the present one, he told them, who refuted the claim that the Church was hostile to the intellectual life. Still, Father Bourke instructed the students to avoid certain university classes — the Bible as literature, "natural religion," and apparently nearly every course in philosophy. "If you need this," he told them, with reference to philosophy, "get it in your own schools."[46]

There was more to Catholic intellectual life at Michigan, however, than prohibitions and apologetics. The Newman Club sponsored numerous study groups and lectures — the social encyclicals were popular topics in the 1930s — and in the 1930s especially a number of distinguished Catholics spoke on campus, among them G. K. Chesterton, Etienne Gilson, Msgr. John A. Ryan, and the Catholic Worker's Peter Maurin. The *Catholic Worker* itself was a feature of the pamphlet rack at the Student Chapel by 1937, where it joined the likes of *Commonweal* and *America.* And there was a growing interest in the liturgical movement: the Newman Club was experimenting with the dialogue Mass by 1939. St. Mary's was never an influence on the intellectual life of the campus as a whole; Michigan was as secular in its preoccupations as most large state universities. But it did provide those students who were drawn to it with at least an introduction to a generous range of Catholic thought.[47]

The Newman movement in the Archdiocese of Detroit was not confined to the University of Michigan. A Newman club had been founded at the City College of Detroit by 1933, when a Basilian father was its spiritual director. Father Leo Andries of Holy Rosary parish in Detroit assumed the post in 1936; he found "a very fertile field" of work at what was now Wayne University. "From the short conversations I had with the various students there," he told the Chancery, "I find that some of the teachings, especially in psychology, are a far cry from the Catholic Doctrine." Archbishop Mooney, as we have seen, was equally worried about the contents of the Wayne curriculum, and in 1940 he managed to secure the Paulist Fathers for the Newman apostolate there. (The Paulists, who were based at "Newman Hall" on the fringes of the campus, remained at Wayne until 1971.) There was also a Newman Club at Michigan State Normal College in Ypsilanti by the 1940s, although a "Catholic Students' Club" had had at least a brief existence at the school at the time of the First World War. But a campus chapel for what eventually became Eastern Michigan University was not achieved until 1965, when there were apparently more than 1,000 Catholic students on the campus.[48]

It was clear by then that Newman work needed to be greatly expanded, and not only in the Archdiocese of Detroit. Catholic college enrollments were still growing in 1965, but there were nearly three and a half times as many Catholic students on secular campuses as there were in Catholic colleges. The national chaplain of the Newman Apostolate in 1965 — he was Monsignor John Bradley, rector of St. Mary's Student Chapel in Ann Arbor — was finding his a veritably "impossible position." "At the present, there are 198 full-time priests on secular campuses," he noted with reference to the national scene, "while more than 3000 priests, nuns, etc., are on Catholic campuses." His unenviable task, as he saw it, was "trying to sell the bishops, priests, nuns, religious orders, faculty and friends on the urgency of visualizing Catholic higher education wherever you find Catholic people and not just on campuses under Catholic auspices."[49]

Monsignor Bradley's mission was so difficult, in large part, because Catholic education had been an astoundingly successful enterprise for at least the past half-century. Detroit was a typical diocese in this regard: parochial school enrollments there had grown dramatically after 1920, and the quality of the Catholic schools had increased substantially. Lay support for Catholic education, moreover, was stronger than it had ever been before, especially with regard to the secondary schools, where the growth in enrollment since 1920 had been particularly impressive. There were still many Catholic children, to be sure, who were not in Catholic schools. But many of them — perhaps most of them, in the Archdiocese of Detroit — were in the public schools because there was no Catholic school available locally or because the parish school was filled to capacity. Even in 1965, it seems safe to say, a substantial majority of Catholic parents wanted — and expected — to see the parochial systems expanded to serve the needs of the newest suburbs. For the parochial school was, for a great many Catholics, an integral part of the religious world in which they had been raised. Loyalty to that school was widely seen as an essentially religious obligation.

By 1965, however, the parochial schools had acquired some formidable Catholic critics. Pope John had called for a greater openness to the world on the part of Catholics, these critics argued. Was it right for American Catholics to continue a policy of institutional separatism, especially at a time when racial segregation in the schools was more and more a troubling issue? And Catholics were no longer a heavily immigrant population; their educational needs were very much those of other Americans. The recent election of a Catholic president was often cited as conclusive proof that Catholics had arrived, and not just economically. Accepted now as fully American, the critics asked, were Catholics justified in maintaining a system of schools that had its origins, at least in part, in nineteenth-century intolerance? Might the abolition of the parochial schools be a necessary gesture in support of ecumenism? And there were financial questions too, ones that troubled even the supporters of Catholic education. Building and maintaining schools was an increasingly costly business, too costly, indeed, for Catholics to look toward a system of parochial schools that would serve the needs of every Catholic child — or even a sizable majority of Catholic children. Under the circumstances, might Catholic resources not be better invested — perhaps more charitably invested — in other ways?[50]

The Catholic audience for critics of this sort was never large, even at the height of post-conciliar disaffection. There was then — and still is — substantial support among the laity for the idea of Catholic education. The crisis in parochial education was fundamentally an economic one: many parishes simply could not afford to pay a sufficient number of lay teachers to staff a school. But the rising tide of criticism almost certainly contributed to the economic crisis, for that crisis was caused most immediately by an abrupt decline in the number of teaching Sisters. And that decline had to do in part with a growing doubt in many orders about the importance of the educational mission to which most American Sisters had historically been committed. There were growing doubts among the clergy too, especially among the younger men. Service to the poor — most of whom were non-Catholics — seemed to an increasing minority of the clergy to be more Christian than the work of parochial schooling. And more and more priests were frank about their desire to work almost entirely with adults. These changing attitudes, it might be noted, had more than symbolic meaning: there were not many parishes in the 1960s where a troubled school could survive without the full support of the pastor.

The crisis in parochial education was but one in a series of crises in the post-conciliar Church. But it was surely among the most important. For American Catholics have been decisively shaped, as a community, by the parochial school. It was the schools that were largely responsible for the surprising solidarity of what was, after all, a multiethnic and economically diverse population. It was the schools that made it possible for even assimilated Catholics to live in partial isolation from the larger society. The steady decline in parochial school enrollments has already had important effects on the Church, as Andrew Greely, among others, has shown. And it will continue to do so, as more and more Catholics come to maturity in a world whose institutional and theological boundaries are no longer clearly drawn.[51]

ILLUSTRATIONS

Weinman Settlement House, League of Catholic Women, in the early 1920s.

Baseball in Detroit's St. Rose parish. Father Herman P. Fedewa, at left, and Father Edward J. Taylor, probably in the mid–1920s.

A class at St. Rose High School in Detroit in the mid-to-late 1920s.

Bowling in St. Margaret Mary parish, Detroit, during World War II.

Confraternity of Christian Doctrine (CCD): an after-school class in the catechism, probably in the early 1950s.

Confraternity of Christian Doctrine (CCD): a home visit near Erie, probably in the early 1950s.

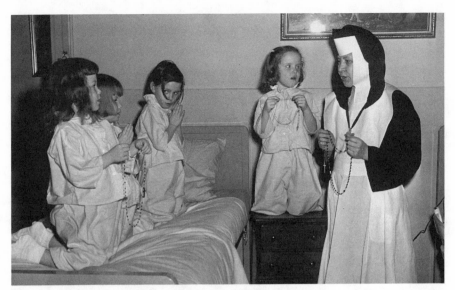

Guardian Angel's Home, Detroit, in the care of the Felician Sisters, probably in the early 1950s.

Holy Name Society men in 1951. The Society's national convention was held in Detroit that year.

Mrs. G. William Goering, president of the League of Catholic Women in 1957, before a portrait of League founder and first president, Mrs. Charles Casgrain.

15

CATHOLICS IN A CHANGING WORLD

The 1920s were a difficult time politically for the Catholics of the Diocese. Anti-Catholicism was a major factor in the politics of Detroit between 1919 and the mid-1920s; this was the case as well in many other Michigan communities. Anti-Catholic organizations in the state, the Ku Klux Klan premier among them, did decline sharply in membership and influence after 1925. But the presidential campaign of 1928 revived the cause, albeit temporarily, and gave anti-Catholic rhetoric a prominence in national political discourse that it had not had since the late nineteenth century. Al Smith did not lose the presidency in 1928 because he was a Catholic, or so it is eminently arguable. The prosperous 1920s were a thoroughly Republican decade. Probably no available Democrat could have beaten Herbert Hoover, who was, in that happy pre-Depression era, a much-admired man. (Smith's chief rival for the Democratic nomination in 1928 was also a Catholic, something that was conveniently forgotten as the campaign passed into the folklore of American politics.) But 1928 was still a blow to Catholic pride, and perhaps especially in Detroit, where Al Smith received only 37 percent of the vote.[1]

There was another side to the 1920s, however, at least in the Diocese of Detroit. Catholics in the city of Detroit made important political gains in that decade, a reflection of their considerable numbers and the growth of the Catholic middle class. These gains set the stage for the unprecedented Catholic successes of the 1930s, when Detroit's Frank Murphy was a rising star in politics, and the Roosevelt White House, wielding enormous powers of patronage, courted Catholics as they had never been courted before. This courtship yielded psychological as well as economic benefits: Catholic political confidence expanded perceptibly in the 1930s and the 1940s, even in an historically Protestant state like Michigan. And that expanded confidence meant, in the prosperous postwar years, something like emancipation for a good many Catholics. Religion ceased to be a divisive issue in the politics of Detroit. (Catholics by then were prominent on both sides of the political divide.) And even in Michigan politics, where Catholics were a distinct minority of voters, the religious preoccupations of an earlier generation had given way to a surprisingly ideological politics.

Catholics arrived politically, in good part, because the Democrats emerged after 1932 as the nation's majority party. (Catholics were still a mostly Democratic population even in the 1950s.) But their political success had to do as well with rising levels of income and education among Catholics, with the increasingly assimilated character of the Catholic population, and with the homogenization of national life that was born of depression and war. Political arrival, then, had not a little to do with economic and social arrival, although many Catholics in the 1950s, perhaps especially the well educated, clung to a sense of themselves as perennial outsiders in American life. There were relatively few Catholics, after all, in the upper echelons of government and industry and on the faculties of the most prestigious universities. And anti-Catholicism had emerged in a newly respectable guise by the late 1940s. No longer a mass movement, it was now the ideology of an urbane elite, who held to a thoroughly secular vision of American culture and democracy. This was certainly an important development. But it does not gainsay the remarkable progress made by a substantial portion of the Catholic population, many of whom were separated by only a generation from the hard realities of immigrant life.

The respectable anti-Catholicism of the postwar years did feed on some serious tensions, not all of which were rooted in the distant past. Catholic schools had long been a source of controversy, and the schools were a principal bone of contention in the years after World War II. But Catholics also found themselves increasingly isolated in their opposition to divorce and contraception. After the early 1930s, it was no longer possible to pretend that a Christian consensus existed with regard to the permanence of marriage and the immorality of birth control, and the Catholic position on these matters was increasingly seen as an eccentric one, admirable in the abstract, perhaps—and fewer and fewer Americans were even convinced of this—but hardly the grounds on which law and public policy could be based. Censorship too was an increasingly divisive issue, and for much the same reason. The Legion of Decency still had Protestant admirers in the 1950s, but the standards enforced by that organization were alien to a growing number of Americans. As for liberal intellectuals, uneasy Catholic allies in a revitalized Democratic party, they deplored what they saw as the Catholic penchant for a too-zealous anti-Communism. The Spanish Civil War had bred a bitterness between these camps that had not been forgotten in the early 1950s, when the rise of Senator Joe McCarthy gave liberal intellectuals new cause to worry about the political values of the large and growing Catholic population.

Many Catholics, of course, gloried in their sense of marginality, even as they resented it. A commitment to separate Catholic institutions grew stronger, generally, as Catholics became a wealthier and more assimilated population. Certainly this was true in the Archdiocese of Detroit, where the network of Catholic educational and social welfare institutions grew impressively in the twenty years after World War II. It was at least partly because of this that the intermarriage rate in these years remained relatively stable, and was lower than it seems to have been for certain years in the 1920s, when Catholics were still a mostly ethnic population.

Prosperity and assimilation, then, did not result in an immediate erosion of Catholic institutional loyalties, although many critics of the Church had hoped that this would happen. For a time those loyalties grew stronger, and were perhaps the more "Catholic" for their being the less explicitly "ethnic." But assimilated Catholics were generally more imbued with the values of the larger society than Catholic spokesmen liked to admit, and powerfully drawn to that society. Many educated Catholics were delighted by Pope John's call for an "opening to the world," and warmly sympathetic to the "secular" theologies that enjoyed such a vogue in the mid-1960s. The walls of the Catholic ghetto were not impermeable; the most enthusiastic Catholic proponents of the new secularism, indeed, had generally been bred within those walls, which they proceeded to attack in the 1960s in a fine display of native optimism. Only thoroughgoing Americans could have been so impatient with the claims of tradition.

Those ghetto walls opened out in the 1960s on a world in political turmoil. For Detroiters, at least, the turmoil had above all else to do with race: the city's troubled and episodically violent history of race relations came to a culmination of sorts in the 1960s, as Detroit moved from an increasingly polarized politics — in which race was the principal issue — to a major riot in 1967. The events of the 1960s had profound effects on the local Church: its members were more seriously divided over issues of social policy than had perhaps ever been the case. And the exodus of whites from the city placed dozens of parishes in financial jeopardy. Detroit's Catholic leaders had been reluctant, for the most part, to address the problem of race relations in the city before the crisis of the 1960s. But even the more conservative among them had undergone a fundamental change of heart on the question in the wake of the Second World War. The Catholic leadership in Detroit was willing to accord a legitimacy to black aspirations in the 1960s that it had not done in 1943, when Detroit was the site of the then-most-deadly race riot in the nation's history. This change of heart was of major importance, especially for the Church but also for Detroit. It is appropriate, then, that the history of racial attitudes among Detroit's Catholics, and the history of race relations within the Church itself, should be a major focus of this chapter. That it occupies the concluding section of the chapter — following sections devoted to marriage and sexuality, to partisan politics, and to the Second World War — is in no way meant to belittle its importance.

Intermarriage, divorce, and contraception

Bishop Michael Gallagher apparently believed that mixed marriage was a problem in his diocese. The Chancery over which he presided was often careless when it came to gathering statistics — *Catholic Directory* figures for Detroit are especially unreliable in the Gallagher years — but the bishop asked in 1925 that a parish-by-parish accounting of mixed marriages be compiled for the entire Diocese. That particular year was a happy choice: markedly fewer dispensations were issued in 1925 than was the case in 1924 or 1926. And the incidence of mixed marriage in that year was lower than it is reported to have been for most years in the 1920s: just under 23 percent of the marriages performed in the Diocese in 1925 had involved a non-Catholic partner. But that figure masked a disturbing trend. Mixed marriages only rarely occurred in the foreign-language parishes: just under 5 percent of the marriages in Detroit's ethnic parishes had been mixed in 1925. In the English-speaking parishes of the city, however, more than 30 percent of the marriages had involved a non-Catholic. Presumably the incidence of mixed marriage could be expected to rise in the future, as mass immigration came to an end and the ethnic populations were assimilated.[2]

But this is not what happened. The incidence of mixed marriage seems to have stabilized in the first half of the 1930s, when from 22 to 24 percent of the marriages recorded involved a non-Catholic. No figures are available between 1938 and 1942, but the rates thereafter generally ranged between 22 and 25 percent. An upward trend is not apparent until the mid-1960s, when the incidence of mixed marriage began a rise that culminated in the highest rates that have ever been recorded for the Archdiocese as a whole. Thirty-four percent of the marriages performed in 1969 were mixed; 38 percent in 1972. Only recently has a modest downward trend been evident.[3]

The apparent stability in the incidence of mixed marriage between about 1930 and the mid-1960s is a rather remarkable phenomenon, given the increasingly assimilated character of the Catholic population. It is perhaps explained in part by the disciplined religious practice that was more and more evident among that population, especially in the middle class. But it probably had more fundamentally to do with the great expansion in Catholic secondary education that began in the 1920s. The parochial high school helped to keep the adolescent's world a Catholic one, and this increased the chances that even thoroughly Americanized youngsters — including the not-particularly-devout — would eventually marry Catholics. The growing number of Catholic youth organizations in the Archdiocese was significant in this respect as well.

The Catholic secondary school was important too as a source of reinforcement for Church teaching with regard to marriage. And reinforcement was needed, at least according to Catholic spokesmen. The incidence of divorce was at record levels in the early 1920s, and continuing its seemingly inexorable rise. Divorce, moreover, was losing much of its stigma, at least in the nation's larger cities. "A few years ago a divorced man or woman lost something of social status and was generally looked at askance, and divorce was regarded as a family disgrace," the *Michigan Catholic* pointed out in 1921. "At present divorce is accepted as a matter of course, having, perhaps, incidental evils but of no inherent wrong." The liberal Protestant clergy were sometimes blamed by Catholics for this dolorous state of affairs, but popular entertainment — particularly the now ubiquitous movies — was a far more frequent scapegoat. The marriage in 1920 of Douglas Fairbanks and Mary Pickford occasioned a series of outraged editorials in the

Michigan Catholic, for both stars had been previously married, and their immense popularity threatened to give divorce and remarriage a romantic legitimacy in the eyes of many Americans. Perhaps at their pastor's urging, the members of the St. Agnes Sodality at Detroit's St. Elizabeth's Church pledged to boycott any film in which either Fairbanks or Pickford appeared. The *Michigan Catholic* praised their "sacrifice," and noted that "a like movement" had recently been inaugurated in Holy Redeemer parish.[4]

The growing acceptability of divorce was evidently of concern to Bishop Michael Gallagher, for he ruled in 1923 that Catholics under his jurisdiction must henceforth have episcopal permission to file for divorce. Such permission had in fact been mandated by the Third Plenary Council of Baltimore, but Bishop Foley had apparently seen no need to have a diocesan regulation to this effect. There is a certain irony here, for Foley's tenure had spanned a period of rapid and dramatic increase in the incidence of divorce, while the Gallagher years were marked by a much more gradual rise, as indeed were the Mooney years that followed. But Gallagher's flock was an increasingly assimilated one, and presumably the more susceptible to shifts in social values. Archbishop Mooney, for his part, was certain that the largely assimilated Catholic population had been seriously affected by the culture's tolerance of divorce. "It is evident even to the casual observer," he wrote, probably in the mid-1940s, "that the evils of civil divorce have lessened the respect our Catholic people should have for the sacred bond of marriage."[5]

There is evidence, in fact, to indicate that this was true, although Catholics were notably different from other groups in their attitudes toward divorce. A 1958 survey found that Catholics in Detroit were much more likely than Protestants or Jews to think that divorce was "always" or "usually" wrong. Two-thirds of the middle-class Catholics questioned were of this opinion, as were 63 percent of the working-class Catholics. (In both groups, respondents were more likely to say that divorce was wrong than that birth control was always or usually wrong.) Still, more than one-third of the Catholics questioned were apparently convinced that divorce was morally acceptable in many cases. But Detroit's Catholics in 1958 had a relatively low incidence of divorce: 8 percent of the Catholics in the sample had been divorced, compared to 16 percent of the white Protestants. Among the Jewish respondents, interestingly enough, only 4 percent had been divorced, although the great majority of those respondents claimed to believe that divorce was not usually wrong.[6]

Catholics, then, were both markedly different from the rest of the population in their views on divorce, but affected too by the tolerant attitudes that prevailed in the larger society. Such, at least, is the picture that emerges from this particular study. Some of the Catholics who did not believe that divorce was wrong were obviously marginal Catholics: those who attended Mass irregularly, the study noted, were much more likely to condone divorce than those who were weekly churchgoers. But there were regular churchgoers too who were tolerant of divorce. Perhaps they knew first-hand of deeply unhappy marriages, or were troubled by the suffering that was an inevitable consequence of the Church's un-yielding stand on the indissolubility of marriage. But whatever their motivation, this minority, which proved to be a growing one, was clearly inclined to a less legalistic view of morality than the Church endorsed. They were obviously sup-ported in this inclination by a pragmatic, broadly tolerant society.[7]

Divorce was not a cause of political conflict between Catholics and Protes-tants in Detroit, despite their markedly different views. Divorce had been legal for a very long time in most American jurisdictions, and Michigan's divorce law was not a notably liberal one. Matters were quite different, however, with respect to contraception, which was increasingly a topic of public debate in the decades after World War I. Catholic spokesmen in Detroit, like their counterparts in other dioceses, were vociferous opponents of efforts to make birth control more freely available; increasingly—and especially after 1930—they were seen as the principal opponents of liberalized laws and policies with regard to contracep-tion. This led to a growing hostility toward the Church on the part of many non-Catholics, who argued that Catholics had no right to impose an essentially sec-tarian morality on a religiously diverse population. (This was, of course, very much the argument that Catholics had used against Prohibition and Sabbatar-ian laws.) The growing isolation of the Church in its opposition to contraception was an important source of the evident sense of "otherness" that prevailed among many assimilated Catholics in the decades after World War I. And it meant that the issue of birth control came to loom almost unnaturally large in the mind of the Catholic community. Opposition to birth control was a veritable badge of tribal membership for growing numbers of Catholics, and a touchstone of loy-alty to the Church.

Still, there were apparently many Catholics who largely ignored the Church's teaching on birth control. The Catholic birth rate in the 1920s declined more rapidly than that of American Protestants, although Catholic families were still, on average, much the larger. But large families were mainly found in the immi-grant generation; native-born Catholics tended to have markedly smaller fami-lies than their immigrant forebears had done, especially when those native-born Catholics lived in cities. It is not certain, of course, that these smaller families were achieved by means of contraceptive practice. But many Catholic spokes-men thought that "sinful artificial causes," in the words of the *Michigan Catholic,* had much to do with the fall in the Catholic birth rate. "Many letters have come to me disagreeing with the attitude I have taken towards Catholic women who persist in limiting their families," one of the paper's syndicated columnists wrote in 1928. "Some of these women have insisted that I am behind the times. Some go so far as to say the Church is narrow."[8]

The editor of the *Michigan Catholic* invariably attributed reactions like these to obstinate bad faith: it was "weak-kneed, so-called liberal Catholics" who suc-cumbed to the siren song of the birth-controllers. But there were those who thought that the problem had more fundamentally to do with the failure of the Church to explain the grounds on which contraception was forbidden. "I know of no Catholic who believes in divorce," a recent Catholic college graduate wrote in 1937, "but I know of innumerable Catholics who have been led to believe that birth control is not only advisable, but absolutely necessary. They do not know why it is wrong; ie, they do not understand the ends of marriage, nor the evils of frustrating a natural faculty, and hence they are practicing various means of contraception, and believing that they are quite within God's law, or at least getting around it neatly."[9]

The Catholic hierarchy and the Catholic press by 1937 had long since abandoned their reticence on the subject of contraception, and it is initially hard to see how Catholics could have remained in ignorance of Church teaching. A part of the explanation may lie in the relatively arcane nature of the Catholic argument against contraception. Most Catholics were not at home with "natural law" concepts, and may well have had trouble understanding the logic of an argument that seemed to ignore pragmatic considerations of individual and social good. Opposition to divorce made eminent sense in a population where social mobility, and even survival, depended on family solidarity; opposition to contraception was perhaps less evidently sensible, for small families were at a clear advantage when it came to achieving security and a degree of social mobility. Then too, it is possible that many priests were reluctant to question penitents closely in the confessional with regard to contraception, thereby encouraging those penitents to think that birth control, at least in their own circumstances, was not gravely sinful. There were venerable grounds in pastoral theology for a prudential practice of this sort, and it was one that would surely have eased the burdens of pastoral life, especially in working-class parishes. Indeed, there were bishops and priests, both in Europe and America, who claimed that this "laxist" approach was common in the confessional. But we have no way to know for certain whether or not this was the case.[10]

We do know, however, that contraception was more and more openly and widely addressed in the American Church in the decades after 1920. It was in the 1920s that birth control began to be acknowledged publicly as a fact of American life, and in this same decade the availability of inexpensive and generally effective contraceptives was greatly increased. It was in the 1920s too that the birth control movement in the United States ceased to be the domain of bohemians and political radicals, and began to acquire a soberly professional aura. Against this tide of social change, the Church in Detroit, like the Church elsewhere, hastened to erect defenses. The *Michigan Catholic* began to editorialize on the evils of contraception, something that it had hitherto done only rarely. Birth control, readers were repeatedly told, was an abominable crime—against the laws of God and of nature. It weakened the marriage bond and promoted immorality. It was a danger to the physical health of the individual and the moral health of the nation. And it meant a diminished ability, on the part of the nation, to defend itself in time of war. (The proponents of birth control, by this logic, were unpatriotic as well as immoral.) How frequently—and how explicitly—the topic was addressed in sermons in the 1920s is something we do not

know, although the priests of the Diocese were obliged by then to follow a prescribed course of sermon outlines that included a sermon on marriage. For the
matter was not an easy one to address, at least in clear and unmistakable terms,
before a large and varied audience. It makes sense, however, to assume that the
growing frankness of the *Michigan Catholic* with regard to contraception had
echoes in the realm of pastoral practice.[11]

It was still possible in the 1920s, if not entirely perspicacious, for Catholics
to believe that their views on birth control were shared by most professing Christians. Only a minority of liberal Protestant clergy were willing to publicly endorse the practice of contraception by married couples. But the situation was
fundamentally altered with the coming of the Great Depression. The terrible
suffering of the early 1930s gave weight to the arguments of liberal theologians,
and a number of Protestant leaders then, and even a few denominations, gave
conditional sanction to contraception. The most publicized of these pronouncements was that of the Anglicans' Lambeth Conference in the summer of 1930:
married couples might licitly use birth control, the conference resolved, if their
desire to avoid pregnancy did not result "from motives of selfishness, luxury, or
mere convenience." A standing committee of the Federal Council of Churches
in the United States gave a guarded blessing to contraception just a few months
later. And numerous local denominational bodies also endorsed the practice.
The Detroit Methodist Episcopal Conference, for example, adopted a resolution
late in 1931 that made the provision of contraceptive information to married
couples an obligation of pastors, who were held to be responsible for the "family
happiness" of their parishioners.[12]

The birth control movement acquired other respectable supporters too over
the course of the 1930s. They included growing numbers of physicians and social
workers, and a variety of moderate to liberal reformers. The General Federation
of Women's Clubs called in 1935 for repeal of the longtime ban on the distribution through the mails of contraceptive information and devices. And the American Medical Association voted in 1937 to recognize contraception as "proper
medical practice." There was growing popular acceptance of the practice too, as
evidenced in part by a sharply diminished birth rate. An equally telling sign was
a widespread tolerance, at least in large cities, for the promotion and sale of birth
control devices, even where this was against the law. "Contraceptive displays are
on view in many Detroit stores," the *Michigan Catholic* noted bitterly in 1935.
"Why can't Catholic organizations here take . . . action to enforce the law?" But
the law itself was under siege by then, for the birth control movement was better
organized in the 1930s than it had ever been before, and well aware that public
opinion was undergoing a major shift with regard to contraception. The Birth
Control League of Michigan, founded in 1931, quickly emerged as a tenacious
lobby for the repeal of anti-birth-control laws at the state and the federal levels.
It was active as well in raising funds for a growing network of "maternal health"
clinics in the state, which provided contraceptive information and devices to a
mostly working-class clientele. (Detroit had four such clinics by 1937, the first

of which had been opened in 1928.) That these clinics had Catholics among their clients was something of which the Chancery was unhappily aware: twenty-two of the fifty-four patients referred to one Detroit clinic in the latter half of 1937 had identified themselves as Catholics, at least according to an anonymous report on the clinic's operation.[13]

Catholic spokesmen were shocked by the seemingly sudden legitimization of birth control, and embittered by what they saw as a Protestant betrayal on the issue. This was clear in the *Michigan Catholic*'s editorials in the early 1930s, and in the numerous opinion pieces that the paper reprinted from national Catholic publications. "The last twelve months have witnessed attacks upon the family emanating not only from pagan sources, but even from groups commonly thought to be Christian," an editorial from *America* asserted in 1931. "The sole defender of the family in this supposedly Christian country is the Catholic Church." The sense of betrayal, and of acute alarm, was not confined to the American Church. Pius XI issued *Casti connubii*, his 1930 encyclical on Christian marriage, at least in part as a response to the Anglican decision to tolerate contraception. The encyclical provided a comprehensive synthesis of Catholic teaching on contraceptive practice, and directed the clergy to enunciate that teaching in clear and uncompromising terms, especially in the confessional. How quickly and extensively the encyclical affected pastoral practice is impossible to determine, but its effects were real and evidently widely felt. "At all events," as John T. Noonan has noted, "its issuance was of immense relevance to the question whether a Catholic could practice contraception in the innocent conviction that it was not a sin. The publicity of the encyclical itself in an age of rapid diffusion of the news made such innocence less likely."[14]

If the particulars of pastoral practice must remain a mystery, we know that the early 1930s saw a much more aggressive Catholic role in the politics of birth control. Numerous Catholic organizations were mobilized in defense of laws that limited or prohibited access to contraceptives. The League of Catholic Women was notably active in Detroit, lobbying against repeal of state and federal birth control laws, and against the provision of public monies to local birth control clinics. The Holy Name Society too issued regular condemnations of the birth control movement and its various legislative goals. Catholics were an important constituency in the Democratic party, and their protests were widely effective: not a single bill endorsed by the National Committee for Federal Legislation on Birth Control was passed by the Congress in the 1930s, and many states retained restrictive laws with regard to contraception. But Catholics paid for these victories, both in terms of revived hostility to the Church and an increasing sense of their own estrangement from a growing population of Americans.[15]

The 1930s was a significant decade on the birth control front for one additional reason. Recent medical findings had made possible a more effective use of periodic continence — the "rhythm method" — as a means of avoiding conception, and these findings were widely publicized in the early 1930s, both in the United States and Europe. There was considerable uncertainty as to the conditions under which "rhythm" might be tolerated or even recommended by a confessor, for *Casti connubii* had not spoken to the question. (Pius XII gave an explicit blessing to the method in 1951.) But the practice was apparently increasingly common in the 1930s and the 1940s. This seems to have been the case in the Archdiocese of Detroit: the Chancery announced a mandatory conference for priests in 1945 on "the morality of artificial birth control and rhythm and the treatment of these matters in the pulpit and the confessional." The two priests who addressed the conference stopped well short of endorsing the rhythm method as morally acceptable for all married couples, but agreed that it might be tolerated by confessors under a fairly wide variety of circumstances. And both asumed that a good many Catholics had attempted to use the method as a means of family limitation, although not always with the proper motives or under circumstances that would warrant a confessor's approval. The more conservative of the two, indeed, was of the opinion that contraceptive practice among Catholics was disturbingly widespread, and that Catholics were often reluctant to admit that such conduct was seriously sinful. "There can be no doubt in the mind of any confessor about the prevalence of the evil of birth control by contraceptive methods," Msgr. John Linsenmeyer asserted, "and his experience proves to him that only a few of those who practice these methods make their acts matter of confession."[16]

It was almost certainly true that substantial numbers of Catholics were using forbidden means of family limitation, even in the 1940s. They were, however, a distinct minority in the Catholic population, at least according to survey data. (A survey done in 1955, for example, estimated that about 30 percent of American Catholic women were using "artificial" birth control.) But a significantly larger minority of Catholics apparently believed that contraception was not necessarily sinful. Only 56 percent of working-class Catholics in Detroit, according to a 1958 study, thought that birth control was "always" or "usually" wrong. Middle-class Catholics were more likely to endorse Church teaching, but fully one-third of these respondents thought that birth control was not usually a sinful practice. Catholics were still much more likely than Protestants or Jews to be opposed to contraception, as this and other surveys indicated. And Catholic opposition to birth control was still a factor in politics. But the changing values of the larger society had clearly had an effect on the Catholic population. Certainly the Chancery assumed, by the late 1950s, that contraception was routinely practiced even by church-going Catholics. It was on these grounds that the archdiocesan director of the CCD was moved, in 1957, to criticize the increasingly popular custom of parents receiving communion with their children on First Communion Sundays. "It seems inconceivable to me," Msgr. Edward Burkhardt wrote, "that, in any given group of First Communicants, there would not be parents who are habitual and unrepentant in their use of birth control, and who, under the pressure of the situation, would not hestitate either to conceal such a sin from a priest or to lie to the priest about his or her dispositions." Cardinal Mooney apparently spoke to the issue at the priests' retreat that year. And in

1959 a Chancery directive forbade all First Communion ceremonies where parents received the sacrament together with their children.[17]

Contraception, then, was a source of division within the Church well before Vatican II. It is true that Catholic attitudes and behavior with regard to birth control changed more rapidly in the decade after the council than they had apparently done in the 1950s. But by the time of the council it was evident that American Catholics, for all their disciplined religious practice, were more and more inclined to a view of sex in marriage that departed fundamentally from papal teaching. Not that this teaching had been static: Pius XII had made an enormously important concession in 1951 when he endorsed the rhythm method for all Christian couples, provided that they had acceptable motives—and these he defined with unprecedented generosity—for avoiding conception. The Pope even expressed the hope that medical science would one day make the rhythm method a truly certain means of family limitation. But Pius XII, like his successors, was deeply ambivalent about sexual expression in marriage: the rhythm method, as Paul VI admitted, was acceptable largely because it imposed a period of continence on the couple, because it required them "to dominate instinct by means of . . . reason and free will." This was a view of married sex that fewer and fewer of the laity were willing to accept. Indeed, before the 1960s had drawn to a close, the growing estrangement of the laity with regard to sexual ethics had done more than anything else to create a crisis in episcopal authority.[18]

POLITICS

The early 1920s saw a resurgence of organized anti-Catholicism that was very nearly national in scope, although its wellsprings were mainly in the South. It was to some extent a continuation of prewar trends. But the anti-Catholicism of the 1920s had a more intensely xenophobic flavor than it had had before the First World War, and an apparently broader appeal. This unsavory chapter in American political history had to do in part with a troubled economy—high rates of inflation and unemployment bedeviled the nation between 1919 and 1922—and with a postwar upturn in foreign immigration. These problems were acutely manifested in Detroit, where unemployment was at crisis proportions in 1921, and where rapid population growth, much of it due to immigration, had caused a serious housing shortage. But the surly political mood of the country had at least as much to do with a soured idealism and a frustrated longing for order. The crusading spirit of 1918 had given way to a bitter sense of betrayal, for it was almost immediately clear that the war had failed to establish a new morality internationally. Nor had America been purified by her first great foreign crusade: a wave of strikes and riots followed hard upon the war, and then an outbreak of the most pervasive lawlessness in the nation's history. (The lawlessness was occasioned by the advent of Prohibition, which was yet another failed crusade. For its advocates had hoped to restore the country to a mythic purity and uniformity.) The politics of the early 1920s, then, were freighted with an almost intolerable burden of disappointed hopes and exaggerated fears. It is hardly surprising that Catholics, along with blacks and Jews and the foreign-born, should have found themselves in the role of scapegoat.[19]

The rising tide of discontent was apparent in Michigan even in 1919. The campaign to outlaw parochial schools was coming by then to resemble a mass-based movement, although it fell well short of majority support within the state. A more disturbing indicator, at least for non-Catholics, was the growth in the state of the Ku Klux Klan, which had only recently been resurrected as a white-supremacist organization. The resurrected Klan, however, was also bitterly anti-Catholic, and it was principally on an anti-Catholic platform that it came to prominence in Michigan and in Detroit. The height of Klan power in the state was apparently achieved in 1924, when a write-in campaign for mayor of Detroit nearly succeeded in placing a Klan-backed candidate in office. That campaign—it was a three-man contest—was a vitriolic one, and the results revealed a deep religious division within Detroit's electorate. But the victor in 1924 was in fact a Catholic, one John W. Smith, who was easily reelected in 1925. Smith was the beneficiary of an enormous Catholic vote in both elections, Catholics being by far the largest minority group in the city. He ran well too among Detroit's growing population of blacks and among Jews, for both groups were even more fearful of the Klan than Catholics were. (The Klan, then, was probably an unwitting engine of Catholic political progress.) Smith's winning coalition in 1924 and 1925 was very much that which had launched Frank Murphy on his Detroit political career in 1923, when he was first elected a judge of the Recorder's Court.[20]

Klan strength in Michigan waned rapidly after 1925, the result in part of well-publicized financial scandals within the national organization. But the decline had to do as well with a change in the national mood: the xenophobic fever of the early 1920s had cooled perceptibly by 1925. This was due partly to a now-booming economy, and partly to the recent success of the nativist lobby in securing the most stringent legal restrictions on immigration in the nation's history. And there was a growing revulsion at the excesses of the various movements that championed the cause of so-called Nordic supremacy. The public did not turn decisively against the assumptions that underlay such movements, although the growing secularity of the culture had already weakened the basis for anti-Catholicism. Nonetheless, as John Higham has written, "the nation's traditional values undoubtedly exercised a quiet brake on xenophobia."[21]

The change in mood was apparent on many fronts by 1925, but perhaps nowhere more so than in the vicinity of Lapeer, where the Church Extension Society had in 1923 begun an experiment in rural evangelization. Lapeer County had been an important center of Klan activity in the early part of the decade, and had twice voted in favor of the anti-parochial-school amendment. By the mid-1920s, however, pastors there were able to report a noticeable thaw in Protestant-Catholic relations. Father John Parker, for example, who came to the village of Davison in 1926, found many Protestants who were eager to be part of a parish musical comedy production, staged to raise money for his tiny congregation. "Half the cast is non-Catholic," he noted. "We have a professional director, a hired orchestra, and almost a Klan chorus. It's going to be some show." By the spring of 1927, Father Parker had lectured locally at the Literary Club and at the high school, and had agreed to hold the high school baccalaureate services for 1927 in the Davison Catholic church. And he was pleased to report that local Catholics had "succeeded in getting the stores of Davison to close for Good Friday afternoon. This stopped a M[ethodist] E[piscopal] supper that was to be given on Good Friday evening." Nor was Father Parker's experience a singular one. His confreres in neighboring villages had similar stories to tell.[22]

Passions had cooled to such an extent by 1928 that it was possible for the Democrats to nominate a Catholic candidate for president. Al Smith's candidacy was inevitably of great symbolic importance for Catholics, and, perhaps just as inevitably, occasioned a groundswell of anti-Catholic propaganda, especially in the South. "The country is being flooded with anti-Catholic literature," the *Michigan Catholic* complained in September. "These spurious, silly and vicious charges have been exploded a thousand times." For its own part, the *Michigan Catholic* had remained above the battle, as had most of the Catholic press. The paper gave only the most limited coverage to the Smith campaign, and, true to its tradition of nonpartisanship—a tradition, at any rate, since the turn of the century— did not endorse the Democratic standard-bearer. The editor, indeed, praised both nominees for their qualifications, pointing out that the election of either would make religious history, for Herbert Hoover was a Quaker, and no Quaker had ever been elected president. But he did see fit to carry a syndicated column, called "Your Ready Answer," which was meant to help Catholics counter the many arguments that were being advanced against Smith on the grounds of his religion. These did not necessarily have to do with theology or Church discipline. On September 13 the column was devoted to the objection that "Catholics are not fitted to hold high office. They haven't the refinement other Americans have."[23]

Smith was not as badly defeated, at least in terms of the popular vote, as the Democratic nominee had been in 1920. Nor had his party fared well in 1924, for it was badly factionalized and seemingly resigned to long-term minority status. But if Smith's defeat looks in retrospect to have been very nearly inevitable, it was still painful for many Catholics. The campaign had been an ugly one, and Catholics were all too aware that Hoover was the first Republican to have broken the "Solid South." This alone seemed likely to doom the presidential aspirations of Catholics for a long time to come. But Smith had run surprisingly well in a number of large industrial cities, although Detroit was not among their number, and he had done better than expected among Western farmers. This suggested an emerging base for a revitalized politics of reform, should the Democratic party overcome its divisions and chart a fresh ideological course. Such a thing seemed unlikely in prosperous 1928. But by 1932, conditions were very different. The party was poised on the verge of the "Roosevelt revolution," and Catholics were about to see their political fortunes altered.

Something like this had already happened, in fact, in the city of Detroit, where Frank Murphy had been elected mayor in 1930 and again in 1931. The 1930 election had pitted Murphy against the incumbent Charles Bowles, whose corrupt administration — shocking even by Detroit's lax standards — had resulted in his recall and a subsequent special election. Bowles had been the Klan-backed candidate for mayor in 1924 and 1925, and there were reform-minded Catholics locally who counseled Murphy not to run. Bowles would surely raise the religious issue with Murphy in the race: "It is his big card," Father John McNichols, SJ, pointed out, and there was "enough small-minded Protestantism in Detroit to make it count." But religion was not an overt issue in the 1930 campaign. Father McNichols had perhaps drawn unwarranted conclusions from Al Smith's defeat in 1928. Or he may have assumed that the advent of hard times meant a resurgence of anti-Catholicism in politics, as it had so often done in the past.[24]

In 1930, however, hard times gave birth to an issue-oriented politics, at least in Detroit. Murphy ran well that year in the city's ethnic neighborhoods and among blacks and Jews — an uneasy coalition of the reform-minded and the dispossessed. And his first year in office produced programs and rhetoric that reinforced the loyalty of this varied constituency. Murphy was an early proponent of what eventually came to be known as New Deal liberalism. "We have been in an era of extreme individualism," he commented in 1934. "It has been best expressed in the industrial order, where it was believed that every man should look out for himself. But this individualism is ruthless and un-Christian, because every man does not have a chance to look out for himself. We shall have to substitute a socialistic sense for this individualistic sense." In a devastated Detroit, where unemployment may have run to 50 percent at the depths of the Depression, talk like this was bound to elicit a response that cut across religious lines. Detroit was indeed a polarized city in the early 1930s, but it was more and more a polarization based on social class.[25]

Still, Frank Murphy was a source of pride for the great majority of Catholics locally, and a powerful symbol of the group's political coming-of-age. The rise of Father Charles Coughlin to national prominence coincided with the Murphy mayoralty, something that strengthened the association of Murphy, then a Coughlin ally, with Catholic political assertion. The superior of the Good Shepherd Sisters in Detroit was presumably typical of a good many Catholics in her response to Murphy's victory in the 1931 primary. "We are all very happy over the results," Mother Patricia wrote from her convent, "and we watched the returns with great interest. During all day Tuesday, Oct. 6th, prayers were being said in our chapel by Sisters, Magdalens and children, and lights kept burning that if it were God's holy will you might be the choice of the people of Detroit." Father Michael Cefai, pastor at St. Paul's (Maltese) Church in Detroit, had also seen the hand of God in the 1931 primary. "Once again the people have spoken," he wrote to Murphy, "and once again, through them, God has manifested His

Will. God wants you to be Detroit's Mayor." Loyalties like these were hardly a secret in Detroit, and there were last-minute efforts to rally the so-called Protestant vote against the mayor. But if this had any effect at all, it probably worked to augment Murphy's impressive margin of victory. Catholics did better than ever before in contests for the City Council, too: when the votes had been counted in 1931, four of its nine members, chosen at-large, were Catholics.[26]

Murphy's career for the rest of the decade was closely linked to that of Franklin Roosevelt, who regarded Murphy as a principal ally in the Midwest and an important liaison to Catholics. Murphy's association with Roosevelt, in turn, strengthened his image as a champion of the poor, and helped to broaden his appeal among non-Catholics. And this helped to undermine the long tradition of religious division in Michigan politics. The state broke with another, albeit related, tradition in 1932, when it gave its electoral votes to Roosevelt — he was the first Democrat to have carried the state since 1852 — and elected a Democratic governor and legislature. Frank Murphy himself ran for governor in 1936, although his religion was widely thought to be a handicap in so heavily Protestant and traditionally Republican a state. That handicap was presumably a major reason that Murphy's victory in 1936 was a narrow one — far narrower than the margin by which a triumphant Roosevelt carried the state. But it was victory nonetheless, and Murphy took office in 1937 as Michigan's first Catholic chief executive.[27]

Governor Murphy's term in office was an eventful one. Michigan was a principal arena of labor strife in 1937, and Murphy gained national notice — notoriety, in some quarters — for his role in mediating the sit-down strikes at General Motors and Chrysler. For a time, indeed, his reputation was such that he was prominently mentioned, and not only in Michigan, as a possible presidential candidate in 1940. Murphy himself was not immune to presidential fever, and made it a point to speak frequently outside the state during his term as governor, although he never ceased to worry that his religion might be a fatal handicap in a national race. The Murphy-for-president "boomlet" came to an end, however, in November 1938, for he was decisively beaten in his bid for re-election as Michigan's governor. A weakened economy had eroded his support, and he may well have paid a price for his prominent identification with the cause of industrial unionism. There were those who thought that this was the case among conservative Catholics. "Many of those who gave *lip-service* to Social doctrines you have enacted into law deserted their own party to vote against you," a leading layman in Detroit informed a disappointed Murphy. "We know that this is true and this kind of defection, in my judgment, had much to do with your losing the election."[28]

The balance of Murphy's career was played out on a national stage. He served as Roosevelt's attorney general from 1939 until 1940, and then as an associate justice of the Supreme Court. But he left behind him in Michigan an important political legacy. Murphy had attracted a coalition of interest groups to his various campaigns that eventually transformed the Michigan Democratic party, and this transformed party, after World War II, made Michigan a genuine two-party state. For the mostly Democratic Catholic population, this meant a greater political leverage than it had ever had before. Murphy, moreover, both symbolized and helped to generate a growing Catholic political confidence. If Michigan's Catholics did not wholly outgrow their defensive mentality when it came to public life, they were notably more at ease in the political arena by the close of the Murphy era.[29]

This heightened confidence is evident in the increasingly systematic attention that Michigan's bishops gave to politics. The state's five Catholic bishops agreed in 1942 to give their joint support to what was in effect a Church lobbyist, who was "to look after our interests in Lansing while the Legislature is in session." In 1944, the bishops established the Michigan Catholic Welfare Committee. Made up of charity and school officials from each of the Michigan dioceses, the committee was expected to monitor state legislative developments and to recommend action, where it was appropriate, to the bishops of the Michigan Province. The committee proved to be an effective lobby on a number of strictly Catholic matters, and it regularly worked with other religious and civic groups on a variety of larger issues. In 1958, for example, the Michigan Catholic Welfare Conference, as it was now known, had a hand in the defeat of a proposal to mandate Bible reading in the schools, worked — unsuccessfully — for a bill to ban most Sunday shopping, and supported successful measures to restrict the sale of "indecent literature." In each of these endeavors, the conference had substantial non-Catholic support.[30]

There was little non-Catholic support, however, for state aid to parochial schools, something that had long headed the Catholic political agenda. Limited gains had been made, to be sure. The Michigan legislature voted in 1939 to authorize local school districts to provide bus transportation to children who attended nonpublic schools. By the 1950s, the parochial schools were the beneficiaries of public health services and government-subsidized milk and hot-lunch programs. There were numerous cases too where parochial school pupils made use of public school facilities. But it was clear that Michigan's voters would not countenance any direct subsidy to parochial education, and Catholic leaders were deeply resentful on this score, as were untold numbers of Catholic parents. Their resentment seems to have grown significantly in the decade after 1945, as the cost of Catholic education began its precipitous rise.[31]

The issue was an increasingly divisive one at the national level too. The Catholic bishops' longstanding opposition to federal aid to education was politically awkward by the late 1940s, as Cardinal Mooney, among many others, was uncomfortably aware. But those bishops who did not object in principle to federal aid were unwilling to support it without provision being made for aid to parochial schools. This demand touched off an acrimonious debate in the late 1940s, one that did considerable damage to Catholic-Protestant relations.

That debate has continued, albeit in generally muted tones, up to the present day, with the federal courts having played a major role in defining the terms of the dispute. For Michigan's Catholics, however, the parameters of the debate were abruptly narrowed in 1970, when a referendum amended the state's constitution to prohibit any public funds from being expended on nonpublic schools. "Proposition C," as it was known, had been opposed by a broad coalition of religious and political leaders, and contested by Catholics with much the same vigor they had brought to the "school amendment" campaigns of the early 1920s. Its passage was a death-knell for a number of financially troubled schools. And it seemed to many Catholics to constitute a repudiation of their rights as citizens — to call into question the political progress that Catholics had purportedly made.[32]

But that progress was real, notwithstanding Proposition C. The proposition, indeed, had been initiated in response to a major Catholic victory in the Michigan legislature, which had voted early in 1970 to make state funds available for the purpose of subsidizing lay teachers' salaries in nonpublic schools. (This form of "parochiaid," as it was popularly known, was subsequently held to be constitutional by the state supreme court.) Some of the considerable support for Proposition C was certainly rooted in anti-Catholic sentiment. Some of it represented an inchoate anger at rising taxes. But there were many voters who genuinely believed that a strong system of public schools was essential to the health and continued political openness of a multiracial and multiconfessional society, and that the state had an obligation to devote its resources to the public schools alone. Perhaps they were wrong; many Catholics thought that they were. But the logic is not inherently anti-Catholic.

War and rumors of war

Relatively few Catholics in the 1930s were much concerned with questions of foreign policy, although the world was clearly in a parlous state. Many leaned to a vaguely isolationist position, hoping to forestall American involvement in a second European war. But the issues that were real to the vast majority of Catholics were domestic issues, unemployment preeminent among them. Domestic issues were of major importance to the hierarchy too and to prominent members of the laity. For Catholic leaders like these, however, the 1930s was also a decade of struggles over foreign policy, struggles that invariably pitted the Church against the forces of secular liberalism. Those forces were triumphant, more often than not: Catholics protests had not prevented American recognition of the Soviet Union nor appreciably altered American policy with regard to Mexico. But Catholics were instrumental in shaping the American response to the Spanish Civil War, an achievement for which they paid a price, both in terms of liberal hostility to the Church and their own sense of alienation.

Archbishop Mooney stood with the rest of the hierarchy in its support of the Franco forces. But he was apparently troubled by the bitterness of the debate that raged domestically over Spain, and by the tendency on both sides to see matters in simplistic terms. Sympathy for the Spanish Republic, he told the Apostolic Delegate in 1941, should not necessarily be taken as an index of hostility to the Church. "For my own part, I am inclined to allow a large margin of error on this matter to non-Catholics in general," he wrote, "and in fact to all who have no exact knowledge of the situation in unhappy Spain." The principal lay supporter of Franco's cause in Detroit was likewise inclined to more modulated opinions in private than he was in public. Arthur D. Maguire, a local attorney, was capable in 1938 of likening Catholic defectors from Frank Murphy's camp to "reactionary Catholics in Spain," who "took all hope out of the hearts of the Common people—that was one of the main causes of the Spanish Civil War." Significantly, perhaps, he wrote these things to his archbishop.[33]

Still, the public campaign in defense of Franco was as uncompromising in Detroit as it was elsewhere. The *Michigan Catholic* was not as extreme in its editorial rhetoric as certain Catholic organs were, but its coverage of the war was lurid and wholly uncritical, and it leveled bitter criticism at the *Catholic Worker* for that paper's editorial stance in favor of neutrality. The war in Spain was a "crusade," the editor pointed out. "If 'The Catholic Worker' is right in its advocacy of neutrality on the Spanish issue, then the Popes were wrong when they encouraged the Catholics to wage war on the Turks at Lepanto and before the gates of Vienna." The principal focus of activity locally was a petition drive early in 1939 in support of a continued American embargo on arms to Spain. Arthur Maguire chaired the drive in Detroit—it was part of a nationwide campaign, orchestrated by the National Council of Catholic Men—and under his direction the work proceeded with apparent dispatch. "The committee has addressed a letter to pastors," the *Michigan Catholic* reported on January 12, "and tens of thousands of petition blanks are being distributed among societies and parishes in the Detroit area. . . . The signed petitions will be picked up Jan. 19 by students of the University of Detroit under the direction of the Rev. Joseph A. Luther, SJ." Before the month was out, Maguire was claiming a total of more than 175,000 signatures. Under the circumstances, this seems to indicate a widespread support among Catholics for the embargo.[34]

That support, of course, may have tapped isolationist sentiment as well as sympathy for Franco's cause. A Gallup poll in 1938 concluded that slightly more than half of American Catholics were either neutral on the Spanish question or partisans of the Loyalists. But in Detroit, as in virtually every other diocese, the Catholic leadership was solidly on the Nationalist side. The one dissenting voice locally was that of Msgr. Joseph Ciarrocchi, whose *La Voce del Popolo* gave a qualified editorial blessing to the Loyalist cause, on the grounds that the Loyalists were fighting a "triple facism"—and against enormous odds. The embargo, in his view, was not neutrality but a dangerous partiality, and he opposed Catholic efforts to retain it. Ciarrocchi's unorthodox position earned him a sharp rebuke from the Chancery early in 1939, after which he promised to be silent on the Spanish question. "But I am sorry . . . that I cannot retract what I have said on the matter," he told Chancellor Edward Hickey, "as I would be an hypocrite and betray principles of Justice as I see them." He had not changed his views a decade later, when he confided to Cardinal Mooney his deep misgivings about what he assumed was the hierarchy's support for American recognition of the Franco regime. "To protect Franco's reactionary and tyrannical regime would be a stain worse than the one coming from the upholding of Mussolini," he warned. "You would probably not experience immediately much damage, but all faux passes are paid in history sooner or later."[35]

Spain and Mexico were distant tragedies, the stuff of propaganda. But the war in Europe was by 1940 the uneasy preoccupation of growing numbers of Americans. The tenor of the national debate over foreign policy grew increasingly shrill in 1940, when Catholics were prominently associated with the anti-interventionist camp, although there was a considerable division on the issue among the national Catholic leadership. Pearl Harbor put an end to the debate, and ushered in four grueling years of war, from which the United States emerged as incontestably the world's most powerful nation, and one with a potentially vast international role. The country was fundamentally changed because of this, and in ways that eventually led to new political divisions among Catholics. In the shorter term, however, the war meant a heightened unity within the multiethnic Catholic population, and worked as well to diminish the distance between Catholics and other Americans. For the war was a powerful agent of national homogenization.

What made the war so effective in this respect was not simply its length or its totality, although these were immensely important. Day-to-day life on the home front meant a consciousness of national purpose and identity that was greater than anything experienced in previous conflicts. Even more significant, however, was the radically egalitarian ideology that was deployed in the struggle against Nazism. The domestic applications of this ideology were widely ignored or even resisted: Detroit is not the only city whose wartime history is scarred by racial violence. But the war years also saw the first federal measures against racial discrimination in hiring, and saw the rise of an unprecedented militancy among Northern blacks—an important new dimension in urban and national politics. And this had meaning for Catholics, although religious bigotry by the 1940s could hardly compare in intensity to hatreds based on race. For anti-Catholicism had since the 1890s been substantially fueled by theories about the genetic inferiority of peoples from Southern and Eastern Europe. Insofar as racist thinking was delegitimized, Catholics stood to benefit. An inevitable by-product of the assault on the racist mentality, moreover, was a celebration of the virtue of tolerance. That celebration was so much a part of American life in the postwar years that some religious leaders — not all of them Catholics — feared for the doctrinal integrity of their respective churches. But there is no doubt that the altered mood meant an easing of religious tensions. Significantly, as we have noted, the anti-Catholicism of the postwar decade was largely an elite concern, and not a mass-based movement.

Detroit and its satellite cities were powerful symbols, during the war, of American industrial might. But they were more troubling when taken as images of the nation's common life, for they were severely congested, wracked by racial and ethnic animosities, and by a rising incidence of delinquency and family instability. It was problems of the latter sort that seem most to have worried the local Catholic leadership, who found it especially hard to bless the wartime employment of married women. "Parents, your responsibility for your children comes before any other consideration," the pastor at St. John the Evangelist warned in 1943, disturbed by a "notable increase in the absentee list of our school." Still, the employment of wives and even mothers was clearly a necessity, for there was an acute shortage of workers locally by 1943. Several parishes, indeed, had wartime day nurseries on their premises, and the Felician Sisters opened a nursery for the children of defense workers at the Guardian Angel Home in Detroit in 1942.[36]

What redeemed such sacrifices, for a man like Archbishop Mooney, were the veritably holy purposes for which he believed the Allies were fighting. "The fate of our country and of Christian civilization hangs in the balance," he wrote to his priests toward the end of 1942, urging them to say a "Victory Mass" each Sunday and to devote the weekly Holy Hour to prayers for local soldiers and the victims of war. In much the same spirit, he assured his priests that the national flag could be displayed in church during Mass and other ceremonies; indeed, it ought to be displayed, if parishioners so requested. The "religious foundations of patriotism" that Mooney commended to his clergy's care have, of course, a venerable lineage. The Archbishop's wartime rhetoric is easily matched by any number of local sermons during World War I. But the Second World War had a demonstrably greater effect on the worldview of most Americans than the much briefer involvement in the First World War had done. The relative restraint of domestic rhetoric during World War II is an ironic witness to this: there was not much doubt at home about the threat or the fundamental evil of the enemy. This unanimity contributed mightily to the sense of national purpose that was so important a product of the war. And it gave to postwar foreign policy a crusading flavor that commended it to most Americans and perhaps especially to Catholics, for whom the apocalyptic vision of a John Foster Dulles bore a kind of tacit imprimatur.[37]

Mobilization meant that Catholic institutions, like most others, were permeated by a consciousness of the war and its apparently imminent threat to the American mainland. Parochial schoolchildren, like their public-school counterparts, had weekly air-raid drills, and Sacred Heart Seminary offered regular lectures on civil defense, where, in the words of the Holy Trinity parish chronicles, the participants "were instructed about what to do when the bombs really come." Marygrove College instituted mandatory "victory courses" for its students in the winter of 1942; "these classes covered every phase of work and study that women might need in a war emergency," the IHMs' historian has explained, "from auto repair to general principles of international law." And there was no parish so small that its life was not colored by the war, its Sunday bulletins filled with news of parish boys in the armed forces, its women's groups given over to Red Cross sewing, its liturgies and devotions directed to the cause of peace with victory. Father Emmet Hannick of St. Rose parish in Detroit was a model wartime pastor: each of the more than 650 parish men who entered the military received his pastor's personal blessing and a rosary and missal, according to a longtime friend of Father Hannick. "He kept in touch with all the boys with personal letters, sending Christmas packages and other gifts from time to time."[38]

The war meant new institutional experiences too. Catholics had provided their own recreational services to soldiers in the First World War, when the Knights of Columbus had regarded itself as a rival of sorts to the Salvation Army and the YMCA. But during World War II, Catholics joined with Protestants and Jews in the United Services Organization (USO). The USO in Detroit had an interfaith executive committee and a presidency that was supposed to rotate among Catholic, Protestant, and Jewish representatives. The first president was a Catholic, who was duly succeeded by a Jew. But Henry Myers was so effective in the job that the executive committee asked him to serve for the duration of the war. "Father Clancy was a prime mover in this," the executive director of the local USO remembered, having reference to Father Raymond Clancy, who served as the committee's Catholic representative. The Detroit USO was an ambitious operation, coordinating the services of nearly 20,000 volunteers. And for many of those who worked closely with it, the experience was a profoundly ecumenical one. "This was the first time in Detroit, I am told, that Catholic, Protestant and Jewish organizations . . . had ever worked together—at such a high level—to supervise such a large organization," the executive director later recalled. "The results were most inspiring, and their wholesome shadow must have been of great help in future programs."[39]

It was an altered Catholic community, then, that emerged from the war: less divided within itself, more fully integrated into American life. It was an altered world as well, filled with unexpected international tensions and, for all the veneer of domestic conservatism, a fundamental restiveness at home. The most consequential signs of the times, domestically, had to do with race: a new black assertiveness, coupled with a delegitimization of racist ideologies, meant a renegotiation of race relations in the United States, beginning—but not ending—with an assault on legal segregation. That renegotiation was a long and sometimes violent process, and one that changed the face of American life. It changed the American Church as well, notwithstanding its relatively small black membership.

CATHOLICS AND RACE

Detroit had only a small black population before the First World War. (There were just under 6,000 blacks in the city in 1910, about 1.2 percent of its total population.) Their small numbers had helped to blunt the worst effects of racism: the city's principal black district was home as well to many whites, and the black elite enjoyed surprising access to white political and business circles. The city's public schools, moreover, had been integrated in 1871, albeit at state behest and only after several years of bitter white resistance. Nor was the color line invariably drawn in public accommodations: many of Detroit's restaurants complied with the terms of Michigan's 1885 civil rights act and served blacks, while the city's theaters in the late nineteenth century were open to all comers. The great majority of blacks, to be sure, were confined to poverty by a segregated labor market, and in no condition to appreciate the relative freedom enjoyed by more affluent members of their race. Still, their situation was freer and more secure than that of blacks in the post-Reconstruction South.[40]

For all the tolerance accorded the local black elite, the vast majority of whites in Detroit before 1914 held unabashedly racist views. (This was true, indeed, as late as the 1940s.) Catholics were no different in this respect from other Detroiters, despite their own experience of bigotry. Catholics, in fact, were widely believed to be more aggressively anti-black than many of their contemporaries, for it was Catholics with whom blacks typically competed for jobs and housing. Detroit's heavily Irish Corktown district was reputed to be a dangerous place for blacks in the nineteenth century, and gangs of Irish toughs harassed black citizens on occasion in the city's principal Negro district. Black leaders, in their turn, were sometimes bitterly xenophobic in their rhetoric, lending support, in the 1890s and after, to proposals for immigration restriction and even, in several notable instances, to the virulently anti-Catholic American Protective Association.[41]

Despite the tension that prevailed between blacks and certain segments of the Catholic community, Catholic spokesmen locally, in the years before World War I, were largely silent on the issue of race. Bishop Foley is not known to have spoken publicly on the matter, nor, evidently, did any of his clergy. The *Michigan Catholic,* on the other hand, ran periodic editorials on the question of race relations, although these almost never had reference to the local scene, and it regularly carried news about the spread of Catholicism among American blacks and in Africa. Longtime editor William Hughes was proud of the universality of his Church, and sensitive to the egalitarian strain in American culture. He was capable in 1890 of applauding a Michigan Supreme Court decision that upheld the public accommodations section of the state's civil rights law and that endorsed "an absolute, unconditional equality of white and colored men before the law." He gave front-page coverage in 1891 to Archbishop Ireland's call for abolition of the color line, including an end to laws against miscegenation. But Hughes was by no means free of the racism that permeated his society, and his editorials endorsing legal equality for blacks were considerably outnumbered by those that argued for segregation in the South and a rigidly limited sphere of equality in the North. "A great part" of the black population, the *Michigan Catholic* declared in 1892, "are essentially as much pagan as their ancestors in Africa." Hence they did not merit the suffrage, not in the South, at any rate, where their numbers were so large. "First make the Southern negroes socially the equals of white, by making them as a class, what they are not now, a moral people, honest, industrious and well-behaved generally, and then political equality will follow as a matter of course, without the aid of constitutional amendments or of political agitation."[42]

Hughes was willing to grant, at least in his more reflective moments, that blacks were potentially worthy of political equality; in this sense his was not a purely racist point of view. But by the mid-1890s, with racist thinking coming more and more to dominate the nation's intellectual life, Hughes spoke increasingly in terms of an ineradicable inferiority. His paper came very close to condoning the widespread practice of lynching—"the law of the land holds no deterrent strong enough to prevent black ruffians from outrages on white females"—and defended laws against miscegenation. There were "ordinances set in man's inner being," the *Michigan Catholic* declared in 1893, "which decree that the races shall not intermingle." For this reason, all but the most perfunctory social contact between the races was impossible. Intimate association with blacks caused "revulsion and disgust" in whites, the paper asserted in 1897, arguing against the appointment of the first black cadet to the Naval Academy. Presumably the same revulsion would justify nearly every instance of discrimination that occurred in Detroit, and perhaps even the illegal practice of segregation in public places.[43]

The *Michigan Catholic* was never again as stridently racist in its editorials as it was in the mid-1890s. The ebbing of racist passions nationally was evident after the turn of the century, and the calmer mood was reflected in the paper's columns. William Hughes could argue with genuine conviction against the evils of lynching by 1906, and he seldom had reference, after 1900, to crime and sexual immorality among blacks. Indeed his paper made no comment at all about the rapid growth of Detroit's black population during and after 1915, despite an ominous increase in racial tensions locally. But it was clear that Hughes and his associates assumed that blacks in the North would live and work, at least for the foreseeable future, almost wholly apart from whites, and that whites were justified in demanding segregation when it came to jobs and housing. "It is not very nice to find out that your across the hall neighbor is a mulatto," the *Michigan Catholic*'s "Rosaleen" wrote in 1911, cautioning her readers against the dangers of even "high-class" apartment houses. Her almost reflexive racism was typical, not only of Catholics, but of white Detroit as a whole.[44]

Churches have historically been among the most segregated of American institutions, and such was the case in nineteenth-century Detroit. Probably fewer than 2 percent of the city's black churchgoers at the turn of the century were members of white congregations. Those black churchgoers, of course, were nearly all Protestants. Detroit had received little immigration from either Maryland or Louisiana—the principal cradles of black Catholicism—and the Church in Detroit had made only the most limited efforts at convert work among blacks. Father Bernard Soffers, the Dutch-born pastor of St. Anne's parish, is the only priest in the nineteenth century who is known to have evangelized in Detroit's black community. He had a "chapel for colored people" in the basement of his church by the mid-1860s, and it was he who encouraged the IHM Sisters to open a "colored school" in Detroit. They did so in 1867, in a modest frame building that was hastily erected behind the then-cathedral. The school survived only until 1870, however. The Sisters "found it impossible to bring the children to religious principles," according to their mission chronicle. "None of them showed any desire for baptism. It was therefore thought proper to close the school."[45]

Father Soffers was transferred to Monroe in 1872, which brought an unceremonious end to the "colored chapel" at St. Anne's. He left behind him a city lot that had been bought for a future black church, and a "Coloured Church and School fund," which survived at least through 1876. But it was not until 1911 that a second "colored chapel" was established in Detroit. Until that time, Detroit's black Catholics apparently worshiped with whites. "We have not a few Catholic negroes who attend the churches nearest their homes," the *Michigan Catholic* reported in 1898, the editor unfortunately neglecting to indicate just which churches these were. We do know, however, that one of the founding members of St. Peter Claver's (Negro) parish had been a longtime communicant at Holy Trinity, notwithstanding the history of enmity between the city's Irish and its blacks. At least one black family were members of the Cathedral parish. And a well-known black attorney was buried from St. Stanislaus (Polish) Church in 1908.[46]

The founding of St. Peter Claver's mission in 1911 signals the beginning of what might be called the era of the "racial parish" in Detroit, an era that ended after World War II. Four parishes for blacks were established in the city between 1911 and 1943, and a fifth — a mission in the mostly black suburb of Inkster — was opened in 1945. Each of these was regarded at the Chancery as something other than a territorial parish; their memberships were defined by race and only secondarily by residence. (Thus, Our Lady of Victory mission "serves the Negroes in Presentation and St. James Parishes," according to its pastor in 1948.) The racial parish was analogous to the ethnic parish in certain respects, although it could hardly be justified, as ethnic parishes were, by the need to provide for people whose native language was not English. (This did not prevent the *Michigan Catholic* in 1926 from including St. Peter Claver's in a list of "strictly foreign-speaking" parishes.) The ethnic parish, moreover, was at least in theory a temporary phenomenon; ethnic parishes were expected eventually to assume territorial status. But there is no indication before the late 1940s that the Chancery saw the racial parish as anything but a permanent part of the city's religious landscape.[47]

Still, the racial parish was widely regarded, at least among Catholics, as a sign of liberality. The appalling poverty in which most blacks lived could be effectively remedied only by means of their moral regeneration, or so most Catholics were led to believe. Support for the "colored missions," then, was a way of expressing concern for the plight of a suffering and despised minority, and of affirming the spiritual equality of blacks. Interest in the "colored missions" seems to have risen perceptibly in the decade after World War I. Such, at least, was the case in Detroit, where the "colored missions" benefited from a growing fascination with missionary work generally and where escalating racial tensions threatened an always-fragile civic order. The *Michigan Catholic* carried a notably increased volume of news about missionary work among blacks in the 1920s, and evinced a cautious interest in the development of black vocations to the convent and the priesthood. This latter was especially significant, for it entailed at least a tacit admission of black equality in the intellectual sphere. Indeed, the drift of mission publicity in the 1920s was toward a warmer, more human image of blacks, one that stressed their dignity as persons fully as much as their purported simplicity and childlike spontaneity. But the paper was far from ready to challenge the color line, either locally or in the South. The *Michigan Catholic* gave no coverage to Detroit's notorious "Sweet case" in the mid-1920s, nor did it make more than passing reference to the anti-black agenda of the Ku Klux Klan. "Bigotry," in *Michigan Catholic* parlance, meant prejudice against the Church.

The Great Depression was a stimulus to Catholic social action, and this in turn meant a greater interest than ever before in the needs of the "colored missions." As we have already seen, a number of Catholic Action groups were attracted in the 1930s to what was more and more often called the "Negro apostolate." It was the Communist party, ironically enough, that gave this apostolate some of its undoubted romance and much of its urgency, for the Party worked hard in the 1930s at organizing urban blacks, and could claim the allegiance of growing numbers of black intellectuals. The Party's militance — and its insistence on a radical equality — was a model of sorts for the more idealistic advocates of Catholic Action. "How can we remain passive in the face of such abomination?" demanded seminarian Donald Hessler in 1934, with reference not only to conditions in the South but to segregationist policies in Catholic schools and hospitals. "The devil thrives on this continued prejudice." Segregation in Catholic institutions came under increasing fire from both lay and clerical activists in the 1930s, although the vast majority of Catholics surely supported such segregation. An important source of criticism locally was Father Leo DeBarry's weekly "Propagation of the Faith" column in the *Michigan Catholic,* where warm support for the "colored missions" occasionally flowered into gentle disapproval of racist policies within the Church. "Why are not more of the potential leaders of 'America's Kindliest Race' admitted to our Catholic colleges and universities?" Father DeBarry not untypically asked in 1934. The *Michigan Catholic's* editor too was willing by 1939 to endorse at least nominal integration at Catholic colleges, and to admit that blacks suffered grievously from unjustifiable discrimination in law and employment and politics. "Traditional thinking on the part of white Catholics must give way to the gospel of charity," he warned. But his paper never spoke directly to the manifold racial problems of Detroit, or to the segregation that still prevailed in many of the city's Catholic schools and hospitals.[48]

The racial parish, then, accommodated a Catholic world that was overwhelmingly segregationist in its mentality. But many black Catholics too, even in the 1940s, wanted parishes of their own, where social life was warm and spontaneous and blacks held positions of leadership. Certainly the founding of St. Peter Claver's parish in 1911 was welcomed by black Catholics locally, although some of those Catholics were part of an integration-minded black elite. Such was attorney Eugene J. Marshall, appointed "special organizer" of the mission at its founding meeting, which assembled in St. Mary's School at the behest of Holy Ghost Father Joseph Wuest. Some of the eighteen persons at the meeting were probably Father Wuest's parishioners, for St. Mary's was a downtown church by 1911 with an appropriately heterogenous congregation, and the priest had an interest in black convert work. (The Holy Ghost Fathers, who eventually had charge of four of Detroit's racial parishes, were an order devoted mainly to missionary work in Africa and among American Negroes.) Father Wuest's interest in St. Peter Claver's mission proved to be important, for the initial membership was much too small to raise the money needed for a church. Outside help was necessary, and it was to this end that Father Wuest established the St. Peter Claver Aid Society early in 1913. The Aid Society, an interparochial women's group, was a principal source of funds for St. Peter Claver's parish in its early years, enabling the congregation in 1914 to buy a modest church. A rectory was acquired in 1917 — the pastor had previously lived at St. Mary's — and in 1915 the congregation opened a fund to build a parish school. It was not until 1936, however, that St. Peter Claver's parish had a school of its own.[49]

Little is known about the men and women who were St. Peter Claver's first parishioners. Black Catholicism is generally said to have attracted a disproportionate share of the well-to-do and the upwardly mobile, and this seems to have been the case in Detroit. A doctor and a lawyer were among the founding members, the most senior of whom was a waiter at Detroit's prestigious Russell House, and hence — by community standards, at least — a man of considerable means. The first church committee included a mailman and a city hall custodian, both of them reckoned by their black contemporaries as solidly middle-class. But the congregation had its share of the indigent too. "The St. Peter Claver Aid Society," according to the "Mission secretary" in 1913, "not content with giving parties, have taken an active part in aiding our needy members." The parish continued to have a varied membership in terms of social class, although it was the well-to-do who dominated its organizational life. In this sense, St. Peter Claver's was similar to the typical ethnic parish.[50]

St. Peter Claver's was virtually indistinguishable from the typical English-speaking parish when it came to its liturgy and parish organizations. Save for devotion to Blessed Martin de Porres, introduced in the late 1930s, there was nothing distinctively "black" about parish worship; indeed the congregation was remarkably responsive to prevailing devotional trends, which may partly account for its interest in the newly popular cult of the Blessed Martin. (A growing militancy is suggested, however, by the establishment in 1943 of an "inter-racial shrine" in the church, where Blessed Martin and St. Peter Claver were enthroned with the Sacred Heart.) Parish societies too were those familiar to nearly every Catholic: an Altar Society was organized at the founding meeting of the parish, and a Holy Name Society in 1915. By 1923 the parish had a drama club, a Young Ladies' Sodality, a St. Vincent de Paul Society, a Boy Scout troop, and junior and senior choirs. Its membership was still quite small—there were 150 communions at Easter in 1924—but evidently the members were an active group, deeply involved in the life of the parish.[51]

St. Peter Claver's differed from other parishes, however, in some important ways. Probably the majority of its members were converts, even in the 1920s. As a consequence, there was a notably smaller proportion of families in the congregation than was the case in other parishes, and a considerably higher incidence of mixed marriage. The congregation looks to have been disproportionately female too: two-thirds of the adults baptized at the church between 1917 and 1932 were women, and slightly more than two-thirds of those confirmed between 1929 and 1938 were women and girls. In each of these respects, St. Peter Claver's was typical of racial parishes in the United States in all but the historically Catholic regions of the South. It was typical too in its relative isolation from the larger Catholic community and its uncertain relationship to the black world around it.[52]

The members of St. Peter Claver's obviously had many fewer contacts with their fellow Catholics than was the case in other English-speaking parishes. Still, the parish was not wholly isolated. White charity was essential to its survival for a very long time, and at least some members of St. Peter Claver's Aid Society took a personal interest in parish life, attending Mass and devotions at the church on occasion, and having apparently warm relations with parish leaders. Whites had charge of religious education at the parish from the beginning, with teachers from the Catholic Instruction League having replaced the Carmelite Sisters by 1923. Devotional life too allowed for at least occasional contact with a larger Catholic world. Pastor Ferdinand Kreutzkampf promoted the church as a shrine to St. Joseph in the early 1920s, and apparently with some success. There was a racially mixed congregation at Tre Ore services on Good Friday in 1922, at least according to William Bradley, president of the Diocesan Union of Holy Name Societies, who was deeply moved by "the manifest devotion of the large crowd of white and negro worshippers." And in the later 1930s, the parish was a center for Blessed Martin devotions.[53]

Certain parish organizations at St. Peter Claver's had occasional contact with their counterparts in other parishes. Holy Name men from the parish went regularly to the quarterly meetings of the Diocesan Union, and the parish had teams in the Holy Name Society's baseball and basketball leagues in 1927 and again in 1933. (The leagues apparently fell on hard times in the late 1920s, and were revived only in 1932.) Sports proved to be an important bridge between the parish and the larger Catholic community in the 1930s and the 1940s, for St. Peter Claver boys were active in the CYO, especially in its widely publicized boxing program. The parish boxing team took the CYO trophy in 1937 and 1938. Women's organizations in the parish, however, seem to have been almost wholly isolated from white Catholic women's groups, with the single exception of the St.

Peter Claver Aid Society. The opening of St. Peter Claver Community House in 1939 did bring the League of Catholic Women into contact with the parish, and led to a growing cooperation between members of the league and leading parish women. But there was a certain inequality of status implied in a relationship like this, no matter how cordial the contact might be, for league women came as social workers and bearers of charity to the black community. There was no real equivalent for black Catholic women to the Holy Name Society or the CYO, where blacks met whites on a formally equal footing.[54]

Even in a setting of formal equality, of course, contact between black and white Catholics was likely to be hedged about by fear and suspicion. Detroit's black Catholics were well aware that they were not welcome in certain of their city's churches nor in the vast majority of its parochial schools. Detroit was not unusual in this regard, nor were Detroit's black Catholics unusual in their resentment at the situation. As early as 1917, a group of black Catholics in the nation's capital had organized a "Committee Against the Extension of Race Prejudice in the Church," their principal grievances having to do with discriminatory practices in certain congregations, with the dearth of schools and colleges for black Catholics, and with the negligible number of black priests in the United States. By 1925, the committee had evolved into the Federated Colored Catholics, with members in a number of northern towns and cities. Detroit had at least one delegate at the 1925 convention, for A. R. Feliciano of St. Peter Claver's parish was elected recording secretary of the group. (Mr. Feliciano was director of the NAACP for Michigan and Ohio in the mid-1920s.) A chapter of the Federated Colored Catholics had been organized in Detroit by 1928 and it was an active one, although its focus seems to have been primarily social, Mr. Feliciano's political connections notwithstanding. The Detroit chapter hosted the group's national convention in 1930, with the economically devastated city a fitting backdrop for speeches on poverty and public health and discrimination in employment. Segregation in Catholic schools and colleges, however, was apparently addressed in a circumspect manner, and the tone of the sessions was far from militant, at least according to the *Michigan Catholic*. "The delegates, by papers and talks, asked their fellow white Catholics to remember that the Negro is a human being seeking to do his duty on this earth so that he may gain his eternal reward," the paper reported. "The delegates requested that their race be not judged by individuals who appear in the crime news and urged their fellow Church members to become acquainted with the better element of the Negro race to appreciate its efforts toward cultural, social and spiritual progress."[55]

The Federated Colored Catholics had been envisioned by most of its founders as an all-black organization, analogous to groups like the Ancient Order of Hibernians and the Polish Roman Catholic Union. In 1932, however, the organization split into rival factions, one of which emerged in the mid-1930s as the National Catholic Interracial Federation. The federation, as its name implies, was open to both blacks and whites, and its long-term goals were frankly integrationist, although it was both apolitical and exceedingly cautious in its rhetoric and tactics. The principal strength of the Interracial Federation lay initially in the Midwest; Detroit had a chapter by 1934, with Charles Rawlings as its president. The group was not a particularly active one, and ceased for several years to function at all. But it was reorganized in 1940, with an interracial slate of officers and an interracial executive committee. The revived Detroit chapter hosted the national convention that same year. It was not until 1942, however, that the Catholic Interracial Council of Detroit was established, although with most of the same personnel as the apparently defunct Federation chapter of 1940. The council was the first Catholic organization in Detroit to speak in a sustained and effective way to the problem of race relations in the Church and in the larger society.[56]

Detroit's blacks by the early 1940s were a notably more militant group than they had ever been before, and the founding of the Catholic Interracial Council was in part a reflection of this change. At least some of the more affluent black Catholics locally were politically active, and all were alert to shifts in the prevailing mood. The rising tide of militancy, however, posed special problems for black Catholics, who lived on the margins of two separate worlds. The church was a natural political vehicle for most black Protestants. But for the congregation at St. Peter Claver's, with its white priests—and they subservient to the Chancery and a religious superior—this easy meshing of racial and religious loyalties was very nearly impossible. Even as moderate a group as the Federated Colored Catholics had met with clerical resistance in the early 1930s, not at St. Peter Claver's but at the recently founded parish of St. Benedict the Moor. And a short-lived movement in the late 1930s to bring a black priest to Detroit had drawn a series of rebuffs from the Chancery. "Loyal parishioners should be willing to support their church financially and to endeavor to give enthusiastic backing to the plans which the Pastor adopts for its welfare," Chancellor Edward Hickey told one petitioner, wholly unmoved by the claim that the Holy Ghost Fathers were "not progressive."[57]

A black priest had in fact been ordained in Detroit in 1926, although he was assigned to the newly created Diocese of Lansing in 1938. This was Father Norman A. Dukette, a native of Washington, D.C., and a graduate of Columbia College in Dubuque, Iowa, and of St. Paul's Seminary in Minnesota. Father Dukette's was something of a late vocation: he was thirty-four at his ordination, and it was perhaps his maturity as well as his evident intelligence that commended him to Bishop Gallagher. Dukette had been the first of his race to attend Columbia College; his record there was apparently an exemplary one, and not only academically. "As I stand now on the threshhold of my graduation morning," he wrote in 1922, "I can truthfully say that never was a boy received more whole heartedly by his professors and fellow students than I was." Seminarian Dukette gave credit for this to "the spirit of Columbia College, so ideally democratic and American, so Catholic in deed as well as in name." But a portion of the credit rests with Dukette himself, for his was a winsome personality and—as his long and difficult career revealed—a graceful patience in adversity.[58]

There was only one other black diocesan priest in the United States when Father Dukette was ordained early in 1926. Nearly all diocesan seminaries were still closed to blacks, most bishops assuming that what black priests there were would be members of religious orders, probably the Society of the Divine Word, which worked primarily in the black community and had opened a Negro seminary in 1923. Bishop Gallagher was presumably of this mind himself, for he never announced that his own diocesan seminary was open to black applicants. (Sacred Heart admitted its first black student in 1946.) Still, his willingness to ordain Dukette set Gallagher apart from the vast majority of his fellow bishops, and suggests a sensitivity on questions of race that his public pronouncements never showed. The Federated Colored Catholics singled out Gallagher and Cincinnati's Archbishop John McNicholas in 1926 for their admirable interest "in the development of a Negro clergy."[59]

Father Dukette was not assigned to a parish immediately upon ordination. He traveled widely about the United States for the better part of a year, ostensibly surveying the progress of Catholicism among blacks, but presumably also marking time while his bishop decided what to do with his new black priest. (The Holy Ghost Fathers were still in charge of St. Peter Claver's, and apparently reluctant to surrender the parish.) Still, it was a year of welcome public recognition for the soft-spoken Father Dukette: he addressed the Negro section of the Chicago Eucharistic Congress and the annual convention of the Federated Colored Catholics, was guest of honor in a number of black parishes, and returned in triumph to Detroit at Christmas for a glorious midnight Mass at St. Peter Claver's Church, in whose rectory the young priest stayed on visits to the city. There were other local honors too: Father Dukette was among the Lenten preachers at St. Aloysius Church in 1927, a rare distinction for so junior a priest. The situation was presumably a difficult one for Holy Ghost Father Charles Kapp, who had been pastor at St. Peter Claver's since 1924. Father Kapp was obviously held in affection by his parishioners, and his tenure in Detroit saw a steady rise in the number of parish baptisms. But there were many in the congregation who hoped that Father Dukette would eventually become their pastor.[60]

Father Dukette was finally given a pastorate in the early spring of 1927, when he was assigned to the newly created parish of St. Benedict the Moor. St. Benedict's was defined as a racial parish, its members to come from the black population on Detroit's west side, a population that was smaller than the population assigned to St. Peter Claver's, but on the whole a wealthier one. Despite its canonical status, however, St. Benedict's was at least initially a biracial congregation. A number of white families who lived near the church attended it for its convenience; some were perhaps attracted by its small size and its personable pastor. But whatever their reasons for attending, whites were indisputably there, and in relatively large numbers. The inaugural Mass found the little church "crowded with negroes and whites," while a typical Sunday in the following autumn saw sixty whites and fifty-eight blacks at the principal Mass. This careful

count, unfortunately, was done by members of a white committee who were trying to persuade the Chancery of "the need of an English speaking church in the
neighborhood," by which they meant, of course, a church that was not shared
with blacks. (This committee enjoyed substantial white support in the area, at
least according to a 1927 petition.) And there was apparently a growing tension
between black and white members of the congregation with regard to control
of parish societies. The Chancery spoke to this in 1932, when it reiterated St.
Benedict's status as a racial parish, where whites were not "parishioners in the
true sense of the term." Whites might occasionally attend Mass at the church.
But they were not permitted to join parish societies, to serve as committeemen, ushers, or Mass servers, or to have weddings, baptisms, or funerals at the
church. The number of whites in the congregation seems to have declined after
this ruling, although some continued to worship at the church. There were still
Polish names among the active members of the Holy Name and the Little Flower
societies in 1933.[61]

If his white parishioners, or a portion of them, were a source of vexation for
Father Dukette, his success among blacks was swift and gratifying. His modest
church was apparently well filled on Sundays, despite the negligible numbers
of black Catholics in the vicinity, and the priest soon established a Holy Name
Society in the parish, as well as a Sodality of the Blessed Virgin and the League
of the Sacred Heart. "Colored Catholics have an especial devotion to the Mother
of God," Father Dukette told the *Michigan Catholic,* explaining his large sodality
membership. "Often even Protestant colored people are so desirous of showing
their devotion to Mary that they wear medals and Rosary beads around their
necks." Evening devotions at the church apparently drew a regular following of
black Protestants. There were numerous Protestants too at the first parish mission, which was preached by a well-known Redemptorist in December 1927.
"This mission was one of the happiest that I have ever given," Father Michael
Pathe wrote at its conclusion, moved by the "enthusiasm and devotion" of the
congregation, by the "splendid singing," and by the crowds that came even to
the early morning Mass. "At the opening Mass the attendance was so large that
people were standing in the aisle and in the vestibule," he recalled. "As the days
went on we found it necessary to fill the sanctuary with chairs."[62]

Father Pathe was not the only white priest to have an affection for the congregation at St. Benedict the Moor and for its young black pastor. Diocesan and
religious order priests regularly preached at St. Benedict's weekly Holy Hour
and at novenas, excited by this missionary endeavor in their midst and by the
success of "the young, zealous and gentlemanly Father Dukette." (The words are
Father Pathe's.) And there was good cause for excitement: despite its poverty,
the congregation was growing rapidly. Father Dukette recorded 103 conversions
in his parish in the first fifteen months of its life. Most of the converts were black
children, many of them recruited through the Catholic Instruction League,
which established a catechetical center at St. Benedict the Moor early in 1928.
Through the children, however, Father Dukette quite reasonably hoped to reach

adults — parents and other family members. Black parishes generally grew in this fashion, with the number of converts rising sharply once the parish established a school.[63]

But Father Dukette did not remain at St. Benedict's to reap his promising harvest. He was removed from the parish, probably in the summer of 1929, and assigned in October of that year to found a "colored mission" in Flint, a city with only a small black population and a history of anti-Catholicism. (Father Dukette said the first Mass at his new mission before a congregation of two persons.) The reassignment was obviously punitive. The reason for it, however, is not known: nothing remains in the Chancery archives that sheds much light on the question. The priest had certainly been judged guilty of a serious offense. And his black parishioners recognized the justice of the verdict, if they did not agree with the sentence. "Now we understand all about Father Duckette," a parish committee wrote to Bishop Gallagher, "but we know that he can do more in St. Benedict the Moor parish if you can in any way forgive and give him one more chance. We too will do the same and try to help him make good."[64]

Bishop Gallagher did not relent. Father Dukette spent the rest of his long career in Flint, quietly building Christ the King into a large and active parish. He was as assiduous in his pastoral duties there as he had been in Detroit, despite the immensely difficult conditions under which he labored — difficult especially in the 1930s, when Christ the King mission was still too poor to have even a chapel of its own. (The mission had "over 100" members by 1939, "most of whom are converts.") Father Dukette became for at least the more militant of Detroit's black Catholics a sign of their subordinate status in the Church. But he never allowed himself to be a focus of public protest, although his career was surely damaged by the Flint assignment, from which he could not play the national role that was potentially his as a black priest in Detroit.[65]

Father Dukette was replaced at St. Benedict the Moor by a member of the Mariannhill Fathers, a German missionary order whose work was primarily in Africa. The new pastor came to a badly divided congregation, and quickly alienated a substantial portion of his black parishioners. "Please send us some person that has not spent his time in Africa and believe[s] that we have no better understanding than some of the heathens of Africa," a parish petition pleaded, probably in 1930. "The man that we have now is absolutely impossible, he doesn't like our children and the young people are the making of the church." The Mariannhill Fathers surrendered the parish early in 1932, presumably at the behest of Bishop Gallagher, who was worried that the dwindling congregation would not be able to meet its debts. St. Benedict the Moor was then assigned to the Holy Ghost Fathers, and the popular Father Charles Kapp was brought from St. Peter Claver's to be its pastor. Under Father Kapp's direction, the congregation began once again to grow, although its financial problems were severe throughout the 1930s. "I can understand why my predecessors catered to a certain extent to the whites," Father Kapp admitted in 1933. "They needed the money, and that was one way of getting it." Partly because of its debt, the parish did not build a school until 1952 — and then only with generous Chancery assistance. Without a school, its growth was almost inevitably limited. The parish had about 500 members in 1940, according to its pastor, compared to some 1,300 at St. Peter Claver's.[66]

The evident health of St. Peter Claver's parish was due in part to the work of Father Henry Thiefels. Father Thiefels, who came to the parish in 1932, was a native Detroiter, having been raised in St. Anthony's parish on the city's East Side. He had an immediate success at St. Peter Claver's: the seventy-three adult baptisms recorded there in 1933 were more than twice as many as any previous yearly total. "A constant stream of converts" was being received into the Church, a parishioner wrote to the *Michigan Catholic* in June of that year. "Two months ago on the Holy Name Sunday, every man and boy received Holy Communion. The church was crowded to the doors and the spectacle was wonderful to behold!" It was Father Thiefels who revived the long-dormant campaign to establish a parish school, pointing to the 150 parish children enrolled in the Sunday school and to the many non-Catholic parents in the vicinity who wanted to give their children a Catholic education. He found willing allies in his Holy Name Society, notwithstanding the Depression. Holy Name member James Gibson "made a fiery plea for cooperation by parishioners" at the opening meeting of the school campaign in 1934, "saying that some of the men were so determined to have a school that, if necessary, they would give their labor as well as every cent they can scrape up for the purpose."[67]

The inaugural meeting was followed by months of assiduous fund-raising. Dances and dinners and bazaars added mite upon mite to the slender balance, with film star Stepin Fetchit making a surprise appearance at an especially memorable card party in the parish hall. "Fetchit is a practical Catholic," the *Michigan Catholic* informed its readers, "and received his early education in a Catholic school." The *Michigan Catholic* gave generous publicity to the various parish events, and this resulted in some limited white support for the undertaking. It was a white businessman who chaired the "second phase" of the school campaign, which opened late in 1934. But there was no help forthcoming from a financially strapped and politically beleaguered Chancery. "We have not received any word from you," two Holy Name men from the parish reminded Bishop Gallagher at the close of 1935, "and to date we have only rumor to inform us that you are in sympathy with our efforts."[68]

St. Peter Claver's School was finally opened in the fall of 1936. Its sixty-four pupils, enrolled in grades one through three, were housed in the converted apartment building where Father Thiefels had his rectory. Their numbers had grown to more than 120 by the following year, when a kindergarten and a fourth grade were added. "There is a fine spirit amongst the children," Father Thiefels wrote then, "and we hope not only to bring many of the little ones into the church, who are non-Catholics but also in many cases the parents as well. . . . The school has been received by the people as a god-send for the reason that many of the public school children in this section have a very low standard of morality."

Father Thiefels was not being bigoted or condescending: respectable black families in segregated Detroit lived side-by-side with petty and not-so-petty criminals. Drugs and prostitution were evident facts of daily life. In a world like this, the discipline and rigid sexual morality that were widely associated with Catholic training made parochial schools immensely appealing to many black parents.[69]

St. Peter Claver's School would not have survived, however, had it not been for the generosity of the Felician Sisters, who donated their services as teachers during the school's first years. And its growth was made possible in good part by Archbishop Mooney's "gift" of the buildings of Sacred Heart parish to the people of St. Peter Claver's. (Sacred Heart, a one-time German parish, had lost nearly all its members by the late 1930s; its closing had been rumored since the early 1920s.) The Mooney "gift" was a gradual and, initially, a tentative one. Sacred Heart school was opened to black children in the fall of 1938, when St. Peter Claver's School was closed. Father Thiefels became pastor of Sacred Heart parish at the same time, although he continued to serve as pastor of St. Peter Claver's too, presumably to oversee the gradual consolidation of the two congregations. Resistance to these changes was expected: the mostly elderly white members of Sacred Heart were known at the Chancery for their fierce insistence on lay authority in the parish, and a group of them did send a bitter letter of protest to the archbishop. ("After building up the Parish to what it is now and then seeing the negroes come in and knock it down is more than we can stand.") But the parish apparently changed hands without serious incident.[70]

The parish plant at Sacred Heart was in a state of near-dilapidation in 1938. It was relatively large, however, and this enabled the former St. Peter Claver's congregation to expand its school. That school had eight grades by 1938, and an enrollment of 390. (Ninety of those students were white; there were whites at the school until 1945.) A ninth grade was added in 1941—"a beginning, please God, of a Catholic High School for the colored in Detroit," in the words of Father Thiefels. There were 515 children in the school by the fall of 1943, when the longed-for high school had become a reality. The physical plant was still a makeshift one, and the school was perennially short of funds. "This year we are teaching chemistry and we have neither chemicals or instruments," Father Thiefels told the archbishop in 1944. But the school enjoyed an excellent reputation in the black community, both for academic discipline and moral training. For despite the large number of non-Catholics in the school, the Felicians maintained a rigidly Catholic regime. The "Happy Mission Helpers" in the school's fourth grade were learning to see the world in much the same terms as youngsters in the neighboring Polish parishes. "This money ($5.00) is for the ransoming of a pagan baby," the fourth grade wrote to the Society for the Propagation of the Faith in 1939. "We wish to call him Martin in honor of Blessed Martin de Porres. We would like to see what he looks like if possible. We are saving now for a baby girl."[71]

The success of the school meant a larger crop of converts than ever before. "Since the school was started four years ago, the Parish has increased its membership threefold," Father Thiefels observed in 1939. The parish was sufficiently large by then to support a mission, which opened in Detroit's "North End" in 1939. The members of the Holy Ghost mission initially worshiped in a private home, and Sisters from Sacred Heart School taught catechism there. There were hardly enough black Catholics in the "North End" to warrant a new parish: "ten Catholic families and about 20 prospective converts" made up the original Holy Ghost congregation, according to Father Thiefels. But the Chancery assumed that neighboring white congregations would not welcome even a limited number of blacks to their churches, and certainly not to their schools. A generous grant from the Archdiocesan Development Fund (ADF) enabled the small congregation at Holy Ghost to build a church in 1944, although it was hardly an imposing one. (A basement chapel, Holy Ghost was too small for any but modest weddings and of no use at all for funerals, because, as Father Thomas Clynes explained in 1955, "there has been no suitable means of ingress or egress for a casket.") It was Chancery generosity too that led to the opening of a parish school in 1949. Largely because of that school, the congregation at Holy Ghost had grown to more than 400 by 1955.[72]

The Chancery continued its policy of establishing racial parishes at least through the end of World War II. Our Lady of Victory mission was opened in 1943, again with generous assistance from the ADF. The mission was intended to serve the black inhabitants of a nearby wartime housing project, the Chancery still unwilling to initiate integration at the several white parishes in the vicinity. It was in connection with Our Lady of Victory that the first black Sisters came to Detroit: two members of the Oblates of Providence, a Negro order based in Baltimore, arrived in the parish in 1948 to work as catechists and home visitors. A parish school was opened in the fall of 1954, just six months after the Supreme Court had ruled against the constitutionality of segregated schooling. If this awkward conjunction disturbed the Chancery, no one said so publicly. Most Chancery officials, like most parish priests, assumed that the vast majority of white Catholics wanted segregation in their schools. "The colored are not welcome in Dearborn," Father John C. Ryan had told the archbishop in 1945, explaining why a "colored mission" was essential in the suburb of Inkster. (Holy Family mission was opened there in that same year.) There was no reason to think that things were appreciably different a decade later.[73]

But there had in fact been important changes with regard to race relations by 1955, notwithstanding the desire of most whites for segregated schools and neighborhoods. The black population of Detroit had grown enormously in the 1940s; by the 1950s, that population was moving into many areas that had hitherto been reserved for whites. "Negroes are building and buying on both sides of us, and that in areas which have heretofore been restricted," the pastor of Holy Ghost parish wrote to Archbishop Mooney in 1950. "God bless the Supreme Court." The Court's striking down of restrictive covenants, however, did not please every city pastor. "This parish is going down," a priest at St. Bernard's quite typically told the Chancery in 1953. "The north part is getting very colored." Men like this were understandably fearful that "white flight" from the city would be the ruin of their large and often heavily-indebted parishes. But the inexorable spread of black settlement meant that even the least socially conscious of the clergy could no longer be indifferent to the problem of race relations. Either Detroiters learned to live together amicably, regardless of race, or a substantial number of Catholic parishes would be in serious financial trouble.[74]

The spread of black settlement had led by the late 1940s to a decline in the congregation at Sacred Heart Church, the principal center of black Catholicism in Detroit. An expansion of the high school there seemed inadvisable to the superior of the Felician Sisters, to whom the project was proposed in 1949. The neighborhood was increasingly home to only the poorest members of the black community, she pointed out; enrollment at the school had already begun to decline. She drew attention as well to the "aversion of the pupils to segregation." That aversion had much to do with the growing political influence of blacks in Detroit, and a corresponding increase in their militancy with regard to civil rights. Black leaders were more and more open about their objections to segregated parishes, with their inevitably inferior facilities, and to the segregationist policies that still prevailed in many Catholic schools and hospitals, even in the late 1940s.[75]

The increasing militance of the black community was complemented in the postwar years by a growing sense among whites that overtly racist policies were morally indefensible. The war itself had much to do with this: Hitler and his death camps had made the evils of racism real in a peculiarly terrible way. Archbishop Mooney seems to have been among those who revised their assumptions about race and race relations during the 1940s. Mooney had come to Detroit with views that were probably typical of many of his fellow bishops. He hoped to see a growing number of black converts in the Church, and to this end he contributed personally to the Catholic Board for Mission Work Among the Colored People, and used archdiocesan resources to aid the struggling black parishes within his own jurisdiction. But he thought almost exclusively in terms of a segregated Church and a segregated city. It was at Mooney's behest that the priests at Blessed Sacrament Cathedral organized a neighborhood "improvement association" in 1941, the purpose of which was to prevent any further movement of blacks into the cathedral parish. (The project was not a success.) The archbishop was understandably anxious to protect his investment in the cathedral, but he seemed oddly indifferent to the plight of Detroit's fast-growing black community, which was more affected than any other by the wartime housing shortage in Detroit. That shortage was a critical factor in the racial rioting that engulfed a portion of the city in the summer of 1943. Mooney, however, was inclined to see black grievances in terms of a "precipitate" Negro leadership. "I am sure that, here in Detroit at least, they are being egged on by agitators with an eye only to their own subversive ends," he told the Jesuit John LaFarge. A "realistic" approach to race relations, in the Archbishop's view, would not "demand intermarriage, full social equality and special 'rights' such as public opinion is not prepared to accept"—this according to Chancellor Edward Hickey, who was a principal Mooney confidant in 1943.[76]

By the late 1940s, however, the now-Cardinal Mooney had clearly begun to think in terms of an integrated Church. He was very much the gradualist: the Cardinal never issued a public statement condemning segregation, and he tolerated overtly segregationist policies in certain of his parish schools, even in the late 1950s. But Chancery sympathies in the postwar years were obviously with those priests who evinced an interest in the "Negro apostolate" and who were prepared to facilitate the integration of their schools and congregations. Father Hubert Roberge, who came to St. Leo's in 1953, assumed—and correctly—that he had Mooney's full support in his efforts to make St. Leo's a model of racial cooperation. Blacks had been attending the church for a number of years when Roberge became pastor; St. Leo's High School had been the first parochial high school in Detroit to admit black students, probably in the late 1930s. But even in 1953 there were no black members in the various parish organizations. Father Roberge set out to remedy this, finding black "volunteers" to integrate the ushers and the Altar Society, appointing a black parishioner to the church committee, and instructing his flock that, as members of Christ's Mystical Body, they were bound in conscience to regard one another as brothers. Cardinal Mooney was genuinely delighted by the progress at St. Leo's—"this all important work," as he wrote to Roberge, "in which you and I are so vitally interested." But he was not pleased when Father Roberge called publicly, in a 1954 article in *Integrity* magazine, for an "authoritative statement" from the American bishops against racism and continued segregation in the Church. The work at St. Leo's was supposed to have proceeded with "as little talk and public announcement as possible," the Cardinal reminded Father Roberge. "We should seek results through our endeavors and not publication of those results or public disapproval of the work of others."[77]

Father Roberge was not alone in his zeal and idealism. A growing number of local priests were interested in the Negro apostolate by the early 1950s, and some had already moved on to a concern for civil rights. Father John Finnegan, pastor of Detroit's St. Patrick's parish, was chairman in 1952 of a citizens' committee that was formed in support of a municipal Fair Employment Practices act. The *Michigan Catholic,* hitherto reticent on the subject of race, condemned racial bias in the Knights of Columbus early in 1954, and greeted the Supreme Court's *Brown* decision with warm approval. "America lived one of its finest hours when the US supreme court voided the 58-year old doctrine allowing 'separate but equal' in the public schools," the editor declared. "The new decision may help to disprove the ancient fallacy that 'you cannot legislate morality.'" And there was a growing commitment to "Negro work" on the part of women religious, something that disposed this important population to an unprecedented support for civil rights. Symptomatic of this was the founding in Detroit in 1949 of the Home Visitors of Mary, an order devoted to catechetical and convert work among blacks and—by force of example—to the betterment of race relations in the city and the Church. The community admitted its first black postulant in 1957, a development that the founders had hoped for from the very beginning. Many of the existing women's orders, moreover, seemed in the prosperous postwar years to find a renewed sense of mission in their work at center-city schools, where enrollments were more and more heavily black.[78]

The Immaculate Heart of Mary Sisters were typical of many orders in their newfound enthusiasm for the Negro apostolate. The IHMs at Holy Trinity School were delighted to welcome a black lay coworker in 1946. "The seventh grade, her homeroom, and the entire school were completely won by her gracious manner and her artistry of conversation," the mission chronicle noted. Holy Trinity had received its first black pupil in 1945, the same year that blacks were first enrolled at Detroit's Holy Rosary, also an IHM school. The grammar school at Holy Rosary was nearly one-third black by 1947, for the neighborhood around the school was rapidly changing hands. The Sisters, however, betrayed no distress on this score. "These pupils are clean, tractable and cooperative, and well liked by all the Sisters," according to the mission chronicle. By 1950, the IHMs had agreed to send Sisters to St. George's in Detroit, which was about to reopen as a territorial parish in an almost exclusively black neighborhood. (St. George's had been a Lithuanian parish until it was closed in 1947.) St. George's School had refused to accept black children even in the 1940s, and there was considerable bitterness in the neighborhood on this account. Perhaps this was one reason that the badly overextended IHMs had agreed to take on the new assignment. The sense of purpose and of quiet excitement that permeates the mission chronicle at St. George's, however, suggests that the Sisters who went there were hungry for something more challenging—and more significant politically—than work in a suburban school.[79]

St. George's School was reopened in the fall of 1950 with an almost entirely black enrollment. Two overburdened Sisters had charge of 109 pupils, enrolled in grades one through four. Most were non-Catholics and all were products of the public schools, to which fact their new teachers attributed the rowdiness of the St. George classrooms. "School becomes a NIGHTMARE for two nuns!" the mission chronicle reported in September. "Silence and study had no meaning to this undisciplined group. . . . Pen and paper could never express what went on during this time." It was not until December that the Sisters won the "struggle for supremacy." Their pupils' parents proved to be natural allies in the struggle: "Almost every family sent a representative either that day or during the week that followed," the chronicle recorded of a "reporting day" in 1951. "The personal interest we took in each child made a lasting impression on the eager parents. . . . 'Sister, I want my child to learn and you make him behave, don't let him fight,' seems to be the general plea whenever you meet them." The St. George neighborhood was poor, with one of the highest delinquency rates in the city. Small wonder that parents were grateful for a school where rules were sternly enforced and perennial troublemakers were invariably expelled. A faculty meeting held early in 1954 was apparently typical of the St. George approach to discipline:

Josephite Father Henry Offer, the much-admired pastor, "went through the complete list of pupils, gave us a background of each family, discussed problems and spotted those who should be dismissed."[80]

St. George's School had a religious as well as an educational mission, and to this end Father Offer insisted that the parents of pupils enrolled in the school attend Sunday Mass with their children and take a course of instruction in Catholic doctrine. Failure to comply meant the expulsion of one's children from the school. And even the non-Catholic pupils at St. George's were required to attend daily Mass and the usual round of devotions. The more devout among the pupils were enrolled each year in the school sodality, where they learned the Rosary and other Marian prayers. "At each afternoon dismissal these little ones assemble before the Grotto of Lourdes for a hymn to Mary and her Son," the Sisters reported. "Some go there for their private devotions." If there were parents who disliked this kind of proselytization, they apparently kept it to themselves. The school's enrollment continued to grow, reaching 214 in 1955, and the school was eventually expanded to include eight grades. There were bumper harvests of converts too, especially among the children. The school was nearly 43 percent Catholic in 1958, by which time the congregation was well accustomed to witnessing the baptisms of large convert classes. "Those Sisters who came when St. George opened really see it growing spiritually as well as intellectually," the mission chronicle noted in the spring of 1956.[81]

St. George's School survived until 1964, when freeway construction resulted in the destruction of the parish buildings and much of the adjacent neighborhood. The children were easily accommodated at nearby parish schools, both of which already had substantial black enrollments, while the Josephite Fathers were "compensated" by being placed in charge of St. Benedict the Moor. St. Benedict's was no longer a juridically "racial" parish, however. "It is my own conviction that a strictly Negro parish is unjustifiable in the Detroit area," Archbishop John Dearden told the Superior General of the Josephites in 1963. Happily, St. Benedict's had a white minority in its congregation at this point. But there was considerable doubt as to its permanence: whites were moving from the city in unprecedented numbers by the mid-1960s, when Detroit's population was perhaps 35 percent black. Integration in Detroit had proved to be an evanescent phenomenon: neighborhoods typically changed hands in less than a decade.[82]

The process by which the various neighborhoods changed hands was rarely a peaceful one. Detroit has a long history of racial violence, and much of it has centered on conflicts over housing. Black-occupied buildings in racially mixed areas were sometimes bombed in the 1920s, as were black-owned businesses and churches. Father Francis Beccherini wrote almost casually to Bishop Gallagher in 1929 about an East Side church that had recently been bought by a black congregation, "and bombed presumably by some Italians." Working-class whites in Detroit were more than usually likely to be homeowners, and the Catholics among them belonged to parishes that had heavy investments in schools, rectories, and convents, not to mention large and sometimes sumptuous churches. They almost inevitably saw the expansion of the black population as an economic threat — indeed as a threat to their way of life. The black population, on the other hand, had grown so rapidly since 1915 that the historically "black" district could not begin to meet its housing needs. And more prosperous blacks were understandably anxious to move away from the noise and congestion and violence of the city core.[83]

The growth of the black population in the 1920s resulted in the integration of a handful of Catholic schools in Detroit. "At least five" of the city's parochial schools accepted black pupils in 1922, according to the *Michigan Catholic*. But they probably accepted only a limited number: the priests at St. Peter Claver's parish in the 1920s and the 1930s assumed that the great majority of their children could not be accommodated at near east side parochial schools. St. Wenceslaus School seems to have been the first with a substantial representation of blacks. The school in this one-time Czech parish was apparently integrated in the mid-1920s. By 1930, 40 of its 110 pupils were black children. The pastor at St. Wenceslaus had presumably integrated his school in order to prevent its closing: the school had only 50 pupils in 1922. But it was with evident pride that he claimed in 1929 to have been the first pastor in Detroit to accept black children in his school. (For all his pride, he was probably in error.) Very different, however, were the attitudes of the neighboring Polish clergy. The East Side Polish parishes were among the largest in the city; their parishioners were fiercely loyal, and unusually slow to abandon their aging neighborhoods. Reluctant to flee to greener reaches of the city, Poles typically regarded the parish school as a final defense against an expanding black population. Their schools, even in decline, remained closed to blacks at least through the 1940s and, in some cases, into the 1960s.[84]

The Depression meant a temporary decline in Detroit's population, and this eased tensions over housing. The 1930s, indeed, were a relatively peaceful decade on the racial front. Certain limited gains were made in the area of parochial school integration, and Marygrove College accepted its first black student in the summer of 1938. The University of Detroit had been nominally integrated for some years — it was among the first of the Jesuit colleges to be opened to blacks — and its dean of men was prepared, by the mid-1930s, to insist that the school's black students be fully included in campus life. Father Joseph Luther, SJ, demanded an immediate end to discriminatory practices in campus-area restaurants in 1934, when the university had six black students. Should any student complain about the nondiscrimination policy, he told one of the offending proprietors, "please give me his name and I shall see that he is called before the Faculty Board on Student Activities, of which I am Chairman, and his intolerant and narrow racial views corrected."[85]

The voices of men like Father Luther were overwhelmed in the early 1940s by rising racial tensions in Detroit. The city's black population grew enormously then, and so did its once-small population of Southern whites. These were war-time migrants, moreover, for whom there were plentiful jobs but very little housing: blacks and whites too were forced to double up with friends and relatives, and not a few families took refuge in garages and even less substantial out-buildings. Government-financed housing projects had begun to alleviate the shortage by 1942, but the projects themselves were a cause of racial animosity. The black population was far too large for the hitherto black areas of the city, and it was necessary to build "black" projects in neighborhoods occupied mainly by whites. St. Louis the King parish, largely Polish, was a principal center of resistance to the Sojourner Truth housing project, which was finally opened to black families in 1942. Poles were by no means the only Detroiters to oppose the project; much of the resistance came from Southern whites. And many Poles lived peaceably in racially mixed neighborhoods — even in racially integrated buildings, as the secretary of the Detroit Urban League pointed out in 1943. "During the June riots," he noted, "there were no race conflicts in these houses." But it was apparent nonetheless that working-class Catholics as a group were deeply hostile to blacks, and deeply fearful of them.[86]

Tensions exploded into violence on June 20, 1943. Three days later, with the U.S. Army occupying portions of the city, more than thirty persons had died, most of them black. Whites had been the principal aggressors in the riot, according to dispassionate observers, and white police were widely blamed for much of the violence. The riot seems to have caught the Chancery off guard: the *Michigan Catholic* took two weeks to come out with a timid editorial deploring the violence. The paper made no reference to the conduct of the police.[87]

Archbishop Mooney, for his part, made no public statement at all. He had been under pressure from black leaders since 1941 to speak to the question of race relations, particularly in view of the escalating tensions between blacks and Poles. But he believed, as he told Father John LaFarge, that black leaders were "naive in their belief in the effectiveness of a word from me and utterly unaware of the complications an injudicious word might cause as well as the difficulty of being both positive and judicious in the circumstances." Mooney had considerable sympathy for the Poles, whose parishes often carried heavy mortgages, and feared that they did not wholly trust their Irish-American bishop. "They are by temperament never phlegmatic," he reminded LaFarge, "and are just now heavy-hearted over what has happened to the homeland and in Russia. . . . Before making any statement I must in conscience consider that any declaration of mine which might have a general apologetic value for the Church among the Negroes would most certain[ly] have a disastrously disturbing effect on the more than two hundred thousand Polish Catholics who are a large part of my direct responsibility." Mooney was more than willing to have the American bishops make a collective statement on the problem of race, as indeed they did, and under his leadership, in the fall of 1943. But certain of his clergy had hoped for more. "As things are now, I believe we are looked upon as one of the most bitterly reactionary elements in the Detroit situation, far behind the Protestants and the CIO," Father John Coogan, SJ, complained in 1944. He wanted Mooney to issue "an authoritative statement on local racial policy," and to do so immediately.[88]

No such statement was forthcoming. Perhaps in part because of this, the racial policies of the various parishes and local Catholic institutions were anything but uniform, even in the 1950s. Most Catholic elementary schools in the central portions of Detroit were accepting black students by the early 1950s. But a number of high schools remained closed to blacks, and the Catholic hospitals locally had only just abandoned their discriminatory policies. The ability of a parish to resist integration seems to have depended largely on its size and its financial health. Father Vitalis Lasota, pastor at SS. Andrew and Benedict Church, was virtually ordered by the Chancery in 1950 to accept black Catholic students in his school. Father Lasota's parish was small, its Slovak founders having mostly left the vicinity of the church. As late as 1957, however, the Chancery was unwilling to insist that the pastor at Corpus Christi (Polish) parish cease his openly discriminatory practices. The pastor's rudeness to a prospective black parishioner had been "unfortunate," the chancellor admitted. But under the circumstances it would be best for her to enroll her children in a public school.[89]

As Detroit became an increasingly black city, its Catholic schools and institutions were more and more likely to be open to blacks. Several of the center-city Catholic high schools had black majorities by the mid-1950s. There were still priests, to be sure, who were openly hostile to blacks: the pastor at St. Theresa's parish in Detroit "has discouraged the acceptance of colored men into the Ushers and men's societies," an assistant at the parish told the Chancery in 1958. "The same goes for the Altar Sodality. He is afraid, he says, of the affect it will have on the remaining white people." But behavior like this was distinctly out of favor at the Chancery, as the young assistant understood. Cardinal Mooney expected his priests to make their peace with integration.[90]

His successor was even more emphatic on this score: Cardinal John Dearden was an articulate proponent of equality within the Church and in his see city, and an ardent supporter of expanded government programs for the poor. For a time it seemed that his generous vision was helping to transform both his city and his Church. Under a young and vigorous Catholic mayor, Detroit was a national showpiece for the War on Poverty in the mid-1960s, and a city often lauded for its progress toward equality in jobs and education. The city's reputation for tolerance, however, did not survive the summer of 1967, when the infamous Detroit riot ushered in a new and troubled chapter in the city's history. The Church has played an admirable role in that chapter, which lies beyond the scope of this book. Still, Detroit is a mostly black city now, and the Catholics of the Archdiocese a mostly suburban population. The problem of race relations has not been solved, but simply evaded—and with predictable social consequences.

ILLUSTRATIONS

National Council of Catholic Women, Victory Bond parade, Monroe, in September 1942.

Father Henry Thiefels, C.S.Sp., and children from St. Peter Claver's School, Detroit, probably during Christmas 1937.

Kindergarten at St. Peter Claver's School, Detroit, during Christmas 1937.
Father Henry Thiefels at rear.

Confraternity of Christian Doctrine (CCD): religious education at Holy Family mission in Inkster, probably in the late 1940s.

St. Francis Home for Boys, Detroit, in 1959, in the care of the Sisters of St. Joseph (Nazareth, Michigan).

EPILOGUE: *FROM 1958 TO THE PRESENT*

To both its adherents and its detractors, the American Catholic Church in the late 1950s looked to be an institution peculiarly exempt from the logic of contemporary history. Apparently uniform and disciplined, very nearly monarchical in its governing ethos, wedded to an utterly traditional theology, that Church was widely regarded, as Garry Wills has phrased it, as "the least changeable part of our religious landscape." There was truth to this perception. The contours of its own history, coupled with a highly centralized teaching authority, had indeed protected the American Church from the more corrosive effects of the century's intellectual revolutions. Still, this particular view of the Church was clearly an exaggerated one, and one that obscured some important realities.[1]

The realities to which I allude have been at the center of this book. Like the American Church more generally, the Church in the Archdiocese of Detroit has historically been a more complex and varied institution than it looked to outsiders, or even to many of its own adherents. It has accommodated a greater diversity in its ranks — diversity not only of ethnicity but also of race and social class — than any other denomination. This made for powerful centrifugal tendencies within the institution, and led to a Church that was far more democratic in its practice than its formal teaching would seem to have allowed. It is true that this democratic practice was eroded over time, for it depended mainly on a constant influx of immigrants. But even in the 1950s, the American Church was not so centralized or so rigidly governed that it was immune to the destabilizing pressures of diversity. That seemingly monolithic Church would be seriously divided in the 1960s, principally along class and generational lines.

If the Church in the Archdiocese was never so disciplined and uniform as observers sometimes imagined, neither was it the changeless institution so dear to conservative Catholic hearts. In many areas of its life, ranging from religious practice to the roles played by women, the Church in the Archdiocese experienced notable, even dramatic, change in the course of its first 120 years. And although the Church did move slowly in these same years towards a greater administrative centralization and an increasingly insulated clerical subculture, the cumulative effects of change were probably emancipatory, at least for the laity.

Lay persons were increasingly engaged in the liturgy in a deeply individual way; the more devout were increasingly likely to pattern their religious behavior on that of the clergy—an essential first step, it might be argued, in claiming their own rights to "priesthood." Women were able to secure for themselves a progressively broadened sphere of competence and responsibility in Church life. Lay activity generally was marked in successive generations by a larger vision of the Church and a greater sophistication in terms of goals and organization. The post-conciliar years were not, then, as abruptly discontinuous with the past as it has sometimes seemed. For that past encompassed substantial change, much of it in a direction consistent with post-conciliar developments.

It would, however, be disingenuous to argue that the pace of change in the Church has not greatly accelerated since the early 1960s, or that all of the changes which have occurred since that time have roots in the pre-conciliar era. Discontinuities do exist; the Church today is in many ways very different from the institution it was in the 1950s. This altered institution, as the reader is aware, is not a principal focus of this book. But it seems right, in concluding, to look briefly at developments in the Archdiocese of Detroit since the Second Vatican Council. Detroit's experience in these years has hardly been unique, though it did enjoy a reputation, during the tenure of Cardinal John Dearden (1959–1980), as an unusually progressive diocese. It is worth noting too that the post-conciliar years have encompassed a traumatic period in the history of the city of Detroit. This had important effects on the Church in the Archdiocese, and on many individual Catholics. Indeed, it makes good sense to begin our post-conciliar survey with a look at the city's troubled recent past.

Detroit in the late 1980s stands at far remove from its earlier industrial vigor. The city's population has declined by more than 40 percent since the early 1950s, and many of its remaining inhabitants are chronically unemployed. The erosion of the city's economic base has made for growing family instability and for an alarming escalation in the incidence of drug abuse and crime. Troubles of this sort accelerated white flight from the city, which since the early 1970s has had a majority black population. In recent years, moreover, increasing numbers of middle-class blacks have also opted for the suburbs—a development that may presage an even more troubled future for an already devastated community.

As Detroit's population was eroding, that of its outermost suburbs was growing rapidly. Much of this new suburban population was Catholic; the city, on the other hand, had by the 1980s a less heavily Catholic population than at any time in its history. Thus it was that scores of churches in Detroit, built for large congregations, were home by the late 1980s to no more than a few hundred Catholics—and sometimes to many fewer. The situation demanded reform—that much was widely conceded. But little agreement existed as to what the nature and scope of the reform should be. Late in 1983 Archbishop Edmund Szoka asked Auxiliary Bishop Patrick Cooney to initiate a study of the problem. This study led, in the fall of 1988, to a recommendation to close churches, a proposal that caused serious division among local Catholics. Opponents argued against the number of closings—more than forty churches were initially recommended to be closed or merged with neighboring parishes, a number that was in fact reduced after subsequent modifications in the reorganization plan. Still, detractors claimed, the scope of the closings would be psychologically devastating to Detroiters. Opponents argued too against the criteria used to gauge a parish's vitality. The small size of many city congregations, they believed, was not necessarily a liability. Reduced numbers could make for an intimate liturgy, for warm and highly personal service to troubled members, and for a strong sense of community. Proponents of the plan had a different perspective. A truly healthy parish, they argued, supported a full complement of sacramental life, afforded its members a wide range of educational and social programs, and worked creatively at the difficult task of evangelization. Under most circumstances, in their view, a parish needed close to 500 households to satisfy these requirements. (The smaller the parish, they cautioned, the more likely it was that its energies would be largely consumed by the demands of fund-raising.) And even with reorganization, proponents pointed out, the ratio of priests to people would be notably higher in Detroit than in the suburban parishes. Nearly all supporters of reorganization, it is fair to say, were genuinely concerned by the pain that such far-reaching change would necessarily cause. "Dying and rising" was a natural metaphor for Cardinal Edmund Szoka to employ in his pastoral letter on the reorganization process. It is perhaps appropriate in this context to note the recent flowering in Detroit of a vibrant black Catholicism. Here, at least, is a sign of resurrection in the city Church.[2]

Detroit's troubled recent past has also meant for the local Church a broader and more ecumenical role in politics and social welfare. Detroit's remaining Catholic schools and charitable institutions have come in recent years to serve a largely non-Catholic clientele, a portion of which has been grievously wounded by the harsh realities of urban life. Partly in consequence, Catholic leaders since the mid-1960s have worked hard to repair the dangerous breach between the city's black population and increasingly suburbanized whites. Success on this score has been extremely modest, but the effort has placed the Church unequivocally on the side of racial justice. And this has meant an unprecedented openness to ecumenical social action, something for which the Dearden years were especially noteworthy. "The Church must be the moral voice of the total community," then-Archbishop John Dearden asserted in 1967. He gave impressive substance to his words a few months later, earmarking no less than $1 million of his 1968 budget for local black organizations and community development projects.[3]

The Dearden gift was deeply resented by a good many Catholics locally, particularly those whose schools were in danger of closing for financial reasons. The bitterness stemmed, in some cases, from unadulterated racism, but often had mainly to do with fear—fear at the pace of social change and at the seeming normlessness of the brave new world of the 1960s. Linked to this fear was a general suspicion of Dearden's increasingly "social" orientation, an orientation shared by many priests and some of the most articulate members of the laity. The archbishop was no radical; he had troubles of his own with activists in the clerical ranks. But his was a world view and a vision of ministry that was wider and more ecumenical than that of many in his flock, and alien especially to those working-class Catholics whose orientation was almost exclusively toward neighborhood and family. As a consequence, the Church in the Archdiocese was by the late 1960s a seriously divided institution.[4]

Politics was not, of course, the only cause of tension. Much had changed within the Church, and in remarkably short order, the Second Vatican Council having come to an end only in 1965. That council gave an unexpected blessing to religious liberty and endorsed a more fraternal approach to the various Christian churches and to Jews. Good citizens that they were, most American Catholics were probably relieved by this. But there were those for whom the old exclusiveness had been a valued source of psychological protection. The Council Fathers adhered to an essentially collegial vision of episcopal—and hence papal—authority, and gave an imprimatur of sorts, by the very nature of their proceedings, to disinterested scholarship in theology and the social sciences. Again, these changes brought Church teaching into closer conformity with dominant American values. But there were those for whom the absolutist claims of the Church had been a principal support of faith. For many others, these reforms prompted expectations of continued change, even visions of a democratic Church. Their disappointment on this score, epitomized by the issuance of *Humanae Vitae* in 1968, led to growing alienation especially but not exclusively among younger and more liberal Catholics.

The most consequential of the changes to flow from the council, however, had to do with public worship. The Mass was said entirely in the vernacular by 1969, and the revised rite had a new "communal" emphasis. The liturgical reforms of Vatican II, as Father Emile Pin has rightly noted, accord "a primordial importance to the active role of the faithful in the sacramental celebration. The faithful must use their intellect and will; they must understand the language and the symbols; they must participate." Most Catholics seemed willing to embrace this new role; at least in the Archdiocese of Detroit, champions of the Tridentine Mass have failed to draw significant support. But for some, the liturgy lost an important dimension of mystery, of holiness. Bereft and sometimes angry— liturgical reform had been, after all, wholly imposed from above—Catholics like these did sometimes leave the Church. For nearly all Catholics, moreover, the revised liturgy reinforced a fundamental tension with regard to Church authority. A hierarchical *ecclesia*, infallible in its teaching, was hardly congruent with a liturgy that stressed the importance of community and of enlightened lay participation.[5]

This tension was heightened, at least for an active minority of Catholics, by the reform agenda of the Dearden Chancery, an agenda that served as a model for progressive Catholics throughout the nation. As early as 1965, Archbishop Dearden was meeting with his priests and with selected groups of laity to chart the course of local "renewal." In the spring of 1966, the archbishop announced his plans for a reforming synod, one that would be preceded by a long and remarkably thorough period of discussion and consultation. The synod was not, in fact, convened until March of 1969, by which time more than 80,000 Catholics had participated in parish "speak up" sessions, where the need for change — and its direction — was vigorously debated. In this way the laity took an unprecedented role in shaping the synod's agenda.

Synod '69, as it was called, transformed the administrative structure of the Archdiocese. In sharp reaction to the trend of previous decades, the synod approved a radical decentralization of Chancery authority — declaring, indeed, that the Chancery had been abolished. In its place was a network of vicariates, twenty-five in all, each headed by an "episcopal vicar" who exercised many of a bishop's functions. In the early stages of this new regime, these vicars were chosen in part by popular election, and their authority was seen as deriving in a principal way from the consent of the people they governed. Those people, in turn, were directed to establish parish councils, whose elected members would play a role in virtually every aspect of parish life. The various parish councils were also involved in setting policy for their particular vicariates, for they sent delegates to serve, along with all the vicariate's priests, on what was known as the vicariate council. Not without justification did Father — now Bishop — Kenneth Untener tell the *Michigan Catholic* that the Church in the Archdiocese was rapidly moving toward "a process of participatory decision-making."[6]

The priests of the Archdiocese were especially affected by this new orientation. It meant a greater liberty for most, and unprecedented opportunities to shape archdiocesan policy. Detroit was among the first dioceses in the country to have a priest's senate, an elected body — albeit a purely advisory one — that met for the first time in December 1966. (The members were initially chosen according to age group, generational tensions afflicting the clergy, at this point, fully as much as the rest of the population.) The Priest's Senate was soon a principal forum for debate on reform of the clerical life, and a source both of pressure and support for the archbishop — the Cardinal after 1969 — as he changed the procedures by which priests were assigned to their posts and moved, with some reluctance, toward a greater tolerance with regard to dress and residence for priests and to the kinds of work that priests might legitimately do. The Senate debated celibacy too — with great heat and at great length — but here, of course, no change was forthcoming. Still, the vision of priesthood that permeated these debates — sharing the whole life of the people, knowing their burdens and their joys first hand — may have been a factor in the strong support that Dearden gave to the permanent diaconate, nearly all of whose members are married. Dearden, indeed, gave his blessing in 1968 to a singularly innovative program, one that originated in Detroit, by which black laymen were trained as "Ministers of Service." Their role in the parish is much like that of the permanent deacon.

The Dearden reforms, taken cumulatively, helped to release great stores of energy, perhaps most notably among the laity but among religious too. Sisters in the Archdiocese, especially, diversified their ministries after 1965, and were more and more identified with the work of social reform. The "activists," whether lay or religious, were disproportionately middle-class — representative of those well-educated Catholics whose numbers had grown so impressively since the late 1940s. They were spiritual heirs of the various Catholic Action movements and of the movement for liturgical reform. But they were also products of the 1960s, of its turbulent politics and its aggressively secular culture. Perhaps it was inevitable, then, that good will and optimism — so much a part of the early stages of reform — should sometimes dissolve in frustration and anger. For by the standards of the 1960s, the pace of change in the Church was slow. There were, moreover, some critical issues that lay beyond the reach of the reformers. Chief among these were official teaching on marriage and sexuality, clerical celibacy, and the role of women in the Church.

By the end of the 1960s, then, the Church in the Archdiocese was at once a vibrant institution, pulsing with life and innovation, and one whose very identity seemed increasingly in doubt. Attendance at Mass had begun to decline, most markedly among the young, and there was a sharp decline, by 1970, in the number of those who went regularly to confession, a trend not reversed by a subsequent reform in the rite — and to some extent, the theology — of penance. The number of priests declined as well: thirty-one diocesan priests left the active ministry in 1969, another thirty-one in 1970. The rate of attrition did slow thereafter, averaging about ten men per year for the rest of the 1970s. But ordination classes were now so small that the shortage of clergy grew ever more acute. (In 1983, there were 187 fewer priests in the Archdiocese, including those in religious orders, than there had been ten years earlier.) As for women religious, their numbers fell so precipitously after the mid-1960s that many parochial schools were soon in crisis. More than 80 percent of the parishes in the Archdiocese had schools in 1965; a decade later, fewer than half of them did.

What emerged — or, more correctly, is emerging — from this welter of change is an essentially voluntary Church, not only in the Archdiocese of Detroit but throughout the nation. A substantial majority of American Catholics today speak the language of individualism when it comes to religion. Their own experience, their own sense of need and of right — this is what Catholics increasingly invoke as they choose with regard to religious behavior and respond to a wide range of moral questions. Catholics are still more regular in their attendance at church than the members of other religious groups, and on certain issues they incline to markedly different views than most Americans. But what is striking, at least to a historian, is less what still distinguishes Catholics from other Americans than the multiple ways in which Catholics today think and act like the other members of their particular class and generational groups. Non-Catholics apparently think so too: save perhaps in the rural South, a candidate's Catholicism sparks little opposition among non-Catholics in the electorate. And the incidence of mixed marriage in the Catholic population is notably higher today than it was in the 1950s. On this score, as on many others, American Catholics look to be more and more like mainstream Protestants — rooted in a particular tradition, but tolerant in matters of dogma and discipline and willing to recognize, at some level of their being, the plurality of religious experience and even of religious truth.

The "voluntary" Church, as it has emerged in recent years, has certain clear strengths. Lay ministries have everywhere proliferated, and certainly in the Archdiocese of Detroit, where lay men and women play important roles in nearly all areas of Church life. The Church has thus succeeded in keeping the loyalties — and harnessing the energies — of some of its ablest and best-educated members. A renewed pastoral emphasis on the primacy of conscience has enabled significant numbers of Catholics to be full members of their Church and still embrace a world transformed by successive demographic and sexual revolutions. A greater tolerance and openness has indeed come to characterize the whole of Catholic intellectual life. And insofar as growing numbers of Catholics are highly educated, it is probably healthful for the Church in this country that its discourse be marked by the critical questioning, the ambiguity, even the doubt that seem to be the legacy of modern education. As for Catholics who are troubled by these developments, they are accommodated, in this pluralist Church, by the remarkable Charismatic movement and by a fair number of parishes where a peculiarly Catholic brand of fundamentalism is supported. The Church has thus maintained a formal unity, despite the centrifugal tendencies of its constituent parts.

This Church, however, is not without its problems. A continued drought in religious vocations is the most visible, and points to even more serious problems in the not-too-distant future, when priestless parishes may be a fact of life in many of the nation's dioceses. (The recent closing of St. John's Provincial Seminary is a poignant local reminder of this.) The "vocations crisis" has many causes, and cannot be wholly explained apart from change in the larger society. But it is not unconnected to the rise of a true theological pluralism within the Catholic community. "The priest, it seems, no longer knows who he is," Father Emile Pin wrote in the late 1960s. "The expectations of the faithful no longer give him a clear idea of what he should be and what he should do." It is true that American Catholics have retained a strong sense of themselves as a Eucharistic people; nearly every practicing Catholic today goes regularly to communion. In this sense the post-conciliar years mesh seamlessly with the developments of earlier decades. But there are many Catholics today who do not speak the kind of theological language that was found in the Baltimore Catechism, and their behavior often suggests that they imagine the drama of salvation in ways quite alien to the pre-conciliar Church. These Catholics lack the eschatological consciousness of their parents and grandparents; the fear of hell is largely gone, and with it the complex synthesis of rules and ritual that once directed souls toward life eternal. The religious world of the younger Catholic is less freighted with guilt than the world his forebears knew. But it is in some ways a less vivid world, and perhaps, for certain psychologies, a less comforting world as well. For nearly all Catholics, moreover, theological pluralism has made for a diminished sense of solidarity, of distinctiveness, even of Catholic purpose. And it has probably made it harder to hold the allegiance of the rising generation.[7]

The increasing fragmentation of the Catholic community suggests one further question. Will that community, precisely because of its divisions, be less and less a distinctive presence in the national life? Given the recent pastoral letters of the American bishops on war and peace and on the economy, one would perhaps be tempted to say no. (The breadth and passion of Catholic social activism since the 1960s might also be offered as evidence here.) But with the fluidity of their new moral universe, many Catholics today find it harder than ever before to articulate a uniquely "Catholic" approach to the nation's manifold problems. Nor are their institutions necessarily imbued with a clearly defined worldview—one thinks especially of the blurred identity of many Catholic schools and colleges. One could argue, indeed, that the much-increased interest of many Catholics in social and political issues flows in part from their loss of theological confidence. The Protestant churches, after all, embraced the Social Gospel as they moved away from creedal certitude.

There is, however, something a bit mean-spirited about this latter argument, and a real danger in assuming that we have, as yet, a balanced perspective on the post-conciliar period. The changes that mark that period have not yet run their course, and we do not wholly know the shape of the Church our children will inherit. A knowledge of history can assist us here, although only in limited and partial ways. (No prudent historian will venture into prophecy!) Our history, for example, would not lead us to expect a resurgence of Catholic institutional separatism, despite the nostalgia of many Catholics for the ordered world of the 1950s. No religious group of any appreciable size has been able to maintain a permanent distance from the dominant American culture, which is of unparalleled seductiveness and openness. Even in the nineteenth century, Detroit's Catholics were powerfully drawn to America's central values—to individualism, materialism, pragmatism, tolerance—and they were increasingly rewarded by economic and social and political success. What is remarkable is that those Catholics maintained a separatist posture for as long as they did.

Our history also suggests that divisiveness and even enmity among Catholics are not necessarily signs of institutional decline. The Church in the Archdiocese of Detroit has for much of its history been a divided institution—a loose federation, in fact if not in theory, of mutually suspicious ethnic camps. Are today's divisions—based mainly on class, ideology, and gender—more likely to cause schism than the powerful emotions connected to ethnic consciousness? Probably they are not, provided that the Church accommodates diversity as sensibly as it did in the polyglot past. (And even on the difficult question of women's status in the Church, the American Church has accomplished a fair degree of accommodation.) Division might even be said to enhance the life of the local Church. The immigrant parishes of the Archdiocese, it will be remembered, have historically been prone to conflict and caused endless headaches at the Chancery. But they nourished a lively Catholicism. Lay ministry flourished in those parishes, although our ethnic forebears would not themselves have used the term.

If the ethnic parish was an ironic force for unity in the Church, it was by no means the only such force. A divided Church was held together in the past in part by its hierarchical structure. The disciplinary potential of that structure was important, especially with regard to priests, but so were its symbolic functions. Detroit's bishops, even the redoubtable Cardinal Mooney, had only partial success at imposing their policies on the Archdiocese. They probably succeeded better than they knew in their powerful symbolic role as shepherds in the global Church. And although episcopal authority has been badly undermined, a bishop is still, for most Catholics, a credible sign of their fundamental unity. Cardinal Edmund Szoka, who came to Detroit in 1980, has a following locally that extends well beyond the Polish-Americans who count him as one of their own. His style and his policies are different, for the most part, from those of Cardinal Dearden, who was himself a widely popular man. But Cardinal Szoka has come to stand for Catholic Detroit, and for the ties that bind the people of the Archdiocese to a larger Catholic world.

Beyond bishops, however, and of even greater importance as a force for unity, has been a common liturgy and the immense significance for Catholics of the Eucharist. Ethnic Catholics in the past were brought to a larger sense of Catholicism in part by liturgical means: the ritual in which they participated was increasingly uniform, and they were more and more affected by an increasingly popular Eucharistic spirituality. Catholic worship today, for all the changes that flowed from the Council, is still firmly centered on the Eucharist. And this has decisive effect on the religious sensibility of nearly every Catholic, no matter how much they may disagree when it comes to the specifics of sacramental theology. At the heart of Catholic worship, then, is an experience of great evocative power. Our past suggests that nothing is of greater importance in defining a people.

ABBREVIATIONS

AACi	Archives of the Archdiocese of Cincinnati
AAD	Archives of the Archdiocese of Detroit
MHC	Michigan Historical Collections, Ann Arbor
MC	*Michigan Catholic*
ND	Archives housed at the Cushwa Center for the Study of American Catholicism, University of Notre Dame
SHS	Sacred Heart Seminary, Detroit
SSIHM	Archives of the Sisters, Servants of the Immaculate Heart of Mary, Monroe, Michigan
SSJ-N	Archives of the Sisters of St. Joseph, Nazareth, Michigan
WSU	Archives of Labor History and Urban Affairs, Wayne State University, Detroit

NOTES

INTRODUCTION

1. The commemorative edition of the *Michigan Catholic* (hereafter MC) is dated Dec. 21, 1933.
2. George Paré, *The Catholic Church in Detroit, 1701–1888* (Detroit: Gabriel Richard Press, 1951; Detroit: Wayne State University Press, 1983).
3. Assumption Grotto, Detroit, Annual report, 1911, AAD, parish files.

1. THREE BISHOPS

1. On the tangled history of the founding of the Diocese of Detroit, see Robert Trisco, *The Holy See and the Nascent Church in the Middle Western United States, 1826–1850* (Rome: Gregorian University Press, 1962), 28–39.
2. Paré, *Church in Detroit,* 399–400.
3. Ibid., 398.
4. Ibid., 372, 387, 390.
5. Ibid., 388, 408.
6. Quoted in Ibid., 404.
7. For the best analysis of the Rese affair, based on the documents in the Propaganda archives, see Trisco, *Holy See,* 344–384.
8. S. T. Badin to "Most Reverend and Dear Sir," Mar. 24, 1840. Copy in AAD, Paré papers, 4:6. Paré, *Church in Detroit,* 425–426. Quoted in Trisco, *Holy See,* 360.
9. Paré, *Church in Detroit,* 399, 412–413.
10. Ibid., 414–418.
11. Ibid., 418–420.
12. Since Lefevere died in 1869, two years before Rese, he never held the title Bishop of Detroit.
13. Paré, *Church in Detroit,* 399, 412–413.
14. Ibid., 436–438.
15. Lefevere to Fr. Stehle, Feb. 12, 1855, AAD, Letterbooks, vol. 2; Quoted in Paré, *Church in Detroit,* 469.
16. Lefevere to "the clergy and faithful," Oct. 24, 1850, AAD. Episcopal Register, vol. 3; Lefevere to purcell, Oct. 26, 1855, AAD, Letterbooks, 2.
17. Lefevere to Bishop Purcell, Nov. 25, 1847, AAD, Letterbooks, 1.
18. Paré, *Church in Detroit,* 441–443.
19. Lefevere to Purcell, March 12, 1867, AAD, Letterbooks, 3.

20. Lefevere to Kennelly, Sept. 8, 1843, AAD, Letterbooks, 1.
21. Paré, *Church in Detroit,* 446–447. A copy of the 1851 regulations is in the AAD.
22. On the 1859 synod, see ibid., 447.
23. Ibid., 447.
24. Ibid., 449–450, 454–457, 530.
25. Lefevere to Carrooll, Dec. 20, 1861, AAD, Letterbooks, 3.
26. Lefevere to Fr. DeNeve, Mar. 12, 1866, AAD, Letterbooks, 3.
27. Borgess to McMullen, July 30, 1881, AAD, Letterbooks, 12.
28. Borgess to "My dearest Sister," Sept. 25, 1882, AAD, Letterbooks, 12. On the Borgess personality, see MC, Apr. 8, 1897, 5:1–2.
29. Rev. Frank A. O'Brien, ms. reminiscences of Bishop Caspar Borgess, undated but probably 1891, SSJ-N, O'Brien papers. Fr. O'Brien was ordained in 1877.
30. Borgess to "Dear Mary," Sept. 30, 1883, AAD, Letterbooks, 12.
31. Borgess to "Dear Mary," Sept. 14 and 17, 1883, AAD, Letterbooks, 12.
32. Borgess to Rev. Aloysius Bleyenbergh, July 24, 1880, AAD, Letterbooks, 13. Four adults were also killed in the accident.
33. Borgess circular letter, Apr. 18, 1881, AAD, Borgess papers, 5:20.
34. Borgess to Fr. Robert Doman, Mar. 10, 1883, AAD, Letterbooks, 11.
35. Paré, *Church in Detroit,* 532–535. Proceedings of the fourth through the seventh synods are in the AAD.
36. Robert Trisco, "Bishops and Their Priests in the United States," in John Tracy Ellis, ed., *The Catholic Priest in the United States: Historical Investigations* (Collegeville, Minnesota: St. John's University Press, 1971), 268.
37. Borgess to Callaert, Oct. 10, 1873, Nov. 5, 1874, Feb. 7 and 11, 1876, AAD, Letterbooks, 6, 8.
38. Borgess to Callaert, Dec. 9, 1876, AAD, Letterbooks, 8.
39. *Western Home Journal,* Mar. 20, 1879, 4:4. Petition forms and relevant letters are found in the AAD, Borgess papers, 4:1.
40. Paré, *Church in Detroit,* 540; Borgess to F. A. Stace, Mar. 24, 1881, AAD, Letterbooks, 11.
41. On the Kolasinski case and its larger significance, see Leslie Woodcock Tentler, "Who is the Church? Conflict in a Polish Immigrant Parish in Late Nineteenth-Century Detroit," *Comparative Studies in Society and History,* 25:2 (Apr. 1983), 241–276. Numerous documents relating to the case are in the AAD, in both the Borgess and the Foley papers.
42. *Detroit Evening News,* Sept. 8 and 11, 1879.
43. MC, Jan. 22, 1891, 5:1–2.
44. Borgess to Elder, Feb. 24, 1887, AAD, Letterbooks, 12. On the Borgess resignation see also Borgess to Maes, Mar. 17 and May 6, 1887, and Borgess to Elder, May 2, 1887, AAD, Letterbooks, 13:5.
45. Borgess to Elder, Mar. 3, 1887, AAD, Letterbooks, 12.

2. THE DIOCESAN CLERGY: THE FIRST FIFTY YEARS

1. Borgess, ms. sermon, "The Priest," 1876, AAD, Borgess papers: sermons, 2:2; MC, Oct. 1, 1891, 5:4.
2. Lefevere to Bishop George Carroll, Dec. 20, 1861, AAD, Letterbooks, 3.
3. "Constitutiones Latae et Promulgatae a Revmo Petro Paulo Lefevere," Oct. 1859, AAD; Borgess circular letter, Aug. 4, 1882, AAD, Borgess papers, 5:20. See also Michael O. Brown, "The Catholic Priest in Northern Ohio: Life-Styles, 1860–1885," *Resonance,* 7:1 (Spring 1972), 53–93.

4. Viszoczky to Leopoldine Mission Society, Mar. 28, 1834, AAD, Paré papers, 8:3; Lefevere to Rev. W. Kennedy, Sept. 8, 1843, AAD, Letterbooks, 1.
5. Olivier Zunz, *The Changing Face of Inequality: Urbanization, Industrial Development, and Immigrants in Detroit, 1880-1920* (Chicago: University of Chicago Press, 1982), 228-231.
6. Dumont to Society for the Propagation of the Faith, Feb. 6, 1860, printed copy in AAD, parish files.
7. Michael MacNamara to Borgess, June 7, 1886, AAD, Borgess papers, 2:5.
8. Lefevere to Rev. Augustin B. Durst, Nov. 13, 1863, AAD, Episcopal Register, 4.
9. Lefevere to Godez, Oct. 7, 1843, AAD, Letterbooks, 1; Immaculate Conception, Anchorville, Annual report, 1868, AAD, parish files.
10. Lefevere to Messrs. Webb and Livering, Oct. 21, 1858, AAD, Letterbooks, 3; Paré, *Church in Detroit*, 417; James Birney to Bridget Birney, Dec. 26, 1860, MHC, Birney-McClear-Hankerd papers; Borgess to W. A. Nevin, Jan. 3, 1881, AAD, Letterbooks, 11.
11. MC, Jan. 28, 1892, 8:3-4.
12. On the parish mission in the United States, see Jay P. Dolan, *Catholic Revivalism: The American Experience, 1830-1900* (Notre Dame, Ind.: University of Notre Dame Press, 1978). Fr. Elliott is quoted on page 75.
13. Quoted in Paré, *Church in Detroit*, 451.
14. Dolan, *Catholic Revivalism*, 40, 44. On the frequency of missions in the various parishes, see the annual parish reports in the AAD.
15. Moutard to James Birney, Apr. 5, 1865; MHC, Birney-McClear-Hankerd papers; Dolan, *Catholic Revivalism*, 49-52.
16. Dumont to Society for the Propagation of the Faith, Feb. 6, 1860, printed copy in AAD; MC, Jan. 28, 1892, 8:3-4.
17. Viszoczky to Leopoldine Mission Society, Mar. 28, 1834, AAD.
18. Viszoczky to Leopoldine Mission Society, Dec. 23, 1834, AAD, Paré papers, 8:3; Rt. Rev. Edward Kelly, ed. and trans., *Correspondence of Rev. Louis Baroux to Rev. M. J. DeNeve* (Ann Arbor: Ann Arbor Press, n.d.), 18. The correspondence, which dates from 1862, was published in France in 1865.
19. Louis W. Doll, *The History of St. Thomas Parish, Ann Arbor* (Ann Arbor: Ann Arbor Press, 1941), 12-13; Maurice Geary, *A Century of Conquest: The Story of St. Alphonsus Parish, Dearborn, Michigan* (Dearborn, Michigan: privately printed, 1952), 21, 23.
20. Moutard to Birney, Apr. 5, 1865, Apr. 3, 1869, MHC, Birney-McClear-Hankerd papers; Kelly, *Correspondence of Rev. Louis Baroux*, 85.
21. Rev. I. F. Durin to Bishop Borgess, Aug. 15, 1885, AAD, Borgess papers, 2:4.
22. Lefevere to Kundig, Mar. 12, 1844, AAD, Letterbooks, 1. Kundig later served as vicar-general of the Diocese of Milwaukee.
23. Brown, "The Catholic Priest in Northern Ohio," 57-58. Lefevere to Fr. Deloul, Feb. 24, 1842, AAD, Paré papers, 9:2; Borgess, ms. sermon, "The Priest," AAD, Borgess papers: sermons, 2:2.
24. Lefevere to Rev. Augustin B. T. Durst, Nov. 13, 1863, AAD, Episcopal Register, 4; Borgess to Rev. E. VanDyke, Jan. 18, 1876, AAD, Letterbooks, 7.
25. DeGryse to Baumgartner, Feb. 6, 1902, AAD, parish files.
26. On the rules governing the fund and on its precarious financing, see "Rule for Mission Fund," undated but ca. 1878, AAD, Borgess papers, 1:2.
27. Borgess to Reilly, Nov. 16, 1883, AAD, Letterbooks, 11; O'Brien to Borgess, Sept. 23, 1886, SSJ-N, O'Brien papers.
28. Borgess to "Rt. Rev. and Dear Friend" (probably Bishop Camillus Maes), Jan. 26, 1887, AAD, Letterbooks, 13.5.
29. These cases are discussed in part II, chapter 6. Baart's papers, including the records of many of his cases, are housed at the University of Notre Dame.

30. *Acta,* Synodi Dioesanae, Detroitensis Sextae, July 1885, AAD, Borgess papers, 3:16.
31. Viszoczky to Leopoldine Mission Society, Dec. 23, 1834, AAD.
32. Lefevere to Rev. J. P. Mackin, Feb. 7, 1850, AAD, Letterbooks, 2.
33. Lefevere to Fr. Chambige, Mar. 20, 1857; Lefevere to Rev. Henri Meuffels, June 20, 1855, AAD, Letterbooks, 2.
34. Annual reports on the seminary collection, which include information on seminarians from the Diocese, are housed in the AAD.
35. "Notes on St. Francis Seminary, Monroe," AAD, Paré papers, 9:10.
36. Minutes, meeting of Diocesan Consultors, Apr. 10, 1889, AAD, minutes and proceedings, 4.
37. On the development of seminaries in nineteenth-century America, see John Tracy Ellis, "The Formation of the American Catholic Priest: An Historical Perspective," in Ellis, ed., *The Catholic Priest,* 5–6.
38. Borgess to Fr. Peter Leavy, Sept. 18, 1886, AAD, Letterbooks, 12.
39. Borgess to Leavy, Feb. 23, 1887, AAD, Letterbooks, 12; Borgess to Rev. A. Zeininger, Jan. 16, 1882, AAD, Letterbooks, 11.
40. On the history of SS. Cyril and Methodius Seminary see Joseph Swastek, *The Formative Years of the Polish Seminary in the United States* (1959; reprint, Orchard Lake, Mich.: Center for Polish Studies and Culture, 1987). See also Frank Renkiewicz, *For God, Country, and Polonia: One Hundred Years of the Orchard Lake Schools* (Orchard Lake, Mich.: Center for Polish Studies and Culture, 1987).
41. Dombrowski to Borgess, Feb. 21, 1884, AAD, Borgess papers, 1:17; Borgess to Dombrowski, Feb. 23, 1884, AAD, Letterbooks, 11; Borgess to R. J. Meyer, SJ, Jan. 6, 1887; Borgess to A. M. Anderledy, Jan. 6, 1887, AAD, Letterbooks, 12.
42. Quoted in Ellis, "Formation of the American Priest," 49; Lefevere to Rev. M. Heiss, Aug. 27, 1863, AAD, Letterbooks, 3; Borgess to Rev. Dr. Magnien, Mar. 19, 1885, AAD, Letterbooks, 12; Borgess to Charles Fix, July 10, 1879, AAD, Letterbooks, 13.
43. Ellis, "Formation of the American Priest," 48.
44. What records survive from the quarterly conferences are found in the Foley papers in the AAD. See also Rev. Frank A. O'Brien to Foley, undated but 1899; Feb. 24, 1900; Nov. 24, 1900; Rev. John Lynch to O'Brien, Jan. 29, 1891, SSJ-N, O'Brien papers; Fr. Ernest VanDyke to Fr. Edward Joos, Oct. 28, 1887, AAD, Ernest Van-Dyke letterbook.
45. MC, Jan. 28, 1892, 8:3–4.

3. RELIGION AND PARISH LIFE: THE EXPERIENCE OF THE LAITY

1. Petition to Lefevere, Jan. 27, 1869, AAD, Lefevere papers, 1:8.
2. Quoted in Paré, *Church in Detroit,* 402–403.
3. Viszoczky to Leopoldine Mission Society, Mar. 28, 1834, AAD, Paré papers, 8:3.
4. Lefevere to Archbishop Purcell, Jan. 28, 1862, AAD, Letterbooks, 3.
5. Paré, *Church in Detroit,* 407 n. 12.
6. Information on the numbers of priests and the Catholic population of the Diocese can be found in the annual *Catholic Directory.* Estimates as to population, however, are notoriously unreliable. One can infer trends from this data, but nothing more. Bolte to Borgess, Oct. 19, 1883, AAD, Borgess papers, 1:16.
7. Lefevere to Fr. DeNeve, Mar. 12, 1886, AAD, Letterbooks, 3.
8. Immaculate Conception, Anchorville, Annual report, 1869, AAD, parish files.
9. St. Mary, Monroe, Annual report, 1870; St. Charles, Newport, Annual report, 1868; Holy Cross, Marine City, Annual report, 1874, AAD, parish files.
10. St. Wenceslaus, Detroit, Annual report, 1878, AAD, parish files. On Czech Catho-

lics in the United States, see Stephen Thernstrom, ed., *Harvard Encyclopedia of American Ethnic Groups* (Cambridge, Mass.: Harvard University Press, 1980), 265–269. Hendrickx to Bishop Borgess, June 18, 1884, AAD, Borgess papers, 2:5.

11. Quoted in Catherine Bicknell, *St. Bonaventure Monastery: A Century of Prayer and Sharing* (Detroit: Fidelity Press, 1983), 29, 31. O'Brien to Rev. Fr. Provincial, C.SS.R., Jan. 6, 1885, SSJ-N, O'Brien papers; "Summary of the Census of 1884 of the St. Augustine's parish, Kalamazoo," undated but ca. 1884, AAD, Borgess papers, 1:17.

12. Paré, *Church in Detroit,* 671. The two newspapers were the *Western Catholic Register,* published for most of 1842, and the *Detroit Catholic Vindicator,* which ran from 1853 until perhaps 1860. For the last four or five years of its life, however, the *Vindicator* was a mainly secular organ devoted to the cause of the Democratic Party.

13. Joseph P. Chinnici, OFM, "Organization of the Spiritual Life: American Catholic Devotional Works, 1791–1866," *Theological Studies,* 40:2 (June 1979), especially 235–255.

14. "Admission into the Pious Congregation of the Sacred Heart of Jesus," Aug. 15, 1842, AAD, Holy Trinity, Detroit, parish file.

15. St. Peter, Mt. Clemens, Annual reports, 1870, 1880, 1905, AAD, parish files.

16. St. Mary, Detroit, Annual report, 1885, AAD, parish files.

17. *Diamond Jubilee: St. Joseph's Liebesbund, 1856–1931* (Detroit, 1931), no pagination.

18. Mrs. Patrick Hankerd, untitled ms. history of SS. Cyprian and Cornelius church, Bunkerhill, undated but c. 1940, no pagination; Bridget to James, Apr. 29, 1858, MHC, Birney-McClear-Hankerd papers.

19. Jane to "Dear Father," undated but 1859, MHC, Birney-McClear-Hankerd papers. The grandchildren included Mother Ruth Hankerd, long-time superior of the Immaculate Heart of Mary Sisters at Monroe, and Monsignor Vincent Hankerd.

20. Bridget to James, Feb. 28, 1843; James to Bridget, Mar. 23, 1843, MHC, Birney-McClear-Hankerd papers.

21. James to Bridget, Mar. 23, 1843; Bridget to James, Feb. 28, 1843. MHC, Birney-McClear-Hankerd papers.

22. Mrs. Patrick Hankerd to Rev. George W. Paré, Nov. 7, 1930, AAD, Paré papers, 1:6; John Birney to James, undated but 1859 or 1860; Bridget to James, Apr. 29, 1858; Jane to James, June 10, 1858; Sarah Ann to James, undated; James to "Dear Daughters," undated; MHC, Birney-McClear-Hankerd papers.

23. James to Bridget, June 17, 1859; Bridget to James, undated but 1859; James to Bridget and children, Aug. 2, 1859, MHC, Birney-McClear-Hankerd papers.

24. Bridget to James, Aug. 25, 1859, MHC, Birney-McClear-Hankerd papers.

25. James to Bridget, Sept. 16, 1860, MHC, Birney-McClear-Hankerd papers.

26. James to Bridget, Oct. 2, 1859; Nov. 1, 1859; Bridget to James, undated but ca. 1859; James to Bridget, Aug. 2, 1859, MHC, Birney-McClear-Hankerd papers.

27. Lefevere to Markey, Jan. 31, 1861, AAD, Episcopal Register, 4.

28. Minutes, meetings of the congregation and church committee, St. Joseph's parish, Detroit, June 14, 26 and 29, July 6, 1857; Jan. 2, 1859, AAD, parish files.

29. John J. Lamott, *History of the Archdiocese of Cincinnati, 1821–1921* (New York: Frederick Pustet, 1921), 215–217; "Rules and Directions of the Administration of the Temporal Affairs of the Church in the Diocese of Detroit," 1862, AAD; Lefevere to Rev. Peter Kindekins, July 10, 1862, AAD, Letterbooks, 3.

30. Borgess to Rev. M. H. Schaeken, Jan. 26, 1871, AAD, Letterbooks, 5 (emphasis in original); "The Regulations of the Diocese of Detroit, Published by the Synod of May 15th, 1873"; "The Regulations of the Diocese of Detroit, Dec. 8, 1875, SHS.

31. "Rules for the Parish of Parisville, Huron Co., Mich.," Jan. 7, 1886, AAD, Letterbooks, 12.

32. Holy Cross, Marine City, Annual report, 1884, AAD, parish files.

33. Our Lady of Mt. Carmel, Emmet, Annual report, 1868; St. Michael, Monroe, Annual report, 1876, AAD, parish files.
34. St. Peter, Mt. Clemens, Annual report, 1870; "St. Mary's Catholic Church, St. Clair, Michigan: 125 Years of Service, 1853-1978"; Our Lady of Mt. Carmel, Emmet, Annual report, 1868; Financial statement, Holy Trinity parish, Detroit, 1884, AAD, parish files.
35. MC, Sept. 17, 1896, 8:2; Borgess to J. W. Malany, Oct. 14, 1881; AAD, Letterbooks, 11; O'Brien to Rev. H. J. Schutjes, Feb. 10, 1886, SSJ-N, O'Brien papers.
36. Minute Book, Catholic Female Benevolent Society of Detroit, 1834-1836; photostat copy in AAD, Paré papers, 6:14.
37. Ibid.
38. Ibid.
39. Ibid (emphasis in original).
40. Ibid.
41. Ibid.
42. Ibid.
43. Information on parish charity groups is found mainly in the *Western Home Journal* and, after 1882, the *Michigan Catholic*. The first St. Vincent de Paul Society in the Diocese was probably organized at St. Patrick's parish in Detroit in 1871, but it seems to have survived for less than a year.
44. Quoted in Paré, *Church in Detroit*, 683; Membership book, Detroit Catholic Temperance Society, undated, SHS.
45. Membership book, Detroit Catholic Temperance Society; Member's card, Catholic Temperance Society of Ann Arbor, signed by Bridget McClear, Aug. 2, 1842, MHC, Birney-McClear-Hankerd papers.
46. St. Albertus, Detroit, Annual report, 1874, AAD, parish files.

4. Catholic education: the foundation years

1. All quotes from Paré, *Church in Detroit*, 294, 621, 377, 382.
2. Ibid., 635-639; Friend Palmer, *Early Days in Detroit* (Detroit: Hunt and June, 1906), 655.
3. *St. Mary's Centennial, Westphalia, Michigan, 1836-1936* (Westphalia, Mich., 1936), 93.
4. The orders brought into the Diocese by Bishop Lefevere were: the Daughters of Charity (1844), the Sisters of the Holy Cross (1844), the Religious of the Sacred Heart (1851), the Brothers of the Christian Schools (1851), and the School Sisters of Notre Dame (1852). On the founding of the IHMs see the excellent history by Sister Rosalita [Kelly], IHM, *No Greater Service: The History of the Sisters, Servants of the Immaculate Heart of Mary, Monroe, Michigan* (Detroit, 1948).
5. Quoted in Paré, *Church in Detroit*, 458-459.
6. Lefevere to Mrs. R. E. Hamilton, Aug. 28, 1854, AAD, Letterbooks, 2.
7. Chronicle of the Mission, SS. Peter and Paul Cathedral, Detroit, excerpted in Sister Rosalita [Kelly], IHM, ed., *Achievement of a Century: The Motherhouse and Missions of the Sisters, Servants of the Immaculate Heart of Mary, Monroe, Michigan* (Monroe, 1948), 55. The IHMs also taught a school for black children in the cathedral parish from 1867 to 1870. See part III, chapter 15.
8. Paré, *Church in Detroit*, 462.
9. Quoted in ibid., 464-465. For the best coverage of the 1853 controversy, see Ronald Formisano, *The Birth of Mass Political Parties: Michigan, 1827-1861* (Princeton, N.J.: Princeton University Press, 1971), especially chapter 11.
10. Lefevere to J. G. Schwartz, Aug. 11, 1850, AAD, Letterbooks, 2.
11. Paré, *Church in Detroit*, 466.

12. Formisano, *Mass Political Parties,* 140, 220–226.

13. Quoted in ibid., 226.

14. Quoted in Sr. Rosalita, *No Greater Service,* 360–361.

15. Borgess, diary entry for May 5, 1872, AAD, Borgess papers, bound volumes; "The Regulations of the Diocese of Detroit, Published in the Synod of May 15th, 1873," SHS; Borgess to Rev. James Pulcher, Jan. 3, 1877, AAD, Letterbooks 8; *Acta,* Synodi Quartae, Detroitensis, 1878, AAD, Borgess papers, 5:18.

16. Borgess to Rev. A. Vandendreissche, Oct. 31, 1882, AAD, Letterbooks, 11.

17. The teaching orders recruited under Bishop Borgess include Sisters of Charity from Cincinnati (1872), the Sisters of Christian Charity (1874), the Sisters of Providence (1875), Dominican Sisters from New York City (1877), the Sisters of St. Agnes (1880), the Felician Sisters (1880), and the Sisters of the Holy Names of Jesus and Mary (1886). The Jesuits arrived in 1877.

18. Sister Rosalita, ed., *Achievement,* 59; *St. Mary's Centennial,* 93.

19. Frs. Friedland and Rohowski to Bp. Foley, Aug. 29, 1889, AAD, Foley papers, 4:1; "Diocese of Detroit, Visitation of the Parish School: St. Joachim school, Detroit," May 16, 1887, ND, Baart papers, 12; Borgess to C. G. Bolte, Mar. 5, 1887, AAD, Letterbooks, 12; Borgess to Rev. J. Theisen, Nov. 10, 1881, AAD, Letterbooks, 11.

20. Mary Lee Anderson, *St. Patrick Church, Carleton, Michigan, 1847–1948* (privately printed, 1947), no pagination.

21. James Burns, CSC, *The Growth and Development of the Catholic School System in the United States* (New York: Benziger Brothers, 1912), 203–204; *Acta,* Synodi Quintae, Detroitensis, 1881, AAD, Borgess papers, 5:18.

22. Sister Mary Janice Ziolkowski, CSSF, *The Felician Sisters of Livonia, Michigan* (Detroit: Harlo Press, 1984), 122; First Annual Report of the Diocesan School Board, 1887, SSIHM: IHM Education, 4; unsigned but Rev. P. A. Baart to Rev. E. Joos, undated but 1888, ND, Baart papers, 1.

23. Hendrickx to Baart, May 16, 1887, ND, Baart papers, 1 (emphasis in original).

24. Minutes, meeting of Diocesan Consultors, Apr. 10, 1889, AAD, minutes and proceedings, 4.

25. Rev. E. Joos to "Rev'd. Dear Friend," Mar. 4, 1875, SSIHM: IHM Education, 4; Joos to Rev. J. Frieden, SJ, Jan. 4, 1888, AAD, Letterbooks, 14; Borgess to Fr. Joseph Seybold, Sept. 21, 1882, AAD, Letterbooks, 12; Borgess to Fr. F. A. O'Brien, Jan. 20, 1885, AAD, Letterbooks, 12. Bishop Foley reaffirmed the age limit of fourteen in response to a query from Fr. Frank O'Brien. See Foley to O'Brien, Sept. 9, 1909, SSJ-N, O'Brien papers. But in Detroit by 1909 there were parish high schools, known to the bishop, that enrolled boys over that age and had them under the instruction of women religious.

26. Herman J. Muller, SJ, *The University of Detroit, 1877–1977: A Centennial History* (Detroit, 1976), 22–26, 61.

27. See the St. Mary's Academy "announcement" in the *Catholic Almanac,* 1847. Piano lessons were an additional $10 a quarter.

28. Announcement of curriculum and terms, St. Mary's Young Ladies' Academy, in *Seminary Report,* July 1877, AAD. For an especially striking contrast, see the same announcement in the *Seminary Report,* July 1901.

29. Borgess to C. J. Roche, Feb. 18, 1879, AAD, Letterbooks, 9.

5. CATHOLICS IN A NON-CATHOLIC WORLD

1. The number of marriages performed by priests in the Diocese each year between 1870 and 1883 could presumably be determined by examining the marriage regis-

ters of each of the parishes then in existence. But since these parishes are now divided among six dioceses and are widely scattered throughout the state, the task was too great to be undertaken for the purposes of this study.

2. Borgess pastoral letter, Feb. 2, 1878, AAD, Borgess papers, 5:20. Evidently the Chancery in these years especially discouraged marriages where the non-Catholic party was the woman. Whatever the putative authority of the man as head of the family, Bishop Borgess assumed that mothers largely determined the religious belief and practices of their children. See Rev. E. Joos to "Dear Sir," Oct. 19, 1888, AAD, Letterbooks, 14.

3. St. Mary, Redford, Annual report, 1879, AAD, parish files; "Summary of the Census of 1884 of the St. Augustine's Parish, Kalamazoo," AAD, Borgess papers, 1:17.

4. Borgess circular letter to the clergy, Aug. 4, 1882, AAD, Borgess papers, 5:20; Holy Cross, Marine City, Annual report, 1874, AAD, parish files.

5. On the Protestant churches and contraception, see David M. Kennedy, *Birth Control in America: The Career of Margaret Sanger* (New Haven: Yale University Press, 1970), 153–171, and also Alan Graebner, "Birth Control and the Lutherans: The Missouri Synod as a Case Study," in Janet Wilson James, ed., *Women in American Religion* (Philadelphia: University of Pennsylvania Press, 1978), 229–252.

6. MC, Feb. 27, 1890, 1:4–5; Nov. 23, 1893, 4:1. For a discussion of contraceptive practice in Catholic Europe in the nineteenth century, see John T. Noonan, *Contraception: A History of Its Treatment by the Catholic Theologians and Canonists* (Cambridge, Mass.: Harvard University Press, 1965), especially chapter 13.

7. Quoted in James C. Mohr, *Abortion in America: The Origins and Evolution of National Policy, 1800–1900* (New York: Oxford University Press, 1978), 73. See also 80–82.

8. Ibid., 219–221.

9. Ibid., 167, 182–196.

10. Borgess circular letter to the clergy, Aug. 4, 1882, AAD, Borgess papers, 5:20; Rev. Louis Cook, C.SS.R., to Borgess, Nov. 20, 1885, AAD, Borgess papers, 2:4.

11. Rev. Edmund Hill, CP, to Borgess, Jan. 15, 1883, AAD, Borgess papers, 1:14; O'Brien to Borgess, Dec. 27, 1883, SSJ-N, O'Brien papers. The pastor at Marine City apparently thought in the 1870s that Catholics sometimes had recourse to abortion. He suggested in 1874 that the Chancery include in the form for the annual parish report the question, "Did any child get killed by a so-called 'Doctor?'" Holy Cross, Marine City, Annual report, 1874, AAD, parish files.

12. On lay "ignorance" with regard to the sinfulness of contraception, see John A. Ryan, "Family Limitation," *American Ecclesiastical Review*, 54:6 (June 1916), 684–696.

13. On the political divide between "pietistic" Protestants and "ritualistic" Protestants and Catholics, see Paul Kleppner, *The Cross of Culture: A Social Analysis of Midwestern Politics, 1850–1900* (New York: The Free Press, 1970), especially chapter 2, and Formisano, *Mass Political Parties*, especially chapters 8 and 15.

14. Formisano, *Mass Political Parties*, 324.

15. Ibid., 203–205.

16. Ibid., 234–263.

17. Ibid., 227–228; Lefevere to "Editor of the *American Celt*," Oct. 24, 1856, AAD, Letterbooks, 2.

18. Borgess to Bp. Joseph Richter, Jan. 14, 1887, AAD, Letterbooks, 12.

19. The Michigan Retreat for the Insane was initially located in Detroit. The facility, known after 1883 as St. Joseph's Retreat, was moved to a rural setting in Dearborn in 1886. The House of Providence became Providence Hospital in 1910.

20. The orders known to have cared for orphaned girls at their convents were the Religious of the Sacred Heart, who were receiving girls as early as 1851; the School Sisters of Notre Dame, whose orphanage in St. Mary's parish in Detroit probably dates

from 1852; the IHM Sisters, who first cared for orphans at the motherhouse in Monroe in 1860; and the Felician Sisters, who took up the work in 1882. The Sisters of Charity and the Sisters of Mercy both established hospitals in the 1870s. But after 1882, these institutions were part of the Diocese of Grand Rapids.

21. MC, Jan. 11, 1894, 5:1–2.
22. MC, Dec. 12, 1889, 8:2. The *Michigan Catholic* made periodic note in the late nineteenth century of Protestant-Catholic cooperation in charity fund-raising.
23. Quoted in Paré, *Church in Detroit*, 690 (emphasis in original).
24. Ibid., 697; *Western Home Journal*, June 4, 1881, 4:3; MC, Jan. 11, 1894, 4:7; Feb. 23, 1888, 4:5–7.
25. Quoted in Paré, *Church in Detroit*, 697.
26. On class and ethnic segregation in late-nineteenth-century Detroit, see Zunz, *Changing Face of Inequality*. MC, Nov. 14, 1889, 8:3; Aug. 13, 1896, 5:1–2.
27. Paré, *Church in Detroit*, 695–696; MC, Mar. 30, 1899, 4:4.

6. THE FOLEY EPISCOPATE

1. MC, Nov. 29, 1888, 4:3–7, 5:1–3.
2. Rev. Earl Boyea, "John Samuel Foley, Third Bishop of Detroit; His Ecclesiastical Conflicts in the Diocese of Detroit, 1888–1900" (Master's thesis, Wayne State University, 1984), 24–29.
3. Ibid., 29–30.
4. On population movement in Detroit see Zunz, *Changing Face of Inequality*. On Detroit's black population before the First World War, see David M. Katzman, *Before the Ghetto: Black Detroit in the Nineteenth Century* (Urbana, Ill.: University of Illinois Press, 1973).
5. Zunz, *Changing Face of Inequality*, 113–128.
6. John Tracy Ellis, *The Life of James Cardinal Gibbons* (Milwaukee: Bruce Publishing Company, 1952), 2:457. Boyea, "John Samuel Foley," 31. On the loss of the Foley papers, see Rev. John A. Donovan to Sister Mary Philip, OP, July 20, 1956, AAD, Chancery records: Religious orders, women.
7. Rev. P. A. Baart to Rev. Francis Kennedy, Oct. 15, 1896, AAD, Foley papers, 8:3; Foley to Keane, Apr. 9, 1897; Keane to Foley, Apr. 10, 1897; Elder to Foley, Apr. 13, 1897, AAD, Foley papers, 5:10.
8. On the founding and the early years of the Apostolic Delegation, see Gerald P. Fogarty, *The Vatican and the American Hierarchy from 1870 to 1965* (Stuttgart: Anton Hiersemann, 1982), chaps. 3–5.
9. MC, Aug. 6, 1908, 1:4; Ellis, *Cardinal Gibbons*, 2:426.
10. Foley to Egan, Dec. 4, 1889, AAD, Letterbooks, 14.
11. Rev. G. Paré to Msgr. William Murphy, Jan. 31, 1938, AAD, parish files; Reilly to Foley, Aug. 26, 1890, AAD, Fr. Charles O. Reilly file.
12. See, for example, Foley to Dennis O'Connell, Sept. 11, 1893, AAD, Foley papers, 5:8.
13. Ellis, *Cardinal Gibbons*, 1:698 n. 114; MC, Nov. 26, 1891, 4:2; Sept. 26, 1889, 5:2; July 18, 1889, 5:1–4; May 25, 1899, 4:1–2.
14. MC, Aug. 28, 1890, 8:1; Apr. 14, 1892, 4:2–5; Apr. 28, 1892, 4:2–3.
15. "To your Eminence must we look for salvation from the wicked wretch, Cahensley, who is striving to undo the work of the Church in our country," Foley wrote to Gibbons in 1891 with regard to the "Lucerne Memorial," which proposed, among other things, a more generous representation for ethnic Catholics in the ranks of the American hierarchy. "You can hardly imagine the feeling among our Western Amer-

icans by the outrage of Lucerne. The Americans are indignant at it. The Poles especially are looking forward to 'national Bishops.' Some decided, and at the same time,
respectful action is demanded. It will not be sufficient to rest upon newspaper protests. There ought to be united, archepiscopal, and provincial action taken at once
to allay public feeling and to enlighten the Holy Father." Quoted in Coleman S.
Barry, OSB, *The Catholic Church and German Americans* (Washington: Catholic University of America, 1953), 150; MC, July 18, 1889, 5:1–4; Sept. 5, 1895, 4:5–6.

16. MC, Aug. 1, 1889, 5:1–3.
17. Handwritten address, untitled, Jan. 19, 1896, AAD, Foley papers, 1:6; MC, Mar.
    24, 1898, 4:2; April 28, 1898, 8:3.
18. MC, Dec. 26, 1907, 2:2–7.
19. Tentler, "Who Is the Church?" 256–264.
20. Ibid., 264–265.
21. Ibid., 266–267, 269–270.
22. Ibid., 244–247, 249–250. The Bay City events, like the principal events in the Ko-
    lasinski affair, were covered extensively by the Detroit press. For a typically colorful
    account of the storming of the rectory at St. Stanislaus in Bay City by the dissidents
    in the congregation, see *Detroit Evening News,* Jan. 5, 1897.
23. Tentler, "Who Is the Church?" 270–272.
24. Ibid., 271–272. Foley's reaction to the Propaganda's decision and the like reaction
    of his consultors is amply documented in the minutes of their meetings between
    Nov. 17, 1893, and Jan. 9, 1894 (AAD, Minutes and proceedings, 4).
25. Tentler, "Who Is the Church?" 272–273; "By-Laws of the Roman Catholic Parish
    of the Sacred Heart of Mary," Apr. 29, 1897, AAD, parish files.
26. Baart to Archbishop Satolli, Nov. 4, 1893, quoted in Boyea, "John Samuel Foley";
    Detroit Evening News, Apr. 11, 1898, 5:1–3; *Detroit Free Press,* Apr. 12, 1898, 10:6.
27. Paré, *Church in Detroit,* 444–445; Rev. Earl Boyea, "A Cathedral or a Church: The
    Church Farm Dispute," unpublished paper, Apr. 1981, 1–3, appendices B, C, D;
    Rev. Christian Denissen, "Deposition," Mar. 14, 1892, AAD, Foley papers, 5:6.
28. "Bill of Complaint," Mar. 14, 1892, AAD, Foley papers, 5:9; "Argument for Com-
    plainant," undated, AAD, Foley papers, 5:16.
29. Foley to Cardinal Ledochowski, Mar. 15, 1897, AAD, Foley papers, 5:9; Foley to
    O'Connell, June 2, 1892, AAD, Letterbooks, 14; "Brief in Support of Defendant's
    Answer," undated, AAD, Foley papers, 5:14.
30. Cardinal Ledochowski to Foley, Jan. 19, 1897, AAD, Foley papers, 5:9; Bp. Keane
    to Foley, Apr. 10, 1897, AAD, Foley papers, 5:10
31. Fr. F. J. Baumgartner to Foley, Feb. 4, 1897; Foley to Bp. Keane, Mar. 15, 1897,
    AAD, Foley papers, 5:9; *Detroit Free Press,* Feb. 6, 1897, 1:8, 2:1–2.
32. Keane to Foley, Apr. 10, 1987, AAD, Foley papers, 5:10.
33. "Brief in Support of Defendant's Answer," Quoted in Boyea, "Cathedral or Church,"
    10; Baart to Fr. Dempsey, May 25, 1892, AAD, Foley papers, 5:7.
34. Foley to Cardinal Satolli, June 6, 1896, AAD, Foley papers, 8:1.
35. Doherty to Kennedy, May 14, 1886, AAD, Foley papers, 8:1
36. Baart to Cardinal Satolli, May 28, 1896, AAD, Foley papers, 8:1.
37. Baart to Kennedy, undated but Aug. 1896; Kennedy to Cardinal Satolli, Aug. 21,
    1896, AAD, Foley papers, 8:1.
38. Baart to Kennedy, Oct. 15, 1896, AAD, Foley papers, 8:3; Kennedy to Foley, Aug.
    31, 1896 (copy); Kennedy to Satolli, Sept. 4, 1896; Foley to Kennedy, Sept. 5, 1896,
    AAD, Foley papers, 8:2; Kennedy to Baart, Oct. 28, 1896, AAD, Foley papers, 8:3.
39. MC, Jan. 17, 1918, 5:1–7.

7. THE DIOCESAN CLERGY: THE FOLEY YEARS

1. Data on place of birth, education, age at ordination, and priests' career patterns was compiled variously from deceased priests' files (housed in the AAD), from newspaper obituaries, and from the *Catholic Directory.*
2. MC, Aug. 22, 1889, 5:3–5.
3. MC, May 23, 1895, 4:2; Apr. 11, 1901, 4:3; Aug. 10, 1916, 4:2.
4. MC, Apr. 12, 1894, 4:5–7.
5. Information on the religion of a priest's parents and the other members of his family in religious life is often found in the deceased priests' files; supplementary information comes from the *Michigan Catholic* and occasionally from private correspondence.
6. MC, Feb. 9, 1911, 1:2–3; May 7, 1914, 4:4–5. The author of "The First Mass" is identified only as J.B.S.
7. My conclusions about the clergy and their economic and social expectations are based on a reading of what correspondence from priests is housed in the AAD and on the sermons, letters, and accounts of clerical life to be found in the *Michigan Catholic.* MC, Dec. 3, 1908, 1:2–4, 5:1–3. Father Kelley founded the Extension Society in 1905, when he was pastor at Lapeer. The society raised money to support mission work, especially in the American South and Southwest.
8. MC, Aug. 22, 1889, 5:3–5; Oct. 1, 1891, 5:4.
9. John Tracy Ellis, "Formation of the American Priest," 47; Michael V. Gannon, "Before and After Modernism: The Intellectual Isolation of the American Priest," in Ellis, ed., *The Catholic Priest,* 328–329; Fr. William E. Randall to Henry F. Brownson, Mar. 31, 1904, ND, Henry Brownson papers; Daniel Murray to Michael Gallagher, Dec. 21, 1890, AAD, Gallagher papers, 12:7. On Roman seminary education see Ellis, "Formation of the American Priest," 23.
10. Leo Knappe to Gallagher, Sept. 28, 1890, AAD, Gallagher papers, 12:7.
11. Rev. William Stang, *Pastoral Theology,* rev. ed. (New York: Benziger Brothers, 1897), 216–217; MC, July 20, 1893, 8:2.
12. MC, July 12, 1900, 8:2.
13. O'Brien to Rev. Lafayette Brancheau, July 19, 1886, SSJ-N, O'Brien papers. Emphasis in original.
14. Gery to "Rev. Dear Father," Feb. 18, 1901; Gery to Bishop Foley, Jan. 11, 1898; Rev. John Command to Rev. F. J. Baumgartner, Feb. 4, 1909, AAD, parish files.
15. Fr. John F. Kramer to "V. Rev. Father and dear Friend," Dec. 2, 1895; DeBever to Very Rev. Fr. Baumgartner, Jan. 31, 1896, AAD, parish files; Sister M. Rosalita [Kelly], IHM, "The Redford Pioneers and Their Pastors, 1833–1919," in *St. Mary of Redford: A Modern Parish with a Pioneer Spirit* (Detroit, 1949), 51.
16. Rev. M. J. P. Dempsey, "Report of Cathedral Parish for the Year 1893," Dec. 31, 1893, AAD, parish files; MC, Feb. 13, 1896, 5:3–4.
17. Rev. T. Slater, SJ, and Rev. A. Rauch, SJ, *Rules of Life for the Pastor of Souls* (New York: Benziger Brothers, 1909), 123–125.
18. Ibid., 65–66. Foley to Bishop Joseph P. Lynch, undated but 1916. This letter, as well as the subsequently quoted report to Cardinal Mooney, is found in the deceased priests' files of the AAD. There were young women serving as rectory housekeepers in the Borgess as well as the Foley years, at least according to a Borgess sermon preached in 1876 and a Borgess diary entry for 1872. Needless to say, the bishop disapproved. But many "good and virtuous priests," as the bishop himself expressed it, evidently believed that custom sanctioned a young woman at the rectory, even if canon law did not. Perhaps for this reason, Borgess was unwilling, or unable, to do very much about the matter, Borgess, manuscript sermon, "The Priest," 1876, AAD, Borgess papers, sermons, 2:2. See also Borgess diary entry for Apr. 25, 1872, AAD, Borgess papers, bound volumes.

19. Rev. Frank A. O'Brien, "Organization and Maintenance of Parish Societies," *American Ecclesiastical Review,* 14:6 (June 1896), 492–493.
20. MC, Nov. 2, 1893.
21. Meuffels to Bp. Foley, undated but mid-1890s, AAD, parish files; Rev. John Kramer to Foley, June 6, 1912, AAD, St. Clement's, Centerline parish file; Seybold to Foley, Mar. 24, 1897, AAD, parish files.
22. Kramer to Foley, May 6, 1895, AAD, St. Clement's, Centerline parish file; Rev. A. Kraus to Foley, Dec. 9, 1914, AAD, parish files.
23. Bertele to Foley, Feb. 16, 1916, AAD, St. Michael, Monroe parish file; DeGryse to Foley, Sept. 18, 1895, AAD, parish files; P. H. Walsh to Foley, Feb. 2, 1899, AAD, Fr. James Gore file; "One who wants to see justice done" to Foley, Sept. 26, 1895, AAD, parish files.
24. "Church of the Immaculate Conception, Lapeer, Michigan, 1890," AAD, parish files.
25. MC, Nov. 1, 1906, 3:5.
26. The *Michigan Catholic* in the Foley years carried many reports of parish celebrations in honor of priests' anniversaries and name-days, which nearly always included an entertainment and the presentation of gifts or a "generous purse." MC, Sept. 19, 1895, 5:3–5; *Monroe Democrat,* Nov. 17, 1905; MC, Oct. 17, 1895, 3:2.
27. MC, Nov. 22, 1906, 8:2.
28. Documentation of a priest's age at death and whether or not he had retired is generally available for the Foley years in the deceased priests' files of the AAD, but the information is not always recorded. Thomas to Bp. Foley, Nov. 5, 1897, AAD, parish files.
29. On the annual stipend, see Foley to Rev. Theodore Muer, Mar. 23, 1892, AAD, Foley papers, 8:8.75; MC, Aug. 18, 1898, 8:1; Minutes, meeting of Diocesan Consultors, May 2, 1919, AAD, minutes and proceedings, 4.
30. Foley to Vandendriessche, Dec. 20, 1892. Fr. Vandendriessche, who died in 1901, presumably retired because of poor health. Laugel to Msgr. John Doyle, Mar. 14, 1924, and undated, AAD, Fr. George Laugel file.
31. Evidence bearing on problem drinking, sexual scandals, and the like is found mainly in the deceased priests' files of the AAD. These records are incomplete in many respects. But I would guess that the files are sufficiently complete to indicate that drinking was in fact a problem brought to Chancery attention far more often than allegations of sexual misconduct.
32. Borgess to Busche, Jan. 6, 1883, AAD, Letterbooks, 11. The career of Fr. Busche is briefly mentioned in a recent biography of Bishop Francis Kelley, who served as pastor at Lapeer from 1893 to 1908. See James P. Gaffey, *Francis Clement Kelley and the American Dream* (Bensenville, Ill.: Heritage Foundation, 1980), 1:75. No information about the 1890 suspension could be found in the AAD.
33. P. Byrne to Rev. F. J. Baumgartner, Mar. 28, 1901, AAD, parish files; Borgess to J.B., Mar. 5, 1881, AAD, Letterbooks, 11.
34. Borgess to J.M., Oct. 9, 1886, AAD, Letterbooks, 12.
35. J.R. to Bp. Foley, Nov. 14, 1896, AAD, deceased priests' files; Borgess to Rev. Vandendriessche, Feb. 11, 1886, AAD, Letterbooks, 12.
36. MC, Oct. 1, 1891, 5:4; July 13, 1899, 8:4–5.

8. THE LAITY: A TIME OF TRANSITION

1. The Third Provincial Council of Cincinnati was held in 1861. On the Council and children's confessions see Rev. E. Joos to Rev. J. Busche, Apr. 13, 1888, AAD, Letterbooks, 14; Stang, *Pastoral Theology,* 184.

2. O'Brien to Bp. Borgess, Feb. 26, 1884, SSJ-N, O'Brien papers.
3. Foley to "Rev. dear Father," Sept. 5, 1909, AAD, Foley papers, 1:13; minutes, meeting of Diocesan Consultors, May 11, 1909, AAD, minutes and proceedings, 4.
4. MC, July 14, 1898, 3:2; June 25, 1891, 8:3.
5. MC, June 17, 1909, 5:3; Oct. 3, 1895, 3:1; Aug. 10, 1899, 4:7; May 11, 1911, 8:2-3.
6. MC, Apr. 19, 1906, 3:1; Apr. 17, 1902, 3:1; Oct. 25, 1906, 3:2.
7. Stang, *Pastoral Theology,* 177.
8. MC, Aug. 12, 1897, 4:6-7; Sept. 26, 1895, 1:4-5, 4:7.
9. Quoted in John A. O'Brien, "Why Not Receive Daily?" (Paterson, N.J.: St. Anthony's Guild, 1944); MC, May 23, 1907, 8:2; Sept. 3, 1908, 8:2.
10. SS. Cyril and Methodius Seminary, "Rules for Students," undated but ca. 1908, AAD, Chancery records—seminaries.
11. Minutes, meeting of Diocesan Consultors, Sept. 20, 1910, AAD, minutes and proceedings, 4.
12. On cultural change in the years before 1914, see James R. McGovern, "The American Woman's Pre-World War I Freedom in Manners and Morals," *Journal of American History,* 55 (Sept. 1968), 315-333. MC, Mar. 2, 1911, 1:3-5, 4:5; Jan. 2, 1913, 4:1-2.
13. MC, May 31, 1917, 4:1-2; Mar. 23, 1911, 4:6; Nov. 13, 1913, 8:5; Feb. 20, 1913, 8:2.
14. MC, July 16, 1914, 4:1; May 13, 1915, 5:2.
15. MC, July 16, 1914, 4:1; May 13, 1915, 5:2; May 31, 1917, 4:1-2.
16. MC, Oct. 12, 1911, 1:6-7.
17. P. J. Hansen to Gallagher, Mar. 10, 1925, AAD, parish files. Even immigrants who spoke English reasonably well were sometimes reluctant to confess in any but their native language. They found it hard in English to describe their sins and difficulties adequately; some apparently believed that an English confession was almost bound to be invalid.
18. Liturgy and devotions at the various parishes are described in considerable detail in the *Michigan Catholic.* Parish reports, housed in the AAD, have information as well.
19. MC, Sept. 26, 1895, 1:4-5, 4:7; June 15, 1893, 3:1.
20. MC, June 11, 1891, 8:1-2; June 5, 1890, 5:5; Nov. 6, 1890, 4:5; *The Glory of Saints Peter and Paul's: The First One Hundred Years* (Detroit, 1948), no pagination; MC, Mar. 22, 1894, 8:1.
21. MC, June 21, 1888, 5:3; June 1, 1893, 3:3-4.
22. MC, July 18, 1895, 8:1; Oct. 19, 1911, 8:1-2; Mar. 12, 1911, 4:5.
23. MC, July 28, 1892, 1:6-7; Aug. 10, 1893, 3:2. The *Michigan Catholic* periodically ran lists of passengers for the Beaupré trip.
24. Bicknell, *St. Bonaventure Monastery,* 37; MC, Dec. 19, 1898, 5:2.
25. MC, May 11, 1911, 3:2.
26. MC, Feb. 18, 1897, 5:4; July 6, 1893, 8:2; July 18, 1895, 8:2; May 10, 1894, 8:4.
27. Stang, *Pastoral Theology,* 80.
28. MC, Mar. 20, 1902, 4:4.
29. MC, Feb. 2, 1888, 4:2; Jan. 29, 1914, 8:3.
30. Information on devotions and church decor is found in the *Michigan Catholic,* particularly in the period before 1920, and in the "Dean's Reports" for 1940, 1948, and 1954, which are housed in the AAD, in the files of individual parishes.
31. MC, Feb. 28, 1907, 4:6.
32. Zunz, *Changing Face of Inequality,* 251-253.
33. Sacred Heart, Detroit, Register of deaths; St. Patrick, Detroit, Register of deaths, microfilm copies in AAD; quoted in Dolan, *Catholic Revivalism,* 95.
34. MC, Nov. 10, 1892, 3:2; Sept. 28, 1893, 3:2; Oct. 6, 1892, 3:1; May 31, 1906, 3:2.

35. MC, Apr. 30, 1896, 3:1; Aug. 9, 1900, 3:1–2; Aug. 4, 1892, 3:2.

36. Information on purgatorian societies is found in the various parish reports, AAD; MC, June 4, 1896, 6:1–4; Nov. 4, 1897, 8:2.

37. Quoted in Paré, *Church in Detroit,* 672; Member's card, Altar Guild, St. Augustine's, Kalamazoo, facsimile printed in Stang, *Pastoral Theology,* 302; MC, Feb. 21, 1901, 8:3.

38. "Rules concerning burials," Nov. 23, 1857 and Dec. 12, 1860, AAD, Episcopal Register, 4; "Circular to the Pastors of St. Ann's, Trinity, St. Mary's and St. Joseph's in Detroit," Feb. 3, 1858, AAD, Episcopal Register, 4; Emmet Larkin, "The Devotional Revolution in Ireland, 1850–1875," *American Historical Review* 77:3 (June 1972), 651; Aloysius Blouigen, OFM Cap., to Rev. M. J. P. Dempsey, Apr. 22, 1890; AAD, Sacred Heart, Roseville, parish file.

39. MC, Oct. 15, 1896, 4:5.

40. MC, Oct. 15, 1896, 4:5; June 1, 1893, 8:1; Nov. 8, 1894, 8:1; Nov. 9, 1893, 8:1–2; May 3, 1894, 5:4; June 17, 1897, 3:1; May 11, 1916, 5:3.

41. Minutes, Conference of the Lansing Deanery, Jan. 30, 1901, AAD, Foley papers, 3:11. The day's recorder was Fr. Mathias Auer.

42. MC, Apr. 18, 1895, 3:1; Dec. 3, 1896, 1:4–5.

43. Changing funeral customs can be traced in the pages of the *Michigan Catholic.* For the St. Gabriel's pilgrimage see MC, Oct. 29, 1931, 8:6.

44. MC, Jan. 5, 1893, 4:2; Apr. 25, 1897, 8:1–2.

45. Information on catechism classes is found in the various parish reports in the AAD and in the *Michigan Catholic.* St. Peter, Mt. Clemens, Annual report, 1870, AAD, parish files.

46. "Acta Synodi Quintae, Detroitensis, 1881," 30–31, AAD, Borgess papers, 5:18; St. Mary, Monroe, Annual report, 1875; St. Alphonsus, Dearborn, Annual report, 1868; St. Joseph, Erie, Annual report, 1890; Our Lady of Mt. Carmel, Emmett, Annual report, 1878, AAD, parish files.

47. MC, May 7, 1896, 1:6–7; Nov. 10, 1898, 8:1; Jan. 10, 1889, 8:3; Mar. 18, 1901, 8:2; Feb. 13, 1902, 4:4.

48. MC, Oct. 19, 1893.

49. MC, Feb. 20, 1896, 5:3–4; Aug. 7, 1919, 5:3; Yale *Record,* Sept. 18, 1903, 3:2–4.

50. MC, May 26, 1892, 3:2.

51. MC, Feb. 11, 1897, 3:2; June 14, 1900, 8:1; Stang, *Pastoral Theology,* 62, 69; Moutard to "Dear Friend," Mar. 21, 1865, MHC, Birney-McClear-Hankerd papers; Handwritten "book of pedagogy," no author, undated but probably mid-nineteenth century, SSIHM, IHM education, 4.

52. MC, Aug. 10, 1893, 3:3; May 11, 1893, 3:1–2; May 25, 1893, 3:4; June 1, 1893, 3:1.

53. MC, Apr. 30, 1914, 8:1; Oct. 11, 1917, 8:3.

54. All quotes from Josephine VanDyke Brownson, *Stopping the Leak* (St. Louis, 1925).

55. Quoted in Walter Romig, *Josephine VanDyke Brownson* (Detroit: Gabriel Richard Press, 1955), 57. On Brownson's difficulties as a laywoman, see 68–69.

56. Commemorative program, 40th anniversary of the ordination of Rev. John G. Cook, AAD, Cook file; MC, Apr. 27, 1916, 3:1; Stang, *Pastoral Theology,* 69, 72.

57. MC, Mar. 6, 1902, 3:2; June 29, 1893, 3:2.

58. MC, July 19, 1894, 3:1–2; Feb. 11, 1892, 3:3; Dec. 12, 1901, 3:2; Feb. 14, 1895, 3:1.

59. MC, July 13, 1893, 8:5.

60. MC, Jan. 18, 1906, 3:1; Oct. 25, 1906, 4:5.

61. MC, Feb. 20, 1890, 4:6–7, 5:1; Jan. 23, 1890, 8:2.

62. The names of parish trustees appear regularly in parish reports and sometimes in the *Michigan Catholic.* Their occupation can often be found in Polk's *Detroit Directories.*

I have not made a systematic study of trustees in the ethnic parishes, save for my work on the Kolasinski affair. Both at St. Albertus and at Sweetest Heart of Mary the elected trustees were usually owners of small businesses or professionals. During the earliest years at Sweetest Heart, however, several laborers served as trustees. See Tentler, "Who is the Church?" 253–254. At St. Peter Claver's parish, the first black parish in the Diocese, the trustees over the years were mainly professionals and businessmen. "St. Vincent de Paul's Church, Pontiac, Michigan: Our Manual," 1896, AAD, parish files; MC, Nov. 5, 1895, 6:2–3.

63. MC, Aug. 13, 1914, 5:6; June 28, 1900, 4:6.
64. MC, Sept. 5, 1895, 3:1–2.
65. MC, July 14, 1921, 4:1–2.
66. On Protestant youth organizations in the late nineteenth century, see Joseph F. Kett, *Rites of Passage: Adolescence in America, 1790 to the Present* (New York: Basic Books, 1977), 189–211. MC, Nov. 3, 1898, 4:3–4.
67. O'Brien, "Organization and Maintenance of Parish Societies," 495, 506.
68. MC, July 6, 1899, 8:1.
69. MC, Dec. 27, 1888, 8:3; Apr. 4, 1889, 8:3, Jan. 30, 1890, 8:1.
70. MC, Feb. 23, 1893, 8:1; Sept. 19, 1889, 8:1; May 3, 1900, 8:3; July 16, 1903, 8:3; Sept. 13, 1894, 1:6–7, 5:1–2; Sept. 28, 1911, 8:3.
71. O'Brien, "Organization and Maintenance of Parish Societies," 492–493.
72. MC, Aug. 22, 1907, 8:2; June 3, 1909, 8:4–5; Feb. 23, 1911, 5:1–3; Jan. 9, 1913, 8:2; Mar. 26, 1914, 8:4.
73. MC, July 15, 1915, 5:3–5.
74. MC, May 2, 1889, 5:1; Sept. 11, 1890, 5:4.
75. MC, Sept. 17, 1914, 8:2; Oct. 15, 1914, 8:2; Mar. 25, 1897, 4:3.
76. MC, Sept. 13, 1894, 1:6–7, 5:1–2; Aug. 20, 1908, 8:2.
77. MC, April 4, 1889, 5:2; May 9, 1889, 8:1.
78. MC, Feb. 7, 1889, 4:5; J. B. Mueller, ms. history of St. Boniface parish, Detroit, 1894, copies in German and in English at St. Boniface-St. Vincent Church, Detroit; MC, Sept. 27, 1888, 4:7; May 17, 1894, 8:2.
79. MC, Jan. 4, 1900, 8:1–2; May 29, 1902, 1:5–7, 8:5–6.
80. MC, Dec. 6, 1900, 5:2.
81. MC, Feb. 3, 1898, 4:3; Nov. 5, 1908, 8:4; Feb. 2, 1911, 11:1–3.
82. MC, Aug. 6, 1914, 1:3–4; Feb. 25, 1915, 1:3–4; June 10, 1915, 5:5. On the history of the Knights of Columbus see Christopher J. Kauffman, *Faith and Fraternalism: The History of the Knights of Columbus* (New York: Harper and Row, 1982).
83. Rev. E. VanDyke to Rev. Louis Cook, CSSR, Dec. 27, 1887, AAD, VanDyke letterbook; MC, Dec. 1, 1898, 8:1; O'Brien, "Organization and Maintenance of Parish Societies," 487–488.
84. MC, Sept. 28, 1899, 4:6; Feb. 20, 1913, 5:3.
85. MC, Dec. 3, 1914, 8:4; Mar. 11, 1915, 4:6; Dec. 27, 1917, 8:3–4; June 29, 1916, 5:5; June 8, 1916, 4:6.
86. MC, Apr. 27, 1916, 5:5; Jan. 8, 1920, 8:1–2. "Tre Ore" services on Good Friday were popularized in the United States after about 1910. It was the Jesuits, apparently, who introduced the service to the Diocese of Detroit during the first decade of the twentieth century.
87. MC, Apr. 27, 1916, 5:5; Mar. 28, 1920, 4:2–3.
88. MC, Apr. 17, 1919, 5:4.
89. MC, Dec. 17, 1931, 1:1.
90. MC, July 13, 1916, 8:5–6; Mar. 22, 1917, 8:3.
91. O'Brien, "Organization and Maintenance of Parish Societies," 494.

92. MC, Apr. 19, 1888, 5:4; Jan. 14, 1897, 8:3; Nov. 22, 1894, 8:2; Aug. 17, 1893, 8:3.
93. MC, June 4, 1914, 8:2; June 2, 1921, 8:4–5; Scrapbook, St. Aloysius Alumnae Association, 1900–1917, AAD.
94. MC, Sept. 19, 1901, 6:2; May 17, 1906, 5:1–2; Nov. 6, 1890, 8:1; Oct. 21, 1915, 8:4; Jan. 19, 1911, 8:6; July 12, 1917, 8:7.
95. MC, Aug. 1, 1901, 1:4–5, 5:3; July 25, 1901, 8:3. Dr. Dunn-Roe, who died in Detroit in 1920, was also active in Irish nationalist circles. She married late in life, and she and her husband, Patrick J. Murphy of Grand Rapids, adopted two children. MC, Feb. 19, 1920, 8:2.
96. MC, Dec. 5, 1889, 1:4–5, 3:1–4, 5:1–2; Dec. 5, 1889, 4:2.
97. MC, Dec. 12, 1889, 4:2. Brownson was the son of Orestes Brownson and the father of Josephine Van Dyke Brownson, founder of the Catholic Instruction League. He was one of the principal organizers of the 1889 congress, serving as chair of the Committee on Papers and helping to draft the congress platform. The *Michigan Catholic* covered both congresses extensively, and the Diocese sent large delegations to each.
98. MC, Jan. 21, 1897, 8:4.
99. MC, Aug. 4, 1892, 5:1. "Most of those here now are women," an observer reported of the Summer School in 1892, "school teachers and students in Catholic schools." For the perhaps incomplete lists of local registrants at the Summer Schools in 1900 and 1901, see MC, July 12, 1900, 3:3; July 11, 1901, 5:5; July 18, 1901, 4:5–6. On reading and debate groups in the Diocese see MC, Feb. 8, 1894, 8:1; Mar. 1, 1894, 8:1; Nov. 15, 1906, 8:2; Jan. 17, 1907, 8:2.
100. The *Michigan Catholic* in the 1890s gave regular coverage to the various reading circles, especially those in Detroit. MC, June 3, 1897, 1:3; Oct. 13, 1898, 8:2; Oct. 12, 1899, 8:2; Sept. 24, 1896, 8:1; Dec. 12, 1895, 8:4; Sept. 26, 1895, 8:2; Jan. 18, 1900, 8:4.
101. MC, May 16, 1895, 8:1–2; Oct. 1, 1914, 8:3; Nov. 30, 1899, 8:5–6.
102. MC, June 2, 1921, 4:2–3.
103. MC, Sept. 28, 1893, 1:6–7, 4:4–6; Apr. 19, 1888, 4:4–5.
104. Correspondence concerning selection of trustees is found mainly in AAD, Foley papers, 2.
105. McManus to "Very Rev. dear Father," Dec. 3, 1908, AAD, Sacred Heart, Roseville parish file; John Mastella to Foley, Mar. 16, 1890, AAD, parish files.
106. Martin Ignasiak et al. to Foley, undated but 1899; Martin Grabawkiewicz et al. to Foley, undated but 1899, AAD, Our Lady of Mt. Carmel, Wyandotte, parish file.
107. MC, Dec. 7, 1899, 8:3.
108. "By-Laws, The Resurrection of Jesus Christ American Polish Catholic Church of Detroit, Michigan," Oct. 8, 1917, AAD, parish files.
109. Krebs to Rev. F. J. Baumgartner, Sept. 27, 1895, AAD, Fr. Clemens Krebs file; "The Committee" to Bp. Foley, undated but 1891, AAD, parish files. The St. Albertus troubles were not mentioned in the *Michigan Catholic* but were extensively reported in the *Detroit Evening News*. See editions for June 11–13, 15–18, 20, 21, 26, and July 13, 16, 19, 1891. MC, June 4, 1891, 4:6; July 13, 1893, 8:4; July 20, 1893, 5:3; *Detroit News*, Apr. 17, 1892, 3:3; *Detroit Evening News*, Apr. 21, 1892, 5:3–4; Oct. 29, 1892, 7:3; Jan. 16, 1893, 4:4; Jan. 18, 1893, 5:3; July 24, 1893, 4:6; "Members of St. Mary's parish" to Bp. Foley, undated but early 1890s, SHS.
110. John Bieber et al. to Bp. Henry Joseph Richter, Aug. 10, 1896; Rev. A. J. Buchsenmann to "The Most Reverend Delegate to the United States," Nov. 3, 1896, AAD, Foley papers, 6:3. The *Michigan Catholic* largely ignored the events at North Dorr, but there are a number of documents relating to the case in the AAD, Foley papers.
111. Rev. John A. Schmitt to Rev. F. J. Baumgartner, July 27, 1897; Anon. to Baumgartner, Dec. 9, 1897 ("I dast not Publish my name as I could not live in this vicinity"), AAD, Foley papers, 6:4.

112. It is not clear why Foley declined at this point to take action against the North Dorr dissidents. The Apostolic Delegate inquired into the case for a second time in the fall of 1897, and the Propaganda conducted an investigation several months later. Perhaps Foley feared censure from Rome if he took firm action, but since the Propaganda ordered the people of North Dorr to submit to their bishop in a ruling dated Feb. 11, 1898, Foley would seem to have had a free hand thereafter. Foley to Archbishop Martinelli, Sept. 18, 1897, AAD, Foley papers, 6:4; Propaganda to Foley, Feb. 11, 1898; Rev. Joseph Ebert to Foley, Mar. 12, 1898, AAD, Foley papers, 6:5.

113. Rev. John Helten to Foley, June 22, 1898, AAD, Foley papers, 6:6.

114. Rev. Joseph Ebert to Rev. F. J. Baumgartner, June 12, 1899, AAD, Foley papers, 6:8; Fitzgerald and Barry, attorneys, to Rev. John Helten, June 8, 1898, AAD, Foley papers, 6:6; Fitzgerald and Barry to Foley, Mar. 28, 1900, AAD, Foley papers, 6:10; Rev. Reynold Kuehnel to Rev. P. A. Baart, Apr. 8, 1903, ND, Baart papers, 3; Foley statement *re* North Dorr school, Aug. 29, 1905, AAD, Letterbooks, 15; Rev. Reynold Kuehnel to Foley, Sept. 8, 1905, AAD, Foley papers, 4:11.

115. Anton Schneider to Foley, Mar. 7, 1899, AAD, Foley papers, 6:8.

116. MC, Feb. 11, 1897, 8:1; Oct. 2, 1890, 8:1; Feb. 13, 1890, 5:5; Jan. 22, 1891, 8:2.

117. On the depression of the 1890s and on charity and municipal relief in Detroit, see Zunz, *Changing Face of Inequality,* 263–279.

118. MC, Oct. 24, 1907, 8:2; Nov. 7, 1907, 8:3; Apr. 2, 1908, 4:5. Late in 1908 a new group was formed in Detroit "to work along the lines similar to those of St. Mary's Aid Society, but in the interest of children and infants of the poor." Both societies were apparently conducted entirely under female leadership. MC, Dec. 17, 1908, 8:6.

119. Minute book, Weinman Club, Apr. 26, 1906–May 6, 1910, has information on the early years of the association and the settlement. See also "Catholic Settlement Association of Detroit, Report, 1911–1913," and for 1913–1915, AAD, League of Catholic Women collection. See also MC, Nov. 12, 1908, 8:2; Mar. 9, 1911, 4:6; June 1, 1911, 8:3; Sept. 14, 1911, 2:3–4.

120. "Catholic Settlement Association of Detroit, Report, 1913–1915," AAD, League of Catholic Women collection; MC, Oct. 30, 1913, 8:4; Dec. 25, 1913, 8:3; Jan. 15, 1914, 8:4–5; Oct. 22, 1914, 8:3–4; May 27, 1915, 8:3.

121. League of Catholic Women, Annual report, 1915, AAD, League of Catholic Women collection; MC, May 9, 1918, 8:4.

122. MC, Aug. 10, 1899, 8:1. The Particular Council in Detroit was incorporated in 1912. MC, Dec. 18, 1913, 8:4–5; Dec. 17, 1914, 8:3; Dec. 16, 1915, 8:3.

123. "Report of the Society of St. Vincent de Paul of Detroit and Its Child Caring Department," Jan. 1914, AAD, St. John Nepomucene parish file; MC, Aug. 29, 1918, 8:3.

124. MC, July 5, 1917, 8:5.

9. Catholic sisters, catholic schools

1. Four hospitals were opened in the Diocese during the Foley years, and the House of Providence had evolved into a general hospital by 1910. Facilities for the care of dependent children were also greatly expanded. But the number of teaching Sisters in the Diocese still dwarfed the number engaged in nursing or social work. Like most American dioceses, Detroit has supported few orders of contemplative nuns. The Good Shepherd Sisters in Detroit inaugurated an enclosed community, the Sisters Magdalen, at the House of the Good Shepherd in 1893, its members drawn mainly from House residents. Bishop Foley was apparently instrumental in bringing the Cloistered Dominicans to Detroit in 1906. They were for many years resident at the Monastery of the Blessed Sacrament.

2. Thaddeus C. Radzialowski, "Reflections on the History of the Felicians in America," *Polish-American Studies*, 23:1 (Spring 1975), 22; Ziolkowski, *Felician Sisters*, 118, 218.
3. Sr. Rosalita, *No Greater Service*, 355, 397–498.
4. MC, Aug. 9, 1917, 8:4.
5. Ziolkowski, *Felician Sisters*, 176; Sr. Rosalita, *No Greater Service*, 749.
6. "Acta Synodi Quartae, Detroitensis, 1878," AAD, Borgess papers, 5:18; Borgess to "Rev. Dear Sir," Aug. 4, 1882, AAD, Borgess papers, 5:20.
7. MC, Aug. 28, 1890, 8:1. Satolli was subsequently made Apostolic Delegate to the United States; his appointment dates from Jan. 1893.
8. Minutes, 22d conference of Detroit Deanery, Oct. 26, 1893, AAD, Foley papers, 3:5; MC, Aug. 24, 1893, 8:4.
9. Atkinson's views on Fr. Bouquillon's pamphlet are found in this interview. *Detroit Evening News*, Apr. 11, 1892, 1:1–2.
10. Ibid. Atkinson answered the critics of his initial interview in a letter to the *News* that appeared in Apr. 22, 1892, 4:4–5.
11. Ibid.; *Detroit Evening News*, Apr. 11, 1892, 1:1–2.
12. *Detroit News*, Apr. 17, 1892, 24:1–3.
13. MC, Apr. 14, 1892, 4:2–4; Apr. 28, 1892, 4:2–3; May 5, 1892, 4:5–6.
14. MC, Aug. 18, 1898, 4:2.
15. The Detroit School Board reported 21,434 pupils in 1886; my thanks to Professor Joellen Vinyard for this information. Catholic school enrollment for 1887 is found in First Annual Report of the Diocesan School Board, 1887, SSIHM; IHM education, 4; MC, Feb. 15, 1917, 4:6.
16. Information on school tuition is found scattered throughout the Borgess and Foley papers and in various annual reports from the parishes. On IHM "music money," see Sr. Rosalita, *No Greater Service*, 471, 565.
17. Minutes, meeting of Diocesan Consultors, Oct. 24, 1911, AAD, minutes and proceedings, 4. On early Italian settlement in Detroit, see Rt. Rev. John C. Vismara, "Coming of the Italians to Detroit," 1918, printed in "Golden Jubilee Program, San Francesco Church, 1896–1946," AAD, parish files. Vismara's parents came to Detroit from Lombardy in 1881. He himself was among the first Italian-Americans to attend Detroit College.
18. MC, Aug. 28, 1890, 8:1; Rev. John F. Kramer to Rev. F. J. Baumgartner, Dec. 19, 1897, AAD, parish files; MC, Apr. 13, 1893, 8:2–3. Enrollments for 1889 are taken from a handwritten survey of schools in the Diocese, listing enrollment and number of teachers, available for selected dates in the 1880s and early 1890s, AAD. Enrollment for 1917 from the *Catholic Directory*.
19. St. Alphonsus, Dearborn, School attendance record for 1895, AAD, parish files; MC, Mar. 17, 1892, 3:3; July 12, 1894, 3:1.
20. Burns, *Catholic School System*, 350; MC, Nov. 8, 1900, 8:5.
21. MC, Apr. 19, 1894, 3:2. School was a favorite topic of the young contributors to the *Michigan Catholic*'s children's page. MC, Feb. 18, 1892, 3:4–5; Apr. 13, 1893, 3:4; Mar. 31, 1892, 3:4.
22. MC, Feb. 11, 1892, 3:3; Feb. 11, 1892, 3:4; Feb. 20, 1896, 5:2; Dec. 1, 1892, 3:1; Oct. 26, 1892, 5:1–2.
23. MC, Nov. 15, 1894, 3:1; Mar. 9, 1893, 3:1–2; May 20, 1897, 3:1–2; Dec. 28, 1893, 3:2; Feb. 2, 1893, 3:2.
24. MC, May 21, 1896, 3:1; Apr. 6, 1893, 3:2; Mar. 1, 1894, 3:3.
25. MC, Sept. 29, 1892, 8:1; Dec. 12, 1895, 8:5; Sr. Rosalita, *No Greater Service*, 374; Mission chronicle, St. Boniface school, especially entry for Jan. 1898, SSIHM, Chronicles, IHM missions. The public examinations at St. Boniface continued at least un-

til the death of longtime pastor Fr. John Schreiber in 1917. "Report re St. Alphonsus School, Greenfield, by John M. Schreiber," May 21, 1895, AAD, St. Alphonsus, Dearborn, parish file.

26. MC, May 7, 1914, 3:1.

27. Quoted in Ziolkowski, *Felician Sisters,* 104–105.

28. Andrew Untener, "The Old Grad Remembers When," in "Holy Cross HomeComing, Holy Cross School, April 24, 1906–1936," AAD, parish files.

29. MC, Nov. 5, 1908, 6:1–2.

30. MC, July 23, 1903, 3:2–3; handwritten "book of pedagogy," undated, SSIHM, IHM education, 4; MC, Apr. 30, 1908, 3:1–2; May 3, 1906, 3:2.

31. MC, Aug. 21, 1890, 4:4; Dec. 19, 1907, 3:1–2; June 6, 1895, 3:1; May 26, 1910, 3:1.

32. MC, July 23, 1903, 3:2–3.

33. MC, Oct. 31, 1901, 3:1; handwritten "book of pedagogy," undated, SSIHM, IHM education, 4; MC, Feb. 20, 1913, 3:2; Jan. 4, 1894, 8:1.

34. MC, June 28, 1894, 4:4; Apr. 7, 1892, 8:1; May 28, 1891, 8:3.

35. Ziolkowski, *Felician Sisters,* 168–169; Burns, *Catholic School System,* 325; Sr. Mary Jeremiah Studniewska, CSSF, *The Educational Work of the Felician Sisters of the Province of Detroit in the United States, 1874–1948* (Livonia, Mich., 1962), 48–49; Zunz, *Changing Face of Inequality,* 193.

36. MC, Oct. 1, 1914, 8:2.

37. "Parish Report of St. Joseph for the year 1913," AAD, parish files.

38. Burns, *Catholic School System,* 325, 327–328; Ziolkowski, *Felician Sisters,* 175–176.

39. Father Kennedy was appointed superintendent in May 1918. It is not clear why or when — or even whether — Bishop Gallagher removed him from office, but Kennedy is not identified as superintendent in the *Catholic Directory* for 1919, 1920, or 1921. He died in 1922, at the age of 56. Sister Arthemise Dalton has claimed that Kennedy was in poor health during these final years of his life and was a mostly inactive superintendent until he was replaced in 1921. Sr. M. Arthemise Dalton, OP, "The History and Development of the Catholic Secondary Schools in the Archdiocese of Detroit, 1701–1961" (Ed.D. diss., Wayne State University, 1962), 69. *Detroit News,* July 20, 1918, 6:2. St. Mary's school in Lansing abandoned the teaching of German in the fall of 1918. MC, Sept. 12, 1918, 8:4. St. Joseph's school in Detroit did so at about the same time. The *Michigan Catholic* was apparently reluctant to publicize the issue, however, and specific information on other German parishes is lacking. On the 1919 law and Catholic efforts to modify it, see MC, Mar. 6, 1919, 4:3–4; Apr. 17, 1919, 4:6. W. H. Ribbing to Archbishop Mooney, Nov. 13, 1944, AAD, parish files.

40. School data for the Foley years comes mainly from the *Michigan Catholic.* It is abundant, but not systematic; hence the uncertainty about the numbers of male and female graduates after ca. 1913. MC, Jan. 15, 1891, 4:5; Jan. 22, 1891, 5:3–4.

41. Bishop Foley's failure to make provision for a central high school is of a piece with the drift that increasingly characterized his administration after 1900. Whether he actively opposed the establishment of such schools, or simply neglected to take the initiative, the surviving evidence does not permit us to say. It is also extremely hard to determine the extent to which the sexes were separated in the primary schools of the Diocese. Some of the larger schools certainly maintained separate classes for boys and girls — at Holy Trinity School, for example, the sex-segregated classroom was not abandoned until the 1920s. See IHM Mission Chronicles, Holy Trinity, Detroit, SSIHM, Chronicles, IHM missions. Other parishes — Holy Redeemer and Sacred Heart in Detroit, for instance — had separate school buildings for boys and girls in the primary grades. But still other schools, not all of them the smaller ones, had mixed classes throughout the course of study. There was apparently no effort

on the part of the Foley Chancery to influence pastors and teaching Sisters in this regard. On St. Aloysius Alumnae Association, see the group's scrapbook, 1900–1917, AAD. On the 1928 survey, see MC, Nov. 29, 1928, 1:3.

42. MC, Sept. 4, 1913, 8:5–6; June 29, 1899, 8:1.

43. MC, June 24, 1897, 1:3–4; MC, June 26, 1902, 8:2.

44. Mother Theresa Carew, RSH, to Henry J. Brownson, Jan. 6, 1901, ND, Henry Brownson papers; handwritten "book of pedagogy," undated, SSIHM, IHM education, 4; MC, Dec. 1, 1898, 8:1.

45. On the growth of Catholic colleges nationally, see Philip Gleason, "American Catholic Higher Education: A Historical Perspective," in Robert Hassenger, ed., *The Shape of Catholic Higher Education* (Chicago: University of Chicago Press, 1967). MC, May 11, 1911, 1:2; June 22, 1916, 1:4–5; Sr. Rosalita, *No Greater Service*, 574–575.

46. *Ann Arbor Courier*, Feb. 10, 1886, reported the results of the survey. The university had 1,331 students in 1886, of whom 1,156 returned questionnaires to the Students' Christian Association. Only 730 of the respondents were identified as "professing Christians" in the *Courier* report. Whether the others had no religion to profess or had failed to complete the questionnaire is not clear. My thanks to Jonathan Marwil for this information, and for information on the 1917 survey, which was reported in the *Michigan Daily*, Mar. 8, 1918. MC, Sept. 12, 1889, 4:6–7; Feb. 10, 1898, 1:4–5; Rev. Michael Bourke, "History of St. Mary's Chapel for Catholic Students," Apr. 6, 1924, typescript, MHC, St. Mary's Student Chapel papers, 1.

47. MC, Sept. 12, 1889, 4:6–7; May 25, 1899, 4:1–2.

48. MC, Sept. 12, 1889, 4:6–7.

49. MC, Feb. 22, 1906, 4:3; Dec. 12, 1907, 4:4; Sept. 6, 1906, 4:3; June 20, 1907, 4:4; Oct. 22, 1908, 4:3–4; April 6, 1911, 4:3; Oct. 29, 1908, 4:5–6.

50. On Catholic students at secular colleges, see John Whitney Evans, *The Newman Movement: Roman Catholics in American Higher Education, 1883–1971* (Notre Dame, Ind.: University of Notre Dame Press, 1980), 32.

51. Ibid., 21–22; MC, Oct. 10, 1889, 4:5–6. Whether the Foley Guild was exclusively male in its earliest years is not known, but it seems unlikely, despite the references in period reporting to the "Catholic boys" in Ann Arbor. The guild was open to all Catholic students, and Catholic women are known to have studied at the university in the 1880s and 1890s. The name of Mary Duffy appears on a guild resolution in 1893, the first clear evidence of female membership; in 1906, two of the four elected officers were women. MC, Dec. 12, 1889, 5:3.

52. MC, Mar. 30, 1890, 4:7, 5:1–5; Mar. 5, 1891, 5:5; Apr. 30, 1891, 8:2; Feb. 10, 1898, 4:1–2. The new St. Thomas Church was dedicated on Nov. 26, 1899. Archbishop John Ireland preached at the Mass. See MC, Nov. 30, 1899, 1:2–6, 4:5–6, 5:1–4.

53. MC, Jan. 22, 1914, 5:4, quoting the *Michigan Daily* of Jan. 17, 1914; Bourke, "History of St. Mary's Chapel."

10. CATHOLICS AND THE LARGER SOCIETY

1. Records of dispensations are in the AAD. Marriages are reported in the annual *Catholic Directory*.

2. MC, Mar. 15, 1906, 2:4–5; Our Lady of Mt. Carmel, Wyandotte, Annual report, 1913, AAD, parish files.

3. MC, Mar. 15, 1906, 2:4–5; Holy Cross, Marine City, Annual report, 1914, AAD, parish files; Gallagher to "Rev. dear Father," June 8, 1934, MHC, St. Mary's Student Chapel papers, 1.

4. William L. O'Neill, "Divorce in the Progressive Era," *American Quarterly*, 17: 2, pt. 1 (1965), 203–217. A good summary of recent research in the history of contracep-

tive practice is found in Carl Degler, *At Odds: Women and the Family in America from the Revolution to the Present* (New York: Oxford University Press, 1980), chaps. 8–10.

5. MC, Feb. 20, 1890, 1:6–7.
6. MC, June 29, 1916, 4:2–3; May 18, 1916, 4:3; Mar. 8, 1917, 8:1; Ryan, "Family Limitation." See also Noonan, *Contraception,* 502–504.
7. Francis C. Lavoy to Bp. Foley, Jan. 20, 1899, AAD, parish files; MC, Feb. 6, 1908, 1:6–7.
8. MC, Feb. 27, 1913, 5:1–2; Aug. 27, 1908, 8:5–7; Sept. 28, 1911, 8:3; July 11, 1907, 1:2.
9. On the changing composition of Detroit's population, see Zunz, *Changing Face of Inequality,* 289–290. MC, Mar. 10, 1910, 4:2–3; Feb. 22, 1906, 4:6.
10. MC, Sept. 3, 1908, 3:6–7; Dec. 1, 1898, 4:3–4.
11. MC, June 6, 1901, 4:2–3.
12. On Detroit and Michigan politics in the latter half of the nineteenth century, see especially Kleppner, *Cross of Culture.*
13. John Higham, *Strangers in the Land: Patterns of American Nativism, 1860–1925* (New York: Atheneum, 1963), 62–63, 80–87.
14. MC, Oct. 20, 1892, 4:2–3; Sept. 14, 1893, 8:6; July 8, 1897, 4:2.
15. *Detroit Evening News,* June 26, 1892; MC, Mar. 8, 1894, 4:3.
16. MC, July 5, 1900, 4:1–2; Sept. 28, 1899, 4:3.
17. MC, Mar. 9, 1893, 4:2; May 25, 1893, 4:5; John Donovan to Bp. Foley, Jan. 10, 1895; P. H. Dolan to Foley, Mar. 15, 1895, AAD, Foley papers, 4:12.
18. Foley to John Donovan, Jan. 10, 1895, AAD, Letterbooks, 14; Donovan to Foley, Jan. 10, 1895, AAD, Foley papers, 4:12; Foley to Rufus Clark, Feb. 2, 1895, AAD, Letterbooks, 14; Rev. F. J. Baumgartner to Bp. John Vertin, Jan. 23, 1896, AAD, Foley papers, 4:12. See also minutes, meeting of Diocesan Consultors, Feb. 25, 1895, AAD, minutes and proceedings, 4. Ternes to Foley, Mar. 15, 1895, AAD, Foley papers, 4:12; *Detroit Evening News,* May 1, 1895.
19. On Pingree's career see Melvin G. Holli, *Reform in Detroit: Hazen S. Pingree and Urban Politics* (New York: Oxford University Press, 1969).
20. Kleppner, *Cross of Culture,* chaps. 8–9.
21. Ibid., 338–368.
22. Ibid., 369–375.
23. MC, Apr. 6, 1893, 4:2; July 8, 1897, 4:2; Nov. 2, 1899, 4:2; Apr. 29, 1937, 1:5–7.
24. Higham, *Strangers,* 175–182. The public selling of the *Menace* and the fear that Catholics were among those who read the paper were frequent topics in the *Michigan Catholic* between 1913 and 1918. For the anonymous foreman's letter see MC, Oct. 16, 1913, 4:5–7.
25. MC, Apr. 29, 1915, 8:2; Jan. 21, 1915, 1:3–4.
26. MC, Mar. 9, 1916, 4:1–2; May 4, 1916, 1:1–2.
27. MC, Sept. 24, 1914, 4:4–5; Higham, *Strangers,* 179–180.
28. MC, Nov. 12, 1908, 4:1.
29. M. Sullivan to Baart, Mar. 1902, ND, Baart papers, 2.
30. MC, Mar. 3, 1898, 4:2; Mar. 24, 1898, 4:2; Apr. 28, 1898, 8:3.
31. MC, May 12, 1898. The letter was ordered to be read in all churches on the following Sunday. MC, June 2, 1898, 3:2; Apr. 28, 1898, 4:6; May 5, 1898, 4:5. The letter writer was Michael Shaughnessy.
32. MC, June 30, 1898, 8:2; June 30, 1898, 8:1.
33. Quoted in James Hennesey, SJ, *American Catholics: A History of the Roman Catholic Community in the United States* (New York: Oxford University Press, 1981), 205; MC, June 7, 1900, 1:4–5; 8:4; Mar. 14, 1901, 4:3.
34. Higham, *Strangers,* 108.
35. MC, Sept. 10, 1914, 8:6–7; Sr. Mary Charitas, SSND, *One Hundred Years for God and Country: The Story of St. Anthony Parish* (Detroit, 1957), 41.

36. MC, Oct. 22, 1914, 8:2; Mar. 25, 1915, 8:2; Mar. 25, 1915, 1:6–7.

37. MC, July 1, 1915, 4:1–2; Oct. 8, 1914, 4:2–3.

38. MC, Apr. 27, 1916, 4:2.

39. MC, Aug. 2, 1917, 5:6–7; Sept. 20, 1917, 8:4. Father McClory is here enunciating a view of the salvific effects of death on the battlefield that was given perhaps its most famous expression during the war in the Christmas 1914 pastoral letter of Cardinal Mercier, primate of occupied Belgium. "The soldier who dies to save his brothers, to protect the hearths and the altars of his country, fulfills the highest form of love," the cardinal wrote. "We are justified in hoping for them the immortal crown which encircles the foreheads of the elect. For such is the virtue of an act of perfect love that, of itself, it wipes out a whole life of sin. Of a sinner instantly it makes a saint." Cardinal Mercier's sentiments did not go unchallenged, however. Cardinal Billot, a Frenchman and an ardent patriot, wrote early in 1915 that Mercier's position "means to substitute the Fatherland for God . . . , to forget what is God, what is sin, what is divine forgiveness." Their differing opinions, and the tradition out of which each comes, are discussed in Ernst H. Kantorowicz, "'Pro Patria Mori' in Medieval Political Thought," *American Historical Review,* 56 (1951), 472–492.

40. MC, May 31, 1917, 1:1; June 14, 1917, 4:6; June 7, 1917, 5:3; July 5, 1917, 5:4.

41. MC, June 13, 1918, 8:3; Sept. 26, 1918, 8:3; Mar. 21, 1918, 8:3; June 6, 1918, 1:1–2.

42. MC, Apr. 25, 1918, 4:3, 8:4–5; Oct. 25, 1917, 4:1; Sept. 26, 1918, 8:3; Dec. 20, 1917, 4:3–6; Mar. 14, 1918, 8:5.

43. Higham, *Strangers,* 200–201; MC, June 20, 1918, 1:4–5; July 4, 1918, 1:3. The Detroit ordinance banned the sale or distribution of any printed matter whose contents defamed a particular religion, denomination, or cult. The city of Highland Park passed a similar ordinance one week later. *Detroit Jewish Chronicle,* July 6, 1918.

44. MC, Dec. 31, 1914, 4:5; Mar. 5, 1914, 8:5.

45. Bishop Foley apparently asked Father Dunigan not to accept the Lapeer nomination in 1912. Such, at least, is the burden of a draft letter in the AAD, presumably a rough copy of one sent to the priest. AAD, Immaculate Conception, Lapeer parish file. On the New Baltimore election see MC, Mar. 19, 1914, 5:2. MC, Feb. 15, 1894, 3:3; Feb. 8, 1906, 5:3; Nov. 15, 1917, 5:2; Jan. 24, 1918, 5:5; Feb. 27, 1908, 8:4; Feb. 20, 1908, 4:6.

46. MC, June 28, 1900, 4:6.

47. MC, Aug. 16, 1894, 1:4–5, 4:4–5; Jan. 11, 1894, 1:5–6.

48. MC, Jan. 21, 1897, 4:3; Oct. 25, 1894, 8:2; Oct. 5, 1916, 1:6–7, 4:5–6, 5:2; May 31, 1917, 5:1. The Irish were the only Catholic group in Detroit to show any significant support for prohibition in the 1916 referendum.

49. James Shuler to Foley, Apr. 29, 1899, AAD, Fr. James Gore file.

50. MC, Jan. 13, 1916, 1:6–7; Rev. F.A. O'Brien to Bp. Foley, Feb. 22, 1895, AAD, Foley papers, 1:6; MC, Mar. 19, 1896, 5:3.

51. MC, July 4, 1895, 3:1; Dec. 3, 1891, 8:2; Sept. 6, 1906, 5:1.

52. MC, Feb. 2, 1893, 8:2; Oct. 2, 1913, 8:4. Mention of Protestant contributions to Catholic building funds in the various small towns of the Diocese appears on numerous occasions in the Foley years in the *Michigan Catholic.*

53. Higham, *Strangers,* 181; MC, May 26, 1898, 5:6–7; May 31, 1894, 8:4.

54. MC, June 6, 1895, 8:1; June 6, 1907, 3:4–5; 6:1–3.

55. MC, Feb. 27, 1890, 5:2–3; Aug. 16, 1894, 1:4–5, 4:4–5.

56. "Heckerism in the Detroit Diocese," *Review,* 5:40 (Dec. 22, 1898). That Baart wrote the article, which is signed "Catholic," is made clear in a letter to Baart from the magazine's editor. Arthur Preuss to Baart, Dec. 17, 1898, ND, Baart papers, 2.

57. MC, Mar. 9, 1893, 4:5–6; Jan. 11, 1894, 1:5–6.

58. MC, Sept. 28, 1893, 8:3; Oct. 12, 1893, 8:2. Virtually every account of the Elliott

missions mentions large crowds; he himself testified that "I had great success in attracting non-Catholic audiences." MC, Jan. 11, 1894, 1:5–6; Mar. 15, 1900, 5:5.

59. MC, Jan. 25, 1894, 5:1–2; Dec. 21, 1893, 4:5; Jan. 11, 1894, 1:5–6; Aug. 16, 1894, 1:4–5, 4:4–5.

60. MC, Aug. 16, 1894, 1:4–5, 4:4–5; Dec. 21, 1893, 4:5. There was no resident priest at Vermontville in 1893, and Mass was said there only once a month. MC, Nov. 23, 1893 6:4.

61. MC, May 24, 1894, 8:3; Feb. 11, 1897, 1:4–5; Apr. 25, 1907, 5:3; Jan. 30, 1908, 5:1; Feb. 13, 1908, 5:4; Dec. 31, 1908, 8:5.

11. Maturity: the Gallagher and Mooney Episcopates

1. Quoted in Fogarty, *Vatican and the American Hierarchy,* 376.
2. MC, Jan. 21, 1937, 1:1–2.
3. MC, Jan. 21, 1937, 1:1–2.
4. Fannie to "My Dear Brother," Oct. 8, 1890, June 6, 1891; Kate to "My Dear Brother," Mar. 3, 1890, AAD, Gallagher papers, 12:7.
5. Rev. Thomas L. Whalen to Gallagher, Dec. 2, 1891; Kate to "My Dear Brother," Dec. 14, 1891, AAD, Gallagher papers, 12:8.
6. Patrick J. McCooey to Gallagher, Nov. 1, 1894, AAD, Gallagher papers, 12:11; McCooey to Gallagher, Mar. 18, 1895, AAD, Gallagher papers, 12:12.
7. Daniel M. Murray to Gallagher, undated but 1890, AAD, Gallagher papers, 12:5.
8. Richter to Gallagher, June 1, 1891, AAD, Gallagher papers, 12:8.
9. Minutes, meeting of Diocesan Consultors, Feb. 13, 1919, AAD, minutes and proceedings, 4.
10. "A Convert" to Bp. Gallagher, Nov. 7, 1920, AAD, Gallagher papers, 1:2. On change in the Cathedral neighborhood, see Bp. Foley to Mother Alice Power, RSH, Feb. 18, 1917, AAD, Chancery records—religious orders, women.
11. MC, Dec. 12, 1918, 4:2. Josephine Byrne Sullivan-Conlon was born in Ontario in 1868. Her career at the *Michigan Catholic* began as editor of the children's page—she was the "Aunt Rowena" to whom young readers sent their letters—but gradually came to include more general reportorial and editorial tasks. She assumed the editorship in January 1917, at the death of William Hughes, and served as editor until her own death in 1920. Mrs. Sullivan-Conlon was by no means the only woman of her generation to have been a Catholic journalist. Prominent as they were in Catholic literary life, women were frequent contributors to Catholic periodicals and, by the end of the nineteenth century, were even moving into editorial positions. The novelist Katherine Conway edited Boston's *Pilot* from 1905 until 1908, and in Detroit the editorship of the *Angelus,* a literary and devotional weekly, was held for a time by Charlotte O'Loan.
12. MC, May 6, 1920, 1:2–5; June 17, 1920, 1:1–2; March 10, 1921, 1:1–2.
13. Albert Kolch, "Twenty-Five Years," in Sacred Heart Seminary, Silver Jubilee commemorative booklet, Detroit, 1944, AAD, Chancery records—seminaries.
14. Minutes, meeting of Diocesan Consultors, July 13, 1920, AAD, minutes and proceedings, 4.
15. Fr. Koelzer's reminiscences are in "Silver Jubilee: St. Margaret Mary Parish," Detroit, 1945, AAD.
16. Gallagher to Most Rev. Peter Fumasoni—Biondi, Nov. 27, 1925, AAD, Fr. Sigmund Dziatkiewicz file.
17. Gallagher to Most Rev. Pietro Fumasoni-Biondi, Jan. 8, 1925, AAD, Gallagher papers, 1:4; clipping, Detroit *Free Press,* undated but 1925, AAD, Fr. Sigmund Dziat-

kiewicz file. Msgr. Stephen Woznicki was named Auxiliary Bishop of Detroit late in 1938, and later served as Bishop of Saginaw. Joseph Plagens was named Bishop of Marquette in 1935 and Bishop of Grand Rapids in 1940.

18. Vismara to Bp. Gallagher, Dec. 21, 1923, AAD, parish files.
19. Charles D. Maginnis, memo: Detroit Cathedral, June 23, 1922, AAD, Gallagher papers, 6:8. Documents relating to the site purchase are also in this file.
20. Doyle to Maginnis and Walsh, Feb. 8, 1933, AAD, Gallagher papers, 6:8.
21. Gallagher to Mother M. Evangelista, Sept. 11, 1920, AAD, Chancery records— religious orders, women.
22. The *Michigan Catholic* was purchased in July 1920. Minutes, meeting of Diocesan Consultors, July 13, 1920, AAD, minutes and proceedings. 4.
23. Quoted in "History of Santa Maria Church, Vol. 1: 1919-1936," typescript, no author, AAD; Hayes to Bp. Gallagher, Aug. 19, 1933, AAD, parish files. On the Capuchin Soup Kitchen see Catherine Bicknell, *Breaking Bread and Mending Spirits* (Detroit: Fidelity Press, 1979).
24. Sidney Fine, *Frank Murphy: The Detroit Years* (Ann Arbor: University of Michigan Press, 1975), 202-203, 328-329.
25. Ibid., 247-248, 328, 339; IHM Mission Chronicles, Holy Trinity, Detroit, entry for June 10, 1932, SSIHM, Chronicles, IHM missions; MC, Mar. 19, 1931, 1:4-5.
26. For Murphy's career in Detroit see Fine's excellent *Frank Murphy*.
27. MC, Dec. 24, 1931, 8:1; Quoted in Fine, *Frank Murphy*, 454-455; MC, Feb. 25, 1932, 1:3-4; Hayes to Gallagher, Aug. 19, 1933, AAD, parish files.
28. St. Boniface "Parish Items," Oct. 1, 1930, AAD, Fr. Michael Esper file; "Roman Catholic Diocese of Detroit: Description of Constituent Parishes and Rating as to Ability to Service Existing Debt," Dec. 31, 1935, AAD, Gallagher papers, 8:3.
29. "Description of Constituent Parishes"; MC, Jan. 29, 1931, 1:3-4.
30. "Description of Constituent Parishes," 1935; Doyle to C. A. Pfaffenberger, Feb. 25, 1933, AAD, parish files.
31. Koelzer to Msgr. John Doyle, Nov. 6, 1934, AAD, Msgr. John Koelzer file; Hayes to Rev. Albert Hebert, Nov. 14, 1940, AAD, parish files.
32. St. Rose *Messenger*, Feb. 22, 1931, April 19, 1931; Rev. Malchy M. Walker to Bp. Gallagher, Sept. 10, 1930, AAD, parish files; MC, June 30, 1932, 1:4-5.
33. "Chancellor" to Rev. Joseph Folta, Dec. 17, 1931, AAD, parish files; Rev. Dennis Hayes to Gallagher, Aug. 19, 1933, AAD, St. Peter, Mt. Clemens parish file; MC, May 23, 1935, 1:8, Sept. 3, 1936, 1:8.
34. Mother Mary DeSales to Archbishop Mooney, Sept. 27, 1937; Mooney to Rev. Constantine Dziuk, June 1, 1939, AAD, Chancery records—religious orders, women.
35. Minutes, meeting of Diocesan Consultors, Dec. 2, 1932, AAD, minutes and proceedings, 4; Rev. Daniel J. Ryan to Gallagher, Dec. 28, 1933, AAD, Chancery records—seminaries; MC, Sept. 28, 1933, 1:4; Minutes, meeting of Diocesan Consultors, Oct. 16, 1935, AAD, minutes and proceedings, 4.
36. Correspondence between LeBlanc and the Chancery is in AAD, Gallagher papers, 8:2. LeBlanc devoted the better part of 1936 to the search, which was cut short by Gallagher's death.
37. The text of the Gallagher telegram was reprinted in the Nov. 9, 1936, issue of *Social Justice*, a weekly that Coughlin founded in 1936.
38. The most extreme argument for the importance of Gallagher's "Austrian connection" in his own political development (and hence for Father Coughlin's career) is found in Forrest Davis, "Father Coughlin," *Atlantic Monthly* 156 (1935). MC, Mar. 4, 1920, 5:1.
39. MC, Aug. 5, 1920, 1:3; Dec. 2, 1920, 1:5-6.
40. MC, Apr. 12, 1917, 4:6; June 19, 1930, 1:7-8; Nov. 14, 1935, 1:2-3, 9:8.

41. From Gallagher's introduction to Louis B. Ward, *Father Charles E. Coughlin: An Authorized Biography* (Detroit: Tower Publications, 1933); MC, Dec. 10, 1936, 1:5; Apr. 25, 1935, 1:6–8, 2:1–4.
42. Relatively little is known about Coughlin's life before the 1930s. For brief biographical sketches, see Alan Brinkley, *Voices of Protest: Huey Long, Father Coughlin and the Great Depression* (New York: Vintage, 1982) and Charles J. Tull, *Father Coughlin and the New Deal* (Syracuse: Syracuse University Press, 1965). MC, Feb. 7, 1918, 5:4.
43. Brinkley, *Voices of Protest,* 89–90.
44. Ibid., 90–91.
45. Ibid., 92–93.
46. *Father Coughlin's Radio Sermons Complete,* October 1930–April 1931 (Baltimore: Know and Leary, 1931), 57.
47. Ibid., 130. Brinkley, *Voices of Protest,* 99–100.
48. Brinkley, *Voices of Protest,* 103, 110–112.
49. Ibid., 107–110.
50. Ibid., 124–125, 133–140.
51. Ibid., 198–203, 258–260.
52. McNicholas to Archbishop John J. Cantwell, Feb. 10, 1937, AACi: MA, Cantwell, John J. My thanks to Rev. Earl Boyea for this and subsequent citations from the Archives of the Archdiocese of Cincinnati.
53. Fumasoni-Biondi to McNicholas, June 30, 1930, AACi: MA, AD, 1935; Fumasoni-Biondi to Gallagher, Oct. 1, 1932, AAD, Gallagher papers, 3:9; McNicholas to Gallagher, Jan. 22, 1935, AACi: MA, Gallagher-McNicholas correspondence re Fr. Coughlin; McNicholas to Mooney, Feb. 28, 1936, AACi: MA, Mooney, Edward; Rochester, 1935–1937.
54. McNicholas to Cicognani, Apr. 13, 1935, AACi: MA, AD 1935; Mooney to McNicholas, Mar. 5, 1936, AACi: MA, Mooney, Edward; Rochester, 1935–1937.
55. McNicholas to Msgr. Egidio Vagnozzi, Aug. 14, 1936, AACi: MA, AD, 1936.
56. Tull, *Father Coughlin,* 105, 134–138, 148–149.
57. Ibid., 143–144; Cicognani to Gallagher, Sept. 29, 1936, AAD, Gallagher papers, 3:9.
58. Sheldon Marcus, *Father Coughlin: The Tumultuous Life of the Priest of the Little Flower* (Boston: Little, Brown, 1973), 131.
59. Tull, *Father Coughlin,* 171–173; McNicholas to Cantwell, Feb. 10, 1937, AACi: MA, Cantwell, John J.
60. Hurley to Hickey, Oct. 27, 1958, AAD, Mooney papers. Because the Mooney papers had not been catalogued when I did my research, I can give no more precise location for documents from this collection. The papers have since been catalogued, and an excellent finding aid is available.
61. Cardinal Mooney to Sister Counsel, Apr. 27, 1949, AAD, Mooney papers.
62. Bp. R.O. Gerow to Bp. Joseph Hurley, Jan. 8, 1959, AAD, Mooney papers.
63. Fogarty, *Vatican and the American Hierarchy,* 242.
64. *Rochester Courier-Journal* (N.Y.), Nov. 7, 1958.
65. The decree raising Detroit to an Archdiocese was dated Aug. 3, 1937.
66. Mooney to O'Hara, Oct. 4, 1946, AAD, Mooney papers; *Rochester Courier-Journal,* Nov. 7, 1958.
67. Mooney to Spellman, Mar. 27, 1942, AAD, Mooney papers.
68. Msgr. William Murphy to Coughlin, Aug. 17, 1937, AAD, Mooney papers; Coughlin to Msgr. John Doyle, Feb. 5, 1937; Doyle to Coughlin, draft dated Feb. 6, 1937; Mooney to Archbishop Cicognani, Oct. 29, 1937, draft dated Nov. 27, 1937, AAD, Mooney papers.
69. Tull, *Father Coughlin,* 181; MC, Oct. 7, 1937, 1:5; Oct. 14, 1937, 12:4; Mooney to Cicognani, Oct. 29, 1937, AAD, Mooney papers.

70. Many of these letters are in the AAD, Mooney papers. Tull, *Father Coughlin,* 182–183; Mooney to Cicognani, Oct. 29, 1937, AAD, Mooney papers.
71. Cicognani to Mooney, Nov. 3, 1937; Mooney to Cicognani, Nov. 4, 1937, AAD, Mooney papers; MC, Nov. 25, 1937, 1:2–3.
72. "KAL" (Msgr. William Murphy) to Mooney, Nov. 17, 1937; Cicognani to Mooney, Nov. 27, 1937, Dec. 3, 1937; Mooney to Cicognani, Dec. 4, 1937, AAD, Mooney papers.
73. Coughlin to Mooney, Nov. 30, 1937, AAD, Mooney papers; Tull, *Father Coughlin,* 185; MC, Dec. 9, 1937, 1:4.
74. Mooney to Cicognani, Dec. 10, 1937, AAD, Mooney papers. The Mooney-Coughlin agreement re *Social Justice* is in the Mooney papers, bearing the face-saving but obviously incorrect date of Dec. 6.
75. Tull, *Father Coughlin,* 197–198. The AAD has a nearly complete run of *Social Justice.*
76. On Coughlin's pre-1938 anti-Semitism, see William E. Leuchtenberg, *Franklin D. Roosevelt and the New Deal* (New York: Harper and Row, 1964), 103n. On the Coughlin-Fahey connection see M. Christine Athans, "The Fahey-Coughlin Connection: Father Dennis Fahey, C.S.Sp., Father Charles E. Coughlin, and Religious Anti-Semitism in the United States, 1938–1954" (Ph.D. diss., Graduate Theological Union, 1982).
77. Mooney to Cicognani, Dec. 18, 1938, AAD, Mooney papers. The censors' copies of the various broadcasts and *Social Justice* columns are in the Mooney papers.
78. Gillan to Mooney, Nov. 21, 1938; Rev. John A. Donovan to Prof. W. H. Albright, Dec. 1, 1938. These and related letters are in the AAD, Mooney papers.
79. Mooney to Ready, Dec. 2, 1938; Mooney to Cicognani, Mar. 8, 1940, Nov. 26, 1938, AAD, Mooney papers.
80. Mooney to Ready, Dec. 2, 1938; Mooney to Cicognani, Dec. 18, 1938, AAD, Mooney papers.
81. Mooney to Cicognani, Nov. 26, 1938, AAD, Mooney papers.
82. Mooney to Cicognani, Dec. 18, 1938; Mooney to Cardinal Eugenio Pacelli, Jan. 17, 1939; Cicognani to Mooney, Feb. 13, 1939; Mooney to Cicognani, Feb. 20, 1939; Cicognani to Coughlin, Mar. 1, 1939, AAD, Mooney papers.
83. Mooney to Cicognani, Feb. 20, 1940, AAD, Mooney papers.
84. Msgr. Joseph Ciarrocchi, editor of Detroit's *La Voce del Popolo,* was reproved by Mooney in 1940 for that paper's endorsement of Roosevelt. Ciarrocchi accepted the reprimand as an "obedient servant," but offered a justification for the endorsement that was as revealing as it was ingenuous. "I have been under the impression that advocating the Roosevelt candidacy would not have been mixing in forbidden politics for a priest, as it was done for a general purpose of common benefit, not with any partisan spirit." Mooney to Ciarrocchi, Nov. 2, 1940; Ciarrocchi to Mooney, Nov. 5, 1940, AAD, Msgr. Joseph Ciarrocchi file.
85. Mooney to Coughlin, Apr. 15, 1939, June 10 and June 21, 1939, Aug. 18, 1939; Mooney to Smith, Dec. 7, 1939, AAD, Mooney papers.
86. Mooney to Cicognani, Feb. 20, 1939, March 9, 1940; Coughlin to Mooney, May 16, 1940; Mooney to Coughlin, May 23, 1940, AAD, Mooney papers.
87. Mooney to Cicognani, June 5, 1940, Sept. 20, 1940, AAD, Mooney papers.
88. Spellman to Mooney, Mar. 25, 1942, AAD, Mooney papers; MC, Apr. 2, 1942, 6:1; Coughlin to Mooney, Apr. 20, 1942, enclosing a copy of his press release, AAD, Mooney papers.
89. Mooney to Coughlin, Apr. 23, 1942; "Notes on Fr. Coughlin's Interview of Archbishop Mooney, April 28, 1942"; Mooney to Cicognani, May 12, 1942, AAD, Mooney papers.
90. The negotiations are summarized in Mooney to Cicognani, May 12, 1942; Mooney to Roosevelt, May 9, 1942, AAD, Mooney papers.
91. Mooney to Coughlin, Sept. 29, 1942, Oct. 1, 1942; Mooney to Cicognani, Oct. 3,

1942, AAD, Mooney papers; Rev. Joseph Sielski to Msgr. John Donovan, Dec. 10, 1951, AAD, Chancery records — religious orders, men; Memo, J. A. Donovan re a Coughlin talk to the First Friday Club of Detroit, Dec. 4, 1953, AAD, Mooney papers; Rev. Raymond B. Schlinkert to Bp. John Donovan, June 29, 1957, AAD, Chancery records — organizations and societies.

92. The institute's first directors included Fathers Frederic Siedenburg, SJ, Sebastian Erbacher, OFM, Vincent M. Borkowitz, Clare Murphy, and Raymond Clancy. The board was subsequently expanded to include lay members: Paul Weber of the Newspaper Guild; Leo Keller of the Brotherhood of Maintenance of Way Employees; Elmer Milliman, from the same union as Keller; and W. L. Whitney of the International Typographical Union. Minutes of early board meetings are in WSU, Fr. Raymond Clancy papers, 1:14. "Report on Labor Discussion meetings Conducted by St. Leo Parish," undated but spring 1939, WSU, Clancy papers, 1:17.

93. Attendance data for 1940 is in WSU, Clancy papers, 1:18. "Student reaction questionnaire," May 1939; "Report on Labor Discussion Meetings Conducted by St. Leo Parish," WSU, Clancy papers, 1:17.

94. Memo, Hubble to Cardinal Mooney, undated but ca. 1955, WSU, Association of Catholic Trade Unionists' papers, 4. Mooney was initially opposed to the organization of an ACTU chapter in Detroit. "He said it appeared to him that we were going to have an effect similar to that of the Jewish War Veterans — simply to introduce a division along lines which would make for the isolation of our people," Paul Weber remembered. Weber changed the archbishop's mind, however, and Mooney was generous thereafter in his assistance to the group. Weber, who served as Detroit ACTU president from 1938 through 1948, was a leading figure in the Newspaper Guild in Detroit. See Paul Weber, "Memorandum to ACTU-NY re Intra-Union Organization," undated but early 1940s, WSU, ACTU papers, 2. Thomas Doherty to Victor LoPinto, May 8, 1941, WSU, ACTU papers, 25. The *Wage-Earner* was originally known as the *Michigan Labor Leader.* It is not clear when the paper began to receive its subsidy from the Chancery. A 1951 letter seems to refer to "several years" of a monthly subsidy of $400; this was about to be increased to $450. See Fr. Raymond Clancy to Cardinal Mooney, July 6, 1951, AAD, Chancery collections — organizations and societies. The eight-week "ACTU Basic Training Course" was apparently first offered in 1943, when Fr. Clement Kern was educational director of the organization. Notes, "ACTU-CIO Conference," Jan. 25, 1944, outline ACTU strategy with regard to the UAW factional struggle (WSU, ACTU papers, 2). On ACTU-Detroit membership, see letter (unsigned carbon copy) to Napoleon Raymond, Jan. 27, 1940, and Thomas Doherty to "Mr. Chairman and Fellow Actists," Apr. 18, 1940, WSU, ACTU papers, 2, 3.

95. St. Vincent's *News,* Sept. 3, 1939. The text of Fr. Clancy's broadcast is in WSU, Clancy papers, 4:2. These papers contain much of interest with regard to Clancy's career. "Hamilton" to Clancy, Nov. 16, 1939, WSU, Clancy papers, 4:2.

96. M. E. Coyle to Mooney, Jan. 3, 1940, AAD, Mooney papers.

97. Philip Murray to Mooney, Sept. 25, 1941; Mooney to Knudsen, Dec. 5, 1939, AAD, Mooney papers. A printed copy of Mooney's speech is in the Mooney papers. Emphasis in original.

98. Mooney to Bp. Walter Foery, Dec. 13, 1945, AAD, Mooney papers.

99. Mooney to Foery, Dec. 13, 1945, AAD, Mooney papers.

100. Mooney to Foery, Dec. 13, 1945, AAD, Mooney papers; Minutes, meeting of Diocesan Consultors, Dec. 6, 1939, July 13, 1940, Jan. 11, 1941, AAD, minutes and proceedings, 4.

101. Rev. Andrew Jacobs to Mooney, Sept. 4, 1945, AAD, parish files. Mooney to Foery, Dec. 13, 1945, AAD, Mooney papers.

102. Mooney to Foery, Dec. 13, 1945, AAD, Mooney papers; Memo, John A. Donovan, re St. Monica parish finances, July 6, 1954, AAD, parish files.
103. "Annual Statistics on Religious Instruction," undated but ca. 1950, AAD, Chancery records — CCD.
104. Mooney circular letter, Jan. 16, 1943, AAD, Mooney papers.
105. St. John's *Bulletin,* Apr. 7, 1946; St. Margaret Mary *News,* Apr. 20, 1958, copies in AAD, parish files.
106. The canonical visitation forms — or "Dean's Reports" — for 1940, 1948, and 1954 are in the AAD, parish files. "Archdiocese of Detroit: Canonical Visitation of Holy Cross (Hungarian) Parish, March 15, 1940"; "Archdiocese of Detroit: Canonical Visitation of St. Francis Parish, Nov. 26, 1948."
107. The updated regulations are found in *Proceedings of the Eighth Diocesan Synod,* Dec. 1944, copy in AAD. Mooney convened a second synod — the ninth diocesan synod — in 1954.
108. Constitution, Federation of Catholic Charitable Agencies, undated but 1943, AAD, Chancery records — Catholic Charities of Detroit; "Report of the Family Committee of the Federation of Catholic Charities," undated but 1945, AAD, Chancery records — Catholic charities of Michigan; MC, May 15, 1958; Catholic Charities of Michigan *Newsletter,* 1:1 (Apr. 6, 1959).
109. Sister Josephine to Mooney, Jan. 4, 1948, AAD, Mooney papers; Msgr. Suedkamp circular letter, Oct. 10, 1960, AAD, Chancery records — Catholic charities of Michigan.
110. Mother M. of St. Denis to Mooney, Oct. 11, 1945, AAD, Mooney papers.
111. "Chancellor" to Mother Mary Gerald, OP, July 21, 1958, AAD, Chancery records — religious orders, women.
112. On the Mooney-Stritch-McNicholas triumvirate and its influence in the NCWC see Fogarty, *Vatican and the American Hierarchy,* 347–348.
113. Hurley to Mooney, July 13, 1941, AAD, Mooney papers; Fogarty, *Vatican and the American Hierarchy,* 271–276; Mooney to Cicognani, Mar. 24, 1941, AAD, Mooney papers.
114. Mooney to Myron Taylor, Dec. 13, 1943, AAD, Mooney papers.
115. Mooney to Taylor, Dec. 13, 1943; Mooney to Roosevelt, Feb. 23, 1944; Mooney to Cicognani, Aug. 27, 1943, AAD, Mooney papers. See also Fogarty, *Vatican and the American Hierarchy,* 295–306.
116. Mooney to Most Rev. Bernard Griffin, Mar. 31, 1945; Mooney, Stritch, and Spellman to Roosevelt, Dec. 14, 1944, AAD, Mooney papers.
117. Mooney to Cicognani, draft dated Mar. 10, 1952. See also Edward Heffron to Mooney, Sept. 24, 1948, AAD, Mooney papers.
118. Fogarty, *Vatican and the American Hierarchy,* 348–358, 368–383, 390–399. There is not much correspondence between Mooney and Murray in the AAD, but what little there is confirms their cordial relationship. See, for example, Murray to Mooney, Apr. 13, 1954, AAD, Mooney papers.
119. Recollections of Cardinal Mooney, written by Msgr. Edward Hickey for Bp. Joseph Hurley, undated but ca. 1959, AAD, Mooney papers.
120. Mooney's copy of this speech is in the AAD, Mooney papers. Mooney to Very Rev. Pierre Girard, Feb. 26, 1954; James Cusack, "Pastoral Lectures of Cardinal Mooney," undated but spring 1956, AAD, Mooney papers.
121. Casey to Mooney, Nov. 23, 1951, AAD, Mooney papers. Mooney's copy of his speech is in the AAD.
122. The following men served as auxiliary bishops of Detroit during the Mooney episcopate: Stephen Woznicki, consecrated in 1938; Allen Babcock, consecrated in 1947 and named Bishop of Grand Rapids in 1954; Alexander Zaleski, consecrated in

1950 and named Coadjutor Bishop of Lansing in 1964; Henry Donnelly and John Donovan, both consecrated in 1954. None has personal papers in the AAD.

123. On Mooney's attitude toward closing the more marginal churches see Rev. Edward Majeske to Archbishop John Dearden, undated but ca. 1959, AAD, St. Vincent, Detroit parish file.

124. My tentative conclusions about Cardinal Mooney's views on liturgical reform are based on his hesitant and sometimes disapproving responses to requests from his clergy to try certain quite limited liturgical innovations in their parishes. He would surely have understood the pastoral arguments for the vernacular Mass. But as an excellent Latinist and a man with a lively sense of the world-dimension of the Church, the demise of the Latin Mass would almost certainly have been painful for him.

125. IHM Mission Chronicles, St. George, Detroit, SSIHM, Chronicles, IHM missions. The Cardinal's remains were transferred to Holy Sepulchre Cemetery in 1987.

12. THE DIOCESAN CLERGY

1. Place of birth from deceased priests' files in the AAD, supplemented on occasion by the *Michigan Catholic*. Those priests who were assigned to the Diocese of Lansing at its creation in 1938 do not have files in the AAD. But they were more likely to be native-born than priests who served in and around Detroit, for there were relatively few foreign-language parishes in the mostly rural Lansing Diocese.

2. Cusack, "Pastoral Lectures of Cardinal Mooney," undated but spring 1956, AAD, Mooney papers.

3. The uncertainty with regard to the exact number of ordinations in the 1940s and the 1950s stems from the Chancery's failure to record, at least in systematic fashion, those ordinations that took place abroad. Once a priest dies, his personal file, including the date and place of his ordination, becomes a part of the AAD. These files are a useful supplement to the record of local ordinations, and it is because of this that my figures for the 1920s and the 1930s are probably exact. Based on archival sources alone, we get the following totals: 164 ordinations between 1920 and 1929, 228 between 1930 and 1939, 199 between 1940 and 1949, and 195 between 1950 and 1959.

4. Mooney to Archbishop Cicognani, Oct. 31, 1941, AAD, San Francesco parish file.

5. "Priest Members of the Third Order of St. Francis," undated but ca. 1933, AAD, Chancery records — religious orders, men.

6. Fr. Robert Begin, "Some preliminary thoughts on becoming Pastor of St. Margaret Mary," June 7, 1970, AAD, parish files.

7. Albert Kolch, "Twenty-Five Years," in Sacred Heart Seminary, Silver Jubilee commemorative booklet, Detroit, 1944, AAD, Chancery records — seminaries; Student report card, 1921, private papers, Msgr. Clement Kern.

8. Quoted in Kolch, "Twenty-Five Years"; Diary, Clement Kern, entry for Mar. 13, 1921, private papers, Msgr. Clement Kern; Minutes, Advisory committee to the Bishop in the matter of planning Sacred Heart Seminary, Apr. 6, 1921, AAD, Chancery records — seminaries.

9. Notes from a conference on seminary rules, undated but probably spring 1921, private papers, Msgr. Clement Kern; "Sacred Heart Seminary: Regulations, Curriculum, Register of Students, 1929–1930," AAD, Chancery records — seminaries.

10. Hayes to H.P.M., July 12, 1921, AAD, deceased priests' files; Kern diary, entry for Mar. 25, 1921, private papers, Msgr. Clement Kern; Rev. Dennis Hayes to M.H., June 3, 1922, AAD, deceased priests' files.

11. "Tom" to "George," Mar. 10, 1929, AAD, deceased priests' files.
12. Leo. J. Trese, *Tenders of the Flock* (New York: Sheed and Ward, 1955), 117.
13. Minutes, meeting of Diocesan Consultors, Aug. 18, 1920, AAD, minutes and proceedings, 4. "Sacred Heart Seminary: Regulations, Curriculum, Register of Students, 1929–1930," AAD, Chancery records—seminaries; Frank Kullman to Archbishop Mooney, Sept. 20, 1945; Fr. Arthur Reckinger to Mooney, undated but ca. 1948, AAD, Chancery records—organizations and societies.
14. Kolch, "Twenty-Five Years."
15. "Sacred Heart Seminary: Regulations, Curriculum, Register of Students, 1929–1930"; Kern diary, entry for Apr. 19, 1921, private papers, Msgr. Clement Kern.
16. "Sacred Heart Seminary: Regulations, Curriculum, Register of Students, 1929–1930"; Rev. Dennis Hayes to "Dear Friends," Oct. 17, 1925, AAD, deceased priests' files.
17. Student essays are found in the *Gothic,* a quarterly magazine first published in 1925. A nearly complete run is located at Sacred Heart Seminary, Detroit. On the annual Forty Hours devotion see "Letter Home," *Gothic,* 28:2 (Feb. 1952), 19. Quoted from Joseph C. DeWindt, "The Ordinations," *Gothic,* 3:6 (Nov. 1927), 10.
18. MC, Dec. 22, 1921, 8:3; "Sacred Heart Seminary: Regulations, Curriculum, Register of Students, 1929–1930"; "Mission Notes," *Gothic,* 3:5 (Oct. 1927), 16.
19. Henry Offer, "Active Catholic Action," *Gothic,* 14:4 (June 1938), 48–49.
20. "Labor Problems," *Gothic,* 29:4 (June 1953), 47; "Interracial Education," *Gothic,* 28:4 (June 1952), 45; "Fair Employment in Detroit," *Gothic,* 28:3 (Apr. 1952), 5, 56–57; "The 'Old Fashioned' Catholic," *Gothic,* 28:2 (Feb. 1952), 4.
21. Mooney, draft letter re SS. Cyril and Methodius Seminary, no salutation, undated but probably 1943, AAD, Mooney papers; Mooney to Bp. John O'Hara, CSC, Aug. 21, 1945, AAD, Chancery records—seminaries.
22. Rev. Lyman Fenn, SS, "First Annual Report to the Bishops of the Province of Detroit," Mar. 15, 1950; Minutes of the Meeting of Bishops of the Province of Detroit, Dec. 14, 1948, AAD, Chancery records—seminaries.
23. Minutes of the Meeting of Bishops of the Province of Detroit, Dec. 14, 1948; IHM Mission Chronicles, Holy Trinity, Detroit, entry for Feb. 22, 1951, SSIHM, Chronicles, IHM missions. Rev. Lyman Fenn, SS, "Sixth Annual Report of the Rector to the Bishops of the Province of Detroit," May 11, 1955, AAD, Chancery records—seminaries.
24. Rev. Lyman Fenn, SS, "First Annual Report to the Bishops of the Province of Detroit," Mar. 15, 1950; Fenn, "Sixth Annual Report," May 11, 1955. It was in the spring of 1955 that John Tracy Ellis delivered his famous attack on anti-intellectualism among American Catholics. Reprinted in *Thought* later that same year, the Ellis speech gave rise to a lively debate among Catholic educators. But Father Fenn's report preceded the Ellis speech.
25. Cusack, "Pastoral Lectures of Cardinal Mooney."
26. Fenn, "Sixth Annual Report of the Rector to the Bishops of the Province of Detroit," Fenn, "First Annual Report."
27. Archbishop Mooney to Most Rev. Ralph L. Hayes, Jan. 3, 1938, AAD, deceased priests' files.
28. Jacobs to "Rt. Rev. Dear Monsignor," Feb. 1, 1934, AAD, Fr. Andrew Jacobs file; Pomponi to Bp. Gallagher, Dec. 12, 1935, AAD, Fr. Robert Pomponi file.
29. Donovan to Msgr. John Doyle, Nov. 23, 1932, AAD, Bp. John Donovan file. On the conservatism of the Roman seminaries see Ellis, "The Formation of the American Priest," 23.
30. Finnegan to Msgr. John Doyle, Mar. 7, 1924, AAD, Fr. John Finnegan file; Flynn

to Doyle, Apr. 29, 1931, AAD, Msgr. Francis Flynn file; Levasseur to Doyle, June 7, 1933, AAD, Fr. Gerald LeVasseur file; Maurice Enright to Michael Gallagher, Oct. 2, 1889, AAD, Gallagher papers, 12:6; Paquette to Doyle, Dec. 8, 1929, AAD, Gallagher papers, 11:8.

31. Levasseur to Doyle, June 22, 1933; Fr. Martin M. Lenk to Doyle, Nov. 18, 1934, AAD, Msgr. Martin M. Lenk file; Flynn to Doyle, Jan. 19, 1929, AAD.
32. Lenk to Doyle, July 29, 1933; Donovan to Doyle, Jan. 8, 1934, AAD.
33. Flynn to Doyle, Jan. 8, 1931, AAD.
34. Trese, *Tenders of the Flock,* 118.
35. Minutes, meeting of Diocesan Consultors, June 27, 1922, AAD, minutes and proceedings, 4; Rev. John Koelzer to Msgr. John Doyle, Oct. 8, 1934, AAD, Msgr. John Koelzer file.
36. Rev. Vincent Hankerd to Archbishop Dearden, Oct. 31, 1960, AAD, Msgr. Vincent Hankerd file.
37. John A. Donovan, memo, Nov. 27, 1941; C.A.U. to Edward Hickey, Mar. 14, 1943; to Archbishop Mooney, June 6, 1943, AAD, deceased priests' files.
38. Cusack, "Pastoral Lectures of Cardinal Mooney."
39. Minutes, meeting of Diocesan Consultors, Feb. 13, 1919, AAD, minutes and proceedings, 4.
40. R.J.C. to Bp. Gallagher, Feb. 25, 1919, AAD, deceased priests' files.
41. Fourth Annual Report of St. Philip Neri Mission, Lapeer, undated but ca. 1928, AAD, Immaculate Conception, Lapeer parish file.
42. Fourth Annual Report of St. Philip Neri Mission; Rt. Rev. Francis C. Kelley, "The Mission House Plan for Country Missions," NCWC *Bulletin* (May 1928), 5; Fr. Albert George to Mooney, Aug. 6, 1938, AAD, Fr. Albert George file.
43. Dillon to Bp. Gallagher, Nov. 19, 1924, AAD, Fr. David Dillon file; B.F.C. to Msgr. John Donovan, Oct. 14, 1931, AAD, deceased priests' files.
44. Rev. William A. Graebner to Cardinal Mooney, July 21, 1947, AAD, parish files.
45. F.J. to "Dear Bishop," Dec. 15, 1955, AAD, St. Mary's, New Baltimore parish file.
46. Trese, *Tenders of the Flock,* 3.
47. Mrs. Mary E. Brothers to "Rev. M. J. Galeger," Mar. 30, 1925, AAD, deceased priests' files; Roberge to "Rev. and dear Father," Dec. 12, 1935, AAD, Fr. Hubert Roberge file.
48. Kern to Cardinal Mooney, July 21, 1950, AAD, parish files. A draft of Msgr. Higgins's 1983 article is in the AAD, Msgr. Clement Kern file.
49. Kern to Mooney, July 21, 1950. Fr. Kern's "we" has reference to all the priests in residence at Holy Trinity—there were five in 1950. IHM Mission Chronicles, Holy Trinity, Detroit, entries for Dec. 1945–Feb. 1946, Sept. 5, 1950, SSIHM, Chronicles, IHM missions.
50. Kern to Mooney, July 21, 1950; July 10, 1951, AAD, parish files; Kern to Rev. Joseph Breitenbeck, Mar. 28, 1952, AAD, Msgr. Clement Kern file.
51. MC, May 12, 1898, 5:3; May 1, 1919, 4:4.
52. Mooney to Cardinal Francis Spellman, draft undated but 1952, AAD, Mooney papers; Mooney to Msgr. Patrick J. Ryan, Apr. 1, 1958, AAD, deceased priests' files.
53. Trese to Mooney, Oct. 11, 1942, AAD, Fr. Leo Trese file.
54. Collins to Archbishop Mooney, July 11, 1943, AAD, Fr. Michael Collins file; Dion to Mooney, Nov. 14, 1943, AAD, Fr. Joseph Dion file; Dzienis to Mooney, June 30, 1943, AAD, Fr. Stephen Dzienis file.
55. Myrick to Archbishop Mooney, Oct. 6, 1943, AAD, Fr. R. Vincent Myrick file; Maino to Mooney, Oct. 3, 1944, AAD, Msgr. Hubert Maino file; Downing to "Dear Bishop," July 7, 1945, AAD, Fr. John J. Downing file.

56. Poznanski to Archbishop Mooney, Mar. 29, 1944, AAD, Fr. Boguslaus T. Poznanski file; McElgunn to Mooney, Dec. 1, 1944, AAD, Fr. Joseph McElgunn file; Maino to Mooney, Oct. 3, 1944; AAD, Msgr. Hubert Maino file.

57. Frank McGinnis, "The Life Story of Austin Ripley," undated draft in AAD, Chancery records—Guest House; Austin Ripley to Msgr. John Donovan, Feb. 4, 1954, AAD, Chancery records—Guest House.

58. McGinnis, "Life Story of Austin Ripley."

59. Mooney to Bp. John Treacy, Dec. 20, 1953; Mooney to Austin Ripley, Nov. 11, 1953, AAD, Chancery records—Guest House.

60. Ripley to Msgr. John Donovan, Feb. 4, 1954; Mooney to M.F. Cudahy, Dec. 22, 1954; Donovan to Rev. Edwin J. Thome, July 21, 1953, AAD, Chancery records—Guest House.

61. McGinnis, "Life Story of Austin Ripley"; William H. Brady to Cardinal Mooney, Jan. 7, 1954, AAD, Chancery records—Guest House.

62. Memo, unsigned and undated, but from Guest House and ca. 1960; "Parish and Personal Contributions from Pastors in the Archdiocese of Detroit, Jan. 1, 1960 to and including Dec. 30, 1960"; Archbishop Dearden to Bp. Martin D. McNamara, Jan. 3, 1962; Ripley to Dearden, May 24, 1967, AAD, Chancery records—Guest House.

63. Joseph H. Fichter, *The Guest House Experience, 1956–1974* (Guest House, Inc., undated); Dearden to Bp. Martin D. McNamara, Jan. 3, 1962, AAD, Chancery Records—Guest House.

64. Cusack, "Pastoral Lectures of Cardinal Mooney."

13. THE LAITY

1. Ternes to Bp. Gallagher, July 4, 1922, AAD, parish files; MC, Dec. 20, 1928, 6:5–6; St. John's *News*, Nov. 16, 1930.

2. MC, Mar. 20, 1930, 8:1; "History of Santa Maria Church," AAD.

3. Gerhard Lenski, *The Religious Factor* (New York: Doubleday Anchor, 1963), 47–48; Jarzembowski to Archbishop John Dearden, May 11, 1960, AAD, St. Joseph, Pontiac parish file; Archdiocese of Detroit, Canonical Visitation of Most Holy Trinity Parish, Apr. 5, 1954; Kern to Msgr. E. J. Hickey, June 25, 1949, AAD, parish files.

4. Numerous letters requesting permission to establish Nocturnal Adoration Societies are found in the parish files of the AAD, most of them dated from the early 1940s to the early 1950s. On the First Friday Club, see Rev. John T. Reid to Archbishop Mooney, May 24, 1941; Oct. 11, 1946; May 14, 1952, AAD, Chancery records—organizations and societies.

5. MC, June 19, 1930, 1:8, Jan. 9, 1930, 1:5, 10:3–4, Apr. 10, 1930, 8:4, March 29, 1934, 1:4–5, Oct. 22, 1936, 1:6; Rev. G. A. Fitzgibbons, SJ, to Cardinal Mooney, May 21, 1946, AAD, Chancery records—organizations and societies.

6. "First Annual Report, St. Philip Neri Mission," undated but ca. 1924, AAD, Non-Chancery records—institutions, societies and parishes. The Church Extension Society provided funds for the first year's work and "loaned" two priests to the Diocese of Detroit.

7. "First Annual Report, St. Philip Neri Mission"; St. Philip Neri Mission House, Lapeer: Weekly Reports, 1923–1929, Carey entries for Nov. and Dec. 1923, AAD, Non-Chancery records—institutions, societies and parishes.

8. St. Philip Neri Mission House, Davison: Weekly Reports, Dakoske entry for week of Oct. 4, 1924; St. Philip Neri Mission House, Oxford and Romeo: Weekly Reports, Gorman entry, undated but 1924; St. Philip Neri Mission House, Imlay City and Allenton: Weekly Reports, Grady entry for week of May 31, 1924, AAD, Non-

Chancery records — institutions, societies and parishes; "First Annual Report, St. Philip Neri Mission."

9. St. Philip Neri Mission House, Lapeer: Weekly Reports, Carey entry for Mar. 21, 1925.

10. St. Philip Neri Mission House, Imlay City and Allenton: Weekly Reports, Grady entry for week of July 26, 1924; St. Philip Neri Mission House, Lapeer: Weekly Reports, Carey entry for Nov. 14, 1925.

11. "Fourth Annual Report, St. Philip Neri Mission," undated but ca. 1928, AAD, Immaculate Conception, Lapeer parish file; St. Philip Neri Mission, Lapeer: Weekly Reports, Dakoske entry for Dec. 1928.

12. Sr. Rosalita, *No Greater Service,* 596; MC, Jan. 7, 1932, 1:7; Rev. Clarence Doherty to Archbishop Mooney, Mar. 26, 1945, AAD, parish files.

13. MC, Sept. 8, 1921, 8:1, Sept. 29, 1921, 8:4; Sister Ellen Clanon, IHM, *Not Built on Sand: Holy Redeemer Parish, 1880-1980* (Detroit, 1980), 45; MC, Apr. 13, 1933, 1:6-7, 4:5-6, Nov. 23, 1933, 1:4, Sept. 28, 1933, 1:6. See, for example, MC, Apr. 16, 1931, 8:2; St. Rose *Messenger,* Nov. 22, 1931, Dec. 13, 1931.

14. MC, Aug. 6, 1931, 8:3, Nov. 26, 1931, 8:3, Sept. 7, 1933, 6:4, May 26, 1938, 10:2-3, Jan. 19, 1939, 12:5, Nov. 15, 1934, 1:8, Mar. 19, 1936, 12:5.

15. MC, Apr. 13, 1933, 1:6-7, 4:5-6, May 21, 1931, 1:5, May 26, 1932, 1:6-7, May 25, 1933, 1:3, May 24, 1934, 1:2-3, May 21, 1936, 2:6, Aug. 17, 1939, 1:5; St. Margaret Mary *News,* Apr. 13, 1952.

16. Popular interest in the Fatima cult is evident in many parish newsletters as well as in the *Michigan Catholic.* The Holy Name Society announcement is taken from St. John's *Bulletin,* Oct. 3, 1948. Emphasis in original.

17. MC, Aug. 16, 1928, 8:1.

18. MC, July 25, 1918, 1:1, Aug. 21, 1919, 8:1, Aug. 5, 1920, 8:4, July 9, 1931, 8:1, Aug. 3, 1933, 6:5, May 25, 1933, 1:4-5. Father Solanus still has many devotees in the Archdiocese, although he died in 1957. Efforts to have him canonized have long been underway.

19. Gallagher to "Dear Children of the Laity," in St. Rose *Messenger,* Sept. 20, 1925; *Centennial History: St. Patrick's Parish, Detroit* (Detroit, 1962); St. John's *News,* Mar. 1926; MC, Sept. 4, 1930, 10:2, Nov. 13, 1930, 10:3.

20. MC, July 3, 1930, 8:2, Oct. 23, 1930, 8:3, July 20, 1933, 6:6, Aug. 10, 1933, 1:3; Archdiocese of Detroit, Canonical Visitation of St. Dominic parish, Feb. 20, 1945, AAD, parish files; MC, Sept. 6, 1934, 8:4.

21. MC, Sept. 3, 1931, 8:4, Nov. 21, 1935, 10:3-4, Mar. 13, 1930, 2:4, Feb. 26, 1931, 1:7.

22. St. John's *News,* May 26, 1935; see, for example, MC, Aug. 3, 1933; MC, Sept. 15, 1932, 1:3.

23. St. Rose *Messenger,* Apr. 4, 1956.

24. Rev. E. W. Allor, CSB, to Archbishop Mooney, July 5, 1939; Rev. E. J. Hickey to Allor, July 10, 1939, AAD, St. Anne, Detroit parish file.

25. *Orate Fratres,* a monthly first published in 1926, was the principal organ of the liturgical movement, whose national leaders were drawn largely from the Benedictine order. Sr. Rosalita, *No Greater Service,* 596.

26. MC, July 31, 1930, 4:1, Nov. 18, 1937, 1:7, Dec. 1, 1938, 1:8; Rev. D. B. Kuntz to Msgr. Alexander Zaleski, Nov. 12, 1947; Zaleski to Kuntz, Nov. 19, 1947, AAD, St. Vincent, Pontiac parish file; Rev. Bernard Kearns to Rev. Erwin J. Bauer, May 19, 1951, AAD, parish files.

27. Rev. John Donovan to Rev. Peter Walkowiak, Dec. 21, 1953, AAD, St. Florian, Hamtramck parish file; Rev. Bernard Kearns to Fr. Declan, CP, June 5, 1953, AAD, Chancery records — religious orders, men; Rev. Emmet Crane, C.SS.R., to Bp. John Donovan, Mar. 15, 1956, AAD, parish files.

28. *Commonweal,* 63:13 (Dec. 30, 1955), 319.

29. *Commonweal,* 61:1 (Jan. 12, 1945), 333-334, 61:15 (Jan. 26, 1945), 381-382.

30. "Report of Programs of the Gateway Grail Center, 1955-1956," AAD, Chancery records—organizations and societies.

31. Betty Ford, "Motor City Gateway: Detroit's Grail Center," reprint from *Today,* undated but ca. 1956, AAD, Chancery records—organizations and societies.

32. The *Michigan Catholic* in the immediate postwar years offers ample evidence of the greatly heightened interest in the foreign missions.

33. MC, Dec. 23, 1920, 5:4; Sr. Rosalita, *No Greater Service,* 650, 653; MC, Oct. 23, 1930, 3:5-6.

34. *Gothic,* 7:5 (June 10, 1931), 31, 34, 7:4 (Apr. 15, 1931), 9, 3:4 (June 1927), 37-38; MC, Aug. 24, 1939, 10:2.

35. MC, Mar. 22, 1934, 1:6-7, Aug. 1, 1935, 3:4-5; Richard J. Roche, OMI, *Catholic Colleges and the Negro Student* (Washington, D.C.: Catholic University of America Press, 1948), 50; MC, Feb. 20, 1936, 2:1-3.

36. MC, Mar. 6, 1930, 2:1-7, Jan. 6, 1955, 1:1; Sr. Rosalita, *No Greater Service,* 662-663.

37. MC, June 18, 1931, 1:6, June 17, 1937, 1:2-3.

38. MC, Dec. 8, 1932, 1:4-5. Jesuit Father Louis Weitzman spoke to the CIL on "rebuffs and apparent lack of success" at the annual Communion breakfast in June 1932. MC, June 23, 1932, 1:4, June 25, 1936, 1:2-3.

39. MC, Oct. 2, 1930, 8:3, Feb. 15, 1933, 1:8, 5:4-5.

40. MC, Feb. 7, 1935, 4:2, Oct. 10, 1935, 1:7-8; Rev. Leo DeBarry to Msgr. John Doyle, Nov. 4, 1937, AAD, Chancery records—CCD; Ziolkowski, *Felician Sisters,* 311.

41. "Annual Statistics on Religious Instruction, 1937-1949," AAD, Chancery records—CCD; "Annual Report, Confraternity of Christian Doctrine: 1943-44," AAD, Mooney papers; Mooney memo re "vacation work for seminarians," undated but ca. 1958, AAD, Chancery records—Catholic deaf and blind. The CIL was incorporated into the CCD in 1939, although the name of the former organization was used locally until 1953. Josephine Brownson died in 1942.

42. Information on the work of the Victory Noll Sisters (more formally known as Our Lady of Victory Missionary Catechists) and on the Mission Helpers of the Sacred Heart is in the AAD, Chancery records—religious orders, women. On the Home Visitors of Mary, see chapter 15.

43. "The Status of the Confraternity of Christian Doctrine in Michigan, 1965," AAD, Chancery records—CCD.

44. Quoted in Fogarty, *Vatican and the American Hierarchy,* 394; Lenski, *Religious Factor,* 47-49. The Detroit findings with respect to Americanization and church attendance were subsequently confirmed in a study employing data from a national sample.

45. "1925 Calendar of St. Elizabeth Parish," AAD, parish files; Mooney to Archbishop John D'Alton, draft undated but Dec. 1948, AAD, Mooney papers; Minutes, meeting of Revs. John Doyle, A. J. Sheridan, CSSp, and members of the St. Joachim parish building committee, undated but 1934; Archdiocese of Detroit, Canonical Visitation of St. Joachim's parish, Nov. 16, 1948, AAD, parish files; MC, Apr. 8, 1920, 8:1.

46. Mrs. Patrick Bruder to Cardinal Mooney, May 9, 1947; Rev. Francis Van Hout to Msgr. John Donovan, Feb. 2, 1953, AAD, parish files.

47. Detroit's Maltese population was at least 6,000 in 1920, according to Father William Hennigan of Holy Trinity parish. Bishop Gallagher thought the number was closer to 4,000. MC, June 10, 1920, 4:4; Gallagher to Very Rev. Nicholas J. Vasey, OSA, July 19, 1920, AAD, Holy Family, Detroit parish file. As for the Mexicans, there were as many as 8,000 in Detroit by the late 1920s, with an unknown number scattered about the rural parts of the Diocese. A good many left for Mexico in the early 1930s, some of them having been forcibly repatriated.

48. Emmanuel Vella to Rev. Alexander Zaleski, Nov. 26, 1938, AAD, parish files.
49. "The Croatian Church Building Fund Committee" to Cardinal Mooney, undated but 1953, AAD, St. Jerome parish file. Evidence of conflict is found in the files of a number of ethnic parishes.
50. References to the election of trustees are scattered throughout the files of the newer ethnic parishes. The Chancery's muted response is also evident there. Gallagher to Rev. Joseph Cizauskas, Mar. 30, 1927, AAD, Divine Providence, Southfield parish file; "By-Laws of the Ukrainian Church of St. John the Baptist of Detroit, Michigan"; Rev. Alexander Pope to Bp. Gallagher, Jan. 2, 1925, Jan. 19, 1927, AAD, parish files.
51. Mooney to Archbishop Cicognani, Mar. 12, 1955; Rev. Louis Kovacs to Bp. Gallagher, May 24, 1927; see also Archdiocese of Detroit, Canonical Visitation of Holy Cross (Hungarian) parish, Mar. 15, 1940, AAD, parish files.
52. Archdiocese of Detroit, Canonical Visitation of St. Hyacinth parish, undated but 1948, AAD, parish files. The 1940 and 1948 visitation forms asked pastors whether they had had any trouble with their church committees. The 1954 form omitted the question. Minutes of the St. John's parish council for 1947 and 1948 are in the parish files of the AAD. The council may have continued after 1948, but no records exist beyond that date. Like many other parishes in the Archdiocese, St. John's organized a "parish council" in the late 1960s. Trese, *Tenders of the Flock,* 109.
53. "1930 Annual Report, Society of St. Vincent de Paul of Detroit," AAD, Chancery records — organizations and societies; MC, Dec. 12, 1935; unsigned memo "re St. Vincent de Paul," Oct. 10, 1950; Evangeline Sheibley to Cardinal Mooney, Dec. 21, 1950; Mooney to B. A. Seymour, July 8, 1955, AAD, Chancery records — organizations and societies.
54. MC, Nov. 15, 1928, 1:8, Feb. 18, 1932, 7:4; Holy Name *Bulletin,* Summer 1956.
55. MC, June 24, 1920, 1:1-2, 5:3-5, Sept. 23, 1920, 1:1-2, Oct. 28, 1920, 1:5-6, Dec. 23, 1920, 1:3-4; St. Rose *Messenger,* June 20, 1926; MC, Feb. 9, 1933, 1:7-8, Jan. 17, 1935, 1:6-8, Jan. 12, 1939, 1:8, Jan. 26, 1939, 1:4-5, Feb. 9, 1939, 2:4.
56. MC, Dec. 15, 1921, 1:1-2, June 25, 1931, 6:5-6. See, for example, MC, Feb. 5, 1953, 4:1-2; St. John's *Bulletin,* Mar. 4, 1945; St. Margaret Mary *News,* Feb. 13, 1955, Sept. 29, 1957, Dec. 1, 1957. Fr. Chateau's rebuke is in St. Rose *Messenger,* Oct. 19, 1952.
57. "Bureau of Catholic Welfare, Report for 1930," AAD, Chancery records — Catholic charities of Michigan.
58. MC, Dec. 15, 1921, 1:3-5. The Big Brother program was removed from the jurisdiction of the Holy Name Society in 1927, when the "Big Brothers of the Diocese of Detroit" was formed as an independent organization, and one that was partially financed by the Detroit Community Fund. This new group did maintain close ties to the Holy Name Society. On the evolution of Big Brother work in the 1930s and the 1940s, see Father Ronald Heidelberger, "History of Catholic Charities — Boys' Division — Archdiocese of Detroit" (Master's thesis, School of Social Work, Wayne State University, 1960). MC, May 18, 1933, 4:1. The CMAA was mainly devoted to the promotion of parish softball teams.
59. MC, Jan. 2, 1930, 3:1, Sept. 29, 1932, 8:4, Apr. 11, 1935, 1:6, Jan. 23, 1936, 1:3-4.
60. MC, Apr. 8, 1937, 9:1-2, April 21, 1938, 11:3-4, Aug. 27, 1937, supplement, 151, Feb. 10, 1938, 1:8, Sept. 22, 1938, 9:5-6, Apr. 27, 1939, 9:3.
61. MC, Feb. 5, 1920, 4:4, July 3, 1930, 7:1-2; Nov. 21, 1935, 2:6-7; "Annual Report, Catholic Youth Organization, Year Ending December 31, 1939," AAD, Chancery collections — organizations and societies.
62. MC, Feb. 6, 1919, 8:3-4.
63. MC, Nov. 11, 1920, 8:4, May 27, 1920, 8:1, May 19, 1921, 8:4.

64. MC, Sept. 2, 1920, 8:5, Nov. 24, 1921, 5:1, Jan. 30, 1930, 1:1, May 8, 1930, 5:5.
65. MC, Mar. 25, 1920, 8:3, Sept. 23, 1920, 8:3, Dec. 22, 1921, 8:4.
66. See, for example, the chronicle of league activities at St. Rose parish in the 1920s: St. Rose *Messenger*, various issues, 1925–1927, copies in AAD, parish files. Bp. Gallagher to Agnes C. Regan, Feb. 9, 1935, AAD, Gallagher papers, 11:3; MC, May 11, 1939, 10:5.
67. "Detroit Archdiocesan Council of Catholic Men, Annual Report, Year Ending March 31, 1950"; Minutes, annual meeting, Detroit Archdiocesan Council of Catholic Men, June 3, 1953, AAD, Chancery collections — organizations and societies; Detroit Archdiocesan Council of Catholic Women, *Faith and Service* (Nov. 1947), AAD, Mooney papers.
68. MC, Oct. 27, 1932, 1:2–3, Nov. 7, 1935, 12:7. "The annual report of the Federation of Catholic Study Clubs reveals a substantial gain over the preceding year in the total number of units organized. The season ended with 3,000 members enrolled in 214 study circles. Study clubs were organized in 75 parishes of the archdiocese, and 58 of these clubs were in metropolitan Detroit" (MC, May 26, 1938, 10:5–6).
69. The Detroit Council of Catholic Organizations was organized in the fall of 1933, "in response to Bishop Michael J. Gallagher's call for concerted Catholic Action against vicious movies and literature" (MC, July 13, 1933, 4:1). The legion pledge first administered in Detroit included "a paragraph concerning immoral books and magazines." MC, Apr. 19, 1934, 1:6–8; MC, Dec. 6, 1934, 1:7–8.
70. On Protestant response to the Legion of Decency, see MC, May 10, 1934, 1:2–3, May 17, 1934, 1:8, May 24, 1934, 2:3–4, May 31, 1934, 1:2; MC, Oct. 10, 1935, 7:2; MC, July 14, 1938, 1:2, Dec. 8, 1938, 1:1, Apr. 28, 1938, 1:2–3, 2:7–8, 7:1, Mar. 2, 1933, 1:1; MC, May 18, 1933, 4:1–2.
71. MC, Mar. 26, 1936, 1:7.
72. Women were cofounders of both the original Catholic Evidence Guild in Great Britain and of the influential Catholic Truth Guild in Boston. Marius Risley, a founder of the Detroit group, had worked with the Boston organization. On Risley's Boston connection, see Debra Campbell, "David Goldstein and the Rise of the Catholic Campaigners for Christ," *Catholic Historical Review*, 72:1 (Jan. 1986), 46. MC, May 17, 1934, 7:4–5, Nov. 22, 1934, 8:8, May 9, 1935, 10:8, May 16, 1935, 10:2, July 25, 1935, 1:8, July 18, 1935, 8:5, July 4, 1935, 8:4, Aug. 4, 1938, 8:2, June 23, 1938, 10:4.
73. MC, Aug. 19, 1937, 8:2–3, Sept. 9, 1937, 1:7–8; Thomas Doherty to Napoleon Raymond, Oct. 1, 1940, WSU, ACTU papers, 2.
74. There are only occasional references to the Detroit Worker house in the various histories of the Catholic Worker movement. But see Sr. Mary Benedicta, FSSJ, "The Catholic Worker in Detroit, 1937 to 1968: A Selected Study" (Master's thesis, Marquette University, 1968).
75. MC, Nov. 18, 1937, 1:4, Mar. 31, 1938, 12:3, May 5, 1938, 10:5; Sr. Mary Benedicta, "The Catholic Worker in Detroit," 69.
76. The "communal" aspects of St. Benedict Farm eventually led to conflict, as was the case at virtually every Catholic Worker farm. The Detroit troubles were finally resolved by dividing the farm among the various members of the ill-fated commune. Interview, author with Justine L'Esperance Murphy, Detroit, Sept. 7, 1984; *Catholic Worker*, May 1940, 9.
77. Hickey to Wayne County Local Board No. 23, Mar. 3, 1942, AAD, Chancery collections — organizations and societies; interview, Justine L'Esperance Murphy.
78. Kern to Msgr. E. J. Hickey, July 9, 1946, AAD, Chancery collections — organizations and societies.
79. *Catholic Worker*, Dec. 1952, 8, March 1957, 4.

80. Memo re ACTU, undated but 1951, WSU, ACTU papers, 4; Nellie Passmore to Cardinal Mooney, Sept. 5, 1952, AAD, Chancery collections—organizations and societies.

81. MC, Jan. 16, 1936, 2:4; Kern to Msgr. E. J. Hickey, July 9, 1946; A. Patrick Madgett, SJ, to Archbishop Mooney, Jan. 29, 1942; "Chancellor" to Marion H. Meehan, Jan. 30, 1947, AAD, Chancery collections—organizations and societies. Father Madgett writes that the Catholic Evidence Guild "was in a moribund state" by the fall of 1940.

82. The mostly female membership of the sodality movement locally is clear in the *Michigan Catholic*'s coverage of that movement in the 1930s. Marguerite Gahagan, president of Detroit ACTU from 1949 to 1952, was a former newspaperwoman and a court reporter. MC, May 14, 1931, 8:8.

83. Mariette Wickes to Cardinal Mooney, Apr. 10, 1957, AAD, Chancery collections—organizations and societies.

14. Catholic education

1. Horkan to Archbishop John Dearden, undated but 1959, AAD, Chancery records—school office.

2. Horkan to Cardinal Mooney, June 23, 1958, AAD, Chancery records—school office.

3. Quoted in *The Michigan Public School Amendment* (no editor or place of publication given, no date but probably 1920), AAD, Gallagher papers, 9:9. On the school amendment controversy see Timothy Mark Pies, "The Parochial School Campaigns in Michigan, 1920–1924: The Lutheran and Catholic Involvement," *Catholic Historical Review*, 71:2 (Apr. 1986), 222–238.

4. Documents relating to the Association for Educational Freedom are in AAD, Gallagher papers, 9:3–4. On the Lutheran "school inspectors" see *Detroit News*, June 21, 1918. Public reaction to the proposed amendment is documented in a scrapbook of news clippings from 1918, AAD, oversize box 19. Fr. McClory was quoted in the *Detroit Times*, June 3, 1918. Bishop Kelly made much the same argument in a letter to the *Detroit News* in March 1918. See MC, Mar. 28, 1918, 4:5.

5. *Detroit News*, July 15, 1918; MC, Dec. 12, 1918, 1:1–2, Aug. 21, 1919, 4:2; *Catholic Vigil*, Dec. 1918; MC, Aug. 19, 1920, 4:2.

6. MC, May 1, 1919, 2:3–6. Each of the Michigan dioceses ran its own campaign. The lack of episcopal cooperation was later attributed, by Msgr. John Doyle, to the division of the state between two ecclesiastical provinces. Detroit was then part of the Province of Cincinnati; Grand Rapids and Marquette belonged to the Province of Milwaukee. See Pies, "Parochial School Campaigns," 226 n. 16.

7. MC, Feb. 13, 1919, 4:3–4, Sept. 16, 1920, 4:2. On the League's role see MC, Mar. 25, 1920, 8:3, Apr. 29, 1920, 8:2, July 29, 1920, 8:2, Sept. 3, 1920, 8:3, Oct. 14, 1920, 5:2. Gallagher to Rev. and dear Sisters, Oct. 9, 1920, SSIHM, IHM Education, 4; MC, Apr. 22, 1920, 8:4. Copies of the 1919 petitions are in the AAD, Gallagher papers, 4:5–7. These petitions come only from the Diocese of Detroit. Those originating in places outside the city of Detroit, however, have a smaller proportion of women's signatures than those from the city itself. One would thus not expect the heavily rural dioceses of Grand Rapids and Marquette to produce results that would support the bishop's claim.

8. MC, June 24, 1920, 1:1–2, 5:3–5, Sept. 23, 1920, 1:1–2, Oct. 28, 1920, 1:5–6.

9. MC, Sept. 9., 1920, 1:7, Sept. 16, 1920, 6:3, Oct. 21, 1920, 1:4, Nov. 4, 1920, 1:1–2, 4:6. See also "Official Program, Parade and Field Mass," AAD, Gallagher papers, 9:9.

10. Election returns by diocese are found in the 1920 "Official Report of the Diocese of Detroit," AAD; Minutes, meeting of Diocesan Consultors, Nov. 15, 1920, AAD, minutes and proceedings, 4.

11. On the Chancery debate see Pies, "Parochial School Campaigns," 232-233 and especially n. 48. On the Klan in Detroit see Kenneth T. Jackson, *The Ku Klux Klan in the City, 1915-1930* (New York: Oxford University Press, 1967), especially chapter 9. The Oregon school law was declared unconstitutional by the U.S. Supreme Court in 1925.

12. The various Protestant denominations conducted their campaigns independently; there was little formal cooperation between Protestants and Catholics. See Pies, "Parochial School Campaigns." Diocesan School Committee to "Dear Sir or Madam," Oct. 16, 1924, AAD, Gallagher papers, 9:9.

13. Gallagher to "Beloved Brethren of the Clergy and dear Children of the Laity," Oct. 15, 1924, AAD, Paré papers, 1:14. The 1924 results do show a growing polarization on the school question between urban and rural parts of the state. Nineteen counties supported the amendment in 1924 as compared to seven in 1920. All were largely rural.

14. Sr. Arthemise Dalton, "History and Development of Catholic Secondary School System," 72; MC, Mar. 6, 1919, 4:3-4, Apr. 17, 1919, 4:6; Bp. Gallagher to Rev. dear Father, Apr. 28, 1919, AAD, Gallagher papers, 9:1.

15. Sr. Rosalita, *No Greater Service*, 556.

16. Minutes, meeting of Diocesan Consultors, Aug. 16, 1921, AAD, minutes and proceedings, 4; Dalton, "History and Development of Catholic Secondary School System," 70-71.

17. MC, Apr. 19, 1933, 5:1-2; Sr. Rosalita, *No Greater Service*, 565; Sr. Silvestris to Bp. Gallagher, June 7, 1934, AAD, parish files.

18. "The School System," no author or date given, but 1941, AAD, Chancery records — school office; MC, June 11, 1936, 1:6-7, 2:3-6, May 23, 1935, 1:8.

19. Gallagher to Mother M. Bonaventure, Oct. 18, 1924, AAD, Chancery records — religious orders, women; Gallagher to Rev. Joseph Herr, Jan. 14, 1922, AAD, St. Albertus parish file; Memo re Our Lady Help of Christians School, undated but mid-1920s, AAD, parish files; Rev. John B. Hewelt to Very Rev. Stephen Woznicki, Dec. 3, 1925; Fr. Garner Legg to Rev. John M. Doyle, Feb. 11, 1925; "Sanitary Conditions—St. Stanislaus School, Detroit," Feb. 6, 1925, AAD, parish files.

20. Quoted in Dalton, "History and Development of Catholic Secondary School System," 106-108; Sr. Rosalita, *No Greater Service*, 524-525; MC, May 23, 1935, 1:8, 8:1-2.

21. Sister M. Agatha to Rev. James Downey, June 28, 1934, AAD, Immaculate Conception, Anchorville parish file.

22. MC, Nov. 29, 1928, 1:3; see, for example, MC, Jan. 16, 1930, 1:2, 3:5-6; IHM Mission Chronicles, Holy Rosary, Detroit, SSIHM, Chronicles, IHM missions.

23. MC, Feb. 6, 1930, 1:5, Feb. 27, 1930, 2:4; Gallagher to "Reverend dear Father," June 16, 1927, AAD, Paré papers, 1:14.

24. MC, Dec. 8, 1921, 8:4, Jan. 24, 1935, 7:4-5. Attrition was apparently greater in the Catholic high schools of Detroit than it was in the public schools in the 1930s.

25. Dalton, "History and Development of Catholic Secondary School System," 116-117.

26. Ibid., 36. Inteview, author with Sr. Amadeus Dowd, IHM, Monroe, Mich., Oct. 1, 1984.

27. MC, Apr. 5, 1934, 8:4-5, May 10, 1934, 7:8, May 23, 1935, 1:8, 8:1-2. Deady also announced in 1934 that high school teachers, whose preparation was not governed by the Dacey law, would henceforth be required to have completed four years of college before they began to teach.

28. MC, May 23, 1935, 1:8, 8:1–2; interview, Sr. Amadeus Dowd, IHM. Sister Amadeus served as a school supervisor for her order from 1939 until 1944.

29. "Annual Report on the Schools of the Archdiocese, 1939–1940," AAD, Chancery records — school office; interview, Sister Amadeus Dowd, IHM.

30. "Annual Report on the Schools of the Archdiocese, 1939–1940"; MC, May 18, 1939, 1:6, May 23, 1935, 1:8, 8:1–2.

31. Harlan C. Koch to Sr. Mary Michael, IHM, Jan. 21, 1938, SSIHM, IHM Education, 5. Other, similar letters are scattered throughout the IHM education files. "Course of Study in High School Literature," Archdiocese of Detroit, 1939, SSIHM, IHM Education, 5.

32. Minutes of the Educational Policy Board are in SSIHM, IHM Education, 5. Quotes from meetings of Nov. 17, 1945, Feb. 24, 1945, Apr. 21, 1945.

33. Minutes of the Educational Policy Board, especially entries for Apr. 21, 1945, Feb. 23, 1946; *Manual of Information: Parochial Schools, Archdiocese of Detroit,* undated but 1940s, copy in SSIHM, IHM Education, 1; "The School System," AAD. "We should not allow more than fifty pupils in a classroom," Msgr. Horkan was explaining to a small-town pastor as late as 1958. "When we go beyond this figure the class as a group suffers and the teacher is overtaxed." Msgr. Vincent Horkan to Rev. Charles J. Wettstein, July 10, 1958, AAD, St. Augustine, Richmond parish file.

34. Msgr. Vincent Horkan to Archbishop Dearden, undated but 1959, AAD, Chancery records — school office; Paul F. Maher to Archbishop [sic] E. Mooney, Oct. 13, 1955, AAD, St. Mary, Rockwood parish file.

35. Sr. Rosalita, *No Greater Service,* 747.

36. "Memorandum," Deady to Mooney, Dec. 15, 1950, AAD, Chancery records — religious orders, women. Ninety-one percent of the elementary school teachers in the IHM order had college degrees by 1959, as did all the IHMs who taught in high schools.

37. The Sister Formation Conference was known initially as the Sisters' Educational and Professional Standards Commission; the name was changed in 1954. On the conference and its antecedents, see Mary Schneider, "The Transformation of American Women Religious: The Sister Formation Conference as Catalyst for Change, 1954–1964," Working Paper Series, 17:1 (Spring 1986), Cushwa Center for the Study of American Catholicism, Notre Dame University.

38. Ziolkowski, *Felician Sisters,* 413–414; Msgr. Carroll Deady to Cardinal Mooney, July 30, 1953; Mother Mary Simplicita, CSSF, to "Reverend Father," Sept. 12, 1952, AAD, Chancery records — religious orders, women. Other, similar documents can be found in this collection.

39. Gleason, "American Catholic Higher Education," 18–19. St. Joseph College became Siena Heights College in 1939.

40. Quoted in William Halsey, *The Survival of American Innocence: Catholicism in an Era of Disillusionment, 1920–1940* (Notre Dame, Ind.: University of Notre Dame Press, 1980), 51.

41. George Hermann Derry, "The Marygrove Idea," in *Eighty-Second Anniversary: A Souvenir Volume* (1927). Marygrove College was accredited by the North Central Association of Colleges and Secondary Schools in 1926. See Sr. Rosalita, *No Greater Service,* 611.

42. Derry, "The Marygrove Idea"; quoted in JoEllen Vinyard, "The History of Marygrove College: A Brief Overview," unpublished paper, 1974. Professor Vinyard discusses the purposes of the Marygrove curriculum as it existed before the late 1960s. MC, Sept. 29, 1921, 5:1.

43. MC, Feb. 5, 1920, 8:5.

44. MC, Feb. 5, 1920, 8:5, Sept. 20, 1928, 1:8, Mar. 31, 1938, 1:7–8; Mooney to Arch-

bishop Cicognani, Mar. 10, 1952, Draft copy in AAD, Mooney papers. "It has been my policy as a bishop to decline the honor of receiving degrees from secular colleges and universities," Mooney wrote to Father George B. Ford in 1943. "This is based on my concept of the duty we have of not giving positive approval to a type of education which is so little in consonance with Catholic principles." Mooney to Ford, Dec. 24, 1943, AAD, Mooney papers.

45. MC, May 15, 1919, 5:3. Newman Club membership is found in the club's minutes, MHC, St. Mary's Student Chapel papers, 7. Estimated figures on Mass attendance are scattered throughout this same collection. St. Mary's Student Chapel, "Sunday Announcements," 1921–1926; "Sunday Announcements," 1926–1932, MHC, St. Mary's Student Chapel papers, 1.

46. "New Student Problems," outlined sermon, undated but apparently mid-1920s; see also St. Mary's Student Chapel, "Sunday Announcements," 1926–1932, entry for Sept. 18, 1927, MHC, St. Mary's Student Chapel papers, 1.

47. Study groups, speakers, and the contents of the pamphlet rack are mentioned in the St. Mary's "Student Announcements," bound volumes 1926–1932, 1932–1936, 1932–1942, MHC, St. Mary's Student Chapel papers, 1. See also Newman Club minutes, same collection, box 7.

48. MC, Dec. 7, 1933, 6:3; Andries to Msgr. John Doyle, Dec. 12, 1936, AAD, Fr. Leo F. Andries file; MC, May 18, 1916, 5:7; Fr. Leo Broderick to Archbishop Dearden, Mar. 10, 1962, AAD, Chancery records — Newman centers. St. John Fisher Chapel at Oakland University also dates from 1965.

49. Bradley to Rev. Arthur Valade, Apr. 27, 1965, AAD, Chancery records — Newman centers. Archbishop Dearden appointed Msgr. Bradley the director of Newman Clubs in the Archdiocese in 1961.

50. The best known of these "critiques" is probably Mary Perkins Ryan's quite moderate *Are Parochial Schools the Answer?* published in 1964.

51. See, for example, Andrew M. Greeley, *The American Catholic: A Social Portrait* (New York: Basic Books 1977), chapter 9.

15. CATHOLICS IN A CHANGING WORLD

1. Paul A. Carter, "Folklore of the Campaign of 1928," in Frank O. Gatell et al., eds., *The Growth of American Politics* (New York: Oxford University Press, 1972), 2:390–302; Samuel Lubell, "Revolt of the City," in ibid., 320.

2. The results of the 1925 study are found in the AAD, Gallagher papers, 1:1.

3. Dispensations for mixed marriages are in the AAD, the number of marriages is listed annually in the *Catholic Directory.*

4. MC, Dec. 29, 1921, 4:1–2, Apr. 29, 1920, 5:1.

5. The Gallagher regulation is referred to in a circular letter from Fr. Henry Kaufmann to the members of the Ephreta Society, May 16, 1923, AAD, Chancery records — organizations and societies, Catholic deaf. Mooney to "the Catholic Lawyers of the Archdiocese," undated, AAD, Chancery records — organizations and societies.

6. Lenski, *Religious Factor,* 165–167.

7. Ibid., 196.

8. See review of Warren S. Thompson's *Ratio of Children to Women: A Study of the Differential Rate of Natural Increase in the United States* in MC, Dec. 17, 1931, 1:3, 2:5; MC, Feb. 4, 1932, 4:2, Aug. 9, 1928, 5:5–6.

9. MC, Mar. 26, 1931, 4:1, July 8, 1937, 6:1.

10. See Noonan, *Contraception,* especially 492–513.

11. Linda Gordon, *Woman's Body, Woman's Right: A Social History of Birth Control in Amer-*

ica (New York: Grossman, 1976), 225. On sermon policies see MC, Feb. 5, 1920, 4:2.

12. Quoted in Noonan, *Contraception,* 486–487; Kennedy, *Birth Control in America,* 154–155; MC, Oct. 1, 1931, 4:1.
13. MC, June 24, 1937, 6:1, Jan. 19, 1933, 4:1; memo re "Neighborhood House," Mar. 23, 1938, AAD, Chancery records—uncatalogued.
14. MC, Apr. 30, 1931, 4:2; Noonan, *Contraception,* 512.
15. MC, Nov. 3, 1932, 4:1, June 13, 1935, 1:8, June 18, 1936, 1:6–8, Oct. 12, 1933, 4:1; Gordon, *Woman's Body, Woman's Right,* 321. Michigan's otherwise restrictive statutes exempted physicians in medical practice.
16. Noonan, *Contraception,* 522–532; Rev. Edward J. Hickey to "Dear Reverend Father," June 4, 1945, MHC, St. Mary's Student Chapel papers, 2. Copies of the Linsenmeyer paper and a companion piece by Fr. Chester Ropella will also be found here.
17. Jay P. Dolan, *The American Catholic Experience: A History from Colonial Times to the Present* (Garden City, N.Y.: Doubleday, 1985), 435; Lenski, *Religious Factor,* 165–167; Burkhardt to Bp. John Donovan, May 28, 1957, AAD, Chancery records—CCD.
18. Noonan, *Contraception,* 530–531; quoted in Garry Wills, *Bare Ruined Choirs: Doubt, Prophecy, and Radical Religion* (Garden City, N.Y.: Doubleday, 1971), 185.
19. Higham, *Strangers in the Land,* 265–270.
20. On the Klan in Detroit and the 1924 campaign, see Jackson, *Ku Klux Klan,* chapter 9. The 1924 election had been called to fill the unexpired term of an ailing incumbent.
21. Higham, *Strangers,* 329.
22. St. Philip Neri Mission House: Davison and "Michigan Home" Weekly Reports, 1923–1928, Parker entry for Oct. 2, 1926; see also weekly reports for Imlay City and Allenton, for Lapeer, and for Oxford and Romeo, AAD, Non-Chancery records—institutions, societies and parishes.
23. MC, Sept. 13, 1928, 4:1, Sept. 20, 1928, 4:1, July 5, 1928, 4:1, Sept. 13, 1928, 5:3–4.
24. Quoted in Fine, *Frank Murphy: The Detroit Years,* 212.
25. Quoted in ibid., 253.
26. Mother M. Patricia to Frank Murphy, Oct. 7, 1931, MHC, Frank Murphy papers, 4:55; Cefai to Murphy, Oct. 7, 1931, MHC, Frank Murphy papers, 4:54. On the role of religion in the 1931 campaigns, see Fine, *Frank Murphy: The Detroit Years,* 435–439. MC, Nov. 5, 1931, 1:8.
27. On the 1936 campaign, see Sidney Fine, *Frank Murphy: The New Deal Years* (Chicago: University of Chicago Press, 1979), chapter 6.
28. Arthur D. Maguire to Murphy, Nov. 10, 1938, MHC, Frank Murphy papers, 22:9; Fine, *Frank Murphy: The New Deal Years,* 323–325, 483–485, 508–515.
29. Ibid., 523–524.
30. "Kal" (Bishop William F. Murphy) to Archbishop Mooney, Dec. 20, 1942, AAD, Mooney papers; Minutes of the meeting of the Bishops of the Province of Detroit, Sept. 7, 1944, Chancery records—seminaries; Rev. Robert F. Allen to Cardinal Mooney, May 9, 1958, AAD, Chancery collections—organizations and societies.
31. Bp. Joseph Albers to Archbishop Mooney, Dec. 22, 1938, AAD, Mooney papers. Bishop Albers was not entirely happy with the 1939 school bus law. "We may look upon this bill as a gesture to placate us so as not to demand a part of the primary school interest fund and other taxes for education to which we are entitled in justice as taxpayers. Part II Chapter II Sec. 20 seems to preclude any chance of getting a portion of this money."
32. The campaign against "Proposition C" was generously covered by the *Michigan Catholic* in the fall of 1970.
33. Mooney to Cicognani, Mar. 24, 1941, AAD, Mooney papers; Arthur D. Maguire to Mooney, Nov. 6, 1938, MHC, Frank Murphy papers, 22:3.

34. MC, Aug. 9, 1937, 6:2, Jan. 12, 1939, 1:8, Jan. 26, 1939, 1:4–5.
35. Rev. E. J. Hickey to Ciarrocchi, Jan. 31, 1939; Ciarrocchi to Hickey, Feb. 1, 1939; Ciarrocchi to Mooney, May 13, 1949, AAD, Msgr. Joseph Ciarrocchi file.
36. St. John's *Bulletin*, Mar. 14, 1943; Ziolkowski, *Felician Sisters,* 341.
37. Mooney to "Dear Reverend Father," Oct. 21, 1942, Oct. 21, 1943, AAD, Mooney papers.
38. IHM Mission Chronicles, Holy Trinity, Detroit, 1941, SSIHM, Chronicles, IHM Missions; Sr. Rosalita, *No Greater Service,* 610; Gerald Burns to Cardinal Mooney, Nov. 27, 1948, AAD, Fr. Emmet Hannick file.
39. George F. Pierrot to Cardinal Dearden, July 26, 1971, AAD, Fr. Raymond Clancy file.
40. On blacks in nineteenth-century Detroit, see Katzman, *Before the Ghetto.*
41. Ibid., 44, 101, 121–123.
42. MC, Oct. 16, 1890, 4:4, Jan. 22, 1891, 1:6–7, 5:6, Sept. 29, 1892, 4:2–3.
43. MC, July 10, 1897, 4:3, Dec. 28, 1893, 4:2–3, Apr. 22, 1897, 4:2–3.
44. MC, Aug. 23, 1906, 4:3, Oct. 26, 1911, 3:5.
45. Katzman, *Before the Ghetto,* 136. Father Soffers came to St. Anne's in 1853. The *Catholic Directory* lists a "colored chapel" at St. Anne's between 1869 and 1872, but it evidently was opened in the mid-1860s. Sr. Rosalita, ed., *Achievement of a Century,* 65–66.
46. C. P. Rabaut to Very Rev. Peter Hennaert, Dec. 4, 1872, AAD, Borgess papers, 5:16; MC, Dec. 8, 1898, 4:1–2, Aug. 16, 1917, 8:2, Jan. 14, 1915, 8:1, Aug. 20, 1908, 8:2.
47. Archdiocese of Detroit, Canonical Visitation of Our Lady of Victory Mission, Nov. 16, 1948, AAD, parish files; MC, Jan. 28, 1926, 8:2.
48. Donald L. Hessler, "America's Real Forgotten Man," *Gothic,* 10:2 (Mar. 1, 1934), 19, 32; MC, Feb. 15, 1934, 5:2–3, Oct. 3, 1939, 6:2, Sept. 21, 1939, 6:1–2.
49. MC, Sept. 7, 1911, 8:3–4, Mar. 6, 1913, 8:5. The fund-raising activities of parishioners and of the Aid Society were regularly covered in the *Michigan Catholic.*
50. MC, May 29, 1913, 8:6.
51. MC, Nov. 11, 1943, 12:1–2. News about parish organizations appeared regularly in the *Michigan Catholic.* For an account of the Easter Mass in 1924 see MC, Apr. 24, 1924, 8:4.
52. Sacramental registers (St. Peter Claver) at Sacred Heart Church, Detroit.
53. The School Sisters of Notre Dame began catechetical classes at St. Peter Claver's mission in 1912; they were succeeded by the Carmelites. MC, Jan. 2, 1913, 8:3, Jan. 27, 1921, 8:2, Nov. 22, 1923, 8:4. Father Kreutzkampf's promotion of "St. Joseph's Little Shrine at the Corner" can be traced in the *Michigan Catholic* between 1919 and 1922. On Tre Ore services in 1922 see MC, Apr. 27, 1922, 5:1.
54. MC, Nov. 17, 1927, 6:4, May 4, 1933, 2:2. St. Benedict the Moor, the second black parish to be organized in Detroit, also had teams in these leagues. MC, Apr. 27, 1937, 9:1–2, Apr. 21, 1938, 11:3–4. Applications for the CYO's annual boxing tourney asked the race of the applicant in the 1930s, but no evidence suggests that blacks were not equitably dealt with in the event itself.
55. On the Federated Colored Catholics see Marjorie Nickels, "The Federated Colored Catholics: A Study of Three Variant Perspectives on Racial Justice as Represented by John LaFarge, William Markoe and Thomas Turner" (Ph.D. diss., Catholic University of America, 1975); MC, Sept. 4, 1930, 1:8, 9:4–5.
56. Nickels, "Federated Colored Catholics," 119–125, 200–201; MC, Mar. 1, 1934, 8:6, June 13, 1940, 1:4; Charles L. Rawlings et al. to Archbishop Mooney, June 20, 1942, AAD, Sacred Heart, Detroit parish file.
57. James Gibson et al. to Archbishop Mooney, Nov. 23, 1938; James M. Burrell to Archbishop Mooney, May 5, 1941; Hickey to Burrell, May 8, 1941, AAD, Sacred Heart, Detroit parish file.

58. MC, Dec. 3, 1925, 1:7, June 8, 1922, 4:4–6.
59. MC, Dec. 16, 1926.
60. MC, June 10, 1926, 7:3–4, Mar. 3, 1927, 7:3, Aug. 12, 1926, 8:6, Dec. 23, 1926, 12:1, Feb. 10, 1927, 10:3–4.
61. MC, Mar. 10, 1927, 10:5, May 19, 1927, 10:7; Elmer A. Pillon to Bp. Gallagher, Oct. 18, 1927; Petition, undated but 1927, AAD, St. Leo's parish file (St. Benedict's was located on the fringes of St. Leo's parish); Msgr. Stephen Woznicki to Rev. Charles Kapp, C.S.Sp., Mar. 11, 1932, AAD, St. Benedict the Moor parish file.
62. MC, June 2, 1927, 10:1, June 9, 1927, 10:1, June 23, 1927, 12:6, May 26, 1927, 10:2, Dec. 29, 1927, 8:3–4.
63. MC, Dec. 29, 1927, 8:3–4, May 23, 1929, 1:6.
64. A. R. Feliciano and James A. Doston to Gallagher, Sept. 4, 1929; James Burrell et al. to Gallagher, undated but 1929; petition addressed to Gallagher, undated but ca. 1930, AAD, parish files. Fr. Dukette's name was often misspelled "Duckette."
65. MC, Nov. 1, 1939, 10:5.
66. MC, Dec. 19, 1929, 8:2; petition addressed to Bp. Gallagher, undated but ca. 1930, AAD, parish files; MC, Mar. 24, 1932, 8:4; Rev. Charles A. Kapp, CSSp, to Msgr. John Doyle, Aug. 8, 1933; Doyle to Rev. Charles J. Diehl, CSSp, Mar. 2, 1953; Diehl to Cardinal Mooney, Mar. 7, 1953, AAD, parish files.
67. MC, June 29, 1933, 6:5, July 12, 1934, 8:3–4.
68. MC, Feb. 28, 1935, 11:5, Nov. 15, 1934, 8:8; James Gibson and Charles R. A. Smith to Gallagher, Dec. 1, 1935, AAD, parish files.
69. MC, Aug. 20, 1936, 1:5–7, Nov. 19, 1936, 1:6, Feb. 3, 1938, 6:5; report, undated but late summer 1937, by Rev. Henry Thiefels, CSSp, AAD, parish files.
70. Rev. J. M. Lundergan, CSSp, to Archbishop Mooney, Aug. 8, 1938; Mooney to Rev. Henry Thiefels, Aug. 20, 1938; Mooney to Very Rev. C. J. Plunkett, CSSp, July 27, 1939; "The Parishioners of Sacred Heart Church" to Mooney, Aug. 7, 1938, AAD, parish files.
71. Ziolkowski, *Felician Sisters,* 293–295; Rev. Henry Thiefels, CSSp, "Report to the Commission for Negro and Indian Missions," Sept. 1938; Thiefels to Archbishop Mooney, Sept. 16, 1944, AAD, parish files; MC, Jan. 19, 1939, 4:2–3.
72. Thiefels to Rev. E. J. Hickey, Sept. 7, 1940; Thiefels, "Report," undated but 1939, AAD, Sacred Heart, Detroit parish file; MC, May 11, 1939, 10:6, May 4, 1944, 1:5–7; Thiefels to Mooney, May 5, 1944, AAD, Chancery records—religious orders, men; Rev. Thomas J. Clynes, CSSp, to Cardinal Mooney, Mar. 27, 1955; Clynes to Hickey, Dec. 16, 1949, AAD, Holy Ghost parish file.
73. MC, Oct. 7, 1943, 1:1–4; Rev. John C. Ryan, "Proposed Projects, CCD," Apr. 13, 1943, AAD, Chancery records—CCD. The parish school was financed in part by a "gift" from neighboring Presentation parish, whose all-white congregation had no wish to see integration at the Presentation School. Our Lady of Victory and Presentation schools were later consolidated. Memorandum, Msgr. John A. Donovan, Apr. 26, 1954, AAD, Our Lady of Victory parish files; Ryan to Mooney, Sept. 26, 1945, AAD, Holy Family, Inkster parish files.
74. Rev. Thomas C. Clynes, CSSp, to Mooney, Aug. 14, 1950; Rev. W. J. O'Rourke to Msgr. John Donovan, Nov. 27, 1953, AAD, parish files.
75. Mother M. Januaria to Rev. J. F. Zehler, CSSp, Nov. 26, 1949, AAD, parish files.
76. "Bill" to Archbishop Mooney, May 31, 1935, AAD, Mooney papers; Rev. Arthur D. Reckinger to Mooney, Aug. 19, 1941, Nov. 27, 1941; Rev. E. H. Hickey to Reckinger, Sept. 8, 1941, AAD, Blessed Sacrament parish files; Mooney to LaFarge, draft undated but June 1943, AAD, Mooney papers; Rev. E. J. Hickey to Rev. Franklyn Kennedy, Sept. 3, 1943, AAD, Chancery collections—organizations and societies.
77. The *Detroit Tribune,* a black weekly, reported in Oct. 1940 that St. Leo's High School

accepted seven black students per class. No other parochial high school was yet open to blacks. Rev. Hubert Roberge, "Integration — It's Here," *Integrity*, 8:7 (Apr. 1954), 11–17; Mooney to Roberge, Apr. 21, 1954, AAD, Fr. Hubert Roberge file.

78. Exclusionary policies in Catholic fraternal groups was the principal raison d'être of the Knights of St. Peter Claver, a national black fraternal society founded in 1909. The first Detroit chapter of the knights dates from 1931. MC, Mar. 11, 1954, 4:1–2, May 27, 1954, 4:1–2. For information on the founding and early work of the Home Visitors of Mary, see AAD, Chancery records — religious orders, women. Cardinal Mooney gave generous financial support to the fledgling community, which did not achieve canonical standing in Rome until 1969.

79. IHM Mission Chronicles, Holy Trinity, Detroit, entry for Sept. 17, 1946; IHM Mission Chronicles, Holy Rosary, Detroit, entries for Sept. 6, 1945, Dec. 20, 1946, Sept. 5, 1947, Sept. 8, 1949, SSIHM, Chronicles, IHM missions; Mother Mary David to Cardinal Mooney, Nov. 21, 1946, AAD, Divine Providence, Southfield parish file. The former St. George (Lithuanian) congregation eventually re-established itself as Divine Providence parish in suburban Southfield.

80. IHM Mission Chronicles, St. George, Detroit, entries for Sept. 11, 1950, Feb. 26, 1951, Mar. 19, 1954, SSIHM, Chronicles, IHM missions.

81. IHM Mission Chronicles, St. George, Detroit, entries for June 1952, Sept. 22, 1952, June 16, 1955, SSIHM, Chronicles, IHM missions; IHM *Elementary Sodality Bulletin*, Mar. 1951. The religious "requirements" at St. George were common to many black Catholic schools in the 1940s and the 1950s. See "Winning Negro Converts" and "Harvest in Harlem" in John A. O'Brien, ed., *Winning Converts: A Symposium on Methods of Convert Making for Priests and Lay People* (New York: P. J. Kenedy and Sons, 1948).

82. Dearden to Rev. George F. O'Dea, SSJ, Apr. 9, 1963, Aug. 5, 1964, AAD, Chancery records — religious orders, men.

83. Beccherini to Gallagher, Nov. 6, 1929, AAD, San Francesco parish file. On race relations in Detroit in the late teens and early 1920s see David Allen Levine, *Internal Combustion: The Races in Detroit, 1915–1926* (Westport, Conn.: Greenwood Press, 1976).

84. The schools listed were Blessed Sacrament, SS. Peter and Paul (Jesuit), Sacred Heart, and St. Mary's. St. Francis Orphan Home was also said to accept black children. The *Michigan Catholic* was replying, rather testily, to a recent claim in the *Chicago Defender* that no parochial schools in Detroit would accept black Catholic pupils. MC, Apr. 6, 1922, 8:4–5, Sept. 25, 1930, 3:4–5; *Detroit Free Press,* Sept. 27, 1929. The enrollment at most of the near east side Polish schools had begun to decline by the late 1920s.

85. Luther to Mrs. Tyrell, Mar. 1, 1934; the letter was reprinted in the *Interracial Review* and quoted in Roche, *Catholic Colleges and the Negro Student,* 164–165. The University of Detroit was apparently open to blacks by 1922, for seminarian Norman Dukette mentioned it in that year, along with Fordham, Marquette, and St. Thomas College in Minnesota, as Catholic colleges that currently had black students. My thanks to Sister Claudia Carlen, IHM, for the information on Marygrove.

86. "Survey of Racial and Religious Conflict Forces in Detroit," Sept. 10–Sept. 30, 1943, WSU, Civil Rights Congress of Michigan papers, 71; see also Dominic Capeci, Jr., *Race Relations in Wartime Detroit: The Sojourner Truth Housing Controversy of 1942* (Philadelphia: Temple University Press, 1984).

87. MC, July 1, 1943, 4:1–2.

88. LeRoy G. White to Archbishop Mooney, Nov. 14, 1941, AAD, St. Ladislaus, Hamtramck parish file; Mooney to LaFarge, draft undated but June 1943, AAD, Mooney papers; Coogan to Rev. John Donovan, May 31, 1944, AAD, Chancery records — Catholic colleges.

89. Fr. John Coogan, SJ, discussed the extent of segregation in Detroit's Catholic schools and hospitals as a member of a 1947 symposium sponsored by the Urban League. See "Editorial Roundtable: Catholic-Negro Relations," *Opportunity*, 25:3 (Summer 1947), 136–149. Rev. E. J. Hickey to Rev. Vitalis Lasota, Sept. 6, 1950, AAD, parish files; Christine Hill to Cardinal Mooney, Aug. 20, 1957; Rev. John Donovan to Hill, Aug. 21, 1957, AAD, parish files. The offending pastor was transferred not long after this, but for unknown reasons.

90. Rev. Ray Maiberger to Msgr. Joseph Breitenbeck, June 22, 1958, AAD, parish files.

EPILOGUE

1. Wills, *Bare Ruined Choirs,* 1.
2. The modified recommendation, tendered by the same committees that had drafted the original plan and subsequently accepted by Cardinal Edmund Szoka, gave three of the affected parishes an unconditional lease on life; twenty-five others were given an additional year to make progress toward "viability." Thirty churches were slated to be closed as of June 30, 1989.
3. Archbishop John Dearden, "Challenge to Change in the Urban Church," address delivered in Kansas City, Mo., undated but 1967, copy in AAD, St. Margaret Mary parish file.
4. On local division with regard to social and political questions (and with regard to theological and liturgical questions as well), see results of the comprehensive survey, *Insight: Our Faith Today* (Detroit: Archdiocese of Detroit, Office of Planning and Research, 1971).
5. Emile Pin, SJ, "The Priestly Function in Crisis," in Karl Rahner, SJ, ed., *The Identity of the Priest* (New York: Paulist Press, 1969), 48.
6. MC, May 8, 1969, 1:3–6, 9:1–4. On the Dearden reforms see John C. Haughey, "Detroit: Evolution of a Revolution," *America* (Apr. 19, 1969), 475–478.
7. Pin, "Priestly Function," 46–47.

INDEX

Leslie Woodcock Tentler is a professor of history at the University of Michigan—Dearborn. She holds the Ph.D. degree from the University of Michigan.

The manuscript was edited by Christina Postema. The book was designed by Selma Tenenbaum. The typeface for the text is Baskerville. The display face is Berling. The text is printed on 50-lb. Glatfelter text paper and the book is bound in Holliston Mills' B-grade Roxite vellum over genuine binders' boards.

Manufactured in the United States of America.